An Archaeology of Australia Since 1788

CONTRIBUTIONS TO GLOBAL HISTORICAL ARCHAEOLOGY

Series Editor:

Charles E. Orser, Jr., New York State Museum, Albany, New York, USA

AN ARCHAEOLOGY OF AUSTRALIA SINCE 1788
Susan Lawrence and Peter Davies

AN ARCHAEOLOGICAL STUDY OF RURAL CAPITALISM AND MATERIAL LIFE: The Gibbs
Farmstead in Southern Appalachia, 1790-1920
Mark D. Groover

ARCHAEOLOGY AND CREATED MEMORY: Public History in a National Park
Paul A. Shackel

AN ARCHAEOLOGY OF HISTORY AND TRADITION: Moments of Danger in the Annapolis
Landscape
Christopher N. Matthews

AN ARCHAEOLOGY OF MANNERS: The Polite World of the Merchant Elite of Colonial
Massachusetts
Lorinda B.R. Goodwin

AN ARCHAEOLOGY OF SOCIAL SPACE: Analyzing Coffee Plantations in Jamaica's Blue Mountains
James A. Delle

DOMESTIC ARCHITECTURE AND POWER: The Historical Archaeology of Colonial Ecuador
Ross W. Jamieson

HISTORICAL ARCHAEOLOGY OF GENDERED LIVES: Historical Archaeologies of Social
Relations in Deerfield, Massachusetts ca. 1750-ca. 1904
Edited by Deborah Rotman

THE HISTORICAL ARCHAEOLOGIES OF BUENOS AIRES: A City at the End of the World
Daniel Schavelzon

HISTORICAL ARCHAEOLOGIES OF CAPITALISM
Edited by Mark P. Leone and Parker B. Potter, Jr.

A HISTORICAL ARCHAEOLOGY OF THE OTTOMAN EMPIRE: Breaking New Ground
Edited by Uzi Baram and Lynda Carroll

MEANING AND IDEOLOGY IN HISTORICAL ARCHAEOLGY: Style, Social Identity, and
Capitalism in an Australian
Heather Burke

RACE AND AFFLUENCE: An Archaeology of African America and Consumer Culture
Paul R. Mullins

RURAL SOCIETY IN THE AGE OF REASON
An Archaeology of the Emergence of Modern Life in the Southern Scottish Highlands
Chris Dalglish

A SPACE OF THEIR OWN: Lunatic Asylums in Britain, South Australia, and Tasmania
Susan Piddock

TE PUNA: A New Zealand Mission Station
Angela Middleton

A Continuation Order Plan is available for this series. A continuation order will bring delivery of each new volume immediately upon publication. Volumes are billed only upon actual shipment. For further information please contact the publisher. For more information about this series, please visit: www.Springer.com/Series/5734.

Susan Lawrence · Peter Davies

An Archaeology of Australia Since 1788

Springer

Susan Lawrence
Archaeology Program
La Trobe University
3086 Bundoora Victoria
Australia
s.lawrence@latrobe.edu.au

Peter Davies
Archaeology Program
La Trobe University
3086 Bundoora Victoria
Australia
peter.davies@latrobe.edu.au

ISSN 1574-0439
ISBN 978-1-4419-7484-6   e-ISBN 978-1-4419-7485-3
DOI 10.1007/978-1-4419-7485-3
Springer New York Dordrecht Heidelberg London

Library of Congress Control Number: 2010937185

Printed on acid-free paper

Springer is part of Springer Science+Business Media (www.springer.com)

For William and James

Acknowledgements

This book is the product of many years of teaching, doing and generally talking about the archaeological record of Australia's history, in the process of which we have accumulated numerous debts both general and specific. Colleagues around the country have been generous in allowing us access to dissertations and unpublished reports and we are grateful in particular to Peter Birt, Alister Bowen, Alasdair Brooks, Mary Casey, Adrienne Ellis, Sarah Hayes, Ted Higginbotham, Estelle Lazer, Jon Prangnell, Kate Quirk, Jeremy Smith, Lindsay Smith and Katrina Stankowski. Staff at the Albury City Museum, Birregurra and District Historical Society, the National Library of Australia, the State Library of South Australia and the State Library of Victoria have all helped with enquiries over the years.

Images have been provided by Tim Anson, Alister Bowen, David Frankel, Rodney Harrison, Geoff Hewitt, Greg Jackman, Maddy Maitri, Richard Mackay, Tim Murray and Mike Nash. Some or all of the text has been read in draft form by Alister Bowen, Martin Gibbs, Sarah Hayes, Edwina Kay, Beatrice Ngo, Alistair Paterson and Kate Quirk. Undergraduate classes past and present have provided the catalyst for developing many of the ideas presented here and have been the guinea pigs on whom we tried them out, and we have learned much from the honours and postgraduate students we have supervised.

Time for Susan to work on the manuscript has been provided by Outside Studies Program leave and teaching relief grants through the Faculty of Humanities and Social Sciences at La Trobe University, while Professor Brian Kooyman, Head of the Archaeology Department, University of Calgary, provided quiet space in which to write.

Teresa Krauss at Springer recognized the need for this kind of book and Graham Connah showed the way in the first place. We are grateful to Teresa and to Katherine Chabalko, also at Springer, for their patience and assistance. We are also grateful to the anonymous reviewers of the proposal whose suggestions have helped us to focus our discussion more clearly, even when we disagreed. At La Trobe University Ming Wei and Rudy Frank have produced and improved many images and maps for us over the years, including those reproduced here, and Katherine Katsoris has helped with logistics.

We continue to be inspired by ongoing conversations about history, archaeology and material culture with Penny Crook, David Frankel, Grace Karskens, Angela

Middleton, Tim Murray, Anita Smith, Ron Southern, Mark Staniforth and Linda Young. Our families and friends, some of whom have nurtured our love of the past and some of whom are perplexed by it, give us support and perspective while our children William and James are constant reminders that we do not own this past, we are merely custodians.

Susan Lawrence
Peter Davies

Contents

List of Figures

List of Tables

Chapter 1
Introduction

When people think of archaeology in Australia, they generally consider two things. One is the rich record of sites and artefacts that provide evidence of Aboriginal existence in this land for more than 40,000 years, the study of which has added immeasurably to general understanding of Australia's past. The other is the legacy of the Western historical tradition around the Mediterranean and in the Middle East, such as the wonders of Pompeii, the Acropolis, the pyramids and ancient Mesopotamia. Most people are surprised to learn that there is also another kind of archaeology with meaning for Australians, which is the archaeology of Australia since permanent white settlement began in 1788.

Sites, places and artefacts have been created continuously ever since and reflect every aspect of society from the first convict settlements through pastoral expansion, the gold rush, Federation, the First and Second World Wars and the persistence of Aboriginal culture. Even though there is abundant written documentation of this period, the archaeological record still has much to tell. This is particularly true where those involved were not literate or did not leave written evidence behind. In those cases much of what we know is based on documents created by outside observers, some of whom were sympathetic and others who were not. Most information about the convicts, for example, was written by colonial administrators or by the upper classes. There are few documents made by the convicts themselves, but there are many buildings and structures that they built, places where they lived and worked, and objects they used and lost or threw away. The same is true of Indigenous people after white settlement. White settlers recorded what they saw of Aboriginal society, which was often about its disintegration, but white observers only saw a fraction of Aboriginal life, much of which took place beyond the settlers' gaze. Other marginal groups have been similarly regarded. The poor, especially those resident in inner-city neighbourhoods that deteriorated into "slums" as the nineteenth century progressed, the Chinese who came in large numbers during the gold rush and even women and children of all social classes and backgrounds have left few first-hand written records but abundant material remains.

It might seem then that there is little to be learned from the archaeological study of well-documented groups like the middle classes and the colonial elites, but here too archaeological evidence can provide new perspectives. Documents record what

S. Lawrence, P. Davies, *An Archaeology of Australia Since 1788*,
Contributions To Global Historical Archaeology, DOI 10.1007/978-1-4419-7485-3_1,
© Springer Science+Business Media, LLC 2011

people thought they were doing and why they were doing it, but the physical remains provide evidence of what they actually did. This is particularly relevant in the realm of daily life, where the archaeological evidence preserves information about activities that were simply too mundane to seem worthy of documentation. The everyday routines of working, eating, playing, mending clothes and keeping clean, are seldom things that we deem fit to record when we are in the midst of them, yet over time there have been profound changes in all of these domains that are worthy of archaeological attention. Their familiarity, and the fact that change is often gradual, makes any shifts in daily routine seem minor, yet it is because they so profoundly shape many aspects of our lives that they are significant.

Just as many activities were too commonplace to record, some places were too ordinary to notice. Farmhouses and outbuildings, shops, mines, mills and factories were all just part of the landscape. They were built, rebuilt and removed to suit the needs of the day, and individually such places may have had little to distinguish them. Collectively, however, they represent ways of doing things that have often vanished or have been considerably altered. Every town once boasted a blacksmith's shop and livery stables, but these have now almost entirely disappeared, superseded by changing technology. The study of such places has much to reveal about those earlier societies and ways of being. In other cases, like the gold rush, the novelty of events and ways of doing things was widely recognised at the time, but settlement moved so quickly that it was difficult even for the authorities to document what was going on. Here the abandoned mine workings and cottages preserve valuable information about a unique period in world history.

For all these reasons people have begun to recognise that it is worth paying attention to the archaeology of the last 200 years of settlement in Australia. The study of these physical remains has been formalised as historical archaeology, a discipline that shares a great deal with more traditional archaeology and with the broader cultural heritage movement. This book presents an overview of the material evidence (artefacts, buildings and landscapes) of Australian post-contact history and the conclusions reached by historical archaeology. We have chosen to focus particularly on information that provides insight into the day-to-day life of Australians. Although industrial processes and technologies are included, our emphasis is on the environments of daily life, whether it be on pastoral stations, farms, whalers' camps, goldfields, emigrant ships, convict stations or urban neighbourhoods. The different conditions experienced by various groups of people are also considered, including rich and poor, convicts and their administrators, Aboriginal people, women, children and minority groups.

The themes included here reflect prominent issues in Australian history, the range and nature of archaeological studies that have been carried out and our own interest in daily lives and living conditions. Chapters have been structured to facilitate broad geographic and temporal coverage, while also reflecting the nature of the archaeology that has been done. Social themes such as gender, status, ethnicity and identity inform each chapter, reflecting our belief that these are integral to every part of life and cannot be separated from archaeologies of industry, urbanisation or culture contact.

The limitations of a single book inevitably mean that some material has been excluded. Although there are strong links between historical archaeology in Australia and New Zealand, and the two countries share much in terms of history and culture, material from New Zealand has for the most part not been included here. There are points, however, at which the history and especially the archaeology intersect in important ways, and in those cases we describe the New Zealand evidence. This is particularly relevant in the industries of sealing, whaling and gold mining, where there was considerable movement of people and technologies between the two countries and where archaeologists in New Zealand have been influential in shaping Australian practice.

Temporally, the book focuses on the period from 1788 to 1945. This reflects the beginnings of modern Australia on the one hand and what is old enough to be considered "archaeological" on the other hand. It takes as its starting point the beginning of permanent British settlement at Port Jackson (Sydney) and its end point the conclusion of the Second World War. The starting point thus excludes the period of European exploration, marked archaeologically by the Dutch shipwrecks in Western Australia and interaction between Aboriginal people and Macassan voyagers in northern Australia, although we make some reference to both. Ending with the Second World War reflects the rolling 50-year date used by some heritage agencies to determine what is covered by heritage legislation and also marks a watershed in Australian culture and society. While pre-war Australia was largely Anglo-Celtic and strongly British, the post-war period was characterised by the immigration of significant numbers of southern Europeans, and the nation became more culturally and politically oriented towards the United States. It seems appropriate to leave detailed discussions of the implications of these shifts to a future date, particularly as archaeologists are only just starting to grapple with the material evidence, and instead to foreshadow them in the concluding chapter.

The site-specific material evidence we discuss in this book is contextualised within wider themes and debates. Engagement with a range of contemporary discussions within Australian society and the international discipline of historical archaeology gives meaning to individual sites and case studies. The material presented is inherently part of the global processes of colonisation and the creation of settler societies, the industrial revolution, the development of mass consumer culture and the emergence of national identities. Archaeology is most relevant to modern society when it provides different perspectives on these themes. Our starting point, however, is the material evidence rather than historical narratives, and some issues of great concern to historians play a smaller role in this book because they have not yet been the focus of archaeological inquiry.

Community engagement with archaeology and with heritage places is widespread and demonstrates the continuing relevance of the past. Many of the places discussed here include ongoing public interpretation through signage, tours, websites and museum displays, and site tours and volunteer programmes are popular features of many excavations. Public engagement, however, is neither passive nor one-way. Community groups, both large and small, have been instrumental in driving the study and excavation of places they care about, from the work at Wybalenna in Tasmania (Birmingham 1992) and on Dutch shipwrecks in Western Australia (Green 1989), which were some of the earliest historical and maritime archaeology projects carried out in Australia, to more recent projects such as the excavation of sites associated with the bushranger Ned Kelly at Glenrowan in Victoria (Hayes 2009). On other occasions projects have generated heated public debate about the heritage values of particular places and the way that work should be carried out, debate that has altered the outcomes for those sites (e.g. Bickford 1991; Casey 2005b; Emmett 1996). More subtly, popular perceptions of the past have been forces that shape research projects and heritage management, elevating some themes, such as convictism and pastoralism, to prominence and consequently attracting research and resources, and pushing others, such as post-contact Aboriginal places, into the background (Ireland 1996, 2002; Jackman 2009). Archaeologists have not always been conscious enough of these influences and of the role of archaeology in challenging common assumptions about the past. In the chapters that follow this complex relationship will be apparent in many areas.

In writing this book we have drawn on a combination of published and unpublished sources. Journals such as *Australasian Historical Archaeology*, the *Bulletin of the Australasian Institute for Maritime Archaeology* and *Australian Archaeology*, together with numerous monographs and edited volumes, provide a wealth of published data. At the same time, high-quality research has been done as consultancy projects and higher degree dissertations. This material is often unknown to non-specialists, and we have tapped the insights of these sources as well to make them available to a wider audience. Technology is increasingly fulfilling its potential for distributing reports and dissertations, and we have relied extensively on internet sites and CD-ROMS for access to this material. Inevitably, however, there have been gaps in what we have been able to gain access to, and there will be sites and case studies that have been missed and which should have been included, and for this we apologise.

In the remainder of this chapter we present information that helps to contextualise the book. To begin with there is a very brief consideration of Australian history, aspects of which will be expanded upon in the relevant chapters. There then follows a review of the development of historical archaeology as a discipline in Australia, which explains some of the approaches and emphases in the work that has been carried out. First, however, there are some terms and usages that require explanation. Botany Bay was the initial landing place of Captain James Cook in his voyage of exploration in 1770, and that name was informally used for the penal colony established in 1788, although the official name of the colony was New South Wales. While the British first arrived at Botany Bay, they quickly realised it was unsuitable for a town and moved a few kilometres north to Port Jackson, now called Sydney Harbour, where the town of Sydney was established. When referring to the early years of the colony, Botany Bay, New South Wales, Port Jackson and Sydney were and are used interchangeably.

Until Federation in 1901 Australia was comprised of separate colonies, each of which was independently governed, and "Australia" as such did not exist. After 1901 Australia became a commonwealth, a term frequently used for the federal level of

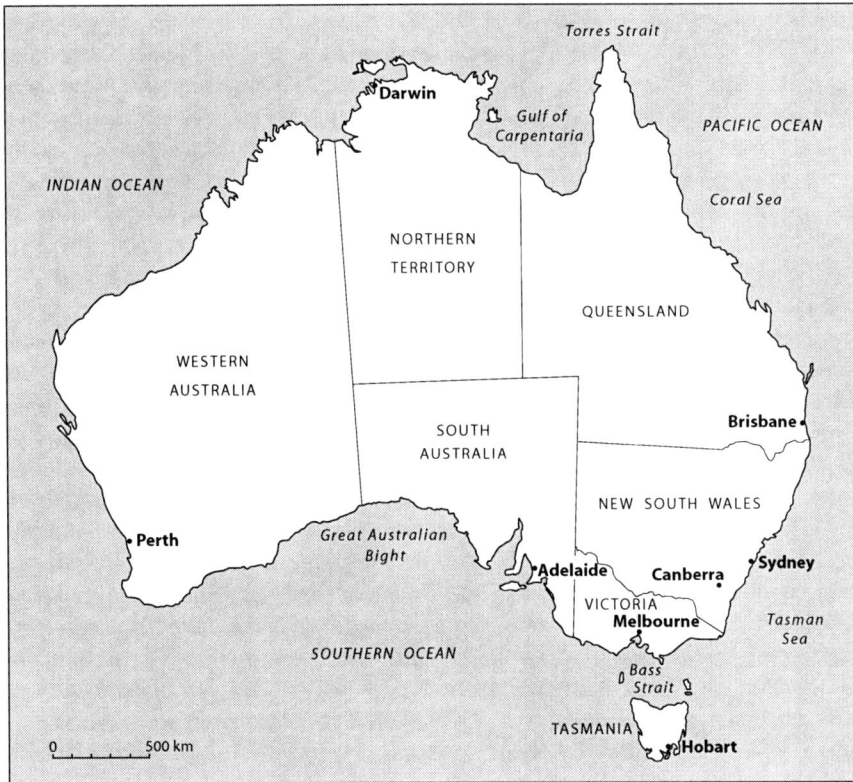

Fig. 1.1 Australian states and capital cities

government. The colonies kept their previous names but became states, and we have used the terms "colony" and "state" according to the period discussed. Each colony had a capital city which dominated that colony politically, economically and demographically (Fig. 1.1). Until the gold rush of the 1850s Sydney was the single most important colonial city, but from the second half of the nineteenth century its dominance was continually challenged by Melbourne. The capital of the new nation of Australia was a new city, Canberra, created specifically for the purpose, following the American model of Washington, DC. Canberra is located roughly halfway between the rival cities of Sydney and Melbourne in the Australian Capital Territory. What is now the state of Tasmania was originally known as Van Diemen's Land. The name Tasmania was adopted in 1853, when transportation of convicts to the colony was abolished, in the hope that the new name would erase the memory of the convict association. We refer to Van Diemen's Land in terms of pre-1853 historical events and to Tasmania for the later period and in relation to archaeological places. The Northern Territory became a separate jurisdiction in 1911 after its separation from South Australia. "Australasia" refers here to Australia and New Zealand and reflects the close historical ties between the two countries.

When referring to the Indigenous people of Australia, it is correct to capitalise the word Aboriginal, whereas the lowercase aboriginal refers to indigenous peoples more generally. When referring to the non-indigenous inhabitants of the continent several terms have been used, including "British" and "white". All of the Australian colonies were established by the British, and thus most colonists were British, encompassing a mix of English, Scottish, Irish, Welsh and Cornish migrants in different proportions at different times for a variety of reasons. Being from Britain, most colonists and their Australian-born offspring were also white. Both "British" and "white", however, are convenient shorthand for a population that was from the beginning much more mixed. African-Americans from the Caribbean were among the British subjects transported to the colonies as convicts, while other African-Americans along with Pacific Islanders and Azores Islanders came as crew on whaling ships. Significant groups of German settlers went to the eastern colonies in the 1840s, and following the discovery of gold in the 1850s large numbers of people, mainly men, came from southern China. Other European migrants included Poles, Swiss and Italians who also came and stayed as a result of the gold rush. From the 1860s large groups of Melanesians were "blackbirded" or brought as quasi-legal indentured labourers to work on sugar plantations in Queensland. Despite the local significance of all these groups, "whiteness" and "Britishness" overwhelmingly dominated Australian society demographically and culturally until well after the Second World War. From the 1890s until the 1960s this status was formally enshrined in the White Australia Policy, legislation explicitly intended to restrict and control non-white immigration. While united by colour, however, religion created a significant divide in Australian society until the 1960s, with mainly Irish Catholics on one side and Protestants on the other.

Australia on the World Stage

The white settlement of Australia has been a quintessentially global, modern process. At every stage local developments have been facilitated by new international discoveries and inventions, and in turn events in Australia have played a role on the world stage, driving large-scale population movements, the international exchange of information and technology, and the production and distribution of commodities. However, while British colonisation was deeply embedded in global processes, the arrival of the British in 1788 did not suddenly liberate a lost continent. Australia has always been closely integrated with the world around it, even if this has not always been recognised by western Europeans. It has close neighbours in the Torres Strait Islands, New Guinea and the Indonesian archipelago and shares much with them in terms of their human, plant and animal populations. Through them Australia is linked directly to south-east Asia. The oceans that isolate Australia have always provided highways along which life has travelled, from the first plants and animals to the earliest human inhabitants and generations of subsequent visitors and settlers over the millennia. White settlement changed the primary focus of engagement from island south-east Asia to Western Europe and then North America and substantially increased the degree of external engagement, but these changes can be seen as part of a long continuum of human and natural history on this continent.

The first Australians probably arrived here sometime between 40,000 and 60,000 years ago (Flood 2004:9). Lower sea levels during the last glacial period meant that Papua New Guinea and Tasmania were then part of a larger southern continent called Sahul. The new arrivals nevertheless had to travel across 100 kilometres of open sea to reach Australia, an extraordinary achievement and one that would not be equalled elsewhere for thousands of years. The best available evidence indicates that the ancestors of the Aborigines first spread around the coastal margins and up the inland rivers, reaching southern Tasmania around 36,000 years ago, before finally spreading across the dry interior of the continent. Aboriginal people developed a rich artistic and ritual life centred on the Dreaming, the stories that encoded law and tradition, with subsistence based on hunting and gathering. With some regional variation and alteration as population numbers increased and climatic conditions changed, this way of life was so successful that it survived intact until white colonisation.

By the time the British arrived in Australia they had extensive experience in dealing with indigenous people, gained in North America, India, the Caribbean, West Africa and elsewhere. Over 200 years they had developed clear, if informal, guidelines on how land was to be acquired (Banner 2007:10–20). Indigenous ownership of land was acknowledged, and it was expected that this land would have to be purchased, however duplicitously, if colonisation was to proceed. Land could be taken by conquest, but ultimately this was assumed to be more costly than outright purchase, and the latter was preferred. Contrary to this policy, the British government made a calculated decision that in Australia the land could simply be taken, and so the instructions issued to Governor Arthur Phillip for establishing the colony of New South Wales explicitly excluded any reference to purchasing land. The decision was made based on evidence about the Aboriginal people provided by the explorers James Cook and Joseph Banks, the only Englishmen to have visited the continent, and on evaluating that evidence against previous experience. According to Banks and Cook, Aboriginal people did not cultivate the land, making it difficult, but not impossible, for the British to recognise ownership, but equally importantly, they apparently did not understand trade, and therefore could not be negotiated with. Further, they were few in number and had no significant weapons so they did not constitute a military threat and would not be able to defend themselves. Australia was effectively empty, and the legal doctrine of *terra nullius* governed all subsequent acquisition of land on the continent. The property rights of Aboriginal people were not recognised and so they were dispossessed of their land (Attwood 2009:72–101). In the wholesale transfer of lands from indigenous to white ownership that was occurring all over the world at this time, global experience provided precedent, but local conditions dictated outcomes.

Much of this book is the story of the exchange of people, plants, animals, ideas and goods between Australia and the rest of the world after 1788. While the historical figures and the sequence of local events may be unfamiliar to non-Australians, the broader context of exploration, industrialisation and colonisation are themes that were being played out in many parts of the world at the same time. Migration and the emergence of new societies and national identities, interactions between settlers and indigenous peoples, technology transfer and adaptation and environmental influences are all areas in which comparisons can be drawn between Australia and other white settler societies such as the United States, Canada, South Africa and New Zealand (Belich 2009; Griffiths and Robin 1997). These show the closest parallels and may be the most illuminating, but there are also potential gains to be made from comparison with Hispanic societies in Central and South America and with parts of the world where Western hegemony was more successfully resisted such as the Islamic world, China and India. Finally, Australia's closest historical ties were with Great Britain, and comparison with that culture, and Western Europe more generally, necessarily provides context for Australian history but also provides a prism for exploring the nineteenth century in the metropolitan centre of a global empire.

Settlement generally was a manifestation of broad global themes, but specific events also had very direct links to what was happening elsewhere. Both the beginning and the end of convict transportation, for example, were such events. Transportation to Australia began because of the American Revolution in 1775, when the 13 British colonies in North America severed ties with Britain, which had included the transportation of convicts. British authorities needed a new solution and they found it at Botany Bay (Frost 1994). Transportation ended (against the wishes of many settlers) partly because of changes in penal reform philosophies in Britain, partly because of the Abolition or anti-slavery movement and partly because of the discovery of gold in California (Hirst 1983). In the 1830s and 1840s penal reformers wanted to see incarceration and closer supervision of prisoners in order to reform their behaviour, rather than punishing them with banishment and hard labour, and Australia was inappropriate in this new model. British Abolitionists agitating for the end of slavery in the United States saw uncomfortable parallels with the convict system and created an environment in which forced labour was no longer socially acceptable. The discovery of gold in California in 1848 was followed soon after by the discovery of gold in Australia, and as goldseekers rushed to the colonies, providing a free ticket for felons seemed like a poor deterrent to crime.

The Australian gold rush that started in 1851 was thus another event with obvious links to events elsewhere (Blainey 1978; Fetherling 1997). Many Australians had gone to California in search of gold, and the observant ones noticed similarities between the landscapes of California and Australia. They returned home and began prospecting, with the result that gold was discovered near Bathurst in New South Wales in February 1851 and a few months later at several locations in Victoria, all discoveries made by the returning 49'ers. These were rich surface alluvial finds and their discovery triggered an enormous gold rush that redistributed the existing population and drew hundreds of thousands of migrants from all over the world, fundamentally changing the direction of Australian history. While the gold rush was sparked by outside events, it also influenced events elsewhere. The most direct was in New Zealand, where experienced Australian diggers discovered gold at Otago on the South Island in 1861. The rush there, while smaller than those in California and

Australia, had a similar effect on migration, the economy and the course of New Zealand history. Discoveries around Australia in the 1870s, 1880s and 1890s kept mining skills and gold fever alive for another generation, ultimately playing a role in the great South African and Klondike rushes at the end of the century.

By the 1850s the Australian continent was firmly British, but this was the result of decades of judicious planting of colonial outposts around the coast, directly stimulated by imperial ambition and frequently as counter-moves in response to actions by imperial rivals. Botany Bay was a convenient solution to the convict problem, but it also served to establish British territorial claims and encouraged trade to reinvigorate a British economy devastated by war with the American colonies (Frost 2003). Captain James Cook, who charted the east coast of Australia in 1770 as part of his Pacific voyaging, was one of a long line of European explorers to the region. The first Europeans to see and record Australia were Dutch sailors who explored the Indian Ocean early in the seventeenth century. From 1606 Dirck Hartog and others charted the north and west coasts of the continent, and in 1642 Abel Tasman and his crew sailed further east, becoming the first Europeans to see Tasmania and New Zealand, and leaving Dutch names on the charts in their wake.

Although Australia seemed to have little to offer them, the Dutch were a major force in south-east Asia at that time. The Dutch empire was at its height, with major colonies on the southern tip of Africa at the Cape of Good Hope and in Sri Lanka and Indonesia (Batavia, now Java). The real power in the Pacific, however, was the Spanish Empire. Spain had claimed the Pacific in the Treaty of Tordesillas of 1494, and while their main activity was further to the north in the Philippines, they also sent out exploration parties throughout Melanesia at the end of the sixteenth century and to Australia and the Pacific at the end of the eighteenth century.

By the middle of the eighteenth century Britain was ready to challenge the Spanish in the Pacific. Cook's voyages were a deliberate and considered part of British strategy, and transporting convicts provided a convenient excuse for establishing a colony that gave Britain direct access to the Pacific. The new colony was settled just in time, because France was also beginning to challenge Spanish claims, and a party of French explorers led by Jean-François de La Pérouse arrived at Port Jackson only days after the convicts in the First Fleet landed in January 1788. Although ultimately overtaken by the French Revolution, France continued to be interested in the region, sending another exploration party under Bruny D'Entrecasteaux in the 1790s that charted much of the coast of Van Diemen's Land. As this coincided with the discovery of Bass Strait between Van Diemen's Land and the mainland, a discovery made as a result of the wrecking of the merchant ship *Sydney Cove*, the British were again eager to assert their claims to territory. More convicts were quickly dispatched southwards, and after an unsuccessful attempt to settle at Port Phillip Bay (later Melbourne), settlements were established in Van Diemen's Land in the south (Hobart) and north (Launceston) within months of each other in 1803–1804 (Lawrence and Shepherd 2006:76–77; Robson 1983).

Other settlements were also established around the coast to secure imperial interests. Renewed Dutch activity in south-east Asia following the end of the Napoleonic Wars prompted another burst of colonising activity (Allen 2008:105–110). Various outposts were established along the north coast at Melville Island and on the Cobourg Peninsula between 1824 and 1849. Unlike the southern settlements, however, which were intended as colonies, these were military establishments. They were placed in strategic locations to control the surrounding waterways, were fortified and were staffed almost exclusively with military personnel. The heat and humidity, however, made them inhospitable to the British and most were short-lived, being abandoned once British sovereignty had been established.

Britain gradually outpaced its imperial rivals and colonial settlement continued to expand. The colony of New South Wales spread northwards to Moreton Bay (Brisbane) by 1824, where the separate colony of Queensland was declared in 1859. Van Diemen's Land became a separate colony from New South Wales in 1825, and on the west coast of the continent an independent British colony was established at the Swan River, later Perth, in 1829. A few years later, in 1836, the colony of South Australia was established with its capital at Adelaide. Victoria was settled from two directions, as an offshoot of the colonies in New South Wales and Van Diemen's Land. The government in New South Wales sent a party to establish Melbourne on Port Phillip Bay following overland exploration in 1835, but the officials found a group of entrepreneurs from Van Diemen's Land already in occupation. The authorities eventually prevailed and the Port Phillip District was formed as an extension of New South Wales before being granted self-government (as the colony of Victoria) in 1851.

Fifty years after the first British colonisation of Australia's east coast, imperial strategy formulated in the context of global rivalries with other European powers had resulted in a process of settlement that was quite different to that which occurred in North America. Instead of spreading gradually outwards from the starting point of Sydney until the continent was filled, the British claimed the coastal fringe almost simultaneously, leaving a thin line of occupation along the shore with only limited use or exploration of the inland. As a consequence, the moving frontier that had such a dominant place in American history played a much smaller role in Australia.

While external events and forces have influenced processes here, Australia has also been a laboratory for social experimentation, the results of which have been exported to the world. The convict system is probably the best-known example of this. From the beginning the Australian colonies were used to trial new philosophies of penal reform. One of the first model prisons built on the revolutionary plan of the radial penitentiary was constructed in Launceston in 1832 (Casella 2002:29; Kerr 1984:94). The apparent success of Australian transportation encouraged French authorities to try a similar scheme, and when they set up their convict colony on New Caledonia in the Pacific they adopted many of the systems that had been in use in the Australian colonies (Smith and Buckley 2007). Another area for experimentation was colonial settlement itself. Social reformer Edward Gibbon Wakefield had devised a colonisation scheme in which the carefully regulated sale of land would both fund further migration and create a society which replicated the English class system. Setting the sale price for land sufficiently high would restrict the number of landowners, while the assisted migrants would form a class of free labourers. British parliament approved of the scheme and established the colony of South Australia for its implementation. While the colony eventually succeeded, Wakefield's system did not provide sufficient income to fund the migration he intended. Despite this failure, authorities supported the establishment of similar Wakefieldian settlements in New Zealand.

Democratic institutions were also established early in the Australian colonies, and their development later served as a model for other countries to emulate. Universal male suffrage, for example, was achieved in 1855 in South Australia, 1857 in Victoria and 1858 in New South Wales, many years before it was established in Great Britain. Votes were cast using the secret ballot, a method that came to be known as the "Australian" ballot in England and the United States and which was eventually adopted as a standard feature of democratic elections around the world (Wright 1992:20). Payment of parliamentary representatives was also established in Victoria in 1870, which permitted working men to stand for office. In South Australia, women were granted the right to vote in local government elections as early as 1861 and to vote and stand for parliament in 1894, one of the earliest jurisdictions in the world to achieve this.

In the twentieth century Australian participation in a series of overseas wars further altered Australian perspectives at home and abroad. Although colonial troops had been sent to New Zealand in the 1860s to fight in the war between Maori and British settlers and to Sudan in 1885 after the death of General Gordon at Khartoum, the first Australian troops to fight overseas were those sent to South Africa to fight in the South African (Boer) War of 1899–1902. This was but a prelude to the First World War (1914–1918) in which hundreds of thousands of Australian men enlisted. They served with distinction on the Western Front in France and Belgium, but for most Australians the First World War is most closely associated with the battle for Gallipoli, in Turkey. Here in 1915 Australian and New Zealand Army Corps (ANZAC) units served alongside British troops in one of the allies' most ignominious defeats. The enormous casualties brought home the realities of war to a country previously without experience of large-scale armed conflict, while the sense of British betrayal and abandonment contributed to an emerging sense of Australian nationalism and identity (Chapter 12). The "Anzac spirit" of mateship and courage under adversity is still a powerful ideology and continues to be used by some to characterise Australia even today.

The Second World War (1939–1945) also quickly entangled Australians as part of the Allied Forces, but for the first time it also saw Australia itself under direct threat. German ships patrolled the coastline, Japanese midget submarines attacked Sydney Harbour and Japanese planes bombed northern Australia. Australian soldiers fighting in Papua New Guinea to slow the Japanese advance were directly defending their own country only a few kilometres to the south. As in the First World War, Australians felt betrayed by the British government which was slow to release Australian troops from service in North Africa and the Mediterranean in order to defend Australia. With the Japanese bombing of Pearl Harbour, the United States entered the war and took a more active interest in the Pacific. The United States used Australia as a staging post for its Pacific battles, basing thousands of troops here and establishing headquarters for its commander, General Douglas MacArthur, in Melbourne. Combined with the sense of British betrayal, closer contact with the Americans brought about by the war was decisive in turning Australia's attention towards the United States, introducing a new source of influence that would reshape Australian cultural and economic life for the rest of the century.

Historical Archaeology in Australia

There have been many reviews of the development of historical archaeology in Australia (e.g. Egloff 1994; Ireland 2002, 2004; Ireland and Casey 2006; Jack 2006; Mulvaney 1996; Paterson and Wilson 2000). We provide here a brief summary, with further discussion of the intellectual development of the field presented in the relevant chapters. The discipline of historical archaeology in Australia began in the 1960s. As part of the general expansion of universities at the time, a new generation of young academics, most of them trained in the United Kingdom, were appointed to posts in archaeology departments around the country. Several, including Judy Birmingham at the University of Sydney, Bill Culican at the University of Melbourne and John Mulvaney at the Australian National University in Canberra, initiated excavations at historic sites, mainly to provide excavation experience and dissertation topics for their students (Allen 2008; Birmingham 1992; Culican and Taylor 1975; Macknight 1976; Mulvaney 1996). The choice of sites was circumstantial but all reflected themes that were to be of lasting interest. Two of the sites, James King's pottery at Irrawang in New South Wales and the Fossil Beach Cement Works near Melbourne, were industrial sites, while others, including Wybalenna in Tasmania and Port Essington and Macassan sites in the Northern Territory, focused on what is now called post-contact archaeology. In the same period, museum-based maritime archaeologists in Western Australia were beginning the excavation of seventeenth-century Dutch shipwrecks off the Australian coast.

Interest was strongest in Sydney, where the National Trust had established a Committee for Industrial Archaeology and where students formed the Sydney University Archaeology Society. Both of these initiatives resulted in the recording and excavation of many historic sites in New South Wales. The Australian Society for Historical Archaeology (ASHA) was formed in Sydney in 1970, 4 years before prehistorians formed the Australian Archaeological Association (Jack 2006:23). In 1974 Judy Birmingham introduced the first undergraduate subject on historical archaeology in the country, which she did with the help of Ian Jack, a historian who was also an ASHA member and Dean of the Arts Faculty at Sydney University, and with geographer Dennis Jeans. Interest was also growing in other parts of the country. In Victoria, the government established the Victoria Archaeological Survey in 1975 and its Director, Peter Coutts, a New Zealander who had completed his Ph.D. on New Zealand colonial whaling sites, immediately began the survey and excavation of early colonial sites in Victoria including Captain Mills' Cottage, Corinella and Sorrento (Coutts 1981, 1984, 1985).

The mainly British origins of these early figures were influential in shaping the new discipline. They came from backgrounds in Classical and Near Eastern archaeology and from history, rather than from anthropology, and while they were influenced by the New Archaeology (Ireland and Casey 2006:12), the approaches and methodologies they developed strongly reflected their British training. Open-area excavations, field survey of standing structures, aerial photography and the methods of finds analysis used are all features of the discipline here that have their origins in British archaeology. From the beginning, however, there was also close contact with historical archaeologists in the United States, where the discipline was also slowly emerging at that time, and the influence of American develop-ments in theory and method specific to historical archaeology was also felt. Another characteristic of historical archaeology as it developed in Australia was its multi-disciplinary nature. Participants in early fieldwork conducted by the University of Sydney included historians, geographers and soil scientists, while elsewhere architectural historians and engineers were also involved.

During the 1970s there was a growing public recognition of the value of historic places. In 1973–1974 the Federal Government directed the Hope Inquiry to report on the nature of Australia's heritage, and several archaeologists participated, including Judy Birmingham and John Mulvaney. This led to the formation of a committee of archaeologists to advise the government on the formation of what was to become the Australian Heritage Commission and the inclusion of historic sites on the Register of the National Estate (Mulvaney 1996:6). Many of these same individuals were influ-ential in drawing up the provisions of the Burra Charter, the Australia ICOMOS document that sets out guidelines for the conservation and management of historic places. The passage of Heritage Acts in Victoria (1972), New South Wales (1977) and South Australia (1978) recognised the importance of heritage at a state level and resulted in the rapid growth of cultural heritage management archaeology (Ireland 2002). In Tasmania there were numerous studies of convict sites and provision was made for long-term conservation funding at Port Arthur, which included the employ-ment of an historical archaeologist. Summer field schools at Port Arthur throughout the 1980s trained another generation of archaeologists from around the country, while their procedures manual (Davies and Buckley 1987) provided guidelines that were widely used. Although Tasmania did not have heritage legislation until 1995, several historical archaeologists were employed at the Tasmanian Parks and Wildlife Service from the 1980s onwards. In Queensland a strong group of scholars based at James Cook University documented the industrial and architectural heritage of the Palmer River goldfield (Bell 1987).

Although practitioners were still few, research increased, most of it produced by people working in heritage management (Egloff 1994). In addition to the growing number of conservation studies and consultants' reports, ASHA began produc-ing a newsletter in 1970 which published research on artefacts, field methods and reports on projects and also published monographs such as Maureen Byrne's (1976) work at Ross in Tasmania, Eleanor Crosby's (1978) work at Fort Dundas in the Northern Territory and Marjorie Graham's (1979) research on Australian ceramics. Judy Birmingham, Ian Jack and Dennis Jeans collaborated on two books docu-menting industrial heritage (Birmingham et al. 1979, 1983), and Graham Connah began publishing research on pastoralism (Connah et al. 1978). Half a dozen

Ph.D. dissertations were completed in the 1970s and early 1980s, most of which were published in full or in part (Allen 1973; Holmes 1983; Macknight 1976). By 1983 there was sufficient activity to support a journal and the first issue of *The Australian Journal of Historical Archaeology* (later *Australasian Historical Archaeology*) appeared, and in 1988 Graham Connah published a comprehensive synthesis of the field.

By the late 1980s historical archaeology was well-established within academia. Graham Connah, a British-trained Africanist, introduced the subject at the University of New England in Armidale, and it was also introduced at La Trobe University in Melbourne with the appointment of Sydney graduate Tim Murray to the country's first dedicated post in historical archaeology. New doctoral research was undertaken at these and other institutions, and by the 1990s there were also historical archaeology students at the Australian National University, and new posts in historical and maritime archaeology at Flinders University in Adelaide, at the University of Western Australia and the University of Queensland.

Consulting archaeology was also well established by this time due to the growth in heritage legislation. "Big Digs" were becoming more common, following on from the large and well-publicised excavations in Sydney at Hyde Park Barracks and First Government House in the early 1980s. In 1988 Melbourne saw the excavation of much of a city block in the downtown core with the first part of the Little Lon project, the largest excavation in Australia up to that time (Murray 2006). Urban excavations were held in Adelaide at the Queen's Theatre and Destitute Asylum sites and in central Hobart. Sydney had the first of many "Big Digs" in 1994 when the Cumberland/Gloucester Streets site was excavated in the Rocks. The pace of urban development in Sydney particularly, and the integration between heritage and planning legislation, means that large-scale urban excavations in Sydney are now regular events.

The beginning of the twenty-first century has been marked by continuing consolidation of the discipline. There have been ever-increasing numbers of undergraduates and the completion of numerous Ph.D.s from all parts of the country. Although many projects remain as grey literature, consulting projects continue to produce important research. Publication of all kinds has intensified and numerous monographs and edited books have joined the journals and reports on library shelves, while Australian sites and projects regularly feature in international journals and edited collections. In addition to the increasing quantity of work done, it is also apparent that the field has become more methodologically and theoretically sophisticated. Large urban sites are excavated routinely and practitioners have become expert in dealing with the logistical issues involved, developing streamlined processes for excavation, record-keeping and the documentation of finds. The analysis of finds from rescue projects continues to be problematic with insufficient funding still to be dealt with, but here too progress has been made. In some cases older collections have been re-analysed with significant results (e.g. Crook et al. 2005; Hayes 2007; Murray and Crook 2005) while other practitioners have demonstrated that it is possible to combine comprehensive and meaningful finds analysis with commercial viability (Carney 1999a; Casey 1999, 2004, 2005a, b). Just as importantly, there is now a large body of research on artefacts from Australian sites, ranging from bottles and ceramics to bricks, buttons and toys, and this is drawn upon by students and experts alike.

The themes and questions being investigated have broadened significantly as more people have entered the field and as basic methodologies have been established. In addition to describing the kinds of sites, landscapes and artefacts that can be found in Australia, researchers have used the data to investigate issues of culture contact, gender and ethnicity. A range of different theoretical approaches have been used and are now commonplace, including domination and resistance, style and ideology, creolisation, consumer theory, gentility and respectability, and technology transfer and adaptation. Studies of gender and of indigenous contact have become important areas of research and have profoundly influenced the ways in which historical archaeology is carried out. With consolidation has come increased confidence as a discipline, and the once determinedly separate organisations of ASHA, AIMA (the Australasian Institute for Maritime Archaeology) and AAA (the Australian Archaeological Association) now regularly gather for joint conferences.

By the late 1990s all Australian states had enacted heritage legislation that recognised historical archaeological sites, although the degree of protection afforded under these laws varies considerably. In Victoria, for example, there is blanket protection for all archaeological sites more than 50 years old, while in other states protection is applied to "significant" archaeological sites. As the legislation has been increasingly incorporated into local planning provisions, the amount of archaeological work has also increased, resulting in literally thousands of surveys, assessments, management plans and excavations around Australia. This process has occurred in other countries as well and has led to much debate about the role of public archaeology, heritage management and the construction of knowledge about the human past. It also reflects, however, changing attitudes to both tangible and intangible heritage, those things and places from the past that we value the most. Historical archaeology speaks to that yearning to know where we come from. It is an expression of our ongoing fascination with the past, revealing forgotten details about people's lives, about things familiar and strange, mundane and exotic. As practitioners of archaeology, we stand at the threshold between the present and the past, privileged to explore and interpret the physical remains of so many things lost, abandoned and forgotten, as the basis for re-imagining past individuals, families and communities. We hope that this book provides a worthy testament to these humble riches of Australia's past.

Chapter 2
Convict Origins

Convicts have an iconic status in Australian history. Many modern Australians take pride in claiming descent from convict ancestors, although this was not always the case in the past. Convict ancestry provides a colourful and immediate link with the origins of white settlement in this young, settler society, and for many non-Australians, convictism is the one part of Australian colonial history with which they are familiar. The convict past that lives in popular understanding, however, is often at odds with scholarly research on the subject. There are many stereotypes of convict life that appear and reappear in popular culture. Typically, convicts were almost exclusively male and always adults. Female convicts are imagined as prostitutes, or at least sexually promiscuous. Most convicts, both male and female, were transported as a result of manifestly unjust punishment for trivial acts such as theft of food or clothing that a harsh and inequitable society forced them to commit in order to survive. Once in Australia, convicts were locked in gaols and barracks, kept in chains and flogged frequently and horrifically. They were so brutalised that they resorted to anything in order to escape, including mutiny, cannibalism and suicide.

These stereotypes are perpetuated in best-selling books, television programmes and even in museum displays and interpretive centres around the country. There is undeniably some truth in this version of the convict past. Most convicts were adult men, some had committed trivial offences and some were confined in barracks and locked in dehumanising solitary cells. Brutal floggings were endured, and there were instances of mutiny, suicide and even cannibalism. This is not, however, the whole story of Australian convictism, nor is it the only story. As a range of archaeologists and historians have now demonstrated, for most convicts their experience of transportation was quite different, and for a variety of reasons (Casella 2002; Connah 2007; Hirst 1983; Karskens 1997, 2009; Nicholas 1988; Oxley 1996).

What happened to convicts in Australia depended first on their age and sex. Almost 25,000 women were transported to the colonies, comprising almost 16 percent of the total of 157,261 convicts sent out in the 80 years the system operated. Young boys were also transported as convicts, some as young as 9 or 10 years of age (Fabian and Loh 1980:23; Holden 1999:205). Convict experience also depended on the period when individuals were transported. The convict system, and Australian society, had changed greatly by the time transportation ended in 1868 from what it

S. Lawrence, P. Davies, *An Archaeology of Australia Since 1788*,
Contributions To Global Historical Archaeology, DOI 10.1007/978-1-4419-7485-3_2,
© Springer Science+Business Media, LLC 2011

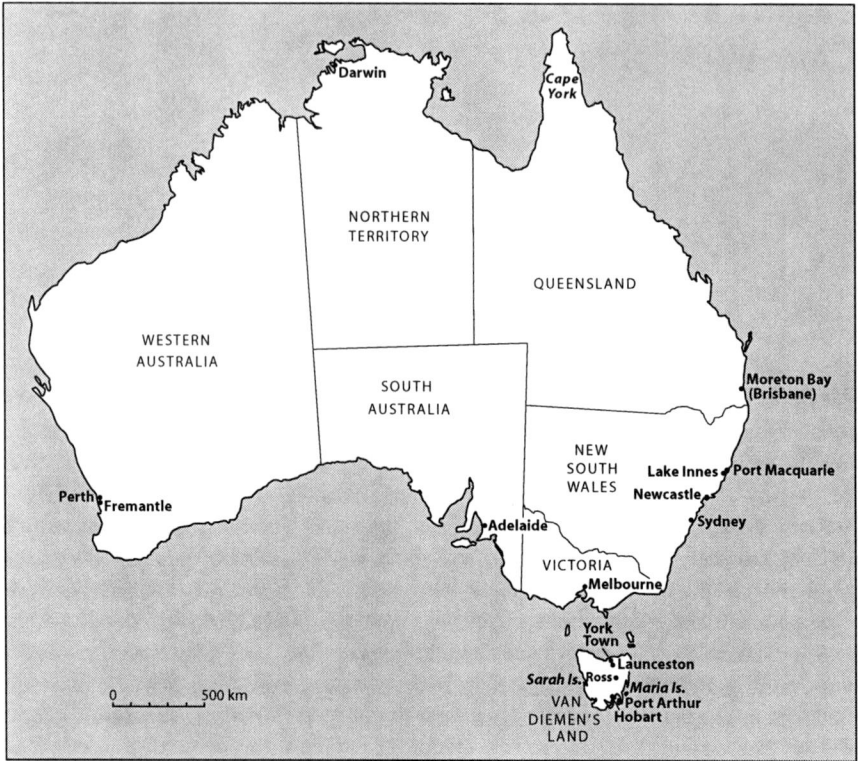

Fig. 2.1 Location map of archaeological sites relating to convicts in the Australian colonies

had been in 1788. Convict experience was also determined by which colony individuals were sent to, as New South Wales, Van Diemen's Land, Western Australia and Queensland all accepted convicts (Fig. 2.1). Finally, and perhaps most significantly, it depended on their own actions once they arrived. The worst and most stereotypical experiences, the chain gangs, solitary cells and floggings, were punishments reserved only for those who committed further crimes or offences in the colonies. The majority of convicts were not subjected to any of them, instead serving out their sentences, obtaining tickets-of-leave or pardons and becoming integrated with the rest of society. Archaeological evidence of convictism spans both of these extremes and much of the middle ground, from the chain gangs along the Great North Road and the solitary cells of Sarah Island, to the assigned servants' quarters at Lake Innes, the boys' prison at Port Arthur's Point Puer, the Female Factory at Ross and the convict-owned homes and businesses in Sydney's Rocks.

Convict places have a high profile in Australia's heritage landscape. There is a strong attachment to places where convicts lived or worked, both among those who have convict ancestors and those who do not. Public interest in convict places has been a significant factor in their preservation and community involvement has taken many forms. It has created powerful lobby groups that saved the remains of sites such as First Government House and the convict-built road at the Conservatorium of Music in Sydney. Convict tourism at Port Arthur, Sarah Island and other places in Tasmania makes heritage an important part of the local economy, ensuring ongoing political support for heritage conservation. On the central coast of New South Wales local community organisations have taken responsibility for management of the convict-built Great North Road, and in 2008 the Australian Government nominated 12 convict sites for World Heritage status (Australian Government 2008). All of these instances demonstrate the different ways in which the wider community interacts with archaeological sites.

Crime, Punishment and Penal Reform

For the first 30 years of Australian colonisation the transportation system was based on traditional understandings of crime and punishment. Gaols were for debtors and vagrants rather than criminals. Punishment for crime was directed at the body of the criminal, and sentences of death, transportation or flogging were carried out quickly with little need for long-term incarceration (Ignatieff 1978:24). Once in Australia, convicts were made to work, and the system was directed towards that end. It was their value as workers that made convicts desirable in the colonies and which led to both contemporary and subsequent identification of transportation as a system of slavery. Nevertheless, although convicts endured forced labour, they were not slaves. They retained significant rights in law, including the right to own and transfer property, their sentences were generally of limited duration and their children, unlike those of slaves, were born free (Nicholas 1988:111–113).

Initially all convicts worked for the government, clearing and cultivating land and building roads and public buildings, and they lived in the community in private accommodation (Hirst 1983). After military officers were granted land and free settlers arrived, convicts were also assigned to private masters. Whether in government or private service convict workers quickly managed to make task-work rather than set hours the norm, enabling them to complete their day's work early and leaving afternoons and entire days at the end of the week free for their own purposes. The enterprising used this time to take extra work for payment or to build up their own homes and businesses, while others used it for leisure, with many complaints about gambling and drinking. If new offences such as theft or drunkenness were committed in the colony, the punishment was flogging or the withdrawal of rations.

As Robert Hughes (1986) has graphically reminded us, flogging was a cruel and inhuman treatment. Historian John Hirst argued, however, that flogging was ineffective as a deterrent and noted that it consistently failed to produce either obedience or hard work (Hirst 1983:51–53). Stephen Nicholas (1988:180–183) has placed the flogging of convicts in the context of how workers were generally treated at the time, when whipping was widespread in England and soldiers and sailors in particular were subjected to floggings both worse and more frequent than those administered to convicts. However brutal, inefficient or commonplace, flogging and the lash was another manifestation of the immediate and physical emphasis on the body

Fig. 2.2 Interior of Crank Mill, Norfolk Island, installed ca.1838 as a punishment site for male convicts in irons (photo P. Davies)

as the site of punishment which characterised responses to criminality at this time (Fig. 2.2). Transportation was an extension of this philosophy, where the criminal was physically removed, or banished, from the wider social body.

Transportation had co-existed with flogging for many years. More than 50,000 British convicts were transported to the American colonies between 1640 and 1776, but this practice ended following the American Declaration of Independence. Alternative sites of transportation for British convicts included Barbados, Belize and Ghana (Bogle 2008:7–19). In deciding to send convicts to Australia it was the location, not the punishment, which was new. Moreover, the new location offered clear imperial advantages beyond simply dealing with the prisoners, a point strongly argued by historians Alan Frost (1994:42–86) and Geoffrey Blainey (1966:16–37). New South Wales was selected in preference to the south-west coast of Africa, which was the other candidate for a replacement penal colony, partly because the former appeared to offer a supply of badly needed naval stores such as timber for masts and flax for sails and because it was always the British government's intention that transportation would be, in the words of the Home Office, "reciprocally beneficial" to both convicts and the State (Frost 1994:43). In addition to the immediate economic benefits, New South Wales also offered longer-term benefits that were strategic as well as economic (Frost 2003). As part of general imperial ambition in the region, an Australian colony afforded the British government a base for furthering its interests in the Pacific and on the west coast of the Americas, countering long-standing Spanish claims and more recent French interest. Many British mercantile interests also intended that in the longer term an Australian colony would provide a new base for trading into India and China, thus opening up a trade long monopolised by the British East India Company (Broadbent et al. 2003).

For several decades after 1788 the transportation system in Australia continued in the established manner, with convicts living largely in the community and labouring at tasks for government and private employers. By the 1820s, however, the growing prison reform movement in Britain led to changes in the way male, female and eventually child convicts were treated. At the heart of the changes lay a shift in focus from punishing the body of the convict to reforming his or her mind and behaviour. Inspired in part by the philosophies of Jeremy Bentham and John Howard, and in part by the morality of evangelical Christianity, reformers believed that the appropriate physical environment would help to direct the hearts and minds of offenders into other and more socially acceptable paths. Specifically, convicts both in the United Kingdom and in the Australian colonies were to be held within purpose-built accommodation that would enable segregation by age, gender and the seriousness of the crime. They were to be employed within the facility as much as possible, and they were to be observed and monitored at all times.

To achieve the necessary level of surveillance, segregation and discipline, it was believed by some that prisons should be built along the lines proposed in the late eighteenth century by the prison reformer John Howard (1973), the architect William Blackburn and by the philosopher Jeremy Bentham in his *Panopticon* (Bentham 1962). In the panoptical design prisoners were to be housed in individual cells arranged around a central observation area. This central guardhouse permitted surveillance of any individual prisoner at any time, to monitor his or her behaviour. Interaction between prisoners was to be controlled and limited, reducing the opportunity for criminal fraternisation (Brodie et al. 2002:58–59; Casella 2007:26; Ignatieff 1978:109–113; Markus 1993:118–129). John Howard advocated separate cells for prisoners arranged in blocks, with separation of prisoners according to the nature of their crimes. An early adaptation of this model, built on a radial design, was constructed to house female convicts in Launceston in 1832 (Casella 2001c:51–52), and similar principles informed the design of the Separate Prison at Port Arthur and the New Gaol on Norfolk Island, both completed in 1847 (Fig. 2.3). Although Bentham's specific designs were not widely applied, his ideas and those of John Howard were influential and their reforms contributed to significant changes in the Australian convict system.

The first dedicated convict barracks in Australia was built in 1803 at the Castle Hill Government Farm, north of Parramatta (Wilson and Douglas 2005). The stone building was around 104 feet (32 m) long and 24 feet (7 m) wide, built on sandstone foundations. Following the Castle Hill uprising in 1804, when a group of mainly Irish convicts rose up unsuccessfully against the authorities, no further convict barracks were built until 1817, when construction of the Hyde Park Barracks commenced.

Fig. 2.3 New Gaol, Norfolk Island, completed in 1847, built on a radial plan with five cell blocks and 10 yards (photo P. Davies)

Governor Macquarie insisted that male convicts working on government projects in Sydney had to live at the Barracks and were no longer allowed to board in the community or to undertake task work. The Barracks initially housed about 600 men, although in later years more than 1,000 were accommodated in the complex. As the number of convicts increased in the 1820s and 1830s, well-behaved inmates and those with families were often permitted to maintain their own houses in town, with more refractory convicts held in the Barracks. Similar places of confinement were also constructed in other major centres, and thereafter convict freedoms were greatly curtailed. At the same time, places of secondary punishment were also being established. These were prison complexes deliberately located in isolated places at some distance from the main areas of settlement and included Sarah Island, Maria Island and Port Arthur in Van Diemen's Land; Port Macquarie in New South Wales; Moreton Bay in Queensland; and Norfolk Island, almost 1,500 km away in the Pacific. Convicts who committed new offences once in the colonies would now be sent to these places for a further period of incarceration with hard labour. These developments marked the introduction of a new regime of graduated levels of punishment and reward (Kerr 1984:61). Newly arrived convicts entered in the middle of the system. If they worked well and behaved appropriately, they were rewarded with increasing levels of freedom, eventually earning their ticket-of-leave. If they re-offended, however, they moved down the ladder and freedoms were gradually

Fig. 2.4 Hyde Park Barracks, established in 1819 by Governor Macquarie to accommodate male convicts working on government gangs in Sydney (photo P. Davies)

removed, until the worst re-offenders ended up in the solitary cells of Port Arthur or Sarah Island, or on the gallows.

Significantly, despite the new emphasis on reforming the minds of convicts, all of these stages had an accompanying physical component. The new residential barracks and the penal settlements were all large-scale capital works, and many have survived at least in part to the present day. Because they have survived and because they are so imposing, it is these structures and complexes that have largely shaped contemporary understanding of what convicts experienced. Many, like the Hyde Park Barracks and Port Arthur, have become museums or official historic sites and are now open to the public (Fig. 2.4). For tourists interested in convicts, these are the most popular destinations. When confronted by the sheer scale and power of a complex like Port Arthur it is easy to forget that comparatively few convicts were ever held there. The ruins at Port Arthur have become the popular face of the convict past. These, and the remains of the other institutionalised components of the convict system, have similarly dominated archaeological approaches to convictism.

Convict Archaeology

Convict archaeology encompasses both research into the convict past and the management of heritage places with extant physical evidence. Archaeological approaches to convictism are informed by the nature of the sites that have survived and by the desire to conserve the heritage values of these places. Archaeologist Martin Gibbs (2001) has noted that in Western Australia convict sites generally fall into three categories, and this system can be applied more broadly to convict sites elsewhere in Australia. The first category is that of the convict system itself, comprising the places where convicts were housed, punished and worked. This includes barracks, gaols, probation stations, penal settlements, factories, mines, quarries and shipyards. Sites in the second category are those associated with the administration of convicts, including offices and quarters for the military and civilian personnel who managed the system. The final category includes places that were constructed with convict labour, such as roads, bridges, jetties and public buildings.

Sites in the first category tend to be the most visible and prominent evidence of the convict past and have received the most archaeological attention. Their association with convicts is clear and unambiguous and the remains themselves often include large buildings and complexes, such as the Hyde Park Barracks in Sydney, Fremantle Gaol or the buildings at Port Arthur. Sites in the second category are not as obviously connected with convictism and, unless part of a complex like Port Arthur or Norfolk Island, may simply be identified as early colonial or administrative sites. The site of First Government House in Sydney, for example, is valued as the site of the earliest permanent structure in the colony and because of its role in early government. That it was built and staffed by convicts is a less evident, though equally important, part of the story. Likewise, the products of convict labour are not always self-evident. A convict-built road or bridge need not look any different to those built by free labour. In colonies such as New South Wales, Van Diemen's Land and Queensland, however, where virtually all labour was initially provided by convicts, much of the early infrastructure is also part of the convict system.

As a result of the kinds of sites that have survived and the need to conserve and manage convict heritage for the community, much of the archaeological work that has been done has inadvertently privileged a particular kind of convict experience. It has focused on the experience of adult male convicts and particularly those who came during the later, post-penal reform period of the 1820s onwards. In New South Wales the focus has been on urban convictism rather than on convicts who lived and worked in rural areas, while conversely, in Tasmania it has been the story of convicts outside Hobart and Launceston that has predominated. Women, children, assigned servants and those transported before 1820 are not well represented in archaeological research to date.

Denis Gojak has noted that archaeologists have contributed a great deal to our understandings of punishment and penal institutions and to details of the daily shape of convict life such as diet and health (Gojak 2001). He argues, however, that archaeologists have not sufficiently addressed broader questions about the nature of colonial society as a convict society. The first 50 years of British settlement in Australia were underpinned by reliance on convict labour, a situation unique in the history of the British Empire and paralleled only by those colonies reliant on slavery. This raises important questions, such as the relationship between convictism and other forms of forced labour and migration. There are indications that archaeologists are beginning to address these gaps and to contribute alternative perspectives on convictism. Recent research on early Sydney sites, female factories in Tasmania, the Point Puer boys' reformatory at Port Arthur and the rural estate of Lake Innes in New South Wales all demonstrate the potential of archaeological remains to produce new insights that can inform general understandings of convict experiences.

As historical archaeology has developed as a discipline over the past 30 years, approaches to convict sites have also changed considerably, and at the same time convict archaeology has contributed significantly to the development of the field. Some of the first historical sites excavated in Australia, such as Elizabeth Farm, had convict components (M. Byrne and Jack 1979). At the time of excavation, however, these associations did not receive much attention, as the sites were not overtly part of the convict system, and then, as is still frequently the case, they were not thought of as "convict" sites. At more recognisable convict places such as Norfolk Island (Allen and Lennon 1978; Wilson and Davies 1980), Port Arthur (Egloff 1984), Hyde Park Barracks (Crook et al. 2003a), First Government House in Sydney (Proudfoot et al. 1991) and Ross Bridge in Tasmania (Byrne 1976), all of which were excavated as a result of conservation and development processes, the emphasis was primarily on description of the structural evidence of punishment and incarceration.

Other studies, such as Grace Karskens' work on sites along the convict-built Great North Road between Sydney and Newcastle, sought to place the archaeo-logical evidence within a broader historical and social framework, exploring how individual sites fitted into the wider convict system (Karskens 1984, 1986). By the end of the twentieth century it was more common to acknowledge convict involvement in a wide range of sites, including the early homes and businesses in Sydney's Rocks district, rural sites such as Lake Innes and settlement sites in Western Australia's wheat belt (Connah 2001; Gibbs 2001; Karskens 1999). The definition of convict site has grown beyond institutions of incarceration to encom-pass all those places in which convicts lived or worked. As the field of historical archaeology has matured in recent years, more ambitious theoretical approaches have also become influential, with issues of gender and power informing work by Eleanor Casella at Ross (Casella 2000a, b, 2001b), while consumer theory has been important in work by Fiona Starr (2001) and socio-economic status has shaped Graham Connah's work at Lake Innes (Connah 2001, 2009). Archaeologists have also started to reflect on the general contributions of convict archaeology, as shown by several of the essays in a collection edited by Eleanor Casella and Clayton Fredericksen (2001).

If disciplinary maturity has altered the ways in which archaeologists think about convict places, it is also true that ongoing work on convict sites has enriched histor-ical archaeology and enabled the field to develop. Public interest in the Hyde Park Barracks and First Government House generated the first large-scale urban archae-ology projects in Australia and brought the archaeological evidence of Australia's colonial past to a wide and influential audience (Bickford 1991; Fig. 2.5). These digs played a significant role in developing greater awareness of the need to leg-islate for the protection of archaeological sites generally and helped to consolidate archaeology within planning and development processes. The extent, complexity

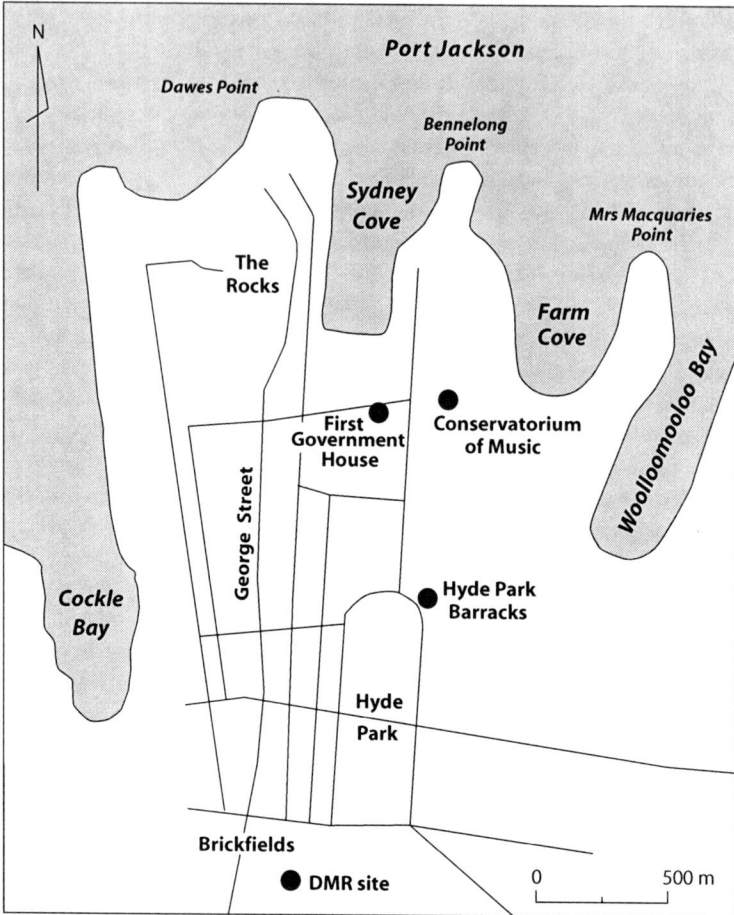

Fig. 2.5 Map of Sydney showing archaeological sites associated with convicts

and significance of the remains at Norfolk Island and Port Arthur have ensured ongoing federal government support for conservation projects at these places, of which archaeology has been an important component (Ireland 2004).

Over this period relationships between convict archaeology and the public have also become more complex. Public interest has always been, and remains, an integral part of convict archaeology. Convict descendants were instrumental in saving the remains of First Government House from development in the 1980s, spearheading a protest that led to a major archaeological project and eventually to the construction of a new museum, The Museum of Sydney on the Site of First Government House, to interpret the architectural remains and manage the artefacts (Emmett 1996). More recently, on the central coast of New South Wales an alliance of local communities has taken responsibility for the management and interpretation of archaeological sites along the Great North Road (Convict Trail 2003). Their work involves conservation of the sites, tourism initiatives and historical research on individual convicts and the iron gang system. Relations between archaeologists and community groups, however, are not always cordial or straightforward. In the late 1990s, when evidence of a convict-built road was uncovered during construction of the Conservatorium of Music in Sydney, archaeologists were taken aback by the nature of public feeling about the site. The archaeologists and heritage professionals involved considered the remains to be of limited heritage value as the road was only partially intact and was one of many such roads in and around Sydney. Members of the public responded more immediately to the remains as direct physical evidence of convict forbears and demanded that the road be preserved. Accommodating the remains as an essentially decontextualised object in the new building cost several million dollars and resulted in continuing government disquiet about the value of archaeology (Casey 2005b; Gojak 2001; Greer et al. 2002).

Mary Casey's (2005b) report of the events surrounding the Conservatorium controversy demonstrates how evidence about the nature of physical remains can be manipulated to serve a variety of interests. This was a particularly emotive case, but it is only one of many instances where heritage values are seized on as a way of preventing development even when the heritage significance of the fabric may not warrant preservation. The strength of community feeling elicited can indicate other values, such as social significance, that are not as apparent to heritage professionals. It illustrates the ambiguous position of archaeology that destroys sites in order to preserve information and the pragmatism of a profession in which practitioners are often involved in facilitating development to which as community members they might otherwise be opposed.

Partially in response to the prominent involvement of descendant groups and the growth of heritage tourism, archaeologists are becoming more thoughtful about the ways in which archaeology is presented to the public and at times appropriated to serve other agenda. In contrast to previous generations of white Australians who wished to ignore and forget the country's convict origins, today convicts are embraced as individual and collective ancestors and convict places and relics are playing an important part in that re-invention. Themes of belonging and forming a new country with a distinctive Australian consciousness play a prominent part in the stories presented at convict museums around Australia (Casella 2005). One local community in Tasmania now has a programme for people to purchase a brick bearing the name of a convict, often an ancestor, which is then laid as part of a continuous trail down the main street. In 2004 Hobart's Cascades Female Factory was the site for a "muster" of descendants of female convicts attended by 800 people, and one of Port Arthur's most popular interpretive programmes invites visitors to identify with a particular convict individual as part of their experience at the site. Greg Jackman, senior archaeologist at Port Arthur, argues, however, that such incorporation is not unproblematic

> Archaeology is at risk of being driven to the fringe as subjective interpretations of the past based on the consumerist desires of visitors and social/spiritual claims of ethno-nationalists begin to divert political and economic support from evidence-based explorations of the meanings and legacies of the convict system (Jackman 2009:109–110).

The Early Years: York Town and Sydney

Convicts and their military guards were pioneers at the beginning of a new settlement, much like pioneers anywhere else in the British Empire. They all had to
cut clearings in the forest, build huts and establish crops and gardens, simply to
ensure their own survival. They met Aboriginal people, sometimes on a friendly
basis and sometimes with fear and violence. They watched out to sea for the next
sail to appear over the horizon, bringing news and supplies from home. Today one
of the few places where we can still get a clear sense of this early, anxious period is
at York Town on northern Tasmania's Tamar River. It does not look like much now,
and it probably did not look like much when the first convict settlers stepped ashore
in November 1804. A few years earlier a member of the exploration party wrote,
"The land is low and very even, but sandy and not good, being full of the dwarf
Grass tree – The timber is large but not very good . . . the Shore is a Black Stone
rock, in some places the landing is very good. . .Very good fresh Water was found at
the head of the Arm. . ." (Macknight 1998:72–73).

Today bush has largely reclaimed the site, but the casual visitor can still see faint
traces of the settlement. Fragments of handmade brick poke through the pebbly soil,
and the occasional piece of black bottle glass can be found. A faint depression in
the grass shows where the commandant, Lieutenant Colonel William Paterson, had
his house. In 1805, it was all much more substantial. York Town (also known as
Port Dalrymple) was a sprawling settlement, housing nearly 300 convicts, military
and civilian officials, and their families. In addition to Paterson's house, the settlement had accommodation for the soldiers and the convicts, a parade ground, several
private farms occupied by the officers, a quartermaster's store, a gaol, brickmaking pits, stockyards, a mill and all the other facilities required for self-sufficiency
(Fig. 2.6). The settlement, however, was abandoned in 1808 due to its poor shipping
access and limited agricultural prospects, and most of the residents relocated further
up the Tamar to Launceston, which became the capital and focal point of northern
Van Diemen's Land. After that the land was sporadically farmed but has remained
largely undisturbed for 200 years.

In 2006, archaeological excavations were carried out by Adrienne Ellis, a Ph.D.
student at La Trobe University. She investigated the remains of the soldiers' huts
and the foundations of Paterson's house. Status was an important feature of life in
the British military, and the size and layout of the buildings at York Town indicate
a similar preoccupation, despite the small size and remoteness of the site. The soldiers' cottages were small one- or two-roomed dwellings, made of local wattle and
daub, about 3.5 by 5 m across, and located at one edge of the settlement. The commandant's house, on the other hand, was a prefabricated timber building imported
from England and set on foundations of locally made brick. It was also spacious,
measuring almost 10 by 4 m, with a cellar, glass in the windows and plastered internal walls (Hayes 2004:32–36). Moreover, it was in the centre of the settlement, at its
literal and figurative heart. Immediately adjacent was the parade ground and flag-
pole where convicts and soldiers both assembled at daily musters and the Union
Jack flew boldly over all.

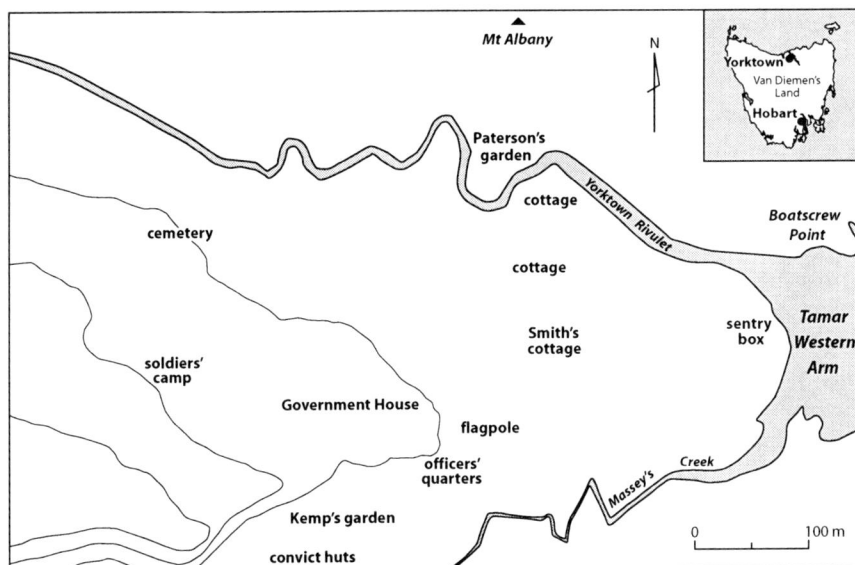

Fig. 2.6 Plan of York Town in northern Van Diemen's Land, occupied from 1804 to 1808 (after Dent 2002; Kostoglou 2003)

While the settlement lasted, the convicts and their military guards at York Town lived cheek-by-jowl, separated from each other by status and topography, but otherwise sharing similar conditions. Single soldiers lived in shared barracks, as did single male convicts. Married soldiers lived in separate cottages with their wives and children, and convict families too lived in their own homes. Seen from a distance, the cottages would have looked similar, and as a whole, with children playing outside, paling fences and struggling plants by the front doors, the settlement must have looked much like all the other uncertain new colonies the British planted around the world at the end of the eighteenth century. York Town was abandoned before it had the chance to become firmly established, but further to the north in New South Wales other settlements that had also once struggled were becoming more secure.

In Sydney the tents and huts were becoming proper houses in the early decades of the nineteenth century. Convicts, ex-convicts and their locally born children, people like George Cribb and the Byrnes family in the Rocks (Karskens 1999:40, 2009:76–78), Catherine Lindsey in the Brickfields (Casey 1999), and William Hill and Mary Johnson in Pitt Street, Sydney (Lydon 1996:156), were able to establish businesses and build comfortable homes. Years of archaeological excavations have provided detailed evidence of buildings, gardens, consumer habits, diet, work and socialising and a developing urban landscape of streets and lanes.

Those excavations have demonstrated that convict houses were generally single-storey cottages and their placement reflects local geography more than urban planning. Until the 1830s and 1840s houses in the Rocks were built along the sandstone ridges or facing the water of Sydney Harbour rather than along the as-yet irregular roads. Some cottages, like those of William Hill and Mary Johnson and of Catherine Lindsey, were wattle and daub with packed-earth floors, but a comfortable size, 10 m long and 5 m wide, and set well back from the street on large allotments. In the Rocks, George Cribb prospered sufficiently as a butcher to build a stone house to which he later added a second storey. He too had a large allotment, and built his house back from the street, but the adjoining shop was right on the street frontage. His neighbours Richard and Mary Byrne had a weatherboard house, but quite a substantial one for the day with a shingled roof, glass windows and three fireplaces. Like the others, the Byrnes' house was set back from the street on a large allotment.

The allotments were an important feature of the young towns. People used them to grow food and as places to work. Traces of fence lines show that William Hill and Mary Johnson kept stock in their yard, as did Catherine Lindsey in the Brickfields. Pollen grains recovered from Catherine Lindsey's house show that she placed cut flowers in her house, possibly from her own garden. Pollen grains from other sites show that George Cribb and his wife Fanny Barnett grew peas, beans, lemons and apples on their allotment, while their neighbours the Byrnes also had a large fenced garden with paths, vegetables and fruit trees. As had been the case in England and Ireland, business was often conducted at home, and the allotments provided valuable workspace. Catherine Lindsey worked as a laundress after her husband died, leaving heavy stains of blueing for archaeologists to find around her well. George Cribb used his yard for slaughtering and butchering stock, leaving offal, horn and bone to rot (see Chapter 11). Across the street, George Legg built a baker's oven on his allotment. At the DMR site in the Brickfields, an unknown woman or women had a home dairy in which she used a wide range of locally made earthenware pans and bowls for making butter and cheese.

The many artefacts found in and around these houses reveal the household goods and personal possessions acquired by this early generation of convicts. Strikingly, what they owned and what they ate was plentiful and of good quality. In the words of historian Grace Karskens, "the archaeology of convict Sydney sketches out not a prison, but households. . .and a culture of consumerism" (Karskens 1999:48). In the earliest years the convicts had suffered the general privations of everyone else in the struggling colony, but by the 1810s and 1820s they, like the colony, were becoming comfortable and even prosperous. Fashionable tea and breakfast dishes, china figurines and religious plaques were commonly recovered from convict homes of this period. George Cribb and the Hill family had tea dishes of Chinese porcelain, and the Byrnes had a very up-to-date and fine-quality meat platter. Catherine Lindsey, a single mother, was able to provide her children with special plates decorated with the alphabet. The Byrne children played with limestone marbles and a painted bisque doll.

The archaeological record of convict meals shows abundant evidence of meat. Both salt and fresh beef were popular, along with pork, goat and chicken. Butchered sheep bones made up 40 percent of the table-waste, indicating that mutton was also highly favoured. Native animals were apparently eaten only rarely by the convicts and appear hardly at all in the bones excavated. Fish were caught in the waters along the shore of Sydney Harbour, and shellfish were collected as well. Sites around Sydney from this time contain substantial quantities of shells from Sydney rock oysters and mud oysters, indicating that they were a common foodstuff. Pollen evidence reveals that local gardens were providing people with a variety of fruits and vegetables, including peas, beans, cabbage and turnip; salad greens such as radish and watercress; and apples, lemons and peaches. Bread does not leave much archaeological evidence, but bakers' ovens have been found in the Rocks and elsewhere. A range of locally made dairying vessels reminds us of the important role of dairy foods in the diet at this time and of the work of the women, both convict and free, who were responsible for producing it.

Assigned Servants: Lake Innes, New South Wales

Most convicts ended up as servants assigned to free settlers, with a large proportion being sent to work in rural areas. An example of this experience is provided by the site of Lake Innes near Port Macquarie in New South Wales. Lake Innes was a property taken up in 1830 by Major Archibald Clunes Innes and his wife, Margaret Macleay Innes. The extended Innes family, members of the colony's self-styled aristocracy, lived there until financial difficulties forced them to move in 1852. At Lake Innes the family created a large and consciously impressive house and stables complex, a boathouse, a servants' village and a home farm (Fig. 2.7). The buildings and the estate were built and run by convict workers until assignment ceased in 1839 and by a diminishing number of assigned and free workers thereafter.

Lake Innes was studied by a team of archaeologists from the University of New England between 1993 and 2001 (Brooks and Connah 2007; Connah 1998, 2001, 2007, 2009). Along with investigation of the main household, which produced few artefacts (see Chapter 6), the team carried out excavations at several sites where the estate's servants were housed. This included the quarters provided in the stable complex for the coachmen, one of the two-roomed terrace cottages in the houseservants' quarters, two of the huts in the more distant servants' village and the home farm. These locations not only reveal some of the living conditions experienced by convicts in rural areas, but also demonstrate that even within a single estate conditions could vary widely. One of Connah's main objectives was to investigate the documentary and archaeological evidence of socio-economic status among residents on the estate. While differences might be expected between convicts working for different masters, in this case it appears that the range in accommodation and material goods reflects differences in rank among the convicts and free servants, and that the differences were related to legal status and personal skills. The story is not a straightforward one, however, because ranking the buildings according to size, building materials and degree of comfort produced some different results than was obtained when the type, quantity and quality of goods in the artefact assemblages were considered.

Closest to the main house were quarters for the stable staff. This consisted of four double-storey gatehouses that were part of the stable complex itself. The buildings

Fig. 2.7 Lake Innes estate,
New South Wales, occupied
by the Innes family from
1830 to 1852

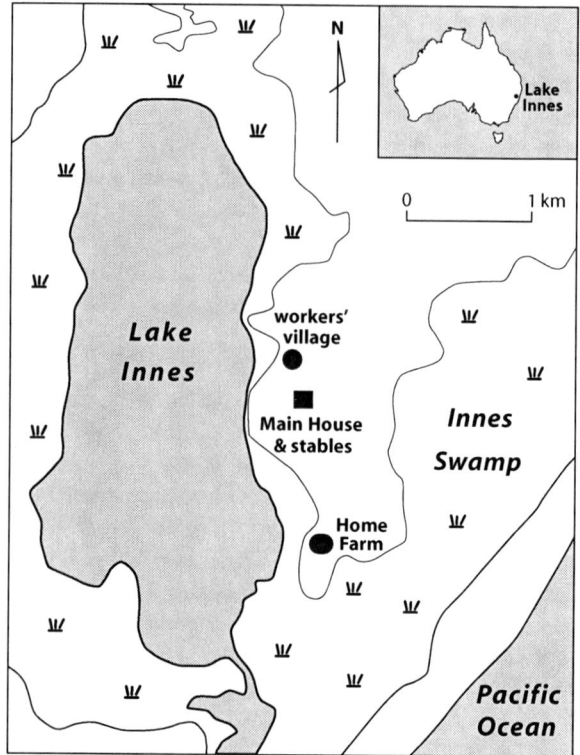

were relatively comfortable as they were built of brick with a kitchen/living area on the ground floor, complete with brick fireplace, and a bedroom upstairs, while both rooms had glass windows. Some of the apartments were shared bachelor quarters but at least one was the home of the married coachman, his wife, and possibly their children. The artefact assemblage here included the largest quantity of the more expensive porcelain, glass stemware and tumblers, and a small number of coins. Both architecture and artefacts indicate that this household was at the top of the estate's servant rank, and Connah suggests that the occupants were probably a free or ex-convict couple.

At the other end of the socio-economic scale on the estate was the servants' village where homes were much less comfortable. The location itself was less pleasant, being in a damp gully near the lakeshore, and the archaeological remains are far less substantial. The first house excavated here had a brick fireplace but was otherwise built of wood, possibly the customary Australian bark slabs with a wooden shingled roof. The floor was earthen and any windows were unglazed, and the artefacts were much less numerous. There were no coins, no glass drinking vessels and only a few ceramics, none of which were porcelain. This dwelling is at the bottom of the rank in terms of both architecture and goods, and Connah believes the occupants were single male assigned convicts, probably unskilled farm labourers.

Between these two ends of the scale the archaeological evidence is more ambiguous. A second home excavated in the distant servants' village was also built of wood, probably bark slabs and shingle roof, with an earthen floor and brick fireplace, but it had at least one glazed window and a much richer artefact assemblage. There was a large quantity of ceramics, of which more than 10 percent was porcelain, and some of which may have been displayed on a dresser, as well as glass stemware and tumblers and a single coin. The proximity of a forge has led Connah to surmise that this was the home of a blacksmith living on his own, possibly a ticket-of-leave holder. While the humble architecture and uncomfortable location indicate low status, the numerous and diverse household goods suggest that the occupant's own perception of his worth was somewhat different.

At the quarters for the household servants, higher quality architecture but a lesser artefact assemblage, particularly ceramics, suggest the opposite story. Near the main house two rows of brick terraces, each row comprising three or four cottages of one or two rooms each, provided accommodation for the household servants. One of these cottages was excavated and found to be two rooms, the larger main room with a fireplace and the second for sleeping, and a small attached structure with washing facilities and bucket latrines, possibly shared with everyone in the row. The bricks were of poorer quality than those in the main house and stables and clay loam rather than lime was used in the mortar, but the walls were finished inside and out with lime render, the windows were glazed and there was a suspended wooden floor in both rooms. The assemblage of artefacts was varied, including the highest number of coins found, glass stemware and tumblers, and the greatest quantity of ceramics, but only a small proportion of the ceramics was porcelain. Connah suggests that this household was also a free or ex-convict family, and while their house indicates that they were of the highest rank of servants, well-regarded by the Innes family, their possessions suggest a lower position.

The evidence from the Home Farm seems to represent a less ambiguously middle position on the scale. Located some 1.5 km from the main house, a cottage had been built for the couple who ran the farm, as well as a separate barracks for the men who worked in the fields. The farm cottage consisted of a three or four room house with timber slab walls and a shingle roof. Unlike the huts in the servants' village, however, the Home Farm house had substantial foundations, wooden floors, a large brick fireplace and glazed windows. The architectural evidence is midway between the household servants and the village, and the artefactual evidence is likewise in the middle. The assemblage included a few coins, glass tumblers but no stemware and a large quantity of ceramics but very little porcelain. The occupants are believed to have been free settlers or ticket-of-leave holders, and it appears that the situation ascribed to them by the Innes' matched their own expectations.

Based on the archaeological evidence Connah suggests that those living in the servants' village experienced "material poverty and ... frugal living conditions", while those in the row houses were treated, materially at least, rather better (Connah 2001:149). In 1837, the Innes family had 91 assigned convicts working for them, although most probably worked away from the main estate. Many of these workers were highly skilled, including the brickmakers, bricklayer/plasterer, carpenter/joiner, glazier, tailors, shoemakers, millers, butchers and magistrate's clerk. The three female servants, a laundress, nursemaid and shoebinder by trade, probably lived near the main house, while the stablemen, grooms, harness-maker and horse-breaker presumably lived near the stables. For the others it is tempting to speculate on how Archibald Innes allocated living quarters and who got the snug brick terrace cottages and who got the damp bark huts. It is also tempting to wonder how the servants themselves saw their homes and whether the wooden floors and plastered walls of the row houses compensated for the close neighbours and watchful eyes of the big house or whether the free-standing houses out of site and sound of the master were worth the damp after all.

While noting the differing housing conditions, Connah also observes that "identifying assigned servants in the archaeological record is not an easy task" (Connah 2001:147). Because all the excavated sites were likely to have been occupied during the period of convict workers as well as after assignment ended, caution must be used in identifying any archaeological evidence as solely that of convicts. What is significant, however, is the way in which both documentary sources and archaeology suggest that while the legal status of categories such as assigned, ticket-of-leave and free was clear, socially and materially the categories were more fluid. As Grace Karskens has argued for early Sydney, hard-working convicts could prosper while lazy, profligate or unlucky ticket-of-leave holders might struggle, and their conditions reflected their characters as much as their legal status. The brick terraces built at Lake Innes resembled the homes of factory workers in England's industrial towns of the same period, while the bark huts are more like those built by many early Australian colonists, whether free or unfree.

Connah (2001) uses the results of his work at Lake Innes to consider the wider ramifications of the convict system in New South Wales, and in particular its relationship with other forms of forced labour in the nineteenth century. He observes that people like Archibald and Margaret Innes aspired to a station in life that would have been impossible for them in Britain, but which was made possible in the colonies by the unfree labour of others. In this Australian society was like that of the American south, where enslaved Africans and African-Americans provided the labour that created a life of conspicuous leisure for others. As we noted earlier, however, there were real and important differences between the two systems. While both convicts and slaves were involuntary migrants made to perform forced labour, convicts could not be bought or sold, served a sentence of limited duration, had rights under the law and did not pass on their servitude to their children. Archaeologically, however, there is at least one similarity between the two groups. Connah found at Lake Innes that it was virtually impossible to tell whether archaeological deposits had been created by convicts, ticket-of-leave men or free employees. Differences in the architecture and in the assemblages seemed to be more closely related to social status and skills rather than to legal status. This has also been found to be the case in the southern United States, where archaeological deposits alone are not enough to determine if the residents were enslaved or free and where cultural identity and social status are greater determinants of the material record (Orser 1988; Singleton 1995:128–129; Stine 1990). This circumstance seems to suggest that in both cases the most obvious social and legal division between free and convict/slave was not the only influence on how the unfree lived their lives, and that those trapped by their unfree status were nevertheless able to recognise and mark more subtle and complex social relationships within their community.

The contrast between the apparent status implied by the buildings and the status implied by the goods lost or discarded by the occupants has also been observed on other historical archaeological sites, most notably the homes of the inner-city poor (Crook 2000). In that case, as at Lake Innes, the built environment was owned by others and the occupants had little control over it. The occupants had much greater ownership and control over their personal and household effects, albeit constrained by factors such as cost and income. The disparity between architecture and goods reflects a disjunction between the status ascribed by outsiders, in this case by Archibald Innes, and the status achieved or aspired to by the occupants themselves. Innes built and allocated the housing as he saw fit and according to his perception of the relative rank of his servants. In asking questions about socio-economic status Connah's problem-oriented research has contributed new understandings about the complexity of convict experiences.

Repeat Offenders: Iron Gangs on the Great North Road, New South Wales

Iron gangs, where groups of men were sentenced to work in chains, were an integral part of the convict system in New South Wales, especially under later governors such as Ralph Darling and Richard Bourke in the 1820s and 1830s. They also typify the dominant image of convictism, with hard physical labour, brutal punishments and frequent escapes. Iron gangs, like penal settlements, were part of the sharp end of the convict system, the destination of the hardened men who continued to offend. The gangs were used to construct main roads in the colony, including the Great North Road between Sydney and the Hunter Valley (Fig. 2.8). For the colonial government the gangs thus had a threefold purpose, as they punished repeat offenders, banished undesirables from more populated districts and extracted useful work out of men who could not otherwise be made productive. Grace Karskens' study of sites along the Great North Road around Wiseman's Ferry illustrates how the iron gangs worked and the value of examining the physical evidence (Karskens 1984, 1986).

Karskens used the archaeological evidence to engage directly with historical debates about the nature of punishment in the convict system, incorporating the work of historian John Hirst, who argues that while flogging and the iron gangs did have a place in the system, incentives such as free time for their own work were far more effective in getting the convicts to work as desired (Hirst 1983). Karskens supports this argument, but notes that Hirst shares the view of both contemporaries and modern historians that iron gangs held violent and hardened recidivists, featured harsh discipline and lax work practices, and ultimately accomplished little.

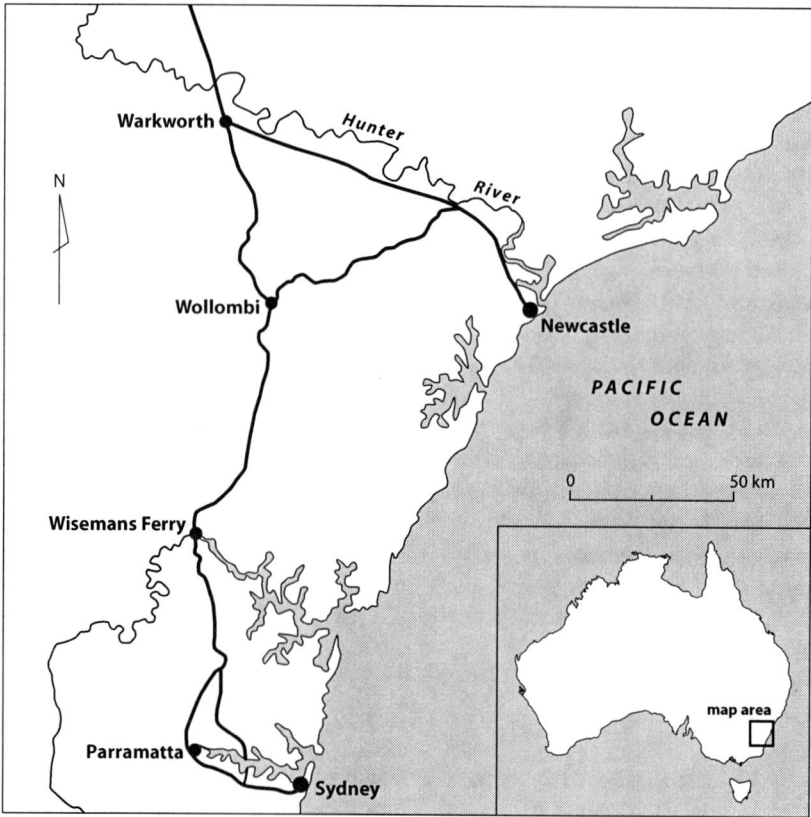

Fig. 2.8 Route of Great North Road between Sydney and Newcastle via Wisemans Ferry, constructed between 1826 and 1836 (after Karskens 1984:18)

Karskens contrasts this document-based perception with the physical results of the gangs' work, the often impressive and monumental engineering of the roads they built. She argues that the iron gangs were a complex environment in which men were deployed according to their degree of skill and application. The rewards that Hirst identified elsewhere in the convict system did not stop when secondary punishment was required but were also used, in different ways, within the iron gangs. Those who worked well were able to acquire considerable skill and could be rewarded with extra rations, seniority in the gangs and eventually tickets-of-leave.

The best evidence of the skills of the men and the labour organization required is in the work they produced. In some sections the stonework is crude, consisting of unshaped and roughly stacked stretches of wall, which would have required minimal skill and comparatively less effort. Other sections are massive and highly technical engineering feats, which required both knowledge and diligence to complete. Here the culverts, retaining walls and bridges show precisely worked and finely finished stone used in expertly designed structures. By comparing the documentary record, including the weekly and monthly reports completed by the government-appointed Assistant Surveyor in charge of the road, Karskens was able to link particular gangs with the archaeological evidence of the sections they built. Some gangs were consistently associated with less demanding sections where the archaeological record shows work of poorer quality. Other gangs were put to work in sections where dealing with steep descents and gully and river crossings required considerable skill and where work was of a high standard. This suggests that both overseers and men were allocated to gangs according to their abilities and willingness to work. While the records show that most of the absconders came from gangs working on the difficult sections, Karskens observed that of the 50 men in a gang, only a few worked consistently on skilled tasks, with the remainder (and those who re-absconded), working on labouring tasks such as clearing brush and debris. As Karskens writes, "The walls they built thus reveal overlaid evidence of their remarkable perseverance and skills, of the diligent supervision of the overseers, and of the ambitious visions of the Assistant Surveyors" (Karskens 1986:27). By combining documentary and archaeological evidence Karskens has been able to demonstrate the mechanisms by which convict labour systems were made to produce the colony's infrastructure.

Women and Children Convicts: The Ross Female Factory and Point Puer, Port Arthur

Almost 16 per cent of convicts transported to Australia were women, with most between the ages of 15 and 30 years (Oxley 1996:110). For the most part they were assigned to private employers, mainly as domestic servants, and because of this their experiences within the convict system have not resulted in monumental archaeological remains. Their lives and their work are represented as layers of meaning in other kinds of sites, such as the great houses of Sydney and Hobart, rather than as sites in their own right. One of the most notable exceptions to this is the site of the Female Factory in the town of Ross in the Tasmanian midlands. The complex was originally constructed in the 1830s as a probation station to house male convicts building a bridge over the nearby Macquarie River (Fig. 2.9), but by 1847 the site was converted into a Factory to house convict women and their children. It was located centrally between Hobart and Launceston and was intended to serve the needs of the free and convict settlers in the area as a hiring depot, lying-in hospital for pregnant women and as a place of secondary punishment. The Factory closed in early 1855, following the end of transportation to Van Diemen's Land, and by the end of the nineteenth century most of the buildings on the site had been demolished. In the 1990s archaeologist Eleanor Casella conducted excavations in the Hiring Class, Crime Class and Solitary Cells areas (Casella 1997, 2001a, c, 2002).

One of Casella's major aims was to explore the role of power within the convict system, including not only forms of control used by the authorities, but also the techniques of resistance employed by the convict women. In this Casella has been able to build on archaeological and theoretical approaches to domination and resistance (Foucault 1977; McGuire and Paynter 1991) and to extend the research of

Fig. 2.9 Ross Bridge in central Van Diemen's Land, built by convicts and completed in 1836. Carvings over the arches depict portraits of individuals and various rural activities (photo P. Davies)

feminist historians who have reinterpreted the history of female convicts (Damousi 1997; Daniels 1993; Oxley 1996). Casella demonstrates that material culture is an important means for recovering the perspective of women who were more often the subject than the object of written history.

For the authorities, control mechanisms in the first instance included incarceration within the Factory itself, with the rules and regulations that applied to inmates. In the second instance, prisoners were disciplined through the removal of privileges, including food, and ultimately confinement in the solitary cells. The architecture of the complex was thus an active part of the disciplinary process, and the structural remains of the buildings, yards, cells and walls represent the institutional power to which the women were subject. One focus of Casella's research was the solitary cells within the Crime Class section of the complex. Parts of three cells were excavated, all approximately 1.2 by 1.8 m in size, with packed-earth floors and thick masonry walls. Window glass was recovered from each, and they probably had small glazed windows immediately below the ceiling to admit light but prevent escape. A unique feature of the cells was the level of the floors, which appear to have been 30–50 cm below the level of the surrounding ground surface, probably necessitating a small ladder or step to enter the cells. Architecture in this case was deliberately designed to reinforce the severity of the punishment – the spaces the women were kept in were small, silent, dimly lit, cold and damp. To underline the point, entering the cells involved a literal descent into the earth, symbolising submission, the moral descent of the prisoner and perhaps even the death and (ideally) rebirth of her reformed character.

In the archaeological deposits within the solitary cells Casella found that the material culture can be read to reveal ways in which the women resisted the force of authority and asserted their own individual wills and personalities. Buttons were found all across the site, most likely associated with the women's work in the laundry and as seamstresses, but the greatest density of buttons was in the solitary cells. As Casella points out, women within the cells were undergoing punishment and were not working at any tasks during that period, so it is unlikely that the buttons were lost accidentally while working. Casella argues instead that the buttons were used as tokens in the illicit economy that operated within the factory, part of a trade that encompassed luxury items, tobacco, extra food rations and sexual favours for both men and women. Their presence in the solitary cells, particularly in significant quantities, suggests that the women held there, who were often those at the top of the prisoners' own hierarchies, were able to subvert prison authorities by bartering for extras that helped to mitigate the deliberately onerous conditions of their punishment. This interpretation is bolstered by the discovery of a deliberately concealed pit within one of the cells, which contained sheep bones, a kaolin pipe stem, a bottle base and a ferrous artefact, possibly a food tin.

The authorities withdrew food as a punishment, and the women resisted by using their own illicit networks to supply and procure food. The authorities withdrew interaction with others, and the women resisted by maintaining casual and more intimate sexual relationships. These have left discernible traces in the archaeological record, and there were other forms of resistance as well that have been recorded in the documentary evidence. Women shouted and jeered when assembled to be addressed by visiting dignitaries, rioted, destroyed property and on occasion set fire to the factories in which they were being held.

Studying the archaeology of convict women has only just begun, and the work at Ross is literally scratching the surface. So far Casella's work has brought to light a specific dimension of female convict experience that was rebellious, independent and anti-authoritarian. However, there were other aspects of the experiences of women at the Ross Factory and places like it, and other stories that may be told. One is the archaeology of mothering and childhood, because the female factories in Van Diemen's Land and New South Wales played an important role as lying-in hospitals and nurseries. The convict system criminalized unwed mothers, sending assigned servants back to the factories for incarceration as secondary punishment for the "offence" of becoming pregnant out of wedlock. Mothering and childhood are growing areas of research in historical archaeology (Davies and Ellis 2005; Vermeer 2009; Wileman 2005; Wilkie 2000, 2003), and the archaeological analysis of places like Ross can contribute substantially to this area, in terms of new perspectives on both childhood and on convict women. Perhaps unsurprisingly it is this aspect of the convict women that has drawn public attention, especially among genealogists and convict descendants, even though scholarly attention has lagged behind (Female Factory 2009).

The experiences of convict children have also been investigated archaeologically at the Point Puer settlement at Port Arthur, a site established in 1834 for the reception of juvenile convicts transported from Great Britain (Austral Archaeology 1997; Jackman 2001). The settlement was created during a period of ongoing debate in Britain and elsewhere over crime, punishment and reform, which intersected with changing notions of childhood morality and responsibility. English law recognised that "infants" up to the age of 7 years could not be guilty of a felony, but those older than this could be convicted and even hanged (Holden 1999:3). Attitudes were changing, however, and increasingly children and young people were beginning to be classified as a separate category of prisoner in terms of their criminal punishment and potential for moral reform. Until the 1820s, about one-quarter of convicts transported were juveniles, that is under 18 years of age. Demand for juvenile labour in the Australian colonies, however, was low in this period, as settlers generally preferred to be assigned adult servants without the "encumbrance" of children. This left authorities with large numbers of teenage male convicts to house, feed and clothe. There were also calls for the segregation and retraining of young offenders in this period, to prevent their corruption at the hands of older convicts and to make them more useful and productive members of colonial society. In Sydney this resulted in the transfer of juvenile convicts from the Hyde Park Barracks to the Carters Barracks around 1820 and in Britain the establishment of Parkhurst Prison for juveniles on the Isle of Wight in 1838. Point Puer was thus one of the first "juvenile prisons" in the British Empire.

The settlement was established on a narrow promontory, with a road across it serving as a line of demarcation patrolled by soldiers to separate the juveniles from contact with adult convicts. The ruins of the establishment include numerous terraces and stonewall footings, which reveal how the geography of discipline exerted over the youths changed through time. The scattered location and ad hoc nature of the prison arrangements, however, meant that constant supervision was difficult, and this allowed the boys to communicate freely with each other and to maintain their own prison culture in defiance of the authorities (Humphery 1997:6–7). A rough timber barracks was built in the first instance, which provided an all-purpose dormitory, mess-room, schoolroom and chapel for the 66 boys first brought to the settlement. Adjacent workshops were also established, where instruction was provided in trades including blacksmithing, carpentry, tailoring, boatbuilding and nail making. Limited resources, however, meant that at least half the inmates spent their days in farm labour, quarrying stones and sawing timber. They endured a 14 h day, with 7 h of work, 2 h of school and the rest in prayers, meals and musters (Fabian and Loh 1980:24). Meals, however, were better than the food served to factory children in Britain, with a daily ration of flour, fresh or salt beef and green vegetables. Most boys spent at least 4 years at Point Puer, some learning to read and write, and most learning a trade of some kind, before passing out into colonial society (Hooper 1967:10–11).

Buildings were erected that gradually increased the degree of surveillance and control exercised over the juvenile convicts. Gaol cells were built at the south end of the settlement, and around 1839 a large timber building was constructed on a stone platform in the middle of the settlement. Used as a schoolroom and chapel, the building was located symbolically midway between the workshops representing industry and reward at the north end of the promontory and punishment in cells to the south. The cells were tiny, 1.6 m long and 0.9 m wide, and were used for the solitary confinement of boys who had escaped and hidden among the rocks and caves below the peninsula. At its peak there were 730 boys held at Point Puer. The settlement closed in 1849, as part of the growing opposition to convict transportation, with more than 2,000 boys having passed through its doors. Careful study of the archaeological remains within their physical setting helps to reveal the evolution of juvenile justice in this period and social transitions from childhood to adulthood and casts light on contemporary debates on juvenile detention and reform.

Conclusion

In 30 years convict archaeology has been transformed from the recovery and description of remains associated with convict men to a diverse and conceptually dynamic field that encompasses a range of convict experiences and theoretical perspectives. Archaeologists have become increasingly engaged in broader discourses with historians and community groups. Evidence from sites where convicts lived and worked is increasingly being used to gain new insights into the material aspects of convict life and through these into their social worlds, their economic situations and even the politics of their resistance. Convicts were more often written about than writing themselves, and as is often the case in historical archaeology, the physical evidence they created themselves shows a richer, more complex and more surprising world than the documents alone have suggested.

Chapter 3
Aboriginal Dispossession and Survival

The archaeology of Aboriginal people since European settlement, or post-contact archaeology, is a dynamic and highly contested area of study. It has a deep resonance in modern Australian life and is charged with significance for many people in the wider community who often have differing agenda. Far from being a dry academic pursuit, research in post-contact archaeology carries great emotional and political weight and has the power to affect major legal decisions with ongoing economic and cultural ramifications. It is also an area that has seen great change since the first work was done in the 1960s. It has grown from a narrowly focused study of Aboriginal people as subjects of European mission activity to a wide-ranging field that encompasses issues of identity and community history, long-term cultural and environmental change and understandings of colonisation as a process which is centrally engaged with contemporary political and legal issues around native title, the nature of history and what it means to be Australian in today's society.

Current archaeological work is driven by these issues and is shaped by two related aspects of disciplinary practice. One is the gulf seen to exist between prehistoric and historical archaeologists, a divide observed by many of those working in the field both in Australia and overseas (e.g. Colley and Bickford 1996; Harrison and Williamson 2004; Lightfoot 1995; Silliman 2005; Torrence and Clarke 2000). Until the mid-1990s it was common for most practitioners trained in prehistoric archaeology to be uninterested in sites or layers within sites that exhibited signs of "contamination" with post-contact artefacts such as bottle glass or clay pipes. Such occupation was obviously comparatively recent and was seen to be of little relevance to research concerned with establishing early occupation dates or describing lithic technologies. At the same time, historical archaeologists were generally more interested in evidence of settler activities such as the convict system, the gold rush or the growth of cities. Aboriginal people of the colonial period were not of much interest to archaeologists, although historians and anthropologists were active researchers (e.g. Beckett 1987; Reynolds 1982, 1989). This situation has begun to break down as the teaching of historical archaeology has increased in Australian university departments and more archaeologists have graduated with training in both areas and as research interests in prehistoric archaeology have enlarged to encompass other issues.

S. Lawrence, P. Davies, *An Archaeology of Australia Since 1788*, Contributions To Global Historical Archaeology, DOI 10.1007/978-1-4419-7485-3_3, © Springer Science+Business Media, LLC 2011

The second factor shaping the growth of post-contact archaeology has been the work of Aboriginal people themselves and the impact this has had on the way archaeologists operate. As Aboriginal people have become more politically empowered they have insisted on exercising greater control over who is able to work in their traditional country and the kind of work that is done. They have insisted on much greater control of their heritage. This has resulted in the development of a number of community-based archaeological projects in which the research questions are established in consultations between the archaeologists and the Aboriginal community (e.g. Greer et al. 2002; Paterson et al. 2003; Smith and Beck 2003). Frequently the material of greatest interest to communities is that which relates to their immediate past and to the lives of their parents and grandparents. Archaeologists who might once have considered themselves primarily prehistorians are thus being increasingly drawn into research on post-contact sites.

Converging interest among prehistorians, historical archaeologists and Aboriginal communities is creating a strong and diverse body of expertise. Historical archaeologists bring with them knowledge of European building techniques and the range of artefacts found on colonial sites, but just as importantly they bring familiarity with colonial history and its sources. They know where to find relevant documentary sources and usually have some skills in the critique of written records. Prehistorians bring skills in interpreting environments and landforms, site survey techniques, and the analysis of stone tools and plant and animal remains. Aboriginal communities are custodians of oral histories, traditions and dreaming stories that direct research and make the results more meaningful. Collaborations between these groups produce archaeologies of contact that are providing new insight into one of the most important aspects of Australian history (Fig. 3.1).

Approaches

Students of post-contact archaeology approach the field from a number of intersecting perspectives. Aboriginal historical sites were among the first colonial archaeological sites to be excavated in Australia, but interest in them arose out of their historical significance to the settlers rather than because of any potential insights into Aboriginal life. The earliest work in the field was done by Jim Allen at Port Essington in the Northern Territory (Allen 1969, 1973, 2008) and by Judy Birmingham at Wybalenna, a mission station on Flinders Island, Tasmania (Birmingham 1973a, b, 1992). Allen chose to work at Port Essington because it was a short-lived British military outpost in the northern coast of Australia. By chance he uncovered artefacts associated with Aboriginal people who were also at the site, but this did not form a major part of his research. Birmingham's approach to the fieldwork at Wybalenna was also characteristic of the general attitude to living Aboriginal people, and Aboriginal history (as distinct from prehistory), at the time. Birmingham's work later expanded beyond models of adaptation and assimilation to reposition Aboriginal people as central actors and shifted to consider resistance

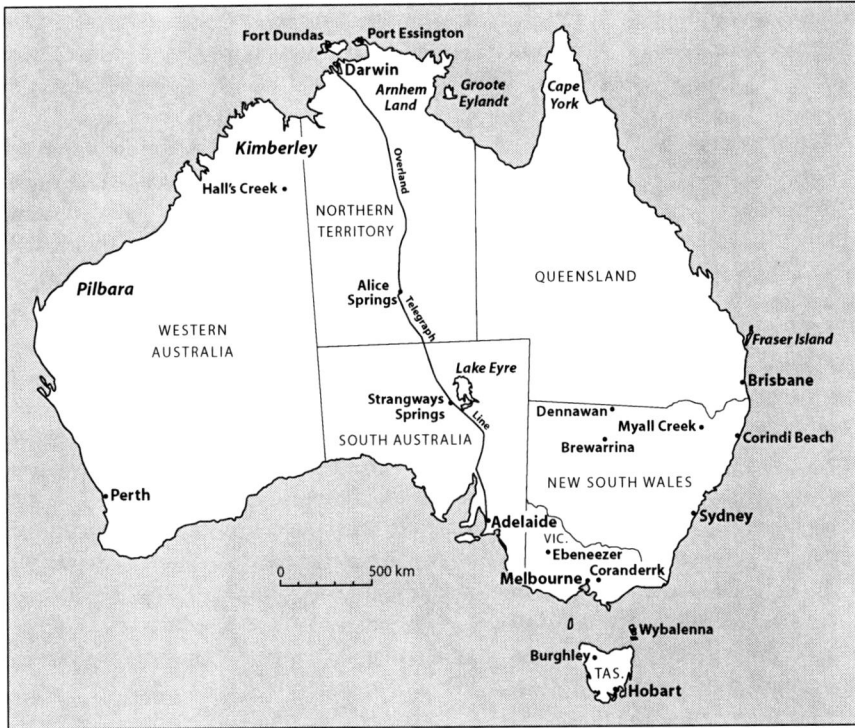

Fig. 3.1 Location map of Indigenous archaeological places discussed in text

to colonisation. This evolution reflects the general development of more nuanced understandings of the survival of Aboriginal people and their participation in all areas of contemporary Australian life.

Wybalenna was established in 1835 by George Augustus Robinson, a Methodist lay preacher to whom the colonial government gave the task of negotiating with Tasmanian Aboriginal groups. There had been an escalating cycle of violence in Van Diemen's Land as Aboriginal groups sought to hold back the advance of British settlement. By the 1820s, there had been hundreds of deaths on both sides and the situation was openly described as one of war. Robinson travelled around the island to speak to all the Aboriginal groups whose lands had not yet been taken, a process described at the time as "reconciliation". Some have seen his trips as the effort to bring "wild" Aborigines into civilisation, but more recent interpretations by historian Henry Reynolds have described it as a formal treaty-making process in which Aboriginal lands on mainland Tasmania were ceded for unfettered use of Flinders Island in Bass Strait to the north (Reynolds 1995). As a result of Robinson's efforts more than 150 Aboriginal people had travelled to Flinders Island by 1835, but rather than being left to pursue their own lives in their own ways as they had anticipated, they were forced into the settlement at Wybalenna, a mission run by Robinson with the intention of training Aboriginal people to become part of white society. Living in close, damp quarters with inadequate food and clothing, the people died rapidly and only 13 years later the settlement was closed and the 47 survivors moved to mainland Tasmania (Ryan 1996:180, 203).

When Birmingham began work at Wybalenna she did so at the invitation of the local branch of the National Trust, which had already been conducting informal digs on the site. Birmingham's role was to formalise and extend these amateur efforts, and it was only by accident that the part of the site where the Trust members had been working was a row of terrace cottages built for and occupied by Aboriginal people. It might just as easily have been one of the other buildings in the settlement such as the store or the commandant's residence. The excavations that Birmingham carried out were aimed at understanding Robinson's efforts to "civilise" the Aborigines and the gradual assimilation of Aboriginal people. As was common in archaeology at the time, there was no attempt to contact members of the Aboriginal community and there were no community members on site at the time of the excavations. This reflected a widespread perception among white Australians, echoed in official government policy, that there was no Aboriginal community to consult in Tasmania because the community had been extinguished with the death of the last Tasmanian Aborigine, Trugannini, in 1876. Throughout Australia, Aboriginal people remained largely invisible, unless as the subject of prehistoric studies into the deep past or anthropological studies into a lingering stone age culture.

The full report and analysis of the excavations was completed in the early 1990s, and in the interim both Australian society and Birmingham's intellectual approach had changed considerably. Across Australia Aboriginal people had become vocal in proclaiming their survival and pro-active in claiming legal recognition (they were belatedly declared citizens in 1969), a range of civil rights and ownership of their own past. Consultation and community representation in archaeological work was becoming commonplace and even legally mandated. Tasmanian Aboriginal people played key roles in spearheading this movement for change. Many were descendants of Aboriginal women and British sealers who had lived on the Bass Strait islands in the early years of the nineteenth century, and they fought vociferously and successfully for land rights and for the repatriation of ancestral skeletal remains. Australian historians were writing more fully and honestly about post-contact relations with Aboriginal people (e.g. Reynolds 1982; Ryan 1981). Historical archaeology was also becoming more sophisticated, influenced by post-processualism and the emergence of new Marxist-informed approaches to social dynamics that encompassed resistance as much as domination and also by new research into gender as a fundamental social category. In her analysis Birmingham successfully integrated these new approaches, producing an interpretation that revealed both subtle and profound Aboriginal challenges to the hegemony Robinson sought. Spatial analysis of small finds showed people interacting out-of-doors in preference to within the cottages, while faunal remains showed a continued preference for wild meats, the implication of the latter being that people left the settlement on a regular basis for food gathering and for ceremonies.

Birmingham's work at Wybalenna established post-contact archaeology as a central theme within Australian historical archaeology and one which illustrates the continuing development of research in this area. Alongside new research into other aspects of post-contact archaeology, an interest in colonisation has continued. One recent example is the work by Alistair Paterson on sites in the Northern Territory and Western Australia (Paterson 2008). Also taking as a point of departure the nature of the colonial project, Paterson has explored how the British desire for grazing land was met by Aboriginal groups in arid Australia. While also sometimes violent, contact there evolved in a way that enabled settlers and Aboriginal people to share resources to a greater extent and to develop a society that involved some level of mutual dependence. As their traditional lands and foods were taken over by the graziers, Aboriginal people began to work on the stations in exchange for rations. Graziers benefited from Aborigines' superior knowledge of country and climate and Aboriginal people maintained personal access to their country and carried out ceremonies. Growing initially out of a project directed by Birmingham, from its inception Paterson's work was built on strong working relationships between archaeologists and Aboriginal people. This is reflected in both his use of new data sources including oral history and his attention to sites beyond the buildings of the whites. Paterson was also able to draw on the skills and techniques of prehistoric archaeology in order to investigate fully the lithic and environmental evidence that predominated in the Aboriginal campsites located around the pastoral structures.

Colonisation is also of interest to Tim Murray, who has advocated new ways of approaching post-contact archaeology that incorporate global perspectives and comparisons of how European and indigenous societies have interacted around the world (Murray 2004b). He argues that better understanding of the diversity of post-contact experiences in settler societies is a first step in writing an archaeological account of contact and its consequences on a global scale (Murray 2004a:3). Part of this understanding is the renewed realisation that contact is a process rather than an event or even a time period, and that it is a process of cultural transformation for both indigenous and settler societies (Murray 2004a:11). To help facilitate such a project Murray identified several significant variables for comparison. The first variable, the timing of colonisation, is relevant to the technological, economic and ideological resources of the invaders, while the nature of the indigenous society helped to shape interactions in regard to treaty-making, violent resistance, access to land and resources and religion. Both of these factors of timing are related to the second variable, the intentions of the colonisers, which could include resource extraction, population settlement, strategic importance *vis-à-vis* other European powers and religious conversion. Demographics, the third variable, have played a crucial role, from the impact of disease to the movement of large numbers of European settlers and enslaved or otherwise involuntary migrants and the kinds of creolised societies that have resulted. The final variable identified by Murray is the duration of colonisation, which ended in the eighteenth century for the United States, the nineteenth century for parts of Latin America, and is still continuing today in parts of Africa and the Pacific. Murray's framework provides a way of identifying the kinds of large-scale forces that were being played out in the minutiae of daily interaction at any given place and which consequently have helped to shape archaeological sites. In this sense, places such as Wybalenna and outback pastoral stations can help illuminate not only the white settlement of Australia, but also some of the ways in which European expansion has shaped the modern world.

While colonisation models have been a useful way for placing post-contact sites within a broad global perspective, for other archaeologists, examination of long-term culture change has proven to be a means of situating post-contact sites within a deeper temporal perspective, creating links between the pre-contact and post-contact periods. One of the leading proponents of this approach is Christine Williamson. Based on her work in north-western Tasmania, Williamson has argued that factors such as environment, technology and a society's history and values all contribute to trajectories that can be followed through time (Williamson 2004a:177, 192). By tracing trajectories across the pre-/post-contact period, continuities and changes in Aboriginal culture can be identified and used to write new kinds of histories.

Explaining both colonisation and long-term culture change are ultimately goals identified closely with academia and are examples of what has been described as "consent-based archaeology" (Greer et al. 2002). Such research requires the consent of communities and when completed may produce results of direct interest to Aboriginal people, but this outcome is neither assured nor necessarily sought. In contrast are projects that explicitly address the needs of the community from the outset and which are driven by community members themselves. Community archaeology projects create detailed local histories of a community's relationship with place which may contribute to its sense of identity and to empowerment, but which may also be associated with pragmatic matters of land claims and native title. While the approaches used are equally applicable in historical archaeology (and indeed Birmingham's work at Wybalenna, at the behest of the National Trust, could be seen as an early example), they have been more widely associated with Aboriginal prehistoric and post-contact archaeology.

The line between consent- and community-based approaches can be ambiguous, but in general a central component of community archaeology is collaboration and interaction with the community rather than reaction by the community to proposals (and results) presented by archaeologists (Colley 2002:92–104; Davidson et al. 1995; Greer et al. 2002:268). As Shelley Greer and her colleagues explain, in collaborative research projects community interests directly shape both research questions and the methodologies used and community members participate fully in all aspects of the project. Researchers may employ techniques drawn from other disciplines including anthropology and geography. Ethnographic interviews, oral history, workshops, and participant observation may all be used to draw out stories of significance in the community and to identify places and landscapes. This process helps to define the areas of interest to the community that can best be addressed using archaeological methods. It also provides access to intangible elements of heritage such as memory and attachment, adding layers of richness and meaning to interpretations of physical evidence. Archaeological sites are visited, recorded and at times excavated with community members, but "places" where there may not be any material evidence are also mapped. This includes places of conception and birth, the locations of bush foods, dreaming tracks and trails and lines of movement used in the recent past.

In combination these techniques add a number of new dimensions to research results. They may provide alternative ways of interpreting typical archaeological sites such as shell middens or scarred trees within the context of the contemporary cosmologies in which they are embedded, as Greer found in coastal Cape York (Greer 1995). Working with Aboriginal and white communities on pastoral stations in western New South Wales, Rodney Harrison has shown that detailed mapping can integrate tangible but discrete sites and intangible places along with memories, stories, tracks and activities into a coherent and meaningful system (Harrison 2004b). Community perspectives bring to light sites that have been unimportant and even invisible within the heritage system and where there has been little or no archaeological interest, as was the case in a community project on the north coast of New South Wales co-ordinated by archaeologists from the University of New England (Smith and Beck 2003). Sites such as the fringe camps on the margins of country towns were centres of Aboriginal life after contact, but these may have low visibility as Aboriginal places using traditional archaeological methods alone. Materials, building styles and artefacts used may all derive from mainstream Australian society, leaving only subtle artefact signatures with no obvious "Aboriginal" evidence. It is only when the techniques of community-based approaches are used that such sites can be understood and appreciated.

Native Title

One of the most explicit intersections of post-contact archaeology with community interests is in the area of Native Title claims. Post-contact archaeology is emerging as a more relevant source of evidence than traditional prehistoric archaeology because the legal basis for determining the validity of claims rests on the assessment of what took place after the arrival of the British. The concept of native title emerged from a High Court decision in 1992 that recognised the possibility of continued Aboriginal cultural ties with land and which overturned the doctrine of *terra nullius*, that at the time of European settlement the Aboriginal people had no claim to their land. According to the *Native Title Act* (1993) and its 1998 amendments, claimants must be able to demonstrate continuity of association with land according to traditional laws and customs (Harrison 2000:35). Archaeology can contribute to this process by providing evidence of the ongoing use of sites and the maintenance of activities into and through the post-contact period, potentially by demonstrating that while customs may be adapted to accommodate changing circumstances they are nevertheless traditional (Lilley 2000).

This must be done, however, within the constraints of the legal system, an arena with which archaeologists have had little familiarity until recently and where there can be fundamental differences in underlying philosophies. The ways in which the legal system operates with regard to Native Title have been explored by Libby Riches (2003, 2004), who has noted several issues of which archaeologists need to be aware. One is the formal rule determining what can be presented as evidence, with anything deemed unreliable or irrelevant being ruled inadmissible. Another is the practice of using expert witnesses such as archaeologists, anthropologists, geographers and historians to "translate" Indigenous knowledge in a way more accessible to judges and lawyers. The testimony of the experts will not be taken on face value, however, as it is assessed on the basis of professional skills, logic, methodological reliability and impartiality. It may be found wanting and rejected in any or all of these regards. Most significant of all, however, is the reliance of the judiciary on "facts" as they relate to underlying truth. As Riches points out, within the social sciences the very notion of "truth" is one that has been significantly destabilised, particularly by post-modern philosophies of knowledge. The courts, however, have little patience for subtleties of academic argument and interpretation when it comes to making determinations on the "facts" of Aboriginal dispossession.

Another issue of concern for those involved in Native Title is that cases generally rely on existing archaeological evidence and do not commission new research specifically in support of the claim being made (Fullagar and Head 2000:32). Whether or not the archaeological work that has already been done in a region is of the kind that is most likely to be useful to claimants is a matter of chance. In some instances previous studies would have recorded post-contact as well as pre-contact materials, but that may not always be the case, particularly given the nature of archaeological enquiry in Australia. Fullagar and Head (2000:34) have argued that Australian prehistoric archaeology's privileging of environmental and evolutionary explanations, and the search for sites of increasing antiquity, rather than pursuing questions related to culture history, have inadvertently created a situation in which coherent regional sequences are unavailable. This is problematic for Native Title claims because it is precisely this kind of sequence on which the claims can most successfully draw. Fullagar and Head (2000:24) also note the general problem of addressing ethnicity in the archaeological record. As this is an area in which historical and post-contact archaeology have generally been more successful, it may be another reason for post-contact archaeology to have great potential in this area of research.

The 1998 amendments to the *Native Title Act* have made provision for negotiated Indigenous Land Use Agreements, which operate outside the court system and are therefore open to more fluid definitions of tradition (Murray 2004c:214). This is helping to address some of the issues surrounding interpretations of Native Title, but the challenges of providing effective evidence nevertheless remain. Research on post-contact sites, particularly when integrated with studies that trace long-term patterns of land use in a region, has the greatest potential to contribute to claims for justice regarding land. In Western Australia, archaeological evidence that demonstrated the presence of glass and metal objects in the upper layers of middens that had been in use for 18,000 years were an important part of the successful Miriuwung-Gajerrong case (Fullagar and Head 2000:24). As Harrison (2000) has argued, post-contact archaeology can demonstrate the continuity of use required under Native Title law, and it can also challenge the notion of the unchanging nature of pre-contact life.

It has been argued that the divide between prehistoric and historical archae-ologies in Australia has contributed to the culture of forgetting Aboriginal people because it has perpetuated a lack of interest in post-contact Aboriginal experiences and denied the authenticity of their identity as Aboriginal people (see Barker 2007; Byrne 1997; Harrison 2000:38). Post-contact archaeologies that contribute to writ-ing new histories of the colonial and post-colonial periods, what Murray (1996) calls *shared* histories, can help to address this failure. The creation of shared histories of the post-contact era is a necessary part of the project of reconciliation between Aboriginal and non-Aboriginal Australians. Shared histories that bring to light and acknowledge past events, especially those that have been most hurtful, help white Australia to understand Aboriginal experiences of colonisation. This can lead to healing on the part of Aboriginal people and to the assuaging of guilt and shame on the part of white society (Murray 2004c). Murray describes one example of this process in action at the construction of a memorial at the site of the Myall Creek Massacre in New South Wales, where descendants of the Aboriginal victims and the white perpetrators have been able to come together for the first time in 150 years (see Chapter 12). At the national level, Prime Minister Kevin Rudd's apology to the Stolen Generations in 2008 has had a similar effect, providing space for stories to be told and healing to begin.

Archaeology, with its emphasis on physical evidence and place, can play a crucial role in making Aboriginal experiences visible to the wider society. One mundane but powerful step is the greater inclusion of post-contact Aboriginal sites in local heritage studies (Byrne 2004). At present the way that heritage studies are conducted in many parts of Australia is symptomatic of disciplinary divides between prehistoric archaeologists, historic archaeologists, architectural historians and historians. Prehistorians record archaeological sites associated with the deep past before European colonisation, and non-Aboriginal sites from the "historic" period are dealt with by architectural historians, historians and historical archae-ologists. None of the sites used by Aboriginal people after contact are recorded by either group, which both denies the ongoing presence of Aboriginal people in com-munities and disconnects contemporary Aboriginal people from their distant past. A similar situation exists in many parts of the Old World where archaeologists have spent considerable time and money reifying evidence of the Classical and ancient worlds, while simultaneously ignoring the more recent archaeologies of the com-munities still living there and effectively disempowering them (Baram and Carroll 2000; Silberman 1989). Filling in the gap by recording the archaeological sites of the intervening years makes that time visible and positions it within the heritage of the wider community, re-connecting contemporary Aboriginal people with their past and empowering them as part of the modern community.

Methods

In addition to the problems created by disciplinary divides, those interested in more recent Aboriginal archaeology face the challenge of actually identi-fying sites and artefacts (Byrne 2004:143). Because European materials were frequently "brought over" by Aboriginal people in unaltered form, even while being radically recontextualised, it can be difficult to identify Aboriginal use of a site from the material evidence alone. Better background research using archival sources and oral histories is one part of the solution as it points to the places that Aboriginal people were using, but archaeologists are also rising to the challenge by developing more subtle ways of analysing artefactual evidence and by expanding the body of evidence considered and the techniques used to study it.

One of the first forms of evidence that archaeologists were able to recognise was distinctive breakage patterns on bottle glass. In the 1960s, it was apparent to Jim Allen at Port Essington that base and body fragments from bottles were being purposefully flaked by Aboriginal people in order to form tools (Allen 1969). This was evidence that glass was being sought as a raw material and used in a traditional manner similar to any other lithic raw material. Since then other researchers have observed flaked glass at many sites, including predominantly non-Aboriginal places such as shepherds' huts at Burghley in Tasmania and in Victoria's Western District (Porter 2004; Williamson 2004b; Wolski and Loy 1999), pastoral stations in the Kimberley and Central Australia (Birmingham 2000; Gibbs and Harrison 2008; Harrison 2002c; Paterson 2008:59–128; Smith 2001) and at Aboriginal places such as rock shelters on the south coast of New South Wales (Colley 1997), and middens on Groote Eylandt in the Northern Territory and in central Queensland (Clarke 2000b; Ulm et al. 1999). Glass tools have also been found at campsites in the Queensland rainforest (Ferrier 2004:29), at missions in South Australia (Brockwell et al. 1989; Hemming et al. 2000) and Tasmania (Allen and Jones 1980; Birmingham 1992) and fringe camps in New South Wales (Smith and Beck 2003). Flaked glass is thus one of the most ubiquitous and easily recognisable forms of evidence for Aboriginal use of a place in the post-contact period. Its presence also helps to destabilise and break down the conventional distinctions between "Aboriginal" and "non-Aboriginal" places, where site use and occupation has been variously contested, alternated or shared.

Researchers have begun to explore what the glass artefacts can reveal about activities on the sites. Some have carried out residue and use-wear analyses on the tools, demonstrating that they were used for processing tuberous plant foods and for woodworking. Significantly, detailed analysis by Nathan Wolski and Tom Loy (1999) has shown that use-wear and residues are not confined to glass that was deliberately flaked. Rather, they have also found evidence of use on sherds that otherwise appear to be the product of normal or random bottle breakage. This has led them to argue that flaking patterns and traditional lithic analysis based on technology and form are not sufficient for identifying glass used as tools on Aboriginal sites. The absence of flakes and cores alone should not be taken as evidence that glass tools were not used, as even unmodified glass was a desirable resource. Other glass objects, such as the elaborately worked Kimberley spear points of Western Australia, are obviously and unambiguously the deliberate product of Aboriginal labour. Going beyond their obvious association with Aboriginal people, Harrison (2002c) has argued that they can also be interpreted as evidence of changing definitions of Aboriginal masculinity in the post-contact period.

Other European objects such as buttons, metal and clay tobacco pipes are commonly found on post-contact sites, but have not received as much archaeological attention. Courtney and McNiven (1998) have analysed three clay pipes from Fraser Island, noting that the numbers observed archaeologically are much fewer than the historical documentation would predict. They suggest that parts of the island were characterised by different patterns of use during the latter part of the nineteenth century. The western side of the island, where the pipes were found, was a core habitation area while the eastern side, where the European observers recorded extensive smoking, was used for large inter-group gatherings featuring a range of social, economic and ceremonial activities. If tobacco use was restricted to ceremonial occasions, as was traditionally the practice elsewhere in northern Australia, fewer pipes on the west coast of the island would be consistent with less smoking on a regular daily basis.

One of the few archaeologists to analyse metal objects is Harrison (2002b), who points out that unlike glass, which was used in a way that followed ancient technologies, metal was either used in unmodified forms (e.g. axes) or processed in ways that are clearly new technological developments. For example, horseshoes were alternately heated and beaten to produce iron spear points and knives. Truck springs were ground and beaten to make adzes similar in use to traditional "tula" adzes. "Wires" were made of any long, thin metal object such as nails, screwdrivers or fencing wire and were themselves tools used to pressure-flake bottle glass when making Kimberley points. Bedsprings were remade into fishhooks and tobacco tins were made into pull-along toy cars. Empty food tins were used as lamps, billies and drinking cups, while kerosene tins were used as furniture or flattened out and added to shelters (Fig. 3.2).

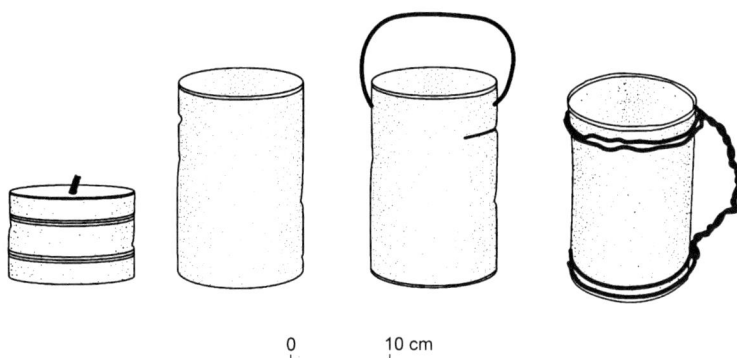

0   10 cm

Fig. 3.2 Tin-can artefacts from Old Lamboo Station in the Kimberley including (**a**) lamp with wick; (**b**) drinking vessel; (**c**) billy and (**d**) drinking mug from Brewarinna Mission in western New South Wales (Reproduced with permission of Rodney Harrison)

While Harrison writes about metal within Aboriginal culture, Philip Jones (2007:102–129) considers the moments of cultural exchange when metal first passed from European to Aborigine. A metal axe, ground down from part of a saddle and hafted in a traditional manner onto a wooden handle, is one of the objects in the collections of the South Australian Museum. Jones suggests that hybrid objects like the axe have the "double patina" of the frontier, with potent histories in both Aboriginal and white culture. Looking beyond this object, Jones uses explorers' accounts to describe the wide circulation of metal in central and northern Australia well in advance of regular contact with Europeans. Aborigines sought out iron of every kind, particularly axes and tomahawks, bartered them, stole them and salvaged the metal from the supply depots and abandoned equipment of white explorers. It is apparent that some explorers, such as Charles Sturt and especially Thomas Mitchell, had at least some understanding of the protocols for entering country and were able to use the axes as items of barter to facilitate their travels. Bartering tomahawks for information, ethnographers Frank Gillen and Baldwin Spencer also used metal to gain entry to Aboriginal society.

Despite the widespread use of metal, Harrison argues that we should not assume unmodified artefacts either have not been used, or have not been recontextualised by Aboriginal people. For Aboriginal informants, items that were or are used by Aboriginal people are, by definition, Aboriginal objects, regardless of their point of origin. Even ordinary items may have particular significance or additional layers of meaning within an Aboriginal context. Teacups and tobacco tins speak to the valued grocery items that station people "came in" from the bush in order to obtain. Buttons and buckles conjure memories of stock work and the station owners' use of clothing and other goods to denote varying levels of prestige. These levels of meaning were accessible to Harrison because his work was done in collaboration with Aboriginal informants who had lived on the site. Others working on twentieth-century fringe camps have also noted that very few of the remains in the sites would be identifiable as Indigenous without the input of the Aboriginal people who lived there and who collaborated in the research (Hemming et al. 2000; Smith and Beck 2003). Such close associations are not possible when working on older, colonial sites, but nevertheless work such as Harrison's points to ways that similar items on older sites may also have held meaning for those who used them.

As archaeologists have begun to recognise the multiple layers of meaning embedded in even seemingly everyday objects, new kinds of theory-building have been required. Older models that employed acculturation and assimilation as ways of explaining culture contact and interaction are increasingly being rejected. Objects do not have to be labelled as either "Aboriginal" or "European", and there is no longer an expectation that a greater number of "European" objects on a site imply a greater loss of culture among the Aboriginal users of the objects. There is no inevitable trajectory followed after contact by which Indigenous groups will gradually become fully assimilated into white society, losing all of their traditions, language, beliefs and material culture in the process. In seeking new ways to understand the material record of post-contact experiences, archaeologists are increasingly being informed by research on other kinds of cross-cultural interaction (Clarke and Paterson 2003; Torrence and Clarke 2000). Some researchers have begun to explore processes of creolisation that take place in post-contact situations where new forms of society emerge that draw on both Indigenous and settler practices (Birmingham 2000; Russell 2005). Others have argued for more subtle, context-dependent interpretations that draw on new understandings of ethnicity and the creation of social identity in colonial contexts (S. Jones 1999; Thomas 1991). As we discuss in Chapter 10, ethnicity, whether Aboriginal or otherwise, is not a fixed, immutable construct. If one element of ethnicity changes, it does not follow that the entire ethnic identity is threatened. Rather, ethnicity is fluid and changeable, evolving as circumstances change, adopting new elements and discarding others. It is only because of its dynamic nature that ethnicity remains a meaningful part of identity. This perspective is closer to the experience of most Indigenous people who maintain a strong and vibrant Aboriginal identity despite 200 years of contact.

Issues of identity and creolisation are much more prominent when working with Aboriginal people themselves. Collaboration also foregrounds the use of oral history, a technique that archaeologists are increasingly using when working on post-contact sites. Oral histories can illuminate how artefacts were made and used and the meanings they held. They can also lead to the location and identification of sites in the landscape and of tracks and pathways between sites. Oral histories are also a way in which people can record the significance that specific places have had in their lives or in their families (Beck and Somerville 2005). These histories may be gathered in a number of ways. Informants may be interviewed individually or in groups, and objects and photographs may be used to stimulate discussion. Maps and aerial photographs may be used for recording information such as the location and names of campsites, birthplaces, ceremonial places or places where bush foods were obtained. Ideally the archaeologists and the Aboriginal people also visit the sites together so that additional information may be recorded. GIS provides a means of spatially integrating oral information with archaeological, environmental and documentary information, and separate layers can be created for each informant and type of information. This technique has been successfully used in studies of the pastoral industry, missions and fringe camps.

Other archaeologists are also turning to new sources of evidence that have not previously been used to study post-contact archaeology. These include rock art, museum collections of objects collected by early explorers and ethnographers and even photographs. Rock art on Groote Eylandt in the Gulf of Carpentaria, for example, depicts Macassan *perahu* engaged in the sea cucumber trade. The images are highly accurate depictions in the X-ray style, revealing the contents of the ships, and indicate an intimate knowledge of the industry on the part of the Aboriginal artists (Burningham 1994; Clarke 2000b; Clarke and Frederick 2008). In the Sydney region, however, the opposite situation prevailed. Jo McDonald (2007, 2008) has recorded an extensive corpus of petroglyphs (stone carvings) and pictographs (pigment art) in the Sydney basin, produced over the last few thousand years. In the first years after contact, however, the amount of traditional art depicting European subjects was very low. More than half the images were of ships, drawn simply as if observed from a distance. McDonald suggests that the low frequency of European subjects indicates that the fabric of Aboriginal society disintegrated quickly soon after contact occurred, limiting their opportunity to communicate and comprehend the outsiders and their culture. In Central Australia, Aboriginal people continued to produce rock art after contact as part of maintaining country, but they did not incorporate European-derived imagery (Frederick 1999, 2000). However, changes in the materials used (charcoal rather than wet ochre), as well as increasing complexity and use of detail in the designs, reflect the shifting contexts in which the art was produced. Fewer sites came to be used more often after contact, indicating a shift from the expansive use of landscape to a more concentrated use of a restricted landscape.

Museum collections of objects collected in the early twentieth century by the Swedish ethnographer Eric Mjoberg have been analysed by Åsa Ferrier and integrated with more traditional archaeological research as a means of gaining insight into material culture in the Queensland rainforest during the immediate post-contact period (Ferrier 2004). The museum objects are particularly significant because they were collected at a time when the Jirrbal people were in the early stages of directly encountering Europeans. Many of the items they were using were still closely associated with their traditional use of the rainforest and its resources. Additionally, because the ethnographic objects are made of organic materials that do not preserve well in the archaeological record, they provide information on practices to which archaeologists do not normally have access, such as fishing with torches and the use of wooden spears and shields in ceremonial combat.

Jane Lydon has analysed photographs of Aboriginal people taken by white photographers to examine ways in which both whites and Indigenous people manipulated imagery in the process of cultural exchange (Lydon 2004, 2005). For her study Lydon used nineteenth-century photographs taken at Coranderrk Aboriginal Station near Melbourne, a reserve established for the Kulin peoples in 1863. Lydon considered the subject matter of the photographs as well as the contexts in which they were later used and displayed. She argues that the same photographs took on significantly different meanings in differing contexts. Portraits of individuals that were displayed in a large panel that was exhibited at the Intercolonial Exhibition in 1866 and the Paris Universal Exposition in 1867 were arranged to wordlessly convey the group's eventual disappearance. The same portraits placed in the family album of the white manager at the station, a man extraordinary at the time for his genuine sympathy and friendship for the Kulin, depict individuals with affection. While white society used the photographs to construct narratives of civilisation, Lydon also argues that the Kulin were able to influence the content and use of the images for their own purposes. They re-enacted historical events for the camera, a visual form unknown in European practice at that time, but common in traditional Aboriginal art in the area. The resulting photographs, which depict the procession of the Kulin onto their new reserve, are stylistically reminiscent of older forms and also make a powerful statement about rights to land.

Aboriginal Experiences

Research on post-contact sites has enabled archaeologists and Aboriginal people to begin to document the archaeological record of processes of contact in Australia. Murray (2004a) has suggested that the nature of contact experiences around the world will differ based on the timing of contact, the nature of Indigenous and settler societies involved and the objectives of each group. On a smaller scale the same differences can be observed within Australia. Aboriginal people in the temperate, south-eastern parts of the country were the first to have sustained encounters with British settlers and generally suffered greater disturbance to traditional life than those in more isolated outback areas where British colonisation did not begin until the second half of the nineteenth century. Aborigines in many places knew about Europeans long before they actually saw them. Trade networks that criss-crossed the interior for the exchange of ochre, shell and stone tools, also distributed fragments of glass, strips of cloths and scraps of iron. Word of the new arrivals also passed quickly over the trade routes, while domestic animals, including cattle, horses and dogs, strayed away from European settlement and into the interior. Exotic diseases, such as smallpox and influenza, crossed the continent in all directions with devastating impact, well in advance of the newcomers themselves. The first British colonists at Port Jackson observed Eora people with skin marked by smallpox, which had probably come ashore with Macassan fishers in Arnhem Land (Campbell 2002).

As Europeans began to exploit the land, conflict with Aboriginal people arose quickly, often over water and stock feed. Aborigines saw the mobs of sheep and cattle as a slow and vulnerable source of prey. They used their hunting skills and intimate knowledge of terrain to take sheep and drive them out of reach of their European owners. Access to large amounts of beef and mutton also changed the pattern of Aboriginal gatherings, with larger groups meeting for longer. Colonists often responded with murderous "dispersals" of Aboriginal people. Aboriginal society, while it suffered enormously under the white invasion, did not collapse completely, but adapted in numerous ways to the foreigners arriving from over the horizon. In the following section several case studies serve as windows into aspects of Aboriginal experiences of colonisation in different parts of Australia at different periods.

Ancient Trajectories

As we noted previously, when sites used after contact are considered as part of the suite of sites in a landscape, they have the potential to reveal the nature of long-term culture change and continuities in a region. This is the case on the Cobourg Peninsula in the Northern Territory, where Scott Mitchell has studied regional exchange networks before, during and after contact (Mitchell 1994, 1996, 2000). In this case, contact seems to have begun in the first half of the eighteenth century, when Macassan fishers from Sulawesi began regularly voyaging to Arnhem Land in order to harvest sea slugs (trepang) for sale to China, a trade which continued until outlawed by the Australian government in

1907 (Bowdler 2002; Clarke 2000a; Knapp and Sutherland 2004; MacKnight 1976, 2008). Sporadic visits were also made to the Kimberley coast up to the twentieth century (Crawford 2001; Morwood and Hobbs 1997). By the mid-nineteenth century the British had also established a permanent presence in the region through the construction of a number of military forts (Fort Dundas, Port Essington and Fort Wellington) that collectively were occupied from 1824 to 1849.

Both the Macassans and the British at that time were based on the coast and did not venture far inland. As Mitchell has been able to document, however, the effects of their presence spread across Arnhem Land, hundreds of kilometres from where they themselves ventured. Ethnographic accounts from the region suggested that exchange networks in the region had intensified significantly in the region as a result of foreign contact, stimulated by the desire for trade goods such as iron and cloth. Mitchell has used archaeological evidence from 45 middens on the Cobourg Peninsula to investigate the nature of exchange in the region prior to contact. As the region is lacking in readily available stone sources, Mitchell used the quantity and diversity of non-local stone as an indicator of the extent of trade. Of the middens used prior to contact, some of which dated to 3100 BP, only two contained non-local stone. Of the post-contact middens, 41 percent contained non-local stone of several different varieties. This indicates that there was a significant increase in trade after foreign contact.

Mitchell observes that the exchange appears to have been driven by the need to maintain social obligations, as favoured objects such as iron and cloth were readily traded away from the coast and, in the case of cloth, torn into smaller and smaller pieces. He argues that while contact provided new and desirable objects, it also created a situation in which there was an increased need for the resolution of conflicts between groups. Foreigners carried a range of fatal diseases such as smallpox, which spread rapidly into the interior of the continent with devastating effect (Campbell 1983, 2002). In Arnhem Land as elsewhere, women and children were particularly vulnerable, resulting in a population where women were scarce. This increased conflict among the men, a situation also documented by European observers. Among the implications that Mitchell draws are that fighting was not necessarily traditional, pre-contact behaviour, and that the elaborate exchange networks observed ethnographically were mechanisms devised in the recent past to resolve inter-group tensions.

Killing Times

In Van Diemen's Land the process of contact was much more rapid, immediate and violent. The first massacre of Aboriginal people occurred within months of the British landing at Risdon Cove in 1803 and establishing what was to become Hobart. The following year a second British settlement was established in the north of the island. More killings followed quickly, and conflict between Aboriginal people and settlers spread throughout the island. By the early 1830s, at the end of a decade so violent it was called "The Black War", the colonial government employed George Augustus Robinson as an envoy to approach all the Aboriginal people still living in their traditional lands with an offer of peace. According to the government, if they surrendered their lands on the mainland of Tasmania they would be looked after at a settlement on Flinders Island in Bass Strait. Having a different understanding of what was being offered, the tribes agreed and Wybalenna was established to receive them.

In 1989–1990, working at the site of a Van Diemen's Land Company outstation at Burghley, Tim Murray uncovered archaeological evidence of one family group who for a brief period eluded Robinson and continued to live on their land (Murray 1993). The outstation, a slab hut that was the base for shepherds looking after the Company's sheep, had been abandoned by the Company in 1839 and subsequently destroyed by fire, but Murray found evidence of Aboriginal occupation after the fire. A number of stone tools were found both inside the hut in front of the fireplace and on top of the charred flooring. Additionally, closer analysis of the glass assemblage revealed that many pieces had been flaked (Williamson 2004b). Although the hut was abandoned well after the conclusion of Robinson's trip, closer reading of the documentary record indicated that one last family was not brought in until 1842. The family consisted of John Lanna or (Lanne), his wife Nabrunga and their five sons between 3 and 20 years of age. The identification of this family and their life at Burghley has added poignancy because while most of the family was dead by the end of the year, one of the little boys, William Lanne, survived into adulthood, achieved fame as a member of a whaling crew and became a leader of the remaining Aboriginal community. His death in Hobart in 1869 was associated with one of the most shameful episodes in a shameful story, when his body was illegally exhumed and dismembered, the hands and skull being taken for "scientific purposes" by the Royal Society of Tasmania and the Royal College of Surgeons in Edinburgh.

Burghley itself was also a place of violence, as were all the Company's holdings in north-western Van Diemen's Land. Van Diemen's Land Company records contain reports of many outrages on both sides, including shootings, rapes and murders. The shepherds at Burghley kidnapped Aboriginal women and held them prisoner, and in response the Aboriginal people retaliated on many occasions, once succeeding in driving off the occupants. None of this is evident in the archaeological record, which instead reflects the persistence and continuity of the Lannes as their world crumbled around them. Christine Williamson's analysis of the assemblage indicated that the stone was heavily worked and that locally available raw materials present on other sites in the area were absent. Likewise, only three small pieces of ochre were present even though the most important quarries on the island were also in the vicinity. From this Williamson argues that by this period the movements of the family across the landscape were restricted and they were unable to obtain stone from their usual sources. Retouched glass was found across the site, particularly in the dump area in association with what may have been hearths. Large quantities of bones from native animals such as wallabies, bandicoots and possums were also found in front of the hearth in the hut, and Murray has suggested that the fire which destroyed the hut was accidentally caused by not cleaning the chimney, as is indicated by the accumulation of bones and fine ash in its lower levels. From this evidence it is apparent that the Lannes were using the site on a regular basis, returning to it before and after the hut was destroyed, and making use of the European materials they found there.

The Missions

Mission stations were established by church groups and government authorities throughout Australia. While the missions served as a focus for attempts to convert Aboriginal people to Christianity, prosyletisation was never a driving concern for the white authorities, who saw the missions primarily as vehicles for acculturating Aborigines into colonial society. Ironically, while early church authorities in Port Jackson were consciously turning their backs on the local Eora people, Sydney served as a base for the Church of England's Church Missionary Society activities in the Pacific. In New Zealand, Angela Middleton (2008) has studied the archaeological remains of Te Puna Mission, the successor to the first CMS mission set up by the Reverend Samuel Marsden, Chaplain for the colony of New South Wales, in 1814. Unlike later missions in Australia, the New Zealand missions were domestic missions based on the household of the missionary family, and Middleton has found that that while the missionaries were connected materially and emotionally to New South Wales, they were also highly dependent on their Maori hosts who remained autonomous until the more intensive British colonisation of the 1840s.

In New Zealand the missionaries were the first white settlers but in Australia the missions frequently followed colonisation and its disruptions. One consequence was that as Aboriginal people were denied access to their traditional country, they became increasingly desperate for food and were forced to seek out the missions because of the rations available there, especially flour, tea, sugar and tobacco. Once there, white authorities controlled their lives to a greater or lesser degree. Some, such as Coranderrk near Melbourne, which was established at the request of the Wurundjeri people, were relatively mild. Others were not. By the twentieth century missions and reserves were the only lands left to Aboriginal people in many parts of the country, particularly in the south-east where dispossession has been more extensive. They became the focal points for disparate communities comprised of traditional owners and groups relocated there by government policy. They became home and are now places of great significance for many Aboriginal people, associated with childhood, parents and grandparents. These are places where community archaeology, with its combination of oral history and spatial mapping, has much to offer.

One place that illustrates the range of approaches taken in the archaeology of missions, and the interests of the Aboriginal community, is that of Ebenezer Mission near Dimboola in north-western Victoria. Ebenezer was established in 1859 by Moravian missionaries, becoming one of six Victorian missions (including Coranderrk) for the confinement of Aboriginal people managed by the Central Board for the Protection of the Aborigines. The number of residents dwindled due to government policies that expelled "half-caste" people from the missions, and Ebenezer was closed in 1904 and the land opened for selection. The National Trust took control of the site in 1968 and transferred ownership to the Goolum Goolum Aboriginal Cooperative in 1991. The site is of considerable importance to the local Indigenous community whose parents and grandparents were born there, who have lived or camped there themselves since its closure and who have relatives buried there. Since 1990, the Goolum Goolum and the Victoria Archaeological Survey (later Aboriginal Affairs Victoria) have initiated a number of studies at Ebenezer (e.g. Brown et al. 2004; Du Cros 1997), and it has also been the subject of academic research in cooperation with the Goolum Goolum and the Wotjobaluk Native Title Claimant Group (Lydon et al. 2004; Zipfel 2002).

The various studies have used different methodologies according to their aims, but all have worked closely with community members who have initiated the work, guided its direction and participated in its completion. One of the most important matters for the community was the identification of the mission's cemetery, which was not formally gazetted or marked and whose location was lost when the mission was closed (Brown et al. 2004; see Chapter 12). Over a decade archaeologists have used a number of strategies to relocate and mark the cemetery which is believed to include burials that both pre- and post-date the mission period as well. Documentary records were used to carry out a new survey based on a plan of the mission drawn in 1904, and oral history has revealed the burial of people in the cemetery in the early twentieth century. Ground penetrating radar and magnetometer surveys have been used increasingly to relocate historic cemeteries in Australia. One of the earliest geophysical applications was the use of earth resistivity in 1986 to identify the location of the Aboriginal burial ground at Wybalenna in Tasmania (Ranson and Egloff 1988:59–64). At Ebenezer the magnetometer was the most useful, locating around 75 probable or possible burials. Another technique that has indicated the location of individual burials was a botanical survey of plants with particular attention to exotic species. The site was surveyed four times at different times of year and the location of exotics such as iris bulbs mapped. A micro-topographic survey was also carried out that used minute variations in the ground surface to identify depressions, and the two techniques in combination revealed around 80 possible grave locations. These results have enabled the community to manage the cemetery more effectively by erecting fences to redirect foot traffic, to erect a memorial cairn to those buried there and to use the cemetery for new burials without disturbing existing ones.

Other work at Ebenezer has used a variety of archaeological techniques alongside those of other disciplines to address a range of research aims. One study used oral history and GIS to investigate the place of the mission within the lived landscape of living members of the community (Zipfel 2002). Another study has used the excavation of the mission house and the analysis of pictorial evidence to situate Ebenezer within a broader landscape of Moravian and government missions in Victoria and Aboriginal responses to them (Lydon 2009; Lydon et al. 2004). Jane Lydon is interested in comparisons between Ebenezer, the Moravians' other mission at Ramahyuk and the Coranderrk and Lake Tyers stations. In each place the

authorities used visual depictions and spatial arrangements as part of a total programme of imposing control on Indigenous people. The detailed study of Ebenezer
provides more specific information on how life on the mission was experienced by
different groups, including the missionaries, Aboriginal children, family groups and
fringe campers. It thus contributes to more nuanced understandings of the process
of cultural exchange within one set of colonial circumstances.

Station Times

Archaeologists have studied the interactions between Indigenous people and
European pastoralists in a number of outback regions, including the Kimberley
and Pilbara of Western Australia (e.g. Harrison 2002a, 2004a, 2006; Paterson 2006;
Smith 2001; Smith and Smith 1999), the north-west Northern Territory (Head and
Fullagar 1997), the Lake Eyre basin (Birmingham 2000; Paterson 2005, 2008) and
western New South Wales (Harrison 2003, 2004b). In moving beyond the old "wool-
sheds and homesteads" model, these studies have recognised the shared nature of
frontier history, and that the pastoral industry was where Aboriginal people in much
of Australia first had sustained contact with European settlers. "Dispersal" gradually gave way to "rationing" as more personal relationships developed between
Aboriginal groups and settlers (Harrison 2004b:115; Rowse 1998:7). Historian
Henry Reynolds argues, "cattle stations probably provided more congenial work
for Aboriginal men than any other European undertaking" (Reynolds 1982:172).
Remaining "on country", they could use their traditional skills to track stock, hunt
and live off the land and become expert horsemen, forging new cultural identities in
the process.

One archaeological study of the pastoral industry is the work done at Strangways
Springs Station by Alistair Paterson (2003, 2005, 2008). The station was established
in the far north of South Australia during the 1860s, in a dryland environment
that featured a mosaic of salt lakes, sand dunes, grassy plains and artesian springs.
Archaeological evidence indicates that Aboriginal people had settled in the immediate area during the last few thousand years. Paterson's archaeological investigation
of the station landscape identified a range of sites relating to sheep husbandry,
including the head station, camps for shearing and scouring, stone sheep yards and a
number of outstations. In the first phase of British occupation (1860–ca.1882), structures were small, in keeping with the precarious balance of climate, feed and water.
Outstation buildings were simple huts constructed from local timbers, brush and
grass and hand-wrought nails. The head station was also a repeater station for the
Overland Telegraph from 1872 to 1896. In 1882, the first bore was drilled into the
artesian basin, providing abundant water and bringing a new phase of pastoral activity to the station. The use of local materials was replaced with imported metal tanks,
troughs and windmills. Sheep were moved out into the semiarid pastures, and large
wire-fenced paddocks were established, watered by bores, which reduced the need
for residential (Aboriginal) shepherds. Aboriginal workers remained in demand,
however, as boundary riders, fencers, wool scourers and shearers. By the 1890s

the property was known as Anna Creek Station, and as sheep were replaced with cattle, it eventually became one of the largest pastoral leases in Australia (Paterson 2008:133–134).

One of the lessons from such an investigation is the degree of cooperation between European pastoralists and the local Arabana people. Many of the latter were involved in the region's sheep industry from the start and provided knowledge and labour that underpinned the longer-term success of European pastoralism. When Europeans arrived, Aboriginal people gained ready access to new sources of food, clothing and tobacco, as well as metal and glass, which they modified into new kinds of tools. Station workers also negotiated continued access to their traditional country, at a time of enormous social and environmental upheaval. As the head station became more important, it became the favoured location for large Aboriginal campsites. Arabana people working on the station set up camps near the station buildings while those who remained outside the pastoral industry set up neighbouring camps nearby, so that family and community ties could be retained.

Nevertheless, ambiguities remained, with Europeans providing rations to maintain a workforce and Aboriginal people receiving them as part of a broader subsistence strategy (Rowse 1998:19–20). Aborigines also had to modify their movements and traditional residential patterns to accommodate the seasonal demands of Europeans and their livestock. Periods of work at outstations provided an opportunity to visit remote areas and maintain connections to country before returning for the lambing and shearing season. There was thus a significant degree of reciprocity between Aboriginal people and pastoralists at Strangways. Europeans gained a cheap and knowledgeable labour force with which to develop a successful livestock industry. The Arabana people maintained connections with their country and traditions, and a sense of stability, and gradually redefined their cultural identity during a period of dramatic transformation. However, not all Aboriginal people chose to work on the stations, and many others worked there only periodically. At other times they followed their traditional ways of life outside the pastoral system, many not "coming in" until the 1920s and 1930s.

Similar patterns were identified by Rodney Harrison at Old Lamboo Station, located in the south-east Kimberley near Halls Creek. The run was established at the turn of the twentieth century by Frederick Charles Booty and occupied until the 1960s. Harrison (2002b, 2004a) analysed archaeological, historical and oral evidence to explore how black/white relationships and identities developed at the site. Aboriginal people set up a fringe camp to the south of the station homestead, with a shifting seasonal population of 70 or more. Many were employed as stockmen and domestic workers and were paid with the usual rations of food, tobacco and clothing. Archaeologically, the camp area included numerous hearths and dense scatters of flaked stone, glass and metal artefacts. Excavation revealed postholes of a substantial building (6 by 2.5 m), used as a dwelling by Old Lamboo fringe campers. The high density of artefacts at the camp reflects the "semi-sedentary" discard of a large group of people living in close proximity (Harrison 2004a:130). Traditionally, Aboriginal people preferred not to camp so close together. The Old Lamboo camp thus reveals a major change in domestic arrangements for

Indigenous people, compared with bush camps, which would have been much more spread out.

A large assemblage of metal artefacts, manufactured and used by Aboriginal people, was also identified at the station (Harrison 2002b). These included knives and spear points forged from horseshoes and adzes hammered from truck springs. Numerous other items, such as belt buckles and tobacco tins, had not been modified, but were nevertheless perceived as "Aboriginal" by informants. Where Aboriginal people have incorporated western items into their own experiences of place and time, the conventional distinction between "Aboriginal" and "European" breaks down, a process Nicholas Thomas (1991) terms "entanglement". In re-imagining and re-contextualising such objects, they take on meanings and significance beyond their simple forms.

There were also differences observed in the spatial distribution of stone raw materials, defined by the main station fence lines. Station boundaries and fences helped maintain an Aboriginal sense of belonging as station workers, as "insiders", distinct from the bush "outsiders". At the same time, however, there was a great deal of movement across these boundaries, especially during the wet season, when there was little work on the stations and many Aboriginal people moved back to the bush for extended periods. Nevertheless, Aboriginal people expressed much of their identity through their work and life on the pastoral station. Their attachment to the land and to each other was re-negotiated but remained intact, mediated through traditional practices and patterns of social and material life.

Harrison's (2003, 2004b) study of Dennawan in New South Wales has revealed a different kind of relationship between Aboriginal people and the pastoral industry. Dennawan functioned as a labour camp that serviced the surrounding pastoral properties. Europeans began taking up pastoral leases along the Culgoa River in the far north-west of New South Wales in the 1850s, in an environment dominated by coolibah and brigalow woodland. Originally known as Bourbah, Dennawan began in the 1880s as a white settlement around a pub and a post office, at the junction of two travelling stock routes. The local Muruwari people camped nearby at Tatala and went out to work at surrounding pastoral stations. The area was declared an Aboriginal reserve in 1912 and grew into a substantial settlement, with more than a dozen extended families living at the site. The reserve was abandoned in the early 1940s, when the Dennawan post office and store closed.

Archaeological survey of the Dennawan camp recorded a complex array of material discard on the surface of low sandhills beside a lagoon. This included at least 18 bush houses on the reserve, with remains of timber posts, iron sheeting and flattened kerosene tins. There were also thousands of glass bottle fragments, about one-quarter of which had been flaked into tools for cutting meat and scraping wooden tools (Harrison 2004b:172–175). Fragments of ceramic tableware had also been worked into flakes. Hundreds of tin cans, originally for food, tobacco, matches and kerosene, had been remade into other useful items, such as buckets, billies, cups and toy cars. Personal items included clay pipes, a brooch and pieces of a pocket watch. Fragments of old vinyl records and harmonica pieces indicate the importance of music in life at the camp, while car parts reveal the ability of residents to acquire vehicles and their fondness for visiting family and friends along the Culgoa River.

The physical remains indicate a degree of personal affluence at odds with the common view of Aboriginal people in New South Wales during this period as relatively impoverished. Arthur Hooper, an Aboriginal informant, noted that people working on the pastoral stations "...had money to spare – [but] they had nowhere to spend it. ... Some were very, very careful with their money too" (Harrison 2004b:192). At least some Aboriginal people working on the stations were clearly able to purchase a range of manufactured goods, avoided reliance on station rations and maintained a greater degree of personal autonomy. In spite of the closure of Dennawan more than half a century ago, the site continues to have great importance for the district's Muruwari people today. This "lost place", with its deep layering of material culture and living memory, has become an important place of pilgrimage in the surrounding landscape (Harrison 2003:20). Frequent returns to visit (and touch) the relics help to nurture and create memories and recreate relationships with country and the ancestral past (Read 2000). Ancestors and place retain a vital spiritual role in the hearts and minds of the Muruwari and speak to the abiding attachment of Aboriginal people to their pastoral heritage and ancestral lands.

Fringe Camps

Denis Byrne reminds us that Aboriginal heritage cannot be isolated at missions and remote pastoral stations (Byrne 2003a, b; Byrne and Nugent 2004). Aboriginal people have always been part of every local community, and their places are a significant part of local heritage. In urban areas Aboriginal places may be buildings indistinguishable from their neighbours, but with particular relevance to the Aboriginal community. Examples include the segregated swimming pool in Moree in New South Wales that was barred to those on the Freedom Ride of 1967, or the building in Fitzroy, Melbourne, where a group of Aboriginal people met in the 1930s to form the Australian Aborigines' League. More broadly, Byrne argues that places of significant Aboriginal heritage may be the lockups in country towns where Aboriginal people were incarcerated and often died and the white homes where girls from the Stolen Generations were kept as servants. A distinctive type of place associated with Aboriginal people also includes the fringe camps that were established in vacant land adjacent to country towns. Many fringe camps were occupied for short periods of time and have left little in the way of historical documentation. Homes were generally expedient structures made of readily available material scavenged from European sources such as tips and obtained from the bush. As such, they deteriorated rapidly after abandonment and have left few archaeological traces. Although the material culture may closely resemble that of marginal white people, these are special places to Aboriginal people, and through the combination of oral histories and mapping their layers of meaning may be drawn out.

This has occurred at No Man's Land, a fringe camp at Corindi Beach on the mid-north coast of New South Wales (Smith and Beck 2003). Research at the site was undertaken as part of a community studies project with the Yarrawarra Aboriginal Corporation and directed by a team of archaeologists from the University of New England. It is not known exactly when No Man's Land was established. It was declared a racecourse reserve and road reserve by the local council in 1890, establishing its status as "public" land, and between the 1920s and 1960s the council issued a series of permissive occupancy leases to Aboriginal families enabling them to build huts and gardens. A fence next to the racecourse created a strip of land between the racecourse and the sea, and it was here that the Aboriginal people established their homes. In the 1980s, part of the land was returned to the community under the NSW *Land Rights Act*.

Drawing on oral histories, documents and landscape studies, the team identified five sites (or camps) for detailed survey and excavation. Even though the camps had all been occupied in the twentieth century, with the oldest possibly in use in the 1890s and all definitely in use by the 1930s and 1940s, little in the way of structural remains had survived. The only standing structure to survive is at the Old Camp, last permanently occupied in the 1980s and still used as an occasional residence. It is made of posts either recycled from other structures or obtained from the bush, clad with galvanised iron sheeting. Occupants take advantage of the flexibility of these materials by periodically reconfiguring the arrangement of doors, windows and internal walls, a process that can only be done with difficulty in the brick houses where most community members now live.

Although all of the camps were occupied on more than one occasion, excavations showed little stratigraphy, and most artefacts were either on or immediately below the surface. The artefacts consisted primarily of building materials such as nails and iron sheeting, broken bottle glass, crockery and marine shell from the nearby estuary. Community members observed that the lack of material remains was due to "cleaning up" the sites when they were abandoned. At one camp, Armi's Camp, there was a more diverse assemblage which included cans, a kerosene stove, a harmonica, parts of gramophone records, parts of shoes and clothing and a plastic toy, most of it associated with occupation in the 1950s. According to the oral histories, many of the items, particularly crockery and metal objects, were recycled and reused from other sources including old camps and tips. Found objects were valued for their raw materials as well, one example being lead from car batteries that was used in fishing sinkers. Exotic plants were a feature at all the camps and were planted by the Aboriginal people who lived there, as were some native plants. Favoured plants were chosen for either their decorative appeal, such as gladioli, bamboo, roses and lilies, or for the food provided, such as fig and lemon trees and native bush cherries. Vegetables as well as flowers are still grown in gardens at the Old Camp. The gardens and the shellfish reflect the value of the land for providing food and beauty and a self-sufficient diet that incorporated new foods while continuing to value traditional ones.

Place provided the anchor for information from a range of sources in the project at No Man's Land. No single data set overshadowed the others. Oral histories shed light on life at the camps and the objects found there, while objects mapped and recovered archaeologically stimulated memories and story-telling. The process identified a number of characteristics in the camps that may be relevant for studies of fringe camp sites elsewhere, including thin archaeological deposits, the reuse of objects and the presence of exotic plants, particularly flowers and fruit. The project also sheds light more broadly on the experience of life in these places, which are not just pre-contact sites with new materials. They represent an adaptation to changing conditions and the use of local knowledge to maintain independent communities that nevertheless intersected with the non-Indigenous community for work, school and other activities.

Conclusion

Recent archaeological studies into black/white relations represent some of the most compelling and methodologically advanced approaches to historical archaeology conducted in Australia. They confidently combine the use of traditional surveys and excavations with oral history and other evidence to achieve subtle understandings of people in landscape that are sensitive to changes in the relationships between people, place and things through time. They remind us of the enduring strength of Indigenous cultural traditions and the ability of individuals and communities to negotiate new ways of dealing with the dominant settler culture. The archaeology of Indigenous/European interactions is also a powerful reminder that Aboriginal people did not merely fade away into the outback before the tide of white settlement. On the contrary, they held on where they could, maintaining families and communities in the face of wider social apathy, ignorance and hostility. These places, on the physical, social and economic fringes of white Australia, served as places of refuge, support and memory to those who lived in them. Camps and homes at pastoral stations, in quiet forest areas, urban neighbourhoods and former mission stations provided a place of retreat from the indignities of dispossession, while at the same time reinforcing cultural marginalisation. Such places may not always be "visible" in the normal archaeological sense, but this in no way lessens their importance to contemporary Aboriginal communities. The growth of collaborative projects has begun to provide common ground where archaeological research intersects with the needs of community members, each approach informing the other, to generate richer and more satisfying understandings of Indigenous lives in the recent past.

Chapter 4
Shipwrecks and Maritime Trade

Despite its preoccupation with the bush and outback, Australia has always been a maritime country, reliant on the sea for survival. From the first Aboriginal occupants to the most recent arrivals, all migrants have crossed the sea to get here. The bulk of colonial settlement took place within a narrow coastal fringe only a few hundred kilometres wide, a trend which accelerated through the twentieth century. As a result, transportation of goods and people within Australia and between the colonies also relied on the sea, particularly before the development of rail networks, good roads and the automobile. The oldest parts of many Australian cities, and the places where much urban archaeology has been done, were port towns built around shipping and maritime industries. The Rocks in Sydney, Wapping in Hobart, Port Adelaide in South Australia and Fremantle in Western Australia were all home to many people who worked on shore in maritime industries and temporary homes to the sailors who arrived on ships that passed through the ports. Their populations were outwardly focused and often well-travelled and were more ethnically mixed than in other parts of the colonies.

In this chapter we examine some of the archaeological evidence for shipping and coastal infrastructure and discuss the field of maritime archaeology that has made these topics its speciality. Maritime industries such as sealing and whaling, which drew on the sea itself as a resource, are the subject of Chapter 5. In two chapters, however, it is impossible to offer a comprehensive review of the richness and diversity of maritime archaeology in Australia. Instead we provide here a broad indication of the work that has been done, while referring interested readers to the many publications available for further detail. Our review of shipwreck archaeology describes changes in the technology of shipbuilding, the wide variety of cargoes carried and life on board for crew and passengers. We also consider industrial and river shipping and the recent discovery of the *HMAS Sydney*, destroyed off the coast of Western Australia during the Second World War. Site formation and shipwreck survivors' camps have also emerged as important issues in maritime archaeology, along with the coastal infrastructure of wharves, ship yards and ships' graveyards.

S. Lawrence, P. Davies, *An Archaeology of Australia Since 1788*,
Contributions To Global Historical Archaeology, DOI 10.1007/978-1-4419-7485-3_4,
© Springer Science+Business Media, LLC 2011

Maritime Archaeology in Australia

Maritime archaeology in Australia had its origins in Western Australia during the 1960s, with the discovery of four Dutch East India (VOC) ships that were wrecked in the seventeenth century. Their discovery was the catalyst for establishing the legislative and disciplinary frameworks that have subsequently shaped the field. The VOC wrecks were discovered by amateur divers and historians, and their importance prompted the Western Australian government to enact legislation in 1964 to protect the sites (Hosty and Stuart 1994). By 1976, efforts to protect archaeological shipwrecks had become national in scope, when the Commonwealth passed the *Historic Shipwrecks Act*, which applied to sites in all Australian territorial waters. Alongside state-based legislation, the Act provides blanket protection for all shipwrecks over 75 years of age. The discovery of the wrecks led to the employment of several maritime archaeologists in Western Australia, first Jeremy Green and then others, and to the establishment of the Western Australian Maritime Museum. The WAMM later developed a Masters degree programme in conjunction with Curtin University that was at the heart of maritime archaeology in Australia for many years, training the first generation of graduates who would go on to work around the country. Today the largest university programme in maritime archaeology is at Flinders University in Adelaide.

Maritime archaeology in Australia originally began with a primary focus on shipwrecks, an emphasis which has resulted in the listing of more than 7,400 wreck sites known in Australian waters on the National Shipwrecks Database (2009). Wreck sites can reveal details about the design and construction of ships and adaptations to local conditions and available materials. Living conditions on board for passengers and crew can also be reconstructed, while cargoes reveal the commodities traded and the systems of commerce in operation. The field of maritime archaeology has expanded considerably over the years to include a wide array of underwater materials and associated shipping infrastructure. The subject covers archaeological remains in lake and river systems, harbours and jetties, shipbuilding yards, shipwreck survivors' camps and ships' graveyards, as well as maritime landscapes more broadly.

Alongside scholarly study of maritime activity, archaeologists have also engaged in heritage management in a wide variety of ways. They have worked closely with recreational divers for many years, teaming up to investigate maritime sites; using artefact amnesties to record artefacts that have been illegally retrieved from wrecks; and providing education through short courses modelled on those developed by the Nautical Archaeology Society in the United Kingdom (Moran and Staniforth 1998; Souter 2006b). Terrestrial and underwater heritage trails have been developed to provide public interpretation of sites, and museum displays have highlighted major projects such as the excavations of the *Batavia*, the *Sydney Cove* and the *Pandora* (Hosty 2006; Jeffery 1990). In some states maritime archaeologists are also taking a more active role in development planning, overseeing heritage surveys in advance of building ferry terminals along the Parramatta River in Sydney and the dredging of Port Phillip Bay in Melbourne (Anderson et al. 2006). As Martin Gibbs (2005b) argues, however, there are ambiguities in the ways in which shipwrecks are considered as part of the national heritage. Shipwrecks are at once artefacts, sites, graveyards and places to be experienced, and more discussion is needed about the implications of the significance of each of these entangled roles.

At the same time, maritime archaeology has also become more theoretically sophisticated, looking beyond shipwrecks to what they can reveal about aspects of life in colonial society, a move originally stimulated in Australia with the publication of Richard Gould's *Shipwreck Anthropology* in 1983 (see also Gould 2000). Mark Staniforth (2003, 2009), for example, has explored issues of capitalism and consumerism in colonial society by analysing cargo assemblages using an approach influenced by the *Annales* school of history. One of the key elements in this approach is Braudel's three historical scales. These range from the short term, concerned with individual people and events (*événéments*), to medium-term processes and social time (*conjunctures*), and long-term geographic and environmental structures (*longue durée*). Staniforth argues that shipwrecks represent specific "time-capsule" events and thus relate to Braudel's "short-term" history. The wreck site and its associated assemblage, however, also provide the opportunity to incorporate the archaeology of the event into the study of larger processes, such as consumerism and capitalism, as well as the transfer of cultural attitudes from Great Britain to the Australian colonies. Using such material as ceramics, alcohol, foodstuffs and tobacco from four different wrecks, Staniforth concludes that objects can reveal deeply held cultural beliefs, and that people use such objects to define and validate their place in the world.

Some of the more dynamic studies have occurred at the interface between maritime and terrestrial archaeology. Iain Stuart (1998), for example, used the idea of seascapes, or maritime cultural landscapes, in his study of sealing and whaling in Bass Strait. The landscape concept unites not just the physical environments of land and sea, but the human perception and use of natural resources as well (see Chapter 5). Brad Duncan (2004) has extended the notion of maritime landscapes with the concepts of perception and risk management to analyse how these affected the distribution of shipwrecks in Gippsland, Victoria, in shaping the maritime cultural landscape of the region.

The boundaries of maritime and terrestrial archaeology were also blurred in Campbell Macknight's investigation of the Macassan fishermen who once sailed to northern Australia from Sulawesi (Indonesia) to collect and process trepang, or sea slugs (Macknight 1976, 2008). The archaeological remains of their activities included stone fireplaces on the beach, scatters of pottery and tree stumps where the fishermen had collected wood for fires. Macknight located the Macassans within a complex trading network linking tropical Australia through south-east Asia to China, a theme of regional interaction that has become prominent in Australian maritime archaeology. In recent years these exchanges have also been explored on the Cobourg Peninsula and Groote Eylandt in the Northern Territory (Clarke 2000b; Mitchell 1994, 1996, 2000) and on the Kimberley coast of Western Australia (Morwood and Hobbs 1997).

The beach, as historian Greg Dening (2004) has noted, is a liminal zone where conventional codes of understanding and behaviour are subject to challenge and renegotiation. This zone of interaction, between land and sea, was a vital point of first contact between Europeans and Indigenous groups. Notions of conflict and resistance on the beach have been explored by Kostoglou (1998) in the Tasmania shore whaling industry and by Anderson (2006) at the site of an Aboriginal massacre on the beach at the Convincing Ground in Portland, Victoria. The beach was also a place of crisis, when the survivors of shipwrecks fought their way to shore and began to deal with the breakdown of traditional shipboard discipline (Gibbs 2003a). Survivor camps were also sites of early interaction between European and Indigenous groups, often before regular contact was made.

The Archaeology of Shipwrecks

Ships carried cargo and passengers between Australia and Great Britain and Europe, the Americas and in the "country trade" around India and south-east Asia. As the nineteenth century progressed, an extensive maritime commerce also developed between Australian colonial ports, while paddle steamers were used on major river systems from the 1850s, to carry wool to the coast and bring food and supplies back to the inland. With so many vessels and people travelling by ship in the nineteenth century, ships were bound to strike poorly charted coasts from time to time. Shipwreck has been described as "the dark undertow of nineteenth-century voyaging" (Terry 2005:76), and shipwrecks have often been portrayed as events of high drama – towering waves, shrieking winds and the awful grinding of timber on rock, as the sodden crew fought valiantly to save the vessel, its passengers and cargo. There is much truth in these images, but also many elements that are missing. Why and how, for instance, did so many ships come to grief on the Australian coastline? What were they carrying and who were their passengers? How did the technology of shipping change over time? What did this mean for the duration of sea voyages and conditions on board? Maritime archaeology seeks to answer these and other questions by investigating the numerous wrecks and maritime sites around the Australian coast. Case studies discussed here shed light on the nature of the cargoes carried and the conditions on board for passengers and crew, as well as on industries that relied heavily on shipping, such as the lime industry in Victoria and the wool trade along the Murray River (Fig. 4.1). In addition, the study of shipwrecks has included the analysis of related subjects such as site formation processes on wrecks and the archaeology of survivors' camps.

Shipbuilding Technology

One of the areas of greatest interest to maritime archaeologists is the history of shipbuilding technology. Sailing ships of the eighteenth and nineteenth century were both beautiful and immensely complex creations, but as relatively few have survived intact, wrecks provide an excellent source of first-hand information on the materials and techniques used in their construction. One example of eighteenth-century shipbuilding is the *Sydney Cove*, which was wrecked in 1797 on a voyage from Calcutta to Port Jackson. It was carrying a speculative cargo of rum, Indian goods and livestock when it was wrecked on Preservation Island in Bass Strait. After an epic trek

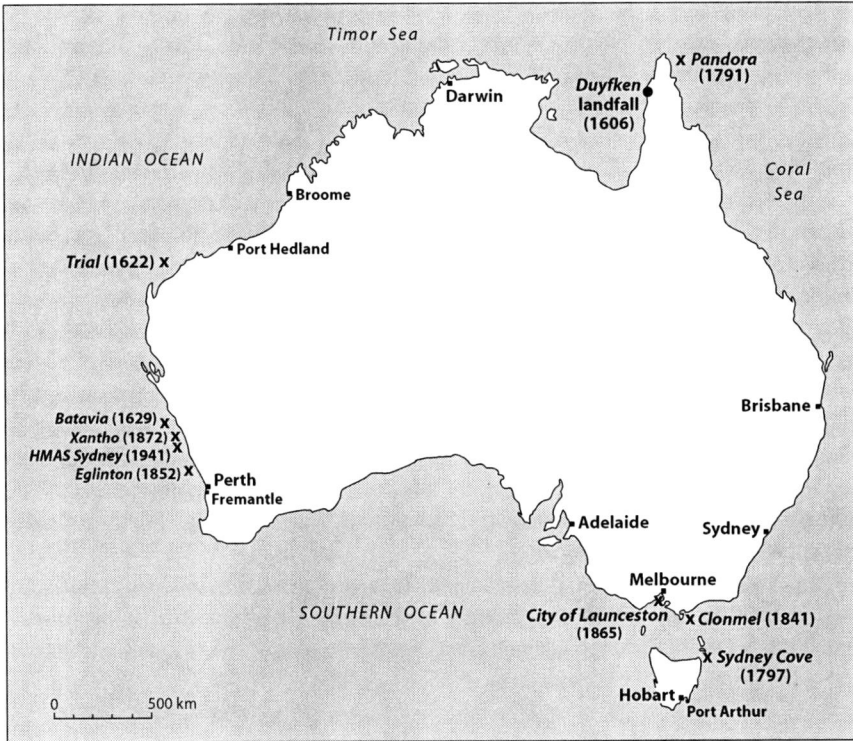

Fig. 4.1 Location map of shipwrecks discussed in text

by several of the crew up the coast of the Australian mainland, most of the survivors and much of the cargo was salvaged, and the rescue efforts led to the discovery of Bass Strait and the establishment of the sealing industry in the area (see Chapter 5). The wreck was relocated in 1977 and archaeological fieldwork continued until 1994, much of it led by the Tasmanian Parks and Wildlife Service (Nash 2001, 2009; Staniforth and Nash 1998; Strachan 1986). The main aims were to survey and record the remains of the ship, recover artefacts and stabilise the wreck site. Most of the keel, frame and hull planking were exposed and recorded. Items were recovered from the ship itself, including pieces of the wooden hull, sheathing materials and rigging elements, along with anchors and cannon. Cargo consisted of hundreds of glass bottles, leather footwear and thousands of fragments of Chinese porcelain, along with timber, bamboo, hessian and straw *dunnage*, or packing materials to hold the cargo securely (Nash 2001:79–96; Strachan 1986).

Excavation of the *Sydney Cove* revealed important details about shipbuilding and design at a time of rapid change in the assembly of wooden sailing vessels, in a region where builders kept few written records of their work. Shipbuilders in India had been influenced by European practices since the late sixteenth century. They admired the military capability of European ships and their ability to remain at sea for long periods. By the 1770s, timber shortages and rising labour costs in Europe had prompted the East India Company to commission vessels directly from Indian shipyards. These ships, used for the country trade from Calcutta (see below), were generally smaller and more lightly built than those from British shipyards and were designed for speed in carrying cargoes of rice and later opium. They also had a shallow draft to allow sailing up the Hooghly River to the city of Calcutta itself.

Evidence from the *Sydney Cove* reveals the influence of European designs and technology combined with Indian materials and construction techniques. The frame of the ship, for example, was built from local sisso and teak timbers, the latter especially valued by shipbuilders for its strength, resistance to rot and ease of working (Fig. 4.2). There is also evidence in the bow for the use of a heavy hardwood, originating from tropical Africa. The vessel may have made a voyage to east Africa at some stage and undergone repairs, or else it was repaired in a port or region nearby which received wood as an export item from Africa (Strachan 1986:24–25). As with most European ships of this period, the *Sydney Cove* was carvel built, with the outer and inner planking shaped to form a smooth face with no overlapping timbers. Hull timbers were fastened with iron spikes, rather than "tree nails", or timber fastenings that rotted in tropical conditions.

Ropes on the *Sydney Cove* were made from coir fibre, obtained from the outer husk of the coconut, which was brought from the Maldives and the Malabar coast. The fibres were soaked and beaten, then twisted into long skeins of yarn and sold to

Fig. 4.2 Water dredge used to uncover hull timbers on the *Sydney Cove* (Tasmanian Parks and Wildlife Service)

rope makers. Although not as strong as rope made from manila, hemp or sisal, coir rope was flexible and light and was widely used throughout India. It also floated when wet and was much cheaper than imported European cordage. There were also numerous wooden pulley sheaves, blocks and deadeyes used in rigging the ship. The sheaves were made from *Lignum vitae*, a West Indian timber preferred for its hardness and smoothness over Indian timbers (Nash 2001:108–110).

Local wood and textiles were thus used for the construction of ships, but items such as sheathing, anchors and cannon were imported from Europe. European ships sailing in warm tropical waters were subject to damage by marine borers such as the *Teredo* worm. Indian shipbuilders had traditionally used sacrificial planking and various coatings, such as fish oil, tree resins and pitch, to prevent borers and to improve waterproofing. European shipbuilders applied similar techniques, but in the eighteenth century they began to use copper sheathing as well. Copper sheathing provided a physical barrier to marine borers, and its toxicity prevented the growth of weeds and barnacles on ships' hulls that normally slowed their sailing. Eastern shipbuilders quickly adopted the new technology, and excavation revealed that the hull of the *Sydney Cove* was protected by a combination of both Indian and European techniques. First, the ship's timbers were covered with a thin layer of sacrificial planking, to which a lime resin was also applied. The planking was then covered with wool felt that had been treated with dammar, a plant resin obtained from Sumatra or the Malaysian Peninsula. Over this was placed sheets of copper, secured with copper alloy tacks.

The *Sydney Cove* also had three iron long-shank anchors, commonly used on both naval and merchant ships in this period. They ranged in length from 2.9 to 3.8 m, and the largest weighed more than 800 kg. The presence of pirates and foreign warships throughout the northern Indian Ocean also meant that country traders such as the *Sydney Cove* were armed with deck guns and small arms. Four iron cannon were located during excavation of the wreck, along with several weights of shot.

Archaeological evidence from the *Sydney Cove* thus reveals important elements of ship design, construction and fitting for the vessels trading from India to Europe, China, Africa and Australia in the late eighteenth and early nineteenth century. European technology was joined with local Indian materials and construction techniques to create sailing ships suited to the needs of their masters and the sailing conditions they would normally meet. The *Sydney Cove* was well adapted for coastal voyaging around India but less suited to the heavy seas of the Southern Ocean. The archaeology of the wreck thus reinforces the speculative nature of such voyages and the lack of knowledge about its intended destination.

In contrast to the *Sydney Cove*, the *Xantho* was a nineteenth-century iron-hulled ship, which sank in 1872 off Port Gregory, near Geraldton in Western Australia. Iron hulls began to be used on ships in the early part of the nineteenth century. They were stronger than wooden hulls and provided greater storage, safety and durability. Michael McCarthy's (2000, 2007) detailed study of the vessel demonstrates that the archaeology of such wrecks can reveal hidden stories not only about frontier technology and colonial capitalism, but also about the people involved and their motivations for behaving in the ways they did.

The *Xantho*'s owner, Charles Broadhurst, was born in Manchester in 1826 and emigrated to Victoria in 1843. He joined his brother on a large pastoral holding north of Melbourne and soon became a successful grazier in his own right. By the 1860s, however, Broadhurst turned his attention to the newly opened lands of north-western Australia. Arriving in 1865 with his pregnant wife Eliza and two small sons, his initial grazing venture in the region failed badly. Broadhurst then looked to the potentially lucrative pearl shell industry to rescue his fortunes. In 1871 he travelled to Britain to buy a ship that he hoped would transform the pearling industry.

Around the same time, the *Xantho,* originally built as a paddle steamer in 1848, was being modified in a Glasgow shipyard. Scrap-metal merchant Robert Stewart had the ship converted from paddle to screw propulsion, and the paddle engines were replaced with a 60 horsepower horizontal engine. This provided more space in the hold and made the ship more attractive to potential buyers. Broadhurst purchased the ship in October 1871 and arrived at his base near Port Hedland in April 1872. He intended to use the ship in the new pearling industry around Broome, as well as for whaling, fishing and as a general purpose carrier through a vast region extending from Fremantle to Batavia (Jakarta; see Chapter 5). Only 7 months later, however, the *Xantho*, having taken on a load of iron ore at Port Gregory, sank in shallow water on the night of 16 November 1872.

Having been extensively salvaged soon after it went down, archaeological investigation of the *Xantho* paid particular attention to the hull and the engine. One of the aims was to study the effects of corrosion and the rate of decomposition of the iron hull and the role this played in the accidental or deliberate loss of the ship. The ship's engine was excavated and removed from the seabed, disassembled and extensively conserved. The process aimed to test the idea that Broadhurst was naive and that the ship was inadequate for use in the waters off Western Australia.

The kind of ship needed to operate in such waters was ideally simple and robust, requiring low maintenance and the economical use of fuel coal. Instead, by the time the *Xantho* reached Australia, it was an ageing and decaying vessel. Its hull was designed for much more sheltered waters, and its poorly maintained engine was ill-suited to such a vessel. The wrong kind of propeller had been fitted which required the engine to run in reverse, dramatically increasing engine wear and posing a significant risk to the engineer (McCarthy 2007:167). Was Charles Broadhurst, then, a victim of his own eccentricity and self-confidence, or was he a visionary and innovator, using family money and great personal energy to open up a new commercial frontier in a remote corner of colonial Australia? McCarthy concluded that in spite of his failures, Broadhurst was hard-working and resilient, recovering from repeated business failures to tackle new opportunities. His purchase and operation of the *Xantho* shows a man keen to take advantage of new technologies, but one who lacked the practical ability and business sense to transform his ideas into a viable enterprise (McCarthy 2000:194). Shipwrecks like the *Xantho* and the *Sydney Cove* provide evidence of technological processes rarely preserved in other sources, and as these case studies demonstrate their careful interpretation can shed light on the social and economic networks of which the ships, their builders and owners were a part.

Cargoes

Artefact studies of shipwreck sites have demonstrated the wide variety of cargoes carried on vessels. Examples include that of the *Sydney Cove* (1797), a cargo illustrating the nature of the country trade in the early colonial period, the *Eglinton* (1852) and its cargo of goods ordered from England by colonists in Western Australia and the *Clonmel* (1841), which traded between Sydney and Melbourne. Consumer goods, including those from wrecks, are discussed in more detail in Chapter 11 in terms of colonial behaviours and customs, while a selection are considered here in relation to trade and commerce.

The *Sydney Cove* was owned by the British merchant house of Campbell and Clark of Calcutta, which was keen to exploit the possibilities of trade with the infant colony of New South Wales. The merchants assembled a cargo of goods from China, Europe, Malaya and India which they hoped to sell at Port Jackson for a large profit. The main cargo was alcohol, especially rum. The *Sydney Cove* was a "country ship", licensed to sail and trade in the monopoly area of the East India Company. This vast region extended from the Cape of Good Hope eastwards all the way to Cape Horn, and the Company had exclusive British rights to trade within it. Country ships could sail in the monopoly area, but could not go beyond it, such as return to England (Hainsworth 1981:14). Ships of other nationalities, of course, were not bound by these rules, and a clandestine but thriving trade with European ports was run by British traders under foreign flags, until the trading restrictions were lifted in 1813 (Broadbent et al. 2003:42–61).

Following the wreck of the *Sydney Cove* in 1797, salvage attempts managed to retrieve about 60% of the original cargo, but the remainder was abandoned. Archaeologists found cask heads, wooden staves and iron hoops from barrels left behind on the sea floor. Until the late nineteenth century, most bulk commodities were stored and transported in wooden casks and only distributed into individual portions at the retail level. Apart from alcohol, casks were also used to carry flour, salted meat and tobacco. The *Sydney Cove* was carrying at least four different sizes of casks, including pipes (108 gallons), hogsheads (54 gallons), barrels (36 gallons) and kegs (9 gallons). The identification of cask timbers as oak and the standardisation of sizes suggest that many of the barrels originally came from Europe (Nash 2001:124). There were also hundreds of dark green bottle glass fragments recovered from the wreck. Most were either square-section case bottles or cylindrical "beer and wine" bottles. All were handmade and sturdy, suitable for long distance transport. Some had been sealed with red wax stamped with the initials "CC" (Campbell and Clark), the firm trying to prevent the dehydration of its product in a warm climate.

The quantity of alcohol on the *Sydney Cove* indicates the scale of production and trade and the assumed demand for rum, brandy and wines in Australia. Alcohol

was an everyday part of life in New South Wales and was available from several
sources. Government authorities rationed out small quantities of rum to those on
public stores, and illegal stills produced inferior spirits. The first beer was brewed
in the colony by James Squire in 1793, followed by John Boston in 1795 (Deutsher
1999:16). Most alcohol, however, entered on ships like the *Sydney Cove* from India,
Cape Town and Mauritius (Nash 2001:126).

In spite of the rapid improvement in agricultural production during the 1790s,
about 70% of the inhabitants of Port Jackson were still drawing public rations. Much
of this was in the form of salted meat, arriving in barrels stored in the damp holds of
ships, often several years old and crawling with vermin. Writing in 1793, Captain
Watkin Tench described the available rations:

> The pork and rice were brought with us from England: the pork had been salted between
> three and four years, and every grain of rice was a moving body, from the inhabitants lodged
> within it. We soon left off boiling the pork, as it had become so old and dry, that it shrunk
> one half in its dimensions when so dressed. Our usual method of cooking it was to cut off
> the daily morsel, and toast it on a fork before the fire, catching the drops which fell on a
> slice of bread, or in a saucer of rice. (Tench 1961 [1793]:165)

Excavation of the *Sydney Cove* yielded 385 whole and fragmented animal bones.
Most of these were from cattle (78%) and pig (10%), with the remainder from sheep,
birds, fish or unidentified. The majority of the cattle bones were from the small
Indian breed *Zebu* that was commonly imported to the colony from Bengal during
the early period. Most of the cattle and pig bones came from large cuts of ribs,
mostly butchered from older animals. By the time it reached its destination, such
meat would have been in bad condition – bony, poorly pickled and foul smelling.

There were also 242 pieces of leather footwear recovered from the wreck, mostly
heels and soles, and their archaeological context indicates that they were not personal items belonging to members of the crew. The shoes had been stored in bundles,
mostly in the stern of the ship, and were part of the cargo intended for sale. Detailed
analysis has revealed that the shoes had been fully assembled prior to despatch,
and that the thin leather of the uppers had mostly rotted away. The shoes range
from 215 mm to 285 mm in length, generally indicating a male footwear size. The
shoes have a narrow instep and are flat and relatively low heeled. All of the shoes
are "straight", i.e. made to fit on either foot, as individual left and right shoes did
not become standard until around the 1830s. The soles consisted of four layers of
leather, stitched together with hemp; the layers of the heels were joined by small
wooden pegs. A welt, a narrow strip of leather, was then used to join the heel and
sole to the upper of the shoe. A strap across the top suggests the shoes were intended
to be fastened with a buckle, although no buckles were found during excavation.

The shoes were probably made in India, in spite of the religious stigma attached
to leather products in Indian society. The uneven quality of the heels, for example,
suggests that the footwear was made by novice shoemakers in India's cottage industry, which had only begun in the late eighteenth century. The quality of these shoes
did not match that of European manufacturers, where shoemaking had long been
considered a highly skilled trade. In addition, the leather for the shoes came from

goat hides, rather than cattle, and the red colouring or staining on many of the shoes is consistent with the use of plant extracts used for tanning leather in India.

Shoes were rare and valuable in New South Wales in the 1790s, and the loss of footwear from the *Sydney Cove* would have been hard felt, quite literally, by soldiers and convicts often forced to go bare foot. Shoes wore out quickly in the rough conditions, and they were difficult to replace given the infrequent arrival of supply ships, the shortage of cattle for hides, the lack of a local tanning industry and the shortage of skilled labour. Footwear (and clothing) thus became a form of currency, and theft from houses and storerooms became common. The stolen articles were gambled away, or sold privately or at illegal auctions, part of a black market in personal goods in the colony. There are also reports of convicts being caught, convicted and executed for theft of clothing (Collins 1975 [1798] (I):70, 273).

Excavation also recovered about 250 kg of hand-painted Chinese export porcelain (Staniforth and Nash 1998). Most of the material was in fragments, with only some of the heavier water flasks and chamber pots surviving intact (Fig. 4.3). Teawares and plate fragments made up the bulk of the collection. Such material provides important information about the trade networks linking India, China, Britain and Australia and reveals some of the cultural patterns taking root in the new colony.

Porcelain was originally developed in southern China between the second and third centuries AD and had been brought overland to Europe in small quantities since the thirteenth century. Made from fine "china clay" or kaolin and petuntse

Fig. 4.3 Archaeologist with Chinese export porcelain washing water bottle from the *Sydney Cove* (Tasmanian Parks and Wildlife Service)

(feldspar), porcelain is hard, white and vitrified, or glassy, usually with a clear glaze. Vessels were thrown on a wheel or pressed from moulds. Specialised, large-scale production permitted a large export trade in Chinese porcelain from the sixteenth century. While European traders obtained most of their supplies from the port of Canton, the centre of production for export porcelain was the city of Jingdezhen (Ching-te-Chen). By the eighteenth century, European potters began to develop their own forms of porcelain as well (Gleeson 1998).

Porcelain from the *Sydney Cove* was of two kinds. The most common had decorations hand painted in cobalt oxide blue pigment. This was then covered with a transparent glaze (thus "underglaze") and fired at around 1,350°C. The other kind of porcelain was painted with additional enamel colours over the glaze and fired again to fix the enamel. The decorative floral and landscape motifs on Chinese underglaze blue and white porcelain had a major influence on European pottery during the eighteenth century. At the same time, European demand prompted Chinese potteries to incorporate many "Western" vessel forms and decorations. This interaction resulted most famously in the development of the "Willow Pattern" transfer motif by British pottery makers.

Items recovered from the *Sydney Cove* included toiletry wares such as chamber pots, wash basins and washing water bottles. The chamber pot was unknown in China prior to contact with the West, and these were made to meet foreign demand. They were decorated with landscape scenes which included lakes, mountains, islands, trees and buildings. Tablewares recovered from the ship included more than 180 dinner or soup plates, also decorated in blue underglaze landscape designs. There were also several dozen octagonal hot-water dishes or warming plates, where hot water was poured through a hollow handle into the interior cavity of the dish. Introduced to China during the eighteenth century, these dishes reflected the British preference for keeping food warm at the table. Teawares on the *Sydney Cove*, however, consisted of cups and saucers in the traditional Chinese form – tea bowls without handles and saucers without the indentation to hold the cup. None of the other elements normally associated with a tea set, such as teapots, milk jugs or sugar bowls, were found on the ship. There were also large quantities of "nested bowls" that came in five to a set, ranging from 6.5 to 11 inches (16.5–28 cm) in diameter. These had once been decorated with polychrome overglaze motifs, but two centuries underwater meant that most of the original colour was lost from the surface of the bowls.

Chinese ceramics were popular partly because their "orientalising" motifs had an exotic appeal and also because they offered a good alternative to metal plates and to poorly made local wares. Chinese porcelain arrived in Australia not only via India, but also from other ports that received goods from China, such as Batavia, Manila, Penang and the Cape of Good Hope (Nash 2001:153). As well as trade stocks, ceramics were carried to Australia by government officials, free settlers and on store ships chartered from Britain. American ships engaged in sealing, whaling and trading in the Pacific also arrived at Port Jackson with crates of porcelain to sell. Even at this early stage, the colonists in New South Wales were clearly part of, and dependent on, trading networks that reached around the world.

Decades after the *Sydney Cove* sank, settlers in the young Swan River colony of Western Australia were equally dependent on imported goods. The *Eglinton* was carrying a general cargo from London to merchants in Western Australia when it sank in 1852, and its loss was a major blow to the colony (Stanbury 2003). Many goods were salvaged at the time, including £15,000 in coin destined for the colonial treasury. Much still remained, however, when the site was excavated by a team from the Western Australian Maritime Museum in the early 1970s. The goods reflect the full range of items required in a growing colony dependent on agriculture. There was farm equipment such as ploughs and cart wheels, and iron and steel bars for making nails. Leather shoes in the cargo were marked with the government arrow, indicating that they were intended for the convicts who had begun arriving in the colony in 1850. There were a wide range of copper household fittings such as doorknobs and light fixtures in fancy designs to improve the comfort and refinement of homes and ceramic water purifiers to filter the brackish local water. Transfer-printed tablewares were represented in quantity, particularly the flow blue pattern "Anemone", made by Mintons particularly for export. Makers' marks on the "Anemone" dishes indicate that some of them were finished as recently as January 1852, the month before the *Eglinton* sailed.

The cargo of the *Clonmel*, a steamship wrecked on its maiden voyage between Sydney and Melbourne in 1841, illustrates the changing nature of inter-colonial shipping in this period (Harvey 1999; Sikari 2003). The ship was a wooden-hulled paddle steamer, built in 1836 in Birkenhead, England. It was the first of its kind in Australia, and the speed and safety it offered were greeted with great excitement in the colonies. The wrecking of the ship on a sandbar near the mouth of the Port River was a factor in the discovery of a viable port for Gippsland and led to the British colonisation of that region, but it was a disaster for the Sydney merchants who had loaded the *Clonmel* with goods required to open shops in Melbourne. Excavation of the site in 1996 by teams from Heritage Victoria recovered a wide range of lost stock, demonstrating what was available in Sydney and what they thought would be in demand in the new settlement at Port Phillip. Ginger beer bottles were prominent among the artefacts recovered and included examples imported from Britain, as well as bottles made by convict potters in New South Wales. Cylindrical glass bottles used for wine and champagne were also recovered. Among the glassware were a number of chandelier lustres which were probably intended for a drapery shop and then the home of one of Melbourne's early wealthy families. Very few domestic ceramics were excavated, indicating that those found were probably for use on board the ship rather than part of the cargo.

Life on Board

On some shipwreck sites it is possible to distinguish between items of cargo, items that were part of the ship's fittings and the personal possessions of those on board. In such cases we can gain some idea of what life was like for those on board. The wreck of the *City of Launceston* reveals the luxury of passenger travel for those who could afford it, while the wrecks of the *Sydney Cove* and the *Pandora* show aspects of the crews' experiences.

Like the *Clonmel*, the *City of Launceston* represented the apex of coastal travel in its day. An iron-hulled steamship built in Clyde, Scotland, it made the crossing from Melbourne to Launceston in only 19 hours, a vast improvement on the voyages lasting from 10 days to several weeks that had been necessary under sail. The gold rush had made Melbourne prosperous, and the ship was carrying goods and passengers from Victoria to Tasmania when it sank after a collision in Port Phillip Bay in 1865. Artefacts recovered from the site during excavations by Heritage Victoria indicate the comfortable, even luxurious, arrangements made for the passengers (Sikari 2003; Strachan 2000). In the dining rooms passengers ate from whiteware plates and tea sets specially commissioned for the ship and decorated with the logo of the Launceston and Melbourne Steam Navigation Company. The ship had lavatories with running water and flushing toilets, a luxury in itself as this technology was virtually unknown on land. The lavatories were included for all classes of accommodation on board, including steerage, and were fitted with built-in, marble-topped wash-stands and flushing toilets with transfer-printed earthenware bowls.

Conditions for crew members were not nearly so comfortable. Most of the crew on the *Sydney Cove*, for example, were anonymous Indian seamen, commonly known as lascars, a mistaken European use of the Persian or Urdu "lashkar", a term for army or a band of followers. Employment of lascars was common in the country trade because they were typically paid less than one sixth of the wage paid to European seamen. During the voyage of the *Sydney Cove* from Calcutta, five of the lascars died of scurvy exacerbated by the cold and exhaustion brought on by the constant pumping required in the vain attempt to keep the ship afloat. Fragments of their pottery were recovered from both the wreck and from the survivors' camp on Preservation Island (Nash 2006; Strachan 1986). The fragments included pieces from thick-walled, grey-bodied storage vessels, thin-walled, grey-bodied bowls and small and large bowls made from coarse red earthenware, some of which had lids. All of the bowls were slipped on the inside but none were glazed. The vessels were all earthenware fired on open fires rather than in kilns and are typical of the cheap utilitarian wares produced in India at that time.

Excavation of the *Pandora* has focused on the quarters of the ship's officers, revealing evidence for diet, navigation, medicine and hygiene and for individual trade with Pacific Islanders (Gesner 1991, 2000, 2007). The *Pandora* was a 24-gun warship under the command of Captain Edward Edwards, sent in search of the *Bounty* mutineers in 1791. When it arrived at Tahiti, the mutineers still on the island either gave themselves up or were hunted out. They were locked away in a makeshift prison, referred to as "Pandora's Box", built on the ship's quarterdeck. After spending 3 months searching fruitlessly for the remaining mutineers (who had gone with Fletcher Christian to Pitcairn Island), the ship ran aground at the northern end of the Great Barrier Reef. It sank the next day, drowning 31 crew members and four of the prisoners. The wreck of the *Pandora* was rediscovered in 1977 where it lay on a soft, sandy seabed. The location meant that, rather than being broken up near the surface by waves and tides, the wreck remains one of Australia's best preserved shipwreck sites. In 1983 a team led by archaeologists from the Queensland Museum began excavations on the site, with the aim of understanding what life was like for officers and sailors on board a British warship engaged on a long voyage to the Pacific during the late eighteenth century.

Archaeologists recovered large quantities of artefacts from the site during the 1980s and 1990s. These included many items from the officers' cabins, such as a gold and silver filigree fob watch, toiletry brushes, glass ink pots, creamware plates and wine glasses. An ornately modelled brass fireplace was also found that probably came from the cabin of Captain Edwards. Weapons included iron and lead shot, firearms, sword fragments and several cannon. There were also about 150 intact ceramic jars found, which may be the "spruce jars" referred to in the ship's log. The jars were wheel-thrown earthenware with a lead glaze, generally 100–140 mm in height. Essence of spruce was used to make spruce beer, an important source of vitamins on long sea voyages (Campbell and Gesner 2000:107–109). In addition, a number of Pacific sea-shells and Polynesian tools and weapons were recovered, such as war clubs, fishing lures and hooks, stone adzes and a stone food pounder. These were probably acquired by one of the officers of the *Pandora* with the intention of selling them as exotic curiosities back in England, or they may have been confiscated from the *Bounty* prisoners. Such objects were in great demand among collectors of exotic items and unusual natural specimens (Campbell 1997; Fallowfield 2001).

Some of the most revealing evidence from the *Pandora* comes in the form of medical equipment, probably belonging to the ship's surgeon, George Hamilton (Pigott 1995). The surgeon's chest of instruments would have contained the standard set of equipment and drugs required by the Royal Navy's regulations at the end of the eighteenth century. One of the items was a screw tourniquet made of a copper alloy, which had originally been fitted with a linen or canvas strap to encircle a limb. The device was used to apply pressure over arteries in arms or legs injured in battle and could be easily adjusted during amputation to ease pressure and reveal spurting arteries. Naval surgeons were required to carry at least six tourniquets on ship. In a naval battle, there could be a number of seamen with injuries awaiting surgery, and the pressure applied by a tourniquet to limb injuries could help prevent death by blood loss. The amputation of limbs was the most common operation in naval surgery in the era before effective anaesthesia. Patients, however, were not generally expected to survive, and often did not: shock, blood loss and acute infection frequently resulted in death.

An ivory syringe from the wreck site would have been used to irrigate the ears or nose with fluid, or irrigate ulcers and wounds and wash away pus (the hypodermic syringe for drug injection was only developed in the mid-nineteenth century). Alternatively, treatment of gonorrhoea, a venereal infection, involved irrigation of the male urethra through the penis, using a small syringe, to mitigate the pain. Several small glass apothecaries' bottles originally contained small quantities of drugs and were usually stored in medicine chests, while a marble mortar was used to crush roots and herbs in the preparation of medicines. A wooden comb fitted with very fine teeth was used to remove lice from human hair.

Surgical artefacts from the *Pandora* demonstrate that medical treatment at sea in the late eighteenth century was a crude business. The status of surgeons was low, and medicine itself was still fairly primitive. Operations were limited in scope, agonising for the patient and frequently fatal. Drug treatments included many preparations now known to be useless. Genuine, effective treatments were few (see Chapter 11). Nevertheless, the surgeon on board the *Pandora* had the responsibility of maintaining the ship's company in good health in the face of outbreaks of infectious disease, preventing nutritional diseases such as scurvy and dealing with terrible injuries in battle.

Industrial Shipping

Most ships were much less glamorous than the *City of Launceston* and less notorious than the *Pandora*. Coastal and riverine trade required basic, sturdy craft that were suited to local conditions. The early lime industry in Victoria, for example, was dependent on such craft, as were the graziers and others along the Murray-Darling river system.

Lime was an essential product for the building industry in the nineteenth century (see Chapter 8). Before the development of railways, shipping was the most cost-effective way of transporting heavy cargoes like lime, and as a result most lime kilns in Victoria were located around Port Phillip Bay and in other coastal regions (Harrington 1996). The remains of jetties can still be seen adjacent to the kilns at several places, including Bell Point and Walkerville. Lime companies owned ships in order to guarantee transport, and as early as 1849 there were at least 25 vessels in the district dedicated to the lime trade. Carrying lime was a hazardous business for ships, however, as lime is chemically volatile and if water is added (or "slaked"), a reaction is triggered that generates heat, and the temperature can become hot enough to set fire to surrounding wood. This happened several times, resulting in the loss of both the cargo and the ship. One of the best documented lime wrecks is that of the *Joanna*, a wooden two-masted schooner wrecked in Port Phillip Bay in 1857 (Harrington 1996:21). The lime cargo is still readily identifiable on the wreck site as solidified lumps in the shape of the bags that once held it. Many personal artefacts associated with passengers and crew have also been recovered, providing rich insight into the domestic lives of the captain's family who appear to have lived on board the ship.

Although much of inland Australia is arid, river traffic was important where conditions permitted. Some of the shorter, coastal rivers in New South Wales, such as the Hunter, Macleay and Manning Rivers, for example, were used to transport logs of red cedar and other timbers (Nutley 2003; Vader 1986). The Murray-Darling river system supported an extensive river trade that spanned the 1850s to the early twentieth century. The river network is Australia's largest, draining the inland slopes of the Great Dividing Range and inland New South Wales and entering the sea

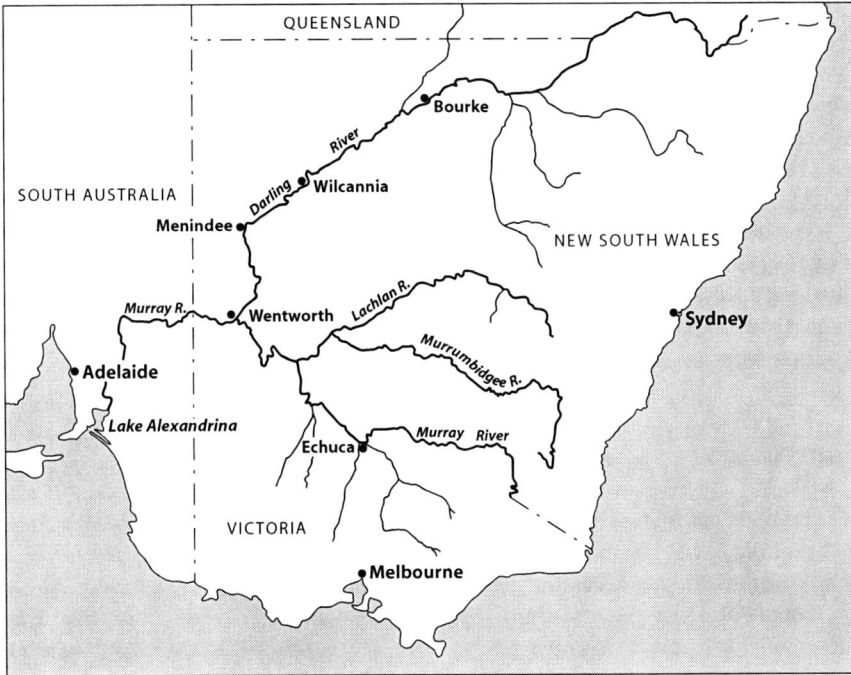

Fig. 4.4 Murray-Darling river system in south-eastern Australia

at the Murray Mouth in South Australia (Fig. 4.4). The terrain is flat, and the river meanders widely. As early as 1861, there were more than 30 vessels on the river, transporting almost 5,000 tons of goods a year (Buxton 1967:33; Phillips 1980). Substantial towns developed to service the river traffic, including Echuca, Wentworth, Menindee and Bourke. Paddle steamers served numerous purposes on the Murray-Darling, transporting goods, people and mail to inland stations and settlements, as well as being used for irrigation projects. Barges towed by the steamers hauled heavy produce such as wool, timber and stone. Small fishing schooners supported a major fishing industry in the lower lakes of the Murray River in South Australia, while ferries or punts provided a way across rivers before the construction of bridges.

Archaeological surveys in the 1990s identified more than 120 wreck sites along the river system in New South Wales, Victoria and South Australia (Kenderdine 1992, 1993, 1994a, b, 1995). Archaeological evidence for inland river shipping is extensive and includes wharves and jetties, navigational markers, landings and slipways, cranes and customs houses, locks, weirs and boatbuilding yards. Wreck sites include paddle steamers, barges, punts and ferries. The physical evidence helps to reveal how the waterways were navigated, the establishment and growth of major inland ports and the dynamics of the river trade, including regional economies and settlement patterns.

River boats varied in design and construction, but the shallow, meandering course of the river meant that several characteristics were common. The steering wheel, for example, was placed high and forward to allow watch for snags and sand bars. A flat bottom and shallow draft aided navigation through low water. Side paddle wheels were also common, in contrast to the stern wheels of Mississippi steamers, to help with manoeuvring through twists and turns in the river. Analysis of hull dimensions of river boat wrecks reveals that, over time, the general length and breadth of boats increased, while draft decreased (Kenderdine 1992:10). River traders modified their vessels in light of the costs of construction, growing knowledge of the river and the changing nature of goods transported. As the river trade slowly died in the early twentieth century, small creeks and tributaries near the inland ports became graveyards for vessels that were no longer needed on the river.

Ships of War

Warfare has not been a prominent part of Australian archaeology because most of Australia's wars have been fought elsewhere. In some cases, however, it is possible to investigate Australian participation in overseas engagements with the co-operation of foreign governments. This occurred with the remains of an Australian submarine, *AE2*, lost in combat off the Turkish coast in 1915 during the Gallipoli campaign of the First World War and relocated by a team of Turkish archaeologists in 1998 (T. Smith 2000). Both countries have an ongoing interest in managing the site, and such work requires a high degree of sensitivity, even though no crew were lost and the site is not a War Grave.

During the Second World War Australian territory itself came under direct attack from German and Japanese forces. Colin De La Rue (2005) has investigated the terrestrial archaeological evidence for the air raids and military bases in the Northern Territory, and shipwrecks from the period have also recently been relocated for the first time since their sinking. Two discoveries in particular have attracted widespread attention: the wreck of *HMAS Sydney* in the sea off Geraldton, Western Australia, early in 2008 and the discovery in 2006 of the wreck of a Japanese midget submarine off Sydney's northern beaches. Both wrecks have been the subject of considerable historical research and it has been this, combined with developments in sidescan sonar technology, which has at last enabled them to be found. Both wrecks are protected as historic sites (and grave sites) which will be left undisturbed on the seabed, but the discoveries have brought greater closure to the families of those involved and have helped to solve enduring mysteries about what happened when the vessels disappeared.

The *HMAS Sydney* was Australia's most celebrated cruiser in 1941, freshly returned from battle in the Mediterranean and assigned to new duties protecting the Australian coast from German raiders known to be in the region. On the afternoon of November 19, 1941 it approached the *Kormoran*, a raider disguised as a merchant ship. In the ensuing battle both ships were heavily damaged and eventually sank, but while most of the *Kormoran*'s crew was eventually rescued there were no survivors from the *Sydney's* 645 crew and no witnesses to report what had happened to them. The scale of the tragedy and the mystery surrounding it have kept the *Sydney* alive in the national consciousness ever since. In March 2008 searchers found first the *Kormoran* and then the *Sydney*, and photographs taken by remote cameras revealed for the first time the full extent of the damage suffered (Finding Sydney 2008; Mearns 2009). The bow of the *Sydney* had completely and catastrophically broken away, which must have caused the ship to sink rapidly. It lies on the seabed at a depth of 2.5 km. Several lifeboats were found on and around the ship and all had been destroyed by gunfire from the *Kormoran*. Together, the speed of the sinking and the lack of lifeboats made it impossible for any crew to survive.

The Japanese submarine *M24* had a much smaller crew, consisting of only two men, and they too were killed when their vessel sank (Smith 2008). The *M24* was one of three midget submarines on a secret mission to torpedo American warships anchored in Sydney Harbour. On the night of 31 May 1941, the *M24* surreptitiously entered the harbour, evading the watch and the anti-submarine netting. The crew fired their torpedoes but missed their main target, the *USS Chicago*, instead hitting and sinking an Australian naval depot ship, killing 21 men. Only the *M24* escaped from the harbour, as one of the other submarines, the *Ha-14* became caught in the anti-submarine netting and the other, the *Ha-21*, was destroyed when it surfaced the following morning. According to the mission plan, all three submarines were to rendezvous southwards along the coast near Royal National Park, where they were to be picked up by their ship. The meeting never took place, however, and it was not known what had happened to *M24*. When the submarine was rediscovered, staff at the New South Wales Heritage Branch found that it lay along the bearing of an alternative rendezvous to the north. It is not known exactly what happened. The submarine was at the end of its 12-hour capacity for being underwater, but surfacing during daylight would have meant almost certain discovery by the Australian military. Inspection of the wreck recorded by Remote Operated Vehicle indicates that the crew did not leave the vessel as the exits had not been used. There is no damage to suggest that the submarine was deliberately scuttled or that the descent to the seabed was uncontrolled. It therefore seems likely that the crew remained inside and either committed suicide or were overcome by mechanical failure.

Now that the location of these vessels is known, official commemorations have taken place. Religious ceremonies have been performed at each, and family members have visited the area and left flowers and mementos at the site of *HMAS Sydney*. At the *M24* site the brother of one of the crewmen poured *sake* on the waters, and families of both crew members were presented with samples of sand from the site to be interred in family shrines in Japan. Many shipwrecks are also grave sites, but these two cases have taken on special significance. Both sites have been protected under Commonwealth historic shipwrecks legislation, and both will be left in situ, in accordance with the wishes of family members and the governments concerned.

Maritime archaeologists have also recently begun to study the underwater remains of aircraft, especially military aircraft, from the Second World War (McCarthy 2004). The aim, as with shipwrecks, is not only to identify the aircraft, but to understand site formation processes and to place the craft within a broader context of modern transportation systems. Silvano Jung (2005), for example, has investigated the remains of two Catalina flying boats wrecked in Darwin Harbour in 1942, to try to identify the specific vessels brought down by Japanese attacks during the Second World War. A similar project in 2001 by archaeologists from the Western Australian Maritime Museum located the remains of 20 Second World War flying-boat sites in Roebuck Bay at Broome in Western Australia (Souter 2003). The aircraft had been sunk while moored, in a Japanese attack on March 3, 1942 that killed between 70 and 100 people. The integration of archaeological material with the oral testimony of servicemen allows a much more nuanced and detailed understanding of an event that drew Western Australia into the war for the first time and changed the way people in the multicultural town saw themselves within the wider region. Elsewhere, Julie Ford's (2004) survey of aircraft losses in Victoria during the Second World War identified 75 wrecks which had been lost during training exercises. Her study reinforces the scale of the aviation industry in this period and the risks involved not only in prosecuting the war, but in simply preparing for it as well.

Theorising Shipwreck Archaeology

While the focus of much shipwreck archaeology concerns individual vessels, others consider wreck events as a whole, to try to understand better what happens when wrecks occur. A team working on data from the *Pandora* (Ward et al. 1998, 1999), for example, has built on earlier theories of site formation processes to explain how a wrecked ship is transformed into an archaeological site and the various factors that affect its preservation. They begin by distinguishing between the wreck itself and the processes forming the wreck site and identify the distinct physical, biological and chemical factors involved. They also note that excavation introduces new conditions that can contribute to further deterioration. In their model, physical factors such as wave action and currents play the dominant role in the early stages of wreck disintegration, while biological action by organisms such as marine borers and fungi and then chemical factors, primarily corrosion, become more important in later stages. All of these factors interact in a complex and dynamic system that creates constantly changing conditions on the wreck site.

Martin Gibbs (2006) has noted the increasing interest in sites that overlap maritime and terrestrial themes, which has been instrumental in developing broader theoretical approaches that go beyond describing particular events and attempt to explain broader cultural processes. The camps occupied by survivors of shipwrecks are an example of this maritime/terrestrial interface. The lengthy and sparsely settled coastline of Australia meant that even if survivors from wrecks made it to shore, they were often still far from safety, and in some circumstances they had to establish temporary camps on the beach. Nevertheless, survivor camps, particularly those surveyed archaeologically, are comparatively rare. Nash suggests that only 1 or 2% of all shipwrecks in Australia resulted in camps that were occupied for a week or more (Nash 2005:9). Gibbs strongly advocates an approach to these places that, in the first instance, treats the wreck site and the camp as related phenomena and then develops a comparative perspective to facilitate the analysis of survivor responses over time and in different circumstances (Gibbs 2006:75–76). Gibbs argues that survivors have an impact on wreck sites through their activities in salvaging goods and materials to aid their own survival. The organisation of shipboard cultures, he suggests, including the complement of crew and passengers, and whether the vessel was a military, merchant, or passenger vessel, will influence the responses of survivors and the nature of the camp they build. It is these differences in the personnel involved, the purpose of the voyage and its culture of origin, and the nature of the cargo, that create the potential for comparative analysis to shed light on broader questions about human behaviour and culture.

The circumstance that links camp and wreck site is the wrecking of the ship, and Gibbs reminds us that for those involved it was a crisis event of the worst kind (Gibbs 2002, 2003a). Gibbs has drawn on research into the psychology of human response to crises, as well as on the arguments outlined above, to formulate a model for the comparative archaeology of survivor camps. He notes that while shipboard hierarchy and authority structures may be re-established on shore and may shape the social and material dimensions of the camp, these structures may also be challenged by individual responses to disaster and perceptions of whether or not those in charge react effectively or even have the appropriate abilities to reassert control. In some circumstances, such as the aftermath of the wrecking of the VOC ship *Batavia* off the Western Australian coast in 1629, new leaders may gather support based on their personal charisma (see Chapter 12). Gibbs' model for investigating survivor camps identifies categories for analysing physical relationships between the wreck and the camp, authority and social structures within the camp, subsistence strategies, material culture including salvaged and foraged supplies, shelters and structures built, the health and mortality of the survivors, the development of a rescue strategy, salvage activities and the psychological influences of the disaster on behaviour patterns. Gibbs also notes that survivor camps were frequently places of contact between European and Indigenous groups, and that interaction, whether hostile or co-operative, may be evident in the material culture and even in the genetics of contemporary Indigenous populations (see McCarthy 2008; Nutley 1995).

This approach provides a framework for interpreting archaeological sites like Preservation Island, the camp occupied by the *Sydney Cove* survivors for up to a year following the wrecking of the ship in 1797 (Nash 2005, 2006). Michael Nash led a team from the Tasmanian Parks and Wildlife Service and Flinders University which excavated the camp site in 2002. He compared material from the wreck and the campsite using documents regarding the cargo and its salvage, as well as the analysis of material excavated archaeologically from the wreck. One of the patterns Nash identified was that the campsite material does not fully represent the cargo from the ship, and, following Gibbs' model, the conscious selection of material for the camp can be interpreted as part of the survival strategy of the crew. Though the crew were engaged in salvaging cargo for the owners, much of this was stored on another nearby island. What they brought back to the camp was to meet their own immediate needs and they deliberately sought out items that would be most useful to them. Ceramics found at the camp consisted of porcelain wash basins from the cargo and Indian-made coarse earthenwares that were also excavated from the wreck and identified as personal possessions or equipment for the crew. Notably absent from the camp were other ceramics from the cargo, including the porcelain plates and water bottles that made up much of the shipment. For the predominantly Lascar crew, the large bowls were evidently more useful than plates for their traditional cooking methods, and these were presumably chosen to replace vessels that had been lost in the wreck.

Faunal remains also indicate that cargo items were salvaged and used where convenient. While most of the bone from the site was in poor condition, both native and non-native bones were identified. All of the non-native bone identified consisted of cattle, pig and sheep bone that had been butchered in ways identical to that recorded for the casks of salt meat in the cargo. Most of the faunal assemblage, however, was local indigenous species, predominantly the short-tailed shearwater or "mutton-bird" which is abundant on the islands of Bass Strait and was a favoured food of Tasmanian Aboriginal groups. Hoop iron found on the island indicates that casks were retrieved from the wreck, so that the contents of salt meat and alcohol could be consumed by the survivors, with the casks reused for storing water and other goods. Other materials from the ship were salvaged to build shelters on the island. These included iron fastenings, timbers from the ship's frame and bricks from the galley that were brought ashore to build a hearth.

For the *Sydney Cove* survivors, the psychological phases of disaster response, including confusion and fragmentation that occur once the immediate threat to life has receded, may account for the poor choice of location for the initial shelter and the failure to provide adequate rations. The wreck event was gradual and planned to some degree, and this helped to shape subsequent salvage operations and the rescue plan. The crew were able to return to the ship over a period of several weeks, recovering many personal items and objects of immediate use, as well as salvaging goods from the upper parts of the ship's hull. This meant that they were able to send the ship's longboat to the mainland to alert the authorities, as well as utilise canvas from the sails, bricks from the galley and food from the stores; and they were ultimately able to build a substantial structure to provide shelter on the island over the winter months. Investigation of the survivors' camp, by documenting the responses of the crew and the effects of salvage operations on the wreck itself, has added considerably to our understanding of this important early site.

Maritime Infrastructure

Excavating shipwrecks has been the high-profile side of maritime archaeology, but attention is increasingly turning to other aspects of the considerable infrastructure needed to support the shipping industry. Archaeologists have begun to investigate sites associated with the whole life-span of ships, from the shipyards where they were built to the dry-docks where repairs and maintenance were carried out and finally the ships' graveyards where decommissioned ships were systematically abandoned. Equally important are the wharves and jetties required for loading and unloading cargoes and passengers.

Shipbuilding and Maintenance

One of the main centres of shipbuilding in colonial Australia was the convict settlement of Port Arthur, located on the Tasman Peninsula in south-east Tasmania, which operated from 1830 until 1877. The rugged terrain of the area is surrounded by water and connected to the mainland only by a narrow spit of land at Eaglehawk Neck. The sea was both a prison wall and a highway of communication with the outside world. Archaeological investigation, sponsored by the Port Arthur Historic Site Management Authority, has focused on the maritime infrastructure of the area to understand how the sea shaped relationships between Port Arthur and its outstations around the peninsula and with the world beyond (Tuffin et al. 2004).

The waterfront at Port Arthur was the interface between the penal settlement and the outside world. Bulk shipments of flour, meat, sugar and tea were brought in, while the products of convict labour, including timber, coal, bricks and worked stone, were sent out. Sails and steam-driven ships linked the outstations to Port Arthur and Port Arthur with Hobart. A dockyard at Port Arthur was established in 1834, and convicts were set to work building lighters, whaleboats, schooners and barques – sturdy craft that served government and commercial users well.

The dockyard precinct quickly grew to include slipways and boat sheds, an overseer's hut, a blacksmith's shop, sawpits, "steamers" for shaping timbers and a house for the master shipwright (Nash 2004:41–43). The workers built not only a variety of vessels from scratch, using local timber and imported fittings, but repaired visiting ships as well. The first large vessel built at the dockyards was the 97-ton government schooner *Eliza*, completed in 1835. Along with such large vessels, over 140 small boats were also built at Port Arthur between 1834 and 1844. With the expansion of the commercial boatbuilding industry by the late 1840s, however, the Port Arthur dockyard closed in 1848, although small-scale building and repair continued for a number of years.

Today, the most obvious maritime features of all this activity include the remains of jetties, wharves, tramways and ballast heaps at various sites around the peninsula. These elements provide the modern physical context of the once-vital connections between land-based convict labour and sea-based transport. Jetties and other coastal facilities reveal changes in technology and the structure of activity over the life of the penal settlement. The first phase, in the 1830s and 1840s, saw decentralised industrial centres around Carnarvon Bay, with small craft criss-crossing the bay to carry people, raw materials and finished goods to waiting ships (Coroneos 2004:97). The second phase, which lasted until the closure of Port Arthur in 1877, saw the closure of the dockyard and several other facilities, the centralisation of works around Port Arthur itself and the increasing use of steamships for maritime transport.

Ships' Graveyards

Ships were not always wrecked on reefs or in storms. In many cases owners would deliberately abandon and scuttle a vessel at the end of its useful working life, and as Nathan Richards notes, this is an important distinction with implications for understanding the archaeological record and human behaviour (2008:7–8). Abandoned ships were often sunk in shallow, inter-tidal zones, or deployed as breakwaters or jetties. Old sailing ships could also be converted for use as coal bunkers or prison hulks. Abandoned watercraft have been widely documented around the Australian coastline and along coastal rivers (Richards 2005, 2008). The Garden Island grave-yard in Port Adelaide, for example, contains the remains of 25 vessels, mostly built in the later nineteenth century and abandoned up to 50 years later (Richards 1998). In Victoria, a ships' graveyard just off Port Phillip Heads was used as a dumping ground between 1913 and 1971. It contained the remains of at least 42 vessels, including steamships, coastal traders and four First World War J-Class submarines (Fig. 4.5; Heritage Victoria 2000). The remains of such places can provide important information not only about the individual ships, but also about changing technolo-gies, the working lives of ships and how the processes of scuttling, demolition and salvage affect the archaeological record and maritime heritage. In contrast to the sudden disaster of a shipwreck, abandonment is planned and takes place over many years, with the disposal of ships serving as a mirror to changing technological, economic and social forces (Richards 1998:80).

Richards (2008:11) argues that deliberate abandonment is best understood as a process rather than an event. Vessels may undergo salvage for a prolonged period of time and by different parties and/or may deteriorate over many years due to expo-sure to the elements. There may also be interventions in the process when a ship is refloated and reused, or a discarded ship may be deliberately abandoned in such

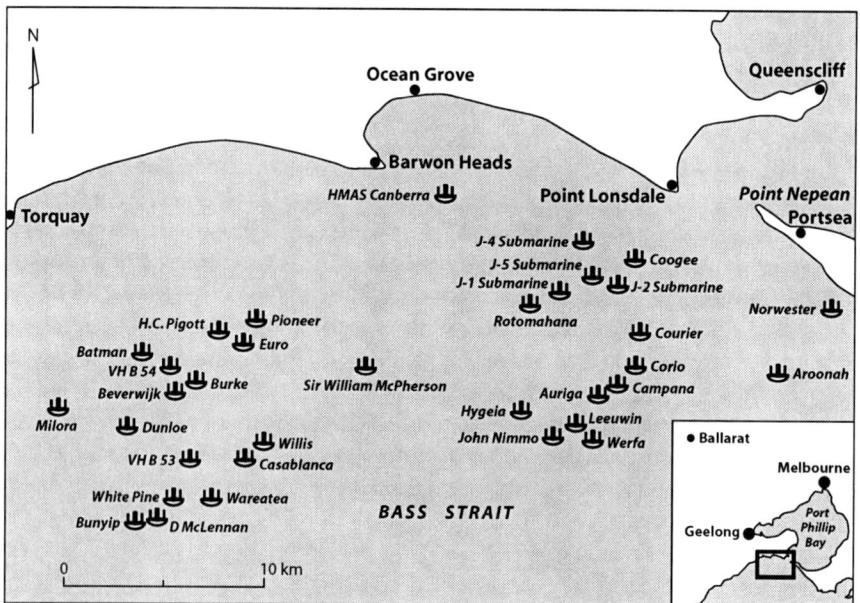

Fig. 4.5 Ships' graveyard at the entrance to Port Phillip Bay, Victoria (after Heritage Victoria 2000)

a way as to create a new kind of function, such as marine habitat. All of these factors present challenges when determining a date of abandonment. By examining abandonment as a type of discard event, Richards has identified national trends in the disposal of watercraft and correlated them with historical and economic events. This provides a perspective for discard beyond vague reasons such as a ship being "worn out", including more general factors that lead a ship owner to this conclusion. During wartime, for example, the demand for shipping keeps old vessels in service, while in post-war periods large numbers of vessels are discarded (Richards 2008:80). Richards has also investigated ships' graveyards as archaeological sites, analysing the environmental and technological factors that have determined their location. Places for the safe disposal of ships must be close to areas with high concentrations of shipping activity, but at the same time they must be located where they will not constitute hazards to shipping (2008:85). All of Australia's major ports have associated graveyards, while many of the minor ports have isolated abandoned ships. In many cases the graveyards are in inter-tidal areas near shipbuilding facilities that can be used to break up the ships and make use of salvaged materials (2008:89).

Jetties and Wharves

Jetties and wharves were essential for the transfer of cargo and passengers. The remains of these structures around the coastline and along navigable rivers is compelling evidence for the importance of shipping in the days before rail and road transport. One archaeological study has documented jetties built to serve the convict probation stations of the Tasman Peninsula in Tasmania (Bullers 2005). The jetties were originally constructed in the 1840s as part of the convict system, but they served two quite distinct communities. They were used by ships that brought in stores for the convicts and took away the products of their labour, mainly timber, coal and vegetables. Most were substantially built on a T-plan with long narrow necks and a shorter head where the ships tied up. The jetties were constructed of wooden trestles and decking and had stone abutments on shore. They had to be long enough to reach deep water (over 600 feet [183 m] at Cascades) and wide enough to accommodate tramways and horse carts. With the end of the convict era in the 1870s, land on the Tasman Peninsula was sold to free settlers who used the jetties to export their own goods. From the 1880s to the 1950s, when the cargo steamers stopped running, the jetties were repaired and upgraded to provide facilities for shipping agricultural produce. The main crop in the region was apples, and sheds to store the fruit were built alongside and on the jetties.

Conclusion

In recent years the excavation of shipwreck sites in Australian waters has become much less common. This is partly due to the very high expense involved, with vessels, equipment and personnel committed to weeks of time on the water. Costs are exacerbated by the need to conserve materials brought suddenly from salt water to a dry land environment. Major advances in remote sensing and site mapping have also lessened the need for manual survey and excavation, with much of the work now done from the surface (Green 2004). In addition, there has been a growing emphasis on site management and public education, to minimise disturbances to wreck sites that might otherwise require salvage excavation. As we have demonstrated here, the field of maritime archaeology in Australia has matured significantly. It now incorporates a range of theoretical approaches that have widened the emphasis from individual shipwrecks, to consider such issues as site formation and taphonomy, consumerism and capitalism, and the psychology of shipwreck survivors. Importantly, the old distinction between archaeology on land and on sea has become blurred, and the two environments are now more commonly regarded by archaeologists as intimately connected. Events and processes on the land and in the water influenced each other in profound ways, and it is in the exploration and understanding of these relationships that maritime archaeology adds so much to our knowledge of Australia's past.

Chapter 5
Sealing, Whaling and Maritime Industries

The sea was a means of transport for colonial Australians but it also held valuable resources. Although wool and gold were Australia's best-known exports during the nineteenth century, sealing and whaling played a vital and much earlier role in the development of colonial industry and commercial activity. Before the resources of the inland were well known, people still looked to the sea for the riches they could draw from it. In an era before petroleum oils, the oil rendered from seal and whale blubber was used extensively for industrial lubrication, as lighting fuel and in the manufacture of paints and soap. Later in the nineteenth century the lucrative fish-curing operations run by Chinese businessmen on the eastern seaboard supported many coastal fishing communities, while pearling developed as an important industry on the remote northern coast of Western Australia. Study of the material remains of these industries has been an important area of collaboration between terrestrial and maritime archaeologists. The survey and excavation of coastal sites has been accompanied by the study of associated wreck sites, and this has led to approaches focusing on the social and economic networks that crossed colonial boundaries. Researchers have also identified distinctive maritime cultural landscapes in coastal regions where overlapping networks of activities and associations meld the sea and the land into a single unified horizon.

This chapter builds on the discussion of ships and shipping activities provided in Chapter 4, especially in the links between terrestrial and maritime archaeology. Here we review the archaeological evidence for sealing in southern Australia and describe shore-based whaling stations and the living conditions of the crewmen. It is evident that there were broad similarities around Australia in the positioning of stations within the local landscape as well as in the activities of the crewmen themselves. Other maritime industries, such as fish-curing and pearling, were established later and operated within distinct ethnic contexts. We conclude by describing maritime cultural landscapes in South Australia and Victoria.

Sealing

Archaeological surveys have revealed that the surviving physical evidence for sealing is generally slight. Sealing groups were small and opportunistic, leaving

S. Lawrence, P. Davies, *An Archaeology of Australia Since 1788*,
Contributions To Global Historical Archaeology, DOI 10.1007/978-1-4419-7485-3_5,
© Springer Science+Business Media, LLC 2011

few traces of their activities behind. In Victoria and South Australia, for example, detailed archaeological investigations of coastal sites have shown few clear links with sealing, in spite of historical reports to the contrary (Davies and Lawrence 2003; Kostoglou and McCarthy 1991; Stuart 1989a; Townrow 1997). The Aboriginal/sealer communities on the Bass Strait islands and Kangaroo Island in South Australia are exceptions, but the archaeological remains there have not been well documented (Stuart 1997b; Russell 2005). In a few places, sealing may have overlapped with whaling. On the Isle Du Phoques, for example, off the east coast of Tasmania, the well-preserved remains of sealers' huts may also have been used as a look-out post by whalers (Kostoglou 1995:36–38).

Captain William Raven demonstrated the potential profit of sealing in southern waters as early as 1792, when a crew he left at Dusky Bay in New Zealand gathered 4,500 skins. The hunting of seals for fur in Australia itself began after the sinking of the *Sydney Cove* in 1797 (see Chapter 4), when the rescue parties returned to Sydney with news of large seal colonies in the Furneaux islands off the north-east coast of Tasmania. Captain Charles Bishop set out in 1798 in the *Nautilus* to explore sealing opportunities in the area and returned to Sydney with 5,200 seal skins and about 350 gallons (1,575 l) of seal oil. The tempo of sealing increased quickly, with large catches made on King Island beginning around 1801, while sealers were also established on Kangaroo Island by 1802. The main Australian sealing grounds extended from the island groups of Bass Strait to King George Sound in the south of Western Australia. Between 1805 and 1810, however, catches declined and sealers moved further afield to Macquarie Island and Heard Island in the Southern Ocean. Nevertheless, the industry continued on sporadically in the Bass Strait area until around 1850 (Plomley and Henley 1990; Stuart 1997b).

The New Zealand sealing grounds, which included offshore islands such as Stewart Island, Macquarie Island and Campbell Island in the sub-Antarctic, were also a major destination for Sydney merchants from this time (Fig. 5.1; I. Smith 2002:4). There were no permanent European settlements in New Zealand and the Sydney sealing gangs were among the first white people to have regular contact with Maori, playing an important role in the post-contact history of the country. Because the sealing industry was regional in its scope, with Sydney serving as a base for activity throughout the southern oceans, studies of sealing in New Zealand can also shed light on the operation of the wider industry.

Two types of seal were hunted. The elephant seal (or southern walrus) was killed principally for its oil, while its hide could also be tanned for shoe leather. The fur seal was killed for its skin, which was exported to England, India and China and made into hats and other clothing. Cantonese furriers in particular were skilled at removing the coarse guard from seal skins to leave the soft inner fur (Russ 2007:169). With skins selling in China for up to £1 each, there were enormous profits to be made (Whitaker 2004:55). Poor curing methods and glutted markets, however, often depressed prices. Sealing was largely a seasonal occupation, usually confined to the spring and summer months when seals were breeding on their island rookeries. Seal hunting took little equipment or skill, other than physical strength and a strong stomach. The seals were clubbed or stabbed to death while they were

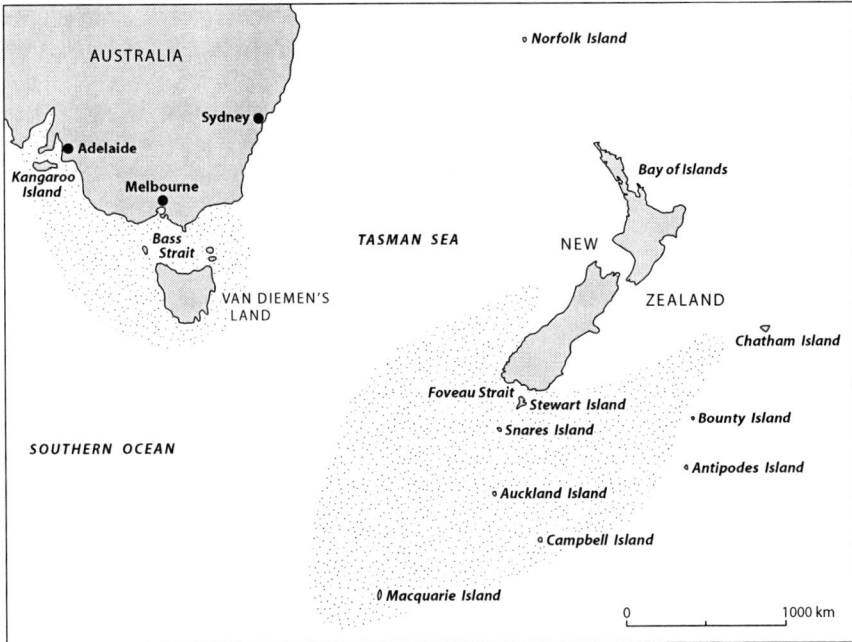

Fig. 5.1 Seal fishery in southern Australia, New Zealand and sub-Antarctic islands (after I. Smith 2002:2)

coming ashore or asleep, with skins salted or pegged out to dry. Extracting oil from the carcass meant boiling the blubber in large iron kettles and storing the oil in casks.

The Australasian sealing industry was mainly run by merchants and sea captains based in Sydney, Hobart and Launceston. Early entrepreneurs such as Simeon Lord, Henry Kable and James Underwood used their ships to drop crews of 10–15 men on remote islands (Hainsworth 1981:244–245). The ships sailed away to trade other cargoes such as sandalwood from Fiji and pork from Tahiti and returned months later to collect the men, skins and oil. Between 1800 and 1806 more than 100,000 skins were obtained from the Bass Strait area.

Men joined the sealing gangs for various reasons. Many were unskilled and hoped for the profit from a big catch, while others wanted to escape wives and family responsibilities. Some simply enjoyed the "work and bust" way of life. The sealing crews were paid on a lay or share system, i.e. a fixed percentage of prof-its per man. Ordinary sealers received from a 75th to about a 100th lay, while an overseer might receive a 25th lay (Hainsworth 1981:141). The system encouraged hard work, with the men profiting directly from their efforts, while the entrepreneur needed only to provide advances for slop clothing and stores for the gangs, which were deducted when the men were paid at the end of the season. The pay was still poor, however, and came with a large element of risk. If the catch was poor, or the supply ship foundered, or the gang was forgotten (as sometimes happened), the men could soon descend into a miserable condition. Joseph Murrell and six companions, for example, spent 3 years on Kangaroo Island from 1806, nearly the whole time without provisions (*Sydney Gazette* 16 April 1809).

The use of shore gangs has been reasonably well documented, in part due to newspaper coverage of cases like Murrell's and because this was probably the most common strategy used in Bass Strait (Fig. 5.2). In addition, archaeologist Ian Smith (2002:27–29) has identified several other sealing strategies that were used in New Zealand and perhaps elsewhere, which were probably more common there than the shore gangs. The first was the use of the ship as a base from which gangs were sent out for short periods of time in open boats. This was a mobile, flexible strategy ideally suited to the rapid discovery and exploitation of new seal colonies, and Smith suggests that it was particularly common on the west coast of New Zealand's South Island in the period 1803–1807. As this strategy would have left very little in the way of physical evidence, there are obvious implications for the archaeological record. The second strategy identified by Smith was favoured particularly in the 1820s, by which time organised sealing had largely ended in Australian waters. This also relied on a combination of ships and open boats, with the boats sent off for slightly longer periods, briefly camping on shore as they worked their way along a stretch of coast before rejoining their ship. The final strategy, and one which also came to dominate in Bass Strait and on Kangaroo Island, involved men who deserted their gangs and remained to live permanently at the sealing grounds, often with Indigenous women

Fig. 5.2 Lithograph of sealers' camp in Western Port, Victoria, ca.1833 (picture collection, State Library of Victoria)

and eventually children. Both of these strategies, and particularly the latter, would potentially have left a greater archaeological signature than the transitory ship-based gangs.

Crews were made up largely of the British-born, but there were also Portuguese, Lascars, Maori and others involved, while American sealers were active in Australian waters from at least 1803 (Wace and Lovett 1973:9). American sealers were bitterly resented, as their crews sometimes assaulted local gangs, and the American captains often lured sealers away from service with Sydney masters. The advantage lay with the Australian colonists, however, because they could operate much smaller boats closer to home and did not have to hold station off dangerous shores for months while the crews worked. Sealing also provided employment opportunities for young native-born men who lacked the capital or training to establish themselves as farmers or tradesmen (Little 1969:112–113).

By around 1810 the pattern of sealing in Australia began to change, as the number of seals remaining could only supply a small-scale industry on the Bass Strait islands. The organised commercial crews were replaced by small groups of adventurers, often escaped or former convicts, who lived on the islands permanently. Some were deserting sailors attracted to the remoteness of the islands and the chance to live free from authority. They built small huts of rough timber, bark and grass; fenced and cultivated gardens and grew small patches of wheat, onions and potatoes; and raised goats, pigs and poultry. The sealers met Aborigines who were hunting mutton-birds and shellfish along the coasts. Soon they were exchanging seal and kangaroo skins for tobacco, flour and tea. Some Aboriginal women elected to stay with the sealers, while others were abducted. The sealers and the Aboriginal women became the founders of a dynamic Straits community and the ancestors of today's Tasmanian Aboriginal people (Murray-Smith 1973; Plomley 1987:191–192; see also Russell 2005; Ryan 1996; R. Taylor 2002).

Archaeological evidence for sealing on the Australian coast is fairly limited but in New Zealand several sealing sites have been located in the remote inlets along the west coast of the South Island. However, there are a number of problems for identifying sealing sites. The processing of skins left little physical trace, so the main archaeological features are habitation sites. In New Zealand caves were occupied, with or without internal structures, as well as purpose-built huts. The huts, however, were generally rudimentary and the supplies the sealers were left with, primarily casks of salt meat and flour, have also left little archaeological evidence. Compounding this is that Maori also lived or camped in both huts and caves and used European goods after contact. The identification of small campsites with only a handful of European goods, usually pieces of metal, as sealers' camps is thus highly conjectural.

Despite these difficulties, Ian Smith (2002:54) has identified more than a dozen sites with likely sealing associations. The most promising locality is the Open Bay Islands, midway up the west coast (Smith 2002:57). There is good documentary evidence for shore gangs in the area, the strategy with the largest archaeological signature, and several hut structures, including one made of stone, have already been confirmed there. At Cape Providence, on the south-western tip of the South Island, there is evidence of a more complete landscape of sealing that includes a lookout, dwelling sites and a possible location where oil was rendered. The dwelling sites include at least one cave from which European artefacts have been recovered, and there is good documentary evidence for the presence of shore gangs.

The best archaeological evidence of sealing, however, comes from the sub-Antarctic islands, which were worked by gangs from Australia as well as from Britain, the United States and France. Heard Island, for example, is one of the remotest specks of land in the world, located about 4,000 km south-west of Australia. Archaeological survey on Heard Island identified more than 30 sites, including hut ruins and tryworks, relating to American sealers based on the island between 1855 and 1880. At least 14 ships were wrecked in the waters around Heard Island as well (A. McGowan 2000; Hughes and Lazer 2000; Lazer and McGowan 1990). Survey on the island revealed a range of archaeological features and materials that permitted the identification of both domestic and industrial sites. Platforms of stone and timber, for example, were found at several coastal locations, which were used to provide an elevated foundation for processing the seals. Remains at the platforms included trypots, scrap blubber, blubber forks and skimmers and butchered seal bone. Numerous barrels were also recorded across the beaches of Heard Island, used to store food and coal and to transport blubber and oil. Ruins of huts, with stone footings and upright wooden posts, were also found, originally with roofs of canvas sail, seal skins or grass thatch nailed over wooden or whale-bone rafters. Domestic items from around the huts include clay tobacco pipes, domestic ceramics, bottle glass, clothing remains and pieces of cast iron stoves. Several lava caves around the island had also been adapted for dwelling places, with timber pieces showing attempts had been made to improve the available shelter (McGowan 2000:67).

Sealing also occurred on Macquarie Island, located about 1,500 km south-east of Tasmania. The island was discovered in 1810, and within a few years there were half a dozen sealing stations in operation, rendering elephant seal blubber for oil. The industry waned around 1830, but picked up again in 1873 and continued until 1920. Excavations by Karen Townrow (1989, 1990) at seven sites on the island attempted to assess the lives of the sealers. Structural remains of wooden huts were common, although associated domestic debris was generally restricted to some glass, ceramic and leather fragments. Industrial items included trypots from the earlier period and iron boilers and digesters from the later period, the latter used to render elephant oil and penguin oil. Barrel staves and hoop iron were common, as casks were used as containers for both food and coal and for storing rendered oil.

Comparison of hut sites indicated that the size of dwellings increased through time. Construction began with site levelling, either by removing beach cobbles or adding foundation posts. Timber was imported for the purpose or scavenged as driftwood. Later huts were also made slightly more comfortable, with insulation such as hessian (burlap), canvas or malthoid (bitumen tar-paper) added to the walls and linoleum on the floors. The ramshackle nature of the huts meant that older sites were scavenged for materials, rather than being rebuilt, as it was easier and more efficient to start again when reoccupying an area. The built-in obsolescence of the huts reflects the nature of the industry. The sealers never intended to settle on the island, only to exploit the local fauna for skins and oil.

Whaling

Whaling is another maritime industry which has been of great interest to archaeologists. This may seem surprising in view of common stereotypes about whaling depicted in novels such as *Moby Dick*, where the work involved lengthy sea voyages with few landfalls. These images, however, are drawn from deep-sea whaling in pursuit of sperm whales, rather than earlier forms of whaling which had extensive shore-based components. Shore whaling was an important industry in the early days of the colonies and unlike sealing has left an extensive archaeological record. Shore whaling stations were established all along the southern coast of Australia, from Twofold Bay in New South Wales to Dampier in the north-west of Western Australia, and along the south and east coasts of Tasmania. The remains of many of the more isolated stations have survived and have been studied by archaeologists interested in the technology of whaling and in the living conditions experienced by the crews. Extensive surveys of the coastlines of Western Australia (Gibbs 1995), South Australia (Kostoglou and McCarthy 1991), Victoria (Townrow 1997), New South Wales (Gojak 1998; Pearson 1985) and Tasmania (Kostoglou 1995; Nash 1998) have been carried out in order to identify and record whaling sites. Several sites have been excavated (Davies and Lawrence 2003; Gibbs 1998, 2005a; Lawrence 2006a, b; Staniforth 1998; Staniforth et al. 2000) and the wrecks of whaling ships have also been identified and surveyed (Anderson 2004; Nash 1990; Nash and Anderson 2007; T. Smith and Weir 1999). Most of the documentary records available are about deep-sea (pelagic) whaling, so the archaeological evidence is an important source of information about this lucrative early industry.

Whales have been hunted for their oil since at least the sixteenth century. Crews from English, Spanish, Dutch and Norwegian ships scoured the waters of the north Atlantic in search of whales to kill. By 1790 the whalers had expanded into the south Pacific, and within a few years there were dozens of ships involved in the industry (Mawer 1999; Whitaker 2004:54). Whale hunting took two basic forms. In pelagic whaling, the ship served as a factory base for the smaller whaleboats and crews. Captured whales were brought back to the ship for processing, and ships would often remain at sea for several years at a time. British, French and American ships were all active in deep-sea whaling in the Pacific and used ports in Hawaii, Tahiti and the Bay of Islands in New Zealand for refitting and supply (R. Richards 2002). Shore whaling, however, involved hunting whales near the coast, with a base camp set up on land. The camp, or station, included all necessary facilities, including the lookout, tryworks, crew quarters, workshops and oil storage. As shore whaling required less capital, it was favoured by colonial entrepreneurs in Australia.

Sperm whales yielded the finest quality oil, but as this species generally kept well away from shore it could only be hunted at sea. The southern right whale, or black whale (*Eubalaena australis*), was the "right" whale for the shore whalers to

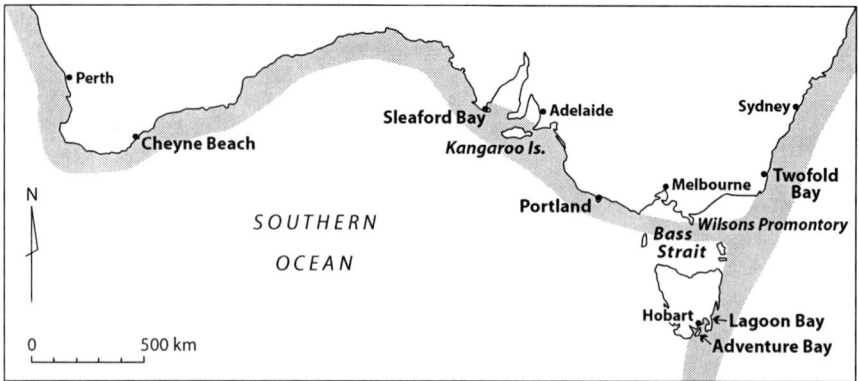

Fig. 5.3 Migration route of southern right whale in Australian waters, with sites mentioned in text (after Nash 1998:21)

hunt: it was a slow swimmer that migrated through coastal waters; it floated when killed; and it produced abundant oil and whalebone (baleen) which was used for springs and women's corsets. The right whale was the most common species hunted in Australian coastal waters in the nineteenth century (Fig. 5.3). Adult whales grew up to 18 m in length and weighed anywhere between 55 and 95 tonnes. The peak period of shore whaling was 1835–1839, when around 12,000 whales were taken in Australian waters, producing exports worth £100,000 annually (Nash 2003:111–114). Hobart and Launceston were the principal home ports for this industry. Although their crews worked around Australia and in New Zealand, most of the ship and station owners were based in Van Diemen's Land and it was there that they signed on crew members, bought supplies and sold their oil. Smaller shore industries operated out of Perth and Adelaide, while most Sydney whalers were engaged either in the pelagic industry or in shore whaling in New Zealand.

The right whales spent the summer in Antarctic waters feeding on plankton and migrated northwards in the winter to breed and calve. They passed up the east coast of Tasmania and then moved either westwards along the coast of Victoria and on to South Australia and Western Australia or further north along the New South Wales coast. Shore whaling was thus a seasonal, winter activity, from April to October. The whalers effectively targeted breeding females and their young, decimating whale populations in the process. By 1850 the southern right whale had been hunted to the brink of extinction, and the whaling industry in Australian waters quickly declined. Some ship owners lost everything, but others adapted by refitting their ships and sending them out into the Pacific to hunt sperm whales. Later in the century new technologies meant that humpback whales could also be hunted from shore and a few stations were set up in New South Wales, Western Australia and Norfolk Island, all of which operated sporadically until the 1960s (Fig. 5.4; Gojak 1998:18–19).

Pelagic and shore whaling used similar methods and technologies. A lookout was stationed to keep watch for the whales, which were chased by crews of six to eight men in open whaleboats. Once the whales had been harpooned and killed, they were

Fig. 5.4 Whale Digester at Cascades, Norfolk Island; from the 1950s (photo S. Lawrence)

towed back to the ship or to the station and the blubber was removed or "flensed" using a variety of knives and spades (Pearson 1983). The blubber was chopped up and put into large iron trypots set over fires, where it was melted into oil. The oil was then sealed into wooden casks for storage, while the remains of the carcass were abandoned in the shallow water adjacent to the station.

Whale oil was measured in "tuns", a large barrel of 252 gallons (1,295 l) capacity. The amount of oil extracted from a whale depended on various factors, including size, species and sex. Keepers of ships' logs often kept good records of the whales caught and the amount of oil they yielded. In the late 1830s, for example, the average value of southern right whales killed in the Van Diemen's Land fishery was around £100 each, increasing to around £150 during the 1840s. On average, each whale yielded around 6 tuns, or more than 7,500 l of oil each (Chamberlain 1988:3; Nash 2003:24). In this period, ships would take anywhere from two to a dozen whales in a season, resulting in good profits for the station owners.

Whale crewmen, however, were among the lowest paid workers in colonial society. Lays or shares paid to men in the Van Diemen's Land whale fishery were fixed at the start of the voyage. In the 1830s a harpooner or carpenter received a share of 1/60 of the catch, while an ordinary seaman received 1/120 portion. If a seaman was careful with his expenses he could expect to earn up to £15 from a whaling voyage, around half the pay received by a farm labourer (Chamberlain 1988:232–235). If, however, he bought items from the slops chest he might even end up in debt. The low pay contributed to discipline problems and a high turnover in the industry. The hope for a large lay attracted men to whaling, but the stiff competition for whales at sea, the decline in numbers by the late 1840s and variable prices for oil meant that large lays were rarely achieved.

Aboriginal people were also involved in the whaling industry. Prior to European settlement they had been accustomed to use beached or stranded whales as a food source. When the whalers arrived, the blubber was processed but the meat was discarded as a by-product, creating a feast for local Aboriginal people (Staniforth 2008). Interactions between whalers and Indigenous people have been documented by archaeologists at a number of places around Australia. In Western Australia, for example, local groups would camp for several months at a time near the whaling stations. Martin Gibbs suggests that a form of reciprocity developed, where whale meat was exchanged for other game as a means of supplementing the whalers' diet (Gibbs 1995:85–88). The Nyungar people of the south coast also incorporated whaling into their ceremonial life in the post-contact period (Gibbs 2003b). At Twofold Bay in New South Wales, Aboriginal crews were employed as boat crews and received equal pay for their work (Gojak 1998:17).

Archaeological Evidence

Several archaeologists have studied the distribution of whaling sites, identifying particular characteristics that were most favoured for establishing a station (e.g. Gibbs 1995, 1998; Kostoglou 1995). The archaeological evidence at stations around the country is remarkably similar, indicating that no matter where they worked, the whalers were considering the same factors. They were guided by the physical environment and the requirements for taking and processing whales, as well as the customs that many shared because of their origins in the Van Diemen's Land industry. The sites chosen invariably had a sheltered anchorage away from the prevailing wind and a gently sloping beach for hauling out whaleboats and blubber (Fig. 5.5). Nearby trees or a headland for the lookout was important, as was level ground on which the tryworks and crew quarters could be built. Most stations also had a source of water and firewood. Although some contemporaries stated that land for gardening and grazing animals was important, little archaeological evidence of this has been found in Australia (Kostoglou 1998). Such self-sufficiency was more common in New Zealand where the whalers often lived with Maori, marrying local women and employing the men in the boat crews (Prickett 2002:9). Proximity to the home harbour was also relatively unimportant, as Hobart ship owners sent their crews as far as the west coast of South Australia and to the North Island of New Zealand. For these men the sea was their highway and their natural environment, and they went wherever they had to in order to hunt for whales.

The coastline of southern Australia varies widely in providing suitable sites and anchorages for shore stations. Victoria, for example, has few locations that offer shelter from the prevailing south-westerly winds. The most useful areas were found at Portland and Port Fairy along the west coast and at Refuge Cove on Wilsons

Fig. 5.5 View of the Adventure Bay whaling station on Bruny Island, Tasmania, looking northwards across Storm Bay to Mount Wellington. The site was occupied from about 1829 to 1842 (photo S. Lawrence)

Promontory. The South Australian coast provides numerous harbours where stations were built, while in New South Wales, the deep shelter of Twofold Bay (modern Eden) provided a base for several operations run by Benjamin Boyd, the Imlay brothers and the Davidson family (Gojak 1998; Howard 1998; Pearson 1985). The vast coastline of Western Australia has only patchy evidence of a dozen or so whaling sites (Gibbs 1998). The eastern and south-eastern coastline of Tasmania, however, is studded with bays and inlets, where the archaeological remains of more than 50 shore whaling stations have been identified (Nash 2003). The southern and eastern coastlines of New Zealand were also well-suited to shore whaling, and Australian whale crews were among the first non-Maori settlers to arrive (Coutts 1976; Prickett 2002).

Archaeologists have identified a common layout of features at the stations. Tryworks were located on the foreshore just behind the beach with associated workshops nearby for the cooper and blacksmith. Huts for the crews were generally a bit further back and upwind of the tryworks. At most stations the remains of three or four huts were identified. Stations usually had three or four whaleboats operating, each with a crew of six to eight men, so it is likely that each crew was housed together in its own separate barracks. At several sites in Tasmania, Parry Kostoglou found that the huts were in two precincts. He argues that this indicated status differences within the crews, with the headsman or station manager living apart from the common seamen (Kostoglou 1998:107).

Excavations at the Adventure Bay and Lagoon Bay stations in Tasmania by teams from La Trobe University have also demonstrated this pattern, with two huts excavated at both locations (Lawrence 2006b:124–131). In each case one of the huts was of substantially better quality than the other, with a larger fireplace and more solid construction. At Adventure Bay one hut was a large stone cottage 12 m long, with a flagstone floor and a well-made fireplace at each end (Fig. 5.6). The cottage was divided into two halves and in one half the space had been further subdivided with a

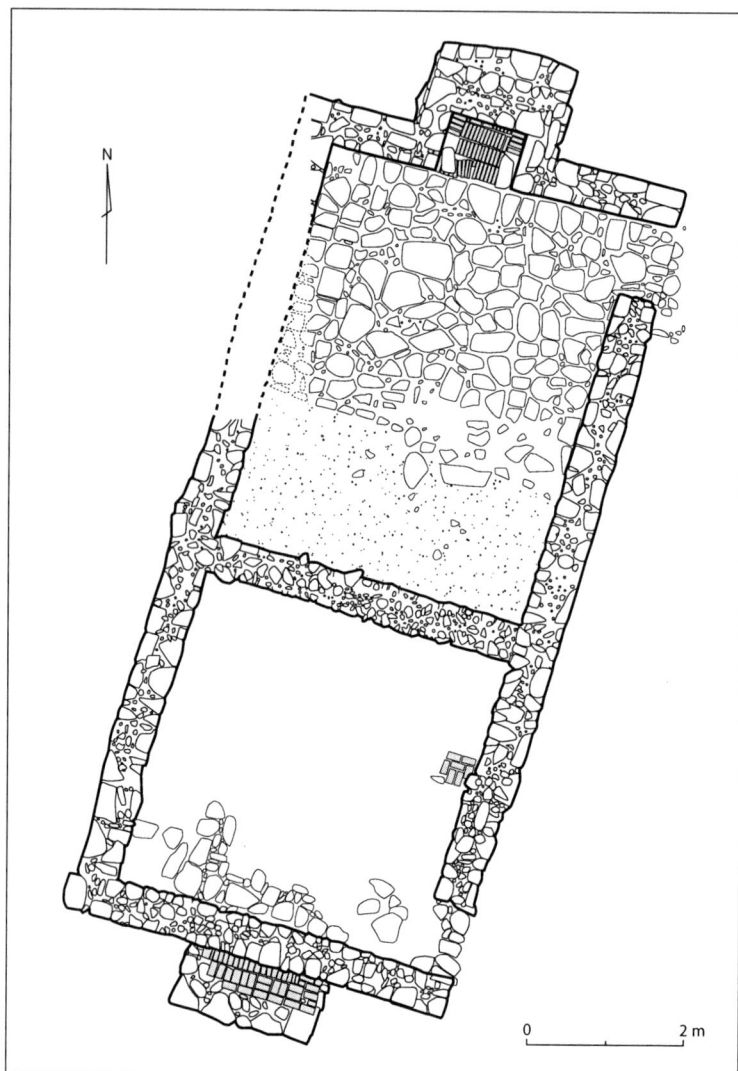

Fig. 5.6 Plan of the stone house at the Adventure Bay whaling station on Bruny Island

wooden partition to form a private apartment with a main room and separate sleeping quarters. The other hut was a much simpler structure built of bark or slabs with a dirt floor and a smaller, more crudely built fireplace. At Lagoon Bay the buildings were all built of bark or timber slabs, but one of the buildings was also clearly divided into two rooms, the inner one with an imposing stone and brick fireplace, and the inner walls were also plastered. The floor plan of the other building was harder to discern, though it may also have had two rooms. There was no sign of plaster on the walls, however, and the fireplaces were also smaller and simpler.

The tryworks built on the stations show the adaptation of maritime technology on terrestrial sites. Archaeologists in Canada and the United Kingdom have excavated tryworks from sites associated with earlier forms of whaling. At Red Bay, in Newfoundland, sixteenth-century Basque whalers used local beach cobbles to build a row of circular hearths for trying-out (Tuck and Grenier 1989). One hundred and fifty years later, British whalers working in the Arctic around Spitsbergen brought the blubber back with them to London to workshops along the Thames at Rotherhithe. There the blubber was rendered in immense circular copper boilers encased in brick and housed indoors in enormous sheds (Douglas 1999). By the time the Australian shore stations were set up, whalers on long voyages to the Pacific had begun trying-out on-board ship. To protect against fire the shipboard tryworks consisted of a brick structure containing one or two bricked-in iron trypots, with a small firebox and flue at the base. The colonial whalers learned their skills from the British, French and American whaling ships that worked in Australian waters, and the archaeological remains at the stations show how they transferred the technology to the shore stations they built.

Tryworks on Australian sites look much more like the shipboard tryworks than the earlier land-based versions. Excavations conducted by staff and students from Flinders University at Sleaford Bay in South Australia (Paterson 2004), and at Adventure Bay in Tasmania by the authors, have revealed tryworks that are similar in design. The remains at each site consisted of a rectangular brick platform approximately 2 m long and 1 m wide. Only a few courses of brickwork survived in each case, surrounded by a shell of local beach cobbles (Fig. 5.7). At both sites encrustations of burnt oil and soot on the bricks indicate that the tryworks housed a pair of trypots, each with its own firebox and flue. Brick was used for the floor of the firebox and for the piers that supported and enclosed the trypots. Although brick was a more expensive material, it was less likely to crack under high temperature than the local stone. The compact, efficient design of the tryworks and the use of brick both suggest that the builders were experienced whaling men as well as masons and that they were familiar with proven technology.

Food on the Stations

Artefacts shed important light on the diet of the whaling crews (see Chapter 11). Meat and bread were staples, but they also had vegetables flavoured with

Fig. 5.7 Stone and brick foundation of tryworks at the Adventure Bay whaling station with charred blubber residue at the base. Two iron try pots originally sat at the back with cooling tanks to each side. The stonework at the rear surrounded the flues, while the flagstones at the front formed a platform for the men (photo S. Lawrence)

condiments, all washed down with sweet tea and occasionally with alcohol. Food for the crewmen was agreed in a contract and counted as an advance on their lay or share of the profits. Men working for Hobart ship owner James Kelly, who also owned the stations at Adventure Bay and Lagoon Bay, were each supplied weekly with 12 pounds (5.4 kg) of bread or flour, 12 pounds of meat, two pounds (0.9 kg) of sugar and 1/3 pound (150 g) of tea. At a time when a convict's meat ration was one pound (450 g) per day, the extra food received by Kelly's men reflected the demands of their heavy physical labour and the long hours worked in difficult conditions. The meals eaten by the whalers also reflect the kinds of food available to colonists at the time and the sources of groceries and fresh food.

Excavations at the Adventure Bay and Lagoon Bay sites yielded thousands of fragments of animal bone (Lawrence and Tucker 2002). Most of the bone came from cattle and sheep, although pig and rabbit were also represented, along with native mammals, birds and fish (Fig. 5.8). Whale vertebrae were recovered, but whale meat was probably not eaten, as nineteenth-century Europeans thought that it had a strong, unpleasant taste. At both sites sheep were represented by all body parts, including cranial and hoof elements, suggesting the local slaughtering of live animals and the supply of fresh lamb and mutton to the sites. With pigs, however, the absence of head and foot elements indicates that slaughtering was done elsewhere, and portions of salted pork were brought in. Evidence for cattle reveals a

Fig. 5.8 Quantity of
identified bones (NISP) at the
Adventure Bay and Lagoon
Bay whaling sites

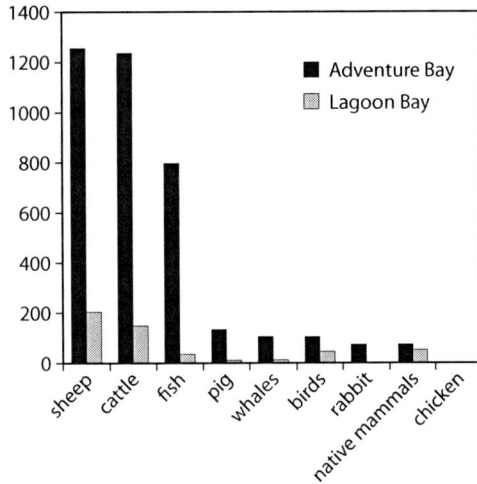

combination of both local and off-site slaughter, with some pelvic, head and foot elements present, along with forequarter cuts including ribs and vertebrae.

Numerous species of native animals, birds and fish were also represented, but in very limited quantities, suggesting a more opportunistic and experimental approach to hunting by members of whaling crews. Gibbs (2005a) documented a similar pattern at the remote Cheyne beach whaling station on the south coast of Western Australia, where sheep provided most of the meat, along with quokkas (small wallabies) and shellfish. These patterns reflect both taste preferences and the nature of the men's employment – they were there to hunt whales and were provided with food and a cook to prepare it. Regular hunting for food would have taken time away from the far more important tasks of whaling and oil production.

Although archaeological evidence for bread has not survived, documents suggest that the flour or bread provided by James Kelly to crewmen was probably in the form of ship's biscuits. This was hard, unleavened bread that could be baked in advance and stored for months at sea in watertight wooden casks. Fresh bread was also probably baked regularly at the shore stations – a visitor to one Van Diemen's Land station recorded that damper baked in wood ash and doughboys fried in boiling whale blubber were both eaten regularly (Evans 1993:45). Fresh vegetables may have been grown at some stations, although rations of potatoes, onions and split peas probably represented a more efficient means of supply.

In contrast to bread and vegetables, there is ample archaeological evidence for the use of condiments on whaling stations, but almost no written evidence. Fragments of glass bottles and stoneware jars would have contained pickles, sauces and powders. Pale green bottles with simple rolled lips and a cork stopper probably contained powdered spices such as mustard or cayenne pepper, both of which were commonly mixed with water or vinegar at the table. The stoneware jars probably held olives, walnuts, gherkins, onions or capers. Condiments helped to enliven the blandness of bread and meat, and vinegar and mustard were especially favoured with salted meats (Lawrence 2001c:219). Numerous ceramic plate fragments also indicate that the men ate their meals from decorated crockery. Tin plates may also have been used, as on ship, but these have either corroded away or were more resistant to breakage and were taken away (Lawrence 2006b:110–111).

Fish-Curing

Another little-known but significant maritime industry was that of the Chinese fish-curers, recently the subject of Ph.D. research by Alister Bowen (2004, 2006, 2007). In the days before adequate refrigeration or rapid transportation, the fish-curers were an important market that helped to sustain many coastal fishing communities. The fish-curers preserved the fish by drying and/or salting it, producing a commodity that was much in demand by Chinese communities on the goldfields and which was also exported to China. Bowen identified a network of fish-curing establishments around the coast of Victoria and then excavated the best-preserved example, the site of Chinaman's Point near Port Albert in Gippsland (see Chapter 10). The men at Chinaman's Point cured fish they caught themselves and also purchased fish from non-Chinese fishers. The size of the Chinese fish-curing industry was enormous. While the total annual volume of fresh fish sold through the Sydney and Melbourne markets in the 1860s and 1870s amounted to just over 200 tonnes, Chin Ateak, a merchant in Sydney, sold up to 300 tonnes of cured fish himself, and he was just one of many Chinese merchants in the fishing trade in Melbourne and Sydney (Bowen 2007:116–120).

Archaeological excavation at Chinaman's Point uncovered the remains of the industrial precinct, including a jetty, fish drying racks and a system of drainage ditches for drawing water away from the swampy, low-lying ground (Fig. 5.9). Two rows of pilings indicate that the jetty ran across the shallow tidal flats to deeper water where fishing boats could anchor when delivering their catches. Behind the jetty was a level area 20 × 20 m in size where a grid of post holes is now all that remains of the fish drying racks. The posts were made of local tea-tree, placed in pre-dug holes forming four rows, each 15 m long. The finished structure would have held several tonnes of drying fish (Bowen 2007:143–145). Remarkably, despite the quantity of fish that must have passed through the site, very little fish bone or scales was found during the excavations. Although this may be the result of preservation, it may also be because the fish was prepared elsewhere on the site before being taken to the drying racks.

Some of the artefacts recovered included equipment indicating that the site's occupants were fishing themselves as well as buying fish caught by others. Lead sinkers from the nets used to catch bream and mullet were found in varying stages of production across the site. Copper nails used in boat-building were also found, as were three masses of hardened oil-based paint used to protect marine timbers. One particularly interesting type of artefact was a group of specially modified glass bottles. At least 30 aqua green cylindrical bottles had had their bases deliberately removed. The bottle bases were all 75 mm in diameter, and Bowen argues that they were used as lamp chimneys on kerosene lamps or candles. The lamps could have

Fig. 5.9 Reconstruction of fish-curing camp at Chinaman's Point in south Gippsland, Victoria, based on archaeological excavation conducted by Alister Bowen (2007). The site was occupied from around 1860 and abandoned soon after 1900 (reproduced with the permission of Alister Bowen and Blake Cunningham)

been used for domestic purposes, but Bowen observes that anthropological and historical accounts refer to Chinese fishers working at night, particularly for squid, a prized catch. The lights were used to lure the fish, and out on the boats the fragile lamp chimneys would have broken easily so the sturdier bottles may have been preferred.

Pearling

Mother-of-pearl shell (*Pinctada maxima*) was widely used by Europeans to make buttons for clothing, along with combs, knife handles and other products. For centuries the major sources of shell were the Red Sea, the Persian Gulf and Ceylon, but overfishing by the nineteenth century had drastically reduced the known shell beds. Discovery of high-quality shell in the waters of north-western Australia in the 1850s and 1860s prompted a rush to exploit the new resource. The early industry was based around the shell, rather than the pearl inside, which made up only a small fraction of pearling profits.

Aboriginal people in the Kimberley region had long been accustomed to collect the lustrous mother-of-pearl shell from tidal mudflats and used it to manufacture decorative ornaments which were widely traded across Australia. Initially, the European pearling masters exploited Aboriginal divers, who swam to retrieve the large shells from the seabed. By the 1870s, however, the shallow beds were worked out and the industry moved further north to waters around Broome and across to the Torres Strait (Ganter 1994; Grimwade 2004; McPhee 2001; Yu 1999). Australian pearling luggers also operated in the Aru Islands between Timor and New Guinea, until forced out by Dutch colonial authorities in 1893 (Mullins 2001). Workers were brought in from Japan, Singapore, Kupang and Manila to collect the shell. They wore a diving suit and copper helmet connected by a rubber hose through which air was pumped from the ship on the surface. By 1904 there were more than 400 pearling luggers working out of Broome, but overharvesting in later years forced the price of shell down and the number of luggers declined quickly (Edwards 2007:81). The development of plastic buttons, cheaper and stronger than mother-of-pearl, also depressed the industry.

In spite of the "get rich quick" mentality of most in the pearling industry, there were a few who saw the need to invest in cultivating the pearl shell, rather than simply harvesting and exhausting the known beds. Around 1902, Thomas Haynes, with backing from London jeweller and entrepreneur Edwin Streeter, prepared an experimental shell pool on the Montebello Islands, north of Exmouth Gulf on the Western Australian coast. Although he later claimed to have successfully reared young shell, a range of legal, technical and financial problems, along with cyclone damage in 1911, forced the abandonment of the works. Archaeological survey of the remains of the operation identified the shell pool and several camps (Stanbury 1994). Evidence from the camps reveals the importance of collecting and storing water and the need to be self-sufficient in supplies, given that the islands were small, dry and very remote. The tidal pool included a masonry dam across the narrow entrance of the inlet and an embankment further back to maintain a certain level of water at low tide. The scale of the operation reveals the confidence of the men in the profits to be made if they could determine a reliable mechanism to cultivate the valuable pearl shell. Their failure to do so underlines the great difficulty in establishing a new industry in a remote location, far from outside help, but also reinforces their energy and willingness to find new ways to exploit a commodity in high demand.

Maritime Cultural Landscapes

Maritime archaeologists have also drawn on concepts used in cultural landscape studies to develop a holistic approach to interpreting the physical remains of maritime activities (Duncan 2004, 2006; Kenderdine 1993; Stuart 1998; Westerdahl 1992). The landscape approach, discussed further in the next chapter, explores interactions between people and the environment and locates archaeological sites within a network of less tangible elements of human activity, such as place names, oral history and memory. Maritime cultural landscapes extend this focus to consider the interface between the land and the sea and the activities and perceptions that encompass both environments. In addition to conventional methods of site recording and documentation, this approach also acknowledges the importance of maritime environmental features as important contributing elements, such as currents, prevailing winds, types of shorelines, depths of water, shoals and reefs, anchorages and marine life such as fish and plants. It is the intersection of natural features and cultural activity that creates sea routes and fishing grounds, ports and harbours, and all the ancillary systems required to support maritime industries and to minimise danger. Two recent studies demonstrate this approach, one in South Australia and another in Victoria. Each identifies significant maritime themes within a single coastal community, including port/harbour facilities, navigation, fishing and recreation. These themes are then used to interpret the relationships between archaeological sites, natural features, oral history, memory and ritual that together have created a changing cultural landscape.

Aidan Ash (2007) surveyed the maritime cultural landscape of Port Willunga, a small coastal settlement south of Adelaide on the Fleurieu Peninsula. For a few decades in the mid-nineteenth century the settlement was a flourishing port, the second busiest in South Australia, exporting wheat to the Victorian gold rush and building slate to Adelaide. Both of those industries were in decline by the end of the century and the town saw little development until the growth in holiday homes in the late twentieth century. Ash carried out underwater and land surveys to identify maritime and coastal features, which he integrated with existing knowledge of significant historic sites in the study area. These sites included several shipwrecks, the remains of two jetties, caves dug in the cliffs by the beach, hotels, guest houses, a store in the town and buildings on a coastal farm.

Although the area is not an active port today and there are no obvious signs of maritime industry, Ash was able to identify both places names and several surviving buildings in the town, such as a store and a hotel used by ships' crews, that indicate the town's maritime connections. Ash also noted the absence of navigational aids such as buoys and lighthouses in the area, which indicates the relative lack of shipping hazards such as reefs. He argues that the main hazard to shipping was the winds, and that the port provided little in the way of natural shelter. By examining patterns in the location and circumstances of the wrecks, he determined that the ships were lost because they had been pushed on-shore by strong south-westerly winds. The winds and swells were so destructive that they also eventually caused the abandonment of the first jetty at the port and the construction of a second one further south in 1867.

A second study in maritime landscapes involves research carried out by Brad Duncan (2006) at Queenscliff, a small town on the Bellarine Peninsula southwest of Melbourne. In addition to the fishing community, the strategic location of Queenscliff at the entrance to Port Phillip Bay resulted in the establishment of a military base for coastal defense in 1860. The town has also been the base for the pilot service that guides ships into and out of the Port of Melbourne since 1839, as well as a popular tourist destination since the nineteenth century. Wealthy graziers and colonial governors maintained holiday homes in Queenscliff, while day-trippers came on steamers from Melbourne. These different economic activities resulted in the formation of distinct communities within the town. Duncan found some overlap and co-operation between them, but also evidence of longstanding animosities and rivalries, with each group maintaining its own precinct within the town, including housing, places of worship and recreational facilities.

Duncan also found spatial correlates in the different ways each group used the surrounding maritime environment. One example of this was the sea routes favoured by local fishers compared with other maritime users. Following the fishing stocks and with detailed local knowledge, fishers favoured small, manoeuvrable boats, particularly the distinctive "couta boat". The toponymy used by the fishers included their own names for currents, shoals, fishing grounds and navigational markers and their own folklore about the use of the sea. The pilots and military used the official names for features as recorded on charts and maps of the area. Interviews with local divers and archaeological survey also revealed a distinctive artefact patterning associated with the use of different parts of Port Phillip Bay. In the West Channel, which was initially the favoured route up the bay to Melbourne, artefacts fell into two groups: bottles and ceramics from Great Britain dating to the period 1840s–1870s and bottles from local manufacturers in the towns around Port Phillip Bay. In the South Channel, which began to be used by the larger ships later in the century because it was deeper and had fewer sand banks, the bottles and ceramics were a combination of international items and those from other Australian colonies and other coastal towns in Victoria, but few items local to Port Phillip. This pattern is further evidence of the use of the West Channel by those with local knowledge of the more dangerous conditions there and the use of the safer South Channel by people from elsewhere.

Conclusion

Most people in colonial Australia had an understanding of the sea that recent generations have lost. Many had spent months on a ship to migrate here, and the majority settled within a short distance of the coast. The sea was not only a wide and dangerous place to cross over, but also provided food, exports, profits and jobs. Whaling and sealing were important industries in the early decades of settlement in Australia, offering investment opportunities for colonial businessmen and employment for those willing to take a chance at sea. The need for watercraft stimulated the local boat-building industry, while jetties and wharfs were needed for loading and unloading cargo and passengers. In later years fishing and fish-curing, and in northern Australia pearl-diving, emerged as significant local coastal industries as well. Most of these activities were conducted on the geographic and social margins of colonial life, often by all-male communities or communities of settler men and Indigenous women, and involved people who left few if any written traces of their daily lives. These same activities, however, resulted at times in substantial archaeological remains at the interface between land and sea. Detailed study of this material from around the country is gradually revealing the complex relationships between workers and bosses, between Europeans, Chinese and Aborigines, and between people and the sea itself.

Chapter 6
Pastoralism and Agriculture

Familiar food was in short supply in the first years of British settlement at Sydney Cove. Lack of experience with the local climate and soils meant that early crops failed, while valuable stock wandered off into the bush. Colonists were forced to rely on dwindling supplies of salt meat, flour, peas and rice, supplemented with wild game and fish from the harbour. The "hungry years", however, did not last long. As early as August 1790, the colony's chaplain, Reverend Richard Johnson, who humbly called himself only "$\frac{1}{2}$ a farmer", had already cut two crops of wheat, barley and oats from a patch of land beside his cottage in Sydney and harvested more than 1,000 cucumbers and many other vegetables (Symons 2007:16). By 1792, only 4 years after the First Fleet arrived, the worst threat of famine had passed, and by 1805, in spite of droughts, blights and floods, the colony was self-sufficient in basic European foodstuffs, with more than 12,000 acres under cereal cultivation and many thousands of sheep, pigs and cattle at hand (Jones and Raby 1989:158).

Conventional historical accounts have stressed the failure and neglect of agriculture in the first 5 years of settlement, with the importation of inadequate farming models to an essentially alien landscape (e.g. Blainey 1982:139; Walsh 1963:22). This view has influenced the development of archaeological approaches such as the Swiss Family Robinson model of colonisation, with its emphasis on early trial and error (Birmingham and Jeans 1983). Recent historical work, however, reveals a more positive picture of early attempts at food production. Historian Angus McGillivery (2004) argues that a regime of mixed farming, with animal husbandry integrated with intensive cultivation, was understood by authorities as vital to the development of colonial interests. Along with a menagerie of livestock, the First Fleet carried 39 casks of vegetable seeds for year-round agriculture and horticulture, together with a spade and three hoes for each of 700 men. The hard labour of convicts with spades and hoes, together with European plants and seeds, was creating a substantial harvest even before the take up of land by officers in 1793. Moreover, as McGillivery points out, in the late eighteenth century cultivation by hand was not backward and primitive, but well adapted to improved husbandry on light sandy soils with an ample supply of convict labour and the need to generate quickly an agricultural food supply for several thousand people.

S. Lawrence, P. Davies, *An Archaeology of Australia Since 1788*,
Contributions To Global Historical Archaeology, DOI 10.1007/978-1-4419-7485-3_6,
© Springer Science+Business Media, LLC 2011

While abundant food soon became available, it was very much an imported, and British, conception of nourishment, based on flour, meat and tea. Awareness of local bush foods was limited, and remained so, at least in part because of its association with Aboriginal Australians. Aborigines traditionally ate fresh foods gathered daily, with seeds and roots collected and prepared by soaking, pounding or grinding (Isaacs 1987). Small animals were trapped and larger ones were hunted. Ignorance, and perhaps disdain, however, meant that European settlers were reluctant to use Aboriginal foods, or perhaps were unable to gather them in sufficient quantities.

The need for fertile, well-watered farmland soon pushed settlers inland along the flats of the Parramatta, Nepean and Hawkesbury Rivers, while large Government Farms worked by convicts were established at Rose Hill, Toongabbie and Castle Hill (Jack 1986b; Karskens 2009:84–90). The navigability of the Hawkesbury, where ships could sail upstream more than 200 km, provided cheap transport for farm products when road cartage was prohibitively expensive (Hainsworth 1981:122). Former convicts received land grants of up to 30 acres, while larger land grants of 500 acres or more were available to military officers and free settlers arriving with substantial capital. They used convict labour and their own resources to establish successful farms. By 1801 Sydney had become a busy port, with ships arriving every week or two with cargoes of supplies and livestock (Cumpston 1964:37–40). Many homes had gardens of potatoes, cabbages, pumpkins and watermelons. As the food crisis receded, it was realised that the real wealth from the soil would be won not only from agriculture, but also from pastoralism and the production of wool.

The process of stocking and farming rural land to produce food and fibre was thus fundamental to the colonisation of Australia. Trading was volatile, and many saw the land as a more promising source of wealth. Early land grants to convicts, along with tools, rations and supplies of seed, were early expressions of the "yeoman" ideal in Australian rural history, based on the notion of a sturdy, independent peasantry of a kind that had largely disappeared from England. James Ruse, a First Fleet convict, embodied this ideal, successfully growing maize and wheat on a 30-acre plot at Parramatta known as "Experiment Farm" and later being celebrated as Australia's "first farmer". The yeoman ideal reappeared throughout the nineteenth century and beyond in various guises, with selectors in the 1860s–1880s, the Homestead Associations in the 1890s and soldier settlers after the First and Second World Wars. The concept often obscured the enduring tension between farming as a moral way of life and farming as a market-driven enterprise (Frost 2001:226). Nevertheless, governments saw it as their duty to support settlers in the "colonising project", opening the way to rural (and national) development by providing the necessary infrastructure, supervision and financial support (Karskens 2009:101).

Settlement of "the bush" has assumed an almost mythological significance in Australian history and culture, taking central place in narratives of nation-building alongside convicts, gold and ANZAC soldiers at Gallipoli (Ireland 2002; Ward 1958). The concept has much in common with the "pioneer" legend identified by historian John Hirst (1978), which embodied the hard work and perseverance of the first farmers and pastoralists in settling the land. "The bush" is a catch-all phrase that encompasses both specific areas of forested land and more generally all the rural territory between the cities and the "outback", the latter being the stereotypically harsh and thinly inhabited centre of the Australian continent. Neither metropolitan nor wilderness, the bush is the region of farms, forests and mines, provincial towns and villages that support Australia's primary industry and exports. More than this though, the bush has iconic stature as the "true" Australia and the source of what it means to be Australian. This is despite the fact that Australia is one of the most urbanised countries in the world, and that since the first British settlement in 1788 most of its population has lived in cities located along a narrow coastal fringe.

Writers and artists of the 1890s glamorised life in the bush and made heroes of drovers, shearers and other rural workers. A. B. (Banjo) Paterson and other authors idealised the bushman and his apparent freedom and egalitarian spirit and contrasted these qualities with the drabness and routine of life in the cities, immortalising the bushman in works such as "Waltzing Matilda" and "The Man from Snowy River". Artists of the Heidelberg School such as Tom Roberts and Frederick McCubbin endowed images of Australian pioneering history with integrity and dignity. Journalist and historian of the First World War C. E. W. Bean argued that the finest Australian soldiers came from the pastoral inland, "the real Australia" (Bean 1963 [1910]:44). Later, historian Russel Ward (1958) famously identified the outback bushman as the "typical" Australian – a rugged individualist, courageous and loyal to his mates. Ward traced his model from its convict origins to gold miners, shearers and bushrangers and ended with the "diggers" who fought in the Boer War and the First World War. As a white, male archetype, the bushman ideal explicitly excluded women, children, Aboriginal people and other ethnic groups, a position that has been subjected to considerable scholarly critique (e.g. Davison 1978; Goodman 1994; Lake 1986; Schaffer 1988). The bushman ideal results in a narrative that is predominantly about isolated white men and their struggles to tame the land. Implicit in this telling is the symbolic conceptualisation of the landscape as feminine, the opposite of the white masculine hero, empty and available to be subdued by him.

Tracey Ireland (2002, 2003) has argued that while archaeology has the potential to de-stabilise these kinds of nationalistic and exclusionary narratives, the practice of archaeology has in fact become complicit in supporting them, however inadvertently. Much publicly funded archaeology has been shaped by the requirements of cultural heritage management, which itself has favoured an investigative approach based around historically significant themes. The relative significance of these themes, and hence the sites and places investigated, is frequently a product of the degree to which they conform with existing myths of nationhood. The most significant themes, and those which receive the most funding and attention, are those associated with widely accepted versions of Australia's past. Archaeology and heritage management are thus drawn into reproducing and sustaining historical orthodoxies.

There can be no doubt that archaeologists have been active in investigating Australia's pastoral heritage, although they have paid less attention to the nation's agricultural development. Following Ireland's argument, this may stem in part from the relative place of the two activities in the national story. Today pastoralism is associated with the memory of wide open spaces, mobility and the freedom from domestic constraints. The same mythos disparages farmers who cultivate the soil as mere grubbers in the earth. Ironically, this retrospective valorising of pastoralism inverts the views expressed by colonial voices. In the nineteenth century the independent yeoman farmer was the ideal on which a prosperous society was to be established. Pastoralists and squatters were loathed capitalists who locked up the land and prevented the "small man" from getting ahead.

In this chapter we examine archaeological evidence for both pastoralism (the grazing of sheep and cattle on large-scale pastures) and the cultivation of cereal crops and gardens (agriculture and horticulture), and we also review archaeological evidence from the outback more broadly (Fig. 6.1). Other aspects of the archaeology of rural Australia, such as the role of Aboriginal people in outback settlement and other types of rural industries such as dairying, are examined in other chapters. Here we draw on a wide variety of archaeological techniques, ranging from the traditional excavation of domestic sites to landscape survey and the botanical analysis

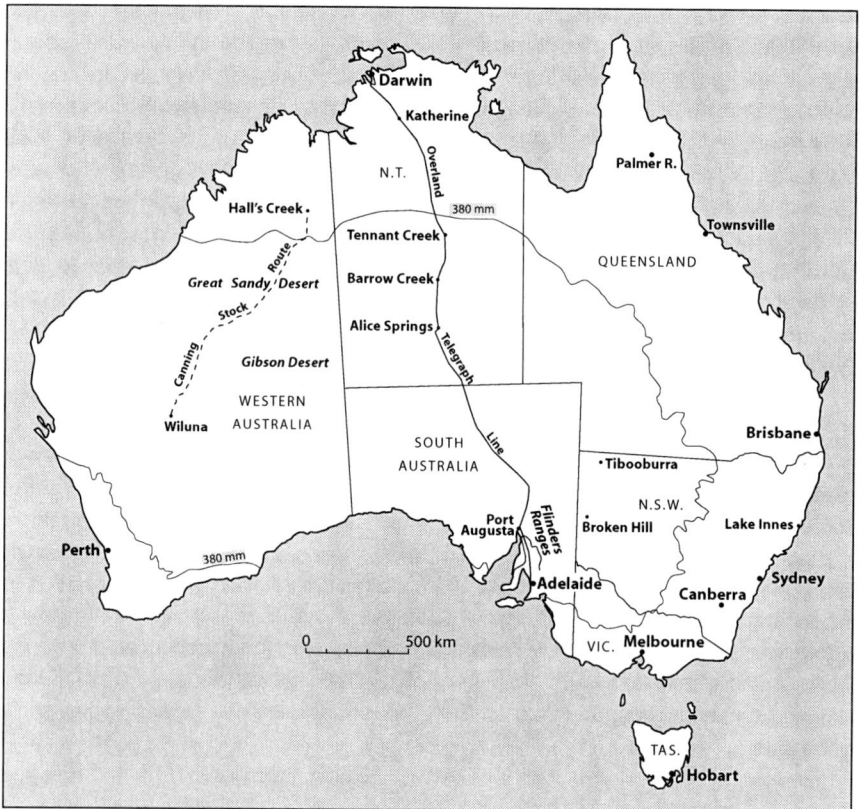

Fig. 6.1 Location map of sites mentioned in text, with 380 mm (15-inch) rainfall line indicating margins of agriculture

of pollen and phytoliths. Places discussed include sites and landscapes such as Regentville and Lake Innes in New South Wales, the Monaro region near Canberra and Holowiliena and Moran's Farm in South Australia. We also describe the process of land clearance, landscapes of water management and the role of survey and selection during the nineteenth century. Horticulture was another important activity, with market gardens established by Chinese migrants in the vicinity of many goldfields. We conclude by examining the farming of some everyday indulgences, including tobacco, wine, hops and chicory.

The Bush as Cultural Landscape

The notion of cultural landscape is important in understanding not only the scale of agriculture and pastoralism in colonial Australia, but also the fundamental relationships between people and the natural world and how these changed through time. Cultural landscape is both a way of seeing the world and a social product, the result of collective human activities in transforming nature (Cosgrove 1984:13–14). It is a thread that brings together archaeology, anthropology, history and geography, linking social processes to changes in the physical world (Gosden and Head 1994:113). An environment becomes a landscape when it is regarded as such by people, especially when they begin to modify and shape it according to their needs and desires (Seddon 1997:111). Landscape thus involves the transformation of natural *space* into recognised, utilised, human *place*.

The concept, derived from geography, has been widely applied in archaeology around the world. It facilitates the integration of historical with archaeological evidence at different scales, including artefacts, buildings, settlement patterns and technology, and acknowledges the role that cognitive perception plays in shaping the cultural environment (Duncan 2004:12). Landscape can also be a way of appropriating the world (or a portion of it) through media such as maps and paintings, while naming places helps to create and project a sense of memory and social meaning (Tilley 1994:18–19). Other approaches to cultural landscapes advocate consideration of the roles of ideology, power and resistance and the ways in which people signify social relationships with nature and with each other (e.g. Leone 2005). Cultural landscapes are thus complex, dynamic, contested and often untidy, understood in different ways according to the social, economic and political perspectives of individuals and groups (Bender 2001).

In Australia much work has been done about landscape use and development, but there has not been a consistent focus on cultural landscape as a theoretical perspective. Its influence in historical archaeology goes back to the beginnings of the discipline here and the work of historical geographers such as Denis Jeans (Jeans and Spearitt 1980). The approach is beginning to influence maritime archaeology (see Chapters 4 and 5) and has recently attracted renewed attention by terrestrial archaeologists. Iain Stuart has explored the idea in detail in his archaeological work on the squatting landscapes of Lanyon and Cuppacumbalong near Canberra, where squatters and selectors struggled for respectability, often on the same piece of land

(Stuart 1997a, 1999, 2007). Cultural landscape theory drawn from anthropology and cultural ecology has informed archaeological work in the Hills Face Zone Cultural Heritage Project in Adelaide (Piddock 2007; Smith and Pate 2006; Smith et al. 2006), and the papers published in a special volume of *Australasian Historical Archaeology* (2007) illustrate the application of cultural landscape approaches to cultural heritage management and research.

Perceptions of landscapes are mediated by ethnicity, gender, age, class and status. Different observers perceived and experienced the same physical places in very diverse ways, most vividly demonstrated by the work of historian Rhys Isaac (1982:52–57) in eighteenth-century Virginia, but equally applicable in colonial Australia. Government surveyors, for example, observed lines of sight and trigonometrical problems, their heavy labour of measurement superimposing a grid of property boundaries and property values over the natural terrain. Convicts saw fields and huts and fences, a landscape of banishment and reluctant *work*, but they also knew the wooded spaces between the farms, where in their free time they could escape their bondage for a few hours to enjoy a bottle with friends. They also knew the marginal places they could claim for themselves to work for their own profit or stash stolen goods. The small farmer saw the same relentless labour in the trees and fields and animals, but recognised in them the prospect of independence, if the weather was kind, if prices held and a crop could be taken to market. For women on the land the house was the centre of their working lives, and journeys much beyond it were uncommon except for occasional visits to church and neighbours. The squatter enjoyed a loftier view, perhaps from the shade of his verandah or the seat of his horse. He saw and understood a wider terrain, much of it his own legal property. He noted feed and water for his stock, the growth of wool and the potential for profit and loss. Once comfortably established, his wife and daughters made social calls and interspersed colonial visits with returns to Great Britain. Aboriginal people were gradually pushed to the fringes, dispossessed from the landscapes to which they so intimately belonged.

Squatters and Pastoralists

In the Australian vernacular any man (and they were almost exclusively men) who owned a large number of grazing animals and occupied the large area of land on which they grazed was known as a "squatter". Squatting began as unauthorised grazing on vacant Crown land, land that had been claimed by the British but not yet formally occupied by British colonists. By the 1830s, sheep and cattle owners were pushing their growing flocks and herds far beyond the official frontier of the "Nineteen Counties" in New South Wales, moving northwards to "squat" on the Liverpool Plains and on land to the south beyond Yass and Gundagai (Gale et al. 2004). The lure of better country further out was a magnet for those who saw their fortunes and futures in wool and hides and who welcomed the freedom of life beyond the settled districts. To the north, the Australian Agricultural Company received a grant of one million acres in 1832 to grow fine wool, on country extending from the central coast back to the New England tablelands. By the early 1840s, the Darling Downs in south-east Queensland were occupied as well. Out west, runs were scattered along the Murrumbidgee, Lachlan and Darling Rivers. When Major Thomas Mitchell explored overland to the south in 1836, he labelled the country "Australia Felix" (literally "Australia the bountiful") because of its perceived capacity for pastoral richness, but he found the Henty brothers and other whaling parties already well-established at Portland Bay, and the parties of Batman and Fawkner had built sod huts on the future site of Melbourne the year before. Across Bass Strait, the Van Diemen's Land Company had received large land grants in the north-west of the island as early as 1826.

Colonial authorities responded to the outwards flow of settlement by setting an annual £10 licence fee on squatting lands, providing de facto recognition of the landholders' possession. Squatting as an unauthorised activity was mostly confined, however, to the eastern mainland. In Western Australia, massive land grants, a tiny local market and low stock numbers delayed the need to graze Crown lands, while in South Australia, the application of Wakefield's principles of systematic agricultural settlement (see below) meant that squatting remained a marginal activity. In Van Diemen's Land, generous freehold grants on the island and the accessibility of the Port Phillip District across Bass Strait effectively removed the need for squatting. Pastoralism flourished in all of these places, however, and whether squatters or graziers, the social systems established, techniques used and landscapes created had much in common.

The early pastoralists were mobile, opportunistic, independent and ruthless. With stock, horses and a dray full of supplies, they set out to establish a run of their own. Much of the land they occupied was ideal for wool-growing: open grassy plains and thin woodlands. In the early stages, insecure tenure discouraged squatters from undertaking more than the most basic material improvements of erecting a bark and slab hut and fencing rough yards for the animals. They survived on a monotonous diet of tea, mutton and damper and employed shepherds to protect their sheep from dingoes and other threats.

There were few white women, especially in the early days, as the squatters were determined to establish themselves before starting a family. Niel Black described his fellow squatters as "Money-making bachelors...half-savage, half-mad" (Kiddle 1963:57). Women who joined their husbands on the run at this time worked endless days, tending poultry and vegetable gardens, making butter and cheese, sewing and mending clothes, grinding flour and numerous other tasks. Children could be a pleasure and a help, but many died young, far from medical aid. As a result of their arduous lives, women were responsible for most of the improvements around the homesteads and created a vital sense of home in the bush (Isaacs 1990).

Historian Keith Hancock explored squatter pastoralism in detail, in his work on the Monaro tablelands of south-eastern New South Wales (Hancock 1972). Beginning with the arrival of Europeans in the 1820s and 1830s, and the effective destruction of local Aboriginal society, Hancock's study integrates history, ecology, geography and archaeology to explore the dynamic interactions between pastoralists and the natural environment and the formation of a distinctive cultural landscape. In the Monaro, a territory the size of Wales, the processes of squatter pastoralism and the alienation of Crown land for closer settlement resulted in tensions and conflicts that were repeated in many other parts of rural Australia in the colonial period (Buxton 1967; Powell 1970, 1973; Stuart 1999; Williams 1974).

The Monaro consists mostly of alps and tablelands and has long been sheep and cattle country, with little land suitable for cultivation. By the 1840s, most Crown land had been taken up, and disputes arose over the boundaries of runs. The Orders-in-Council of 1847, however, issued under the imperial Waste Lands Occupation Act, imposed some order on the jostle for land and consolidated the position of squatters in the region. Annual licences were replaced with 14-year leases, with pre-emptive purchasing rights over one square mile of land on each station. Compensation was also now payable for improvements such as buildings and fences. The position of the squatters looked secure, even with the spike in labour costs caused by the gold rush to the area (see Chapter 7). Calls to open up land throughout the colony for "sturdy yeoman" farmers, however, resulted in legislation for closer settlement in the 1860s, which in turn prompted alienation of most leasehold land in the Monaro by the squatters themselves. They bought up as many freehold acres as they could afford and selected properties on conditional purchase in the names of family members and willing servants. The practice, known as "dummying", strengthened the squatters' position in the Monaro and elsewhere and led to the aggregation of many smaller properties into fewer, larger ones. In the process, the squatters formed an increasingly wealthy and influential group as the nineteenth century progressed. By 1883 in New South Wales, 96 pastoralists owned a total of 8 million acres. While they replaced their makeshift huts with substantial homesteads, however, the hard times of the small selectors often came to be marked by the rubble and timber of their ruined homes (Hancock 1972:106; Stone and Garden 1978:97).

In the settled districts, pastoralism was a means for some to live lives of comfort and wealth and to emulate the social systems of the English aristocracy. From the outset pastoralism was a large-scale enterprise aimed at producing goods for export and requiring large amounts of capital. The squatters thus came from and formed the upper echelons of colonial society and included among their ranks the sons of British gentry and retired military officers. Such men were welcomed in colonial society for their wealth and social connections "back home". Many received substantial land grants and assignments of convict labour to develop their pastoral holdings (Fig. 6.2). The Macarthur family of Camden Park (Atkinson 1988) and W. J. T. "Big" Clarke of Sunbury in the Port Phillip District are well-known examples (Hill 2003; Peel 1974:51–57). Several of these landholders, including Sir John Jamison of Regentville and Major Archibald Innes of Lake Innes, have been the subject of major archaeological studies. Large agricultural companies, including the Van Diemen's Land Company (Murray 1988, 1993) and the Australian Agricultural Company (Bairstow 2003), have also been the focus of archaeological investigation, with particular emphasis on relations between Aboriginal people and Europeans.

Sir John Jamison was born in Antrim, Ireland, in 1776, the eldest son of Thomas Jamison, who had arrived in Australia as surgeon's mate with the First Fleet.

Fig. 6.2 Elizabeth Farm homestead at Parramatta was built in 1793 by John and Elizabeth Macarthur. The family developed extensive wool and pastoral interests over thousands of acres in the early decades of settlement in New South Wales (photo P. Davies)

Knighted by both the Swedish and the British governments for curbing a serious outbreak of scurvy in the Swedish navy, Sir John arrived in Australia in 1814 to take control of the pastoral holdings of his father, who had died in 1811. In the following years he extended his land holdings to the Hunter Valley and the Liverpool Plains. By the 1820s he was one of the richest men in the colony and a leading figure in New South Wales society. By the early 1840s he also had squatting leases on the Namoi River in northern New South Wales of almost 130,000 acres (Fletcher 1979:3).

Jamison began building his famous country house, Regentville, in 1823. Located 50 km west of Sydney, the house became the centre of a large estate that eventually extended over 9,000 acres. He built a home to impress visitors and to express how he saw his role in colonial society. The complex consisted of a large, two-storey dwelling built on a low promontory overlooking the Nepean River. At the rear of the house was a walled courtyard which enclosed servants' quarters, kitchen and stables (Wilson 1988:125; 1999). Jamison also cleared 600 acres adjacent to the house and laid the area out as a park and pleasure ground. By 1830 he had 40 settlers working as tenant farmers on the river flats.

Excavation of the homestead site in the 1980s by Judy Birmingham and Graham Connah aimed to investigate international trade networks and the place of major land owners and occupants in colonial society (Connah 1986; Wilson 1988). Among the artefacts recovered were fragments of a Mason's Ironstone dinner service. The pieces probably arrived as part of a large table service of 140 items. The service was part of Jamison's attempt to furnish his new home in a fashionable and lavish manner, in keeping with his role as "the hospitable Knight of Regentville". Sir John enjoyed entertaining and extended his hospitality especially to overseas guests, partly as a way of promoting the prospects of the colony and countering its penal reputation. Although often derided as vain and ostentatious, Jamison was nevertheless a keen innovator in agricultural science. He cleared the land, improved pastures, practiced manuring and crop rotation and imported English horses for breeding (Connah 1986:30). His Regentville estate included a windmill, a winery and a steam pump for irrigation, along with a four-storey brick woollen mill. The estate included a village of carpenters, a blacksmith, a stonemason, a millwright, a cooper and other tradesmen. Jamison thus tried to re-create an English country estate in colonial New South Wales, mixing traditional social structures with modern farming practices, and promoted a free economy in place of a penal one.

Sir John Jamison lost his fortune in the drought and depression of the 1840s and died in 1844. His financial decline was due in large part to the collapse of the Bank of Australia, in which he was a major shareholder. But it was also through the failure of his view of settlement and society, which conceived a British-style landed gentry in Australia, benevolently watching over a subsidiary class of tenant farmers. In the economic malaise of the period, those who could adapt to the changing circumstances of land ownership, trade and the end of convict transport would survive. Those committed to the old model of landed proprietorship failed.

A similar notion of colonial grandeur was expressed at Lake Innes, near Port Macquarie in northern New South Wales. Like Regentville, the Lake Innes estate flourished for a while but eventually failed. Graham Connah conducted an extensive programme of archaeology at Lake Innes from 1993 to 2001 (Connah 1997, 2007, 2009). One of the aims was to test ideas about the visibility of socioeconomic differences in the archaeological record (Connah 2007:24). Excavations were carried out at various features of the estate, including the bathroom and entrance hall of the main house, the gatehouse of the stables and four huts occupied by servants. The archaeology of the servant huts is described in Chapter 2. Here we examine the ruins of the house and stables, which provided the main surviving physical evidence of the Innes estate.

Archibald Clunes Innes was born in Caithness in north-east Scotland. As the sixth son of a minor landholder, his prospects in his native land were poor. He joined the army in 1813, serving in the 3rd Regiment of Foot, "The Buffs". In 1822 he arrived in Sydney as captain of the guard on the convict ship *Eliza*. He then served in Van Diemen's Land and returned to Sydney in 1825 as Aide-de-Camp to the Lieutenant-Governor of New South Wales, thus gaining access to the upper echelons of colonial society. He briefly held the post of Commandant at the penal settlement of Port Macquarie before retiring from the army in 1828. In 1829 he married Margaret Macleay, daughter of Alexander Macleay, the Colonial Secretary of New South Wales, and in the following year Innes and his wife took up land grants at Port Macquarie (Flowers 1967).

The couple began construction of a house that grew substantially over the next decade, eventually resulting in a 22-room mansion that included suites of rooms for guests, a library, drawing room and even a bathroom with hot and cold running water. Archibald Innes wanted to create for himself the sort of social and economic position he could never have achieved in Britain. He used the house to impress and entertain visitors and to display what he regarded as his important status, as part of an emerging Australian aristocracy (Connah 2001:141). The large brick residence became the centre of a large estate, which included stables and accommodation for numerous convicts and free servants. Much of the land was heavily timbered, however, and required extensive clearing to sculpt a rural landscape with views to the "wild" country beyond.

The garden was an important part of daily life for the Innes family and featured exotics such as giant bamboo, roses and mysore thorn (Connah 1998:19). The home farm produced pigs and poultry, along with oats, lucerne and maize (Herman 1965:69). Innes' pastoral enterprise also expanded rapidly, supplying food to the government store at Port Macquarie and acquiring sheep and cattle runs of more than 30,000 acres by 1843 (Connah 2007:6). He planted a vineyard and bred horses for export to India. Innes was also largely responsible for building a road from Port Macquarie to the New England district, known after him as the "Major's Line". The success of the Lake Innes estate relied heavily on convict labour. By 1837 there were 91 assigned servants on the property, many with useful skills such as brickmakers, a carpenter, a plasterer, a painter and glazier, grooms, dairymen and others. Along with free servants, they lived and worked at the main house, at the home farm and at the estate workers' village.

The economic depression of the 1840s that had brought about the downfall of Sir John Jamison also affected the ambitions of Archibald Innes. The end of assigned convict labour in New South Wales from 1840 meant that Innes had to employ free labour, which was in short supply, especially on the margins of European settlement. Long in debt and with expensive tastes, most of his assets were heavily mortgaged, and by around 1850 he was financially ruined. He left Lake Innes House in 1852 and took paid employment with the government, before dying at Newcastle in 1857. The house had several occupants until the 1870s, but by the end of the nineteenth century it was abandoned and derelict and was destroyed by fire soon after.

Archaeological excavations revealed that the house featured a well-planned water supply and drainage system. Water drained from the roof into a 17-m-deep brick-lined well or cistern, located at the rear of the building. Lead pipes were installed to deliver water for flushing the toilets and to take the waste away. A boiler provided hot water for the bathroom, and box and barrel drains diverted stormwater from the house itself. Fragments of a Wedgwood toilet bowl featured a blue transfer pattern known as Blue Chinese Temples, while there were also pieces of ceramic ewers and chamber pots, all imported from England (Connah 2007:45, 97–98). Clearly, a great deal of effort and expense was invested in the cleanliness and hygiene of family and guests at Lake Innes House.

The Lake Innes estate was one of the finest residences in rural New South Wales during this period. Archibald Innes presented himself as a Scottish laird, a landed proprietor and used his home, his furnishings and the rural landscape he created to promote his status and demonstrate his importance. He built his house on a hill overlooking the lake which bore his name, with views to the mountains beyond. The bathroom and toilets were of the highest quality but they were located discretely away from the bedrooms, while the kitchen and other facilities were at the rear of the house, out of the way of guests and visitors. Domestic servants resided close to the house, while more menial workers lived further away. Innes thus created a landscape of privilege for himself and his family on a distant edge of European society, but also assumed responsibility for the dozens of convict servants under his command, ensuring some degree of comfort in their accommodation.

The house was not only a place of display and entertainment for visitors, but of domestic calm and retreat for the Innes family as well. It included a library, a dining room and a drawing room at the front, opposite the main entrance. Such spaces and their use were characteristic of genteel family life in the mid-nineteenth century. Historian David Goodman has written of the "quietness" prized at this time, and the desire for peaceful reflection, amid the "busyness" of life (Goodman 1994:190). The drawing room provided an important space for quiet family gatherings, especially in the evenings, when music, sewing, reading and conversation could be practised and displayed. The Lake Innes drawing room, with its French doors, yellow satin damask, mirrors and paintings, would have served these purposes admirably.

A much less grandiose residence was developed by the Clarke family at Plover Plains in the Port Phillip District in the 1840s. Located about 30 km north of Melbourne, the property was owned by William J. T. Clarke and occupied by his brother Lewis Clarke and his wife Rachel, between 1842 and 1852. W. J. T. "Big" Clarke was one of Melbourne's earliest squatters, and his ruthless business dealings enabled him to build up vast land holdings and wealth, which generated widespread notoriety and antagonism towards the Clarke family in the process. Lewis Clarke, however, was much less ambitious and was generally content to follow the bidding of his larger-than-life brother. Social acceptance only came many years later for the family, after W. J. T. Clarke's eldest son Will had built several mansions and was bestowed with the hereditary title Baronet of Rupertswood in 1882.

The remains of the homestead at Plover Plains were excavated in 2001 by Valerie Hill (2003) to explore the nature of pastoral settlement in the Port Phillip District, at a time when this region was part of the pastoral frontier in Australia. Excavations revealed hearths and cobble flooring and wall footings of basalt up to 2 feet (60 cm) thick, built in random rubble style with mud mortar. Little or no ground preparation had been carried out, however, suggesting a degree of haste in constructing the buildings to accommodate the arrival of the Clarke family and their servants. There were just two main buildings at the site, the main homestead of about 70 m^2 and nearby a building for workers of about 50 m^2, while artefacts were dominated by bottle glass and sheep bone. Building locations were determined by practical considerations, including the availability of water and shelter from prevailing westerly winds. Hill notes that the overall impression provided by the structural evidence is of "a life filled with hardship" (Hill 2003:264). Lewis and Rachel Clarke raised nine children in rudimentary conditions, and when the chance came, after 10 years at the homestead, they moved to a more spacious home at a nearby station. The life of the squatters was as often one of hardship and isolation as of comfort and gentility. Those who endured the droughts and economic crises, and profited from the gold rush and expansion of settlement, could perhaps after years of toil pass some kind of legacy to the next generation.

The Outback

Despite the successful expansion of the squatter pastoralists throughout the inland plains, it was the outback of Australia that became the focus of the colonial dream in the second half of the nineteenth century. The outback, however, is as much an idea as it is a place; an idea of immense distance, shimmering heat haze, of scrub, sand and rock. For much of the nineteenth century few Europeans really knew what was "out there". Until explorers like John McDouall Stuart, Ernest Giles and Augustus Gregory had criss-crossed the continent and proven otherwise, there lingered the hope that all the emptiness might yet contain a great river or inland sea (see Cathcart 2009:84–98). But if not water, what other riches might be hidden in the outback vastness? Many tried to find out, risking health, fortunes and sometimes even their lives, on the promise of wealth "just a little further out". A few succeeded, others retreated, defeated, while the occasional lonely grave marks the final resting place of those whites who ventured into the outback and stayed there forever.

The story of Europeans and the Australian outback has long been dominated by two main industries: mining (see Chapter 7) and pastoralism. Both industries have been constrained by the lack of water and the difficulties of transport and communication over huge distances. In responding to these problems, miners and pastoralists slowly came to terms with both the physical reality of inland Australia and its Indigenous inhabitants. Even today, only a tiny portion of Australians reside in the outback. Many others visit, as tourists, miners or officials, before retreating to the comfort of coastal areas.

Pastoralism in the outback presented many challenges, including isolation, thin grazing and limited rainfall or surface water. Conflict with Aboriginal people and then Aboriginal involvement in the pastoral industry were also significant features of life in the interior (Chapter 3). The movement of information and commodities was aided by construction of the Overland Telegraph in 1872 and the arrival of Afghan cameleers in the 1860s. The Australian Inland Mission, established in 1929, provided a vital health service in outback South Australia. While we use no formal definition of "outback", the 15-inch (380 mm) rainfall isohyet is an approximate guide to the limits of agriculture and the zone of limited and sporadic rainfall in the interior (Fig. 6.1).

Holowiliena, in the Flinders Ranges of South Australia, provides an example of an outback pastoral landscape. Geographer Monte Woodhouse (1993) has used standing structures, the natural environment and documentary records to describe a pastoral station as it was in 1888 when it was visited by the government surveyor, Alexander Goyder. Water appears as a consistent focus on the property, emphasising the aridity of the environment. All the paddocks had seasonal watercourses as well as springs, wells and dams, and stock were watered by using whims to draw water into wooden troughs. The Home Paddock was also the best watered, with three wells in addition to the seasonal streambeds. The scale of the property brought its own challenges, and a subsidiary set of buildings in the furthest paddock, some 20 miles (32 km) from the main house, housed the family of the man who was responsible for managing the far end of the station. Isolation meant that locally available materials were relied on for construction. The main house and the manager's house were built of the local quartzite, while other buildings such as the kitchen, smithy and stockmen's quarters had walls of local pine. By the 1880s, however, most of the buildings had roofs made of corrugated iron, brought across the ranges by cart from Port Augusta. Already in 1888 the station was nearly 40 years old and showed evidence of changes in the pastoral industry over that period. Several of the outlying paddocks featured abandoned stone chimney butts that had once been used as base camps for the shepherds in the era before fences. In the 1860s shepherds were displaced by post-and-rail fences and by the time of Goyder's visit these too had been replaced by galvanised wire fences. A distinctive landscape was created at Holowiliena which characterised pastoralism in the outback, with limited rainfall and sheep grazing on sparse vegetation, set against the rocky backdrop of the Flinders Ranges.

Huge numbers of sheep were also bred for wool in the semi-arid plains of outback New South Wales and Queensland. Wool not only drew Europeans into inland Australia, but tied Australia to Europe, and crucial parts of preparing the wool for market were the washing and shearing processes. Shearing sheds are familiar reminders of the importance of the pastoral industry throughout Australia, but sheep washes and wool scours are often less prominent. Wool is relatively lightweight, compact, durable and valuable, all vital qualities for a commodity which had to be transported thousands of miles to textile mills in Britain. One of the problems faced by graziers, however, was that about half the weight of shorn wool was grease and dirt. Brokers in London complained about the grit and burrs in Australian wool, compared to English and German sheep, which came from much smaller flocks and provided cleaner fleeces. Washing the sheep or scouring the wool meant a cleaner product, but graziers had to weigh up the costs of processing and transport against fluctuating sale prices (Pearson 1984:39–40).

For much of the nineteenth century, sheep washing prior to shearing was the main way of cleaning the wool. The simplest method involved washing the sheep by hand in a pool or trough of water and rubbing and squeezing the wool to remove dirt and droppings. This was labour intensive and required men to stand in water all day long. A more effective washing method was developed later which involved hot water (at about 110°F, or 43°C) to dissolve the greasy lanolin in the fleece. The sheep were first soaked with cold water in narrow pens and then washed in hot water to which soda was added. They were then rinsed from overhead spouts, allowed to dry for three days and then shorn. Stations in semi-arid outback areas, however, often had difficulty finding enough water for sheep washing. By the 1880s, washing was gradually replaced by wool scouring. Scoured wool was thought to be not only cleaner, but less labour-intensive and cheaper to ship.

Wool-scouring involves washing the fleece after it has been shorn from the sheep. The archaeological remains of large-scale mechanical scouring establishments near Geelong are typical of the operations that were set up near towns (Cummins 1989), but station-based manual scours also operated in some areas. Michael Pearson (1984) investigated one such enterprise at Mount Wood Station, near Tibooburra in north-western New South Wales. The station was taken up as a lease in 1883 and covered approximately 500,000 acres. The wool scour complex was probably built around 1897, just as the effects of the disastrous "Federation" drought were beginning to be felt. The owners of Mount Wood contracted a camel driver from Broken Hill, Abdul Khalick, to cart the wool to the river port of Wilcannia on the Darling River. By the 1920s, however, motor vehicles had begun to replace camel teams, station-scoured wool declined and the Mount Wood scours were soon abandoned (Pearson 1984:42).

The station is located in a low rainfall area (214 mm, or $8\frac{1}{2}$ inches per annum), so water management was crucial to the success of the operation. Water came from a dam built across a small, intermittent creek. Archaeological investigation provided detailed understanding of the wool scouring process (Fig. 6.3). The site consisted of an array of tanks, pipes, a boiler, drainage channels, timber posts and pumping equipment. Wool was delivered to the site and piled into one of two hot scour tanks containing hot soapy water. The wool was agitated by fork and then transferred into an adjacent rocking drainer. From there the wool was forked into a "William's box", a circular perforated tub, where it was washed with a broad jet of water to remove all the residual dirt. The rinsed wool was then allowed to drain, before being put through a hydro-extractor, and then spread out in the drying yard. Once dry, the wool was pressed into bales and loaded onto camels or drays for the trip to Wilcannia.

Pearson notes that wool scouring was a water-intensive process. At Mount Wood, water was recycled where possible, with the drainage from the fleeces allowed to flow back through channels to the dam for re-pumping. In a region of unreliable rainfall, the station owners persisted with this technique for several decades, suggesting the value of scoured wool generally outweighed the risks of climate and the costs of long-distance transport. While much of the equipment used, such as the engine, pump and drainage boxes, were purchased from manufacturers, the way they were put together and used suggests a strong degree of bush workmanship and improvisation. The components were adapted to local conditions to create an effective mechanism for scouring wool, one which answered the needs of a remote pastoral station for many years.

Another perspective on outback pastoralism is provided by research at Old Kinchega Station in western New South Wales (Allison 2003). Archaeologist Penelope Allison focussed on the manager's homestead and the experiences of those who lived there, rather than on the operation of the station. The homestead was occupied from 1876 to 1955, and Allison was able to use a combination of survey techniques, surface collection, excavation and documentary and oral history to

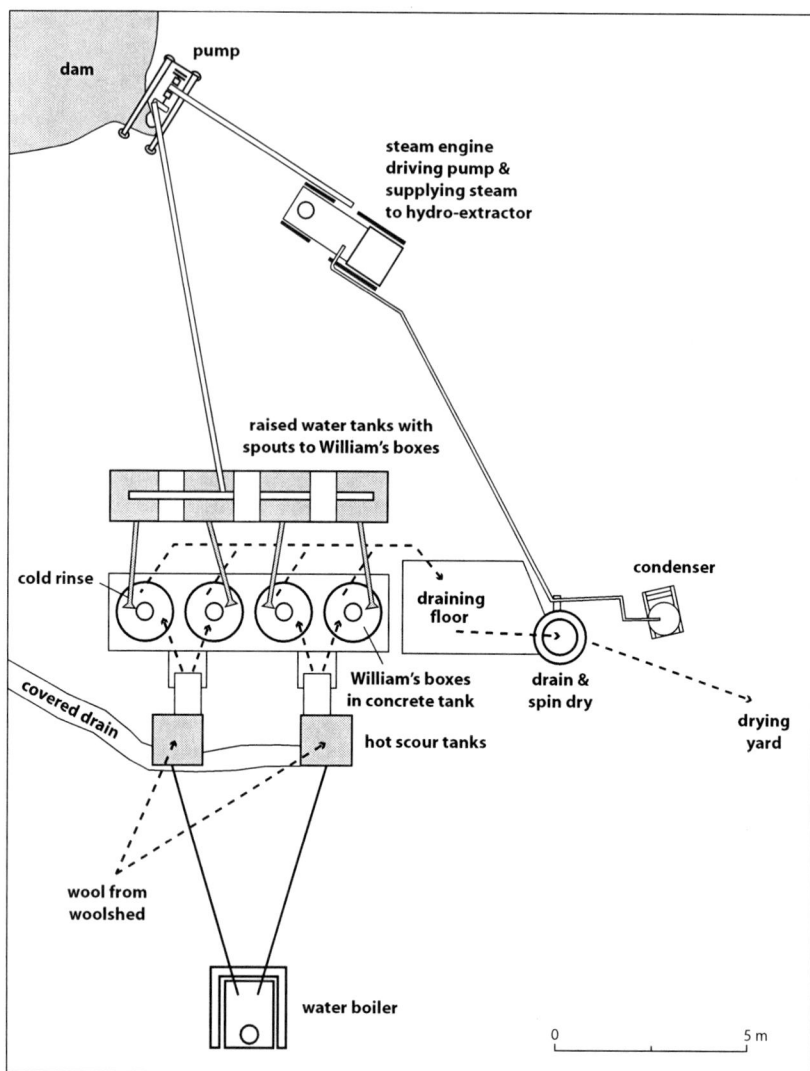

Fig. 6.3 Schematic plan of Mount Wood wool scour, near Tibooburra in north-west New South Wales (after M. Pearson 1984:48)

investigate the activities of the women and children who were the families of the managers. Artefacts found included children's toys, writing slates, lace-making and needlework tools, as well as teawares made of porcelain and bone china. They were concentrated in the verandah area on the north-eastern side of the house; a cool, shady place in the afternoons for schoolwork, playing and working. The variety and quality of the goods reflects the peculiar geographic situation of the station as well. Although deep in the outback without any near neighbours, Kinchega was nevertheless only 130 km from Broken Hill, a large mining centre that was on the railway from 1885. Even before that, Kinchega exported wool via the steamer trade on the Darling River. The archaeological evidence indicates that consumer goods were readily available through the same network.

The places and industries described so far illustrate some of the problems of distance and isolation that have long been crucial factors in Australia's development. Historian Geoffrey Blainey suggested that distance is "as characteristic of Australia as mountains are of Switzerland" and argued that Australia's isolation not only limited the movement of people and goods, but played an important role in developing the national character (Blainey 1966:viii). John Hirst (1975) challenged this view, arguing instead that people, materials and ideas have always been highly mobile in Australia. The movement of information and commodities is not related primarily to distance, but to the nature of goods produced, markets for them and the means and costs of transport. Until the end of the nineteenth century, the means of transport and communication in outback Australia were very limited. It was only with the arrival of the Afghan cameleers and construction of the Overland Telegraph, examples of ancient and modern technology respectively, that outback isolation began to be overcome.

Direct communication between the settled areas of southern Australia and the rest of the world meant laying a telegraph cable across the interior of the continent. The telegraph had been developed by Samuel Morse in the late 1830s, and the technology soon spread as its potential was recognised. In Australia, great distances had to be threaded with wire to facilitate the transmission of messages. Adelaide, Melbourne and Sydney were joined in a telegraph network as early as 1858, and Brisbane joined in 1861. As the mainland network expanded during the 1860s, there were proposals for Australia to join the international cable network that was approaching through south-east Asia. When the British Australia Telegraph Company offered to extend its cable from Java to Port Darwin, South Australia began to build a line north from Adelaide across Australia to meet it (Livingston 1996; Moyal 1984; Taylor 1980).

The main architect of the overland telegraph was Charles Todd. The 3,200 km line was built in three sections: a southern section of about 800 km, commencing from Port Augusta; a northern section extending from Port Darwin to the Roper River and a central section linking the two ends. In spite of the huge logistical problems of arranging men, supplies and transport, the line took only 2 years to build and was completed on 22 August 1872. It cost the lives of eight white men. Historian Ann Moyal has called its construction the greatest engineering feat carried out in nineteenth-century Australia (Moyal 1984:42; Taylor 1980).

The route traversed arid country that had been occupied by Aboriginal people for millennia, but to Europeans it was extremely remote and mostly unknown. Aboriginal people found the line useful. They broke and flaked the porcelain insulators into tools, made fishhooks from the wire and fashioned axes from the footplates at the base of the poles (Moyal 1984:54). Construction crews built repeater stations along the route every 200 or 300 km to boost the weak signal, at places like Katherine, Daly Waters, Tennant Creek, Beltana and Alice Springs. The stations were built solidly of stone, with windows facing an inner courtyard and gun holes in the outer walls, in defence against Aborigines resisting encroachment on their land. In 1874 at Barrow Creek, four white men were speared by Aborigines, with one killed. A punitive party ranged over hundreds of square kilometres, reputedly killing every Aboriginal man, woman or child found (Moyal 1984:54–55).

The repeater station established at Todd River (Alice Springs) was built beside a permanent waterhole in the bed of the river. Apart from the defensive barracks, there was also a stable and wagon shed, a battery room, a residence for the officer-in-charge, a blacksmith's hut and a separate kitchen. The stations were remote and self-contained. Once a year supplies were replenished when a camel train arrived from the railhead in South Australia. The stations also aided the white colonisation of outback Australia. Based on a natural water supply, each served as a base for supplies, communications and law enforcement. The wire between the stations acted like a safety net in the outback vastness. The telegraph stations were physically isolated, yet ironically they were instrumental in helping to overcome the tyranny of distance endured by people in the outback.

While the telegraph provided communication across the great distances of inland Australia, it was camels and their drivers that often provided transport linking the remote outback with coastal ports and emerging railway lines (Chapter 9). Horses and bullocks were not suited to work in these regions, due to the lack of water and extremely high temperatures. Camels, however, were much better suited to the conditions, thriving on brackish water and the saltbush and mulga that grows across vast stretches of arid and semi-arid Australia. The camel trains travelled swiftly and quietly, often at night, and with the soft pads of the camels' feet they could take short cuts across sandy country and make good time in difficult terrain. Camels played a vital role in the construction of the Overland Telegraph, both in the early survey stages and later in carrying much of the building materials and supplies. They were also crucial in providing supplies to pastoral stations in the arid interior, sustaining the remote settlements until the arrival of motorised transport in the early twentieth century.

The telegraph carried information and the camels carried goods, but the flocks and herds that underpinned the pastoral industry in the outback travelled by foot. A persistent feature of the outback was the long-distance droving of cattle and sheep as animals were brought in to stock new regions and were later taken out to market. Archaeological remains of the Canning Stock Route in Western Australia provide evidence of the challenges this presented (Grimwade 1998). The Canning Stock Route extends for 1,700 km through some of the most isolated desert country in Australia. It crosses the Great Sandy Desert and the Gibson Desert, from Halls Creek in the north to Wiluna in the south, passing through extensive regions of sand dunes, salt lakes and spinifex plains. Surveyed and constructed in 1906–1910, the route provided access to southern markets for cattle bred in the Kimberley region of north-west Western Australia. It was used sporadically until 1959, and since the 1970s it has become a popular four-wheel-drive recreational track.

The region had attracted the attention of explorers in the nineteenth century, but it was the development of the Kimberley cattle industry from the 1880s that spurred calls for an overland route to the south. In 1906, Alfred Canning, a Government

Surveyor, was commissioned to find a suitable route. He headed a team that included cameleers, well builders and Aboriginal guides. They needed to find drinkable water at shallow depths, at intervals of about 25–30 km. Canning later admitted to keeping the Aboriginal guides shackled to prevent them running away; the party completely relied on these men to find water and to preserve all their lives (Grimwade 1998:71–72). Construction began in 1908, and by 1910 more than 50 wells had been sunk. Over the next half century, about 35 mobs of cattle were driven along the route.

Archaeologist Gordon Grimwade (1998) has surveyed the surviving archaeological evidence along the route, along with the modifications made by more recent visitors, to understand better the challenges of moving cattle through such vast outback distances. Each well was numbered sequentially from south to north, with the well shafts measuring 1.8 by 1.2 m across, similar to mining shafts of the time. The depths varied from 2.5 m at Well 11 to almost 32 m at Well 5. Local timbers were used to shore up the walls of wells where necessary. The wells were also fitted with metal doors to reduce evaporation and to prevent animals falling in and polluting the water. Each well was equipped with a hand windlass and a timber winding drum to retain the wire cable. Attached to the end of the cable was a riveted metal bucket, generally with a capacity of 30–40 l. Larger quantities of water could be lifted with whip poles. A heavy wooden post set at an angle over the well shaft was fitted with a winding wheel. Animals could then haul at ropes which ran over the wheel and lift 200-l canvas buckets from the well, with the water poured into nearby metal troughs.

Along the stock route there are also a number of graves of colonists who perished from violence or accident. A pile of rocks at Weld Springs, for example, marks the site of a fortification built by the explorer John Forrest in 1874, after his party encountered local Aboriginal people. The physical remains of the Canning Stock Route reveal the tenacity and resourcefulness needed to survive in such isolated terrain. The importance of the route lies in its initial surveying and construction, the challenges of moving cattle for a thousand miles along its length and the evidence for personal and racial conflicts that arose during its period of use.

Selectors

Archaeologists have paid little attention to the physical evidence of farming, but agriculture played a significant role in colonial Australia. By the middle of the nineteenth century there were important changes occurring in colonial society. The gold rushes and the end of convict transportation brought a huge influx of migrants and a growing demand to "unlock the land" in settled districts. Attitudes to land ownership and farming began to shift, from the old model of squatter pastoralists with servants and tenants, towards a more egalitarian model of independent family farms or "yeomen" smallholders (Buxton 1967; Powell 1970, 1973; Waterson 1968). The struggles of the selectors had begun.

The Selection Acts introduced by colonial governments in the 1860s were intended to break the squatters' monopoly on pastoral land. Initially, however, they had the opposite effect, and squatters became owners of land they had previously leased. Smallholders faced the disadvantage of having less capital and often poorer land and struggled to get their produce to markets until inland railways were developed from the 1870s. They responded by taking seasonal employment, working as shearers and drovers for the squatters, as well as having family members, including children, take up neighbouring selections, thereby securing enough land to create a viable farm (Waterhouse 2005:88–89). Changes to legislation also gradually made it easier for small farmers to acquire land. Terms for repayments became more generous, administrative oversight more careful and dummying became harder. One of the developments fostered by these processes was the growth of wheat farming by selectors in Victoria and South Australia in the 1870s, and the ideal of closer settlement gradually became a reality.

The experiences of selectors varied enormously. Many struggled with drought, disease, lack of capital and insufficient acreage and were often forced to abandon their leaseholds and homes. Writers like Henry Lawson and "Steele Rudd" (A. H. Davis) famously described their hardships and "endless sorrow" in stories like *The Drover's Wife* and *On Our Selection*. Others endured, scraping by in the bad years and catching up in the good, buying blocks from neighbours and gradually establishing successful mixed farms of grazing and crops. The mechanisation of agriculture in the second half of the nineteenth century also favoured larger farms, with the capital needed for harvesters and threshers effectively excluding many small selectors.

One of the few archaeological studies of a family farm is that of Moran's Farm, near Melrose in South Australia, a site typical in many ways of the selectors' struggles. Its archaeological study has revealed important aspects of social and domestic life on a selection and the process of generational change (Lawrence 2001b). The pattern of land settlement in South Australia, however, was different from the other colonies. It was based on the idea of "systematic colonisation" developed by Edward Gibbon Wakefield. The scheme involved orderly settlement based on the controlled release of land after survey, in contiguous blocks at a fixed price. The aim was to create stable and permanent communities based on family farms. Squatters were discouraged because they promoted a mobile and landless workforce. Revenue from land sales was to be used to assist further immigration. Although many elements of Wakefield's plans were soon abandoned, the principle of controlled land release remained, with pastoral leases only permitted beyond surveyed areas.

Until the 1870s the bulk of surveyed agricultural land in South Australia was within a 100 km radius of Adelaide. Growing demand, however, led to the opening of new lands, especially in the north (Fig. 6.4). One of the "Hundreds" (a rural land division similar to parish or county) proclaimed in 1875 was that of Willowie, 270 km north of Adelaide on the flat plains east of the Flinders Ranges and a short distance from the town of Melrose. The area was just beyond Goyder's Line, which by the 1870s had come to define the northern limit of reliable rainfall for agriculture (Meinig 1962:44–46; Sheldrick 2005). The return of dry conditions in the

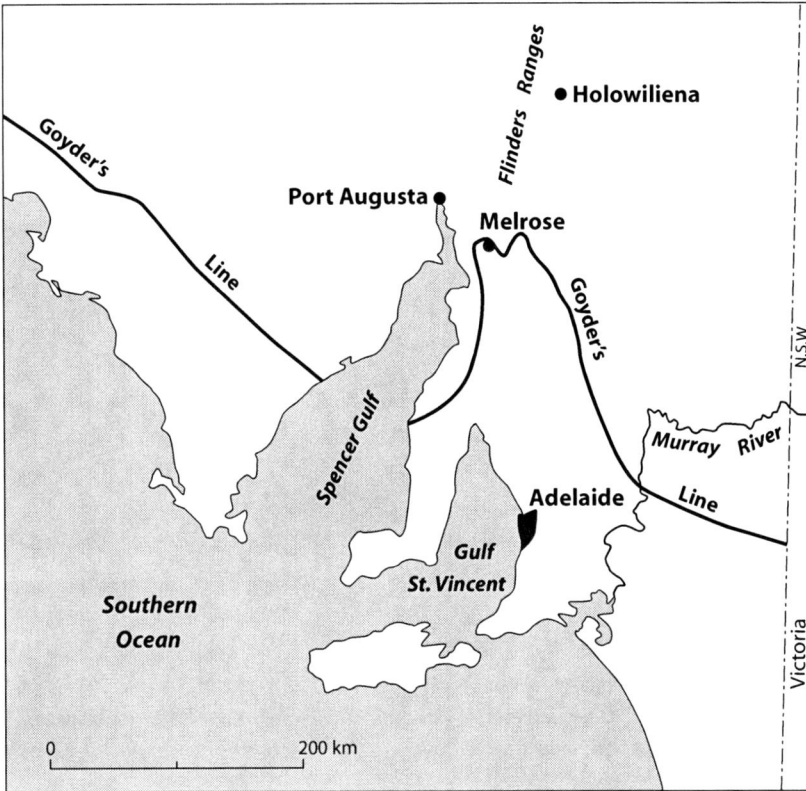

Fig. 6.4 Goyder's Line of reliable rainfall for agriculture in South Australia. Good rains in the 1870s encouraged selectors to take up land north of the Line, but the return of dry conditions in the 1880s brought ruin to many

1880s, however, meant that many selections in the district were abandoned or subsumed into larger pastoral runs. Today the cultural landscape beyond Goyder's Line is marked with hundreds of ruined stone cottages and deserted towns (Fig. 6.5).

Melrose had originally been settled in the 1850s during a short-lived copper-mining venture at the nearby Mount Remarkable mine. By 1866 the town had 250 residents, with a post office, several stores, three hotels, two schools and an Anglican church. Thomas W. Moran was a well-known farmer and businessman in the town. Irish by birth, Moran was posted to Melrose as a police constable in 1853. He married Alice Neagle the following year, and in 1855 their only son, George, was born. Moran then left the police and pursued several ventures, including land speculation and running two local hotels. He also ran sheep, bred horses and was one of the first in the district to grow wheat. The drought of 1864–1865 reduced him to insolvency, but he recovered enough in the following years to start again, and in

Fig. 6.5 Ruins of Kanyaka Homestead in the Flinders Ranges of South Australia, dating from the 1850s. In good seasons the station employed 70 workers and their families, with the main homestead at the centre of a small pastoral village (photo P. Davies)

1875, at the age of 59, he selected 740 acres at Willowie. He obtained full title to the land in 1881, around the time he began construction of a small house on the property.

Excavation at Moran's Farm in 1994 and 1995 revealed both the nature of the house and intimate details of the lives of those who lived on the edges of colonial society. While Moran himself was a colourful and well documented local figure, the activities of other family members are more prominent in the material evidence. The house began as a simple two-room structure, with walls built from local granite, timber and clay. The basic hut indicates the financial distress he experienced at this time, when a man of his local standing might have been expected to construct a more substantial stone residence. Extensions some years later added a third room and cellar and then a fourth room. Despite the local tradition associating the house with Thomas Moran, artefacts associated with women and children suggest that the house was occupied by Moran's son George, his wife Cicely and their nine daughters.

The artefacts reveal various aspects of the Morans' family life. Rosary beads, for example, confirm the importance of private prayer and spiritual belief, mirroring Thomas Moran's public support of a campaign to build a Catholic church at Melrose. Patriotism was also important. A pierced copper disk inscribed "British Transvaal War" was one of about 200,000 such tokens issued to school children in 1900 to promote the courage of Australian soldiers. Pins, needles and thimbles were used in sewing and mending, skills passed on to the little girls by their mother and grandmother. Alice and Cicely laid the table with a decorative but inexpensive

Rhine dinner service and took tea with other ladies of the district using unmatched cups and saucers decorated with many different colours and patterns rather than a dedicated tea service.

Melrose did not have a railway connection to Adelaide until 1913, so all these and other goods came over the ranges by bullock dray from Port Pirie, as they had done for 50 years. Despite their physical isolation, the family's possessions indicate their connections with the wider world. They had dolls from Germany, perfume from France, clay pipes from Scotland and dishes from England. Clothes had buttons stamped with the names of Adelaide tailors and bottles came from an Adelaide glassworks. Selecting on the agricultural frontier was risky, but the Morans were able to call on their experience and contacts throughout the district to briefly overcome the hardships of a new selection. After the deaths of Thomas in 1904 and George in 1915, Cicely left the farm, taking the girls to live in Adelaide, and the house was abandoned.

Creating Rural Landscapes

The creation of rural landscapes was a deliberate and ongoing process. It involved clearing the land, fencing it, constructing houses and other buildings and the widespread introduction of exotic plants and animals. It also involved, however, important psychological processes of framing and representation, as we have seen at Regentville and Lake Innes, where the environment was shaped to conform to European ideologies of class and production (Leone 1988; Stuart 1999:15–33). Iain Stuart (2007) has argued that a crucial figure in this process in Australia was the land surveyor, who interpreted the ideals of land legislation on the ground by pegging out roads, fence lines, farms and townships (see also Wright 1989). The results of these activities can still be read in rural landscapes across Australia today, where the shape of paddocks and the alignment of quiet roads reveal the differing patterns of land settlement over the last 200 years.

One of the great challenges for European settlers was clearing the land of native vegetation. The rural landscape they encountered, however, was anything but uniform. It was instead a mosaic of grassland, hills and river flats, open woodland and thick forest, rocky scrub and swampland, sometimes all within a few kilometres of each other. This patchwork pattern was often a result of Aboriginal burning. Firing the bush encouraged the growth of new grasses, attracting game animals which Aboriginal people hunted. Burning also cleared tracks, opened the country and herded game. Europeans wanted grassland in particular, to graze their animals and plant their crops. Where trees stood in the way, they got rid of them. Many pastoralists regarded trees as simply a nuisance to be cleared to make room for building and farming. Removing the tree cover, they believed, "sweetened the grass". Most open country in agricultural areas today was once clothed in forest or woodland.

Axes and saws were the primary weapon in this "war against the trees" (Bolton 1992). In Gippsland, early selectors spent up to 90 percent of their time in axe work, trying to clear a few acres to grow some vegetables and graze a few cows (Fig. 6.6).

Fig. 6.6 A bush farm in the Gippsland mountains in Victoria, ca. 1900 (Nicholas Caire, nla.pic –
an3128941, National Library of Australia)

To remove the stumps they used horses and bullocks, fire and even dynamite, wasting huge quantities of timber in the process. For many selectors, clearing the land was a condition of their lease. Along with fencing, building a hut or house and sowing a crop, removing the tree cover was taken as evidence of commitment to and thus ownership of the land.

Ring-barking was also widely practised to remove trees. It was simpler and cheaper than clearing by axe and brought pastoralists a quick increase in the acreage and value of grazing land. The aim was to cut a wide strip of bark around the trunk of the tree, severing the flow of water and nutrients to the crown. The tree soon died, leaving a stark grey skeleton and permitting more grass to grow. An expert axeman could kill four or five acres of trees each day. In some districts gangs of Chinese men, no longer able to make a living on the alluvial goldfields, laboured as cheap and hard-working contractors for ring-barking (Frost 2002:121–122).

Ring-barking had a range of environmental impacts, as well as social and cultural consequences. Clearing the trees meant that straight wire fences could be erected, making the cadastral grid a visible, tangible reality on the ground, where before it had only been lines on paper. The loss of tree cover, however, also affected Aboriginal people. Living on the margins of white settler society, their presence and movement became more visible, and they were subject to white surveillance in new and disturbing ways. Denis Byrne argues that Aboriginal people responded by seeking bush cover, retreating more and more to creek and river lines, road reserves and stock routes, places not yet cleared of trees, and voluntarily withdrawing their presence (Byrne 2003a:16).

Land clearance also spread to the Mallee by the 1880s, the dry scrubland in the north-west of Victoria, east of South Australia and central New South Wales. Often regarded by early settlers as "horrid", "waterless" and "barren", settlement increasingly encroached on the mallee lands as better country elsewhere was taken up. The smaller eucalyptus vegetation could be knocked down by heavy rollers pulled by horses or bullocks, with the timber and branches stacked and burnt. The technique was known as "mullenzing", after Mullens, a farmer near Gawler in South Australia. Mallee roots suckered if left in the ground, however, meaning shoots had to be slashed again and again, with the roots and spikes left in the ground taking a terrible toll on the animals. Farmers could partially offset the cost of clearing by sending wagon loads of mallee roots to town as firewood. Sometimes the roots were stacked to make fences, some of which still exist today. Despite the effort and money spent, however, many selectors learned the hard way that the mallee lands were often of poor quality for agriculture and did not pay the cost of clearing.

Having cleared the land, farmers then had to fence it. Fences not only kept stock from wandering, but also created a visual sense of place in otherwise undifferentiated, untamed bush. To begin with, however, pastoralists had very few fences. Instead they employed shepherds, often convicts or ex-convicts, to watch the sheep by day. At night the animals were enclosed within a portable fold of wood or brush, while the shepherd slept nearby in a "watch box". Each shepherd typically watched over a thousand sheep or more. They were on the bottom of the social pile, and there are frequent stories of shepherds growing mad from loneliness, boredom and alcohol (Adam-Smith 1982:39–42). Cheap labour evaporated in the 1850s as the shepherds joined the gold rush, and pastoralists and squatters were forced to fence their runs. One of the consequences was to give squatters a seemingly greater moral right to the land. While the runs remained open it was obvious to all that the squatter grazed his stock on public land. The appearance of fences, however, imposed both a physical and a psychological hurdle for selectors wanting to encroach on the land.

Fences were built according to need and available resources. Graham Connah has described the range of rural fencing developed throughout Australia during the nineteenth century (Connah 1988:87–90; see Pickard 2009). The simplest was the brush fence, consisting of trees cut down along boundary lines. Post-and-rail fences were usually confined to areas immediately around the homestead, while drystone walling was common in western Victoria and parts of Van Diemen's Land and New South Wales, where thin, volcanic soil had to be cleared of rocks. In parts of Victoria and Tasmania "quick" (i.e. living) fences or hedges were also commonplace, as settlers planted rows of dense, prickly shrubs such as hawthorn and broom (Anderson 2002). In areas where there was little timber suitable for fences, wire came to be used instead. The earliest wire, "bull wire" was $\frac{1}{4}$ inch (6.5 mm) thick and very hard to handle. The development of the Bessemer steel process in the 1850s, however, made it possible to produce thinner and stronger steel wire, reducing the number of posts and droppers needed and thus making fences cheaper. Wire fencing rapidly became very popular. In New South Wales in the 1880s more than 1.6 million km of wire fencing was erected. Fences permitted grazing and cropping to expand enormously and created one of the most distinctive features of the Australian landscape: the division of rural land into endless rectangular blocks.

As land was cleared, fenced and sown to crops or pasture, the need for water remained paramount. If a farmer was lucky enough to have a reliable stream or creek flowing through his property, water was less of an issue. Such land, however, was quickly taken up in all areas and jealously held. Away from permanent water courses, various measures were devised to trap and store water. At the simplest level, barrels were used to capture rainwater as it drained from roofs. With the introduction of galvanised iron in the 1850s, larger rainwater tanks gradually appeared. Dams were dug by hand or with horse-drawn scoops, while wells were also excavated, the water drawn up by horse-powered whims, steam pumps and windmill pumps (invented in 1876). Bores were also drilled into artesian water sources from the 1880s, opening up new territory for pastoralists in the north of South Australia and western Queensland and New South Wales, allowing sheep and cattle to be watered regularly.

Detailed archaeological research in the Adelaide Hills has revealed that settlers in the area relied heavily on creeks and permanent springs for water. Farms, orchards and market gardens established in the narrow, fertile valleys supplied fresh fruit and vegetables for the rapidly growing city of Adelaide. The control and management of water was vital, however, in a climate of long dry summers and occasional torrential rains. Recent archaeological survey has identified more than 100 stone features associated with water control in the Adelaide Hills (Piddock et al. 2009:72–75; P. Smith 2006, 2007). These include stone-lined water channels, drains and irrigation races, along with wells, dams and tank stands.

Pamela Smith (2006:72) notes that the dry-stone construction of these features used random walling of undressed or minimally dressed stone, in contrast to more carefully built fences and farm buildings. These water management structures were the legacy of numerous different groups from Britain and Europe, each of which brought their masonry skills to the region. Farmers forced meandering creeks into stone-lined channels, so they could grow irrigated crops along fertile flood plains. Water races for irrigation included in-ground channels and wooden pipes. More than 40 wells and cisterns were also documented, often associated with natural springs in market gardening areas. The survey also identified occasional sluice gates, agricultural terraces and water wheels.

Gradually, however, as the population grew and demand for fresh food increased, the supply of water diminished, and many properties in the area became unviable. As technologies for pumping groundwater became more widely available and transport infrastructure improved, market gardeners and orchardists moved to larger farms on the Adelaide Plains or along the Murray River, leaving behind the water management features they had worked so hard to create.

Market gardens and water systems were also frequently operated by Chinese settlers. Their skills produced cabbage, lettuce, tomatoes and many other vegetables at cheap rates and helped end the reign of "mutton and damper" that had dominated the European diet on the goldfields. Historian Warwick Frost (2002) notes, however, that Chinese farming did not arrive fully formed in the 1850s. Instead there were several decades of adaptation and adjustment to local conditions, with a peak in market gardening around 1880–1900, followed by a decline in the following years. The Chinese succeeded in adapting their techniques of intensive farming to a range of environments, from north Queensland to Tasmania (McGowan 2005). They also worked in partnership with Europeans and even, occasionally, alongside them (Vivian 1985). Chinese market gardeners combined hard work with innovation, entrepreneurship and labour management, to become successful growers of European foods for a largely European market (Frost 2002:124).

One of the first archaeological studies of such places was at Ah Toy's garden on the Palmer River goldfield in far north Queensland (Jack et al. 1984). The field was first rushed in 1873, but its isolation meant that no infrastructure was available, and transport costs were high. By 1877, the European population was down to 1,500, while the number of Chinese had increased to 18,000, making it the largest Chinese community in Queensland. The field was in decline, however, by 1900 when Tommy Ah Toy took over the lease of a garden site along Lone Star Creek. His garden contained fruit trees, including custard apples, and orange and mandarin trees, along with vegetables watered through a complex system of irrigation channels. Ah Toy spent the next 34 years at the garden, mostly alone, before moving to Cairns and dying soon after.

A different social pattern was revealed at Yong Kit's garden settlement on the Loddon River, near Castlemaine in central Victoria. The site was first leased to a man called Li Chun in 1867, then passed on to a series of Chinese men, including Yong Kit in 1903. He abandoned the garden in 1912, selling the cultivation licence to a European. Archaeological evidence from the site reveals a complex system of terraces, vegetation, paths and household debris (Stanin 2004a). Where Ah Toy's garden was a solitary enterprise, Yong Kit's garden was highly communal in nature, and it may have been integrated into the kind of large-scale economic system identified by Alister Bowen near Port Albert (Chapter 9). A large number of partners were involved in the garden, with a high turnover of people as men returned to China or moved to other goldfields. Small huts each housed several men, who endured personal discomfort and a lack of privacy, in return for greater profit. Co-operative work and living thus brought both benefits and problems. Cultural support and labour efficiencies were available, offset at times by the inevitable tensions of competing personalities and aspirations.

Excavation of chimney platforms at the site in 2002 yielded fairly modest household assemblages. Most items related to the storage of food and drink, including Chinese stoneware bottles and jars and celadon bowls and cups (Kitchen Ch'ing). There were few personal items or signs of wealth. The men were not investing their money in personal possessions or in building substantial homes. Instead, they were sending money back to China and accumulating relatively few goods in the process. For these men, transience meant movement, and movement meant that possessions were a liability (Stanin 2004a:28).

Remains of the gardens themselves suggest dependence on traditional agricultural methods, frugality and co-operative labour, similar to the pattern documented for market gardens in suburban Sydney, Perth and Melbourne (Morris 2001; Pullman 2001; Richards 2001). Crops were planted in straight, parallel rows and furrows, dug to the very edge of the property. There were also shallow rectangular wells placed along the furrows, indicating the use of manual watering techniques. There were, however, no internal fences or divisions to show individual ownership – only separate areas devoted to different crops. Plum trees were also common at the site, as they were at many other market gardens on the goldfields. Plums were processed into jam, dried into prunes for use as medicinal products to aid digestion and fermented into alcoholic beverages. They were also symbolically important, as part of a trio of plants known as the Three Friends of Winter, including the evergreen pine tree and bamboo. They represent a model of fortitude in adverse circumstances and an adaptation of Chinese traditions to the local environment. Overall, the planting of trees and the construction of dams, bridges and paths, built up by several generations of gardeners, reflects care and commitment to the place and landscape and the importance of communal labour, in contrast to the simple huts and the paucity of personal possessions. Here, as in other Chinese communities in Australia, co-operation and organisation took precedence over individual needs.

Growing Simple Pleasures

While Chinese market gardeners were instrumental in providing fresh fruit and vegetables for a large proportion of both rural and urban Australians, farmers also produced crops for the simple indulgence of consumers. Wine, tobacco, chicory for coffee and hops for beer were all widely grown and processed in nineteenth-century Australia and have left a diverse archaeological legacy.

James Squire was Australia's first brewer, making beer in Sydney in 1793. He started by using imported ingredients, but soon after 1800 he established the colony's first successful hop plantation for beer production (Deutsher 1999:69). By 1815 there were seven breweries in Sydney, while commercial production began in Van Diemen's Land in 1820, when James Whyte set up the Tasman Brewery in Hobart. As beer did not preserve well without refrigeration, it had to be brewed locally, so many country towns had their own breweries by the mid-nineteenth century. In Victoria, there were 116 different breweries operating by 1870 (Birmingham et al. 1979:168) and 45 in South Australia (Deutsher 1999:207; Shueard and Tuckwell 1993). By the early twentieth century, however, there was rapid consolidation of the industry, with larger city breweries taking over the smaller country ones.

Brewers began the process by heating water with malted barley grains, adding hops and then fermenting with yeast, before cooling and storing the beer in casks or bottles. An important part of brewing beer was thus the addition of hop flowers, which gave the bitter flavour of traditional beer. In the 1820s and 1830s Van Diemen's Land emerged as a centre for growing hops, while production was also well established in Gippsland and north-east Victoria by the 1880s (Pearce 1976). Early hops were dried in the open air, following the traditional German practice, but kiln-drying soon became the rule. Known originally as "oast houses", the kilns were built of timber, brick or stone (Fig. 6.7). Green hops were brought in from the field and spread on the drying floor of the kiln. Gradual warmth and a good current of air were needed to reduce the water content of the hops from 70 percent to around 7 percent, with the process taking about 12 hours. After withdrawal from the drying floor, the hops were carefully shovelled into the cooling rooms and gently turned each day for about a week. They were then taken to a hop-press and pressed into bales. There are a number of well-preserved kilns in Victoria and Tasmania that reveal the scale of the drying process and the geographic extent of the industry. Other physical remains of the hop industry are the distinctive field patterns. Hops are tall slender plants grown on narrow frames. To protect them from damage by winds and frosts, they were planted in small paddocks which were often surrounded by windbreaks of Lombardy poplar trees. Today the windbreaks and the small sheltered fields remain, even though the hops are no longer planted (Birmingham et al. 1979:174).

There was also enthusiasm for wine in early colonial society. Governor Arthur Phillip promoted the "cultivation of the vine" as early as 1788, while the very first issue of *The Sydney Gazette* on 5 March 1803 carried the first of several articles on preparing land for a vineyard. Australia's wine pioneers saw the vine as both a potential export crop and as an alternative in the battle against "ardent spirits". Possibly the first wine was made in 1795 by Phillip Schaffer, a German

Fig. 6.7 Hop kiln (oast house) at Mossiface near Bairnsdale in eastern Victoria (photo P. Davies)

from Rheinhessen, who cultivated land at Parramatta (Beeston 1994:4). In the following years other attempts at wine cultivation were also made, but with little success. These early efforts, however, were largely experimental. Growers relied on European techniques and traditions, but struggled to come to terms with local soils and climate, and the best planting methods and grape varieties.

By the 1820s, many of the large pastoral estates around Sydney featured vineyards, including Sir John Jamison's at Regentville. The Macarthurs were also prominent exponents of the industry. John Macarthur returned to Sydney with his sons, James and William, in 1817. They arrived from Europe with cuttings of about 30 grape varieties. Archaeological study of the soils at Camden Park Estate, the family's property south-west of Sydney, reveals the traditional trenching technique applied to planting vines in this period (Koppi et al. 1985). Trenches were dug in the vineyard to a depth of about 70 cm. The open trenches were then backfilled with topsoil and organic matter at the bottom, then with the clay subsoils, and the surface filled with rock fragments. The result was an inversion of the original soil profile. This practice, advocated by one of the era's greatest winemakers, James Busby, was evidently a success for the Macarthurs, who by the 1840s had achieved considerable renown for their wines. By this time, wine-growing was also well established in several other regions, including the Hunter Valley, around Adelaide where German as well as British vintners were prominent, and in the Yarra Valley north-east of Melbourne.

Another everyday indulgence for generations of Australians was drinking tea. The taste for tea was imported from Britain and flourished in the hot Australian climate. Nevertheless, coffee was also widely consumed in the nineteenth century, available from street stalls, temperance hotels and from shops as "essence of coffee and chicory" (Chapter 11). Much of the coffee available was heavily adulterated with chicory, a root crop looking much like a parsnip. Chicory was widely grown in southern Victoria from the 1860s to the 1960s, with the roots of the plant dried in wood-fired kilns and ground into a fine powder. More than 30 chicory kilns remain in the Western Port district, mostly derelict, indicating the scale and distribution of chicory processing (Davies 2009).

Kilns were typically square in plan, 4–5 m across and up to 7 m in height. They were built from a variety of materials, including pisé (rammed earth), stone, brick and concrete, and enclosed within a corrugated iron shed (Fig. 6.8). Kilns featured a hipped roof, with louvres and a cowl at the top to control the updraft of heat, smoke and steam from the furnace below. The drying floor of the kiln was usually about 3 m above ground level and consisted of heavy iron mesh supported on old iron tram tracks. The largest kilns were built in the 1870s and 1880s, in the early days of the industry, when growers were still discovering the most efficient means of processing, but by the early 1900s kilns were smaller and more uniform in design.

Kilns were always located close to a road and often near the farmhouse as well, making firing and transport easier. There were always more farmers growing chicory than farmers with kilns, however, resulting in the sharing of kilns and equipment

Fig. 6.8 Chicory kiln on Phillip Island, Victoria (photo P. Davies)

during the autumn harvest and the need for negotiation and compromise. Although chicory cultivation was a minor industry in Australian agriculture, usually as a side-line to dairying, it was nevertheless highly labour intensive. Partial mechanisation during the twentieth century relieved some of the effort, but farmers' children still provided valuable help during the harvest. With each kiln burning more than 100 tons of fuel in a season, the industry also contributed significantly to land clearance and the transformation of rural landscapes in the Western Port region.

Tobacco and pipe-smoking was another everyday pleasure for most men and many women in colonial Australia (Gojak and Stuart 1999; Tyrrell 1999:4–6; see Chapter 11). Tobacco was first grown in New South Wales from 1818, but production remained on a small scale. Large quantities were imported from Brazil up to the 1840s, because the area was close to trade routes on the Great Circle route to Australia. By the 1860s, tobacco cultivation in Australia was largely in the hands of Chinese growers, often share-farming with European owners. The American Civil War interrupted supplies of Virginia leaf, leading to a boom and then glut, of local production. For most of the nineteenth century, tobacco in Australia was cured in the open or in sheds, rather than in a kiln. The process took about 6 weeks, and produced a dark "plug" tobacco suitable only for chewing or pipe-smoking, or for applying to sheep with scab. By the 1880s, however, there was a growing preference for brighter, golden tobaccos, used especially in cigarettes, which could only be produced by flue-curing in a kiln. Kilns began to appear in tobacco-growing regions, and by the 1920s, when Italian migrants were joining the industry, the kiln-curing process had become standard (Birmingham et al. 1979:176–179; Verrocchio 1998).

Kiln drying took about 6 days. The tobacco leaves were tied onto sticks that sat on cross beams, eight to nine layers high inside the kiln. Wood fires were lit in furnaces on the outside wall of the kiln or below the floor, with the hot air circulated inside through wide convection tubes. The tobacco leaves changed colour from green to yellow, as chlorophyll was broken down and starches were converted into sugars. Some of the earliest tobacco kilns were built from brick or concrete, while in later kilns corrugated iron was generally the preferred material.

Recent decades have seen a dramatic decline in the tobacco industry in Australia, in response to a profound change in the way we view the product. Many old kilns remain, however, in tobacco-growing regions of Queensland and Victoria. They reveal the changing technologies developed to cure tobacco and represent the strong links the industry had with Chinese and Italian migrants. Clay pipes and tobacco kilns are powerful reminders of how tobacco was once enjoyed in one form or another by all manner of people in Australian society.

Conclusion

The rural landscape first encountered in Australia by the earliest European explorers, pastoralists and settlers was not original, wild and untouched. It was a landscape created by Aboriginal people over thousands of years of careful burning and management. From the fertile coastal areas of the south-east to the dry inland plains and the tropical forests and savannahs of the north, Australia in 1788 was an anthropogenic landscape, one created and maintained by human needs, decisions and activities. When Europeans arrived, they broke the delicate balances between water, soil, climate, plants and animals. Their needs were immediate: to feed themselves and to produce commodities for export. They brought with them a whole new suite of plants and animals and developed new ways of perceiving the landscape. Australia was totally unlike Britain or anywhere else in Europe. It was flatter, hotter, drier and distant, filled with strange animals, upside-down seasons and unknown trees and plants. The new arrivals carried in their heads the idea of what a productive place should be like and set about trying to create it, beginning with the removal of the Aboriginal owners. Archaeology can document the results of their labours, in the fields and fences, stock routes and gardens, cleared forests and woodlands, and can reveal a great deal about what early Europeans thought and how they behaved. In the rural landscapes they created we can read the physical legacy of dispossession and more than two centuries of trying to come to terms with the reality of Australia.

Chapter 7
Gold Rushes and Precious Metals

The discovery of gold in New South Wales and Victoria in 1851 brought dramatic change and upheaval to the Australian colonies. Migrants flooded in from around the world, eager to make their fortunes. Towns and cities grew quickly, bringing with them new industries, amenities and the elements of civic life. With more money available, local manufacturing grew and trade and communications expanded. Gold, via the Eureka Rebellion in 1854, was an important catalyst for political reform and the growth of democracy in the Australian colonies. Mining also had a severe impact on natural landscapes, with forests and woodlands plundered to provide the great quantities of timber demanded by the miners, while hillsides were eroded and waterways silted up due to the mining techniques used.

The search for gold and other precious metals in Australia was stimulated by the California gold rush of 1848–1849 as well as by local economic crises and unemployment. Gold rushes occurred in a roughly counter-clockwise sequence around Australia in the second half of the nineteenth century (Fig. 7.1). Beginning in New South Wales and Victoria in the 1850s, major fields were discovered in Queensland in the 1870s and 1880s at Gympie, Mount Morgan, Charters Towers and Palmer River; at Halls Creek in the Kimberley in 1886; and in the Pilbara and then Coolgardie and Kalgoorlie in Western Australia in the 1890s (Blainey 1978). Australian prospectors and miners were also avid participants in the large gold rushes in New Zealand that began with the discovery of gold in Otago in 1861. Gold, however, was not the only valuable mineral ore mined in Australia. Major deposits of silver, iron, tin, copper, lead and zinc have also been exploited since the nineteenth century. One of the earliest "rushes" in Australia pre-dated gold by a number of years, when copper was discovered at Burra in South Australia in 1845.

Given its significance to so many elements of Australian life, historians have paid a great deal of attention to mining and to gold in particular, analysing such issues as gold's impact on the development of towns and urban centres, immigration and ethnicity, settler/indigenous interactions and the expansion of colonial economies. The study of mining has also been prominent in historical archaeology in Australia, partly because of its historical significance, but also because of the scale of the landscapes created by mining, which even today comprise a considerable proportion of the public land in many areas. The requirements of heritage management have resulted in archaeologists developing considerable expertise in interpreting mining

S. Lawrence, P. Davies, *An Archaeology of Australia Since 1788*,
Contributions To Global Historical Archaeology, DOI 10.1007/978-1-4419-7485-3_7,
© Springer Science+Business Media, LLC 2011

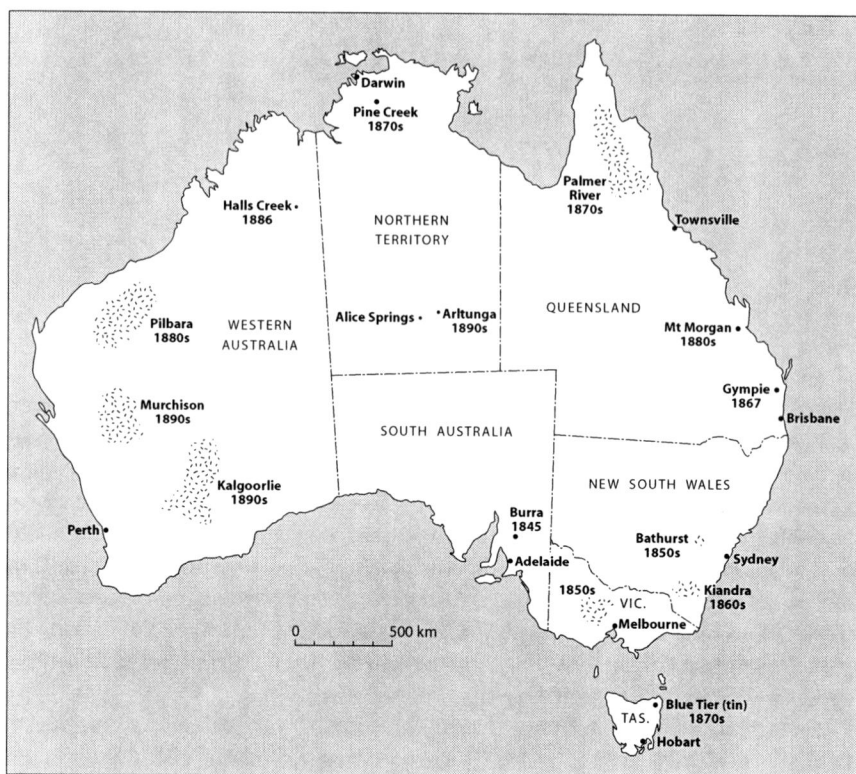

Fig. 7.1 Location of major mineral rushes in the Australian colonies from the 1850s to the 1890s

landscapes and have contributed much to the understanding of Australia's industrial heritage.

The archaeology of mining typifies the study of industrial archaeology in Australia, where the documentation of machines and technologies has been integrated with analysis of the social, cultural, economic and environmental contexts of industry (see Chapter 8). The extensive literature on mining archaeology, much of which is in the form of heritage management reports and postgraduate dissertations, includes studies of the technology of ore extraction and processing, settlement patterns, environmental impacts, Aboriginal contact, ethnicity, class, gender and domestic sites, as well as assessments of the significance of mining heritage and its appropriate management (Pearson 1993a; Pearson and McGowan 2000).

In keeping with the general focus of this book, we concentrate here primarily on the social archaeology of gold and other forms of mining, to examine their impacts on ordinary people and how they responded to the challenges and opportunities of the mining industries. We use case studies of three mining areas – Dolly's Creek in Victoria (Lawrence 1995, 2000), Arltunga in the Northern Territory (Holmes 1983, 1989) and Chinese miners in the south-eastern highlands of New South Wales

(Smith 1998, 2003, 2006) – to examine how miners coped with local conditions and the kinds of communities they formed. These places have been well documented and illustrate some of the patterns characteristic of mining communities around Australia. Dolly's Creek was mined during the 1860s to 1880s and was known as a "poor man's diggings", where subsistence miners independently worked shallow alluvial claims in small groups, avoiding the wage labour of the big mining companies. The same period saw large numbers of Chinese miners forming distinct and segregated communities on the goldfields of south-eastern New South Wales. Around the turn of the century miners battled isolation and dry conditions in central Australia on a field where the available gold could never cover the cost of its extraction. To understand the context of these mining settlements, however, we begin by sketching out the early impact that the discovery of gold had on colonial society, especially in Victoria, and look at the archaeology of various techniques used to extract gold. We also review the formation of goldfields landscapes and consider some of the environmental impacts of mining, many of which remain highly visible even today. We conclude by considering the social archaeology of other vital mining industries, including the copper townships at Burra in South Australia, and tin mining in Tasmania and the Northern Territory.

Major gold deposits were first discovered in New South Wales near Bathurst in 1851, about 270 km west of Sydney. Almost at the same time, even larger deposits were found in several places in Victoria, first near Melbourne and Ballarat, then at Bendigo and Mount Alexander (Castlemaine). When the Cavanagh brothers arrived in Geelong around September 20, 1851 carrying 60 pounds (27 kg) of gold in their saddlebags, cities and towns as far away as Adelaide and Hobart began to empty as able-bodied men rushed to the goldfields. The commercial life of Melbourne virtually halted, as houses, shops and ships lay abandoned. The Mount Alexander goldfield alone was rushed by 20,000 miners in its first three months. In New South Wales the impact of gold discoveries was the same, with Sydney soon resembling a "deserted village" (Pickering 2001:38). Wild excitement greeted the news when it reached England, with reports of gold "actually oozing from the earth" (Dickens 1852a). Six ships arrived in London in May 1852 carrying eight tonnes of Victorian gold, inflaming the frenzy to migrate. In London Charles Dickens observed "legions of bankers' clerks, merchants' lads, embryo secretaries and incipient cashiers; all going with the rush, and all possessing but faint and confused ideas of where they *are* going, or what they are going to do" (Dickens 1852b). In the decade 1851–1861, Victoria's population increased from 77,000 to 540,000 (Serle 1963:382). The new arrivals included 10,000 Germans, 8,000 other Europeans and 2,500 Americans (most from California), as well as around 40,000 Chinese. All were hoping to return home in only a few years with new wealth for the stability and prestige of their families.

For the most part, however, not many diggers actually found their fortunes on the goldfields. Historian Geoffrey Serle estimated that 8 out of 10 made wages or less, and only one in a hundred made enough to retire and live in comfort (Serle 1963:85–86). Those who provided services to the goldseekers, such as storekeepers, publicans and skilled tradesmen were generally in a better position to profit. In the early days of alluvial mining especially, the spoils went to those well-accustomed to hard physical labour. Thousands of others returned to their jobs and lives after a few weeks or months with little more than the experience to show. In later years, when large companies worked deep mines, the profits went mostly to merchants and shareholders. Nevertheless, even the relatively modest quantities recovered by most miners were enough to change lives, enabling them to start a small business or buy a house.

In this period Victoria produced 20 million ounces of gold (more than 560 tonnes), around one third of total world output. Gold replaced wool as Australia's leading export for 20 years and raised Melbourne to equal status with Sydney (Bate 1988:8–9). The newly available capital stimulated local industries, which ploughed the profits back into the local economy. Mining required equipment, including tools, pipes, pumps and engines, which provided work for foundries and machine shops. The miners needed housing, clothes and food, which expanded the construction industry and created large markets for local products (Fig. 7.2). Towns grew overnight and soon acquired fine new buildings and were ornamented with parks and gardens, art galleries and theatres. Australia's first major railways linked Melbourne, Geelong, Ballarat and Bendigo by the early 1860s and improved transport to the goldfields. Gold changed the political landscape, extending the franchise to all white men, and the cultural landscape, with significant numbers of migrants arriving from outside the British Isles. Gold-etched Victoria, and the Australian colonies more generally, onto the mental map of the British Empire.

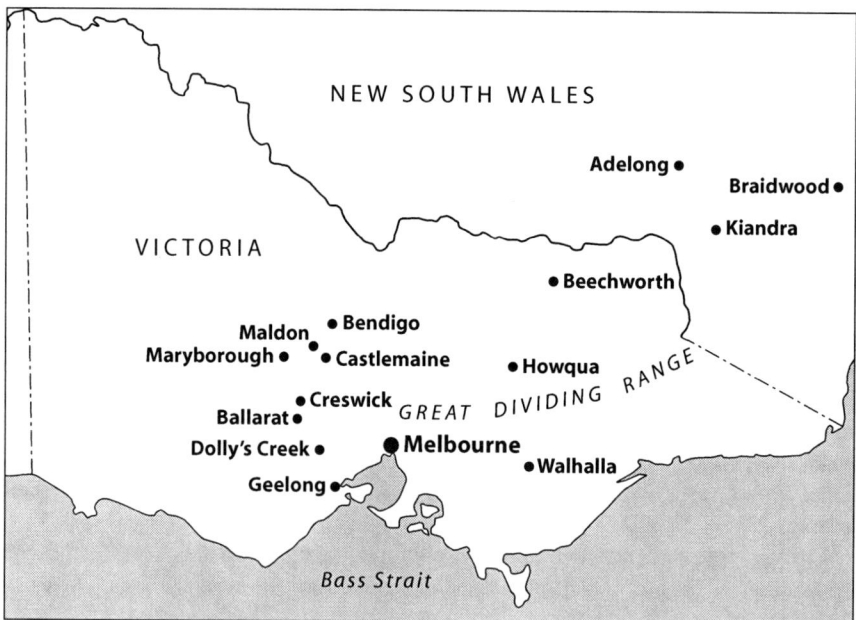

Fig. 7.2 Centres of gold production in Victoria and south-eastern New South Wales during the nineteenth century

Technology

There were several ways to mine for gold. These depended on the nature of the gold deposit and the topography of the goldfield. Gold generally occurred either close to the surface in shallow alluvial deposits or deeper underground, in deep leads or quartz reefs. Once the gold-bearing ore was taken from the ground, it had to be processed to recover the gold from the accompanying rocks and minerals. Each type of mining and processing has left its own distinctive archaeological signature on the landscape. In most cases repeated phases of working and reworking the diggings have created a complex palimpsest of features that must be disentangled to interpret the sequence of activities. To a large extent, different methods of mining and processing characterised different mining eras as more complex methods replaced simpler ones, so that understanding the sequence of activities on a site will also provide a rough chronological framework. However, small miners and prospectors have returned to the goldfields, particularly during the depressions of the 1890s and 1930s, so older techniques may sometimes be used after newer ones.

Alluvial Mining

Alluvial gold occurs as flakes or nuggets, eroded by water into the beds of creeks and streams. Recovering such gold from shallow and geologically recent deposits involved either working the surface soil layers or sinking shafts with pick and shovel up to about 10 m deep. The earliest method for washing gold used a shallow metal pan, in which a little water was swirled around with a shovelful of dirt. The water and soil were poured off until only the gold, being heavier, was left. This method required little specialised knowledge, but could only process a small amount of wash-dirt and much of the gold was lost. Cradles and sluice boxes permitted larger volumes of dirt to be washed. A wooden trough was fitted with a series of bars across the bottom of the box. As water carried the dirt and gravel through the cradle, the gold was washed out and trapped against the riffle bars. Although these methods were cheap and simple, they were inefficient and required large quantities of water to operate effectively.

Shallow alluvial diggings are characterised by a landscape feature archaeologist Neville Ritchie has described as "mullocky ground" (1981:51–69), where numerous shallow shafts are grouped in close proximity, with accompanying mounds of mullock (non-gold-bearing rock) and tailings (processed sands and gravels from which the gold has been removed). On many shallow diggings the ground was sluiced, with the wash-dirt shovelled into nearby ditches or water races, and the resulting tailings forked out. Ground-sluicing leaves behind long tailings mounds where the rocks and gravel have been heaped up, and these mounds often line the watercourses or form other patterns that indicate the manner in which the ground was worked. Dolly's Creek was one such diggings, as were the Lisle Denison goldfields in north-eastern Tasmania and the diggings in the Shoalhaven River area of south-eastern New South Wales (Coroneos 1995; McGowan 1996).

When water was scarce a puddler could be used. This was a ring-shaped trough in the ground filled with water, into which cartloads of dirt were tipped. A post in the centre supported a crossbar from which a wooden paddle was suspended. A horse harnessed to the crossbar dragged the paddle around the trough, mixing the clay and water and loosening the gold. When the water was released through an outlet channel, the gold could be cleaned off the bottom of the trough. If the wastewater was diverted to a dam it could be reused, adding to the efficiency of the system. In the summer when creeks dried up, piles of earth for washing would accumulate and be guarded until the rains came again. Many puddlers are still visible in the drier diggings of the Whipstick Forest, just north of Bendigo in Victoria.

A more complex system of working shallow alluvial deposits was hydraulic sluicing. This process involved channelling a stream of water downhill into a series of progressively smaller pipes, ending in a nozzle. The water pressure that was built up was directed at the deposit, usually the wall of a creek or gully up to 20 m high, which was blasted away. The force of the water loosened the dirt and washed it towards sluicing channels in which the gold could settle. This system required even more water and hills to create the necessary gravity, but dramatically increased the volume of soil that could be moved quickly by a small group of workers. Hydraulic sluicing produced a landscape of dramatic vertical cliffs with tailings mounds below. Because all the topsoil has been washed away, vegetation is usually minimal, even to this day, such as in the Mitta Mitta region of north-eastern Victoria.

The final phase of alluvial mining in some areas was dredging, introduced from New Zealand in the 1890s. Dredges were large "floating factories" that scooped up gravels in a stream bed using a chain of connected buckets, washed it through a system of sluice boxes and discharged the tailings into long mounds at the back. As the sluicing machinery was largely enclosed, dredges looked like large timber buildings floating on a pontoon. They sat in ponds of their own making that advanced along the streambed with the dredge. The process usually destroyed any trace of the previous landscape and resulted in the creation of dredging ponds, tailing mounds and entry channels (Pearson and McGowan 2000).

All these methods of working shallow alluvial deposits involved managing water. In the seasonally dry climate of Australia, water had to be obtained, stored and directed to where it was needed. Dams were built to store rainwater or divert streams, and ditches or races were excavated to carry water from the dams to the workings. The networks created by such systems were extensive and impressive feats of engineering, extending for many kilometres. The races had to follow the contours of the land, skirting hills and valleys and maintaining a slight downwards gradient. The remains of such systems are often preserved in gold-mining regions today. Small, localised systems can be seen as shallow ditches in the ground and may show up best during dry periods when the grass in the ditch will be greener. Larger systems can frequently be traced for considerable distances, cutting slightly across the fall of the land and often as ditches up to half a metre deep and a metre wide.

Deep Lead and Reef Mining

Deep lead mining occurred where former riverbeds had been buried over geological time beneath hundreds of metres of sediment. These were particularly common in the Ballarat region. Reef mining pursued veins of gold-bearing quartz, also often deep underground. The quartz had to be brought to the surface for crushing and processing to recover the gold. The depth of such deposits presented engineering and geological problems for miners. Water accumulating in the gravels had to be pumped out before the ore matrix was hauled up to the surface, and specialised crushing was then needed to process the ore. All of these processes involved sophisticated technology and large amounts of capital. Such ventures were far beyond the means of a few workmates. Deep lead and quartz mining were thus the business of capitalists and engineers rather than independent miners. For the men doing the work, pay was steady and life was settled, but there was little chance of quick fortunes.

Underground mines leave little in the way of visible archaeological remains, but abandoned machinery and footings may sometimes be found, particularly in more isolated regions like the Palmer River goldfields in Queensland (Bell 1987). In other areas such as the mines of the Adelaide Hills (Horn and Fradd 1987) and around Castlemaine the round stone chimneys used with the boilers are still visible. The most distinctive features, however, are the shafts themselves, often only large shallow depressions now that most have been filled in, and the associated mullock heaps which can be 10–20 m high and 100 m around. In the region around Creswick in Victoria, renowned for its deep lead mines, immense mullock heaps are still a prominent characteristic of the landscape, visible for kilometres across the flat grasslands.

In deep mines, water seepage was a problem, and it had to be pumped out. One of the most effective means of achieving this was with beam pumping engines (Milner 1997). Developed in England in the eighteenth century, these engines were capable of raising water from depths of over 500 m. A well-preserved example survives at Fryerstown near Castlemaine, revealing the scale of such operations. The stone engine house and round chimney of the Duke of Cornwall mine, built in 1865, are largely intact, although nothing of the machinery survives. In the copper-mining areas of South Australia several other engine houses have also survived. In addition, winding engines were needed to haul ore from deep mines. Usually, they featured massive horizontal steam engines, heavy wire rope and a tall head frame or poppet (Birmingham et al. 1979:42; Wegner 1995). Initially, such poppet heads were of heavy timber, but by the turn of the century steel was commonly used instead. Examples of these head frames can still be seen in the Bendigo area today and in North Queensland.

Processing

Gold-bearing ore recovered from quartz reefs or deep leads had to be treated to separate the gold from the associated rock and other minerals. This involved several

Fig. 7.3 Twelve-head stamp battery, used by the Kent Tin Mine at Blue Tier in north-eastern Tasmania (photo S. Lawrence)

processes. The most important machine was the stamp battery. It featured heavy stamp heads that were lifted and dropped by a rotating overhead cam shaft (Fig. 7.3). Ore was fed into the box below, along with water, and crushed to a fine powder. Water and fine sand flowed from the box over copper sheets coated with mercury. The gold formed an amalgam with the mercury, which was scraped off at regular intervals.

From the beginning quartz ores were sometimes roasted in kilns to make them more friable and easier to crush and to improve the amalgamation of very fine gold particles. Roasting (calcining) took place in either earth-cut pits (unlined or brick-lined), in free-standing masonry furnaces, or in kilns partially cut into a hillside and completed with bricks or stonework (Davey 1986; Gojak and Allen 2000; Lawrence et al. 2000). The ores were then processed by crushing and separating (Fig. 7.4). In later years new methods were developed where refractory ores were crushed first and then roasted to drive off other compounds. The footings of early calcining kilns have survived in Victoria at Maldon and on the Howqua goldfield, and at Hill End in New South Wales, while examples of reverberatory furnaces survive at the Warribanno Lead Smelter north of Geraldton in Western Australia (Gibbs 1997) and at the Talisker Silver Mine south of Adelaide (Drew 1987).

Stamp batteries and winding machinery were powered by either portable or stationary steam engines. Both required large boilers which needed good supplies of

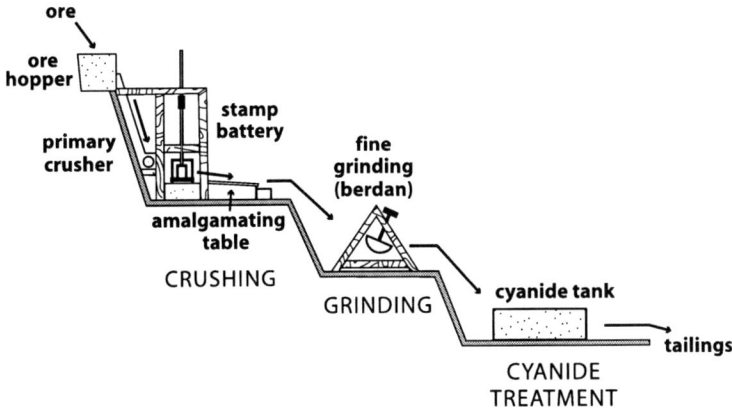

Fig. 7.4 Schematic sequence of ore processing with cyanide treatment (after Ritchie and Hooker 1997:23)

clean water. Water was also needed to mix with the ore beneath the stamp heads. Boiler settings can often be identified on gold-mining sites, usually with two low parallel walls of brick or stone, sometimes with a concave supporting base between. Nearby was usually a chimney to draw the fire, with a flue connecting with the boiler stoke hole. Cornish miners often used hillsides as a sloping chimney, digging a shallow trench *up* a hill and building an arching stone cover over the top. Other physical evidence of such operations includes the often huge mounds of tailing and battery sands dumped below the stamps.

Sometimes waterwheels were used to drive mining machinery instead of steam engines. The Garfield waterwheel near Castlemaine in central Victoria was built in 1886–1887 and drove a 15-head stamp battery (Fig. 7.5). Usually, such waterwheels required a storage dam and water race somewhere above the wheel and a tail race below, and they were more common in the mountainous districts of eastern Victoria and New South Wales. In the typically dry conditions of much of Australia, however, the volumes of water needed to drive waterwheels were simply unavailable, and steam power was harnessed instead (see Chapter 8).

Mercury amalgamation and gravity separation of gold were widely used in the 1850s and 1860s, but neither was very efficient. Subsequent reworking of early tailings, even after the careful sluicing by Chinese miners, was both standard and successful. In later years further chemical and physical methods were developed to recover the gold particles. Processes such as chlorination, treatment with cyanide and sulphuric acid and flotation were all tried with varying degrees of success. Cyaniding involved mixing a finely crushed ore with dilute potassium cyanide in a tank. The solution was then drawn off and the gold content precipitated on zinc shavings. The efficiency of the process meant that it often proved worthwhile to re-process old tailings. Cyanide vats can still be found on goldfields today. They were usually about 6 m across and lined with cement or corrugated iron, located below the stamp battery and boiler, with wooden paddles to stir the ore solution

Fig. 7.5 Garfield Water Wheel near Castlemaine in Victoria, used to drive a large stamp battery in the 1880s (photo S. Lawrence)

(Fig. 7.6). Tailings sands from cyaniding also survive, sometimes in large quantities, and these remain highly toxic and should be regarded with caution. Later mines generally employed several of these methods in combination. The processing works were built on hillsides wherever possible with each step on a different level, so that gravity could assist with moving the ore. Unprocessed ore was fed into the stamp

Fig. 7.6 Cyanide vats for separating gold from finely crushed ore at Steiglitz in Victoria (photo P. Davies)

batteries on the top level, then moved down for finer crushing and then into kilns or tanks for chemical or flotation treatment. Sloping sites often show the evidence of each stage of treatment.

Gold-mining Landscapes

The nature of gold deposits also influenced the way gold-mining landscapes were altered. Before the discovery of gold, colonial economies were dominated by pastoral interests, with dispersed settlement based on scattered sheep stations and river crossings. With the gold rush of the 1850s, natural environments were more intensively disrupted by mining activity, widespread forest clearing and damage to creeks and rivers. When the surface gold ran out quickly, towns were abandoned as soon as they had sprung up. In places where the gold was buried deeper, however, and required more complex industrial processes to extract, towns often grew and thrived. In Victoria, the largest goldfield towns (Ballarat, Bendigo and Castlemaine) quickly became centres of manufacturing as well, with foundries and sawmills to serve the mines and flour mills and brickworks to provide for the needs of the miners. Smaller centres, such as Creswick, Maldon, Maryborough and Beechworth, had stable populations of several thousand people each (Serle 1963:370). Starting out as temporary camps, such places were quickly transformed into solid and respectable towns providing services to surrounding districts.

Townships

The layout of mining towns is often distinctive, due to the nature and timing of mineral discoveries. Peter Bell (1998b) identified three factors that contribute to this distinctive appearance. One is the geology itself: mining towns are located purely and simply where the minerals are found, without regard to climate, topography, or the availability of water, food, or level ground for building. A second factor is the rapid onset of mining rushes. When populations climb almost overnight from a handful of people to several thousand residents, planning is inevitably haphazard and buildings and services develop in an almost random manner. A third factor is the transient nature of mining which inexorably depletes the resource on which it relies. Whether in 5 years or 50, miners and mine owners know that they will eventually be moving on. This has a particularly strong influence on building materials used. Bell has observed that in contrast to farmers and pastoralists, miners rarely used locally available building materials such as stone, bark or local timber. Rather, they relied on manufactured products imported to the mining district along with the supplies for the mines. Thus miners' cottages are made of sawn timber and corrugated iron, often imported from overseas. When the mines were exhausted, all the buildings in town could be relocated to the site of the next rush, as happened at Paradise in Queensland (Prangnell et al. 2005).

Mining towns were sometimes laid out on a formal grid, such as Broken Hill, Kalgoorlie, Moonta and Wallaroo, where government surveyors or company engineers were able to impose order on subsequent occupation. Other towns, however, particularly those of the chaotic early days of the gold rushes in Victoria and New South Wales, were often linear and dispersed. Their layout was determined by the location of mineral resources and water, rather than the ideals of officialdom. By the time surveyors arrived to lay out townships, land was already claimed, mined and occupied. Grid-based town sites had to avoid the mining activity and were thus located adjacent to the diggings, leaving the initial, expedient pattern largely in place.

The modern city of Castlemaine retains evidence of this division between diggings and government town. The official town site was surveyed in 1852. Its long rectilinear grid of streets on both sides of Barker's Creek includes the former Government Camp with its police station, gaol and courthouse high on the hill above the flats where the miners worked. On the high ground across the creek the centre of mercantile and civic activity was laid out with banks, shops, churches, the post office, and, later, the art gallery, mechanics' institute and botanical gardens. The town and Government Camp presented all the features of an ordered and civil society, only a decade after the first miners arrived (Lawrence 2005:286).

Adjacent to the official town site of Castlemaine is Chewton, the straggling town of the miners. Its houses and shops stretch for 5 km along the Melbourne road

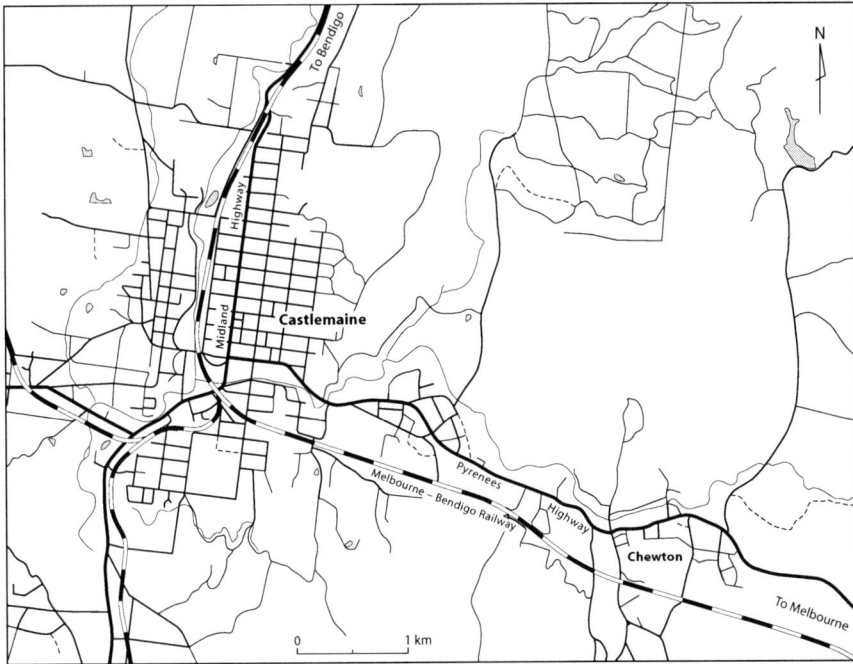

Fig. 7.7 Contrasting town plans of Castlemaine and Chewton in Victoria (drawn by Ming Wei)

running south-east from Castlemaine, following the course of Forest Creek where the gold was found (Fig. 7.7). The road itself is narrow and meandering, quite unlike the broad thoroughfares of Castlemaine. In this area the diggings and miners' rights took precedence over rigid surveys. The main road winds awkwardly around the remains of old mine workings and stamp batteries, and many cottages sit directly beside the road.

This divided layout was no accident. Although less pronounced, it is also apparent in other mining centres such as Ballarat and Bendigo. There too the early diggings were on flats along creeks. Modern streets in those districts are narrower with irregular bends and twists around what were once active mining claims. On the hills overlooking the diggings are the wide rectilinear streets of the surveyed towns, with government facilities such as the police station, courthouse, gaol and post office located on what was once the Government Camp, and the establishment facilities of bank, art gallery and botanical gardens that proclaimed wealth and success. This was a convenient and expeditious arrangement that left the main auriferous ground available for mining, but it was also calculated to provide the authorities with a viewpoint from which the diggings could be easily and comprehensively monitored. In Ballarat today it is still possible to stand behind the art gallery on what was once the site of the Government Camp. Troops were mustered here for the assault on the Eureka Stockade in 1854, and although obscured now by trees and newer buildings, the former diggings in the valley are still easily visible. Even more visible on the opposite hill is the site of the stockade itself, now marked by an interpretive centre and prominent Eureka flag. From their vantage point across the valley the troopers would have kept an even more constant vigil in that nervous December.

Goldfields towns made important public statements about order, responsibility and respectability. Government-surveyed townships were created with enormous public and private wealth in the 1860s and 1870s. Fine buildings in stone and brick featured imposing classical columns, Italianate porticoes, gothic arches and delicate Victorian wrought iron. The city founders who built these structures were creating an impression of respectability and permanence that expressed their social position, energy and good fortune. Their housing, civic institutions and mansions all symbolically expressed the personal and collective progress they managed to achieve in only one generation.

At the same time, the miners' towns with their straggling narrow streets were no less a statement of achievement, because many of the houses and businesses along those streets were owned by their occupants. The miners were not as rich as the mine owners, but many had carefully saved the gold they won and used their savings to build and buy their homes. At a time when the rate of home ownership in England was, at most, 10 percent, in Ballarat East, the miners' town, 90 percent of the homes were owner-occupied (Davison 2000:12–14). The houses they built are still known as miners' cottages – simple, symmetrical double-fronted weatherboard structures – and they are a distinctive architectural style on the goldfields. Their ubiquitousness symbolises the success that could be achieved by ordinary working people on the goldfields and represents the Australian dream of home-ownership to this day.

Environments

Among the many upheavals brought by the gold rush was the impact it had on the natural environment. The effects of mining ranged from erosion and siltation to pollution and deforestation. These impacts were often permanent and are still apparent today in the physical landscape of mining areas. Mining interests, both great and small, were permitted a large measure of control over colonial forests and water sources, at a time when relatively little was known about the full extent of those resources and their future significance (Powell 1976:37–41; Taylor 1998:21–28). Most of the early goldfields in Victoria and New South Wales were located in wooded hills, ranges and valleys which had previously been lightly used or virtually ignored. These ecosystems could scarcely contain the destruction wrought by mining.

When miners rushed a new field, they tore up the ground and destroyed the vegetation, leaving little shelter against wind or dust. They worked streams and rivers for almost their entire length, often several times over and often using different techniques. Sometimes the result was a mass of shallow holes and humps of dirt. In other places huge pits spread over many acres of ground (McGowan 2001). Louisa Meredith, visiting from Tasmania, thought the result "irredeemably hideous"

(Bolton 1992:69). Alluvial gold mining resulted in heavily scoured creek beds and gullies worked down to bedrock. The sludge discharged from puddling machines and sluicing flowed into creeks and rivers downstream. At Bendigo, the slimy sludge from the treatment of gold buried roads, fences, farms and bridges. As waterholes and creek beds were filled in, water levels rose to flood adjacent farmland. Geoffrey Serle described the impact on the early alluvial fields: "The grass was all gone, the trees all slaughtered, everywhere mud and slush, heaps of yellow soil and yellow puddles, the hills turned inside out and honeycombed. . .a by-product of progress, a crime against nature" (Serle 1963:71–72).

Elsewhere, areas subject to hydraulic sluicing resemble massive quarries. At one site along the Shoalhaven River in south-east New South Wales, for example, the sluiced area is more than 300 m long and up to 30 m high (McGowan 2001:89). On other rivers, bucket dredges used a continuous series of buckets to excavate the bottom of streams and creeks, cutting a passage as they went. The excavated gravels were processed on the dredge and then dumped back into the holes made by the buckets. Melbourne's *Age* newspaper called them "desolating dredges", converting fertile land into "a permanent waste of shingle" (9 January 1913). The effect on dredged areas was immediate and seemingly permanent. Parts of streams flowing into the Mitta Mitta and Ovens rivers in north-east Victoria resembled little more than a series of inter-connected dredge ponds along much of their length. With few attempts ever made to reclaim these areas, natural rehabilitation has been very slow.

Mining also had a voracious appetite for timber, deforesting great swathes of countryside. In 1873, for example, timber use on the Victorian goldfields included more than 1.1 million tons of wood fuel for steam engines, along with 2.3 million props and cap pieces, 4.3 million laths and slabs, and more than 8 million sawn feet of building timber (Parliament of Victoria 1874). Newly arrived miners from England and Europe brought with them a tradition of "basic needs", the right to cut forest wood from commons (Wright 1989:88). For many others, cutting down trees was virtually a hobby. Author and traveller William Howitt reported in 1855: "It is amazing what a number of trees they fell. No sooner have they done their day's work, than they commence felling trees, which you hear falling continually with a crash, on one side of you or the other" (Howitt 1972 [1855]:177).

The red and brown stringybarks that grew on the goldfields of central Victoria were well suited to the needs of the miners. The bark peeled off easily to form large sheets which dried into hard boards. These made the walls and roofs of huts, as well as seats and tables. The timber was easily split into posts and rails and slabs for huts, and also burnt well even when green. Immense quantities of these and other timbers were consumed by the gold miners of Victoria. The Bullarook Forest, for example, which extended for 700,000 acres across the Great Dividing Range, had been reduced to one-seventh of its original size by 1880 and was later described as a "ruined forest" (Tucker 1899). Although the impact on forests was dramatic, the ready availability of large volumes of timber helped sustain the development of the goldfields during the nineteenth century. The effects of such damage can be identified in forest and woodland areas today, with a low stump at the base of a cluster of one or more re-growth stems.

Ironically, while mining drastically reshaped the natural environment, in some places it has also helped to preserve native forests. Much of the public land in gold-fields regions was originally reserved from selection in order to protect the mining interests (Wright 1989:154–155). In the 1860s and 1870s the slow decline of mining combined with increasing political pressure to make land available for selection meant that mining reserves and goldfields commons shrank in size as farmland was released around their margins, but sizeable cores remained as government reserves. These have become the national parks that modern generations know as "the bush".

Gold-mining Communities

While much of the archaeology of mining has documented the remains of ore extraction and processing, Australian archaeologists have always been equally interested in studying the communities that arose on the diggings. Definitions of "community" have been intensively debated for many years by sociologists, anthropologists and historians. However, it generally refers to a group of people interacting daily and living in close proximity. Face-to-face interaction is an essential element of community, and the more frequent this personal interaction, the stronger the sense of community. Interaction is facilitated by social institutions such as church and school, by commercial networks such as work and store, and by personal relations including residential proximity and kinship. The spatial organisation of a settlement reflects and structures the kinds of interaction possible between individuals. If a settlement is small, informal meetings take place frequently and easily. However, if a settlement is more dispersed, it may require more formalised occasions to bring people together.

On goldfields the structure of both the settlement and community depended on the nature of the mineral deposit. On shallow alluvial fields small groups of miners could work independently, with settlement scattered over a wide area. This fostered a complex mix of individualism, co-operation and egalitarianism in community relationships (Douglass 1998). Deeper and more complex ore bodies, however, demanded the capital and technology provided by large companies. Shareholding and wage labour created a very different kind of community. Settlement clustered around the mines and ore processing facilities, and social groups were defined more by income and occupational status. In archaeology the smaller communities have been more prominent, both those on shallow alluvial fields and small company towns. This reflects the higher survival rate of sites and material in bush areas, and the more active management they receive from heritage professionals. A great deal of work has focused on Chinese miners, but several non-Chinese communities have also been analysed. Three studies that illustrate the archaeology of mining communities are those of Dolly's Creek in Victoria, Chinese miners in the south-eastern highlands of New South Wales and miners on the dry outback goldfield of Arltunga in the Northern Territory.

Dolly's Creek

At Dolly's Creek and the Moorabool diggings, just south of Ballarat, Susan Lawrence has studied the industrial and domestic remains of a small settlement occupied from the late 1850s into the 1880s (Lawrence 1995, 2000). Through the integration of documentary and archaeological research, she identified a distinctive kind of mining community that formed as the early days of the gold rush gave way to longer-term mining interests. On rich deposits, mining became dominated by large-scale capital works and complex engineering systems. Many people, however, continued to mine for gold at a small, local scale, and the communities they formed were both widespread and persistent, lasting for several decades on diggings around the country. Subsistence miners chose not to become wage labourers for big mining companies, but instead retained their independence by working on "poor man's diggings", forming small communities of individuals and families. Such miners preferred to earn 10 shillings independently rather than £1 as a wage labourer, and clung to the hope that their lucky day would come. They searched for gold, but also worked in seasonal jobs in order to sustain themselves. This mode of life and work involved women and children too; the gardens and flocks they tended provided both food and extra income. Archaeological and documentary evidence at Dolly's Creek and the Moorabool reveals the transformation from rough diggings to settled community, and how the change was negotiated in the demographic structure of the settlement, in the homes built and gardens planted, and in the consumer goods used and the foods eaten.

The industrial remains indicate that the miners on the Moorabool either formed small local companies or held miner's rights. Evidence for the diggings consisted of large areas of mullocky ground and several hydraulic sluices, all typical of shallow alluvial goldfields. Details of the settlement plan and the excavated houses demonstrate how subsistence miners were able to succeed on a field with low returns, and how they used the provisions of the miner's right to their advantage. The miner's right was a product of the Eureka Rebellion, replacing the earlier, expensive mining license with a cheaper (£1 a year) entitlement. The holder of a miner's right could dig for gold, vote at parliamentary elections and draft mining laws at locally elected courts. The holder could also claim a quarter-acre block of land on which to build a house and graze livestock on common land (Armstrong 1901:18; Birrell 1998:72–73; Lawrence 2005:288–289). The miner's right thus made home ownership possible, a proud achievement for men who in Europe had scarcely dreamed of such independence.

Survey of the area documented a widely dispersed settlement, with most of the houses scattered thinly over a network of hills and steep, narrow gullies (Fig. 7.8). Holding a miner's right, those at the Moorabool could build houses on the public land of the Morrisons Goldfields Common, and they did so according to their own preferences rather than according to the systematic plots of a government surveyor. It was a community of neighbourhoods, clustered loosely around the settlements of Morrisons, Dolly's Creek and Tea Tree Creek. Services gradually evolved, such

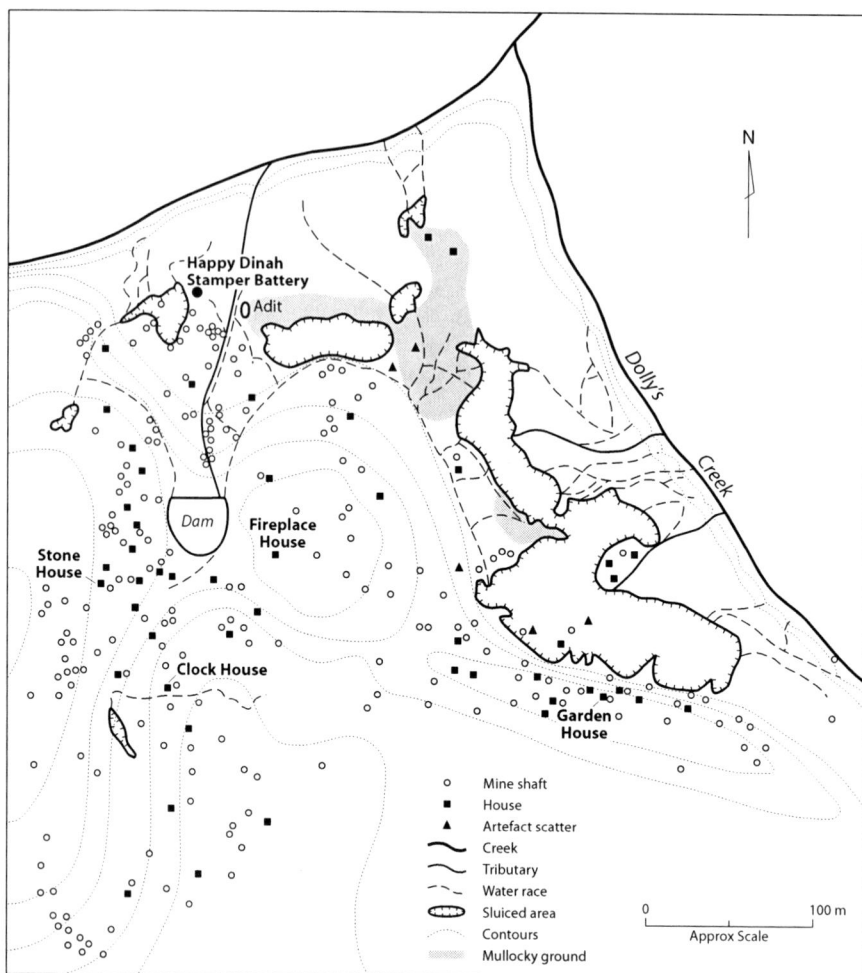

Fig. 7.8 Plan of the "poor man's diggings" at Dolly's Creek, Victoria

as a post office, schools, hotels, churches and a cemetery (Lawrence 2000:55–57). Buildings were dispersed along roads and tracks that linked the district together.

Documentary research at Dolly's Creek indicated that young families were common on subsistence goldfields. Dolly's Creek had a population of around 600 people, mostly men and women in their 20s and 30s. There were large numbers of children present, but very few elderly people. Large kin networks often developed in such areas, as early arrivals encouraged friends and relatives to migrate and as migrants intermarried. Networks of kinship ties provided social support, especially for women, and eased the strain of settling into a harsh new environment. Family members also contributed the labour that made subsistence mining sustainable.

There was little direct evidence of women or children in the four houses that were excavated, but the buildings and assemblages nevertheless demonstrate a way of life that was becoming more settled than the rough-and-tumble of the initial gold rush years. The buildings were mostly made of canvas, typical of the rough, temporary structures generally associated with goldfields architecture. Level terraces had been dug into hillsides, each providing space for a small house of about 16 feet by 12 feet (4.9 × 3.7 m). Square-cut iron nails and round wire nails were used to hold the timber frames together. Brass tacks were used to fasten calico covers in place, although window glass was also found at the houses. Ditches were dug to channel rainwater away from the base of the walls.

Fireplaces dominated the homes, occupying most of one end of the tents. The fireplaces were built of roughly shaped quartzite blocks held together with mud mortar. When the houses were abandoned, the mud washed out from between the stones and the fireplaces collapsed, leaving a mound of stones up to 1 m high. While still standing, contemporary descriptions suggest that the fireplaces would have had chimneys made of wood, corrugated iron or green bullock hides stretched around branches. Sometimes a barrel was added at the top to give extra height.

A fragment of building material from one house at Dolly's Creek reveals a complex story of home improvement. The fragment comprised a multi-layered sandwich of paper, fabric and tin. In the centre was a layer of calico, the original tent. The calico had been strengthened by the addition of several layers of newspaper and cardboard. Sheets of tin had been nailed on the exterior, making the structure snug and watertight. The interior was covered in wallpaper with a delicate foliage pattern, completing the transformation from a temporary tent to a permanent home.

This fragment was recovered from a building of more solid construction than most on the goldfield, with the lower walls built of roughly shaped blocks of stone. It had at least two glass windows, and a solid wooden door with iron hinges, a strong lock and a brass doorknob. It may have been used as a store or pub, with the walls providing some protection for the goods inside, which would otherwise have been vulnerable in a canvas tent to a thief cutting a hole with a knife. As such, the stone building may also have been a residence, used in the same way storekeepers lived in their shops in inner-city areas. The other artefacts found in the building included nails stored in an old pickle jar, a stack of shovels and a cask. While these items belong in a shop, the fireplace for warmth and cooking and the floral wallpaper suggest a home as well (Lawrence 2001a:257–258).

Portable consumer goods surviving within the archaeological record reveal dimensions of goldfields homes that would otherwise be lost or hidden. One such item was a brass mantle clock case recovered from one of the houses at Dolly's Creek (Fig. 7.9). It stood 7 inches high and rested on two curved feet. The space for the central dial is surrounded by a moulded floral motif and the original surface was probably gilded to produce a French ormolu effect. The mechanism itself, probably a 2-inch dial with a white enamel face, was available for separate purchase as a mass-produced and commonplace item. While only the affluent could afford to carry large pieces of furniture with them, smaller household goods like these could be transported more easily.

Fig. 7.9 Brass case of a mantle clock from Dolly's Creek, Victoria (photo S. Lawrence)

The written evidence of goldfields life in the early days of the rush emphasises the almost universal use of metal dishes: a kettle or billy, a dutch oven, a tin plate and mug and a knife, fork and spoon. The archaeological evidence, however, provides a direct and dramatic contrast, indicating that the later subsistence miners had different habits. Quantities of broken crockery were recovered from all four houses excavated at Dolly's Creek, suggesting that ceramic plates and cups were widely used. At least 76 dishes were represented in the Dolly's Creek assemblage – these were the ones broken and thrown away. Each household would have used many others each day. All these dishes were made from common, inexpensive white earthenwares. More than 40 different patterns were found, although Asiatic Pheasant and

Willow were the most common. No household bothered to display matching sets of tableware. Instead, diverse patterns in blue, mulberry, sepia, green, red and black were used. Documentary evidence suggests tin was preferred because it was tough, lightweight and portable. Pottery was fragile, heavy and impractical. Nevertheless, itinerant goldseekers clearly chose to use crockery in their bush settlements, preferring to eat their meals and drink their tea from ceramic plates and cups whenever possible. Miners and their families were trying to create more permanent settlements and to signal their membership of respectable society. Their crockery symbolises a powerful longing for order and domestic predictability, for a secure base upon which to build, accumulate and improve. Perhaps crockery was a tangible way of reaching for what historian David Goodman has called "quietness", a settled peace-of-mind that many outside observers felt was lacking on the goldfields (Goodman 1994:189–192).

The houses built by subsistence miners sought a balance between freedom of movement and basic domestic comfort. Although small in size, they were mostly used for sleeping, storage and cooking; otherwise people lived outdoors. The household goods inside were both expedient and fashionable. Some have been recovered from the excavations, while documentary records suggest what others may have been. Although furniture has not survived, diarists write of bush carpenters making chairs, tables and beds on the spot from odds and ends of branches and posts. They also describe sacking carpets, and chintz wall coverings not unlike the excavated wallpaper fragment. The colours and patterns of the ceramic dishes also served as bright household ornament as well as tableware while fragments of slate pencils, clay pipes, ink bottles and a thimble and needle suggest a rounded life of study, work and relaxation. At night rooms were lit by fires in hearths, supplemented by candles stuck in bottles, or by kerosene lamps; parts of brass lamp bases and glass chimneys were found at two of the houses. In the 1860s kerosene was still a recent innovation which was in the process of displacing whale oil, so the households were very up-to-date in some ways.

Another important characteristic of subsistence mining was the dependence on food the miners produced themselves. By the 1860s the provisions of the miner's right and the establishment of the goldfields common meant it was possible to keep domestic animals and to grow crops and vegetables. From the archaeological evidence at Dolly's Creek, it is clear that mining families were often creative and enterprising in working their land. At three of the houses, fist-sized quartz cobbles had been arranged in deliberate patterns to form pathways and borders around garden beds. Documentary sources reveal that gardens such as this provided a wide range of fruit and vegetables. Scraps of excavated bone came from cattle, pigs, sheep, goats, rabbits and chickens. Grazing animals could have been kept on the commons, tended by the women and children of the family, while rabbits could be trapped there as well. In addition to meat, cattle and goats could provide milk, butter and possibly cheese, while chickens provided eggs. Although popular accounts of life on the Australian goldfields refer to endless meals of mutton, damper and tea, the archaeological evidence from Dolly's Creek reveals both a more varied diet and a more active response to transforming the local landscape.

Legislative changes in the 1860s and 1870s encouraged the selection of small farms in goldfields regions. By the 1880s, subsistence mining had largely been pushed to the margins of colonial life. As it became less viable, farming assumed greater importance. Many of those who took up the newly available land were mining families already settled in the area. Small-scale farming preserved some of the independence that the goldseekers treasured and often allowed part-time mining to be continued on the side.

Although small and obscure, Dolly's Creek was nevertheless part of much wider social and economic networks. The diggings existed because of European industrialisation and international expansion. They were part of a gold rush that was global in scale, with participants involved in one of the largest and most rapid mass migrations in human history. Life on the diggings was shaped by long-term cultural trends towards mass consumer culture. The families at Dolly's Creek may have resisted capitalised wage labour and held onto traditional forms of organisation, but they were also emphatically modern. The industrial and commercial revolutions made cheap, mass-produced goods of all kinds readily available for even working people on the fringes of settler society. Furnishings and household goods are basic consumer items and were acquired enthusiastically at Dolly's Creek. People used accurate, standardised clocks and watches, fashionable corrective spectacles and clean, efficient kerosene lamps. In taking advantage of these consumer goods, however, they had to reconcile their lack of permanence on a poor man's goldfield, and the possibility of moving elsewhere to find gold. They made their choices and acquired items that were small and portable. They built rough, functional houses from local materials, but added touches such as wallpaper to turn houses into homes.

Arltunga

The success of gold mining in Victoria from the 1850s prompted the eager search for new fields in increasingly remote areas. Prospectors pushed far inland with picks and shovels and wheelbarrows, while speculators made and lost fortunes on the Adelaide and Ballarat exchanges. Rich discoveries were made at Kalgoorlie and Coolgardie in the 1890s, and the legend of Lasseter's lost reef was an added incentive to search in the Depression times of the 1930s (McGowan 2006). The harsh reality for most outback miners, however, was hard work with little reward. Machinery, equipment and supplies were hauled laboriously over hundreds of kilometres from the nearest port or railhead and later abandoned when claims cut out or mineral prices fell below the cost of production and transport.

One such place was the Arltunga goldfield, located more than 100 km east of Alice Springs. The field began as a ruby mine in the 1880s, but miners shifted their attention to gold around 1890. Isolation, limited supplies and lack of water were perennial problems at such a remote outpost of European activity. The South Australian colonial government, however, was keen to promote industry in its vast inland territory, and so it commissioned improvements such as wells for water, more frequent mail services, a stamp battery and cyanide works. A small population, usually of around 50 European prospectors, and up to 100 Aboriginal people, made a living on the goldfield. Aboriginal men worked as labourers, and Aboriginal women served as domestics and sexual partners (Birmingham 1997:10). By 1911, when the Federal Government took control of the Northern Territory, the Arltunga field was in decline, and only sporadic mining occurred thereafter. Archaeological recording of the area by Kate Holmes in the 1970s and 1980s showed how residents coped with the demands of living in such an isolated and arid environment (Holmes 1983, 1989).

The Arltunga field covers an area of almost 40 km^2 and features the remains of mines, mullock heaps, wells, buildings and tracks. Stone was widely used for buildings, partly because there was little timber available, but also because most of the miners came from South Australia where building in stone was common (Fig. 7.10). Stone was also cooler in the high summer temperatures. Aboriginal residents constructed curved stone walls that acted as windbreaks alongside their housing. Excavation at one of the police station buildings revealed the remains of a garden bed adjacent to the verandah. The garden was dug out of the underlying bedrock and backfilled with a combination of gravely soil, goat bones, woody material, manure and a fine brown fill. Historic photos reveal the success of this venture, with grape vines growing thickly along the verandah and shading the building from the westerly heat of summer (Holmes 1989:46). Otherwise, however, the lack of water and poor soils made market gardening very difficult. A lone Chinese gardener succeeded in growing vegetables at Arltunga, but in 1896 he was threatened with eviction by European miners fearful of invading Chinese hordes.

Fig. 7.10 Stone house at Arltunga in the Northern Territory (photo G. Jackman)

Excavation of the White Range settlement store at Arltunga revealed a partial basement cut into the bedrock below the stone walls of the store. A 5-m long ventilation tunnel extended south-eastwards from the basement, in the direction of the prevailing winds. Protected from animal intrusions by wire mesh, the tunnel helped with passive cooling of the space below the store. Nearby features included stone wall footings and chimney foundations that appeared to be part of a domestic area. The structures included a large building, 10 × 4 m, with a carefully levelled floor, and walls made from light brush and canvas (Holmes 1983:84). Numerous pieces of slate were also found over the site, which were too thick to have been used as roofing tiles. Instead, they probably came from the slate bed of a snooker or billiard table. Several pieces had holes for counter sunk screws and curves for the pockets. The table was probably brought to Arltunga by Patrick O'Neill in 1903, at the height of activity on the goldfield. Several other people had had similar plans, but the rush was over so quickly that no other tables arrived. The transport of such an unwieldy item over hundreds of kilometres of rough roads indicates tremendous confidence in the future of the field, in spite of its isolation. Such optimism was misplaced, however, and the billiard room remained a forlorn testament to a goldfield that soon faded away.

Chinese Miners in the South-Eastern Highlands

A very different kind of gold-mining community was formed in the highlands of south-eastern New South Wales during the nineteenth century. Chinese miners were active in the region, forming distinct and separate communities from contemporary white settlements, but little of their experiences or contribution has entered the mainstream history of the region. Lindsay Smith (1998, 2003, 2006) has recorded the distribution of the Chinese settlements, mapped their features and carried out excavations in each in order to build up a detailed picture of the organisation of the Chinese community in the region (Fig. 7.11). As there is scarcely any documentary record of this community, Smith's work provides an unparalleled insight into an otherwise unknown group of people.

Chinese people came to Australia in highly organised labour groups, sometimes up to several hundred men at a time, usually under the direction of a leader or "headman" (see Chapter 9). Under the credit-ticket system their passages were paid by a wealthy merchant, for whom they then worked for a set period until the passage money was repaid. Upon the discovery of a new goldfield, merchants would arrange for the set-up of temporary tent camps, with stores and often a temple, to which new arrivals would then be directed. As the Chinese population became more established, tents were abandoned in favour of more durable huts. These settlements functioned as "homogeneous and segregated communities" until the end of the nineteenth century (Smith 2006:2).

By the early 1860s, most of the 13,000 Chinese people in New South Wales lived and worked on the colony's goldfields (Wang 2001:199). In the south-eastern highlands, the miners worked alluvial claims in groups of 10–30 men, lead by headmen

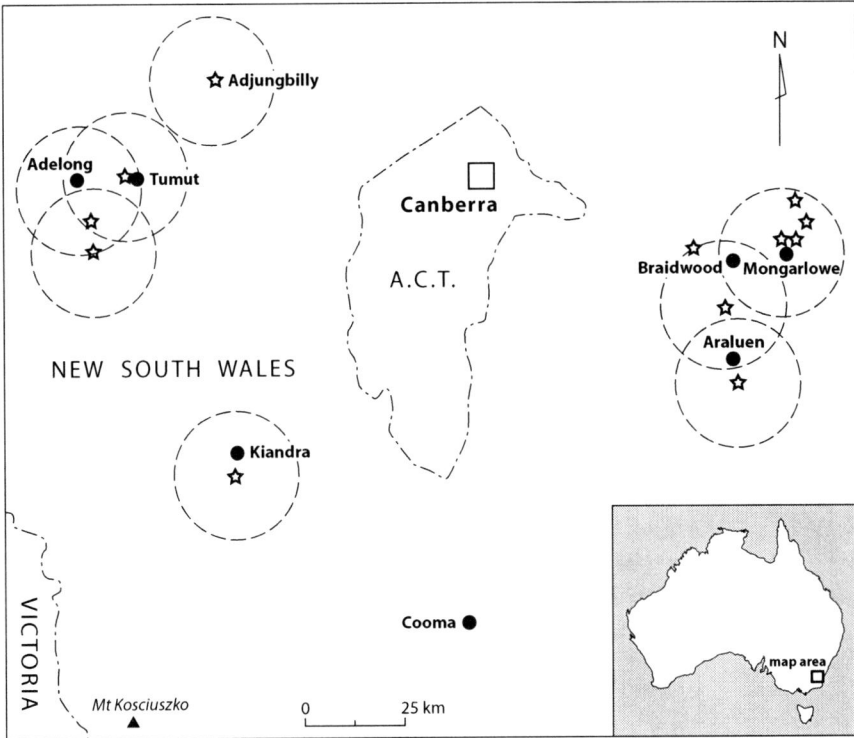

Fig. 7.11 Location of Chinese settlements in the highlands of south-eastern New South Wales, with stars indicating Chinese occupation sites and rings indicating settlement systems (after Smith 2006:233–237)

who acted as brokers between local authorities, the population of Chinese miners, and clan and ethnic organisations in China. Chinese women were generally very rare on the Australian goldfields, partly due to the expense of passage and the humble origins of most miners, along with the preference for women to remain behind in order to maintain family links with ancestral homes. Some Chinese women did make the trip, generally the wives of merchants and headmen, and some Chinese men did form relationships with non-Chinese women in Australia, but on the whole Chinese goldfields settlements were male-dominated places.

Through an extensive programme of survey and excavation Lindsay Smith has been able to identify nine Chinese settlement systems within three areas around Braidwood, Tumut and Kiandra, all in the high country south, east and west of Canberra. At the centre of each settlement network was a self-contained village on a major goldfield, close to but separate from its European counterpart. It contained the essential elements of a traditional Chinese community, including a store, temple, communal oven, cemetery, dwellings and gardens. Associated with each of these villages was a network of smaller work camps, which exploited the alluvial gold along the major rivers and creeks. These camps were much more basic, containing only individual dwellings and a communal oven, and miners depended on the parent village for supplies and social support. Smith found a high degree of similarity between each of the communities in their physical layout, landscape aspect and housing patterns, and identified a transplantation of traditional Chinese material, religious and community structures to the goldfields.

Smith identified more than 180 individual Chinese dwellings in the region, primarily in camps of less than a dozen households. The houses were generally smaller than those of European miners, with only 6–8 m^2 of internal space, and they were clustered tightly together with no concept of "street". Houses had floors of tamped, or packed earth, and wall footings of random rubble masonry, with light timber framing above. The houses had no chimneys, but featured instead an internal hearth next to the doorway. Some of the cooking for Chinese miners was done in communal ovens. These were generally circular in shape and built of large stones, and those in the main villages stood up to 1 m or more in height. Ovens in the satellite camps were smaller, only about 0.5 m high and less solidly built. The village ovens were used for the communal roasting of large animals, especially pigs, which featured prominently at traditional Chinese ceremonial feasts. Similar structures, though with slight regional variations, have also been recorded by archaeologists in other mining regions around Australia where there were large Chinese communities, including the Palmer River in Queensland, Pine Creek in the Northern Territory, and in north-eastern Tasmania (Bell 1995; Gaughwin 1995).

In addition to dwellings and ovens, the larger villages had several other amenities as well. One important facility was the store, and Smith has identified at least 19 Chinese stores in south-eastern New South Wales during the nineteenth century, with several villages supporting two or more. They functioned as focal points for the Chinese communities, and sold familiar Chinese items such as crockery, foodstuffs, beverages and opium paraphernalia. Archaeologically, stores were identifiable because the buildings were generally a little larger than typical miners' huts, rectangular in shape, and built from timber rather than calico. They generally had larger and more diverse artefact assemblages, and the frequency of Chinese materials on the sites, especially ceramics, supports the view that separate trade networks were well established between China and Australia by the 1860s (L. Smith 2003:27; McCarthy 1988). Goods made in China were imported to Australia by Chinese merchants for use by resident Chinese people. Such items were mostly used for the transport, storage, cooking or consumption of food and drink. This pattern has also been identified in other overseas Chinese communities, including California, where it appears that labourers working off their passage money in the mining camps were required to purchase goods at the stores owned by the merchants who had provided their tickets (Praetzellis and Praetzellis 2001).

Most of the villages had a small wooden temple or "Joss" house in order to meet the spiritual needs of the miners. The term "joss" was an eighteenth-century corruption of the Portuguese *deos* (from Latin *deus*) meaning god. The primary function of the temple in the Chinese community is as a building for the worship of ancestors and deities. People visit the temple as needed, rather than as part of a weekly congregation (see Chapter 9). This meant that nineteenth-century Chinese temples were usually small, as they did not need to accommodate large gatherings of people. Temples were built all over Australia, wherever there was a Chinese community, and surviving examples can still be found in South Melbourne, Atherton (Queensland), Bendigo and Sydney (Grimwade 2003; Wegars 2003). Smith has noted that in the New South Wales highlands the temples were located at a distance from other buildings and were positioned to give each site good *feng shui*. In traditional Chinese culture *feng shui* (literally "wind" "water") is a system of spirit influences inhabiting the natural landscape, and the means of dealing with these influences in the position of buildings and graves (see Chapter 12). On the goldfields, the preferred location was one overlooking flowing water and with land sloping upwards behind the structure. From the archaeological evidence Smith has been able to determine that temples were generally larger than domestic huts and were also more substantially built, with weatherboard walls and timber floors in contrast to canvas walls and dirt floors.

The satellite camps were located on the diggings themselves and provided shelter and cooking facilities for the miners. These were not, however, independent and self-sufficient communities like Dolly's Creek. Instead, the archaeological remains indicate that they were organised around traditional Chinese practices such as co-operative working and the preference for communally prepared meals. The occupants of the small camps relied on the larger community centres for their provisions, for social interactions, and for their spiritual needs, and each of the camps was located within a radius of about 10 miles (16 km) of a larger village. The central villages appear to have provided for the wider needs of the Chinese miners. They supplied not only essential daily requirements through the establishment of co-operative stores, gardens and individual dwellings, but also provided for social and religious requirements with their temples, ceremonial ovens and cemeteries. The centres also reinforced traditional Chinese practices, including co-operative working arrangements and social activities, and worship and burial customs. They allowed the Chinese to retain their separateness from their European counterparts and provided focal points for the smaller camps in each region.

In both Chinese and European gold-mining communities, there was thus an important element of interdependence and co-operation, both economic and social, which served to strengthen communal bonds and provide each member with a sense of place and belonging. Connections with the outside world were also vital, not only as a source of consumer goods, but as a reminder of the wider cultural context which gave people's lives meaning. Although the European miners at Dolly's Creek and the Chinese miners in the south-eastern highlands were separated by language and cultural practices, the extent to which they relied on other community members for support was a common element in all their lives.

Copper

The technologies, ways of life and cultural landscapes created by gold mining have parallels in other branches of metals mining. Two industries that were particularly

prominent in colonial Australia were those of tin and copper mining. Copper helped
established the fortunes of South Australia years before gold was to have such a
dramatic impact on the other Australian colonies. In June 1845 a rich copper lode
was discovered by a shepherd, Thomas Pickett, in the dry hills of Burra, 150 km
north of Adelaide. Similar discoveries quickly followed 90 km south at Kapunda
and later in the "copper triangle" towns of Moonta, Kadina and Wallaroo on the
Yorke Peninsula (Fig. 7.12). In the first few years, ore from the Burra was hauled
to the surface, then sorted and bagged and sent by slow bullock wagon to Adelaide,
where it was shipped to Wales for smelting. Only the richness of the Burra ores, containing on average 20 percent copper, allowed such expensive handling. By 1849,
however, Burra had its own smelter, with coal hauled inland from Port Adelaide or
from Port Wakefield, at the head of the Gulf of St Vincent. The "Monster Mine"
employed more than 2,000 men and boys, most of them Cornish, in mining, smelting and carting the ores. Within a few years the value of the copper the copper towns
produced exceeded the value of South Australia's wheat and wool combined, and
by the late 1840s the Burra mine had made South Australia the richest of all the
Australian colonies (Blainey 1978:112). On the eve of the gold rush in 1851 Burra
was Australia's largest inland centre, with a population of at least 5,000 people, but
production declined after 1860, and underground mining ceased in 1867. Arrival of
the railway in 1870 established Burra as a centre for agriculture in the district, but

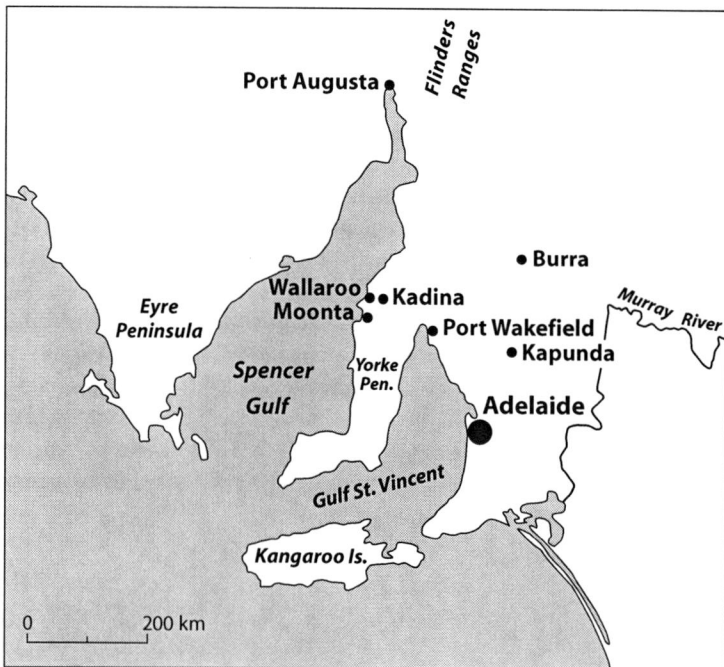

Fig. 7.12 Location of copper-mining centres in South Australia

attempts to work the mine by open-cut methods were mostly unprofitable, and the Burra mine closed in 1877 (Auhl 1980:9; Drew 1988:7).

Considerable evidence of the mines and processing plants survives at all of the copper towns, as does the layout and architectural heritage of the residential and business districts. There has been little excavation, but a number of heritage studies have documented the industrial and architectural remains. Burra is the best known of the towns, in part because it played host to the Australia ICOMOS conference in 1979 that established guidelines for best practice in heritage management, subsequently enshrined in the Burra Charter (Marquis-Kyle and Walker 1992). Surviving buildings and archaeological sites at Burra reflect the influences that shaped the community, including rapid growth, labour and housing shortages, and attempts at corporate control. Architectural historian Peter Bell's (1990) study of one early house reveals some of the difficulties faced in the early years when the burgeoning population meant that building materials were in short supply. The house Bell analysed was a seven-room structure made of stone and timber and built in several stages, starting in 1849. In contrast to common practice elsewhere, he found that the oldest part of the house was the timber section, and that the stone portions were the later additions. Even more remarkable, the timber used to build the house had come from the east coast of North America and from northern Europe. The fabric of the house demonstrates that during the boom, labour was more expensive than materials, and timber, which could be erected quickly and with minimal skill, was a cheaper alternative than stone. In later years as mining declined there was less available cash to pay for expensive imported timber and there was less employment locally so it made more sense to build with the cheap, locally available stone even though it required more skill and was more labour intensive.

Stone buildings are common in Burra, and indeed throughout South Australia where timber is comparatively scarce. Many stone buildings were constructed by the South Australian Mining Association. The company built rows of cottages based on old European designs, with stone walls, earthen floors and no verandahs. The company established a version of corporate paternalism, levying a compulsory sixpence a week from workers' wages to finance a sickness and disability scheme, as well as building chapels, supplying drinking water, running an abattoir and establishing a cemetery, all on company land and at company expense. The town laid out by the company on its land was called Kooringa, but it was only one of several settlements around the mine. Others included Redruth, Hampton, Llwchwr and Aberdeen (Fig. 7.13). The village names reflect the diverse cultural origins of Burra's workers, with specialist miners, smelters, labourers and others arriving from Cornwall, Wales, Scotland, Ireland and Germany. There were also market gardeners from China and muleteers from Chile. Hundreds also worked as wood-cutters, shepherds and bullock drivers. The rapid growth of Burra, however, along with a desire to break the company's monopoly and its high rents, resulted in the Government survey of the Redruth township in 1849, along with the privately surveyed settlements of Aberdeen, Llwchwr and Hampton.

There was also a large settlement along the Burra Creek and its tributaries, where more than 1,500 people lived in caves excavated in the bank of the creek.

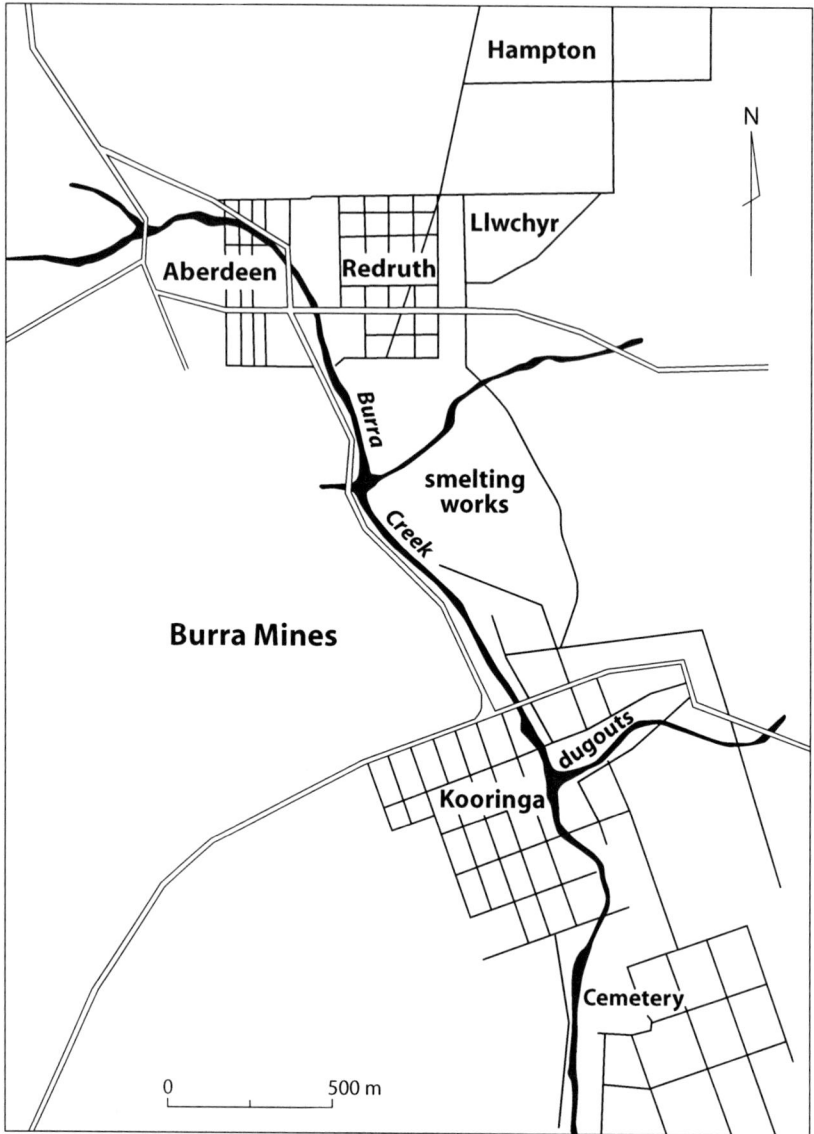

Fig. 7.13 Plan of the Burra township

This appears to have resulted from several factors, including a rapidly increasing population and shortage of housing, as well as the high rents charged by the South Australian Mining Association. Some of the dwellings were simple, one-room dug-outs with holes for doors and windows. Others were more substantial, with weatherboard fronts to keep out the weather, along with glazed windows, timber doors, whitewashed or papered walls, clay-cut shelves and carpets on the floors

Fig. 7.14 Dugout dwellings in the bank of Burra Creek (photo S. Lawrence)

(Fig. 7.14). A hole from the fireplace to the surface carried away the smoke. Most of the occupants were miners and their families. Salvage excavation of a dugout house in 2004 indicated that some of these houses had several rooms, joined by low arched passages, with vaulted ceilings up to 2.20 m high. Artefacts recovered included a clock mechanism, cooking implements, shoe fragments, a woman's brooch, marbles, bottle glass, tin can fragments and crockery decorated with the "Alhambra" transfer pattern (Birt 2005). The people who lived in such houses were not necessarily poor and desperate, but chose to live underground while it was expedient to do so. Their homes were improvised, but as comfortable as circumstances allowed (Birt 2004). Nevertheless, the "huts" were unhealthy, with poor sanitation, and were dangerous when the creek flooded (Rowney 1984). By 1860 the creek settlement was abandoned, mainly due to periodic flooding and migration to the Victorian goldfields.

Burra, like other South Australian mining settlements, was dominated by the Cornish. Copper and tin have been mined in Cornwall since the Neolithic, and the skills of the Cornish miners were eagerly sought in colonial South Australia. Between 1846 and 1850, nearly 5,000 Cornish colonists arrived in South Australia, and most were miners. Driven out by potato crop failures in 1845 and 1846, they were also attracted by the high wages, earning £3 a week in South Australia's copper mines, the equivalent of a month's wages in Cornwall.

The Burra mine was run almost exclusively by Cornishmen and Cornish mining methods were widely applied, with Cornish-built beam pumping engines imported to pump water from the depths of the mines (Connell 1987). Tall Cornish engine houses dominated the skyline of mining settlements, built of untrimmed stone with round chimneys and arched windows, and sometimes finished with a coat of whitewash. The Cornish tribute system of mining was also widely employed. This was neither company wages nor piece-work, but a traditional practice where a group of miners worked a "pitch", and were paid an agreed percentage based on the amount and value of the ore shifted. If the pitch contained rich ore it was possible to make a good living, but "tributing" was a gamble that meant only a basic wage or subsistence for many. Cornish miners thus prided themselves on their practical mining skills, studying the rock formations to extract the maximum amount of ore at the least expense. When gold was discovered, the technology, methods and tribute system of South Australia's Cornish miners provided a strong foundation for the growth of other branches of metals mining in Australia.

In later years the copper triangle towns became known as Australia's "Little Cornwall", and their Cornish heritage is still celebrated (Payton 2001:229). The Cornish accent was distinctive, and native born Cornish people treasured their Celtic background, a heritage not shared by the English. The Cornish banded together in groups based on parish, class or extended family networks. Cornish influence was expressed in wrestling matches, choirs, Cornish food and sayings, while the Cornish heritage was also expressed in social and physical ways. Cornish houses were small and built in stone with low ceilings, reflecting company housing in Cornish towns (Faull 1987). Their Non-Conformist chapels were small and deliberately lacked ostentation, with a simple architectural style developed in contrast to the more elaborate Catholic and Anglican styles. Graveyards also held distinctive tombstones recording the names of Cornish people.

Burra today is one of Australia's largest and best-preserved nineteenth-century mining towns. The settlement illustrates how communities of different ethnic origin could live and work together, and seek to retain important elements of their traditional culture in their housing, neighbourhood structures, work patterns and religious practices. While Cornish people dominated the settlement, in terms of technology, management and mining arrangements, the contributions of English, German, Scottish and other groups characterise the global nature of migration and industrialisation in the nineteenth century.

Tin

By the 1870s copper and another precious metal, tin, were produced in large quantities in the west of Tasmania with the discovery of copper at Mt. Lyell and tin at Mt. Bischoff (Fig. 7.15). In the 1880s the latter was the biggest tin mine in the world and Tasmania accounted for around 18 percent of global production of tin at this time (Blainey 1993:23; Gaughwin 1992:57). There has been little archaeological work at the big mines and their associated settlements, both of which have continued in production intermittently into the present. There has been research, however, on the smaller tin fields of north-east Tasmania, initiated as part of forestry management in

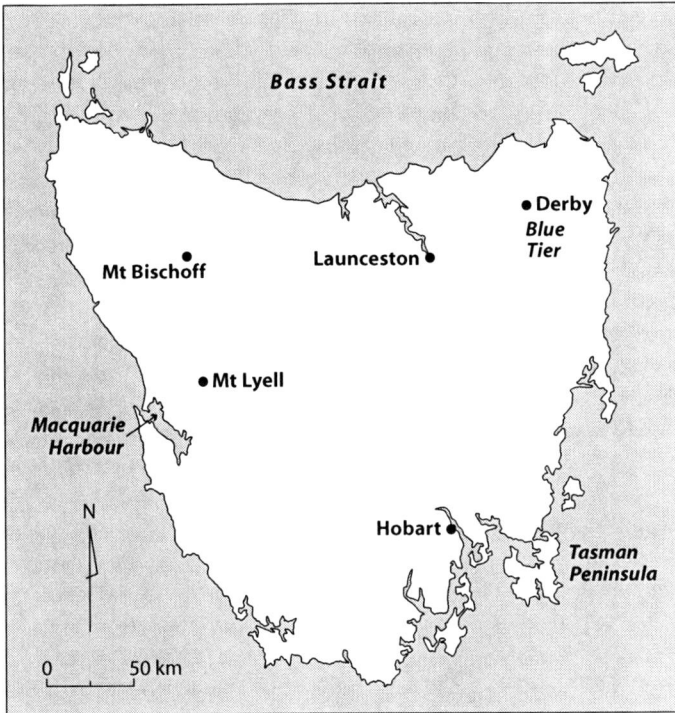

Fig. 7.15 Map of Tasmania showing places associated with tin mining

the region (Gaughwin 1992; Jackman 1995, 1997). These projects illustrate different approaches to the analysis of mining places, each of which contributes insights
into the development of Australian mining and the evolution of cultural landscapes.

Like gold, tin was mined from both alluvial and hard rock deposits. Alluvial
mining was widely spread over most of the creeks and rivers in the north-east, while
lode mining was concentrated in a few areas around Derby, Mt Paris and the Blue
Tier (Jackman 1995). Denise Gaughwin (1992) has linked the development of the
Tasmanian tin industry to changes in the global market for tin. She observes that
the modern landscape of relict mines and timber-getting sites exists across the Blue
Tier as a result of first the growth and then the decline of international markets
for Tasmanian tin, together with distinct characteristics of the local environment
that made it unsuitable for agricultural activity. The remains demonstrate the phases
of mining and the availability of capital which was one influence on the type of
technology used to exploit the deposits.

In both the early (1874–1890s) and late (1890s–1910s) phases small miners made
use of wooden cradles and ground sluices to process the ore raised from shallow
shafts sunk into the alluvial deposits. More complex networks of water races and
sluices and the use of puddling machines and stamp batteries on early-phase sites

indicated that some capital was available. In the later phase some capital was also required for installing petrol or steam-powered winches and for hydraulic sluicing. Housing was more substantial at these sites and there was a greater array of services such as roads, shops and hotels. In both phases there were large mines that indicated considerable capital investment. These had deeper shafts and larger surface workings with machinery such as winding gear in the early phase and airshafts and pumps in the later phase. Processing areas were separate from the mine itself and included complex sluices and retorts. In the later phase processing and mining areas were connected by timber tramways or aerial tramways with machinery powered by petrol or electricity. Substantial towns grew to service these mines with clear status distinctions evident in the kinds of housing available.

Greg Jackman (1995) has expanded Gaughwin's work to explore the social dimensions of knowledge transfer, which also had a significant impact on the choice of technology and mining method. The archaeological and geological evidence of tin mining on the Blue Tier shows the long-term persistence of entrenched approaches to mining based on vernacular understandings of the mineralogy, despite more sophisticated and accurate models being promoted by government geologists. Using the workings of the Moon Mine as a case study, Jackman argues that this inertia is the result of the influence of locally based networks of mine ownership, investment and management that inhibited the adoption of new methods.

Archaeological evidence shows that during the early period of work at the site from 1874 to 1891 workings consisted of ground sluicing with shallow shafts to prospect the granite. As the working face extended it appears that the higher-grade ores were targeted, which provided immediate payoffs but limited the long-term viability of the mine. Evidence of improvements to the crushing plant and to drainage at the site in an attempt to open greater areas of ground relate to the next phase of workings, associated with new owners who were active from 1891 to 1893 before being forced to suspend operations due to the depression of the 1890s. The next phase of activity is represented by four long, narrow exploratory trenches or "costeans" that were dug across the entire workings to explore the full extent and nature of the tin deposit. The high quality and ambitious nature of the work suggests it was carried out between 1905 and 1907 when the leases were held by the Mt Lyell Co. which was briefly interested in extending its operations into the area. Following this prospecting, the remaining evidence of work at the mine reflects small-scale, limited operations that again focused exclusively on extracting high-grade ore.

Jackman argues that most of the work done at the Moon site, as at other mines on the Blue Tier, reflects a generally held belief that the source of the rich alluvial tin deposits in the region would be found concentrated in high-quality veins or lodes within the surrounding granite. He traces this geological model to the influence of Cornish precedent on the field. In Cornwall, which until the nineteenth century had some of the largest known copper and tin mines in the world, lode deposits predominated. Familiarity with, and expectations of, lode mining was brought to Australia by the Cornish miners and mine managers who went to the South Australian copper mines in the 1840s, and then to the Victorian goldfields in the 1850s and 1860s. The first white arrivals to prospect and work the minerals on the Blue Tier had mining experience from Victoria and New Zealand, where they may have encountered this orthodoxy. Others who became managers of the local mines had direct experience in Cornwall and South Australia which they applied in Tasmania. In addition to historical evidence about the prevalence of Cornish practices on the field such as tributing, Jackman also found physical evidence of common Cornish mining techniques at several of the mines. In Cornwall and South Australia the mines were worked in 60-foot (18 m) blocks, with drives extended off shafts at the 60, 120 and 180 foot levels. Where shafts were used on the Blue Tier, similar depths were apparent, further indicating the influence of that body of knowledge.

The expectation of finding the mineral concentrated in lodes, following the Cornish model, distracted local attention from the reality of their deposits in which the tin was actually diffused more widely and unpredictably throughout the granite. The local geology was accurately assessed and reported by the government geologists from the 1890s but as the archaeological and historical evidence indicates, knowledge about the new model was not widely accepted on the field. Throughout the life of the Moon Mine and others on the Blue Tier there is archaeological evidence of repeatedly targeting the richest mineral pockets as a kind of lode while failing to seriously test the extent or viability of the deposit in advance of the working face of the mine. The failure to properly prospect resulted in practices that were unsustainable because they worked the richest spots out too quickly. This failure to recognise the widely distributed but poor quality nature of the ore also resulted in undercapitalisation of the works as the infrastructure developed was insufficient for the scale of workings that would have been required to make the mines pay.

The new water races and costeans still evident at the Moon Mine reflect the brief period around the turn of the twentieth century when prevailing local wisdom was challenged by outside forces. By the end of the nineteenth century the centre of innovation and research in mining had moved from Cornwall to Germany and continental Europe, where large-scale, low-grade ore bodies like that on the Blue Tier were common. The new government geologist appointed in those years had trained in Germany, and the managers and metallurgists who were succeeding spectacularly at Mt. Lyell and Mt. Bischoff also had German training. It appears from both the infrastructure developed in the 1890s and the Mt. Lyell Co. costeans of 1905–1907 that new interests were intending to work the ground following the German model of large-scale extraction and processing. Neither of these new groups ultimately proceeded, and the subsequent workings demonstrate the return to the Cornish lode-style mining model, now being used by the children and grandchildren of the first local syndicates. Jackman argues that early, vernacular approaches became entrenched in the field and that locally controlled syndicates were unable or unwilling to adopt new approaches that threatened existing hierarchies.

Alongside the white mining syndicates, Chinese miners were working and reworking the region's alluvial tin deposits. Originally brought in as cheap labour, they soon established themselves as miners in their own right and also set up market gardens and shops. By the late 1880s the Chinese population in the region had peaked at around 1,000–1,500, largely outnumbering Europeans. The heritage and archaeology of the Chinese tin miners has been documented by historian Helen

Vivian (1985). Most of the Chinese miners lived in isolated camps of small wooden huts or in "long huts" built to house three to six people. The main Chinese centres were at Weldborough and Garibaldi. Each consisted of a main street in which stood one or two "clan" stores, the temple, fan-tan houses and dwellings (Walden 1995:179). A number of communal pig roasting ovens have been recorded in the region as well, some near the isolated claims where miners lived in simple bush huts. As in the New South Wales highlands, dwellings were temporary, as the miners were mobile and most had little intention of remaining permanently in Australia. The collapse of tin prices in the late 1880s, however, along with new immigration laws, prompted large numbers of miners to seek their fortunes in Victoria, or even to return home to China.

Chinese miners were also prominent at a short-lived tin rush at Bynoe Harbour near Darwin in the Northern Territory between 1903 and about 1907 (Mitchell 2005). The field was worked by around 100 Chinese miners, along with smaller numbers of Europeans and Aborigines. Although the tin was a very high-grade ore, the alluvial deposits were small and scattered. Most of the mines were small in scale and were operated by only a few men who had little capital to invest. As the accessible surface tin ran out, the mining community shrank, and by the end of the First World War the area was completely abandoned.

In other mining areas of the Northern Territory, such as Pine Creek, archaeologists have demonstrated that Chinese and European miners lived and worked in separate areas and maintained separate economic and trading networks (McCarthy 1988, 1995). At Bynoe Harbour, however, such divisions were much less obvious in the archaeological remains. Surface artefacts included gin and whiskey bottles and various iron implements, along with more obviously "Chinese" material such as celadon bowl fragments and numerous pieces of brown stoneware rice wine jars. Historical sources also indicate that Europeans and Chinese lived and worked together at the Bynoe Harbour mine sites over the years. In spite of such intermingling, the mines operated at a time when white hostility to Asians was formalised in the White Australia Policy. The presence of simple Chinese pottery on the field hints at the ongoing efforts of the Chinese miners to maintain a sense of cultural identity in the face of wider community hostility. The "poor man's show" at Bynoe Harbour remains a symbol of how the Chinese successfully developed a presence and community in Northern Territory society (Yee 2006).

Conclusion

Australia witnessed one of the great gold rushes of the nineteenth century, and the surviving archaeological evidence of that event has international significance. Gold mining has provided the model for archaeologists documenting other forms of mineral extraction, and the archaeology of mining has been important for establishing the Australian tradition of integrating social and technological approaches to the study of industry (see Chapter 8). Past mining activities created the places and landscapes that continue to provide context for the daily lives of many Australians, from the distribution, layout and physical fabric of towns and cities to the patchwork of surviving bush used for recreational purposes. Minerals mining also remains a foundation of the Australian economy, and thousands of people continue to be drawn to new lives in remote areas following the lure of bright metals. Technologies have changed since the nineteenth century but the essential patterns of prospecting, extraction and processing remain. Post-war mining is also just as vulnerable to booms and busts, and twentieth-century ghost towns have already appeared on the west coast of Tasmania and in parts of Western Australia and Queensland, waiting for future archaeologists to document them. Mining today, however, is emphatically big business, and the great rushes of the nineteenth century are now a thing of the past.

Chapter 8
Manufacturing and Processing

Europeans brought with them to Australia the need and desire for all kinds of manufactured items. Settlers arrived with many goods from home, but others had to be created from materials at hand. Early houses, for example, were built from timber, bark, mud and clay, with more substantial homes constructed of brick and stone. Furniture, from rough bush tables to fine cedar cabinets, was crafted from native forest timbers. Dining tables were laid with Staffordshire crockery, but kitchens, dairies and storerooms needed robust, utilitarian wares provided by colonial potters. As settlement expanded, people needed carts and drays to haul their goods, tools to clear and cultivate the land and utensils to churn butter, mould candles and create the many other necessities of daily life. Flour mills, tanneries, salt works, cordial factories, breweries and many other processors emerged in towns and cities to transform raw materials into consumer goods.

Sources of energy were vital to drive these industrial processes. While coal and steam were transforming Europe, in Australia there was initially a heavy reliance on human muscle power, especially of convicts, to plough paddocks, quarry rocks and build roads. Horses and bullocks were quickly bred up to provide transport and haulage and were a major presence in both rural and urban areas well into the twentieth century. Early views of Sydney featured the sails of windmills which provided the settlement with its first form of industrial power to mill grain, but the future of energy lay underground. Coal deposits were discovered in the 1790s at the Hunter River in New South Wales and on the Tasman Peninsula, but until large-scale extraction began in the 1840s, the main source of fuel for Australian colonists was wood. Felling trees was part of clearing the land for settlement, providing vast quantities of fuel in the process. As the nineteenth century progressed, however, and rail networks improved, colonial coal production expanded dramatically, fuelling thousands of boilers and steam engines. Hydroelectric power was also introduced on a small scale in 1888 (Gojak 1988:3), while water-driven flour mills were developed in northern New South Wales and in Tasmania (Connah 1994; W. Pearson 1996, 1997, 1998). By the 1920s and 1930s, however, steam power was giving way to diesel engines, and coal was used to meet the growing demand for domestic and industrial gas and electricity.

Manufacturing in Australia was built on primary extractive industries such as mining, forestry and wool growing. It became increasingly important during the

Contributions To Global Historical Archaeology, DOI 10.1007/978-1-4419-7485-3_8,
© Springer Science+Business Media, LLC 2011

nineteenth century, due to the great distance of Australia from efficient manufacturing countries such as Britain, Germany and the United States, and the need to process local materials into commodities. The international flow of capital and technology, however, also helped determine the character of Australian industries, by enabling the growth of some and restricting the development of others (Butlin 1994; Jeans 1988). In the first few decades of settlement, manufacturing enterprises were small by international standards, but they played an important role in developing colonial society and economy. Processing industries added value to raw materials to create products such as flour and salt for local consumption, while manufacturers produced finished goods which competed with imports, including boots, beer and pottery. New colonial industries provided employment for workers beyond simple agriculture, and created opportunities for investment with a modest return on capital. They also reinforced the mutual interdependence of local industries. Leather tanning, for example, supported cattle breeders, while salt makers made possible the pork trade with Pacific islands such as Tahiti. Timber-cutters provided material for boat-builders, which in turn encouraged voyages for seal skins and sandalwood.

The study of these manufacturing industries and the sites and landscapes in which they developed are all part of industrial archaeology. This kind of archaeology involves the recording, preservation and interpretation of the remains of industrial activity, which Kenneth Hudson (1976:7) defined very broadly as "making and selling things, and moving goods and people from one place to another". All of these topics have long been a focus of interest in Australia, and while in the United Kingdom and North America industrial archaeology constitutes a separate sub-discipline, in Australia it is firmly integrated within the broader field of historical archaeology (Jack 1979:7). Industrial processes and the impacts of the Industrial Revolution touch on all aspects of the European settlement of Australia, and the archaeological study of industry here is invariably situated within broader social, environmental and landscape contexts (Fig. 8.1).

Eleanor Casella (2006) argues that the integration of industrial with historical archaeology in this country means that Australian research is at the forefront of approaches that have only recently been initiated overseas. Her review of new thematic directions emerging within industrial archaeology in Britain identifies approaches which closely reflect the study of industry in Australia. Outlined below, these broadly include continuity and change, production and consumption, cultural landscapes, gender, class and identity, and internationalisation.

As Casella argues, the tension between continuity and change provides the dynamic in which Australian industry has developed, with the former represented by the importation of overseas technology, capital and skilled labour, and the latter by the development of specifically Australian industries and practices. These include woolscours (Pearson 1984), eucalyptus oil distilling (Pearson 1993b), local potteries (Casey 1999) and the development of vernacular architectural traditions (Bell 1990; Lewis 1977). Numerous detailed studies of primary production industries and secondary manufacturing have also been carried out over the years, all of which combine in different measure continuities from older technologies and

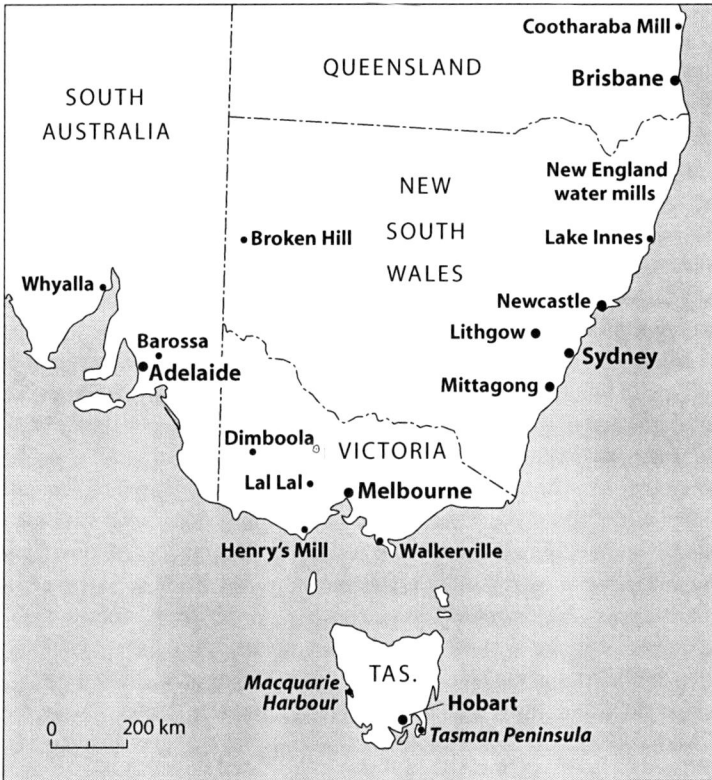

Fig. 8.1 Location of manufacturing sites discussed in text

traditions and innovations to meet changed circumstances and conditions. These range from European and Aboriginal pastoralism (Harrison 2004b; Paterson 2008), whaling (Lawrence 2006b), timber (Davies 2006a) and various forms of mining (see Chapter 7), to iron-smelting (Jack and Cremin 1994), brick-making (Stuart 1989b), textile manufacturing (Stenning 1993) and many others. While studies of production have dominated, studies of consumption, the twin of production, have also flourished in recent years, extending the focus from factories and mills to markets and households (Crook 2000, 2005; Karskens 2003b), and studies of mass-produced artefacts such as bottles, buttons and ceramics have proliferated (Boow 1991; Brooks 2005; Lindbergh 1999). Many of the most successful Australian industries produced consumer goods such as food, beverages and footwear, and the consumption of industrial products underpins the discussion of the material culture of domestic life presented in Chapter 11.

Industrial sites have also been examined as part of wider cultural landscapes, as a way of understanding the complex interactions between people, labour, capital, technology and the natural environment (see Chapter 6). These studies range in scale from the household and settlement to industry-wide regions (Casella 2006:67–68;

Jeans 1984). This emphasis has frequently been overlaid with appraisals of social class and power (Davies 2005b; Taksa 2005), gender and labour (Lawrence 2000; Lydon 1993b), and the role of ethnic identity in technological innovation and community formation (Gaughwin 1995; Smith 2006; see Chapter 9). Finally, the importation of overseas technology and its adaptation to local conditions has also been widely addressed (Jack and Cremin 1994; Milner 1997; W. Pearson 1996), along with the ways in which Australian industries developed within the broader context of the nineteenth-century global economy. Many of the goods produced in these industrial processes are encountered again and again in archaeological contexts, and include bottles and beverages, ceramics, clay pipes, food, footwear and numerous other products.

Social approaches have been significant influences in the archaeology of industry in Australia, and while ethnicity and class are discussed elsewhere (see Chapters 9 and 10 in particular), it is worth considering gender in greater detail here. Since the 1980s when American prehistorians Margaret Conkey and Janet Spector (1984) first drew attention to the issue, gender has been an abiding theme in Australian historical archaeology generally. Researchers were initially concerned with identifying women in the archaeological record and revealing patterns of gendered experience within the discipline and practice of archaeology, but attention soon turned to developing more sophisticated ways of investigating gender as a process that shaped the experiences of men, women and children in the past (Casey 1998; Du Cros and Smith 1993). Alongside research into the activities of women there have also been studies of masculinity (Fredericksen 2005; Lawrence 2003a), "queer" archaeology (Casella 2000a, b), and childhood (Davies 2005a). The analysis of gender has presented a significant critique of traditional narratives in Australian historical archaeology, from convicts and post-contact archaeology to urbanisation and industrial archaeology. It has done so primarily by focusing attention on the social dimensions of these areas, establishing individual agency as a factor in the creation of the archaeological record, and identifying the contingent nature of historical experience which is shaped by gender and age as much as by race or access to power.

Gendered approaches to industrial archaeology have challenged stereotypes of monolithic, male-dominated production in several ways. Researchers have drawn attention to the distinctive demographic composition of industrial settlements in Australia, where women and children were frequently present in considerable numbers (Davies 2006a; Higginbotham 2005; Lawrence 2000; Quirk 2008a). Acknowledging this presence in turn has led to the examination of patterns of work, the close juxtaposition of domestic and industrial activities in small rural settlements, the formation of communities, and the role of kinship networks. Other research has focussed on women's work for income, often carried out within the home, and its implications for site formation and artefact patterning. Archaeological evidence for sewing and dairying, two industries traditionally dominated by women, has been of particular interest (Casey 1999; Lydon 1993b). Gender ideology shaped masculine identities and men's experiences of work just as it did for women. This has been most apparent archaeologically at places where white women were generally absent, such as whaling camps and pastoral stations (Lawrence 2003a), and among prison guards at Darwin's Fanny Bay Gaol (Fredericksen 2005). In these cases archaeological evidence has demonstrated differing constructions of masculinity and highlighted the historically contingent nature of gender.

Gendered approaches have also opened up new areas of inquiry around consumption, the necessary corollary of production. The manufacture of consumer goods such as food, clothing and beverages was one of the mainstays of Australian industry and of the industrial revolution more broadly. Archaeologists and historians have begun to examine the processes by which manufactured products entered the home, including marketing, retail facilities, and the role of markets and second-hand goods (Crook 2000, 2005; Kingston 1994). The acquisition of household goods was frequently a task performed by women, and one weighted with social responsibility because the selection of goods that were appropriate for the family's status and aspirations was a crucial part of negotiating their position in the community.

These broad themes of continuity and change, technology transfer, landscape and social context provide an important framework for understanding the archaeology of manufacturing and processing in Australia. To illustrate them, and to demonstrate their inter-connectedness, in this chapter we describe the archaeology of several major industries that transformed raw materials into usable commodities. These include water mills for flour-milling; timber-getting and other forest activities; the clay industries for bricks and pottery; lime-burning; and the development of coal, iron and steel production. The settlement patterns and landscapes created by these industries were determined by the location and quality of raw materials, the means of transport, availability of labour, capital, and technology, access to markets, government policies, competition from imports, and various other factors. Manufacturing also transformed natural environments, with the constant demand for materials, fuel, water, roads and housing, as well as the industrial operations themselves. The topics discussed reflect those areas that have attracted archaeological attention, and some historically important industries such as the footwear industry have been excluded due to the lack of archaeological investigation.

Water Mills

Water-powered milling technology encompasses many of the themes common to industrial archaeology in Australia more broadly. These include the importation of overseas technology and its adaptation to local conditions, and the development of human, financial and industrial resources. British colonists came from a wet environment (Cathcart 2009:8), and they brought with them the tradition of using water to drive machinery. Hundreds of water mills were used in Australia during the nineteenth century, especially in gold mining and flour milling. In contrast, thousands of such mills were established in Britain during the same period, mostly in support of the textile industry. Warwick Pearson (1996, 1997, 1998) has studied the archaeology of Australian water mills in detail, especially in terms of technology transfer and adaptation. His focus has been on well-preserved flour mills in Tasmania and the

New England tablelands of New South Wales, from the 1820s to the 1870s. Pearson identified a range of variables in the development of water technology, including physical landscapes and climate, resource distribution, the industrial and cultural context, and the availability of engineering skills.

The first successful water mill in Australia was built at Norfolk Island in 1795, but the early settlement and relatively high rainfall of Van Diemen's Land meant that water power was quickly established in the colony, and by 1861 there were 50 water-powered flour mills in use (Fig. 8.2; Pearson 1998:67). In New South Wales, however, drier conditions meant the technology was applied less intensively, and it was supplemented more often by steam, wind and animal power. In the New England region, pastoralism and poor transportation networks meant that each settlement required its own small mill to be self-sufficient in flour. Dispersed population, and the expense and difficulty of transporting grain for processing, thus resulted in the widespread construction of flour mills, generally serving a small, local market. With the coming of railways later in the nineteenth century, however, and the growth of large metropolitan centres, the small mills were replaced with much larger steam-powered roller mills (Pearson 1998:32).

Water mills worked on the principle of moving water that drove buckets or vanes attached to the rim of a wheel, which in turn drove gearing attached to a shaft, with the power transferred, in the case of a flour mill, to a heavy circular grinding stone (Fig. 8.3). Different types of wheel suited different conditions. In areas of abundant water and little slope, undershot or breastshot mills were common, with the movement of water generating motion of the wheel. These were common in Britain, with

Fig. 8.2 Ruins of a water-driven flour mill built in the 1820s on the Supply River in northern Tasmania (photo P. Davies)

Fig. 8.3 Mill stone from Wappan Station in central Victoria, dating from the 1840s (photo P. Davies)

the water supplied direct from nearby ponds or rivers. In Australia, however, overshot wheels were much more common. These mills relied on the weight of a small volume of water falling from a height to generate power. Such mills were often better suited to Australian conditions, with lower and more variable rainfall, and steeper topography in areas suitable for water mills. Overshot wheels in Australia were typically larger and narrower than British versions, with water brought some distance along channels and head races and directed to the mill by a flume (Pearson 1997:54).

Only a small number of water mills in Australia remain even partially intact. These mostly relate to flour milling, as they were constructed for longer operation than those associated with sawmilling and mining. One example is Dight's Flour Mill, built on a sharp bend in the Yarra River near Melbourne in the early 1840s. A weir was built across a rocky fall on the river, along with a head race and return race, to drive an undershot wheel. The original building was constructed of brick imported from Launceston, even though local bluestone (basalt) was becoming popular in the 1840s for building purposes. Frequent drought and flood, however, meant a constant struggle to operate the mill at its capacity. It closed after about 15 years, and was rebuilt in the 1880s using more efficient water turbines. Fire destroyed the mill in 1909, and later dismantling left only the turbine house and stone-lined water races to indicate the operation of Melbourne's first and only water-driven flour mill (L. Jones and P. Jones 1990:28–32, 77–84).

Water power was also used to drive a paper mill on the Barwon River near Geelong in Victoria. The archaeological remains of the mill provide good evidence of a vanished technology, when paper was still made from cotton and linen rags, grass and straw, prior to the use of wood pulp (Hunter 1957:389–394). The mill opened in 1878, comprising a substantial complex of stone buildings and sheds and houses of timber and iron, built on a sloping site beside the river. Machinery included a paper-making machine, rag engines, grass boilers and a rag shredder, all imported from James Bertram and Sons of Edinburgh, even though local engineering firms in Geelong and Ballarat were quite capable of supplying such equipment by this time. The machinery was driven by both steam engines and by a 125-horsepower Fourneyron turbine, probably the only one of its kind installed in Australia (Milner 1985:21). Water was supplied from the Barwon River along a bluestone race more than 900 m long and 3 m wide. The mill produced a variety of coarse brown wrapping papers and finer grade writing and printing paper, but by the 1890s competition from imports had become intense, and the mill eventually closed in 1922. The Barwon paper mill is an important example of a capital-intensive nineteenth-century manufacturing enterprise. It incorporated some of the best available paper-making technology at the time, but also took careful advantage of the site to ensure efficient handling of materials. The introduction of wood pulp and high volume paper imports, however, gradually eroded the viability of the operation.

The successful operation of water-powered mills depended on a range of factors. Perhaps most importantly, climate and rainfall directly affected the flow of water available to turn wheels and drive the mills. Skilled millwrights and engineers were also crucial in the construction and operation of water mills, and Pearson has demonstrated that such men were important agents in the transfer and adaptation of this technology to Australia, with their names often inscribed on preserved machinery. The construction of water wheels also needed iron components, such as wheel frames and gearing. Colonial iron foundries were emerging around the same time as water mills, and played an important role in supplying mills with the necessary parts. Colonial economic conditions were also a significant factor, with small and widely dispersed populations in rural areas resulting in generally smaller mills than those employed in Britain (Pearson 1997:51). British regional influences, however, were still important in the transfer of milling technology. Lowland mills in Britain tended to be larger operations, with storage floors and undershot wheels fed directly by dams, and extensive use of iron machinery. Upland mills, on the other hand, were smaller, with less storage capacity, and were more likely to be powered by overshot wheels fed by long races. Colonial water-powered mills were thus a hybrid technology, combining elements of both upland and lowland traditions. Local conditions generally favoured the British upland model of overshot wheels fed by long races, but the frequent use of iron components and the need for storage space owed more to lowland technology.

Timber Milling

One of the first tasks for convicts when the First Fleet landed in 1788 was to start chopping down trees. Wood was needed immediately for fuel and tent frames, and soon for huts, furniture, carts, tools and numerous other products. The vegetation the colonists met in and around Sydney was mostly a mix of eucalypt forest and woodland, kept open by Aboriginal burning practices (Attenbrow 2002:41–42). Further to the north were extensive stands of red cedar, one of Australia's most beautiful furniture timbers, which formed the basis of a substantial timber industry in northern New South Wales during the early nineteenth century (Vader 2002). As settlement expanded along the coast and inland, many new kinds of trees and plants were encountered. Colonists responded to these forest and woodlands in a variety of ways. For some the trees were simply a nuisance, to be cleared as quickly and efficiently as possible to make way for the plough, farming and "civilisation". Convicts toiled to cut, burn and grub the tough timber which quickly blunted axes and saws. Others were oppressed by the seemingly inexhaustible expanses of grey–green trees rolling away in every direction. They resented that Australian eucalypts were so unlike familiar European trees, shedding their bark rather than their leaves, and offering such thin shade in hot weather. A few settlers, however, learned to appreciate the native forest trees, seeing beauty in their twisted shapes and recognising their endless variety. Their appreciation would eventually blossom into a conservation movement which began to value the natural world for its own sake (Bonyhady 2000). Collectors gathered specimens of flowers, fruits and leaves and sent them back to Britain where they were studied as exotic antipodean curiosities (P. Clarke 2008). For most settlers, however, trees were simply a useful source of raw material, to be exploited more or less at will. Timber-getting thus had a rapid and often dramatic impact on natural landscapes, as trees were cleared to make way for settlement, and create the products that sustained the settlers.

Most archaeological research on Australian forest industries has concentrated on steam technology and the development of timber tramways (e.g. Evans 1994; McCarthy 1993; Tracey 1997). This was augmented during the 1990s when hundreds of archaeological sites relating to the timber industry were documented as part of the Australian Government's Regional Forest Assessment process (Lennon 1998). Recently, however, there has been an increasing focus on the material and social lives of the men and their families who created forest mill settlements. Studies of Henry's Mill in Victoria's Otway forests (Davies 2002, 2006a) and the Cootharaba Mill near Noosa in Queensland (Murphy 2007) have explored community life in isolated forest communities, along with production and consumption, and labour and gender relations.

Forest settlements and landscapes were structured by the nature of forest resources, and the technology available to exploit them. Most archaeological evidence of the timber industry relates to twentieth-century activities, as earlier sites are fewer in number and obscured by erosion, organic decay, forest re-growth and sometimes by later timber-getting. Expansion of roads and railways in the early twentieth century resulted in sawmillers cutting previously untouched forests, with many more mills scattered through the forest. Sites from this later period generally have better preserved archaeological remains, which provide important insight into the distinctive geography of timber-getting activities, including the spatial distribution of the industry and its components, the structure, scale and layout of mills and camps, and the common features that mills shared. Paradoxically, bushfires, which can be so destructive of forest areas, can also reveal in stark detail for a short time the earthworks and arrangement of mill sites and associated settlements and tram networks.

The earliest timber-getting was slow, laborious and repetitive. It involved felling trees with axes and saws, lopping off the branches and cross-cutting the trunk into short lengths. These were then hauled to a sawpit or creek and literally manhandled into position. One man stood above the log and another below, pushing and pulling on a long pit saw to cut the log into timber. The "underdog" below sometimes wore a bag over his head to prevent sawdust getting into his eyes. Sawpits from the nineteenth century are hard to identify in the bush today, usually being overgrown and heavily eroded. When in use, however, they were up to 2 m deep, narrow-sided and carpeted with sawdust. Their memory is often proclaimed in local place names such as Sawpit Gully and Sawpit Creek. A rare surviving example of a large pit-sawing complex has been documented at the Sarah Island penal settlement in Macquarie Harbour in Tasmania (Nash 2007). The settlement operated as a penal station between 1822–1833 and 1846–1847, with up to 380 convicts working at timber-cutting, coal-mining, lime-burning and brick-making at various outstations around Macquarie Harbour. Contemporary depictions show a long open-sided shed with a pitched roof, covering eight separate sawpits. The surviving section is approximately 20 m long, almost 4 m wide and up to 1.5 m in depth. Directly in front of the sawpit was a simple timber wharf for loading the timber onto boats.

Manual sawing in pits was only gradually superseded by other means. One of the first steam engines in Australia, imported to Sydney by John Dickson in 1813, was intended to saw timber but in the end it was used to mill grain (Fletcher 1976:143; Godden Mackay 1992). At Bagot's Mill on the central tablelands of New South Wales, Graham Connah (1994:33–34) investigated a brief experiment with a water-driven sawmill in the 1870s. One of the curious features excavated by Connah and his team was a sawpit at least 1 m deep and lined with a mortared stone wall. The apparent anomaly of a manual pit saw at a powered sawmill is explained by the need to reduce the largest logs down to a smaller size that the water-driven saws could cut.

Steam-driven sawmills were generally introduced in the 1840s and were an immediate success, dramatically increasing productivity. While mechanical milling increased the volume of timber that could be sawn, it only intensified pressure on the other significant limiting factor, that of transport. Sawmilling was essentially a transport industry that needed an efficient means of transferring logs to the mill and timber to market. As only about half the volume of a round log could be converted into square timber, with the rest going to waste, the distance and cost of transporting logs had to be kept to a minimum. Sawmills had to be located close to the supply of timber as it was generally easier to move a mill to the trees than to haul logs for long distances through rugged forest terrain.

Tramways were the favoured means for transporting timber to market from the remote forest mills. Existing roads were frequently unsealed, pot-holed and almost impossible to negotiate in winter conditions. All-weather tramlines, built of timber sleepers (ties) and rails, connected logging areas, sawmills and government railways, and provided an essential means of transport for mill workers and their families, feed for horses, consumer goods, and new tools and parts as needed, bringing in supplies by the tramway that took the sawn timber to market. Horses and steam locomotives were the main sources of power on tramways until the 1920s. Horses were cheap, reliable and well suited to hauling on steep grades (Fig. 8.4). Larger mills served by longer tramlines, however, often invested in small steam locomotives to convey timber to market. After the First World War, trucks and tractors were also used for tramway haulage (Frawley 1993:155).

The reliance on transportation and mechanical milling resulted in a distinctive pattern of land use and industry that evolved over a 100-year period from the introduction of steam power and tramways in the 1840s until the introduction of diesel engines and better roads in the 1930s. Small, temporary sawmills were established in forested areas in the midst of the timber to be cut. Men employed by the timber company, including timber-cutters, mill hands, and their families, lived in small settlements around the mill. The average duration of a mill at one location was around 5 years, although much longer periods at the one location were also common. Networks of tramways connected the mills to the logging areas deeper in the surrounding forest, to other mills and to the nearest railhead or good road.

Sawmill sites have a number of characteristic features. A sloping position beside a creek or river was often preferred, to take advantage of gravity in handling logs and because the mills required a reliable source of water to supply boilers, to lubricate saws, and for domestic consumption. Level ground was also needed for mill

Fig. 8.4 Horse hauling on a log tramline (photo Birregurra and District Historical Society)

buildings and for housing. Saw benches and engines were generally housed under a rough, open-sided shed roofed with palings or corrugated iron. Power was transmitted to the saws by a series of shafts and belts driven by a wood-fired steam boiler and engine. Sawdust was taken away from below the saws by wheelbarrow and dumped in a heap nearby. The mill yard quickly became littered with off cuts, bark, piles of timber, mud and manure. Typical archaeological remains of forest sawmills include pits and trenches for the saws and drive belts, heavy stone or brick foundations for a steam boiler, and a large sawdust heap. The latter are often visible in forest areas as an open space among the trees, as sawdust is a poor medium for plant growth. Domestic materials include chimney foundations and bottles and glass, while cuttings and embankments for timber and log tramlines, often heavily overgrown, lead off into the bush (Fig. 8.5). There are many hundreds of such sites preserved in forest areas around Australia, along with thousands of kilometres of bush tramlines.

Due to the short-lived nature of the mills, the forest tramways were also mostly short-term operations. They were characterised by light and economical construction, using materials close to hand and employing the labour of mill workers or contractors. Once the route was surveyed, the track bed was cleared of timber and then excavated by pick, shovel and horse-drawn scoop. The tramway itself was constructed of wooden rails nailed onto rough timber sleepers and split packing,

Fig. 8.5 Log bridge on tramline near the New Federal Mill in the Upper Yarra Forest, Victoria, from the 1930s (photo P. Davies)

commonly at a gauge of 3 feet (0.91 m). Wooden rails provided an effective braking surface for the iron tram wheels, which featured deep flanges and wide treads. Steel rails were sometimes laid, however, on heavily used sections of track, especially on curves and close to the mill, as timber rails wore out very quickly. A tram repairer was often employed to replace rails, repair bridges and renew packing displaced or broken down by horses.

Most sawmills in eastern Australia between the 1850s and 1930s were owned and operated as small, often family-run businesses. Capital costs for mill and tramline construction were high for such small firms, so that mill plant was often acquired secondhand and sold on again when the operation closed. Large sawmilling companies, such as those that dominated the industry in Western Australia, were rare in the eastern colonies (Mills 1986). Labour needs were high, which meant that sawmills provided valuable employment opportunities in many forest districts. Local markets, however, were generally small and competition from cheap imported softwoods was a constant threat. Eucalypt forests offered large but highly variable log sizes, resulting in the establishment of a large number of small sawmills in frequently remote forest locations.

An example of one such operation is the site of Henry's No. 1 Mill, where Peter Davies (2006a) has carried out extensive archaeological research. Henry's Mill was established in 1904, deep in the watershed of the West Barwon River in the Otway Ranges of south-west Victoria. It was connected by a timber tramline to the railhead at Forrest, 10 km to the north, but the mill's relative isolation meant that a permanent population of around 100 people lived on site. Around half of these were adult workmen and the others were women and children. The mill settlement featured rough timber huts for single men and modest wooden houses for married men and their families, along with a boarding house, billiard room and stables (Fig. 8.6). Children attended the mill school, which opened in 1909, while a post office and store provided further services. In later years the firm of W. R. Henry & Son opened several other mills higher up the valley as well. In 1927 the main mill shed was destroyed by fire, resulting in the gradual abandonment of the settlement. Relatively little historical information survives of Henry's Mill, although Education Department files preserve a rich correspondence relating to the school. Surprisingly, despite the comparatively recent occupation of the settlement, it was not possible to identify any residents still living and oral history is also limited. Archaeological evidence has thus greatly enhanced the understanding of the site and by extension forest communities more generally.

The research emphasised the domestic lives of people at the mill camp as much as the technology of timber-getting, illustrating the capacity of gendered analysis to illuminate issues such as the spatial layout of the settlement and the consumption patterns of residents. Survey and excavation at the site in 1998 focussed on revealing the remains of domestic structures and associated household debris in order to investigate material and social life at the mill (Davies 1999, 2006a). At least eight family houses were built in a small neighbourhood to the north-west of the main mill shed. The limited space meant the houses were only a metre or two apart, with the school building in their midst. Archaeological evidence indicated that a common

Fig. 8.6 Henry's No. 1 Mill in south-west Victoria, occupied from 1904 to 1927 (photo Birregurra and District Historical Society)

plan and materials were used at each house. Construction featured wooden framing and weatherboards, probably freshly sawn at the mill. The general architectural pattern was based on a central front door under a verandah, opening onto a main living area. Two small bedrooms made up the rear part of the house, with a lean-to kitchen at the back. At each house excavation revealed a pair of hearths which showed the layout of the houses and how the space was used. An open fireplace used for light and heat indicated the location of the main living space, while a brick hearth with an enclosed cast-iron oven used for cooking indicated the position of the kitchen to the rear.

Residential space in the settlement was segregated on the basis of gender and marital status. Huts for single men were separated from the family houses by a gully and hill slope, an arrangement that reflected the social and marital division between the two groups. Each hut in the single men's area consisted of a single room about 3 by 4 m across. They were constructed from split palings, with a shingle roof and a large fireplace, and each housed two men. A third form of accommodation was also available at the mill, however, with communal quarters for married workers who lodged their families in nearby townships and visited them on weekends. The marital status of employees at Henry's Mill was thus recognised and expressed in the form and location of accommodation made available to each group.

Space was also used by the mill proprietors to indicate and maintain their separate status. The authority of the Henrys was not expressed overtly in the architecture of their on-site residence but it was nevertheless clearly marked. W.R. Henry and his family lived in Geelong and visited the mill from time to time, and maintained a house at the settlement for their visits. The site of the house could not be relocated but oral testimony from Henry's grandson, who stayed there briefly as a child, provides some details. The Henrys' house was similar in construction to other houses at the site, built of timber and lined internally with hessian and newspaper, but it was also subtly different, with a connection of piped water from a gully behind the house. This probably reflected Henry's earlier training as a plumber and the application of his personal skills to ensure his family's comfort, but it also reflects a significant improvement on the facilities available to his employees. Moreover, the Henry house was isolated from all the other buildings at the southern edge of the mill clearing. Its location at the highest point of the mill, away from all the other huts and houses, provided a clear physical indication of the separation between employer and employees.

Artefacts from the site provided important evidence for consumption patterns among mill workers. While Henry maintained a small store in the camp, employees were not obliged to shop there and it appears to have been mainly used by single workers for the purchase of personal items such as tobacco. Most residents preferred to order staple goods from storekeepers in nearby towns which were then delivered twice a week along the tramline. Makers' marks on the excavated artefacts show that the goods they brought in included numerous items manufactured in Melbourne, with additional goods deriving from Geelong, Ballarat, Adelaide and Sydney. Most overseas goods, including crockery and condiments, came from England. Some households maintained vegetable gardens, while children caught fish in the river and trapped rabbits (Davies 2005a).

There was also substantial archaeological evidence for reuse and recycling. Sawmills frequently acquired equipment, including rails, boilers and engines, second-hand from mining companies or government railways. This resourcefulness extended to domestic contexts as well. Bricks, for example, were scavenged from other mills when they closed or were purchased second-hand in small lots. Knight's bricks from Lal Lal, near Ballarat, used in one of the fireplaces, must have been in circulation for some years before being brought to Henry's Mill, because the brick company went out of business in 1898, 6 years before the mill was established (Jack and Cremin 1994:62). Iron rails were cut into short lengths and fitted as a rough hearth in one of the excavated houses, while another hearth featured an iron fire bar salvaged from a boiler. There were also 11 examples of glass bottles cut down into jars, probably used to preserve jams and sauces made from locally grown fruits and vegetables (Davies 2002:63–64; Stuart 1993). As sawmills were mostly short-term operations, and workers generally rented their housing, there was little reason or incentive to invest heavily in one's residence. Instead, people made do with what was available locally, combining the purchase of mass-produced goods with careful thrift and self-sufficiency.

This way of life in forest areas changed substantially after the Second World War. Fewer workers were willing to endure the isolation and rough living conditions of forest mills, and most wanted better access to community facilities and education for their children. Extension of the electricity grid provided greater convenience, safety and control for sawmillers than steam engines, which enabled the relocation of mills to towns at the forest edge (Dargavel 1995:52). This process was also facilitated by the construction of roads and the growing availability and power of diesel trucks.

Combined with the expansion of wood chipping and pulp mills, an entirely new economy of forest exploitation had emerged by the 1950s.

Minor Forest Industries

Along with sawmills, a range of other processing industries were also based on forest resources. Historical records of such activities, however, are often lacking, and archaeological remains are an important source of evidence for understanding how these industries functioned. Railway sleepers, for example, were cut with axes from river red gum and ironbark woodlands, while palings and shingles were split from straight-grained trees such as mountain ash and messmate. Wood was also cut for domestic and industrial fuel in massive quantities, while black wattle trees were stripped of their bark to provide tannin for use in the leather industry (Searle 1991). Charcoal burning was also carried out in forest and woodland areas, creating a product that burnt at twice the heat of wood, but had negligible weight and was easy to transport (Walker 1979:40). The industry was widespread in the Wimmera and Grampians regions of western Victoria. Burning charcoal involved cutting timber into short lengths and stacking the pieces into a large conical mound. The wood was covered with earth, clay and galvanised iron, leaving only a small hole at the top. It was then set alight, and allowed to smoulder slowly for days or even weeks at a time. The production of good charcoal depended on keeping the air supply low and the temperature high. Constant vigilance was thus needed to prevent flare-ups and to maintain an even burn, so charcoal burners often camped beside their kilns in the bush. When the charcoal was cool, it was shovelled into sacks and sold to blacksmiths and foundries. Old iron drums and boilers were also used as retorts to produce charcoal in some areas (Fig. 8.7). Charcoal burning was widely practised in Australia's forests and woodlands, and archaeological traces include shallow pits, iron kiln fragments and coppice regrowth around old kiln sites (Land Conservation Council 1996:65).

A unique archaeological site in Victoria's Dandenong Ranges is testament to one related but short-lived forest industry. The Kurth Kiln was built in stringybark forest in the hills east of Melbourne to produce charcoal during the Second World War, as a response to petrol shortages. Cars fitted with a "gas producer" could run on charcoal gas as a substitute fuel. By 1941, the huge demand for charcoal to fuel vehicles prompted the Forests Commission of Victoria to build a large charcoal kiln to increase supplies. Based on a model developed by Ernest Kurth, a chemist at the University of Tasmania, it operated on a continuous cycle by the pyrolysis of timber, and produced about 1.4 tons of charcoal every day, which was a major improvement on the standard steel kilns of the day (Catrice 1998; Schmitt 1992). Physical remains of the site show that the Kurth Kiln was built of brick on a concrete foundation and had a working height of 6 m (Fig. 8.8). The brickwork was reinforced with iron bracing, using light rails set vertically in the sides.

The site for the kiln met three crucial requirements: sloping land, running water and ample forest nearby. Gold miners had worked in the area since the 1860s,

Fig. 8.7 Portable charcoal kiln in the Gembrook Forest east of Melbourne (photo P. Davies)

leaving a network of water races and dams. Several of these were adapted to draw water from the Tomahawk Creek nearby, to supply the kiln's cooling system and to drive a water wheel to power a charcoal grader. There was also a ready supply of dry but otherwise useless timber, the result of ringbarking by sustenance workers in the 1930s Depression. "Susso" workers were paid a small relief wage by the government to undertake forest work. The sloping site meant that wood fuel was fed in at the top of the kiln via a ramp at the top of the embankment, and charcoal was recovered from chutes at the bottom of the kiln. The Kurth Kiln operated successfully for several years, producing several hundred tons of charcoal, but the expansion of private production meant the facility was obsolete by the end of 1943, although petrol rationing continued in Australia until 1950 (Davison 2004:12). The kiln represents, nevertheless, an excellent example of change and continuity in Australian manufacturing. It combined traditional forms of technology, including water races, a water wheel, and managed forests, with contemporary chemical engineering to deal with a wartime energy crisis.

Eucalyptus oil was an early and highly distinctive Australian manufacture that has left archaeological evidence in many forested parts of the country. The oil was recognised for its medicinal value almost as soon as Europeans arrived in 1788, but it was not until the 1850s that production began on a commercial scale. Joseph Bosisto, a Victorian chemist, began distilling oil at a small plant in the Dandenong Ranges near Melbourne around 1854. The popularity of eucalyptus

Fig. 8.8 Kurth Kiln in the Gembrook Forest east of Melbourne. The kiln operated between 1941 and 1943 to produce charcoal for use as a substitute motor fuel during the Second World War (photo P. Davies)

oil grew quickly, recognised not only as an effective decongestant and antiseptic, but also as a deodoriser and as an additive to soap. In later years it was also used in mining operations involving the separation of base-metal ores. In 1880 Bosisto joined Alfred Fenton and Frederick Grimwade in establishing the Eucalyptus Mallee Company near Dimboola in western Victoria (Poynter 2003:34). A number of other distillers were also in operation in the area by this time, and production had spread to New South Wales, Tasmania and South Australia.

Eucalyptus oil was commonly distilled from about 20 different eucalypt species, especially from the peppermint and mallee groups. The process was a simple one of steam distillation, in which the leaves were gathered and packed tightly into a large vat or tank. A fire heated water in the vat to produce steam, causing the oil cells in the leaves to burst, releasing the oil as a vapour. This mixture was cooled by water in a condenser, and the oil, being lighter than water, separated by gravity and floated to the surface. It could then be redistilled and refined further, while the spent leaves were burned in heaps to produce a potash residue used as a fertiliser.

The archaeology of the industry, described in detail by Michael Pearson (1993b), reveals a number of standard features, with variations according to the local environment and the scale of operation. A forest or woodland area of at least 1,000 acres was needed to supply the necessary leaf for one still. Trees were cut close to the ground, so that coppice regrowth could be cut again 2 or 3 years later. Distilling sites were normally located near dams or creeks to supply the water needed in the steaming process. A typical arrangement included one or two tanks, often 400 gallon ship-tanks, with the tops cut off and refitted as removable lids. Mud or clay was used to seal the lid when it was bolted or clamped to the tank. A simple crane was used to raise and lower the lid, and to remove the spent leaf. A condenser pipe ran from the top of the tank downhill through a water-filled race, carrying the oil vapour, which was collected in a drum. Sometimes elaborate water races were built to maintain a supply of water, while tanks sunk into brick pits and substantial furnaces were recorded in South Australia (Pearson 1993b:100). The archaeological remains of the industry are widespread but often quite ephemeral, as the equipment was generally removed when an area was worked out. The impact on local landscapes, however, was significant, with distilleries targeting particular species, and transforming the ecology of slow-growing eucalypt communities in the process.

Eucalyptus stills utilised a range of simple, accessible materials, including tanks and drums, corrugated iron, water piping and abundant local wood for fuel. Tools for cutting the leaf included hand axes, small adzes, cane knives and "eucy" hooks, a sickle-shaped knife. A bush hut near the still provided accommodation for the distiller and perhaps for one or two workmates. The industry was popular with small-scale, independent operators, who could acquire the basic equipment and work to their own routine. Larger operations might employ a dozen or more men, some working seasonally between farming jobs, and paid by the volume of leaf they cut (Borschmann 1999:240). The industry suited men who sought independence and flexible work, and required little in the way of skills and experience. The work, however, was very arduous, with constant bending, cutting and lifting, and distilling sites were nearly always in isolated areas.

Bricks

Brick-making was one of the very first extractive and manufacturing industries established in 1788. Even though several thousand bricks were brought out with the First Fleet, local manufacture quickly became a necessity. Within a month or two of landing, settlers had discovered a good source of clay at Cockle Creek, near today's Darling Harbour in Sydney. This area, soon known as the Brickfields or Brickfield Hill, was to be the focus of brickmaking in Sydney until about 1841. The area had good supplies of clay and shale suitable for making bricks, tiles and pottery, and was close to the main road to Parramatta and outlying areas. Several convict brickmakers arrived with the First Fleet, including James Bloodsworth, Samuel Wheeler and John King (Cowan 1998:12–14). Bloodsworth was a bricklayer and builder by trade, and was soon appointed master bricklayer in the settlement. As there were initially no architects in the colony, he was responsible for designing and constructing some of Australia's first government buildings. These included First Government House, a Georgian-style, two-storey building constructed in 1789 as the official residence of Governor Arthur Phillip. Archaeological excavations carried out in the 1980s revealed that brick and stone were used for the foundations, with solid brick walling and stone quoins extending to the roof level (Proudfoot et al. 1991:44–45). Bloodsworth was pardoned in 1790, and later became superintendent of all bricklayers and brickmakers. When he died in 1804, a number of brickworks and potteries were operating at Brickfield Hill, responding to the demand for bricks for private houses and government buildings.

Although sites like First Government House have produced examples of the products of early brick manufacturing, there has been only limited archaeological evidence for the brickyards themselves (Stocks 2008). Recent consulting projects in the Brickfields area, however, have produced more information about the industry. Pits and hollows used as clay sources have been found in the Haymarket area below Brickfield Hill, and waster pits and kiln debris have also been found at several sites. One site, excavated by Casey and Lowe at 710–722 George Street, has been associated with Thomas Ball (ca. 1800–1823) while a site on Wentworth Street excavated by Graham Wilson has been associated with Jonathan Leak (ca. 1820–1839). Ball's waster pits contained numerous fragments of roofing tile and Leak's included pottery and clay pipe fragments as well as building materials.

Parramatta also had an early brick industry, begun by the government in 1790 in order to provide materials needed for the settlement. A series of development projects 200 years later has provided the opportunity to learn much more about this industry. Robyn Stocks (2008) has analysed clay building materials from several sites around Parramatta built in the 1790s and compared them with contemporaneous clay products from Sydney. She identified several types, leading her to conclude that while some tiles used in Parramatta were made in Sydney, others were made locally. Variations in the size, style and quality of the roofing tiles indicate that there were distinct manufacturing differences in the two centres, due to a number of factors including different regional traditions brought from England by the convict brickmakers, the availability of materials in the colony, and local innovation and improvement in methods. In general, the tiles produced in Parramatta appear to have been of higher quality, possibly because of lessons learned in Sydney.

Early brick manufacture was a slow and arduous business. Clay was manually excavated by pick and mixed with fresh water in shallow pits. The raw clay was kneaded (or pugged) with bare feet or tree branches to remove stones and other impurities, after which the clay was covered to settle for a few days. The labour-intensive nature of this method, however, meant pug mills were soon introduced. These were essentially a large wooden tub with a shaft in the centre. A beam attached to the shaft was driven by convicts or a horse, with blades along the shaft slicing and kneading the clay into a plastic texture. Pug mills were much more efficient than manual pugging and produced larger quantities of prepared clay.

Brick moulding was a skilled but repetitive process. The mould was a rectangular wooden box without a top or bottom. A stockboard was fitted to the base of the mould, with a raised "kick" to form the frog in the brick. The frog helped the mortar to bind the bricks more strongly and served to identify the brickmaker. A lump of clay was taken and roughly moulded by hand into the shape of a brick. It was then rolled in sand and thrown hard into the mould (hence "sandstock" brick). The clay was pressed firmly into the corners of the mould, with any extra clay scraped off the top. The mould was then lifted from the stock, and with a sharp tap the brick was loosened onto a board. If the clay stuck in the mould, a thumb or finger mark would be left when the brickmaker pushed it free (Fig. 8.9). Thumbprints may also have been used as tally moulds to record daily quotas (Ringer 2008:16). A skilled moulder, with three or four workers to assist, could produce about 1,200 bricks in a 10-hour day (Bell 1998a:15; Gemmell 1986:6).

The new, soft bricks were carefully stacked in a "hack" for drying, which could take up to a fortnight, depending on the weather. The bricks were then ready for firing, usually in a "clamp" kiln, a temporary structure built adjacent to the brick-works. The bricks were arranged in courses, leaving flues and tunnels for fuel and heat circulation, and the whole clamp was covered in a skin of old bricks and clay. While they varied in size, a clamp often measured around 8 by 6 m at the base, and stood 3–4 m in height. The firing normally took 1–2 weeks, after which the fire was quenched and the clamp was allowed to cool.

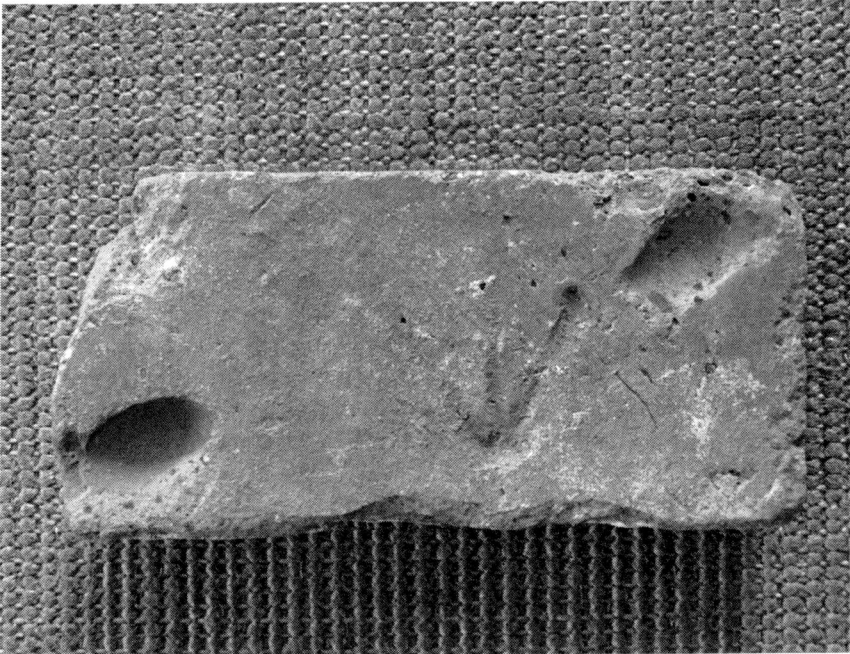

Fig. 8.9 Brick with thumbprints and broad arrow mark indicating government property (photo P. Davies)

Several brick-making sites from the 1830s have been recorded at Lake Innes in New South Wales (Connah 2007:77–84). The sites included clay pits, flat areas for moulding and drying the bricks, the remains of clamps, and at one location an artefact scatter suggesting that the brickmakers had lived on-site. In most cases evidence for the clamps was slight, consisting of scattered bricks and brick fragments and short lines of in-situ bricks partially buried in the ground. The low mounds seem to be the bases of the clamps, and from the lack of surviving material it appears that they were fired successfully and the bricks removed for use. Connah notes that it is highly likely that when firing was successful clamp locations were used repeatedly, making it difficult to judge the quantity of bricks produced. At one of the sites there was also evidence of a clamp that had failed. Here the mound was at least one and a half metres high and several metres long. While many of the bricks were intact, others had weathered back into clay, indicating that for some reason the clamp had not achieved temperatures hot enough or for long enough to bake the bricks sufficiently. From the arrangement of the visible bricks it was also possible to trace the system of vents built into the stack that enabled the hot air to circulate during the firing.

This traditional method required little beyond a good supply of clay, fuel and plenty of labour. It was, however, inefficient, with each kiln having to be demolished to remove the bricks. Archaeological evidence indicates that brick quality was also variable, as it was difficult to maintain a constant kiln temperature. Many bricks were overfired (clinkers), with a glassy exterior and a brittle interior. Others were underfired (doughboys), and were soft and porous. In spite of these problems, clamp kilns remained standard in Australia for much of the nineteenth century (Lewis 2008:6.02.3).

Brickworks were invariably located next to a good source of clay or shale. The blasting, excavating and loading of clay was a substantial industry in its own right, and often resulted in a large clay pit. Bricks themselves were always heavy to transport, especially when roads were poor, so it was generally easier to make bricks at the source of demand rather than haul them long distances by horse and cart. This meant that numerous local brickworks in country areas continued to use traditional methods of moulding and firing through the nineteenth century, when large city brickworks had become largely mechanised. In remote areas, itinerant brickmakers made their rounds well into the late nineteenth century, contracting to make bricks on site (Gemmell 1986:6). As clay soils are very common in Australia, this was a cost-effective building method, used on pastoral properties such as Lake Innes and on isolated industrial sites such as the Howqua goldfield in the mountains of northeastern Victoria, where bricks for the roasting kiln were made on-site (Lawrence et al. 2000).

As the industry expanded during the nineteenth century, permanent kilns were also constructed. The simplest of these was the scotch (or updraft) kiln, which consisted of a large brick box with a chimney at the top and fireholes at the sides. They often had a capacity of about 20,000 bricks. Improvements in firing methods were accompanied by the gradual introduction of steam-powered machinery for clay preparation and brick moulding. Steam engines were used, for example, to drive large crushing mills, which broke down the hard clay shales found throughout the Sydney region (Ringer 2008:44–45). An extruding machine was also developed to produce semi-plastic, wire-cut bricks. In this method, stiff clay was clamped in a box and extruded out of a rectangular nozzle, like toothpaste from a tube. The resulting column of clay was sliced by wires into bricks, at a rate of around 15,000 bricks a day (Ringer 2008:47). This method was especially appropriate for the softer alluvial clays of Victoria, although the bricks were often poorly compressed and slow to dry. Bricks produced this way lack frogs and makers' marks.

A major development in brick production was the dry press method, developed by a number of English firms in the 1870s, including Bradley and Craven, and the Platt Brothers. Finely ground clay was mixed with about 10 percent water and the mixture was placed in a hopper at the top of the press machine. The clay was then fed into brick-shaped moulds below, and a plunger was forced downwards under high pressure to squeeze the clay into a brick. Bricks were ejected mechanically from the mould, which was refilled with clay, and the process repeated again and again. Each press could turn out 2,000 or more bricks per hour. Dry pressed bricks were a great improvement on traditional methods, being denser and more uniform in size (Stuart 2005:83). The dramatic increase in production also meant that brickmakers needed large metropolitan markets to absorb the quantities of bricks they produced. This coincided with the suburban building boom of the 1880s, and the construction of brick terrace housing in Melbourne, Sydney and Adelaide.

This period also witnessed a major change in kiln technology, when a Prussian inventor, Friedrich Hoffman, patented a new type of kiln in 1858 (Stuart 1989b:29). His "continuous" kiln was based on the principle that the fire, unlike in earlier

Fig. 8.10 Interior of Hoffman kiln at the Hoffman Brick Company in Melbourne (photo P. Davies)

kilns, was never extinguished. The Hoffman kiln consisted of one long vaulted chamber, originally constructed in a circle (Fig. 8.10). The chamber was partitioned into smaller apartments, each with an arched opening to the outside. The fire was led progressively around the kiln from one chamber to the next, with the bricks undergoing drying, pre-heating, firing and cooling in turn. The whole process could take several weeks for one batch of bricks, but several batches of bricks would be in the kiln at any one time, each at a different stage in the firing process. Above the kiln was a large shed with rows of firing ports in the floor, through which sweating stokers fed coal to the firing chambers below. Underground flues connected the firing chamber to a tall central chimney. Australia's first Hoffman kiln was installed in 1870 by the Hoffman Patent Tile and Brick Company in Brunswick, Melbourne, but others soon followed. In Sydney, Goodlet and Smith established a new yard at Waterloo in 1876 with a circular Hoffman kiln, while in Adelaide, the City and Suburban Steam Brickbuilding Company erected a Hoffman kiln in about 1882 (Lewis 2008:6.02.11). Although the original Hoffman design was circular in plan, examples in Australia normally had straight sides with semi-circular ends (Fig. 8.11). Hoffman kilns were very fuel efficient and held many thousands of bricks at any one time. They quickly became the dominant firing technology in metropolitan areas and combined with high-powered presses to bring

Fig. 8.11   Hoffman kiln at the Hoffman Brick Company in Melbourne (photo P. Davies)

brick construction into the mass housing market by the end of the nineteenth century (Bell 1998a:22).

Working conditions for brickmakers were often extremely harsh, especially prior to mechanisation. Hot summer winds whipped up clouds of brick dust and grit, while rain turned clay pits into quagmires. Throughout the nineteenth century, labourers extracted clay and shale using only pick and shovel, and transferred the clay with wheelbarrows, or portable tramways at the bigger yards. Men working at the kilns endured thick smoke, fumes and great heat. Brickworkers had a well-deserved reputation for toughness and heavy drinking. Young boys, aged 8–14, were also widely employed in brickyards as cheap labour. They worked 10-hour days and had to keep pace with the brickmoulders, shifting up to 8 tonnes of clay a day, and earning only 10–14 shillings a week (Fitzgerald 1987:146). In the 1880s, brickmakers were still working a 56-hour week, with men earning only a little over £2 per week (Gemmell 1986:10). Technological changes introduced late in the century, however, slowly began to improve working conditions to some extent.

The small scale of most brickworks until later in the nineteenth century means that relatively few traces of them survive, except perhaps for the remains of a small clay pit and scatters of broken bricks from the clamp where they were fired (Birmingham et al. 1983:54). The large metropolitan brickworks, however, were huge operations, often sprawling over acres of ground. With deep clay pits, tram and train lines, moulding sheds, power plants, large kilns and a range of other infrastructure, they were a prominent industrial feature of local landscapes. Such yards often employed hundreds of workers, who generally lived in suburban cottages nearby. The Hoffman brickworks in Melbourne, for example, included numerous brick and pottery kilns, several massive clay holes, a research laboratory, engine house, workshops, storage sheds, and its own railway siding and locomotive (Stuart 1987, 1989b). Highly innovative in its early years, the business became slowly run down during the twentieth century, and eventually closed in the early 1990s. Since then it has been transformed into a housing estate, with industrial remnants including a kiln, smoke tower and moulding shed today sitting uneasily among the modern suburban townhouses. At other suburban brickyards all that remains is a park, the end result of a long process of filling in the clay pits with the local council's rubbish collection and then capping and landscaping the area.

Lime

Bricks needed mortar to hold them together, and a key component of mortar was lime. In the first few decades of settlement around Sydney, the main source of lime was shell from Aboriginal middens. Convict women were sent out to collect shells, which were washed, crushed and burnt in pits. Lime-burning, however, was filthy, unpleasant work, as the quicklime burnt the skin and eyes, and the work was often performed by convicts as a punishment. The quicklime was mixed with water and left for a few days to make slaked lime. Sand (and sometimes animal hair) was then added to make mortar. Shell remained a source of lime in some areas until late in the nineteenth century, often transported in small sailing vessels that loaded directly from the coastal middens. Limestone, however, came into use by the 1820s, and more substantial kilns were constructed as well (M. Pearson 1990:28).

Archaeological evidence reveals that lime kilns took various forms in the nineteenth century, but were generally distinguished by whether they operated intermittently or continuously. The most common type of kiln in New South Wales was the D-shaped, intermittent kiln. It consisted of a curved pit dug into the face of a hill or slope, with a stone wall built across the front to create a D-shaped firing chamber. Ash boxes were built into the floor of the kiln, and covered with brick or iron fire bars, and each had an opening through the front wall with an arched fire hole over the top. The kiln was loaded with alternating layers of fuel and limestone, and firing took from 2 to 4 days. The D-kiln was simple to build and operate, but required a significant amount of fuel and labour. It was also out of operation while cooling and being emptied and refilled (M. Pearson 1990:30).

Lime was also in demand from the earliest days of settlement in and around Melbourne, and by the early 1840s a substantial industry had developed, with production mainly occurring around Geelong and the Mornington Peninsula, where there were good supplies of limestone in close proximity to coastal shipping for transport (see Chapter 4). The building boom that accompanied the gold rush increased the demand for lime, with extra supplies brought in from New South Wales, Tasmania, and as ballast in ships from Britain (Harrington 2000:21–22). Portland cement was also becoming a popular building material around this time. It consisted of a mixture of clay and limestone which was calcined, or roasted, and then ground into a fine powder. Lime kilns in Victoria were often built as vertical shaft, or bottle kilns, and could be fired continuously. The kilns generally comprised a shaft or chimney built into a hill or escarpment, which was enclosed by a front retaining wall with a tunnel providing access to a draw hole at the base. The shaft was up to 9 m deep and usually narrowed into a funnel towards the base, to promote downwards movement of the load. Wing walls at each side ensured the stability of the cut into the hillside (Fig. 8.12). Six of these kilns were built at Walkerville, near Wilsons Promontory, from around 1878, with ships used to transport the lime to market. By the early 1890s there were up to 80 men employed in firing, quarrying and woodcutting for fuel. Around 50 families lived in the area and were supported by the lime trade. Demand gradually declined in the following years, however, as inland quarries opened and the operation was abandoned in 1926 (Harrington 2000:42–44).

Pottery

Pottery was made in New South Wales almost from the beginning of the settlement period. One of the earliest potters was Elijah Leake, a convict who made basins, plates, jars, pipes and similar wares in the early 1790s (Lawson 1971:18).

Fig. 8.12 Limekiln at Walkerville in southern Victoria (photo S. Lawrence)

By 1800, several potteries were established at the Brickfields, including the work-shop of Samuel Skinner. Skinner arrived in the colony in 1801, accompanying his wife Mary who had been convicted and transported for shoplifting. He made glazed domestic pottery and began advertising his wares in the *Sydney Gazette* in October 1803, which included "Flower Pots, Tea-Pots, Cups and Saucers…Ewers, Chamber vessels, Cream Jugs, Muggs, Water Jugs…Children's Tea Sets" and many other items. The pottery appears to have flourished until his death in 1807. Another potter, William Cluer, began making clay tobacco pipes in 1808, which were exported to England and the Netherlands (Lawson 1971:20). Archaeologists have recovered examples of locally made pottery from this period at a number of sites, including sherds of both glazed and unglazed earthenwares from the Gateway Site at Circular Quay in Sydney and from George Street in Parramatta (Higginbotham 1987:17). Early pottery production thus depended on the skill and energy of just a few individuals, and stands in contrast to the industrialisation of pottery manufacture in Staffordshire from the mid-eighteenth century.

In the following years, a number of other potteries were established in Sydney as well. Jonathon Leak and John Moreton were potters from Staffordshire who were convicted of burglary and transported to Sydney in 1819. Both were put to work in the Government Pottery, but within a few years each had established his own workshop. Leak's pottery at the Brickfields included a residence for himself and his family, and three pottery kilns. By 1828 he was exporting coarse earthenwares to Mauritius, and sending shipments of bricks to Launceston. He died in 1838, and the pottery closed the following year. John Moreton, who had worked with Josiah Wedgwood prior to his conviction, had established his own pottery by 1823. Sentenced to work on a quarry gang for 6 years for another burglary, he returned in 1832 to work the Surry Hills Pottery with his three sons, and produced a range of pottery articles and clay tobacco pipes. John Moreton died in 1847 at the age of 70, and the pottery closed a few years later (Casey 1999:8).

Mary Casey's (1999) archaeological study of the DMR site in the Brickfields in Sydney links the local manufacture of pottery with dairying and the role of women in local food production during the early nineteenth century. Home dairies were common in this period, providing an important degree of self-sufficiency and fresh food, including milk, cream, butter and cheese. Milk was left to stand in wide, shallow pans until the lighter cream rose to the surface. This was skimmed off and churned into butter using a hand churn, with the butter packed in salt as a preservative (Gollan 1978:71–72). Until the industrialisation of dairying in the 1880s, most dairy work, which included milking and butter-making, was in the hands of women. Surplus production was sold or bartered to provide extra income (Casey 1999:4).

Excavation of a highly disturbed deposit in 1997 at the DMR site (Area B) in Sydney recovered, among other material, the remains of 57 lead-glazed vessels and 12 self-slipped vessels, all of which were probably of local manufacture. These items included wide shallow pans in glazed earthenware, along with fine yellow wares that appear to imitate the popular "creamware" of this period, and self-slipped vessels that may have been garden pots. The site dates to the period ca.1807–1840s, when most of the area was an open grassy paddock. The building was probably used as a home dairy, based on the high proportion of glazed earthenware pans. Women's dairying activities provided essential fresh foods for both the family and the local community, with the production of a food surplus allowing for the purchase of other goods and services. Insights derived from archaeological projects such as these help to challenge the conventional image of the Brickfields as a place simply of harsh

convict labour and disorderly behaviour, and reveal hidden and unrecorded details
of complex domestic arrangements and gendered work practices.

Archaeological investigation of James King's pottery at Irrawang near Newcastle
reveals further details about pottery manufacture in this period. King (1800–1857)
arrived in Sydney in 1827, having spent a decade studying glass-making and chem-
istry in Scotland. He soon obtained a land grant of almost 2,000 acres on the
Williams River, just north of Newcastle, where he built a homestead and called
it Irrawang. King's main interest was in the wine industry, and he played a major
role in developing viticulture in the Hunter Valley. He also began making pottery
at Irrawang around 1834, relying on imported workmen and their skills to develop
his enterprise. The pottery produced cheap, domestic earthenwares for the colonial
market, and King used newspaper advertising to promote his wares. The shortage of
labour brought about by the gold rush, however, forced King to close the pottery in
1851, and equipment was sold off in 1855.

The site of King's Irrawang pottery was excavated between 1967 and 1974 by
Judy Birmingham (1976). The project revealed two kilns, a crushing mill, a circular puddling ditch lined with palings and a pottery workshop. One of the kilns was
a circular bottle kiln and the other was rectangular in plan with brick walls 2-foot
thick. The workshop included two flues which channelled hot air from the bottle
kiln under the floor to dry out the green wares. The remains suggest that workmen
applied traditional English pottery techniques, while making allowances for local
conditions. Thousands of pot sherds recovered from the site also indicate the nature
of the pottery produced (Fig. 8.13). Shapes included pie dishes, pudding basins,
milk pans, water filters, jugs and ewers. Stoneware jars filled with two gallons of

Fig. 8.13 Pottery stamp of James King, Irrawang (photo D. Frankel)

Irrawang wine sold for two shillings and sixpence, and were returnable for refilling (Birmingham 1976:308). One sherd of blue edge ware was also found, suggesting that King may have experimented with tablewares as well as utilitarian items. However, edgeware was considered old-fashioned by the 1830s and 1840s, and the more modern transfer prints were sufficiently desirable that they could command the higher prices required for imports to be profitable. In the main, the pottery produced a range of functional earthenwares and stonewares with a variety of glazes and decorative mouldings, which were popular in the New South Wales market and could compete with imports on price. Because it was so utilitarian, however, very few complete pieces have survived (Bickford 1971:51).

A pottery and brickworks was also established at Port Arthur in Van Diemen's Land in the early 1830s. The products of the pottery were mostly limited to milk pans and flowerpots, with no evidence of domestic items such as cups and plates ever being manufactured at the site. Almost 200 convicts were transported to Van Diemen's Land over the years who had some training in pottery, but relatively few were given much opportunity to exercise their skill (Queen Victoria Museum 1983:5). The penal settlement closed in 1877 and later, around 1886, James Price established a commercial pottery at Port Arthur, known by this time as Carnarvon. He produced a range of tiles, salt-glazed pipes and unglazed domestic pottery. Most of the pottery was inscribed or stamped "Port Arthur", but this should not be taken as evidence of convict manufacture, as transportation to Van Diemen's Land ended in 1853. The operation closed around the time of Price's death in 1912 (Ford 1995:173–176).

Pottery was also made in South Australia from the 1850s by German Lutheran and Cornish potters. Samuel Hoffmann was a master potter from Prussia who arrived in South Australia in 1845 with his wife Auguste. The couple established a farm in the Barossa Valley and in the late 1850s Hoffmann began making pottery on his property. He built a bottle-shaped updraught kiln, similar to those built in Germany from about 1700, and prepared red clay from a number of local sources. Using a wooden potter's wheel, Hoffmann produced a range of full-bodied vessels of traditional German design, with a lead slip glaze. Noris Ioannou's study of the few surviving Hoffmann vessels, and his archaeological investigation of the kiln site and associated sherd material, indicate that Hoffmann produced numerous functional items, such as pickling jars, jam pots, milk pans, and water and wine jugs (Ioannou 1986:18–37; 1987). He packed his wares in a wagon and sold them to settlers in the Barossa Valley and beyond, meeting a demand among German families for familiar, traditional ceramic vessels. Hoffmann's retention of traditional forms and styles indicates his own sense of cultural identity, as well as a determination among local German settlers to preserve Prussian culture within a new homeland and natural environment. It is a rare Australian example of a pottery tradition based on inherited knowledge and techniques that for a brief period continued to exist alongside the expansion of the industrial mode of production in Britain.

As the nineteenth century progressed, some small-scale potteries expanded into large industrial concerns. The Bendigo Pottery, for example, started by George Duncan Guthrie in 1858, became a major supplier of industrial and domestic ceramics (Scholes 1979), while the Lithgow Pottery became an important part of the industrial landscape of the Lithgow Valley in the 1880s and 1890s (Evans 1980). Enoch Fowler established a pottery at Glebe in Sydney in 1837, where he made up large orders for ginger beer bottles and blacking jars (Ford 1995:27). When the operation was moved to Camperdown in 1863, Fowler began mass production of sewer pipes using mechanical extrusion. Mechanised production techniques were reaching the Australian colonies by this period and dramatically expanded workshop capacity. By the 1870s Fowler's Pottery produced all manner of pipes, paving tiles, chimney pots and bricks. The number of employees rose to 100, and many who began as apprentices spent their whole working lives at the Fowler pottery. The business continued to expand and remains in business today.

Coal, Iron and Steel

Coal, iron and steel have long formed the backbone of Australian industry, and today Australian companies are major producers and exporters of each of these commodities. As early settlement grew, the need for iron products, large and small, became increasingly clear, and interest grew in producing these goods locally. Exploration for coal began in the 1790s, and foundries using pig-iron imported as ballast from Britain were flourishing in Sydney by the 1830s. The first colonial ironworks was established at Mittagong in New South Wales in 1848, and steel was produced at Eskbank in the Lithgow Valley as early as 1900 (Jack and Cremin 1994:97). The historical archaeology of these industries brings out many of the themes common to Australian manufacturing and processing, including the import of overseas technology and capital and their application to colonial conditions, and the development of Australian industries within a global context. Coal, iron and steel have also transformed natural and cultural landscapes, creating a distinctive legacy of industry and settlement at places such as the Hunter Valley, Broken Hill, Lithgow and Port Kembla in New South Wales, at Whyalla in South Australia, and at Gippsland in Victoria. There is also archaeological evidence for short-lived operations where the experiment was tried and failed, including the Tamar Valley in northern Tasmania, the Fleurieu Peninsula south of Adelaide, and at Lal Lal in central Victoria (Jack and Cremin 1994).

Coal

Coal was observed north of Sydney in the Hunter Valley (Newcastle) on several occasions during the 1790s, and in 1801 a convict settlement was established near the mouth of the Hunter River. The settlement was intended to serve as both a coalmine and as an outpost of secondary punishment. Convicts dug horizontal tunnels into the coal seams, and wheeled the coal out in barrows, working up to 12 h a day. By the 1820s, however, Newcastle became less of a place

of banishment, as land was taken up in the area, and trade and industry flourished. The Australian Agricultural Company took over coal mining operations at
Newcastle in 1828. A new mining area was established, with coal skips rolled
down a railway to the company's wharf on the Hunter River. Further operations were developed in the following decades, which included railways, wharf
reclamation and hydraulic steam cranes (Bairstow 1986). The scale of operations at what remains one of Australia's richest coalfields, however, and the
need for constant refurbishment of facilities at Newcastle, means that relatively
few traces remain of the origins of coal mining in the area (Birmingham et al.
1979:100).

Tasmania's coal industry began in 1822, when convicts began mining for coal
at Macquarie Harbour (Tuffin 2008:41). A much more substantial operation began
in 1833, when the Coal Mines Station at Plunkett Point on the Tasman Peninsula
was opened using the labour of convicts from Port Arthur. The mines offered punishment to "refractory" convicts, and provided an alternative to importing coal from
New South Wales. Unlike at Newcastle, however, substantial archaeological remains
reveal important details about living conditions, punishment and mining operations
at the Coal Mines Station. These include the ruins of buildings, mine workings and a
tramway incline. Coal was first extracted using horizontal adits close to the water's
edge, but as workings moved further inland, a series of vertical shafts were sunk
to reach the coal. A steam engine, manufactured at the Derwent Foundry in Hobart,
was installed in 1841 to pump water from the mine, and while neither the engine nor
its chimney has survived, the stone foundations are evidence for the first mechanised
mine in Tasmania. Hand-turned winding wheels, however, were still used to bring
coal baskets up to the surface from the working galleries. The convicts worked in
shifts, and each shift was required to extract 20 tonnes of coal (Tuffin 2008:51). By
the 1840s up to 600 convicts were stationed at Plunkett Point, guarded by a detach-
ment of officers and soldiers. The convicts were first accommodated in huts, but
these were later replaced with cells of stone and brick, while nearby were quarters
for the commanding officer, surgeon and other officials. There was also a chapel,
bakehouse and a large, two-storey commissariat store (Fig. 8.14). Four punishment
cells were built deep in the underground workings, but these were replaced around
1846 by 36 solitary cells built below the Prisoner Barracks. The mine eventually
included an extensive network of underground tunnels, with the convicts working in
two 8-hour shifts. Inefficiency and poor management, however, along with charges
of rampant homosexual vice among the convicts, resulted in the closure of the mine
in 1848, although private concerns continued to mine the coal until ca.1877 (Brand
1993; Tuffin 2008).

Coal was initially used mostly for domestic heating, but coal gas for lighting was
also developed for urban areas in the nineteenth century. The process involved heating coal in the absence of air, in a closed vessel or retort, which gave off a flammable
gas. Gas lighting was first turned on in Australia on May 24, 1841, in a few streets
in Sydney. The new technology was still unavailable in many English towns at the
time, and although the manufacture of coal gas was relatively simple, its distribution

Fig. 8.14 Remains of the Chapel (1838) at the Coal Mines Station on the Tasman Station, which operated with convict labour between 1833 and 1848 (photo S. Lawrence)

was complex and expensive. A law of 1830 required publicans to burn a light outside their premises, but this was a haphazard way to make the streets of Sydney safe at night. The Australian Gas Light Company, formed in 1836, established a plant on Darling Harbour that included coal retorts, a new wharf and large tanks dug into the sandstone to provide a water seal for the gasholders or gasometers (Broomham 1987:22). Lack of local familiarity with the technology meant that the company relied heavily on equipment and skilled workers brought out from England. Coal from Newcastle was unloaded on the dock and shovelled into cast-iron retorts, producing coal gas for storage and distribution through pipes laid beneath the streets. Coal gas was promoted for use in shops and houses for its cleanliness, safety and cheapness over candles and whale oil lamps. Although early acceptance was slow, the 1860s–1880s saw a great expansion of street and household lighting into the suburbs. A similar pattern emerged in Victoria, where gas was first manufactured in 1856, and up to 50 gasworks were eventually built in the colony (Proudley 1987). Most of these were small, and consisted of a retort house, gas condenser, scrubber and purifier, and a gasholder, along with workshops and coal stores. By the turn of the century, however, electric light began to be used increasingly in homes and businesses, with coal gas used more for heating and cooking, while penny-in-the-slot gas meters were introduced as well. Coal gasification nevertheless remained a primary source of energy in Australian cities for much of the twentieth century, with large iron gasometers dominating suburban streetscapes, but by the 1970s it was gradually replaced with natural gas and the coal gasworks were dismantled.

Iron

The value of coal as an export commodity and as an industrial fuel for working iron was also recognised from the early colonial period. Its relationship with iron meant that both became synonymous with manufacturing and processing in the nineteenth century. Iron was cheap and abundant, and a range of technological developments in this period meant that iron came to be used for the production of thousands of domestic and industrial items. Steam engines, railways, bridges and ships were made from iron and steel, and served as symbols of the Industrial Revolution and the emerging modern world (M. Freeman 1999). The Australian iron industry began in the 1840s, and by the 1870s there were numerous ore smelting works in operation. These included three plants on the Tamar River in northern Tasmania, the Hindmarsh Tiers Furnace in South Australia and James Rutherford's blast furnace at Lithgow (Birmingham et al. 1979:90). There were also numerous tin works, brass foundries and wire works contributing to the colonial metal industries. A major challenge, however, was always the distance between suitable sources of iron ore, limestone (used as a flux) and coal. Heavy products needed cheap transport to be competitive, and this calculus of raw materials, transport and markets has long been a factor in Australian iron production. Other problems included securing adequate capital and fluctuating commodity prices on global markets. The early, often faltering steps taken to develop an Australia iron industry, however, were also driven by the need for greater colonial self-sufficiency, and resulted in industrial experiments which heightened awareness of Australia's mineral resources (Jack and Cremin 1994:11–13).

The coal and iron industries in Australia have been the subject of extensive archaeological research over many years, particularly operations at Lithgow (Birmingham et al. 1979:93–98; Cremin 1989; Jack and Cremin 1994) and Mittagong (Godden Mackay Logan 2007). The work of Ian Jack and Aedeen Cremin (1994) shows that most Australian ironworks in the nineteenth century operated in a similar fashion. Iron ore was mined from the earth and fed into the top of a blast furnace, usually a chimney lined with heat-resistant firebricks, with the whole encased in stone or iron. The blast of air, generated by a steam engine, entered near the base through pipes or tuyeres. Fuel was traditionally coal, charcoal or coke (calcined coal), while limestone was added as a fluxing agent to draw off impurities from the ore as slag. The ore took about 12 hours to become molten, when it was tapped from the furnace, and a furnace could remain in blast for months at a time. Molten iron was led out into moulds in a bed of sand, the usual pattern of which was thought to resemble piglets feeding from a sow (hence "pig-iron"). Pigs of iron were then used as the raw material for cast iron, which was hard but brittle, or forged at a hearth and hammered into rods and plates for use as wrought iron by blacksmiths.

At Lal Lal in Victoria the well-preserved remains analysed by Jack and Cremin (1994) reveal the entire operation of an iron-smelting complex. Lal Lal is located about 20 km south-east of Ballarat and the site was closely associated with Ballarat's metal industries. As demand for gold-mining equipment and machinery eased in the 1870s, the slack was taken up by farmers and their enthusiasm for mechanical cultivators and harvesters. Ballarat foundries also made boilers and engines for breweries and factories, while the Phoenix Foundry began producing locomotives in 1873 (Bate 1978:213). A railway line had been completed between Geelong and Ballarat in 1862, with a siding built to Lal Lal to exploit brown coal (lignite) deposits. Lignite is a soft coal with a high water content, which made it a poor fuel for foundries or smelters. The hills around Lal Lal, however, were heavily wooded, and so charcoal was the main fuel used in the blast furnace instead.

The Lal Lal Iron Company was formed in 1873, and the first blast furnace was built in 1875. It consisted simply of an upended boiler lined with firebricks. The furnace operated with limited success, until it was dismantled and replaced with a better model in 1880–1881, the remains of which are visible today. The blast furnace and its associated structures were built on a series of terraces cut into a hillside above the Moorabool River (Fig. 8.15). The furnace and casting shed were on the lowest terrace, while a steam engine to blast the furnace was supported on massive stone foundations on the next terrace up. A smithy and carpenter's shop were built one level higher, while a tramway ended on the top terrace, bringing iron ore, limestone and charcoal to a large wooden shed. These were stored and wheeled directly to the top of the furnace along a wooden trestle bridge.

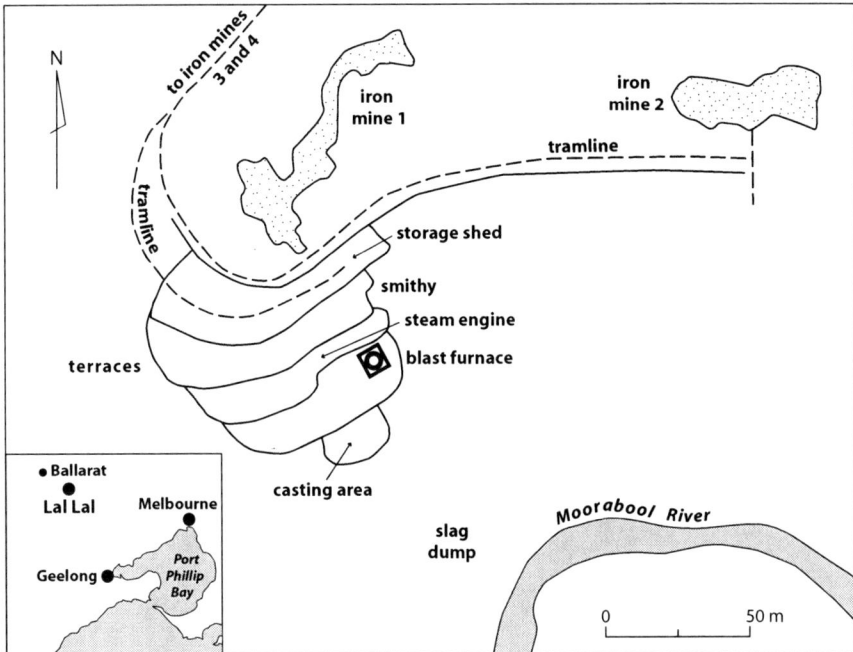

Fig. 8.15 Plan of the Lal Lal ironworks (after Jack and Cremin 1994:68)

The base of the furnace was built of locally quarried stone, with three arched tuyere openings and another for the tap hole. The circular, tapering chimney was lined with firebricks imported from Harris and Pearson of Stourbridge, England, although bricks from the Knights family brickworks nearby were built into the earlier furnace. The whole structure stands about 17 m high (Fig. 8.16). The firebrick lining was surrounded with a 5-cm layer of clay, which was enclosed by stone rubble and the whole encased in worked stone. The furnace was originally square in plan, typical of eighteenth-century furnaces, at a time when circular furnaces in iron and steel had become widespread elsewhere (Jack and Cremin 1994:9). Smoke from the boiler was drawn up the hillside through a stone flue just below ground level, and originally featured a small metal chimney at the top. Other surviving features include the open pits where ore was removed, the remains of the tramlines which

Fig. 8.16 Lal Lal blast furnace (photo S. Lawrence)

carried the ore to the furnace, the slag heap below the casting shed, and the ruins of the cottages that housed the workers and their families.

The fall in price of imported pig-iron, from £10 to £4 10 shillings in 1884, made the Lal Lal operation uneconomic. It had produced several thousand tons of pig-iron in the previous few years, with the ore consistently yielding around 50 percent iron. At its height it employed up to 160 men, as miners, furnace men, charcoal burners, blacksmiths, carpenters and tram drivers (Jack and Cremin 1994:77). These men and their families lived in huts and houses scattered over the hill above the blast furnace area. Some of the children crossed the Moorabool River to attend the school at Bungal. After the furnace closed, the workers moved away and their houses decayed into the bush. All the movable property such as engines, pipes, rails and other equipment were salvaged and sold, and slowly the trees grew back, but much of the site remains as it was abandoned in the late nineteenth century, a monument to the iron industry and the determination to produce iron commodities in the colony.

Steel

The next major development in Australia's iron industry was the production of steel. Steel is essentially an alloy of iron and about 1 percent carbon, and had been produced in England since the mid-eighteenth century. Mass production of steel came about through the work of Henry Bessemer and Robert Mushet in England and William Kelly in the United States during the 1850s. Air pumped into molten pig-iron removed the impurities, while the addition of an iron–carbon–manganese compound restored the carbon content and resulted in low-cost steel. The open-hearth (Siemens-Martin) process, however, developed ca. 1864, also allowed the use of scrap steel, and this became the dominant steel-making process. These and later refinements meant steel could be produced cheaply and in quantity, so that it gradually replaced wrought iron in many applications by the end of the nineteenth century.

Although steel was first produced in Australia at Lithgow, the town initially came to prominence because of its coal deposits. Located just beyond the Blue Mountains west of Sydney, coal mining at Lithgow had begun in the 1850s, but the arrival of the railway in 1869 led to a boom in production. An ironworks was established in 1875–1876 by a group of entrepreneurs including James Rutherford, the American owner of Cobb and Co. The venture was unsuccessful, however, and Rutherford destroyed the blast furnace in 1884 using two carts of gunpowder (Jack and Cremin 1994:100). Around this time William Sandford arrived in Australia from England, and within a decade he had come to dominate ironworking in Lithgow and beyond. In 1900 he bought a 5-ton Siemens-Martin open-hearth furnace to manufacture steel at Lithgow. The furnace was tiny compared to British and American models, and was charged with a combination of imported pig-iron and scrap steel. Loading was done by men pushing barrows and trolleys and throwing the material into the open furnace by hand, risking serious injury from the heat and fumes (Hughes 1964:37). Two more steel furnaces were opened in 1902 and 1906, but they did not pay and all were soon closed, and nothing remains of them (Birmingham et al. 1979:96). Sandford sold out his iron and steel interests to Charles and George Hoskins in 1907. Iron production at Lithgow continued until 1931, but was continually hampered by lack of finance and its poor location relative to materials and markets. By 1915 the Broken Hill Proprietary Company (BHP) opened a major new iron and steel plant at Newcastle, shipping processed ore from Spencer Gulf in South Australia. By the 1930s, when BHP had taken over the Port Kembla steelworks established by Charles Hoskins from his Lithgow plant, the "Big Australian" was set to dominate the industry for decades to come.

Conclusion

Colonial manufacturers developed local industries to meet local needs. Some were small-scale and ephemeral, producing items such as tobacco pipes and eucalyptus oil, while others such as coal, iron and steel grew into major industries that eventually competed in global markets. Development of manufacturing and processing was always determined, however, by a complex array of factors, including the availability of materials, technology, expertise and capital, as well as the means and cost of transport. Colonial industry was often most successful when it focused on producing low cost goods that were sold close to the source, such as wood products, bricks, lime and iron. These commodities were heavy, and cheap transport helped in the competition against imported items. Archaeological evidence reveals the decisions that were made in how to produce goods in the most cost-effective ways. Manufacturers used imported technologies and modified them according to local conditions, such as in water-powered flour mills and steam-powered sawmills. They also created industrial landscapes that integrated elements of the manufacturing process. Archaeological study of the Lithgow Valley, for example, has revealed the mutual interdependence of roads and railways, coal-mining, iron-smelting and steel production, and brick and pottery-making. The timber industry often worked to log and clear native forest ahead of settlement and farming, with timber tramlines later upgraded into local roads. Archaeologists in Australia have documented these and many other industries in considerable detail, combining studies of technological processes with social and economic conditions, to provide new insights into the relationships between people, commodities and the natural environment.

Chapter 9
Migration and Ethnicity

Australia began as a migrant society, with Indigenous Australians first arriving over sea and island from Southeast Asia almost 50,000 years ago. Modern Australia grew out of the arrival of convicts, settlers and soldiers from Britain, sent out to create a new colonial society. English, Scots and Irish dominated these next groups of immigrants, and continued to do so for generations to come. But there were other groups with other ethnic traditions who arrived in those early days as well, including West Indians and Pacific Islanders, all trying to build a life in a strange and difficult place. In later years, new groups included Germans, who settled in large numbers in South Australia and the Riverina, and Chinese, lured by the prospect of gold. The years after the Second World War brought hundreds of thousands of "New Australians" from war-ravaged Europe, thrown together in migrant reception camps to learn the rudiments of Australian identity and how they related to it. Today, Australia is home to hundreds of ethnic groups, including more recent arrivals from Turkey and Lebanon, Iraq, Afghanistan, Sudan, Vietnam and Cambodia, each contributing to culture and society in numerous ways. In this chapter we explore a common theme in archaeology, the relationship between ethnic identities and wider society.

Ethnicity, be it Aboriginal, Irish, or Chinese, is a complex amalgam of learned behaviour, cultural norms, material goods, and personal preference, grounded in the notion of shared descent. It is only one layer of identity that also comprises elements such as gender, class, age, religion and language, categories we address in more detail in Chapter 11. Influenced in part by the New Archaeology of the 1960s and 1970s, the first historical archaeologists to analyse ethnicity regarded it as something mutable and fixed that was irrevocably altered if aspects of clothing, diet or language changed (McGuire 1982; Staski 1990). People and groups, it was believed, inevitably became acculturated to the dominant society, losing their distinctive ethnic identities. This change was measurable in the nature and quantities of objects excavated at archaeological sites, along a continuum from mostly traditional goods and an intact ethnicity to mainly new goods, acculturation, and loss of ethnicity, an approach that has been and continues to be influential in Australia and New Zealand (Ritchie 1986; Smith 2006). These studies have made important contributions to describing a range of goods and practices that were distinct from those of the dominant culture, and in raising awareness of the diversity within colonial society.

S. Lawrence, P. Davies, *An Archaeology of Australia Since 1788*,
Contributions To Global Historical Archaeology, DOI 10.1007/978-1-4419-7485-3_9,
© Springer Science+Business Media, LLC 2011

In the 1990s, archaeologists and other social scientists moved away from mono-lithic views of ethnicity to make ethnic identity itself the subject of analysis. The fluidity of identity has been acknowledged, and ethnicity, like other social cate-gories, is recognised as something that is contingent upon circumstance and social interaction. Archaeologist Siân Jones has drawn on the work of French sociologist Pierre Bourdieu to argue that ethnicity is part of individual and group *habitus* (Jones 1999:226–227). Habitus constitutes all the expectations of behaviour, language, cul-ture, morals and beliefs that become part of the self through socialisation that begins in childhood. Part of this conditioning occurs through exposure to cultural practices and to the material environment. Thereafter, social practice and the material world continue to shape and redefine the habitus. The tension of continuous redefinition through practice makes the habitus a useful basis for understanding ethnicity, while the constitutive role of material culture within this understanding of culture makes it particularly relevant to archaeology. In linking habitus and ethnicity, however, Jones observes that the two are not the same thing. Ethnicity and the objectification of cultural difference are instead a subset of the greater whole of the habitus, which provides a repertoire of objects and behaviours on which individuals can draw to express numerous elements of identity, of which ethnicity is just one. Furthermore, the expression of identity, including ethnicity, is flexible and can be varied to meet the requirements of any situation or historical context (Mac Sweeney 2009).

Habitus in action is illustrated by the work of American archaeologists Adrian and Mary Praetzellis in California (Praetzellis 1999:128; Praetzellis and Praetzellis 2001:648–649), who apply sociologist Erving Goffman's (1959) performance the-ory to explain how the expression of ethnic identity is responsive to context. Individuals are actors who use material goods as props to create the impressions they desire, effectively stage-managing the perceptions that are created in onlook-ers. Both of these approaches share an understanding of identity as situational and contingent, dependent on context for realisation and interpretation. Central to this in both schemes is the existence of an audience which stimulates the creation of an identity from an individual's available cultural repertoire and which views its performance.

Also conscious of the flexible and provisional nature of ethnicity, Australian archaeologist Jane Lydon (1999:1–24) has drawn on the post-colonial theory of Edward Said and Homi Bhaba to situate ethnicity squarely in the domain of colo-nial encounters of all kinds. Lydon points to the ambivalent and ultimately inventive nature of cultural exchange and, following Nick Thomas (1991), to the ways in which objects are "entangled" in that process. One of the key issues raised by Lydon's work is that of representation, and the ways in which objects sit along-side other kinds of cultural productions as forms of communication. She uses the term "pidgin" to describe the new language of practices, ideas and objects that was shared between Chinese and whites in the Rocks and which drew on elements of both cultures.

Linguistic analogy has also informed studies of ethnicity in historical archae-ology, which have examined cultural interaction as a form of creolisation (Dawdy 2000a). For archaeologists, creolisation can imply the combination of new elements within an existing structure, the development of new and distinct cultures within colonial contexts, the emergence of hybrid and syncretic cultures, or some combination of all three. While the terms and definitions originally related to groups who self-identified as "creole", particularly in the American South and parts of Latin America, its use has been extended to others, most notably African-Americans through the work of James Deetz (1977) and Leland Ferguson (1992). Significantly, much of this work discusses communities that have been many generations in forming (Dawdy 2000b:108–110), while most of the work done by Australians on issues of ethnicity concerns the first generation of encounter.

In Australia creolisation has been of greatest influence in post-contact archaeology, where both Judy Birmingham (2000) and Lynette Russell (2004) have used the concept to analyse Aboriginal/European cultural exchange. Russell in particular prefers creolisation models because, she argues, not only is it impossible to distinguish the separate elements of race, class and gender, but to do so would deny the lived reality of post-contact society. In her research on Kangaroo Island in South Australia, the community consisted of descendants of male European sealers and Aboriginal women from Tasmania and the South Australian mainland. Russell suggests that, at least in that time and place, the degree of culture change was such that binary categories of male/female, Aboriginal/European are not meaningful categories for analysing material culture. Drawing also on Homi Bhaba, Russell points to the negotiated nature of identity, and to the potential for *bricolage*, or creative re-interpretation, as a form of resistance to the hegemony of the dominant culture.

Habitus, performance theory, pidgin and creolisation all have much to offer studies of ethnicity in archaeology. The conscious expression of ethnicity emerges in the experience of otherness, and New World settler colonies like Australia that brought together people from all parts of the globe have been fertile grounds for the expression of traditional practices alongside the creation of novel forms of identity that meld influences from many sources. In seeing new ways of doing things people of all backgrounds have become more aware of their similarities with others from the same homeland, at times strengthening those ties through mutual association, and on other occasions embracing the possibilities offered by alternatives. Because identity and ethnicity are fluid rather than fixed, traditional and novel elements can co-exist within individuals and groups. People may simultaneously see themselves as "Chinese" and "Australian", while the perception of others will be shaped by their reading of what is offered during the encounter. Degrees of difference may be expressed and perceived, with people of similar backgrounds recognising subtle and nuanced markers that are hidden to strangers who might only recognise gross, even caricatured signs of cultural affiliation.

The notion of *diaspora* is also important to this sense of identity, the development through migration of dispersed communities that relate both to the host land and to the homeland. Such communities maintain complex senses of belonging through time and space. Diaspora theory draws attention to the tensions and subtleties of how diasporic communities construct and maintain their distinctiveness, alongside their identification with the wider society in which they live (Davidson and Kuah-Pearce 2008; Lawrence 2003b; Lilley 2004; Safran 2004; Terrell 2005). Ethnic identity is created anew in each context, negotiating the use of material culture, language, religion and customs, in the ongoing process of forging personal and group narratives.

As so much archaeological attention over the years has been directed at the Chinese in Australia, we begin here by exploring some aspects of Chinese identity in the Australian colonies, and how this was negotiated in interactions with Europeans. In a recent review of American research into the archaeology of the overseas Chinese, Barbara Voss and Rebecca Allen lament that such work has failed to attract the attention of the discipline as a whole in North America (Voss and Allen 2008:5). This is not the case in Australia, where research on the Chinese has made a significant contribution to other areas including the archaeology of mining, post-contact archaeology and urban archaeology, and where work on the Chinese has been at the forefront of archaeological interests in race, ethnicity and identity. Moreover, while Voss and Allen urge their colleagues to engage more fully with the disciplines of Asian American and Asian studies, such relations have a long history in Australia, where joint conferences have been the norm and interests have tended to develop in parallel. Rather than describing case studies, here we will synthesise the evidence of work in several parts of Australia to discuss patterns of Chinese labour arrangements and settlement patterns, diet and beliefs as they developed in colonial and later society. We draw in particular on research into the Chinese on the goldfields at Braidwood and Kiandra in New South Wales (McGowan 2003, 2004; Smith 1998, 2006), in Central Victoria (Stanin 2004a, b) and in North Queensland (Bell 1995); on urban Chinese in the Rocks in Sydney (Lydon 1999), at Cohen Place in Melbourne (Muir 2008) and at Cooktown in north Queensland (Rains 2003); and at market gardens (Jack et al. 1984; McGowan 2005) and a fish-curing camp in South Gippsland (Bowen 2007; Fig. 9.1).

We also compare the distinctive material remains of German Lutheran settlers in South Australia (Young 1985) with the almost invisible traces of neighbouring settlers from Poland (Stankowski 2004). The Afghan cameleers were another marginal migrant group which left only ephemeral remains of their lives, but recent archaeological research has shown these to be highly revealing markers of the first Muslims in Australia (Parkes 2009). The dominant ethnic identity in the Australian colonies during the nineteenth century, however, was British, and we examine how it formed the foundation of social and material culture, which all other migrant groups confronted and, at times, contested. We conclude by examining the archaeology of migrant reception centres after the Second World War, and how governments of the day responded to the arrival of large numbers of "foreigners", and the ongoing construction of national identity.

The Chinese in Australia

More than 100,000 Chinese people came to the Australian colonies from the 1840s to the 1890s. The discovery of gold was a major attraction, but they were also driven to emigrate by a range of factors in their homelands, including flood, famine,

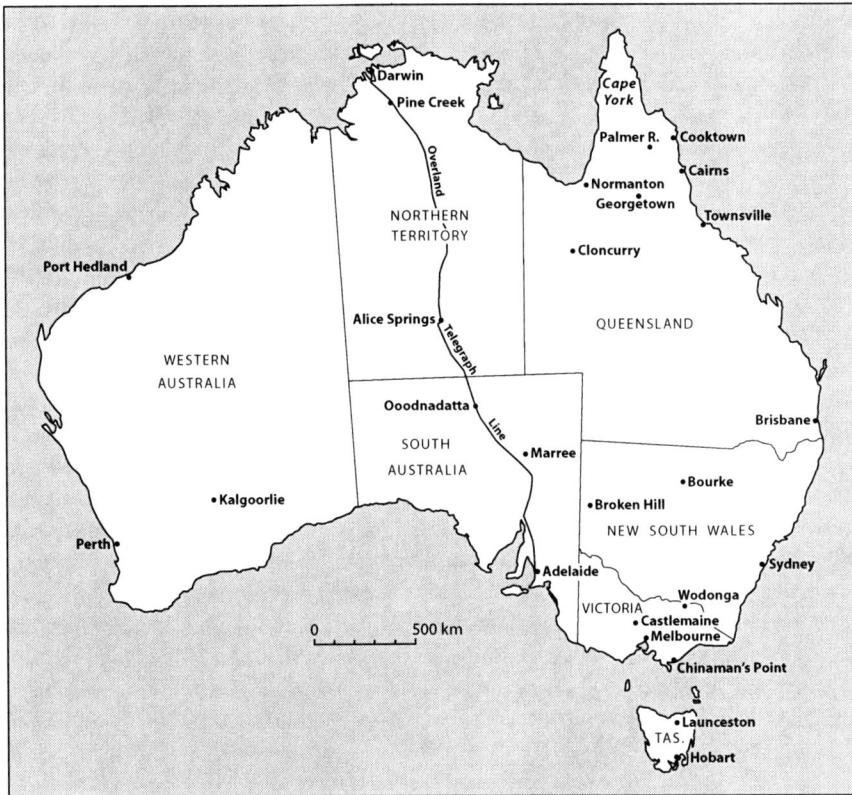

Fig. 9.1 Location of migration sites mentioned in text

rising population, political instability and warfare. Their migration was part of a wider diasporic process, which resulted in the establishment of numerous Chinese communities throughout the Asia-Pacific region during the second half of the nineteenth century.[1] The majority of Chinese immigrants came from the two southern provinces of Guangdong and Fujian. They were mainly poor rural people, who worked as farmers, carpenters, fishermen or hawkers, and arrived in Australia as indentured labourers under the credit-ticket system. Their passage and other expenses were paid by a sponsor, often a merchant, and the immigrant worked for that sponsor until the debt was repaid.

A small number of Chinese began arriving in Australia well before the gold rush. Mak Sai Ying, for example, was born in Canton in 1798 and arrived as a free settler in Sydney in 1818. He anglicised his name to John Shying, bought land at Parramatta, and married Sarah Thompson, an English woman, in 1823 (Fitzgerald 1997:17). The Macarthurs' servants at Elizabeth Farm in Parramatta in the early

---

[1] A similar pattern resulted in the establishment of many communities of Indian migrants around the Indian Ocean rim, from South Africa to South-East Asia, during the same period (Bose 2006).

1820s included a Chinese carpenter and a Chinese cook (Broadbent 1984:39), while two men, named Quong and Tchiou, worked as cabinet-makers in Sydney around 1827 (Gilchrist 1951:103). The First Opium War between Britain and China in 1839–1842 resulted in the Treaty of Nanking, which opened up Chinese ports to trade, and increased the outward migration of indentured labourers and free emigrants. Between 1848 and 1851, around 1,700 Chinese arrived in the Australian colonies, serving as station hands, plantation workers, miners and personal servants. From 1851, the gold rush brought many thousands more Chinese, especially to Victoria and New South Wales, but there were never more than about 40,000 in the colonies at one time (Wang 2001:199). Later in the century, several thousand Chinese also arrived in Tasmania to work in the tin mines of the north-east (see Chapter 7), while others came to the Northern Territory to work in mining and railway construction. Large numbers also joined gold rushes to north Queensland during the 1870s.

By the final decades of the nineteenth century many of the goldfields were exhausted, and Chinese miners found work where they could, in shearing, cooking, market gardening, fruit-picking and scrub-cutting. Many returned to China while others left rural areas to live in and around Sydney, Melbourne, Cairns and Darwin, where they worked as laundrymen, furniture-makers, grocers and market gardeners. Growing anti-Chinese sentiment, however, saw the introduction of the *Immigration Restriction Act* of 1901, which established the White Australia Policy and imposed an effective ban on all non-European migration to Australia. The number of Chinese declined rapidly, from around 30,000 in 1901, to around 6,000 by the 1940s (Yuan 2001).

The hostility and violence experienced by the Chinese in Australia is well documented. European antagonism was driven by racial prejudice, fear of the unknown and a perceived economic threat. Most Europeans were unwilling or unable to acknowledge that the overall numbers of Chinese men in the colonies was relatively small, and that most returned to China after a few years. The small number of Chinese women, limited by restrictive colonial immigration policies, was also regarded by Europeans as unhealthy and immoral. The distinctive dress, language and customs of the Chinese on the goldfields meant that Europeans regarded Chinese immigrants as culturally homogeneous and separate. The identity of individual Chinese, however, was closely aligned with kinship and place of origin, while different dialects were also spoken. District societies (tongs) developed in Australia to provide support for members. They functioned as benevolent aid societies, offering sick and aged care, and sending the bones of the deceased back to China for reburial (Chapter 12). As many as 16 tongs were represented in New South Wales alone by 1891 (Yong 1977:189). These societies played a significant role in the social and community life of the overseas Chinese, reinforcing regional identities, strengthening ties to the homeland and expressing the diversity of cultural attachments.

There has been a strong tradition of archaeological research on the overseas Chinese in Australia and New Zealand, beginning with Neville Ritchie's Ph.D. work on the Otago goldfields of the South Island in the late 1970s (Ritchie 1986, 1993).

In the same period a team led by Ian Jack excavated the market garden of Ah Toy on the Palmer River goldfield in North Queensland (Jack et al. 1984). These studies were characteristic of overseas research at this time in their focus on gold-fields sites and in their theoretical orientation. For many years the archaeology of the Chinese was almost a subset of mining archaeology, as much of it was con-ducted as a result of either an interest in mining or mining-related cultural heritage management projects (Bell 1995; Gaughwin 1995; McCarthy 1988; McCarthy and Kostoglou 1986). From the beginning, however, archaeologists worked closely with historians, museum-based researchers and members of the Chinese-Australian com-munity and participated in several joint conferences (Chan et al. 2001; MacGregor 1995). In addition to establishing a strong corpus of descriptive information on the material characteristics of the Chinese diaspora, much of the work was deeply engaged with contemporary anthropological theories emphasising acculturation and adaptation (Piper 1988; Ritchie 1986).

In the 1990s the growth of urban archaeology resulted in the excavation of Chinese homes and workshops in the Rocks in Sydney and the Little Lon and Cohen Place neighbourhoods in Melbourne (McCarthy 1989; Myers 2002). A major the-oretical development at this time was Jane Lydon's (1999, 2001) work on some of the Rocks material, which introduced new perspectives on ethnicity and drew on notions of cultural entanglement and exchange to suggest more fluid and complex ways of understanding material culture in cross-cultural contexts. In the twenty-first century Chinese archaeology has broadened considerably as a new generation of students have carried out postgraduate research (Bowen 2007; Muir 2003, 2008; Smith 1998, 2003, 2006; Stanin 2004a; Svenson 1994), shifting the focus away from cultural heritage management towards themes such as community develop-ment, gender, and economic structure, and going beyond mining to look at market gardens, fish curing and urban life.

These recent analyses have begun to question the outsider status of most Chinese, recognising instead the diverse and dynamic roles played by the Chinese in Australia. The bounded, enclosed view of the overseas Chinese is being challenged by notions of fluidity, complexity and cross-cultural interaction (e.g. Fitzgerald 1997; P. Jones 2005; Rains 2003). The Chinese also played a vital role in the spread of global capitalism and colonialism from the seventeenth century, establishing enclaves throughout Southeast Asia to transmit goods, capital and labour through-out the region and beyond (Dobbin 1996). As we will see, there were distinctive patterns of work, diet, recreation and belief that were central to the experiences of Chinese people in Australia, but all of these were consciously manipulated accord-ing to individuals' willingness and desire to shape new identities in the Australian colonies.

Labour Organisation and Settlement Patterns

The work of Lindsay Smith, Alister Bowen, and Jane Lydon in particular has focused attention on the material implications of social organisation within the

overseas Chinese community. In attempting to understand more about the archaeological sites they have studied, these scholars have all shed light on the way
the credit-ticket system governed the organisation of work within the overseas
Chinese community, and consequently settlement patterns within a broader white
Australian landscape. While Chinese immigrants often endured racial hostility,
they were also admired for their work ethic and sobriety. Ambrose Bierce's (1996
[1911]:41) sardonic definition of the Chinaman as "a working man whose faults are
docility, skill, industry, frugality and temperance" reflected the quiet perseverance
in toil frequently observed of Chinese workmen in colonial encounters. Chinese
labour practices were quite different to those of most Europeans. Rather than being
autonomous workers, free to advance their own personal interests, Chinese migrants
to the Australian colonies were embedded in a web of custom, rules and obligations.
They lived according to both the support and expectations of family, clan and home
village. Kinship obligations, and a cultural understanding that individuals worked
for a broader common good, limited personal choice but resulted in strong group
cohesion. Group-based labour practices, underpinned by the credit-ticket system
and backed by powerful merchants, thus flourished among the overseas Chinese.

   Under the credit-ticket system, a form of indentured labour, the money for
migrants to journey to Australia was advanced through kinship networks by a merchant or his agent, a headman. In return the migrant worked for the merchant for
a period of time, usually a year, to repay the debt (Cronin 1982:18), and both during that time and thereafter he was also responsible for returning earnings to the
kin group in China. During the period of paying off the debt, the place and nature
of work, accommodation and provisioning were determined by the merchant. The
group-oriented labour relations of Chinese immigrants directed individuals to work
at particular occupations. During the gold rushes in Victoria, New South Wales and
north Queensland, for example a substantial number of the thousands of Chinese
who arrived in the colonies did not mine for gold. Instead, they were sent to build
housing, and to generate supplies of food and equipment to ensure that Chinese
communities could operate largely independently of European economic networks,
thus controlling the degree of interaction with the dominant culture.

   This system had obvious implications for the (lack of) autonomy of individuals,
and it meant that a small number of merchants were in key positions of controlling
large labour forces and serving as gatekeepers between the Chinese and the wider
community (Bowen 2007:73). Planning and control was in the hands of Australian-
based Chinese merchant firms. Prominent merchants, such as Louey Ah Mouy and
Lowe Kong Meng in Melbourne, Way Kee in Sydney and Chin Kaw in Launceston,
played a major role in organising Chinese migration and coordinating business
interests throughout the Australian colonies, New Zealand and beyond.

   By controlling these integrated networks of labour and business, a small group
of merchants were then in positions to amass considerable wealth on behalf of
themselves and the family group and to dramatically improve their own social
status. Although merchants had traditionally been at the bottom of the Chinese
class structure (Wang 1992:310–311), in Australia many were able to direct their
wealth into philanthropy and gain prestige in the process. This was supported by

the notion of *guanxi*, the cultural practice of personal networks based on the reciprocal exchange of gifts and favours (Yang 1994). The *guanxi* system, based around kinship and locality ties, promoted interaction between business endeavours and social networks, and allowed traditional cultural relationships to flourish in a diasporic environment. As Lydon has shown in Sydney and the Praetzellises have shown in California, *guanxi* was also used strategically to reach out to non-Chinese individuals (Lydon 1999:82–85, 147–157; Praetzellis 1999; Praetzellis and Praetzellis 2001:648–649). Gifts were given to white Australian police officers, officials and business leaders, who were also invited to lavish banquets. While the intention may not always have been clear to the white recipients, it is likely that the Chinese were attempting to draw people they perceived as gatekeepers for the wider community into reciprocal *guanxi* relationships. Lydon suggests that *guanxi* may partly explain the presence of Chinese items such as ginger jars found in the archaeological deposits of European households in the Rocks (Lydon 1999:153). Praetzellis and Praetzellis (2001:648–649) have suggested that sets of British tablewares in archaeological deposits from district association boarding houses in Sacramento may be related to historical descriptions of banquets given by powerful Chinese merchants for Sacramento's white business leaders. They echo Jane Lydon in arguing that Chinese businessmen deliberately used material objects to create public personas that were acceptable to non-Chinese.

In many ways the overseas Chinese community was tightly organised, centralised and hierarchical. Lindsay Smith's analysis of settlement patterns among Chinese miners in south-eastern New South Wales is further evidence of this structure (Smith 2006). As we discuss in Chapter 7, Smith identified a number of small, often isolated mining camps in each district with few archaeological features other than basic accommodation structures and mine workings. These satellite camps were the homes and workplaces of the miners, many of whom may have been working off their credit-ticket debts. Each district also had a central place, which generally included a temple, cemetery, pig-roasting oven and a store. In each of these settlements there was a Chinese merchant who probably co-ordinated work arrangements and communications with the Chinese community in Sydney, in addition to providing supplies and accommodation to miners moving between the diggings and other places. Extrapolating from Smith's analysis, it is likely that the archaeological remains of Chinese mining found throughout Australia's mining regions are predominantly related to the lowest tier of workers in a complex social and economic hierarchy.

Alister Bowen (2007:242–245) has argued that Chinaman's Point was a similar outpost of a larger economic enterprise, which explains the modest material remains excavated at the site. His research indicated that the main markets for cured fish were the Chinese miners on the goldfields and export to China and Hong Kong, so by its nature the camp was embedded in wider Chinese networks. Despite the enormous profits generated by the Chinese fish curers there and elsewhere in coastal Victoria and New South Wales, there was no evidence of wealth or comfort in the archaeological record at Chinaman's Point. Bowen suggests that wealth was leaving the camp, partly to the absentee merchants who controlled the operation, partly in payment for the debt bondage of the workers, and partly to kin and family back in China. Market gardens such as those at Vaughn Springs near Castlemaine in central Victoria (Stanin 2004a), in southern and western New South Wales (McGowan 2005) and on the Palmer goldfield in north Queensland (Jack et al. 1984) were probably also part of these larger networks (see Chapter 6).

Jane Lydon's work provides evidence of life in urban centres that were at the apex of these settlement hierarchies. Chinese landlords and tenants like the merchant Hong On Jang provided accommodation and assistance both to newly arrived migrants from China on their way to country areas and to earlier arrivals returning from the diggings and travelling through Sydney on their way back to China (Lydon 1999:82–84). Hong On Jang's occupation of Samson's Cottage on George Street between 1916 and 1924 yielded an array of archaeological material that sheds light on the lives of its Chinese occupants and the way that Hong On Jang and his associates modified the Victorian architecture of the Rocks for their own purposes. Outbuildings were constructed in rear yards to provide more living space, with access via ladders. Basements were closed in, while multiple doors were built in gambling rooms to avoid police control. At Samson's Cottage the rear yard of the premises was expanded over the remains of an earlier cottage demolished around 1920. The yard was then roofed over with a shed, providing extra accommodation for Hong On Jang's guests or boarders. A circular depression in the ground was possibly the vestiges of a traditional Chinese oven built at some point. The Chinese in the inner city created a shared, physical autonomy by isolating themselves within their rental properties. Although this resulted in overcrowding, the Chinese adapted their buildings to defend themselves against an antagonistic white society which sought to monitor and control their lives (Lydon 1999:77–79).

Comparison of the distribution of Chinese artefacts in rural mining and fish-curing camps with Chinese households at Cohen Place in Melbourne's Chinatown illustrates household consumption patterns, trade networks and the degree of control exerted on those workers at the furthest ends of these integrated economic networks (Muir 2008:119). Surprisingly, the rural deposits had far higher frequencies of Chinese items than did the urban households in the heart of Chinatown. Deposits from three households of male cabinet-makers in Leichhardt Street from 1895-ca. 1920 showed less than 50 percent of the ceramics were of Chinese origin, with only 10 percent Chinese in one instance. In each of the deposits related to three family households in Lacey Place, which included Chinese women and children, only 20 percent of the ceramics were of Chinese origin. In contrast, at Chinaman's Point in Gippsland, 77 percent of the ceramics were Chinese and in the mining camps between 50 and 80 percent of the ceramics were Chinese.

Muir (2008:111–112) notes that by the time Chinese people were living in the inner suburbs of Melbourne, all households were sewered and rubbish was regularly collected, which reduced the opportunity for the formation of archaeological deposits. Nevertheless, with access to a variety of Chinese shops and suppliers it is striking that all the households chose British ceramics more frequently. She suggests that the male cabinet-makers may have been eating meals prepared at clan

stores, a practice described in oral histories of the area, and that this is one explanation for the lack of Chinese ceramics in their households (Muir 2008:118). More
documentary information is available for the family households, particularly that
of the Tongs, a household that included the merchant Chin Tong, his wife Sue
Hoe (known as Mrs. Tong) and their eight children. Muir describes Mrs. Tong as
a boundary figure like the merchants Louey Ah Moy and Quong Tart. Mrs. Tong,
who sent her children to the Presbyterian Women's Mission Schools, was herself
a member of the Presbyterian Women's Missionary Union, and entertained non-
Chinese women from the Union and the school at her home (Muir 2008:116–118).
Her use of Chinese and British ceramics was one means for negotiating a place for
her family within Australian society while maintaining Chinese traditions and providing her children with futures in both cultures. When her husband died, Mrs. Tong
returned to China with her surviving children, and when she herself died in 1916,
those children in their turn were able to leave China and return to their Melbourne
friends.

Straightforward equations of Chinese ceramics with Chinese identity not only
implies a static view of identity, but also obscures the variability of access to goods
and the power relations that may be implicit in controlling that access. The high
frequencies of Chinese ceramics in rural deposits, in isolated locations ostensibly
far from sources of goods, demonstrates, on the one hand, the strength of overseas
Chinese trade networks which imported and distributed a wide range of goods to
members of the Chinese community throughout Australia (McCarthy 1988). It also
indicates, however, that workers in rural contexts were highly dependent on trade
and social networks that connected them to their homeland. The men who lived
in these camps probably had fewer opportunities for interacting with non-Chinese
than did their urban counterparts, and probably had few skills in English or literacy,
making them reliant on translators and go-betweens to communicate. Particularly if
caught up in the credit-ticket system, they were also limited in their choices of where
to obtain supplies, so that obligation and reciprocity determined their selection of
goods as much as did cultural familiarity and the desire to maintain a traditional diet.

Adrian and Mary Praetzellis (2001:649) argue that restricting the supply of
European goods to the mining camps was a deliberate strategy on the part of the
merchants that denied the Chinese workers the opportunity to develop identities as
Chinese-Americans. As in Australia, the Praetzellises have observed that ceramic
assemblages in archaeological deposits at isolated mining camps occupied by overseas Chinese are almost entirely dominated by Chinese forms, in stark contrast to
the deposits at the district society boarding houses in Sacramento (Praetzellis and
Praetzellis 2001:648–649). In the satellite camps the workers had little choice but
to use Chinese goods, and consequently had less chance to develop competency in
white American culture and so advance their position in society. The Praetzellises
argue that owning and using non-Chinese items, while keeping them away from
the workers they employed, enabled the merchants to emphasise their own liminal
status as gatekeepers between the Chinese and American communities (Praetzellis
1999:128).

Food

Food was a vital means by which the Chinese asserted their cultural identity in Australia, but here too the archaeological evidence speaks of fluidity and agency rather than simple acculturation. There is much evidence that speaks to the maintenance of traditional diets based on rice, vegetables, fish and tea, with smaller quantities of chicken and pork. Gardens, fish-curing operations and import networks, while manipulated by merchants to exercise control and maximise financial return, also supplied the familiar foodstuffs of the Chinese community. The Chinese goods appear to be unambiguous ethnic markers, but the meanings that derive from contexts of use can be highly variable (Fig. 9.2). Ceramic assemblages from Chinese sites around Australia are dominated by forms such as porcelain rice bowls, spoons, and tea cups (known as Kitchen Ch'ing) and brown-glazed stoneware containers that once held a variety of foodstuffs such as rice, pickled vegetables, soy sauce, vinegar and rice wine (Muir 2003). At the same time, imported Chinese foodstuffs were consumed by Europeans, and fragments of ginger and pickle jars in particular have been found on many non-Chinese sites in the Rocks and elsewhere such as Viewbank and Dolly's Creek in Victoria.

Fig. 9.2 Chinese artefacts from mining sites in Victoria and Tasmania, including stoneware jars, a medicinal vial and a Chinese coin (photo S. Lawrence)

Andrew Piper's (1988) analysis of faunal remains from a Chinese site on New Zealand's goldfields showed that portions had been cut to small, bite-sized pieces. Bones used for marrow extraction and broth preparation were also favoured, both patterns in keeping with traditional methods of food preparation, but the men also ate far more meat than would have been the case in China. The meat included goat, mutton, rabbit, and eel, in addition to the more familiar beef and pork. They also used tinned food, particularly meat and fish, alongside fresh supplies.

A closer look at fish consumption adds another dimension to what is now known about provisioning networks. Because bones were removed as part of the curing and drying processes, this fish is archaeologically invisible, and it is impossible to know how much cured fish might have been consumed on a site. Alister Bowen has demonstrated, however, that cured fish was widely available on the diggings and elsewhere through the same sources that distributed other Chinese supplies. It seems possible that in New Zealand the tins of sardines and the eels the men trapped themselves were a way of obtaining desired foods while circumventing networks that might have been restrictive as well as supportive. At Hong On Jang's boarding house in the Rocks, Jane Lydon found that fish bones dominated the faunal assemblage, mostly snapper and bream fresh from Sydney Harbour, so here too Chinese consumers were seeking European suppliers.

Items of cookware used to prepare the food have also been found on occasion. In the rear yard of Hong On Jang's boarding house archaeologists uncovered a ceramic "sand-pot" buried in a small rubbish pit (Lydon 1999:216). Made from a light, porous fabric, such pots were used for the slow cooking of soups and stews over a low flame, and also for preparing traditional medicines. Rice could also be prepared in sand-pots with an internal glaze. These pots are rarely found outside China, and its presence at Hong On Jang's may be evidence for special care in the preparation of traditional dishes. At Butcher's Gully near Castlemaine in central Victoria, Zvonka Stanin recovered fragments of an iron wok and the handle of a cleaver, both used in traditional cooking methods, but she also found fragments of European-style cooking pots and teapots at the site (Stanin 2004b:40–41). At Chinaman's Point fragments of common colonial cast iron cookware were found, including the spout from a kettle and parts from heavy cast iron pots, and there were also fragments of two porcelain teapots.

The artefact assemblages from these and other sites demonstrate ways in which individual Chinese men and women blended traditional foodways with elements from their new environments. The durability of imported tablewares and containers has drawn attention to ancient customs while local foods such as fresh vegetables are archaeologically invisible and European items in the assemblages tend to be down-played. We have already seen how in the rural, satellite communities access to non-Chinese items may have been restricted while in urban areas many more options were both available and taken up. Even in rural areas, however, there could be fluidity and flexibility in the acquisition, preparation and serving of food.

These ideas have been explored by Kevin Rains, using archaeological material from a dumpsite at Cooktown to interrogate the nature of Chinese identity in far north Queensland in the late nineteenth century (Rains 2003). Cooktown developed as a major port following the discovery of alluvial gold at the Palmer River field in Cape York in 1872 (Comber 1995). Large numbers of Chinese miners flocked to the region, and the Chinese rapidly became integral to Cooktown's commercial activity, with strong support from the local business community. Most of the dumpsite material consisted of large ceramic storage jars, as well as celadon and Kitchen Ch'ing rice bowls. While such an assemblage can be understood in terms of Chinese cultural insularity and long-distance trade networks, Rains uses the material to develop a more nuanced understanding of social relationships among Chinese and Europeans.

Although rural, Cooktown was a major central place for the Palmer River diggings and the Chinese community there included both labourers and a wealthy merchant elite. The artefacts at Cooktown were utilitarian, mass-produced items, related to the consumption of large quantities of food and drink, and probably reflect communal dining and the frugality and poverty of Chinese miners, labourers and gardeners. The numerous alcohol bottle fragments identified at Cooktown can be read in terms of class and gender solidarity, or at least identification. Drinking as an expression of masculine and working-class identity is historically well-documented in Australia (Dingle 1980; Kirkby 1997; Lake 1986). The alcohol need not have been consumed, however, by any one ethnic group, but rather by Europeans and Chinese drinking together. Further, the bottles may represent a change in consumption patterns among Chinese, rather than a simple substitution. Rice wine was consumed rarely in traditional Chinese village society. The availability of large quantities of cheap spirits at Cooktown, however, may have prompted a shift from drinking alcohol at family feasts, to one associated with shanties and grog shops. There may thus have been a shift in both inter-ethnic drinking habits and in the take up of habitual drinking among some ethnic Chinese community members (Rains 2003:37–38).

Inter-relations between Europeans and Chinese in Cooktown were expressed in other aspects of consumption as well. The traditional Chinese diet based on rice and vegetables was altered to some extent by the scarcity of some standard Chinese goods, the ready availability of European products, and new levels of disposable wealth. Flour, for example, became a prominent part of the Chinese diet, along with locally produced beef. At the same time, a range of Chinese goods were eagerly adopted by Europeans, including various foodstuffs, drugs and pharmaceuticals, and household goods. Chinese and European merchants cooperated to exploit the town's complex consumer needs, creating webs of personal loyalty and trust which overcame ethnic suspicion, and promoted a wider spirit of tolerance and mutual interdependence.

Health and Recreation

Artefacts at Hong On Jang's in the Rocks also included the remains of around 40 small glass medicine vials (Lydon 1999:98–101). Similar examples are common to archaeological sites associated with the overseas Chinese in Australia, New Zealand and the United States (e.g. McCarthy 1995:200; Ritchie 1986:195; Wegars 1988:47). The vials included some with Chinese manufacturers' marks on the base, and were used for a variety of medicinal preparations, including tincture of opium. During the nineteenth century, opium was readily available in Australia, and was the basis for most painkillers used by both Europeans and Chinese. While some archaeologists have suggested that those addicted to opium may have sought it in tincture form after opium for smoking was banned in 1901, Jane Lydon believes that the vials are more likely to have been associated with herbal medications, and the persistence of traditional Chinese medicines. Lydon observes that the sand-pot described above could also have been used in the brewing of medicinal teas, and the kettle at Chinaman's Point could also have been put to use in this way.

Evidence for opium smoking has been recovered from many Chinese occupation sites in Australia and New Zealand. For the most part this consists of parts of the pipes, including fragments of earthenware and stoneware bowls and metal pipe fittings. Embossed, rectangular opium cans have also been found along with glass lamp stands. At Chinaman's Point Alister Bowen recorded a number of bases from cylindrical black glass bottles that he believes were specially modified for smoking opium. The bases have had the central section of the pontil chipped away leaving a hole 10–20 mm in diameter. Bowen suggests that a flame was placed beneath the hole in the bottle and opium resin rested on a metal strip placed across the broken edges, creating a plume of smoke that could be inhaled through a tube of some kind (Bowen 2007:228–230; see Wylie and Fike 1993:294–295).

Chinese coins are another ubiquitous find on sites associated with the Chinese. Based on an extensive review of archaeological coins in New Zealand, Neville Ritchie and Stuart Park have argued that the coins were used as gambling tokens or as part of the equipment used in playing *fan tan* (Ritchie and Park 1987; Chapter 11). Gambling and opium smoking were practices that divided both the Chinese community and white Australian society. Some Chinese men gathered to smoke opium and play *fan tan* as a relatively benign form of relaxation and socialising, much as white men might bet on the horses or go to the pub for a drink. Others within the Chinese community, particularly merchants establishing reputations of respectability, were critical of these activities, and actively supported an 1891 New South Wales Royal Commission into Chinese Gambling and Immorality (Lydon 1999:106–118). Chinese gambling and opium smoking were viewed with fear and suspicion by Australian society and were used to demonise Chinese people, but at the same time there were colonials who were attracted to the new and exotic and the element of danger that these activities represented.

Religious Beliefs

Several scholars have drawn attention to the importance of religious belief among the overseas Chinese in Australia, and in particular to its influence in shaping patterns of land use. Temples and cemeteries were important community facilities and mark settlements that were the central places in larger networks. Circular stone ovens were used to prepare communal meals that featured in celebrations and religious rituals. More subtly, principles of *feng shui* have been found to inform settlement plans and building orientation.

Traditional Chinese religious practices were based around the principles of ancient animalistic beliefs including the veneration of ancestors ("classical religion"), and Confucianism, Taoism and Buddhism (De Groot 1967; Smith 2006:37). Temples facilitated practices such as checking horoscopes, prayer and making offerings to the ancestors and to the principal deity of the temple. They were places for meeting neighbours and provided the focal point of major festivals such as New Year, but they were not places for gathered worship in the way that churches, mosques and synagogues serve other religious communities. Temple buildings may thus be small compared to communal worship spaces, but are nevertheless integral to community spiritual and social life. Temples and the sites of former temples have been identified all over Australia. In places that still have large Chinese communities the temples may also still be active, such as the See Yup temple in South Melbourne (Niemeier 1995), but in other places such as the remote Buckland goldfield of north-eastern Victoria, known temple sites are virtually the only surviving evidence of once-thriving communities (Talbot 2004:149–151).

Gordon Grimwade (2003) has reviewed a number of surviving temples and temple sites in north Queensland, while Lindsay Smith (2006:41–53) has extended the search to include all known temple sites in Australia. Each of the Queensland structures consists of a long, narrow building with a porch at the front, a gable end, and two rooms known as the Bell Tower and the Main Palace, one behind the other. At the rear of the front room or Bell Tower is a sunken courtyard known as the heavenly well or Smoke Tower where offerings would have been placed. In Croydon, Georgetown and Atherton in Queensland there were also other structures associated with the main temple building, including a caretaker's residence, meeting hall and circular stone oven. Smith assessed the Australian examples against what is known about the development of temple design in China and has been able to identify several styles of increasing elaboration. Unsurprisingly, those in places with large permanent communities such as the capital cities and regional centres such as Ballarat and Bendigo also had larger and more opulent temples.

There is documentary evidence for nine temples within Lindsay Smith's study area in southern New South Wales, of which he was able to identify archaeological remains for five (2006:215–217). The main archaeological evidence consisted of large postholes from rectangular buildings that seem to have been of the simplest "one-house" form of temple. The buildings were consistently larger in size than the miners' huts recorded in the same study and were made of better materials, being of weatherboard rather than calico construction and with timber rather than earthen floors. While dwellings generally clustered together, the temples were situated at a slight distance from other buildings and were located on large, level platforms. In addition to typical domestic artefacts, some of the temple sites also contained more unusual forms including a ceramic vase, a fragment of cut glass, and a metal incense burner. At least two of the temples had associated buildings in close proximity, which may have been for storage or the accommodation of a caretaker.

Chinese burial practices are discussed in detail in Chapter 12, but it is worth noting here that cemeteries and burial sites were also important places for religious observance relating to veneration of the ancestors. Caring for the graves and leaving offerings on anniversaries and during festivals was believed to confer material benefit on descendants, and these regular and ongoing rituals meant that cemeteries were embedded in the religious life of the community.

Other features with both religious and secular overtones are the circular stone ovens that have been identified around Australia, particularly in mining districts (Bell 1995; Gaughwin 1995; Grimwade 2003, 2008; Smith 2006:50–55; Vivian 1985). These ovens have been called "pig ovens" because they were most commonly used for slow-roasting whole pigs. Roast pork is a particularly favoured offering for the gods and the ancestors, and roasting whole animals was an important part of community festivals. Peter Bell (1995) reviewed archaeological reports from northern and eastern Australia to document the typology and use of the ovens. Although Bell suggested, based on evidence available at the time, that the ovens were confined to communities settled later in the nineteenth century in Queensland, the Northern Territory and Tasmania, more recent research has identified ovens on goldfields mined in the 1850s and 1860s in the Buckland district of Victoria and in south-eastern New South Wales (Smith 2006).

The ovens are sometimes located near houses and sometimes near temples, reflecting their use in both domestic cooking and religious celebration. There is some variation in style and materials used, but the ovens are essentially similar in construction. Each has a central cylindrical chamber about 1 m high and 1 m in diameter, usually at least partially buried, with a superstructure of stone, brick and earth. A fire was built in the oven to heat it while the pig was being prepared. This involved splitting the carcass and marinating it inside and out in a mixture that included soy sauce, garlic and ginger. Once the oven was hot the carcass was suspended on an iron pole and lowered into the oven, the top sealed with corrugated or cast iron and wet sacks, and the whole left to cook for about 2 hours.

There is increasing evidence to show that temples, cemeteries, ovens and homes were all carefully placed according to the principles of *feng shui*, an ancient system for harmonising the energy of individuals with that of topographic features, winds, seasons, hills and constellations so as to confer the most benefit in spiritual and material terms. Archaeologists have been slow to acknowledge the influence of belief in the tangible, material business of erecting structures, but its significance is gradually becoming more widely appreciated, with Lindsay Smith's (2006:17–20) work the most detailed in this regard. Where possible, building sites were chosen to be most auspicious, and where that choice was limited the buildings themselves were oriented in the most auspicious manner. The best building locations were those that featured protective hills curving behind with running water in front. Houses in Australia and New Zealand ideally faced the morning sun. As Smith writes, the perception of the landscape in terms of *feng shui* principles is deeply embedded in Chinese culture. It has persisted for millennia and continues to be of importance in the present day. As such, it should be no surprise that it played a role in the physical shape of the dwellings and settlements that are today archaeological sites.

The cemeteries located in the five major Chinese villages identified by Smith in southern New South Wales all had associations with desirable *feng shui* characteristics (2006:221). In contrast, at Tumut the Chinese were buried within the general cemetery and there was no evidence of *feng shui* influences in the burial practices. *Feng shui* also featured strongly in the location of the temples. All the buildings had a long axis oriented from north-east to south-west and all were on sites overlooking water a short distance in front of the temple. The land behind all the sites sloped upwards and at three of the five temples sloping land enclosed the sites on three sides (Smith 2006:217). The same principles informed the location of the villages and to a lesser extent the mining camps. Most of the villages were close to but separate from major non-Chinese settlements in the area, with the specific locations apparently chosen to take advantage of topographic features. They were located at a break in slope or in the lower foothills of sloping terrain and overlooking rivers or creeks, as were the smaller camps. While the non-Chinese settlements in the study area had regular streets, the Chinese settlements large and small did not, with buildings clustered together and connected by winding paths.

The archaeology of Chinese communities as disparate as those of south Gippsland, Sydney's Rocks, Cooktown and southern New South Wales reveal some of the ways that the Chinese were both independent from, and integrated with, wider colonial society. Individuals, households and settlements interacted in highly complex ways, with each other, with European society and with the Chinese homeland. Although often stereotyped by their clothing, language and customs as alien and unknowable, the Chinese in Australia were diverse and divided. They came from different districts, spoke various dialects and owed allegiance to a wide range of kinship networks. In the colonies, as in other overseas Chinese contexts, individuals were distinguished by gender, occupation, class and clan association. Working to repay their credit-passage, their commitment was as much to strengthening group identity and prestige in their homeland as it was to pursuing individual ambition.

Afghan Cameleers

The hostility and suspicion endured by the Chinese in Australia, and the ways they continually negotiated an ongoing sense of individual and group identity, was also a common experience for a less well-known migrant group: the Afghan cameleers. They were the first Muslims to settle in Australia, and played a crucial role in linking the isolated mines, settlements and stations of the outback. Among the first Afghans to arrive in Australia were three men hired to handle the 24 camels imported for the ill-fated Burke and Wills expedition in 1860, and camels later played a significant role in outback transportation (see Chapter 6). By the 1890s there were about 6,000 camels in Australia, guided by more than 800 Afghan drivers, who lived primarily in fringe communities or "ghantowns" at transportation hubs in the outback such as Cloncurry in Queensland and Oodnadatta in South Australia (Rajkowski 1987:59–65; Stevens 2002:26).

Most of the cameleers were Pathans or Baluchis, semi-nomadic people from the arid hill country of today's Afghanistan and Pakistan. They came to Australia on a 3-year contract, many leaving wives and families behind, after which most returned home (Jones and Kenny 2007:35). Some, however, stayed longer, in some cases setting up a carrying business of their own. A few became successful merchants, including the brothers Faiz and Tagh Mahomet of Maree, Abdul Wade (Wahid) of Bourke, and Mahomet Allum of Adelaide, but most were poorly paid, earning about one-quarter of the wage of a European worker, and endured tough working conditions in extremely remote areas. They were generally feared and hated by Europeans, and their unique communities were always shunned, marginal places within the wider landscape of European society. Europeans were suspicious of the appearance and language(s) of the Afghans, and distrusted their Islamic customs. They also feared economic competition from the Afghans, whose camel trains could more reliably cover longer distances with bigger loads at smaller cost than horse or bullock teams. Afghan men arrived in Australia without wives or children, and prejudice on the part of both Europeans and Aborigines prevented most Afghan men from marrying local women, especially in the early years. Those who did marry women in Australia usually raised their children as Muslims.

Islam was a fundamental dimension of the Afghans' life in Australia. It provided spiritual solace as well as guidelines for every aspect of daily life, including prayer, meals, slaughtering animals and burying the dead (Fig. 9.3). It also defined the Afghans in cultural terms, and set them apart from wider European society. The Afghans were able to assert their cultural and religious identity in Australia in part because of their relatively small numbers, and because they were willing to endure a socially and geographically marginal existence, while maintaining strong links within their own community.

Archaeological research on the Afghans in Australia has been almost entirely neglected until quite recently. Rebecca Parkes (2009), however, has begun a substantial investigation into the sites and landscapes associated with the cameleers,

Fig. 9.3 Afghan Mosque at Hergott Springs (Maree) in South Australia, about 1884 (State Library of South Australia)

including their houses, graves, mosques and camps. She uses the concept of *qibla*, the direction of Mecca, as an organising principle to explore how the Afghans perceived and ordered domestic and communal religious space. Muslims face Mecca for prayer, with a *mihrab*, or alcove, set into the interior of the mosque to indicate the appropriate direction for worship (Insoll 1999:28–31). From an Australian perspective, *qibla* was generally in a north-west direction; the *intention* to face Mecca was paramount, even if the precise cardinal direction was uncertain.

Archaeological survey has indicated that material evidence from the Afghans is often slight. They lived in tents of canvas or hessian to begin with, in camps on the edge of town. As they spent most of their time travelling, permanent dwellings were only used from time to time. The tents were gradually replaced with huts and houses of corrugated iron, with a hard-packed mud floor and an open fire. Water was generally scarce, although gardens and date palms were established when possible. Alcohol containers are recorded only rarely, reflecting the Islamic prohibition of alcohol. Fish tins, however, were common, which may reflect Islamic dietary rules where fish is not subject to *halal* (lawful) measures, and so provided a valuable source of protein for the Afghan Muslims.

Mosques represent some of the best-preserved features of the ghantowns, and are often represented by the remains of stonework floors and foundations, and a *qibla* orientation. Running water for ritual washing was also an important element in the sacred geography of Islamic prayer. Even trees and wells, however, passed regularly on the Afghans' travels, could become "bush mosques", recognised as special, sacred places for worship (Stevens 2002:171–174). Afghan graves are also identifiable by their orientation and marking, and by their position in the north-west of local cemeteries. The deceased were buried without grave goods, placed on their right-hand side facing Mecca, with the head to the north. This differs from the traditional Christian practice of burial on the back with an east–west alignment and a headstone to the west (see Chapter 12). Few Afghan graves have headstones, but many have a simple stone arrangement at the head and foot of the grave.

The Afghan cameleers, as the first Muslim community in Australia, brought with them an array of cultural traditions and practices relating to their religious faith, tribal origins and nomadic lifestyle. Widely regarded as "the untouchables" of Australian society (Stevens 2002:150), they set about adapting their lives and beliefs to local conditions to create a practical setting for their cultural and religious life. Never more than a few thousand in number, the cameleers forged a network of paths that criss-crossed the vast spaces of inland Australia. In spite of all their hardships and effort, however, they remained basically outcasts, clinging to a way of life and spiritual belief on the margins of white Australia.

Polish and German Settlers

Another small group of immigrants who created a home for themselves in Australia were Polish Catholics, who first settled in South Australia in the 1850s. Most came from the Poznán region in western Poland, forced to leave by drought, lack of access to land, and political turmoil. They formed a settlement known as Polish Hill River, about 120 km north of Adelaide, and by the 1880s there were around 400 people living in the area, mostly engaged in farming. The community was based around their church and school, which provided a focus for the practice of faith and customs (Paszkowski 2001:621). The group was closely associated with the much larger German Lutheran community in South Australia, but the Poles maintained a distinct sense of their own identity. Stankowski's (2003, 2004) archaeological investigation of the settlement has revealed, however, a lack of obvious "Polish" material remains, which raises important questions about "the meanings of things" and the maintenance of cultural identity in the broader context of a dominant Anglo-British society.

Survey of the remains of seven house complexes at the settlement revealed that most domestic architecture was built in the Australian vernacular tradition, with verandahs, skillion extensions and fireplaces set into sidewalls. The houses were built of brick, slate, galvanised iron and local fieldstone. Traditional Polish houses normally featured a central hearth and chimney under the roof ridge, but only one house at Polish Hill River included this arrangement. The only other conventionally Polish architectural feature was a niche built into the wall beside several fireplaces, used either to keep pots of food warm, or for display of items such as religious statues. Polish grave markers in local cemeteries show only English inscriptions, while domestic artefacts identified during survey and excavation were entirely typical of later-nineteenth-century Australian rural sites. Thus, while Polish language, religion and customs flourished at the settlement for at least 40 years, supporting a vibrant sense of community spirit, this ethnic identity is not easily accessible through the archaeological record. Stankowski (2004:5) suggests that a distinctly Polish world view was being translated into patterns of non-Polish artefacts, and that the same objects were seen and understood in different ways by different groups of people.

This absence of a readily identifiable "Polish" material culture stands in obvious contrast to the well-known German community of South Australia, most fully documented by the work of Gordon Young and his colleagues (Young 1985; Young et al. 1977) and by Noris Ioannou (1995). Lutheran Germans began to arrive in the late 1830s, mostly from Prussia, Saxony and Silesia, driven from their homeland by religious persecution and drawn to the new colony by economic opportunity. They formed a number of closely related settlements in the Barossa Valley and in the Adelaide Hills, later moving up the Murray River into the Riverina district and to Thomastown in Melbourne's northern suburbs. Many arrived in groups under the leadership of a parish priest, and laid out their townships in traditional patterns. This included the *Hufendorf* settlement, where settlers occupied narrow, parallel farmlets fronting a road or watercourse. Vegetables, pigs and fowls were raised behind the house, while beyond these were vines, then grain crops and finally pasture (Young 1985). German farmers tended to focus on self-supporting subsistence, rather than relying wholly on commercial crops, and thus endured well the vagaries of weather and markets.

The settlers also brought German architectural styles, many examples of which are preserved in the region today. Kitchens, for example, often included complex arrangements of hearths and ovens linked together by a central chimney, while attic rooms for sleeping and storage were built into large roof spaces. Half-timbering was also used to build houses, sheds and barns. A timber frame was erected with vertical and diagonal timbers, and the spaces were filled with wattle and daub or with brick. Other elements of German material culture in the area included cemeteries, where many monuments featured lengthy inscriptions in German, along with traditional clothing styles, food, furniture, pottery and farming equipment. The retention of these traditional cultural products helped to overcome the stress of the migration experience, and contributed strongly to the "Europeanisation" of the Barossa Valley within the wider setting of colonial British culture (Ioannou 1995:14).

The distinctive material signature of the Germans in South Australia is partly the result of numbers, with around 18,000 migrants entering the colony from Germany by 1900. Arriving in groups, they created a close network of settlements populated by farmers, skilled artisans and professionals (Young et al. 1977:47). Each settlement was largely autonomous, but could draw on the skills and resources of neighbouring German villages, thereby controlling the degree of contact with outside influences. The Poles, however, mostly arrived as small family groups, rather than as an entire community. They lacked the resources to be independent of wider British society, and with little or no trade or movement back to Poland, the community was culturally isolated in Australia. Arriving in South Australia later than the Germans, they found a society already imbued with British customs and practices. Where the Germans, arriving only a few years after the founding of the colony, had enjoyed considerable freedom to develop their own ways of life and religion, the Poles began to arrive in the 1850s and had to blend in and adapt to the landscape and society already established. During the 1880s and 1890s, as the settlement frontier moved northward in South Australia, many Poles moved with it, thus diluting their cohesion as a group, and facilitating their gradual absorption into the mainstream of colonial society.

Australian and British Identity

By the late nineteenth century, there was a growing sense that Australia's future was separate from, though still related to, the British homeland. Although around three quarters of the population were Australian-born (Jupp 2001:863), the majority of them were of British extraction. People commonly referred to Britain as "Home", even though most had never been there. There was widespread debate on what it meant to be Australian, and how this might be different from being British. Prior to Federation in 1901, however, Australia remained a collection of separate British colonies, and people remained subjects of the British Empire. Britain continued, by and large, as the main source of ideas, people, capital, customs and technology, reinforcing the Australian colonies as outposts of British life. This notion of "British" identity, however, is far from straightforward. Due to its dominance in colonial Australia, it has been the unexamined measure of normality, the silent "other", against which the non-British are compared in archaeological studies. This unproblematic construction of British identity can easily obscure the multiplicity of identities that constituted a "British subject".

"Britishness" includes elements of language, geography, legal and political structures, cultural habits and moral values. It also comprises a diversity of identities within the United Kingdom, including people of English, Scottish, Irish, Welsh, Cornish and Manx descent, and is frequently contested by regional and ethnic affiliation. Further, non-white citizens of British colonies in Asia, Africa and the Caribbean could and did claim British identities. Britishness, therefore, was a composite ideal, involving juxtaposition of national identities (English, Scottish, etc.), rather than an amalgam, which created something new and distinctive. British identity was, and remains, highly diverse, plural and contested (Lawrence 2003b:2; Porter 2004:20).

This sense of regional distinctiveness decreased as the distance from the United Kingdom increased. In contexts of colonial settlement, including Australia, South Africa and Canada, those who settled the empire experienced a greater sense of unalloyed Britishness than those who stayed at home. English-speaking, colonial-born people of English, Irish, Welsh and Scottish descent could claim a British identity that distinguished them from Dutch, French or Indigenous residents of the same colony. In Australia, Britishness encompassed all the separate ethnicities in the United Kingdom that were blended in the colonies as migrants intermarried, and served as the other against which a new Australian identity was constructed. There was also a sense of pan-British identity that connected settlers with friends and relations in colonies in other parts of the world, and by the turn of the twentieth century this was strengthened by an imperial identity fostered by the growing strength of the British Empire (Merrington 2003; Young 2003). People could still identify as both colonial Australians and British subjects at the same time (Hassam 2000:2–3; Terry and Prangnell 2009). They could also recognise their Irish, Welsh or Scottish heritage without surrendering or denying their Australian or British allegiance. National and ethnic identity in Australia thus remained as fluid and layered as it was in Britain (Fig. 9.4).

Historians have documented the experiences in Australia of many groups from the British Isles (e.g. Hammerton and Thomson 2005; Keneally 1998; O'Farrell 1987; Ronayne 2002; Watson 1984), but archaeological attention has been minimal. In South Australia the Cornish formed a large proportion of the population in the mining regions around Burra and on the Eyre Peninsula as well as in the Adelaide Hills, and there has been some documentation of their distinctive vernacular architecture and their influence on mining technology (Connell 1987; Faull 1987; Piddock and O'Malley 2006; see Chapter 7). There has also been an archaeological study of a settlement of Welsh miners near Castlemaine in Central Victoria (Hill 1998), and the possible identification of an Irish presence at the Sailor's Home in Sydney (Gojak and Iacono 1993; see Chapter 11).

As yet there is little evidence for the transportation to Australia of regional traditions of material culture. It is clear, however, that the Australian colonies were developing a material culture that shared much in common with other British

Fig. 9.4 Houses in Burra in South Australia, built in the traditional stone manner and lacking verandahs (photo S. Lawrence)

colonies while being distinct from that of the United States (Lawrence 2003c). Early colonial houses were built in the symmetrical style of Georgian architecture, but inside many were simple one-or-two roomed cottages. By the 1840s and 1850s, more prosperous builders had begun to favour the eclectic, asymmetrical designs popular in the Victorian era and the unadorned Georgian buildings were considered old-fashioned. The dishes on Australian tables were also different to those of their American counterparts. Australian consumers, like those in Canada, South Africa and Britain itself favoured colourful transfer-printed patterns throughout the nineteenth century, while American consumers preferred moulded white ironstone dishes, particularly after 1850. British manufacturers produced wares specifically to cater to this market, and only briefly, when the American Civil War closed American ports in the 1860s, did these white ironstones appear in any numbers in Australia (Brooks 2005:56–60; Ewins 1997; Chapter 11).

By the 1890s Australians were attempting to articulate a new national identity that co-existed with loyalty to the Empire. They sought to define elements of the Australian landscape and experience that were distinctive, and which could be used as symbols for a newly emerging national identity. The "bushman" was the best-known and most enduring symbol of this period. As we note in Chapter 6, this figure was promoted in art and literature as a rugged individualist, despising authority and ever-loyal to his mates, the stereotype created as a deliberately non-British confection at a time of burgeoning Australian nationalism. The bushman as national archetype, however, has been criticised from numerous perspectives, including its masculinist bias, urban origins and its erasure of Aboriginal Australians (Davison 1978; Goodman 1994; Lake 1986). Lawrence (2003a) has explored how qualities such as domesticity and respectability were also stripped from the bushman ideal, thereby simplifying the complexity of Australian rural experience, excluding women, children and ethnic minorities, and creating in the process an uncomplicated icon to represent a new Australian identity.

This search for distinctively Australian motifs was not confined to mythical men in the bush. People sought unique aspects of life all around them to forge a sense of Australianness that was still compatible with a shared British identity. Australian motifs drawn from native plants and animals, for example, began to appear in architecture and fashion. Moulded plasterwork incorporated Australian designs including waratahs, gum nuts, wattle, ferns, lyrebirds and kookaburras (Capon 1993:49). Between the late 1880s and the end of the First World War, the most popular style of housing in Australia was the "Federation house", a vigorous local adaptation of English "Queen Anne", Arts and Crafts, and Art Nouveau influences (Fraser and Joyce 1986). Motifs from the Australian bush were used extensively in the decorative treatment of exterior woodwork, stained glass, and on interior tiles and wallpapers. At the same time, symbols of Australia were used to sell everything from Billy Tea and Goanna Oil to Rosella Sauce and Emu Brand Rope (Cozzolino and Rutherford 1990). When Australian colonists voted to federate into a single nation in 1901, the process took place as part of a wider cultural assertion of Australian identity. People embraced things that were distinctively Australian, as a way of asserting difference and distance from the British homeland, and a growing confidence in what it meant to be Australian.

New Australians: Bonegilla

One of the first acts of the Commonwealth Government in 1901 was the passing of the *Immigration Restriction Act*, which created the White Australia Policy, and focused immigration firmly on people from the United Kingdom. Between 1901 and 1940, more than 800,000 migrants arrived in Australia, mostly from Britain and Ireland. Several thousand British child migrants arrived as well, especially in the 1920s and 1930s, to live and work at farm-schools run by the Fairbridge Society and Dr. Barnardo's Homes. Most were expected to become agricultural workers or domestic servants (Hill 2007). Local attitudes to immigration in this period, however, were increasingly fraught, contested between notions of imperial attachment and national identity, and economic development and rising unemployment. What did "Australia" actually mean, and what sort of country did people want to belong to and create? By the late 1940s and 1950s, this question took on an urgency rarely seen before or since.

The Second World War transformed Australia's relationship to the rest of the world. It took many thousands of service men and women away to war, while thousands of American service personnel were in their turn stationed in Australia, and it re-oriented Australian foreign policy away from Britain and towards the United States. Near-invasion by Japanese forces had revealed Australia's vulnerability, and the need to boost the population as part of a wider programme of nation building. People from Britain were still the preferred immigrants, but the need for greater numbers and types of migrants forced Australia to turn to other sources. Between 1947 and 1953, the national migration programme included 170,000 Displaced Persons (DPs or "Balts"), refugees from war-ravaged Europe. Their numbers included Poles, Yugoslavs, Latvians, Ukrainians and Hungarians, many unable or unwilling to return to their homelands.

The Australian government established around 150 migrant accommodation centres in all states and territories. These were significant as places of first engagement between Australia and migrant societies. The Bonegilla Migrant Camp was the largest of these centres. It opened in 1947 on the site of a former army camp, located near Wodonga in north-east Victoria (Fig. 9.5). It was an ideal location for the government, because its distance from Sydney and Melbourne limited confrontation between migrants and those Australians resistant to the programme (Sluga 2001:72). Displaced Persons had to sign a 2-year directed-labour contract, and while in camp they received English language training and classes on the "Australian way

Fig. 9.5 The Taczanowski family from Poland at Bonegilla in 1949, where tents were used to relive overcrowding (Albury City Bonegilla Collection)

of life". From the camp the breadwinners were sent away to work out their contracts, usually in remote areas, while wives and children waited in ex-army holding centres.

By the late 1940s, Bonegilla consisted of 24 blocks of army huts, with more than 800 buildings spread out over a wide area. The landscape was denuded of trees, with dust storms, flies and mosquitoes plaguing the inhabitants in summer. The camp was almost a town in itself, accommodating up to 7,700 people, with an additional 1,600 in tents (P. Freeman 1999:41). Different national groups were housed in separate blocks. The huts were built of galvanised iron and timber, and provided dormitory-style accommodation for about 26 people. There was no heating and little furniture, and initially men and women were separated, regardless of marital status (Sluga 1988:7). Migrants worked in the camp as interpreters, cooks, cleaners, nurses and medical orderlies. The specified period of stay was 4–6 weeks, but this varied considerably depending on the wider employment situation.

Recent archaeological "excavation" of photographs, oral histories and archives has yielded important clues about both officials' and migrants' attitudes to national and ethnic identity (Zipfel 2007). British immigrants, for example, retained a favoured status during this period, not having to sign labour agreements, and they avoided the ex-army migrant camps by being sent straight to workers' hostels. For the DPs, however, the camps sent out signals about their transition from Old Europeans to New Australians. The huts and buildings were temporary, re-used, Government-owned, rural, communal and basic. These characteristics linked them to earlier expressions of migration and identity, in terms of colonialism, convictism and life on the frontier. The migrants experienced simple outback living, complete with possums in the roof and snakes under the floor, and a certain degree of hardship and institutionalisation. Starting at the lower end of the social spectrum, they enacted certain migrant experiences common to colonial Australians before working their way up. After passing through this procedure, the non-British migrant would, ideally, be accepted into Australian society.

The migrants were not, however, passive recipients of official treatment. They responded energetically, in numerous ways, to the structures and strictures of camp life. Huts were divided into cubicles, with luggage arranged into "walls" and blankets suspended from ceilings to create private spaces for individuals and families. Women tapped illegally into power sockets to cook meals in the huts, both practices forbidden because of the fire danger and the challenge to camp order. Hut spaces were decorated with paintings, wall hangings and other mementoes of life in the old country, easing the sense of dislocation and distance from the homeland. Resistance hardened into riot in 1952, when Italian migrants damaged some buildings at Bonegilla in protest at not being allocated to jobs. Having been in the camp for several months, they were frustrated at not being able to repay the cost of their passage to Australia.

As the DP programme ended in the early 1950s, the Australian government increasingly sought migrants to meet the specific needs of primary and secondary industry. Migration agreements were signed with the Netherlands, Italy,

Austria, Belgium, West Germany, Greece and Spain. At Bonegilla, changes were made to respond to the new migration patterns. Huts were gradually subdivided, and linoleum was laid on the floors, while windows were curtained, pit latrines were converted to flushing toilets and trees were planted for shade. Increasingly, however, migrant camps and institutional communal living became an outmoded response to the needs of the migrants themselves. By the time Bonegilla was closed in 1971, purpose-built migrant centres had mostly replaced the old migrant camps. Preferential treatment of British migrants ceased, Asian and Middle Eastern refugees were welcomed to metropolitan areas, and a new awareness of Australia's complex, multi-ethnic identity had begun to be embraced. It is beyond the scope of this book and has yet to be adequately addressed by archaeologists, but the transformations that followed these post-war waves of migration have been profound. Language, culture, diet and suburban landscapes have been transformed, and Australia has become a truly hybrid society.

Conclusion

Historian Geoffrey Moorhouse has called Australia the last great social melting pot on earth (Moorhouse 1999:60). Since 1788, people have arrived in this country from almost every other place in the world. Many have been driven from their homelands by war, famine and disease, and drawn to Australia by the promise of peace, prosperity and opportunity. They have typically been met at first with hostility and suspicion, then indifference, and later with toleration and acceptance, as each new migrant group has made a home in Australian towns and suburbs. It is no mere cliché to acknowledge the extraordinary contribution that successive waves of migrants have brought to Australia, not only in obvious ways like food and architecture and language, but also in deeper, subtler measures of transforming what it means to be Australian. In this chapter we have observed the archaeology of several prominent ethnic groups to arrive, with a particular focus on the Chinese as a group which has attracted a great deal of historical and archaeological scrutiny. The old model of calibrating the assimilation of migrant groups in terms of their identifiably "ethnic" material culture has been replaced over the years by a more considered understanding of the ways in which diasporic people relate to their new home and their homeland via the material world. Artefacts need not be a simple reflection of ethnic presence or absence, but symbols of agency, negotiation, and changing identity. The meanings of objects can and do change, depending on time, place and circumstance, and we do well to respect this very active engagement with the material world in exploring the archaeology of migration and ethnicity.

Chapter 10
An Urbanised Nation

Australia has long been a nation of city-dwellers. From the earliest colonial period many settlers were unwilling to move beyond the town centres. By 1891, one third of the population lived in cities, with around a million people equally divided between Melbourne and Sydney and another 300,000 spread between Adelaide, Brisbane, Hobart and Perth (Cannon 1988:10–14). During the twentieth century this trend accelerated even further, with three-quarters of the population living in cities by 2001 (Hugo 2003:187). Cities are thus an important part of the archaeological record of Australia's colonial history, containing a wealth of information about the ways in which many nineteenth-century Australians lived, worked and played. At the same time, due to the nature of the heritage industry in which much historical archaeological work is carried out, archaeology in cities has had a high profile within the discipline and in the wider community. Much historical archaeology is done as rescue archaeology in association with development, and in inner-urban areas archaeology has tended to be more closely integrated with the planning process. The continuous rebuilding of Australia's capital cities over the past 30 years has thus resulted in a great deal of archaeological activity. There is a rich and growing body of data available to answer questions about the history of Australia's cities, and archaeologists are becoming increasingly skilled in dealing with urban sites.

Judy Birmingham published the first major review of urban archaeology in Australia in 1990, with a primary focus on Sydney (Birmingham 1990). This reflected work to that point because, with a few notable exceptions such as the Little Lon dig in Melbourne and the Destitute Asylum and Queen's Theatre projects in Adelaide, very little work had been done outside Sydney to that time. Based on her Sydney experience, Birmingham identified a number of issues, including the relationship between documentary and archaeological data, problems with interpreting stratigraphy on complex multi-phase sites, and the challenges of processing hundreds of thousands of finds in ways that were both efficient and likely to produce useful information. Birmingham's review emphasised the youth of the discipline at that time, which was only beginning to develop the confidence and methodologies to deal with the excavation of large historical sites and the mass of artefacts that were recovered. Writing in the same period, Grace Karskens and Wendy Thorpe turned their attention to the need for more sophisticated research questions to guide

S. Lawrence, P. Davies, *An Archaeology of Australia Since 1788*,
Contributions To Global Historical Archaeology, DOI 10.1007/978-1-4419-7485-3_10,
© Springer Science+Business Media, LLC 2011

archaeological investigations (Karskens and Thorpe 1992). While Birmingham argued that the archaeological record should not be subservient to the documentary record, Karskens and Thorpe countered that when working in the recent past the documentary record cannot be ignored and should be seen as an invaluable resource. They proposed a series of research themes drawn from their knowledge of colonial history which they hoped would enable the experiences of those who lived at the sites to be understood better. Their questions concerned the impact of the industrial revolution, gender, changing standards of living, and the existence of local identities.

A decade later, Tim Murray returned to the problem of what can be learned from the archaeology of cities. Working with his colleague historian Alan Mayne at Little Lon and the team that excavated Casselden Place, Murray has developed an approach that works outwards from individual excavated households to encompass neighbourhoods, the city, and finally to comparisons with nineteenth-century cities around the world (Mayne et al. 2000; Murray and Mayne 2001). They have sought to tell the stories of real people at these sites in order to move beyond stereotypes about urban slums. With his colleagues in the Exploring the Archaeology of the Modern City Project, Murray has further refined approaches to achieving these aims (Murray and Crook 2005). The EAMCP team have used fine-grained historical documents such as rate books and birth, death and marriage records to create profiles of the residents of sites, and have also started to critically analyse the taphonomic processes of archaeological site formation in urban areas. In this way they have expanded the historically driven approach of Karskens and Thorpe but have also responded to Birmingham's challenge about the need to improve our understanding of the archaeological record.

The stories told in this chapter will also be balanced with the archaeological and historical methods used to uncover them. We begin by looking at the kinds of archaeological deposits found in cities and the sorts of urban activities that created them. In the second half of the chapter we look at what archaeologists have learned about life in Australia's colonial cities, examining in turn slums, the wealthy and the suburbs.

These divisions are implicitly based on class, a topic with which archaeologists and historians in Australia have been equally reluctant to engage. Australia has a reputation and a self-image as an egalitarian society, and while there has been a strong tradition of labour history, the notion of class has not been the subject of sustained historical enquiry. It has been considered "un-Australian" to even identify a middle class (Ward 1958:39), and with a few notable exceptions (e.g. Hirst 1988; Russell 1994; Young 1997), any form of class distinction has been resolutely resisted. In parallel with this historical disinterest, and perhaps emerging from a general refusal to recognise class in Australian society, historical archaeologists have paid far less attention to class than to other social structures such as gender and ethnicity. Indeed much of the discussion about class comes out of research into gender, as archaeologists have sought more nuanced ways of understanding the range of domestic goods found in assemblages. Where class has played a role in archaeological analysis, Australians have tended to take what LouAnn Wurst (2006:191) describes as a gradational approach to class, with the emphasis on using class as a social category rather than attempting to analyse conflict between classes or the interplay of domination and resistance.

The most fully developed Australian archaeological study to critically examine issues of class per se is Heather Burke's (1999) study of ideology in domestic architecture in the New England town of Armidale. Burke used architecture as a means of analysing social identity and ideology among different groups, and the ways in which style was used as part of the process of negotiating relationships. This remains one of the few examples of a process-oriented approach to class in Australian historical archaeology, and there has yet to be anything comparable. Australians continue to be more interested in questions of how individuals and families negotiated their own positions within colonial society than in how disadvantage or resistance operated at a systemic level.

Understanding the Archaeology of Cities

In cities as elsewhere, archaeologists work with deposits formed by a variety of natural and cultural processes. Understanding how these processes operated is critical to interpreting what took place at a particular archaeological site. In addition to answering archaeological questions about site formation, studying a site's taphonomy can also shed light on historical questions about the development of urban infrastructure, changes to the physical shape of the land, and changes in attitudes and behaviours towards hygiene and sanitation. Typical urban deposits include fills in pit features such as privies, cisterns and trenches; fills formed by demolition and material brought in to create level ground; structural remains of walls and footings; and surface scatters in open areas such as yards, streets or parks. While some activities created deposits, other activities removed deposits. In cities this happened on small scales when buildings were demolished and their footings removed, and on larger scales when hills were cut away and levelled. Other deposits form inside buildings, usually in rooms where there is a bare earth or wooden floor. Underfloor deposits are typically recovered from ground floor rooms, but in unusual circumstances such as the Hyde Park Barracks in Sydney, these may also be recovered from upper stories (Davies 2010). Work by Mary Casey and Tony Lowe at the CSR site in Sydney has produced valuable insights into the formation of underfloor deposits, which typically date to houses built in the period before the introduction of tongue-and-groove flooring in the late 1870s and which reveal activity patterns within rooms (Casey 2004).

Creating Ground Surfaces: Filling and Levelling

Ground surfaces in cities are subject to significant alteration which affects the kinds of deposits that are created and destroyed, and which archaeological sites survive. Adding fill to the top of the ground can add up to several metres to the depth of a site. The foundations of the site of First Government House in Sydney were buried beneath a metre of fill that included demolition debris, sand and gravel used to create a car park (Proudfoot et al. 1991:109). Fill deposits can help to preserve sites by raising the level currently in use above the older parts of the site. Fill can be local in origin, such as demolition debris from buildings on the site, or it can be brought in from elsewhere and contain artefacts entirely unrelated to activities at that location. Removing large quantities of fill can be a challenge for archaeologists and frequently heavy machinery is used for this task.

The filling-in of low-lying coastal ground has added valuable space to cities, and can result in unexpected archaeological finds. In San Francisco, New York City, and Wellington, New Zealand, disused ships were sunk or beached as part of landfill and are still preserved beneath the streets and skyscrapers of the modern city (Cantwell and Wall 2001; Delgado 1990, 2009; O'Keefe 1999). Both the ships' hulls and associated artefacts are generally in very good condition because they are in waterlogged contexts. At Point Gellibrand in Melbourne, ballast from ships coming from England was used as fill along the shore, which was discovered only when archaeologists working at the site of the old jetty found prehistoric stone tools worked in English flints within the fill. At Sydney Cove, a small embayment was filled in following construction of the Sydney Sailors Home in the 1860s. The earliest material was refuse from the Home, while the new land created was later turned into a garden (Gojak and Iacono 1993). Around Sydney Harbour the heads of bays were filled in to create new land for industrial and recreational purposes.

Levelling and the removal of material from sites can have an equally dramatic effect. Sometimes it is very localised and confined to small areas. The first British builders in the Rocks in Sydney levelled out the sandstone ridges to make flat spaces to build on and dug into the rock to make wells and cisterns (Karskens 1997:28–29). At Camp Street in Ballarat the first white occupants of the site were the government troops sent to control and administer the diggings during the gold rush. They built their camp on a hill high above the miners' town and did not alter the hill itself except to add some crushed mine tailings to keep down the dust in the yard of the barracks. In the 1880s the police who were by now using the site began a major rebuilding project to realign the buildings with the line of the newer surveyed road. They removed the hilltop and used the rubble to fill in the lower ground, creating a much more level precinct (Godden Mackay Logan 2004). At other times the removal of material is widespread and reshapes the entire archaeological record. Batman's Hill, for example, at the western edge of the Melbourne CBD, was removed entirely between the 1860s and 1890s, to make room for the Spencer Street railway complex (Presland 2008:4). The construction of twentieth-century skyscrapers with their deep footings also destroys pre-existing archaeological sites (Fig. 10.1). Archaeologists in London have found that even smaller changes in building practices such as the excavation of cellars, which became more common in the nineteenth century, have caused widespread destruction of the archaeological record of the seventeenth and eighteenth centuries (Egan 1999:61).

Fig. 10.1 Casselden Place in Melbourne. Following archaeological investigation in 2002 and 2003, bulk excavation of the site prior to construction removed not only the remains of houses, yards and factories but also roads and laneways in the neighbourhood. A nineteenth-century horizontal architecture was replaced by the vertical architecture of a twentieth-first-century office tower (photo P. Davies)

Dealing with Waste: Plumbing and Rubbish Disposal

One of the richest archaeological sources of information on life in cities is the kind of deposit that comes from pit features such as wells, cisterns, cesspits, privies and purpose-dug rubbish pits. These pits can contain an abundance of artefacts and remain stratigraphically intact, that is, they have not been disturbed by later activity on the site. It is only recently, however, that archaeologists have begun to closely analyse the ways in which the deposits inside these pits were formed. Essentially, pits were handy receptacles for household rubbish and were filled as people discarded food scraps and broken and unwanted items (Fig. 10.2). Pits were generally filled within short periods of a few days to a few months, and the deposits usually relate only to the very end of the use-life of that feature rather than reflecting the whole period of its use.

Wells and cisterns were both associated with obtaining and storing supplies of fresh water for household use. While they were being used as part of the water supply they were kept clean and rubbish was not allowed to accumulate within them. The pits were full of water but empty of artefacts. It was only when alternative sources of water were found, such as a new well or piped water, that the old

Fig. 10.2 Stone-lined cesspit in the rear yard of 124 Cumberland Street in the Rocks. The house was owned and occupied by John and Catherine Winch from 1834 to 1861. The pit was backfilled with large quantities of domestic debris, mostly pre-dating the 1860s (photo P. Grant, Sydney Cove Authority, Godden Mackay Logan)

and now disused pits were put to a new use as rubbish pits. Similarly, cesspits and privies were only used for rubbish when they stopped being used for their original purpose, holding human waste. Privies and cesspits were self-contained pits, sometimes lined with stone or timber, sometimes not, above which a shelter with seats was built. While in use the pits filled and were emptied on an irregular basis, the "night-soil" being used on market gardens or dumped on vacant land. When the pits were no longer needed they were filled with rubbish. In the case of modern cities this occurred when cesspits were abolished and replaced by the pan system, which happened in Melbourne in the 1870s, or because plumbing had been connected, which happened in Sydney from the 1860s[1] and in Melbourne from the 1890s (Dunstan 1985:157; Fitzgerald 1987:82–83; Wong 1999). The contents of cesspits excavated by archaeologists may therefore contain lost and discarded objects as well as the traces of human waste. The latter may be detected through the presence of ecofacts, such as insect and plant remains from intestinal parasites and tiny seeds that pass through the human gut.

---

[1] Sewerage connection, however, was by no means rapid or uniform. As late as 1960, almost one third of all suburban homes in Sydney still relied on the "nightman" to remove the sewage (Cowan 1998:157).

Detailed analysis of the artefacts excavated from pit deposits can reveal whether the pit was filled all at once or in discrete episodes, and it can also reveal how old the artefacts were when they entered the pit. When combined with documentary evidence about the connection of utilities in the neighbourhood this provides information on when the pits were filled and who the people were who probably did the filling. If the pit was filled very quickly in a single episode, there should be cross-mends between artefact fragments found at different levels. It should be possible to find pieces of teacup from the top of the pit that will match pieces from the same cup at the bottom. If the pit was filled in distinct episodes separated by a period of time, such matches should be rare. Likewise, the dates during which the artefacts were made should be similar from all parts of the deposit if it was formed quickly. Bottles at the top should not be substantially newer than bottles at the bottom.

One detailed study of the contents of pit deposits in Sydney has demonstrated how this kind of analysis can reveal a great deal about activity on the site. The EAMCP team re-analysed artefact assemblages from 10 post-1860s cesspits on the Cumberland-Gloucester Streets (CuGl) site that had originally been excavated by Godden Mackay in 1994 (Crook and Murray 2004; Godden Mackay Logan 1999). One of the EAMCP findings was that most of the artefacts were very fragmentary. No more than 22 percent of the minimum number of vessels in each pit was complete or near-complete. This is in stark contrast to data from the United States, where vessels are often largely intact and appear to be the result of a single household clean-out. Data from the nearby Rocks property occupied by Mrs. Anne Lewis, a boarding-house proprietor, shows a similar "clean-out" pattern, as all the bottles and ceramic vessels in that cesspit were either complete, near-complete or mendable (Lydon 1995). In the case of the clean-outs it seems that pits were filled when people had some reason to get rid of a large portion of their goods: they may have been moving house or had a serious illness or death in the family. In the EAMCP data, however, the rubbish seems to have come from other sources.

For the 10 CuGl assemblages the EAMCP team calculated the *terminus post quem* (date of manufacture, or "date after which" the artefact must have been deposited). In some cases the artefacts had been manufactured as much as 14 years prior to the time when other records indicate the sewage was connected and the cesspits filled. These old assemblages were also the most fragmentary, with less than 2 percent of vessels intact. Other assemblages had TPQs only 3 or 4 years prior to filling, and likewise had more intact vessels, up to 35 percent of the assemblage. This leads Crook and Murray to speculate that some of the cesspits at least were filled with "old" rubbish that had been stockpiled in yards for some years and now provided a convenient source of fill. Their research also indicates that in Sydney there could be a considerable gap between when sewerage became available on a street and when individual properties were actually connected. In some cases landlords connected all their properties soon after the service was available, but in other cases they waited for up to 20 years before making the connection. Leaving the decision to individual property owners was quite different to the case in Melbourne, where the sewage scheme was paid for by a levy on rates and neighbouring properties were connected at the same time.

One reason that disused pits were filled quickly was because most urban dwellers had very few other ways of disposing of household rubbish. In the days before the establishment of municipal tips and council rubbish collection, individual house-holders had to find a way either to store it on their property or pay to have it removed. Many yards must have contained heaps of old rubbish like the ones used to fill the cesspits in the Cumberland/Gloucester Street neighbourhood. Knowing when councils began to regularly collect rubbish is a vital part of understanding how and when archaeological deposits formed in urban back yards. The deposits containing rubbish, which are the ones of greatest interest to archaeologists, were most likely to accumulate before council rubbish collection occurred, as householders had to make their own arrangements. As we have seen, this often included disposal in pits or in heaps in the yard. Dan Astley Gresswell wrote a report on the sanitary condition of Melbourne in 1890, and described how many people simply threw their rubbish into the street, onto vacant lots or into neighbours' yards (Gresswell 1890:10). A related factor was the practice of burning household rubbish to dispose of organic material, leaving mostly non-combustible material behind. After council rubbish collection began, most rubbish (i.e. artefacts) was removed and any deposits formed in yards are more likely to be fill of various kinds used to level the surface.

These taphonomic processes also explain a puzzling feature of the adjacent sites of Casselden Place, Little Lon and Cohen Place in Melbourne (Godden Mackay Logan et al. 2004; McCarthy 1989; Myers 2002). All three sites were in the heart of what was once Melbourne's Chinese district where the homes and businesses of the Chinese community were concentrated (Couchman 1995; McConville 1985). Archaeologists and historians therefore expected that the excavations would produce abundant evidence about this community, but this did not happen. Of the hundreds of thousands of artefacts recovered from the three excavations, only a small fraction was identifiably Chinese. This does not mean that the Chinese people living there had stopped using familiar foods and objects imported from China, which would be particularly strange as many of the businesses in the area were specialist importers and wholesalers who supplied goods from China throughout Victoria. Instead, it reflects the nature of local amenities at the time the Chinese community lived in the area and the ways that the archaeological record forms. The number of Chinese homes and businesses in the neighbourhood was at its greatest from the mid-1890s until the 1930s (Mayne 2006:321). By this time the inner city was fully sewered, so there were no backyard pits to fill. Rubbish collection had also begun so broken and discarded items were put out in the bin every week and not tossed into the yard or under the floor. Despite negative perceptions of the squalor of the area at the time, the archaeological evidence, or rather the lack of it, demonstrates that the Chinese were as careful of their rubbish as anyone else in Melbourne.

The organised collection of rubbish by councils removed refuse from the archaeological record of domestic sites and resulted in the creation of a different kind of archaeological deposit, the tip. Tips are a commonplace feature of the urban landscape and they are frequently the target of activity by bottle collectors. Archaeologists and heritage managers have generally been less interested in their potential heritage significance. The perception has been that because they constitute secondary deposits of uncontextualised material, tips have little value for answering research questions. The data offered by the study of historic tips will certainly have different characteristics to that of more traditional excavations on domestic sites, but there are also sound arguments to be made for treating tips seriously as archaeological sites. The work of William Rathje and his colleagues at the Projet du Garbage in the United States has demonstrated in numerous studies over 30 years that modern tips can offer unique insights into contemporary life (Rathje 1977; Rathje and Murphy 1992), and there is no reason to think that this would not also be true of historic tips. Tips cannot provide answers to fine-grained questions about ethnicity, class, gender or age within a household, but at a broader scale of analysis they do provide data about neighbourhoods and cities that can be usefully compared with information about other places and other time periods. Tips in Melbourne may well be different to those in Sydney or Perth, let alone New York, London or Cape Town, while twentieth-century tips ought to be different to nineteenth-century tips. There may also be differences between tips in capital cities and those in country towns (Bagshaw 2001:68–69). Tips should be rich sources of data on trade networks, local manufacturing, the adoption of new types of consumer goods such as toothbrushes or radios, broad dietary patterns and attitudes to land use and recycling. All of these themes are illustrated in the studies of two major urban tips in Australia that have been the subject of controlled archaeological investigation.

The first case study is that of Turner's Paddock in Adelaide, excavated in 1993 by Susan Lawrence and a team from Flinders University (Lawrence 1993). The tip, in a corner of the Adelaide Parklands adjacent to the Public Cemetery, had been in use between the 1880s and 1910. Redevelopment of the site led to the opportunity for a limited programme of sampling and excavation. One of the issues raised was the role of recycling at the time. Council records show that special contracts were awarded for people to remove rags, bones and bottles from material deposited at the tip. All of these items had particular value for recycling. Glass bottles were washed and refilled (Lucas 2002), rags were used for paper and bones were used for glue and fertiliser. It was expected that few of these items would therefore be found in the tip, but this was not the case. Little cloth was recovered, although that may have been due to organic decay, but both bone and bottles were present in large quantities. Recycling seems to have been valued, but the process was not always efficient.

A second issue raised was that of changing perceptions of public space. The Adelaide Parklands were laid out by surveyors William Light and George Kingston in 1836 as part of their grand design for the city of Adelaide, and they form a wide and almost unbroken belt around the Central Business District. Today they house gardens, open space and sports grounds, and are a valued part of Adelaide's identity. Using part of the Parklands for a rubbish tip would be unthinkable. In the nineteenth century, however, Turner's Paddock was just one of many tips scattered through the Parklands. It was also pocked with quarries for lime and clay, trees were cut for timber, animals were pastured there and the dead were buried in the public cemetery. These varied uses hint at radical changes in what was meant as "park". Today the term implies natural, green space set aside for aesthetic and recreational purposes.

The use of the Adelaide Parklands in the nineteenth century is more akin to that of the English commons, set aside for common use as an economic resource.

The Brisbane municipal dump provides another case study. This site was excavated in 1998 by Archaeo Cultural Heritage Services prior to the construction of a freeway (Harris et al. 2004). As in Adelaide, the tip was situated in a park, with the refuse used to fill in swampy ground and create level sports fields. The tip was in use from the 1880s until the 1920s, and the similar age to Turner's Paddock reflects a growing trend at that time for municipalities to introduce rubbish collection. Data from the excavation of the tip were particularly welcome in Brisbane because few other historic sites of that period have so far been excavated in the city. A number of research themes were identified that could shed light on life in Brisbane at the time and which also suggested comparisons with other cities. These themes included refuse disposal patterns, trade networks and market access, health and diet, and the effects of the depression of the 1890s. They found that goods in the tip with makers' marks were overwhelmingly from Great Britain, and that locally made goods were rare. Most Australian-made goods were from Sydney and Melbourne, reflecting the manufacturing strength of those centres at the time. The effects of the depression were evident in the lack of building-related debris in the tip, while both formal and informal approaches to healthcare were also represented. One group of artefacts identified was associated with the New Brisbane Hospital and included tea and dinnerwares with medical insignia on the reverse, as well as large undecorated basins and pitchers used on the wards. Home treatments for ailments included a range of patent medicines such as Holloway's Pills, Bosisto's "Syrup of Red Gum", and "Barry's Pain Relief".

Changing Neighbourhoods

Urban excavations provide clear evidence of the ways in which the geography of cities has changed. As population density increased, wealthier residents moved on leaving only the poor behind, and industries developed and shifted locations. The lowest levels of urban sites often reveal the rural or semi-rural character of the earliest British settlements. The stumps of two large river red gums, for example, were found beneath the lanes and factories of Little Lon in Melbourne (McCarthy 1989:6). In Pitt Street, the heart of Sydney's towering business district, traces in what had been the yard of the Hill family showed where plots had been fenced off for growing gardens and crops and keeping livestock (Lydon 1996:154–155). Evidence for home dairying has been found in sites in Surry Hills in what is now inner Sydney and in Parramatta, testifying to the rural character of those areas (Casey 1999; Casey and Lowe Associates 2006).

These spacious blocks were gradually subdivided as the population grew. In the 1830s and the1840s in the Rocks, rows of terrace houses were built in what had been open yards and new cesspits were dug (Karskens 1999:77–79). Terraces were also built on what had been the grounds of the First Government House. Evidence for gardening and agriculture-related activities such as slaughtering, tanning and

Fig. 10.3 Lot 42 at Casselden Place at the rear of the Black Eagle Hotel, showing extensive disturbance by later service pipes (photo T. Jenner, Industry Superannuation Property Trust, Godden Mackay Logan/Austral Archaeology/La Trobe University)

dairying disappeared as these industries moved further away from the city. In Melbourne, light industry and manufacturing businesses set up in what had been residential neighbourhoods (Fig. 10.3). By the end of the nineteenth century Little Lon and Casselden Place accommodated engineering works and Chinese cabinet-makers. Morally ambiguous businesses such as brothels also found a base there, contributing to the area's poor reputation (Mayne 2006). In Pyrmont, foundries were built on what had been open ground as the industrial character of the area was established (Casey and Lowe Associates 1995). Nearby at the head of Cockle Bay (now Darling Harbour), reclaimed land was used for industrial and residential purposes during the nineteenth century, and then resumed for clearance and redevelopment into Paddy's Markets in the early 1900s (Crook et al. 2003b). In Adelaide the Rookery neighbourhood of terrace houses and tanneries was demolished and later replaced with the East End Market (Austral Archaeology 1992).

Archaeological Insights on City Life

Urban excavations are often a prelude to the redevelopment of a precinct. The size and dimensions of the area to be excavated are determined by the footprint of the project planned for the site, rather than by any historical boundaries within the precinct. Excavations can encompass the whole of a modern city block, and frequently take in numerous previous allotments and the roads and laneways between them. A single dig can include domestic and industrial sites as well as shops, pubs and schools. Conversely, as the edge of the dig is determined by the boundary of the modern block, it may only include part of a historic place which extends into neighbouring blocks or under roadways. Urban excavation is thus at the scale of the neighbourhood rather than an individual home or business. The research questions developed to address urban projects are also frequently at the level of the neighbourhood. The themes proposed by Karskens and Thorpe (1992) in Sydney are one example of this, as they looked at processes of change in the neighbourhood as a whole. At the Five Points site in New York City, archaeologists have documented how the whole neighbourhood changed over time, as it went from being home to native-born American artisans to housing Jewish immigrants, many of whom were tailors, and then became home to poor Irish labourers (Yamin 1997). In Lowell, Massachusetts, archaeology has revealed some of the tensions between mill operatives and the employers whose control extended into the minutiae of what workers ate, how they dressed and how they spent their leisure time (Mrozowski et al. 1996). This approach is useful as it provides a way of dealing with the large quantities of data that result from urban excavations in a way that is efficient and meaningful.

It is also possible to consider other scales of analysis in urban archaeology. Although excavations are often large in scale, the data can be broken down into smaller packages that reflect individual households. Architecture, spaces and artefacts can be associated with separate buildings and the people who used them. Documentary research using archival sources such as rate books, directories, land title records, birth, death and marriage records, and bankruptcy and court records builds up profiles of the people who lived on the site. Household archaeology combines this information to investigate the lives of known individuals. Many stories of individuals have been teased out of the archaeological research on the Cumberland/Gloucester Streets site in Sydney and at Little Lon/Casselden Place in Melbourne, as well as other sites in the Rocks, Pyrmont, Parramatta, Cohen Place, and Port Adelaide (Briggs 2005; Karskens 1999; Lydon 1995, 1996, 1999; Mayne et al. 2000; Muir 2008; Murray and Crook 2005). This parallels the results of household archaeology in American cities such as New York, Boston and West Oakland (Beaudry 2006b; Praetzellis and Praetzellis 2004; Wall 1991). Combining the analysis of discrete household assemblages from pit, yard and subfloor deposits with fine-grained archival research and even oral histories can reveal more nuanced ways in which particular places were experienced, a process Mayne and Lawrence (1999) have referred to as producing "ethnographies of place".

At wider scales of analysis, urban excavations provide glimpses of cities that can be compared on a world stage. The rapid growth of large urban centres was one of the defining characteristics of the nineteenth century and one that continues to mark the modern world (Briggs 1968; Dyos and Wolff 1973). Old cities mushroomed and new cities emerged all over the world, facing similar problems of providing adequate housing stock and public transport, commercial and industrial facilities, and dealing with issues of hygiene and waste. Archaeological evidence provides one means of investigating how different cities dealt with these and other challenges. Excavations of houses in the Rocks tell us about individual lives but also provide examples of life in Sydney that can be compared with similar situations in Melbourne, Adelaide, New York, London and Cape Town. Such comparisons can reveal what were common experiences and what was particular and unique about the character of life in specific places.

Tim Murray and Alan Mayne (2001) remind us that all of these scales of analysis can exist simultaneously, and that all are relevant to the analysis of a single excavation. Archaeologists move back and forth from household to neighbourhood to city and back to household again. The detail needed to make sense of individual deposits is lost as enquiry moves outwards to investigate wider patterns and is replaced with insights into longer-term historical processes such as industrialisation and mass consumption. But the detail is required to build up the broader patterns, and knowledge of long-term processes in turn contributes to the understanding of locally based experience. The juxtaposition of specific and general analyses at different spatial scales is akin to the temporal rhythms identified by the historian Fernand Braudel, who observed that historical explanation must also move between the immediacy of the event, the longer changes experienced over a lifetime, and the even longer-term fluctuations over the centuries, what he called the *longue durée* (Braudel 1981; Fletcher 1992; Knapp 1992; Staniforth 1997).

Slums

The slum is one of the overriding images of nineteenth-century cities. A wide range of observers, from social reformers, journalists and politicians to novelists such as Charles Dickens have vividly characterised inner-city neighbourhoods in terms of poverty, disease, cramped and collapsing housing, squalid and noxious surroundings, and vices such as gambling, drunkenness, violence and prostitution. There is a host of historical literature detailing the evidence of housing and hygiene, poverty and crime in Australian cities (e.g. Davison 1978; Davison et al. 1985; Fitzgerald 1987; Garton 1990; McCalman 1982; Mayne 1982; O'Brien 1988; Ramsland 1986). The evidence is clear and there can be no question that living conditions in these neighbourhoods were dreadful by any number of measures. Children died young or were stunted in growth. Large families lived in only one or two rooms with no running water and shared outdoor privies with several other families. Sewage ran in open drains in the streets, seeped into the earth and flooded homes when it rained. Diseases such as typhoid and cholera were common, while low and intermittent wages meant that food and clothing were both in short supply.

There is also a growing body of literature pointing out that there was more to these neighbourhoods than deprivation and hardship (Mayne 1993; Ward 1976). They were home to working people with all manner of trade and skill levels. Some were renters but many others owned their own homes or had comfortable bank balances. Wash basins, lice combs and costume jewellery show that people took pride in their appearance despite the constraints of sanitation arrangements over which they had little control. In Australia's colonial cities migrants from all over the world lived side-by-side; Irish and English ex-convicts and their descendants dominated in the Rocks, but it was also home to sailors from Scandinavia, Europe and America, as well as Polynesians, Maori and the Chinese (Karskens 1999:130). In Melbourne, German, Jewish, Indian, Chinese, Italian and Lebanese families lived alongside the English, Irish, Scottish and Australian-born (Mayne 2006). Inner-city neighbourhoods were complex and diverse places, and for those who lived there they were home.

Those who created the documentary record on which later historians have relied were generally middle-class observers, outsiders who did not live in these neighbourhoods and who created the label "slum" as a shorthand term for all that was worst about them (Mayne 1993). The term had a purpose inasmuch as it turned attention and resources to solving structural problems such as housing and sanitation, but it also did the residents a great disservice by stereotyping them as depraved at worst and helpless at best. The "slum" label sensationalised and made "Other" people who only a generation before had been simply working people, some of whom were lazy or dirty or criminals, but many of whom were not.

Archaeologists have been at the forefront of unpacking the complexities of life in slum neighbourhoods (e.g. Green and Leech 2006; Karskens 1997; Mayne and Murray 2001; Sneddon 2006; Yamin 1997). Urban excavations produce concrete evidence about the hardships of inner-city life as they uncover the footings of tiny buildings, cramped yards, leaky cesspits and open drains. But they also reveal the diversity apparent in well-built, modern homes with early sewer connections, ornaments, toys and educational materials for children, grooming aids and dinner services. Case studies from the Cumberland/Gloucester Streets (CuGl) site in Sydney (Fig. 10.4) and Casselden Place/Little Lon in Melbourne demonstrate these contradictions.

At CuGl the archaeologists worked closely with historian Grace Karskens in order to implement a research design built around the four themes of industrialisation, changing standards of living, gender and local identity (Godden Mackay Logan 1999; Karskens 1999). The effects of the Industrial Revolution were apparent in many aspects of the site. One was the shift in behaviours and use of space that occurred as the Rocks changed from a pre-industrial town to a more "modern" way of life. In the early phases at the site homes and workplaces were closely integrated and people used their large allotments for a number of purposes that today would be considered incompatible with residential use. Slaughtering waste in the yard deposits indicate that the ex-convict George Cribb used part of the yard behind his house as a slaughteryard for his butcher shop, leaving the heads and hooves lying in piles or buried in pits. Less noisomely, George Talbot had his baker's oven and mixing troughs in a room immediately behind his house. Many objects from this period were hand-made, irregular and rougher than machine-made items. Sandstock bricks sometimes bore the fingerprints of their makers, nails used in fastening beams were shaped locally from imported iron rods, and houses were built of roughly

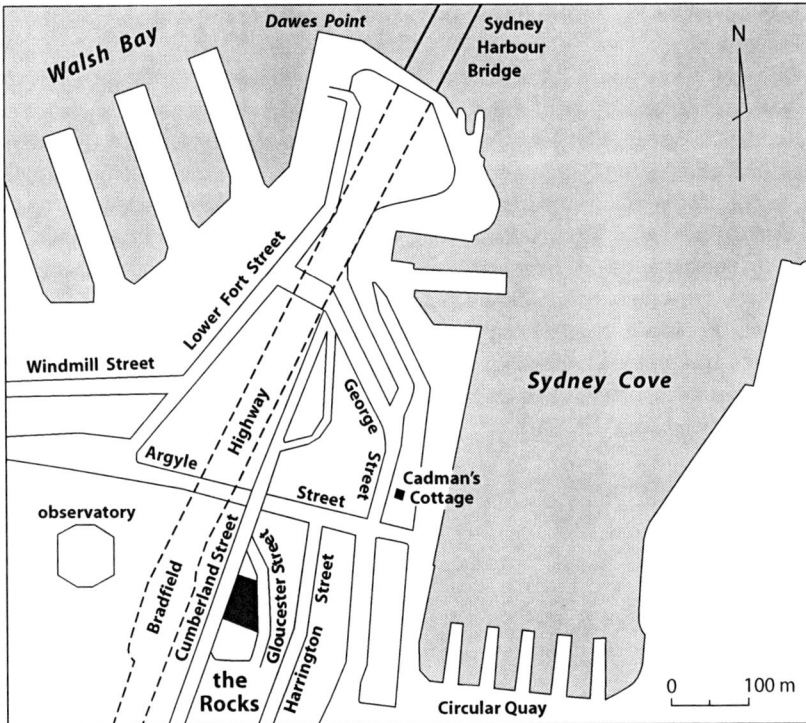

Fig. 10.4 Plan of the Rocks in Sydney, showing location of excavation area between Cumberland and Gloucester Streets

hewn sandstone quarried from the ground where they stood. Faunal remains indicate that there was a preference for dishes cooked slowly in a single dish, such as lamb shanks, "calf's feet broth", and bullocks' head brawn, and many large iron and ceramic cooking pots were found that would have been suspended over an open fire or placed next to it.

Over time these traditional, pre-industrial ways of doing things were replaced by new practices. Bricks and nails were made elsewhere by machine in industrial quantities, new houses were built that faced the surveyed streets and lanes rather than the sea, and open fires were gradually enclosed in iron stoves. One aspect of the Industrial Revolution that was particularly apparent in the artefact assemblage was the increase in the quantity and diversity of consumer goods. Glass bottles and ceramic tablewares are there in abundance by the middle of the century as mass production, marketing, and transportation networks made them cheaper and more readily available. Pressed glass made available a variety of tableware forms such as cruets, salt dishes, jelly cups and decanters. Metal buttons were stamped with manufacturer and retailers' names and pressed glass buttons came in many colours and designs. Women's and men's jewellery, perfume and hair oil became more available and were used by Rocks people, while marbles, dolls and toy china were given to their children.

Archaeologists found that standards of living varied across the site. As time progressed and the houses grew older, many deteriorated and became squalid. From around the 1830s, as subdivision increased, all the houses opened directly onto the streets and lanes with no front yard or footpath. Backyards were small and crowded with privies, a laundry, woodshed and tools (Fig. 10.5). Some yards were paved and swept clean, with few artefacts to be found, while others were damp and covered with debris. In some homes rubbish was deliberately placed under floorboards, including food scraps, meaty bones and even dead dogs and cats. Grace Karskens points out that while interiors might be kept as clean and comfortable as possible, these were not gracious suburban streets, and the efforts to maintain respectability were partly in response to an outside world that was far from clean, safe or respectable (Karskens 2001:80).

Fig. 10.5 Rear yard of house in Collingwood, Melbourne, in 1935 (Picture Collection, State Library of Victoria)

The activities of men and women on the site showed how gender shaped the experiences of residents. One source of evidence was the objects associated with the work done by men and women. George Cribb's boning knife and a spade he may have used for digging the pits to bury the slaughter waste were found in his well, and speak clearly of his hard and dirty labour. Both men and women frequently worked from home. Families lived above or behind shops and pubs, and often it was the women who ran the shops while husbands worked as labourers on the wharves.

Abundant artefacts associated with sewing such as pins, needles, thimbles and scissors all testify to the work that women did in sewing for their families and to bring in an income (Chapter 11). Laundresses worked from home and left pieces of blueing in their yards. Men also worked from home, carving horn and antler, grinding paints and running their businesses as tradesmen. Artefacts show ways that men and women sought to control their work and their lives. One such artefact was a membership token issued by the Sydney Wharf Labourers Union, symbolising the importance of the union movement in improving the conditions of workers.

The lives of many women were more intimately governed by the demands of pregnancy, childbirth and child rearing. In Rocks families where it was common to have 10 or 12 children, pregnancy and breastfeeding could easily account for 20 or more years of a woman's adult life. Controlling fertility was not only about limiting family size, it was also about controlling conditions of work. One artefact bears eloquent testimony to how women in the Rocks were taking steps in this direction by the end of the nineteenth century. It was a bone ring 42 mm in diameter, part of a contraceptive "occlusive pessary", and it probably belonged to Margaret Foy. Mrs Foy spaced her first six children at 3–4 year intervals, and then had no more children until a final son was born 6 years later, perhaps in a way to replace their firstborn son who had died in the intervening years.

The final research question the team addressed was to consider the identity of the Rocks as a convict place within a "gaol town". In the early years of British settlement in Sydney government officials built on the east side of Sydney Cove and the convicts built their huts on the sandstone ridges to the west. There was no indication that convict status materially effected life in those early years. Convicts, ex-convicts, free migrants and colonial-born people lived and worked side by side until the 1820s. Their houses were built and furnished in similar ways, they prepared, served and ate food in the same ways, and they cared for their children in similar ways. Based on the archaeological evidence, the team found no sign of a separate identity among the convicts. Changes that appeared were the result of time and the shift from pre-modern to modern patterns and to higher-density urban living, not the result of a criminal past.

In Melbourne at the adjacent sites of Little Lon and Casselden Place the archaeologists investigated the stories of individual lots and residents as well as broader patterns evident in the site as a whole. Together the sites comprise most of a city block in inner Melbourne. The eastern portion, Little Lon, was excavated in the 1980s by a team lead by Justin McCarthy, and re-analysed by Tim Murray and Alan Mayne in the 1990s. The central portion, Casselden Place, was excavated by Godden Mackay Logan, Austral Archaeology and La Trobe University in 2002–2004. In the projects the archaeologists worked closely with historian Alan Mayne and his students in order to build up a detailed profile of the area's residents using documentary and oral sources (Leckey 2004; Mayne and Lawrence 1998). In addition to the usual sources consulted by historical archaeologists such as rate books and land titles, the historians used a technique called "record stripping" to recover fine-grained details from births, deaths and marriage records, wills and probates, inquests and bankruptcy proceedings, and other such people-centred records. This information was used to create files on individuals, their families and their neighbourhood social networks. Called family reconstitution, this process extends the focus beyond the (usually male) head of household to include the women and children who may also have been at the site. In the United States archaeologists often use manuscript census records in this process as well, but these documents are not available in Australia.

The resulting matrix of case studies that integrated family reconstitution data with the archaeological analysis of space, stratigraphy and artefacts was used to build an ethnography of place, a close-up, insider's view of the neighbourhood that the team hoped would get beyond the slum stereotypes that were generally used to characterise the area (Mayne and Lawrence 1998, 1999). They found that for much of the area's history, from the 1840s until the 1940s, it comprised a mix of residential, commercial and industrial establishments. There were brothels and pubs that slum journalists loved to describe, particularly from the 1880s, but there were also long-term residents who owned their homes and lived there for several decades, as well as young families renting accommodation for 2 or 3 years before moving elsewhere. One property excavated at Little Lon was the home of the Moloney/Neylan family (Mayne et al. 2000:140–143). Irish labourer John Moloney bought the recently built three-room timber structure in 1855 and lived there with his brother and sister. Another brother lived next door and another sister, Margaret Neylan, moved in with them when she was widowed in 1866. In 1886 Margaret, by then the only surviving sibling, demolished the house and rebuilt it in brick, living there for another 15 years until her death. Artefacts in their cesspit, filled in 1886 when the brick house was built, included old pieces of Spode china and decorative Staffordshire figures. The Spode, dated 1829–1833, before the British settlement of Victoria, must have been brought with them from Ireland or purchased second-hand.

Strikingly, the archaeologists found that the goods discarded by this stable, comparatively prosperous family did not differ substantially from goods found in the cesspit of the house across the street, a wooden house rented to a succession of short-term tenants (Mayne et al. 2000:144–147). The tenants in the 1860s and 1870s, the period when the cesspit was most likely filled, included Daniel and Mary Toomey, then William and Jane Pugh and finally William and Eliza Jobb. All were Irish and all had small children, and the men were respectively a labourer, a painter and a blacksmith.

Collectively, the archaeologists were able to identify other patterns when looking at the artefacts from the neighbourhood as a whole. Embossed labels on bottle glass demonstrated consistent preferences for different kinds of products and the dimensions of colonial trade networks (Davies 2006b). Beverages such as beer and aerated water were almost exclusively manufactured locally, reflecting the difficulty in transporting such products long distances before refrigeration and pasteurisation. Most of these were made in Melbourne, some within 3 km of Casselden Place. Milk, which also had to be obtained locally prior to pasteurisation, was also in bottles from greater Melbourne and dairies continued to operate in the inner suburbs into the 1920s (Brown-May and Swain 2005:190–192). Spirits such as gin and cognac,

however, were imported from Great Britain and Europe, as were pickles and preserves, perfume and ink. Products from the United States were notably absent,
as were Australian products from other colonies or even elsewhere in Victoria.
These bottles reflect the broader trade patterns of Melbourne, where the principal
trade links were with Britain and Europe rather than with the United States. Before
Federation in 1901 the Australian colonies were governed independently and inter-
colonial tariffs as well as incompatible railway gauges combined to restrict trade
between the colonies.

The Well-to-Do

Cities were and are home to a wide cross-section of people, and archaeologists
have excavated the homes of the very wealthy as well as the very poor. In Sydney
archaeologists have worked at the homes of several of the colony's most influential families, including Vaucluse House (William Charles Wentworth), Regentville
(Sir John Jamison) and Elizabeth Farm (John and Elizabeth Macarthur), as well as
at First Government House, the home of the first colonial governors, and the stables and rubbish dump from the second Government House. Such work has been
less frequent in Melbourne, but one exception is Viewbank, the home of Dr Robert
Martin and his family. Many of these homes were once country estates and are now
part of the greater urban area. Substantial homes on large, landscaped properties that
were nevertheless within commuting distance of the metropolis followed the ideal
English model for the upper classes (Davison 1978:137). Much of the archaeological record at these homes is associated with the wealth and prestige of the owners.
They were able to purchase the best quality goods, often directly from Britain, to
employ a large number of servants or assigned convicts, and to use their goods and
the labour of their employees to create environments that established and displayed
their social position.

   Landscaping was designed to impress guests, employees and passers-by alike.
From the first days of colonial settlement the grounds of First Government House,
in the centre of Sydney, were laid out to convey status. One of the earliest drawings
of the building, in 1792, shows a formal garden in front of the house complete with
straight paths and flower beds in a symmetrical geometric design (Proudfoot et al.
1991:46). The strict control of the natural world embodied in the garden stands
in direct contrast to the as-yet untamed wilderness beyond the fence and the disorderly nature of early colonial society (Casey 2006). A generation later Sir John
Jamison intended that the sheer size of his home, Regentville, would reflect his status (Connah 1986:30–32). The main range was 78 feet (24 m) long by 45 feet (14 m)
wide with 15 rooms in two stories. Additional outbuildings included kitchens, a
bake house and servants' accommodation. Together the complex covered an acre of
ground, all of which was enclosed by a stone wall 10 feet (3 m) high.

   Viewbank, the home of Robert Martin and his family from 1844 to 1874, was
more modest but also featured extensive landscaping (Hayes 2008:298–299). The
house was built high on a hillside with commanding views across the Yarra Valley

to the distant ranges, and was itself visible for miles around. Visitors entered up a long sweeping drive flanked with exotic deciduous trees, arriving on the central of three terraces in front of the house itself. The terraces were also planted with exotic trees including a pair of Italian cypresses on either side of steps leading up to the house itself (Fig. 10.6). As the drive curved around the hill behind the house, visitors came upon both house and views at the last moment, heightening the effect of each.

Fig. 10.6   Viewbank Homestead, with steps leading to upper terraces (photo P. Davies)

Artefact assemblages associated with dining indicate the expensive tastes displayed when entertaining guests and the elaborate rules of etiquette that surrounded fine dining (see Chapter 11). First Government House (1788–1845) and later Government House (1845–present) in Sydney were the homes of the vice-regal representatives in the colony and hence the pinnacle of society. In the first few years the clearest sign of status was access to food. Unsuccessful early efforts at growing food in the colony and the lack of supply ships meant that rations quickly became scarce. However, the team excavating the site in the 1980s found faunal remains from a rubbish pit that showed that the lower limbs of cattle were being discarded with meat still on them, even though stews, broth, brawn and other dishes were all popular dishes made with boiled "hocks" at that time (Lydon 1996:149; Proudfoot et al. 1991:61–66). At a time when the weekly ration of meat was down to only two pounds of pork, throwing away bones that others might have eaten seems to be a most conspicuous form of consumption. By the 1820s the colony was on a more secure, indeed prosperous, footing. Governor Darling and his wife Eliza entertained frequently and on a grand scale, setting their table with an array of fine china and hand-made cut glass, and, according to the archaeological remains, serving their guests young suckling pig and fine French wine (Lydon 1996:149; Proudfoot et al. 1991:116–122).

In the 1990s, as part of the Conservatorium of Music project, Casey and Lowe excavated rubbish deposits associated with the later Government House from the second half of the nineteenth century (Casey 2005). Much of what they found was similar to the kinds of ceramic and glass tablewares they had excavated elsewhere in Sydney from sites of that era – blue transfer-printed items in the common Willow, Asiatic Pheasant and Albion designs, purple transfer-printed vessels in the Cable pattern, and plain, moulded and banded whitewares. Teawares were primarily heavy, durable semi-vitrified wares or bone china with a gilded tealeaf design, also common at that time. The ordinariness of this assemblage is in striking contrast to a single fine bone china teacup with a green transfer-printed and gilded design that was found in the cesspit, and to some of the services described in inventories of the house made in 1902 and 1908. The services were highly specialised, with separate services for tea, dinner, dessert and breakfast all in use. The services all included a wide range of forms, reflecting the need to serve complex and elaborate meals to the Governor, his family and guests. The services included high-quality names such as Dresden, Crown Derby and Royal Worcester, and featured various decorative schemes in which gold figured prominently. There were several blue and gold dinner services as well as white and gold services and even white and gold toiletry sets for the bedrooms. Mary Casey argues that the materials in the tip and cesspit represent the rubbish of the servants and staff at Government House, and reflects the kinds of serviceable china that was purchased for the servants' hall and kitchen. It seems that the richer items on the inventory were not disposed of with the rest of the rubbish when they broke. Casey notes that the inventories actually included references to items that had clearly been damaged and/or repaired, such as cracked and chipped pieces and even ones repaired with rivets. She also found that broken items present on the 1902 inventory were still there in 1908. They had obviously been carefully stored in the interim, perhaps because no one wished to be held accountable for making the decision to throw away valuable items that were part of the equipment of state.

The Martin family at Viewbank were less prestigious than the colonial governors but were nevertheless wealthy leaders of local society. Dr Robert Martin owned several pastoral runs in Victoria as well as properties in and around Melbourne and was active in the affairs of church and state at the local level. The site of their home was excavated by Heritage Victoria in the 1990s and the artefacts were later analysed by Sarah Hayes (2007, 2008) for her Ph.D. Hayes found that despite the family's wealth, it was the nature of the assemblage as a whole that expressed their social position, rather than any individual object or group of objects. She observed that while not all the goods were expensive, there was a consistently high quality of goods in all areas of activity. As might be expected, the tablewares were both costly and elaborate. The ceramics included 11 matching tableware sets of both expensive and more everyday wares, and suggest that there were enough settings for entertaining on a large scale. The sets included many of the specialised items needed for the complex dining rituals of the upper classes, such as soup tureens, ladles and individual plates of several different sizes, and these were complemented by cut crystal stemware and tumblers. Faunal evidence indicated an emphasis on high-quality cuts of beef as the main source of meat (Howell-Meurs 2000). High-quality goods were evident in less public domains as well. Personal hygiene was important and was achieved with numerous brushes, combs, toothbrushes and toothpaste containers, while matching toilet sets indicated that even the most intimate activities were carried out in as genteel a manner as possible. Mrs. Martin and her four daughters wore good quality clothing and employed themselves industriously in both fancy and practical needlework. Dr Martin and his son likewise dressed in the latest men's fashions. Hayes argues that these goods present a cohesive picture of polite behaviour that extended across all facets of family life and that was supported by sufficient wealth to provide any commodity desired.

The Respectable and the Genteel

Most of the people who lived in Australia's colonial cities would have seen themselves as living somewhere between the very wealthy and the very poor. These were the middle classes, a group, or perhaps a group of groups, that was beginning to emerge early in the nineteenth century and which had become prominent by the 1840s (Cott 1977; Davidoff and Hall 1987; Howe 1975; James 2006). The middle classes have been defined in a variety of ways, as people who had to work for a living (unlike the aristocracy) but who did not perform manual labour (unlike the working classes); as people who earned enough from one household wage (the man's) to maintain the rest of the household (including women and children) as dependants who did not have to work themselves; and as people who employed at least one servant. All of these were characteristics of the middle classes, but perhaps the most definitive was the suite of values, beliefs and behaviours that gave this often disparate group its focus. Central to middle-class culture was a morality based most strongly in evangelical Christianity, a morality that encompassed purity, temperance and self-restraint. The belief in hard work and education was epitomised in the relentless drive for self-improvement and the improvement of others. In the public world they believed in the power of science and technology to solve problems and bring about progress. In the private world they valued domesticity and family life, the home as a haven and place of restoration. The ideologies of these two spheres were consciously separated and became associated with the distinct domains of men and women. Much of this found material expression in the homes, furnishings, dress, food and entertainments with which the middle classes equipped themselves. Indeed, many have argued that the skilful acquisition and then use of appropriate material goods was one of the key ways in which the middle classes affirmed their own status and recognised a kindred status in others (Ames 1986; Flanders 2003; James 2006:3; Young 2003).

Linda Young has made an extensive study of the close links between middle-class ideology, material culture and consumption. She has drawn on the theories of Pierre Bourdieu and his concept of *habitus*, a deeply held understanding of the tastes and behaviours appropriate to one's place in society in which people are socialised from birth, and in which material culture plays a pivotal role (Bourdieu 1984; Young 1997:14–15). Young has identified "gentility" as one such habitus, located specifically at the upper end of the middle class, where the boundaries began to blur into the wealth and power of the upper class. The Martins at Viewbank could be situated at this boundary, one of the colony's leading families, but not ennobled or politically active. As we have seen, the archaeological assemblage from the site indicates that their home was furnished with the full range of goods necessary to fulfil genteel standards of dress, cleanliness, recreation and dining (Hayes 2008:397–398). At the lower end of the middle classes where the situations of small-scale shop keepers, clerks and prosperous tradesmen blurred the boundaries with the working classes, the habitus might be more accurately described as one of respectability and decency (Karskens 2003a:52; Lawrence 2000:127–143; McCalman 1982; Young 1997). Here we find sites such as those at Port Adelaide (Briggs 2005; Lampard 2004), Paradise in Queensland (Quirk 2008b) and Parramatta in New South Wales (Casey and Lowe Associates 2006), which will be discussed below. These households lacked the wealth and social standing of the Martins and their peers, and work played a larger role than leisure in their lives, but they were nevertheless economically secure, they identified with middle-class values and they used consumer goods assiduously in redefining those values to accommodate their own experience. Further analysis of the kinds of goods used in middle-class homes is discussed in Chapter 11.

The genteel and the respectable alike found homes in the suburbs that were burgeoning around Australia's cities. The suburbs were a response to the economic success of the middle classes and the accompanying desire to occupy a detached, single-family home surrounded by its own garden and yard. In Australia home-ownership was widespread, in part because of the wealth and political power of the gold rush generation (Davison 1978:137–142; 2000). This is one of the factors that so effectively blurred the boundaries between classes in Australia and heightened the egalitarian appearance of society. As a result both contemporaries and historians have tended to downplay the role of the middle classes, as Young in particular has noted (Young 1997:11–13; see Hayes 2008:24–27), but the suburbs are quintessentially middle class. Their ubiquitousness has disguised the fact that far from being a classless society Australia is a middle-class society. In the twentieth century this was recognised by politicians such as Robert Menzies and John Howard, who used a middle-class powerbase to become the country's longest-serving prime ministers (Brett 2005:10–15). Archaeologists have yet to adequately investigate the material record of the suburbs, and when they do it will be that of the middle class (Davison 2003; Karskens and Lawrence 2003).

While we lack a full archaeology of the suburbs, glimpses of the middle classes are beginning to emerge from several studies around the country. The most detailed picture comes from work at Paradise, a small gold mining town in Queensland occupied in the 1880s and 1890s. The site was investigated in 2003 by a team from the University of Queensland, which, under the direction of Jonathan Prangnell, carried out a full survey of the abandoned town and excavated 13 of the 97 premises. The analysis of artefacts from eight domestic sites formed the basis of a Ph.D. by Kate Quirk (Prangnell and Quirk 2009; Prangnell et al. 2005; Quirk 2008a, b). The town was based on a number of small mines that attempted to extract gold from quartz reefs in the area and at its peak had a population of over 600 people as well as a range of shops, hotels, churches and government services. The households investigated ranged from the white-collar Shuttleworth and McGhie families who managed or owned mines and the Kirkes who ministered in the Methodist mission, to the Plastows, Turks and Buzzas who ran small businesses, to the Bartletts and McConnells who were miners.

Quirk investigated the degree to which the families may have engaged with the practices of gentility in a strategic manner in order to secure social status. Based on the archaeological evidence, she found that the families varied considerably in their approach. As part of her analysis Quirk measured the presence of goods associated with middle-class ideologies in a range of behaviours which she characterised as the private realms of child-rearing and temperance and the more public arenas of dress, use of ceramics and refuse disposal. The families she describes as middle class, the white-collar Shuttleworth, McGhie, Kirke and Turk families, had goods that indicated they adopted genteel behaviours across both private and public realms. These families had comparatively expensive sets of tablewares with enough forms to serve meals of some complexity. They dressed fashionably and disposed of their rubbish carefully by burying it in pits or hauling it to the town dump. They also purchased toys, special dishes and educational materials for their children and decorative ornaments for their homes, and either abstained from or observed moderation in the consumption of alcohol and tobacco. In contrast, those she describes as working class, the Bartletts, McGonnells and Plastows, seem to have been more concerned with private practices than with presenting a genteel appearance in public. They too had ornaments in their homes and toys for their children, and they too were temperate in their use of alcohol and tobacco. However, both their dress and their tablewares were less expensive and less elaborate, and most strikingly, they were far less concerned about the disposal of rubbish which they allowed to accumulate in the yards around their houses. While following fashion is constrained by income, rubbish disposal was entirely a matter of personal preference and, as Quirk notes (2008b:292), the behaviour of these Paradise families challenges any simplistic assumption that respectability was merely a less costly, watered-down version of what the genteel were doing.

Further evidence of how families at the working/middle class boundary engaged with respectability comes from sites occupied by the Farrow and Mackay families in Port Adelaide (Briggs 2005; Lampard 2004, 2006). Both sites date to the third quarter of the nineteenth century, and were owned by the families who lived in them. The men worked with their hands, John Farrow as a labourer and George Mackay as a sail-maker, but both families also had investments, the Farrows in property and the Mackays in sailing ships. Both families owned several sets of tablewares in the most common and less expensive patterns, such as Albion, Willow, Rhine and Asiatic Pheasant. They had some serving vessels as well as plates of several different sizes, and could set a decent table. They also had a number of bone china matching cup-and-saucer sets with sprigg and gilt decorations. While the Farrows preferred cheap cuts of mutton, including brains, the Mackays spent slightly more to purchase beef and pork which they ate as roasts. For these respectable Portonians, family meals were both possible and important.

By the time Paradise was settled, the middle class was well established as an identifiable segment of society. The site of 109 George Street, Parramatta, excavated by Casey and Lowe in 2004–2005, provides evidence of a much earlier phase in the development of middle-class ideology (Casey and Lowe Associates 2006). The site was occupied by the Hassell family from 1804 to 1834, a period when the old system of status and rank was still influential but some of the defining elements of the middle class were starting to take shape. The Hassells were typical of a group that would become highly influential in the formation of middle-class ideology. Rowland Hassell and his wife Elizabeth had been missionaries in Tahiti before arriving in Parramatta. Members of the Church Missionary Society, they were friends and supporters of the influential Sydney cleric Samuel Marsden, and espoused the kind of evangelical Christianity that underpinned middle-class morality. Rowland operated a store and served as Superintendent of Government Stock, as well as preaching at weekly services he held in his barn and starting a Sunday school.

The Hassells built a two-storey brick house of 13 rooms with a cellar, attic and outbuildings, including a kitchen, dairy and school-room. The size, style and substantial nature of the building suggests that it may have been built for the Hassells in 1814 when Rowland became Superintendent. At a time when many people were living in single story timber homes, this house was large and imposing (Casey and Lowe Associates 2006:116–117). In the yard archaeologists found numerous purpose-dug pits for the disposal of rubbish. Ceramic analysis also revealed differences between the Hassells and their less prosperous neighbours. On archaeological sites of this period in Sydney and Parramatta both Chinese export porcelain and locally made pottery are common. These were also present at the Hassell site but in smaller quantities, representing only 15 percent of the vessel count in each case compared to 35 percent Chinese export wares at the home of Samuel Larkin on the Parramatta Children's Court site (Casey and Lowe Associates 2006:118). Casey and Lowe suggest that the large proportion of British ceramics, including blue transfer-printed pearlware and black basalt, may have been at least partly the result of Rowland's access to trade networks through his store. Other goods that were poorly represented included clay tobacco pipes and black glass bottles, which may be associated with attitudes to temperance in the family.

The Industrialising City

A feature of the archaeology of Australia's nineteenth-century cities is the degree to which evidence for domestic activity and industrial activity occurs on the same archaeological site. This is partly because rescue archaeology usually occurs at the scale of the city block and encompasses a number of earlier allotments and activities. It also reflects the nature of nineteenth-century cities where people had to live close to their places of work. The suburban sprawl that marked the end of the century was made possible by the development of inexpensive public transport, so that even those of modest means no longer had to walk to work. Prior to that, and for the majority of working people in particular, neighbourhoods necessarily included industry as well as residential accommodation.

Some sense of the variety of environments created can be gained by a brief survey of urban-industrial projects. We have already seen George Cribb's slaughter yard and butcher shop behind the houses on Cumberland Street in Sydney. As the density of urban areas increased such activities were moved to designated stockyards on the edges of the towns. Dairying was another semi-rural activity that once flourished within urban areas (Vines 1993a:6–11). At the DMR site in Sydney, Casey and Lowe found evidence of locally made ceramics used for dairy work. Brickyards were also a common operation that gradually moved outwards as land in the inner suburbs became more valuable and clay sources were exhausted. The inner suburb of Brickfields, where the DMR site was located, was one of several areas around Sydney that specialised in brick and pottery manufacture in the first half-century of settlement (Chapter 8). In Adelaide the site of the Rookery, excavated in the early 1990s, included a row of nine brick terrace cottages owned by William Peacock, who also owned the tannery over the back fence. The smells and waste associated with cleaning and tanning hides would have been a particularly unpleasant part of the local environment (Austral Archaeology 1992; M. Jones et al. 1997). Such "noxious trades" were often located along urban waterways until protests mounted about the fouling of the water (Vines 1993b:8).

As some industries were forced out of the inner city others moved in. By the turn of the twentieth century Casselden Place and Little Lon were dominated by industrial premises that had replaced the earlier houses. Prominent among them were Chinese furniture makers who operated in small factories such as the converted Black Eagle hotel and often lived on the premises (Leckey 2004:267–277). Alexander Lugton and Sons' engineering works was another prominent business in Little Lon. The firm was one of Victoria's leading manufacturers of boilers and steam engines whose products still survive in several places around the state. The firm began slowly from small rented premises on Little Lonsdale Street in 1859, and as the business grew the premises also expanded, gradually purchasing several adjacent properties until by 1908 the firm occupied much of the central portion of the site (Leckey 2004:42–44).

Not all industry, however, took place outside the home. Several projects have uncovered evidence of sewing in particular, work that could be easily done at home by either tailors or seamstresses. Costumier William Ford was one occupant of a brick terrace at Casselden Place where a large number of sewing artefacts was recovered. The house also produced several bobbins used in making lace, another source of piecework income (Mayne et al. 2000:144–146). Jane Lydon analysed sewing items such as thread-winders, thimbles, pins, needles and clothing attachments from the site of Lilyvale in the Rocks as evidence of domestic sewing. She argued that variation across the assemblages from the six excavated terraces was due to depositional factors and excavation methodologies rather than to commercial sewing by any of the residents, but as we discuss in the next chapter, comparison with more recent excavations suggests this is in fact a commercial sewing assemblage (Lydon 1993b:132). Nearby at the CSR site in Pyrmont, Casey and Lowe (Casey 2004) have used detailed spatial analysis of underfloor deposits to argue that one of the many tenants was a professional seamstress. Careful excavation and mapping revealed that in all seven of the houses with subfloor deposits, artefacts were concentrated within 1.5 m of the back wall of the kitchen, where a window and a doorway let in afternoon sun from the west. At one house, however, the pattern was particularly strong, with 85 percent of the artefacts found in this location. Most of these artefacts (77 percent) were sewing-related, including pins, buttons, beads, hooks-and-eyes, and tools such as scissors and thimbles. Further, the 2,749 sewing-related items from this house accounted for 50 percent of all the sewing items from the entire row of seven houses. The use of space that favoured well-lit areas, and the quantity and nature of artefacts recovered, is convincing evidence of sewing on a commercial scale.

Conclusion

Cities are the most complex archaeological sites that people have created. Interpreting the multi-dimensioned archaeological record that they represent requires considerable skill, but offers great rewards. Urban archaeology is particularly important for Australians because so much colonial and modern history has occurred within them. One of the most compelling qualities of urban communities and environments is dynamism and change, a characteristic that archaeology has identified again and again. Cities have long been engines of growth and transformation, resulting in a constant tension between old ways and new. As our cities are rebuilt around us, the physical legacy of the past is buried, damaged or destroyed entirely. Former human-scale neighbourhoods of houses, shops and lanes have gradually given way to huge office towers, and the daily surge of city workers and their nightly retreat to the suburbs. Through this constant process of tearing down and rebuilding, archaeologists have sought to recover traces and echoes of the past. Using this material they have addressed a wide range of topics within urban contexts, including gender and ethnicity, class and authority, health and sanitation, and the expansion of industry in the modern era. They have begun to challenge the prevailing ideology of the slum that has dominated conventional understanding about inner-urban neighbourhoods since the late nineteenth century, and revealed instead a more intimate and private landscape of individual and family lives. Archaeologists have also explored the lives of the more prosperous and used the material remains as a prism through which to understand notions of gentility and respectability. In the following chapter we look in more detail at these personal spaces, and the places that Australians called home.

Chapter 11
Australians at Home

Archaeological artefacts have the potential to reveal a great deal about the intimate patterns of daily life. Certain kinds of objects are frequently found on sites due to their material qualities and the ways in which they were acquired, used and discarded. Some of the most common types of objects are those made of ceramic and glass, both of which break easily when in use but then resist decay in the ground. Bone also preserves well in many contexts, leather occasionally, and from the late nineteenth century onwards plastics may also be found. Other kinds of objects are rarer. Iron is very durable and common in daily use, but once in the ground it decays rapidly into often indistinguishable lumps of corrosion. Items made of bronze, lead and precious metals preserve better but are less frequently used. The exception to this is in arid parts of Australia where even iron objects found on the ground surface may preserve very well. Organic materials such as wood, textiles and paper make up the majority of goods in an ordinary household but these break down quickly in the ground and are only found in rare circumstances where the soil has become waterlogged or where they are preserved within cavities in buildings.

The ways in which objects are lost or thrown away also play a role in what archaeologists find. Things that break easily such as ceramic dishes, clay tobacco pipes and glass bottles were more likely to be disposed of than things that do not break, such as tin washbasins. Small items such as buttons, beads, coins and marbles were easily dropped and lost, especially where there were dirt floors or gaps between wooden floorboards. Food scraps were fed to animals or discarded in yards, though the bone may survive as well as tiny seeds, particularly if they have been burnt in a fire or preserved in wet soil. Many other household objects were recycled or re-used. Furniture was sold, given away or broken up for firewood rather than thrown out. Clothing was also re-used by others or recycled into rags. Metal items were salvaged for the metals they contained, particularly during the First World War.

As a result of these various factors, archaeologists excavating floors, yard spaces and pits tend to find fragments of ceramics and glass, pieces of metal that may or may not be identifiable, bone and shell, and "small finds", the tiny lost objects like buttons and coins. Much of what has survived is associated with food and beverages: the remains of the food itself, packaging such as bottles and tins, and the ceramic dishes used in preparing, serving and consuming the food. Different aspects of diet and food consumption have thus been of considerable and on-going interest to archaeologists. Another suite of artefact types are associated with dress and clothing: buttons and other fastenings, jewellery, footwear and tools used for sewing and craft work. Other objects, such as medicine bottles, wash basins and toothbrushes, are related to treating disease and maintaining health and cleanliness. A fourth group of artefacts is associated with children and includes baby feeders, specially decorated dishes, toys and games, and educational materials such as slate pencils. A final group is the archaeological evidence for coins and currency in their various forms in the colonial era, providing evidence of how coinage served as a medium of value and exchange between private and public life.

These artefact groups form the subject of this chapter. All are directly related to the activities of household and family life. We have defined our subject narrowly, leaving out architectural items such as nails, bricks and window glass that are related more to the buildings themselves than to what went on inside them, and we have also excluded tools (with the exception of sewing, writing and food-preparation items) which might be considered part of paid work rather than family life. This is an arbitrary decision and the boundaries could be defined differently, but it reflects our own interests and expertise and the constraints of space. It also reflects the nature of the research done on artefacts in Australia, which has largely been concerned with these domestic matters rather than with architecture or equipment.

The groups of artefacts considered in this chapter are mundane, private and domestic but they provide access to issues that are large-scale and wide-ranging. They shed light on topics such as the rituals and etiquette of dining, dietary preferences and food availability, changing beliefs about medicine and hygiene, attitudes towards children, gender roles, trade patterns within and beyond the Australian colonies, socio-economic status, ethnicity and fashion. All of these were fundamental to Australians' life experiences and all have changed considerably over the period since the first British settlement in 1788.

In the discussion that follows many of the same archaeological sites will recur repeatedly. This is because they have proven to be the most informative about the issues we examine here, with assemblages that have been subjected to rigorous analysis and careful documentation, and because the information is presented in ways that aid comparison. The sites referred to tend to be family households rather than institutions such as the Ross Female Factory and Hyde Park Barracks, because our concern in this chapter is to explore the nature of domestic patterns among the majority of the Australian community and because other kinds of experiences including those of convicts, the Chinese and Aboriginal people are treated in more detail in previous chapters. The sites examined here range from large urban neighbourhoods to small rural households, and they include examples from all the Australian colonies. Temporally, they span the entire colonial period and beyond, from the first convict settlements to the early years of Federation at the beginning of the twentieth century.

Some of the sites have been introduced elsewhere, including the Tasmanian whaling stations (Lawrence 2006b:151, 159), the mining community of Dolly's Creek (Lawrence 2000:131), Viewbank (Hayes 2008:158–159), Casselden Place and Little Lon in Melbourne (Mayne et al. 2000; Murray 2006), Henry's Mill in the Otways (Davies 2006a) and Lake Innes in New South Wales (Connah 2007). The Cumberland/Gloucester Streets data used here come from the initial project (Godden Mackay Logan 1999; Karskens 1999) and from a re-analysis of portions of the site carried out by Tim Murray, Penny Crook and Laila Ellmoos (Crook et al. 2005:79, 152). Other Sydney sites excavated by Casey and Lowe and Associates are also referred to, including the 1804–1834 home of the Hassell family at what became 109–113 George Street, Parramatta (Casey and Lowe Associates 2006), the Conservatorium of Music site associated with Government House between the 1840s and ca. 1913 (Casey 2005a) and working-class homes from the 1860s to the 1930s at the CSR site in Pyrmont (Casey and Lowe Associates 2000). Shipwrecks including the *Sydney Cove* and the *Eglinton* are also discussed in Chapter 4. The two Port Adelaide sites associated with the Farrow and Mackay families analysed by Susan Lampard (née Briggs) (Briggs 2000, 2005; Lampard 2004, 2006, 2009) are included here, as are the eight house sites from the 1890s mining town of Paradise in Queensland, studied by a team from the University of Queensland (Prangnell and Quirk 2009; Quirk 2008a, b:167–284).

Other sites are discussed in detail here for the first time. A whaling station at Cheyne Beach, on the south coast of Western Australia, was analysed by Martin Gibbs for his Ph.D. dissertation (Gibbs 1995). While whaling activities have been discussed in Chapter 5, our interest here is in the artefact assemblage associated with the home of the station owner Captain John Thomas and his family, who occupied the site from 1846 to 1869. Information on rural Victoria is provided by two sites in Gippsland excavated by Susan Lawrence, Alasdair Brooks and Jane Lennon in 2006–2007. The home of the Reverend Willoughby Bean and his family was occupied from 1849 to 1859, while a house on Wellington Street, Port Albert, was occupied by harbour pilot John Thomas and his family from the 1850s to the 1890s (Brooks et al. 2009; Lawrence et al. 2009; Prossor 2008). Despite the coincidence of their shared names and maritime professions, at this point we know of no relationship between the two John Thomases.

Food

What does the archaeological record reveal about what Australians were eating and drinking? The primary sources for this are food and drink containers and faunal and botanical evidence, including the remains of food bones, plant parts and seeds. Documentary evidence tells us that the initial white settlers in each region had a simple diet based on what they could bring with them, and that this diet gradually expanded as settlements became better established. In the early months and years people ate salt meat, usually pork or beef, flour, tea and sugar. Dried peas, lentils or rice might also be included (Gollan 1988:2; Karskens 1999:64–65). For the convicts and their military guards these foods were issued as rations from the government stores in carefully measured quantities. Convicts in Sydney received a weekly ration of seven pounds (3.2 kg) of meat, the same amount of flour, three pounds (1.4 kg) of maize (corn), one pound (500 g) of sugar and one quarter pound (100 g) of tea, while each soldier received five and a half pounds (2.5 kg) of meat, seven pounds (3.2 kg) of sugar and seven pounds (3.2 kg) of bread (Nicholas 1988:184). In the "starving years" of first settlement, when there were not enough ships bringing new supplies, these rations were reduced to less than half those amounts.

These same foods were consumed by free settlers in other colonies and later by pastoralists and shepherds and by selectors pushing out the boundaries of white settlement. They were also ideal foods for those employed in extractive industries and not interested in self-sufficiency, such as miners, sealers and whalers. Although the quantities varied, the foods themselves mirrored the rations issued to sailors and to migrants on the long ocean voyages to Australia, so this was familiar, even comfortable food. It continued to shape preferences in the colonies for many years after initial settlement. Archaeological evidence indicates that the taste for salt meat in particular seems to have persisted for many years. Faunal remains from the wreck of the *Sydney Cove*, sailing for Port Jackson in 1797 (Nash 2001), and from the *William Salthouse*, heading for Port Phillip in 1841 (English 1990), provide evidence of the cargoes of salt meat that were being imported to the colonies within the first few years of settlement (Fig. 11.1). Similar butchering patterns found on bones excavated in the Rocks from early nineteenth-century contexts show that people still chose to eat salt meat even when other foods were available (Karskens 1999:65). Faunal remains from whaling stations excavated in Tasmania and at Cheyne Beach indicate the persistence of salt meat into the 1830s in Tasmania and the 1860s in Western Australia, almost certainly in these cases supplied as rations to men who may also have spent part of their working lives at sea (Gibbs 2005a:119; Lawrence and Tucker 2002; see Chapter 5).

The settlers showed little interest in the local foods that had sustained Aboriginal people for thousands of years. Mark Staniforth argues that resisting these native foods and relying on familiar, imported foods was a necessary part of the colonisation process that helped the settlers to "define, reassure and identify themselves", underpinning the establishment of a society that was in direct opposition to what was there before (Staniforth 2003:37–38). During the starving times at Port Jackson Governor Phillip sampled bush foods, but did not persist. Possums, wombats and emus were eaten at times, but were generally considered inferior to European domesticates (Blainey 2003:206–208). At the other extreme, kangaroo tails were the central ingredient of a popular soup served even in expensive hotels (Fahey 2005:88–89), while birds, including black swans, black ducks, and even parrots and galahs, were so popular that they were soon eradicated from settled areas. Legal restrictions began to be placed on hunting game birds late in the nineteenth century. Archaeological evidence indicates that native meat was never a widespread staple, being invariably either a food of last resort or a delicacy. Very few bones from native animals or birds are ever recovered from archaeological excavations on non-Aboriginal sites, while the bones of cattle, sheep, pigs, chickens and even rabbits are frequent. Of the 125,000 bones catalogued at the Cumberland/Gloucester Streets site in the Rocks, only 2 were from native animals (Karskens 1999:65), and there were none at all among more than 7,000 bones at Casselden Place in Melbourne (Simons and Maitri 2006). On rural sites they are more numerous, but still rare.

Fig. 11.1 Wooden cask head from the *William Salthouse,* wrecked in Port Phillip Bay near Melbourne in 1841 (Reproduced with permission of Geoff Hewitt)

On the Tasmanian whaling stations native mammal and bird bones accounted for 3 percent of the nearly 10,000 bones recovered (Lawrence 2006b:151, 159). Both maritime workers and city dwellers, however, were eating fish, and 800 fish bones were recovered from Adventure Bay and Lagoon Bay. At the Cheyne Beach whaling station in Western Australia native species, mainly fish, accounted for nearly 20 percent of the total weight of identified bone (Gibbs 2005a:118).

Without local food supplies, the rations the colonists relied on were all imported and what could be imported depended on what would survive the long sea journey. This explains the prevalence of salt meat, as salting was the main method for preserving meat before canning methods became widespread in the 1870s and freezing in the 1880s (Farrer 1980:78–81, 195–198). Grains and pulses would last for considerable periods if kept dry, and beef and pork in particular could be salted or cured, but there was no ready method for storing fruits and vegetables. The pastoralists and miners who moved into the outback from the 1870s benefited greatly from the new preservation methods. White people were still dependent on the rations they brought with them, along with meat from the flocks and herds they tended, but rations had expanded to include a wide variety of tinned goods. Archaeological sites in the outback, including cattle stations, the mines at Arltunga and the camps of workers along the Goldfields Pipeline in Western Australia are all marked by piles of discarded tins (Harrison 2004b:178–179). At Arltunga, a goldfield in the Northern Territory occupied from 1887 to 1917, Kate Holmes recorded more than 700 tins at the home of one married couple. These contained meat, fish and vegetables, and Holmes speculated that the unusually large quantity of milk cans observed might be evidence of children in the family (Holmes 1989:47).

The diet gradually expanded beyond rations as colonial settlements became more established and local gardens, orchards, animal husbandry and agriculture were able to supplement or replace imported supplies. Pollen and other plant parts recovered from excavations in and around Sydney indicate that from the very early years colonists were planting vegetable gardens and fruit trees around their homes. By 1800 there is pollen from kitchen gardens, including peas, beans, turnips and cabbages, radishes and watercress for salads, and lemon, apple and peach trees. One of the oldest European features excavated at the Cumberland/Gloucester Streets site was a relict tilth, a prepared soil dating to the 1790s, possibly worked with the hoe recovered from an adjacent cistern (Karskens 1999:33). In Parramatta, location of the first successful government farm, pollen has been found from the orchards planted around convict huts in the 1790s, as well as from vegetable gardens and from broad-acre cereal cultivation (Casey and Lowe Associates 2006:54). Colonial potteries were making basins and pans for separating cream and making butter from 1803, indicating a local dairying industry that required such products. Later examples have been recovered from the DMR site in the Brickfields and 109–113 George Street in Parramatta (Casey 1999; Casey and Lowe Associates 2006:124–125).

From these early beginnings Australians have continued to produce food from the land around their homes. The study of sites at Dolly's Creek in Victoria shows how on the goldfields the wives and children of miners produced a range of foods on their miner's right allotments and on the public commons (Lawrence 2001a). Several of the houses had garden plots outlined with quartz cobbles, while the faunal remains included goat and rabbit as well as sheep and cattle bones. Beef and mutton may have been commercially butchered, but goats and rabbits were probably killed by the family. Goats provided milk, and both cows and goats could be pastured on the nearby goldfields common as part of the miner's right. Goats were common around the South Australian towns built by Cornish miners in the 1840s, but feral goats are now considered pests in many parts of Australia (Blainey 2003:252). Rabbits, another now-notorious pest introduced to Australia near Geelong in 1859, could have been trapped on the commons. Rabbits were a regular part of many Australians' diets until after the Second World War. Eggshell was also found at Dolly's Creek, which suggests that there may have been chickens there as well.

Two generations on from the miners at Dolly's Creek, residents of the isolated forest community of Henry's No. 1 Mill in Victoria's Otway Ranges used a similar range of foraging strategies in the 1920s: growing vegetables, making home preserves, hunting, fishing and keeping a dairy herd (Davies 2006a). It was about using skills and available resources of time, space and materials to make limited cash incomes go further and to add variety and nutrition to a restricted and expensive store-bought diet. At Henry's there was a herd of 28 dairy cows kept by one of the mill workers and plentiful honey and blackberries in the forest. An alignment of stones like that at Dolly's Creek outlined a garden bed near one house and the school children were encouraged to maintain plots in the school yard. Oral histories recall children fishing for the trout, grayling and eels in the mountain streams, while rabbits were avidly hunted, reflected archaeologically by a range of ammunition from shotguns and small rifles and a complete rabbit trap. Cut-down beer bottles were used for home preserves of some sort.

By the 1870s there was abundant local production of fruit and vegetables. Botanical remains from 22 plant species were recovered from Casselden Place (Simons and Maitri 2006), dominated by grape, cherry and plum seeds, while fig and raspberry seeds could have come from jam or fresh fruit. Orchards were well-established in both suburban and country areas by this time, and Victorian producers of jam were competing with Tasmania. Pumpkins and tomatoes were the only vegetable seeds present at Casselden Place but there were several varieties of nut, including peanuts, walnuts, hazelnuts and almonds. Fairbairn (2007) has identified a similar preference for familiar Old World plants at the late-nineteenth-century Mountain Street "slum" in Sydney, including pumpkin, apple, peach and cherry, along with a few exotics such as dates, coconut and lychees.

Even in cities where blocks were smaller, households used their available land to meet some of their own subsistence needs. Writer Peter Timms describes an archaeology of his own yard, the relics of previous landscapes uncovered during his own gardening endeavours (Timms 2006:3–4). He uses the traces he uncovers to write the history of his own garden as well as the broader history of Australia's suburban yards and the uses to which they have been put. Traditionally, front gardens were and are those most on display, while side gardens, if they existed, were for private use, and backyards were utilitarian spaces reserved for activities such as wood-cutting, water collection and storage, waste disposal (including privies and cesspits), laundry and food production, which might include chickens and even goats or cows as well as a vegetable patch and fruit trees. Garden historian Andrea Gaynor notes that livestock and poultry were more popular in working-class suburbs than in middle- or upper-class ones, perhaps because animals were more portable for people renting their accommodation and also because the sale of the milk, cheese and eggs provided a source of income for the household (Gaynor 2006:44–47). After the Second World War electricity and the motor car eliminated the need for many of the backyard's utilitarian functions and leisure equipment such as barbecues and swimming pools began to appear. Australians continued to use the space as a source of food, however, even if it were only a single lemon tree. The New Australians who arrived from southern Europe after the war brought their own traditions of gardening and home food production, planting olive trees alongside the lemons and building enlarged sheds and outdoor sinks that facilitated large-scale preserving and storage of the produce. Disturbingly for many existing residents, front gardens were included in this productivity and were also planted with vegetables and fruit trees (Gaynor 2006:137; Head and Muir 2007; Holmes et al. 2008:195–212).

Archaeological evidence of food is inevitably skewed towards meat, but documentary sources also attest to the popularity of meat in Australian diets. It has been calculated that nineteenth-century Australians ate on average 270 pounds (120 kg) of meat each year, two and a half times as much as the 109 pounds (49.5 kg) consumed annually by the average British person (Gollan 1978:68). Closer studies of the British diet indicate that the disparity was even greater for those on the lower rungs of society. In the decades around the turn of the nineteenth century the weekly diet among working-class Britons in both town and country areas included less than four pounds (1.8 kg) of meat weekly, shared among families that had on average six members (Jackson 2005:16–21). The abundance of meat in Australia was repeatedly remarked on by visitors and new arrivals alike (Blainey 2003:201–202).

Archaeological evidence indicates that from mid-century sheep bones are more frequent than cattle bones, particularly on sites associated with working class and lower-middle class people (Briggs 2000:83; Gibbs 2005a:118; Jones et al. 1997:48; Lampard 2006:24; Simons and Maitri 2006:360; Steele 1999:211). At the Cheyne Beach whaling station, the Rookery and Port Adelaide sites in Adelaide, Casselden Place in Melbourne and Cumberland/Gloucester Streets in Sydney, sheep bone accounts for at least 50 percent of each faunal assemblage and cattle bones less than 14 percent, with the remainder represented by pig, chicken and fish (Fig. 11.2). While mutton or lamb was less expensive than beef, and pork was more expensive again, the relative size of the animals and the kinds of meat cuts must also

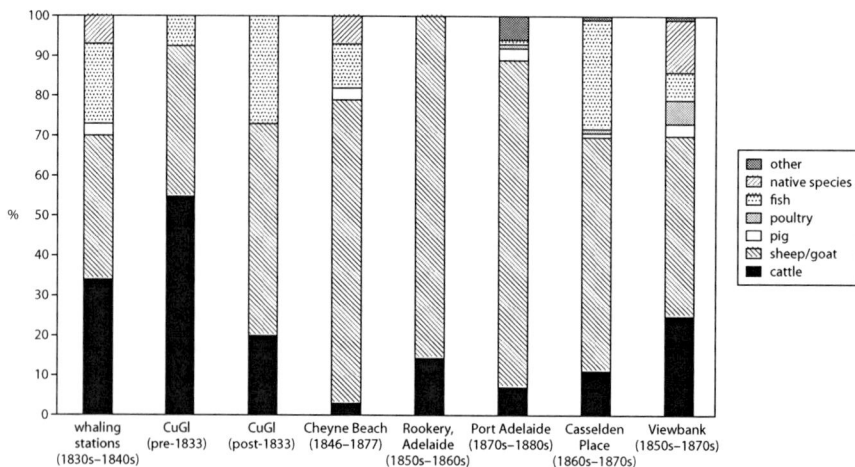

Fig. 11.2 Proportion of bones from selected sites as percentage of total identified specimens (bone weight in grams used for Cheyne Beach)

be considered when reconstructing meat consumption based on faunal evidence. Cattle are much larger than sheep or pigs, so beef bones would come with more meat than corresponding cuts of mutton or pork. Many cuts of beef and pork do not include any bones at all, including some roasts, bacon and sausages. Thus fewer beef *bones* do not necessarily imply that less beef was eaten. However, this later pattern is the reverse of that found on earlier sites such as the early phases at Cumberland/Gloucester Streets, where cattle bone accounted for 51 percent and sheep only 35 percent of the assemblage, and on the Tasmanian whaling stations where the two species were roughly equal (Lawrence and Tucker 2002:27). This suggests that the faunal evidence does reflect dietary patterns to some extent. It is likely that the evidence reflects greater reliance on salt meats in the earlier periods which was replaced with fresh lamb and mutton as the colonial flocks increased.

Cuts of both mutton/lamb and beef tended to be the cheaper, poorer-quality cuts that could be boiled or stewed, and marrow bones were sought for making soups. More expensive cuts such as steaks, however, did not contain bones and these findings must be treated with caution. Roasting cuts were present at all the sites, but it is clear from the archaeological evidence that bones we would discard today were being kept and used to prepare traditional British dishes such as head cheese, brains, tongue and calf's foot jelly. Other offal dishes such as tripe, liver and kidneys were undoubtedly also eaten, but like steak and sausages leave no archaeological evidence.

At Casselden Place the age of the animals killed was analysed in order to understand how colonial flocks and herds were being managed and whether younger or older animals were slaughtered. Most of the sheep bones were from mature animals and would be classified as mutton. Alison Simons and Maddy Maitri (2006:360) point out that while modern tastes are accustomed to the moister, sweeter flavour of lamb, the drier texture of mutton meant that it preserved better without refrigeration, perhaps one reason for its greater popularity in the colonial period. Raising the animals to maturity also increased the number of fleeces that could be shorn. Cattle bones indicate that most animals were between 2 and 4 years old and were probably raised for their meat. Some bones of older animals were also found, which may represent the consumption of draught or dairy animals too old for further work. There was also a considerable quantity of bone from very young animals less than 2 months old, indicating that veal continued to be popular in the colonies.

Fish and shellfish also appear regularly in deposits on inner-city sites in particular, but are not common on rural sites, probably due to problems with transporting fresh fish prior to refrigeration. At Cumberland/Gloucester Streets early deposits contain large, mature specimens of rock oysters and mud oysters, but by the second half of the century mud oysters have disappeared and the rock oysters are smaller in size, which Dominic Steele attributes to increased pressure on the stocks from a growing population and more pollution in the waters of Sydney Harbour (Steele 1999:183). Oysters continued to be abundant at Casselden Place in the 1870s, perhaps because Port Phillip Bay was not yet as intensively used (Simons and Maitri 2006:358, 360). Oysters were one of the foods of the poor in the nineteenth century, and Dickens characterised them as such in his depiction of 1830s London in

The Pickwick Papers. By the 1850s oysters were rare in England, but they remained abundant in Melbourne into the 1880s.

Fish bones made up 27 percent of the identified bones at Casselden Place and were also numerous at Cumberland/Gloucester Streets. The early deposits in the Rocks indicate that flathead, bream and snapper were eaten, all species that could be caught locally in shallow waters. Later deposits at the site include a wider variety of fish, with groper, morwong, wrasse and jewfish also represented. These species frequent deeper waters and indicate that the colonial fishing industry was becoming more established. Interestingly, only five fish bones were reported in the three Port Adelaide households analysed by Briggs (2000:83) despite the maritime connections of that community, although several were found at the Rookery in inner Adelaide (Jones et al. 1997:45).

Based on the archaeological evidence from Viewbank, it seems that wealthier colonists enjoyed a greater variety of meats and also better quality cuts (Howell-Muers 2000). Mutton/lamb was still the most popular and made up nearly half the bones identified. Cattle bones made up a further quarter of the assemblage, but 16 percent were native species including quoll, possum, pheasant, lorikeet, bustard and quail, all of which suggests that the Martins took advantage of their semi-rural location to hunt game for the table. The family evidently favoured poultry, as they were also eating duck, goose and turkeys in addition to chicken. Approximately 8 percent of the assemblage was fish bone, but no shellfish were reported. Sarah Howell-Meurs also analysed the age of the animals consumed and found that most of the sheep and cattle bones were from young adult animals raised primarily for meat. There was a predominance of bones from the upper hind limb of both cattle and sheep, indicating that cuts such as roasts were regularly consumed. Skull and lower limb bones were much less common, indicating that the animals were probably butchered elsewhere, but also that the family was not consuming offal dishes such as head cheese.

The other kind of food for which there is archaeological evidence is condiments. Pickles, sauces and spices were not a major part of the diet but the glass bottles they came in are a significant part of the archaeological record at many sites. This information about the sugary, spicy extras that livened up colonial meals is a unique source of information about a part of the diet that is otherwise little discussed. The challenge for archaeologists is to move from the bags and bags of broken glass to an interpretation of the foods eaten, and as part of this process there are a number of issues about site formation and artefact disposal that must be considered. The first concerns the ways in which bottles were acquired and used. The form and decoration of the bottles is of interest, particularly for those who collect old bottles, but the ultimate purpose of much archaeological bottle analysis is to learn more about the contents of the bottles, how they were made and how they were used. For the most part glass bottles then, as now, are containers and they are useful for what they contain, rather than for their own intrinsic qualities.

One of the objectives of bottle glass analysis is to establish an estimate of how many complete bottles are represented in an assemblage. Glass breaks easily and potentially into many small pieces, so the quantity of fragments is not necessarily a guide to how many whole bottles were once present. Instead, archaeologists use an estimate called the Minimum Number of Vessels, or MNV. To determine the MNV archaeologists first sort all of the glass according to formal attributes such as colour, size, bottle shape, manufacturing technology and so on. Within each formal group diagnostic elements are then isolated, so that bases are separated from necks and rims (called "finishes" as this was the last part of the bottle to be made) and from body fragments. By counting the diagnostic parts it is possible to determine the minimum number of bottles. Bases and finishes are considered diagnostic because each bottle would only have one base and one finish. Thus if there are five bases, there must have been at least five bottles. If there were five bases and seven finishes, there must have been at least seven bottles, as each finish represents a complete bottle, and in this case some of the bases must be missing. It would also be possible to estimate the MNV in other ways, such as piecing together all the glass like a jigsaw puzzle, or weighing it and dividing by the average weight of a single bottle. The first method would be far too time-consuming, however, and the second is generally not reliable because of the great variation in size of bottles that were made by hand. It must also be emphasised that this approach simply indicates the *minimum* that must have been present, and it is almost certainly an underestimate.

Another issue to be considered is that of re-use. Because bottles were containers, they could be used to contain any sort of liquid, including those which were unrelated to the original contents of the bottle (Busch 1987). Until the development of machine production at the beginning of the twentieth century, bottles were often valuable commodities in their own right and empty bottles were even imported into the Australian colonies to be filled with alcohol shipped in bulk (Morgan 1991). The most straightforward kind of re-use was when the bottles were collected, washed and re-filled with the original product, a practice which led to bottlers moulding their names on the bottles and to complex networks of "bottle-ohs", people who gathered empties and then returned them to bottlers (Lucas 2002). The analysis of sealed bottles recovered from shipwreck sites, however, indicates that the contents were often quite different to what the shape of the bottle would suggest (Peters 1997). So-called beer and wine bottles (cylindrical black/olive green bottles) were also collected by cordial makers for the bottling of their non-alcoholic products, as Martin Carney found in his re-analysis of a bottle dump at the Babes on the Wood site in Parramatta (Carney 1999a). In addition to the potential for re-use, bottles were recycled in a variety of ways. A common practice in the early twentieth century, especially in rural Australia, was to remove the neck and finish of bottles and fill the base with home-made jams and preserves, sealing the top with wax (Stuart 1993). Examples of such bottles have been found at Henry's Mill (Davies 2006a:100–101). As we noted in Chapter 3, Aboriginal people also used bottles as a source of raw material for making sharp glass tools and in such cases may only have brought fragments of glass to a site, rather than whole bottles. Bearing all of these possibilities in mind, extreme caution must be used when using bottle glass to interpret diet.

A third issue to be considered is that of time-lag (Adams 2003). Rapid changes in bottle-making technology throughout the nineteenth century, as well as information about manufacturers and bottlers often moulded directly into the glass itself, means that bottles can be readily dated and used in turn to estimate when the archaeological deposit was created. As with other artefacts such as ceramic dishes and clay tobacco pipes, however, what is actually being dated is when the bottle was made, rather than when it entered the archaeological record. On the one hand, because bottles were most important for their contents rather than for their own properties, they could be disposed of quickly once their contents were used and were not curated over many years as tablewares often were. Their disposability was only enhanced by the fact that they broke easily. We would therefore expect that bottles in an assemblage would have been made not too long before they were discarded. On the other hand, because of their potential re-use it is possible and even likely that most bottles were in circulation for some time before they eventually broke, and might in fact be several years old when they entered the archaeological record. The only way to effectively deal with this problem is to date each type of object in the assemblage independently, and to use as many lines of evidence as possible to date the deposit as a whole, including stratigraphic and documentary information.

Despite these constraints, it is possible to use the archaeological evidence as a source of information on what people were eating, and one of the things that glass tells us is that Australians have always liked spicy condiments as part of their meals. Assemblages of bottle glass from sites from the first half of the nineteenth century such as the Tasmanian whaling stations and Cumberland/Gloucester Streets include plain mould-blown containers made of pale green glass, both square and rectangular with chamfered corners, short necks and wide mouths (Lawrence 2006b:79, 86). These bottles were probably sealed with corks and originally contained powdered spices such as mustard or cayenne pepper, both of which were commonly mixed with water or vinegar at the table (Jones and Smith 1985:60–67). In some cases these may have been used to disguise the taste of decaying meat. The cargo of the *Eglinton*, wrecked off the Western Australian coast in 1852, included a variety of glass condiment bottles, some with intact contents which provide valuable insight into what was available in Australia at the time (Stanbury 2003:153–155). The food bottles were moulded in either clear or pale green glass and were cylindrical or square with chamfered corners. One cylindrical bottle contained preserved blackcurrants while another once held stone fruit. James Boow (1991:18) observed that in the early 1800s the price of these goods, at five shillings a bottle, put them into the realm of semi-luxury goods, so their use at the whaling stations and among the convict and ex-convict homes on the Rocks demonstrates a pervasive desire for sweet, spicy and flavourful food and a willingness to purchase it.

Other condiment containers at these early sites include squat stoneware jars, also with short necks and wide mouths sealed with a cork. These probably contained pickled foods such as olives, walnuts, gherkins, onions or capers. Stoneware was particularly favoured as a container because it was far cheaper than glass until the lifting of the British excise on glass in 1845 (Boow 1991:24–26). The *Eglinton* cargo also included a variety of stoneware containers for condiments (Stanbury 2003:80–83). French mustard was packaged in small stoneware jars stamped with the name of the Maille company, which began making mustard in 1747. Fruit preserves, probably gooseberry or raspberry jam, was packed in buff-coloured stoneware jars and sealed with a tin-foil capsule marked with the coat-of-arms of the makers,

Gunter and Co of Berkeley Square, London. Other stoneware jars contained jam made by Hill & Jones of Jewry Street in London, and the Bristol company of William Powell and Sons made jars that probably contained pickles or meat paste.

From 1845 when the British excise on glass was lifted there was a proliferation of glass bottles to contain condiments, and the gradual replacement of powdered spices with proprietary sauces such as Lea and Perrin's Worcestershire Sauce, introduced in 1838. Ornate designs in pressed glass were intended to resemble the more expensive cut glass cruets sets so that the bottles could be placed directly on the table. Cylindrical bottles with long, thin necks held vinegar and salad oils, while pickles and chutneys came in wide-mouthed bottles similar in shape to the earlier ones, but with more elaborate designs pressed into the panels. Mustard and prepared pastes such as shrimp paste and anchovy paste were sold in bright polychrome underglaze ceramic pots (Fig. 11.3).

Fig. 11.3 Small condiment jar from Casselden Place in Melbourne (photo M. Wei, Industry Superannuation Property Trust, Godden Mackay Logan/Austral Archaeology/La Trobe University)

In the Government House tip at the Conservatorium of Music site in Sydney, condiment bottles were the third largest category of food-related artefacts, with at least 69 vessels represented in the assemblage. Most of these contained either oil or vinegar or pickles and chutney. Mary Casey notes that this is a far greater proportion of the assemblage than at other Sydney sites of a comparable date, and she speculates that it may be associated with the food served to the Governors, their families and guests (Casey 2005a:105). The Governor's household, which included large numbers of servants as well as the family, was certainly larger than the average household and this may account for the greater quantity of condiments consumed.

At Casselden Place at least 36 pickle bottles and 31 salad oil bottles were identified among the 2,972 vessels represented, but a further 158 club sauce stoppers probably sealed condiment bottles as well, and many of the 562 unidentified bottles also contained condiments. Products represented included pickles produced by the firms of Batty and Co, Hill and Jones, and George Whybrow, all of London, along with Holbrooks Sauce and Worcester Sauce, and Dundee marmalade (Davies 2004). At the Cumberland/Gloucester Streets site, Martin Carney identified at least 123 different types of condiment bottles and stoppers, which is also an indication of the range of products that were being consumed (Carney 1999b:55).

Beverages

Bottle glass provides evidence of many of the drinks consumed by Australians, but not for the most popular beverage, tea. Tea was well-entrenched as a habitual part of the British diet by the time the first convicts arrived in Australia, so it is little surprise that it was also popular here. Tea and its inevitable accompaniment, sugar, was a major component of rations, alongside salt meat. The whalers were issued one third of a pound of tea each week (150 g) and two pounds (900 g) of sugar (Lawrence 2006b:109), while convicts received one quarter of a pound (100 g) of tea and one pound (500 g) of sugar (Nicholas 1988:184). By the 1850s, Australians drank on average seven pounds (3.2 kg) of tea per year, almost five times as much as people in Britain (Simmonds 1854:88). In a hot climate, vast quantities of tea were consumed both in the city and in the country. In the 1870s, a typical farmer was said to drink four cups with every meal. A thirsty bushman might drink more than 60 l in a week. In the kitchen, housewives kept a kettle full of hot water on the stove, ready to dispense cup after cup of tea. Tea was easy to prepare and cheap and easy to transport (Dingle 1978:243). Boiling water for tea also killed harmful bacteria and thus unwittingly reduced the risk of disease from dirty water.

The archetypal Australian tea is billy tea, made by throwing a handful of tea leaves into a tin of water boiling on an open fire. This was beloved of generations of bushmen, but most Australians probably brewed their tea in ceramic pots and drank it from ceramic teacups. Broken teapots, most with their spouts missing, were one of the notable forms of artefacts recovered from the excavation of the Turner's Paddock rubbish tip in Adelaide. Teapots are less frequent on domestic sites but teacups and saucers are almost ubiquitous. Matching cup-and-saucer pairs are the most common kind of set found and occur even at sites like Dolly's Creek and the whaling stations where the rest of the dishes are a mixed batch of contrasting patterns. Tea drinking was commonplace but it was also a ritual loaded with meaning. Sharing a cup of tea cemented bonds in every social group. Brewing a good cup of billy tea was a sign of a bushman's skills and competence, while taking tea was a central part of the system of "calls" exchanged among middle- and upper-class society women. Numerous teawares recovered from the upper levels of a cistern behind 300 Queen Street in Melbourne, used as government offices from the 1860s, show that even office workers fortified themselves for their work with cups of tea (Birmingham 1984).

In a country of such committed tea drinkers, coffee was always a minor beverage in Australia. The few bags of coffee beans imported in the early days of settlement were dwarfed by the cargoes of tea chests arriving from China and later from India and Ceylon. During the colonial period and well into the twentieth century, most coffee in Australia was drunk as an essence mixed with chicory (see Chapter 6). Blainey (2003:367) described the mix as like a cup of warm brown cordial. Archaeological evidence for domestic consumption of coffee is mostly in the form of bottles of chicory and coffee essence, manufactured by firms including Bushell's, Bickford's, Symington and Brooke's. Coffee was also promoted as a health drink (Bersten 1999), while the temperance movement established coffee palaces as an alternative to pubs, several of which, such as the Federal and the Windsor in Melbourne, became palatial hotels.

The detailed analysis of ceramics from sites all over Australia provides some insight into the objects used in the drinking of hot beverages. It is clear that most people drank tea from matching cup-and-saucer pairs, which are present at almost every site excavated (Table 11.1). Teawares occur in a wide range of decorative types, including transfer prints, hand-painted patterns, simple banded designs, and

Table 11.1 Teawares from selected sites dating from the 1840s to the 1890s

	Matching cup and saucer pairs	Porcelain or bone China teas	Teas that match tables	Matching tea service items
CuGl Glou 101	–	–	–	–
CuGl Glou 97 (2)	–	✓	–	–
QLD-Kirkes	–	✓	–	–
QLD-Turks	–	✓	–	–
CuGl Cara 001	✓	–	–	–
CuGl Cara 005	✓	–	–	–
CuGl Cumb 122	✓	–	–	–
CuGl Cumb 126	✓	–	–	–
CuGl Glou 93	✓	–	–	–
Mrs Lewis	✓	–	–	–
Whaling	✓	–	–	–
Cheyne Beach	✓	✓	–	–
CuGl Glou 97 (1)	✓	✓	–	–
QLD-Bartletts	✓	✓	–	–
Dolly's Creek	✓	✓	–	–
QLD-Buzzas	✓	✓	✓	–
QLD-McGhies	✓	✓	✓	–
QLD-McGonnells	✓	✓	✓	–
QLD-Shuttleworths	✓	✓	✓	–
CuGl Cara 003	✓	–	–	✓
QLD-Plastows	✓	✓	–	✓
CuGl Cumb 124	✓	–	✓	✓
Pt Ad. Farrows	✓	✓	✓	✓
Pt Ad. McKays	✓	✓	✓	✓
Pt Albert	✓	✓	✓	✓
Bean	✓	✓	✓	✓
Viewbank	✓	✓	✓	✓

moulded patterns. Many are on whiteware or white granite, but a large number are on porcelain or bone china, some of which had gilt decoration as well. These better quality wares were also more expensive and Brooks and Connah (2007) have used the presence or absence of these wares as one indicator of status among the servants' sites at Lake Innes in New South Wales. In many of the ceramic assemblages considered here it was only the teawares that were made of this more expensive material. It seems that when households were deciding where to spend more money, they were more likely to spend it on teawares than on tablewares. Drinking cups of tea had a high social value, and was part of the ritual of receiving visitors at all social levels. It was also a cheaper and more manageable way of entertaining than to have guests to dinner, so it is probable that having more expensive teawares was a better way of projecting the family's status than having expensive tablewares. This is consistent with patterns observed in the archaeological record overseas, where archaeologists in New York City in particular have noted that teawares were more likely than tablewares to be expensive and used for entertaining (Fitts 1999; Wall 1991). Issues of quality, cost and value in ceramics, however, are difficult to understand fully (Crook 2005, 2009). While porcelain and bone china are considered better quality, some families preferred to invest in a cheaper ware, such as transfer-printed whiteware, but purchased an entire service rather than a few more costly bone china cups and saucers that required the use of the everyday teapot and slops bowl (for teacup dregs). In the absence of firm information on manufacturers' pricing schemes, it is also possible that the best quality transfer prints were dearer than "seconds" of porcelain or bone china.

At most of the sites for which data are available on the minimum number of vessels and matching sets, the cup and saucer pairs did not form part of a larger matching set, and tea services that also included additional items such as slops bowls, sugars and milk jugs are uncommon. The wealthy Martin family at Viewbank may have had a silver tea service, as Hayes points out (2008:287), but most of the other households discussed here probably had a brown Rockingham teapot, fragments of which were found on several sites. Only eight of the sites analysed had pieces that might have formed part of a tea service. The Thomases at Port Albert and the Winches at Cumberland Street had slop bowls that matched their teacups, while the Martins at Viewbank had at least two tea services that included matching jugs and the Beans had a matching teapot. These were all prosperous households, and it may be that a tea service denotes some higher level of social status. If so, the fact that the two Port Adelaide families, the Farrows and the Mackays, also had tea services supports Susan Lampard's contention that those families were of respectable status despite the reputation of the neighbourhood as a place of poverty (Lampard 2004). The presence of tea service items at the sites of the Plastows at Paradise is more puzzling. Edwin Plastow was a cobbler and their site had the second-smallest ceramic assemblage at Paradise. Quirk (2008b:283) notes that theirs was unlike either the middle-class assemblages (the McGhies, Shuttleworthes, Kirkes, Turks, and upwardly mobile Buzzas) or those of the working-class families (the Bartletts and McGonnells). Other families with claims to middle-class status, such as the

Plastows' neighbours the McGhies, did not have dedicated tea services, so the social meaning of this element of household equipage remains ambiguous.

It was slightly more common for Australian households to have teawares that matched a table service than to have a stand-alone tea service. Half of the Paradise households had teawares that matched other items such as dinner plates and platters, as did four of the other sites, including both the Beans and the Thomases in Gippsland, the Farrows and Mackays in Port Adelaide and the Martins at Viewbank. The Winches at Cumberland Street may also have had teawares that were part of a table service, but this is not clear from the report (Crook et al. 2005). In addition to tea and coffee services, distinguished principally by the size of the cup, by the middle of the nineteenth century specialised services could be had for breakfast, dinner and dessert (Young 2003:184). A full dinner service for a genteel family consisted of up to 120 pieces including different sized plates, serving platters and bowls, lidded dishes and sauceboats. Breakfast services consisted of a range of plates plus large cups and saucers, while dessert services included plates and some serving dishes and stands, and were often more highly decorated. According to Young's research, most genteel households aimed to have at least two of these specialised services.

Using this information about teawares, it is possible to compare artefact distribution patterns between sites, a process that produces further insight. The households can be grouped according to some of their purchasing decisions, to provide one measure of social status, albeit a simple one. In the first group are the sites where matching cup-and-saucer pairs were present but no other matching items, and where the teawares were of earthenware rather than bone china or porcelain. This includes the whaling stations and Mrs. Lewis' boarding house, places where groups of unrelated individuals rather than family members lived together, and where tea drinking was functional rather than symbolic and any creation of group identity was apparently achieved in realms other than the purchase of matching or costly teawares (Lydon 1993a). Half of the Cumberland/Gloucester Streets households are also in this group, which tends to confirm the poverty ascribed to many Rocks residents by the middle of the century. The two Paradise sites in this group are ambiguous because while no matching pairs were referred to in the report, those described were of good quality.

In the second group are the sites at Dolly's Creek and Cheyne Beach, the Bartletts at Paradise and one of the Cumberland/Gloucester Streets assemblages. These households had matching cups and saucers and some better quality wares, but no other matching pieces. These seem to be households without extensive financial resources, and it may be that they desired more elaborate settings but simply lacked the money. Alternatively, they may have had the financial means, but lacked the desire to display social status in that way. The next group consists of most of the Paradise families, the Winches at 124 Cumberland Street, and one of their neighbours. These households had good-quality teawares and either a tea service or a matching breakfast set, enabling them to conduct a slightly grander ritual. The documentary evidence indicates that these households owned assets and had a comfortable income. If they were not clearly part of the middle class, the archaeological evidence demonstrates that they possessed the tea equipment required at such a social level.

In the final group are the assemblages with all four indicators. They not only had matching cups and saucers in good-quality wares, but they also had at least one set each of both a tea service and a breakfast service, enabling the rituals of taking tea to be fully observed at meals and as a separate occasion. The households include the Martins at Viewbank, an indisputably wealthy family, and the Beans in Gippsland, also a family with claims to high social status as a result of the Reverend Bean's position in the local Anglican church. While the good quality and extensive nature of their teawares is perhaps not surprising, what is more interesting is the other families whose teawares place them in this high-status group. The Thomases of Port Albert were friends or at least associates of the Beans according to documentary records, but our understanding of their social position is sharpened by the archaeological evidence. When their tea assemblage is considered in comparison with a wide range of sites from around the country, it clearly ranks above most of the others, showing that the position of John Thomas as a harbour pilot in the town elevated the family above the merely respectable. Likewise, the Farrow and Mackay family assemblages from Port Adelaide certainly appear respectable when analysed in isolation, but our understanding of the families' social status sharpens considerably when looked at comparatively. The Thomases, Mackays and Farrows all appear in the documentary evidence to be respectable but unremarkable families. Their diverse and well-equipped collections of teawares, however, suggest that within their own local communities they were prosperous social leaders.

Soft Drinks and Strong Drinks

Mineral waters had been popular for centuries in Europe as a medicinal tonic, but the development of aerated (carbonated) waters or sodas in the late eighteenth century dramatically increased the market for bottled water. Fruit flavourings and sugar were added for variety of taste, and a new consumer industry was born. Products included cordials, hop and ginger beers, bitters and sarsaparilla, and by the second half of the nineteenth century, most Australian towns of any size boasted a factory for making and bottling aerated waters. David Jones (2009) has documented in lavish detail hundreds of soft drink manufacturers in Sydney, while in Melbourne there were several dozen factories operating by the 1880s, with most producing a range of drinks. The Phoenix Cordial Factory, for example, manufactured ginger brandy, green ginger wine and raspberry wine, cherry brandy, rum punch, raspberry vinegar, lemon syrup, peppermint cordial, milk punch, elder wine and various other products (Arnold 1990:128). There was clearly a strong demand for flavoured drinks in colonial society, beyond the staples of tea, beer and spirits.

Many of these drinks, however, were volatile to store in a bottle, and this resulted in hundreds of patented closures, most based on corks, gravitating stoppers, wire clamps or internal screws. Ginger beer, for example, was made by fermenting ginger with cream of tartar (potassium tartrate), sugar and yeast in water, a composition that required a sturdy container. Stoneware ginger beer bottles (stonies) were commonly used for storage, often stamped or impressed with the name of the drink maker. One of the best known containers, and most distinctive glass bottles, was the Hamilton "blob top" or torpedo bottle. Stored on its side, the cork was kept wet and held tightly against the thick finish. These bottles were mostly clear or aqua in colour, and were frequently embossed with the name of the manufacturer. The first examples appeared in Australia around 1840 (Vader and Murray 1975:33). Another bottle closure was developed by Hiram Codd in Britain around 1870. The Codd bottle used a glass marble under pressure of carbonation to seal against a cork or rubber ring. When the marble was pushed down and the seal was broken, the marble slid into a recess in the neck of the bottle. Numerous variations of the Codd closure were developed, and these bottles remained popular in Australia until at least the 1920s. The marble in the bottle was also an inevitable attraction for children, who often smashed the bottle to retrieve the marble (Carney 1999a:88).

The largest proportion of any glass assemblage is usually comprised of bottles, and particularly bottles associated with alcohol. At Lake Innes, for example, alcohol bottle fragments made up as much as 96 percent of the glass assemblage at some sites (Smith 2007:196). Bottles that may once have contained beer, wine and spirits are ubiquitous across colonial sites, and at first glance would appear to confirm Australians' reputation as hard drinkers. Closer examination shows that the story is more complex and raw fragments counts are deceptive. As already discussed, bottle glass is a dominant artefact category because it was packaging that was frequently discarded and because it breaks easily and preserves well in the ground. Alcohol bottle glass is particularly abundant because the bottles were such useful containers for a variety of liquids. Once the fragments are sorted to establish the minimum number of actual bottles represented, however, the per capita rates of discard can be quite modest. More than 3,000 fragments of alcohol bottle glass at the Adventure Bay whaling station amounts to only 16 bottles, a minute quantity of alcohol to be shared among the 30 men working at the site each winter over 13 years or so (Lawrence 2006b:150). It is also possible, even likely, that at least some of those bottles held other liquids when brought to the site, reducing consumption rates even further. At the same time, we know from other sources that whalers did drink large quantities of alcohol when they had the opportunity, and we also know that James Kelly, who owned the stations, purchased alcohol in bulk in wooden kegs, as did many other colonials with the resources to do so.

The combination of bulk purchasing and bottle re-use means that archaeological bottle glass provides only an imperfect guide to what was actually being consumed on a given site. Nevertheless, as bottle glass is a large component of the archaeo-logical record it is worthwhile to analyse it carefully. Exploring patterns of use and disposal on sites can lead to better information about the life-span of bottles and how soon they were discarded, while scratches and usewear can reveal signs of re-use. It may also be that rates of recycling and time lag vary between different kinds of sites at different times and places. Inter-site comparison can shed light on con-sumption behaviour associated with gender, social position, geography and personal taste. It may also point to new questions about how and where alcohol was obtained and consumed. Recent archaeological research in North America, for example, has drawn on alcohol's functional role as a means fostering sociability and group integration, and as part of escapism in physically or emotionally stressful situations (F. Smith 2007).

Comparison of assemblages from a number of Australian sites suggests that the number of alcohol-style bottles recovered is often quite modest, with most assemblages having fewer than 30 alcohol bottles (Fig. 11.4). Some of the exceptions to this have considerably higher quantities, with well over 100 alcohol-style bottles recovered from Viewbank and from one of the assemblages at Casselden Place. However, allowing for the number of years the sites were occupied or over which the deposits were formed reduces all of these totals and reveals a more complex picture. Calculated on a per annum basis, all of the households discarded fewer than 10 bottles per year, and many disposed of less than one bottle per year (Fig. 11.5). The period of time it took for the assemblages to accumulate is not clear in every case. Re-analysis of the Cumberland/Gloucester Streets site has demonstrated that most of the deposits were probably created within only a few weeks or months (Crook et al. 2005). It is likely that the deposits at Casselden Place were created under short-term circumstances similar to those at Cumberland/Gloucester Streets, but open household tips such as those at Viewbank, Government House and Bean's parsonage probably reflect longer periods of accumulation while those at Paradise are probably the result of much shorter periods of actual residency at the ephemeral mining town.

In spite of this variability, distinctions between sites are clear. Most of the Paradise households, for example, stand out for their relative abstemiousness. This

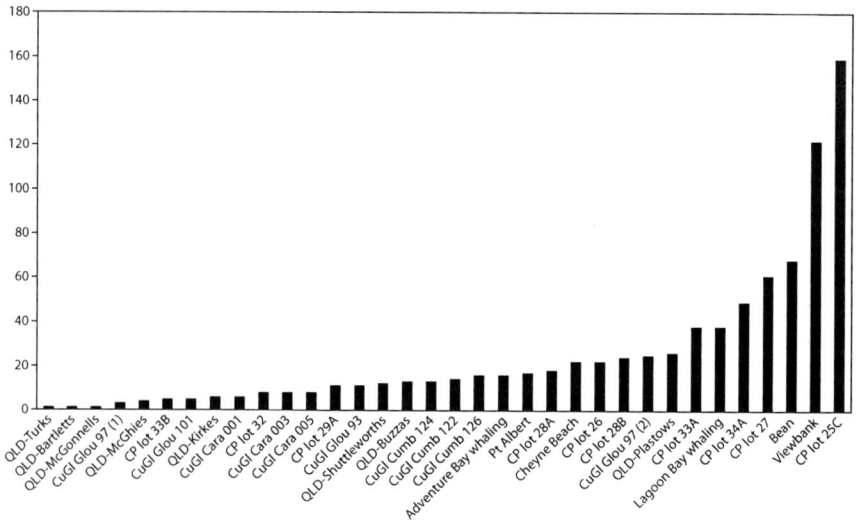

Fig. 11.4 Total number of alcohol-style bottles recovered from selected sites (shown as minimum number of vessels)

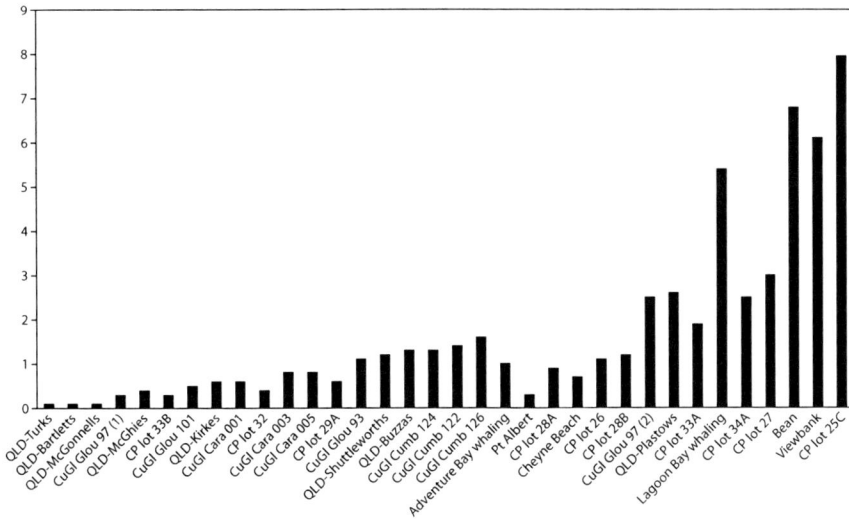

Fig. 11.5 Per annum disposal rates of alcohol-style bottles from selected sites (shown as minimum number of vessels)

supports Kate Quirk's conclusions about the powerful influence of Methodism and temperance within the community, but interestingly, residents were little more abstemious than those at Cumberland/Gloucester Streets. In fact, the Plastows at Paradise had one of the higher per annum disposal rates according to these figures. In contrast, by this measure the households in the working-class inner-city neighbourhood of Casselden Place generally appear to have disposed of more alcohol bottles each year, reinforcing its colourful reputation as a slum. Confounding these neat correlations, however, those at Bean's parsonage had the second highest annual disposal rates, accounting for 6.8 bottles per year, only a few more than the six bottles per year from the Martins at Viewbank. Bean had a reputation as someone who enjoyed a drink (Watson 1984:197), but these figures also point to the complex association between alcohol consumption and status.

Temperate behaviour in all respects was one of the ideals of the middle classes, and the temperance movement that advocated abstention from alcohol was a strong political force, particularly in the second half of the nineteenth century (Dunstan 1968; Hyslop 1976; Kirkby 1997; Wright 2003:152–167). This can lead to the assumption that alcohol consumption was incompatible with respectability and gentility. While temperance was undoubtedly one of the hallmarks of good behaviour, the ways in which this ideal was enacted across lines of class, religion and gender were intricate and must be tested rather than assumed. Among some segments of society temperance meant abstention, and this was particularly true for those with strong evangelical views of Christianity. For others, including Catholics and high-church Anglicans, temperance meant moderation and alcohol consumption continued to be practised. In the United States, temperance was associated with the native-born middle classes, who urged abstinence on the working classes and European immigrants (Reckner and Brighton 1999), but this pattern was less marked in Australia. Thus the Beans and the Martins, both Anglican families, could comfortably drink alcohol without bringing their morality or genteel status into question, while in Paradise, where the evangelical Methodists were a prominent social force, even the higher status families like the McGhies and the Shuttleworths seem to have abstained.

Temperance was largely an initiative of the middle classes that was directed at the working class, but Karskens argues that working people probably drank to suit themselves rather than others, and alcohol was never outlawed in Australia (Karskens 1997:180). Among those who did drink, there were conventions about what was appropriate for whom and in what circumstances. In the United States beer, wine and porter were acceptable drinks even for the temperate, while spirits were considered by their very nature to be out-of-bounds (Reckner and Brighton 1999:76–78). In Australia, spirits were held in higher regard and they were particularly popular in the bush where they were easier and cheaper to transport than beer or wine (Blainey 2003:344–345). Rum (more accurately arrack made from palm sugar in India (Staniforth 2003:81)) was the main spirit in the early years, standing in for currency at a time when money was in short supply and lending its name to the Rum Corps who made their profits from importing it. Blainey (2003:345) claims that by the time of the gold rushes brandy was the most popular drink, while wealthier squatters and businessmen preferred Scotch whisky. Wine was far less popular than today, but nevertheless more was consumed here than in other English-speaking countries, perhaps because from the 1840s it was produced in several regions including the Barossa Valley in South Australia, the Hunter Valley in New South Wales and the Yarra Valley and north-eastern Victoria.

The most detailed empirical study of Australian drinking habits has been carried out by economic historian Tony Dingle (1980). Based on import figures Dingle found that the period of greatest spirit consumption was in the 1830s when New South Wales had an annual per capita consumption of over four and a half gallons (20 l), 80 percent of it rum. The economic depression of the 1840s ended that spree and although spirit consumption rose during the gold rush years (this time mainly brandy) it never again reached those levels. Victorians consumed about a gallon (4.5 l) of wine per person annually throughout the second half of the century, while in New South Wales consumption fell from a high of 3.5 gallons in the 1830s to less than one gallon by the 1890s. Most of the wine consumed was fortified port and sherry, gradually being replaced by lighter, locally made table wines towards the end of the century. Beer consumption is harder to track because statistics on local production were not kept until the second half of the century, but it appears that in New South Wales people drank between two and three gallons per year for most of the century. In Victoria they drank closer to ten gallons per year, and nearly 18 gallons per year from the 1860s until the depression of the 1890s.

Before pasteurisation and refrigeration were developed in the 1870s and 1880s, beer went off quickly, and even after local breweries got underway they were beset by problems with production that made for an inferior brew. Corioli Souter's analysis of cargo from the *Sepia*, wrecked off Perth in 1898, suggests that imported British beers remained popular, even after local production began, because of their superior quality and status associations (Souter 2006a:175). The first colonial breweries were already in operation by 1800, and locally made stoneware bottles for packaging were being made by 1803 (Deutsher 1999:8; Ford 1995:13). Breweries and the glass bottle manufacturers that accompanied them, however, only became widespread in the 1860s. By the 1870s nearly every country town had its own brewery, many of which also made aerated waters and cordials, all with their own distinctive bottles and labels (Arnold 1990). The distinctive markings now beloved of collectors made it easier to get the re-usable bottles returned to the right bottler.

Any or all of these drinks could have been contained in the square case bottles and cylindrical black glass bottles found on archaeological sites. Analysis of the contents of sealed bottles recovered from the wreck of the *William Salthouse* reveals the range of beverages that such bottles held (Peters 1997). In 1994 Heritage Victoria arranged a formal tasting of their archaeological wines by a panel of professional wine tasters, and compared their conclusions with laboratory chemical analysis. Some of the wines tested were from bottles which archaeologists call "champagne-style", tapering green glass containers with a large push-up, prominent mamelon, and applied string rim. Labelling on the corks indicated they had been filled in Ay, a French town in the Champagne region, and further research suggests that they were sold by the House of Gosset, the oldest Champagne house in the world. Analysis of the contents revealed that it was a table wine, but analysis of another bottle, identical in style but with a different cork and found nearby, showed that it was probably a beer. Other contents tested came from cylindrical black glass "beer/wine" style containers that were recovered from intact pine crates whose labelling indicated that they contained muscat, a sweet dessert wine. Cargo manifests from the ship's point of origin, Montreal, and from Melbourne, recorded that another dessert wine, sauterne, was also on board. The initial chemical analysis seemed to show that the wines were sauternes, leading to the conclusion that the crate labelling was incorrect, but subsequent research suggests that the wines were in fact muscats. So champagne bottles held beer as well as champagne, and beer bottles held sweet table wines. All had a place in Australian drinking habits.

Table Settings

Many archaeological sites also provide evidence of the vessels used for serving and consuming these drinks. Ceramic jugs and glass decanters held the beverages at the table. At Lagoon Bay an elaborately decorated whiteware jug with a cream glaze has a moulded design that features a procession of strange animals and people in exotic costumes. On Cumberland Street the Winch family had at least five glass decanters in plain, panelled and ribbed patterns, and three of their neighbours also had decanters. Most of the households analysed also had jugs or pitchers for serving beer or ale (Table 11.2). The Thomases at Port Albert had two decanters, and two glass stoppers from decanters belonging to the Martins were found at Viewbank

Table 11.2 Glass tablewares at selected sites (shown as minimum number of vessels)

	Stemmed ware	Tumblers	Decanters/jugs	Pressed glass
CuGl Cara 005	1	3	✓	–
CuGl Glou 93	1	2	✓	–
CuGl Glou 97 (2)	1	7	✓	✓
CuGl Glou 101	1	1	✓	–
Adventure Bay Whaling	2	4	✓	–
CuGl Cumb 122	2	14	✓	✓
CuGl Cumb 126	2	4	–	–
CuGl Glou 97 (1)	2	7	–	–
CuGl Cara 001	3	3	–	✓
CuGl Cara 003	3	8	✓	–
Conservatorium	4	10	–	✓
Bean	5	3	–	–
CuGl Cumb 124	8	10	✓	✓
Viewbank	25	13	✓	✓

together with a corkscrew. Unsurprisingly, given the apparent lack of alcohol consumption, only one decanter was represented among the Paradise households, which was a glass stopper found at the Buzza property. A cut glass stopper was also found at the Turks' house but it is not clear whether it was from a decanter or part of a cruet set. The *Eglinton* cargo included several different decanter and carafe styles, and Myra Stanbury notes that it was common in the nineteenth century to use decanters and tumblers as water containers in bedrooms as well as at the table (Stanbury 2003:160–162).

The beverages were drunk from tumblers and stemmed glasses, several examples of which were also found on the *Eglinton*. Olive Jones (2000:224–225) states that stemmed glasses were used for wine, champagne, claret and cordial, while tumblers were used for ale, whiskey, soda water, lemonade and iced tea. Presumably, tumblers were also used for other spirits such as the rum and brandy popular in Australia. Rebecca Yamin (1997) suggests that the context of use also mattered, and that stemmed glasses were preferred at the table and tumblers elsewhere. In the early deposits at Cumberland/Gloucester Streets there were very few of either when compared with the quantity of fashionable ceramics. Martin Carney (1999b:84) points to the relative expense of all glasswares before the British excise was lifted in 1845, but Grace Karskens also notes the social context of drinking from a shared glass "circling" among a group (Karskens 1999:72–73). It is also possible that people substituted other vessels such as teacups, mugs and older style cups made of wood or horn, but whatever the explanation it certainly points to a different pattern of behaviour.

At Adventure Bay, only slightly later, the whalers were using both tumblers and stemmed glasses. The four tumblers recovered were all plain and undecorated, while the two stemmed glasses were in popular styles introduced at the end of the eighteenth century. None of the glasses appeared to match in any way but all were hand blown, unlike the *Eglinton* examples of 1852 which were all moulded. The Beans had five stemmed glasses, two of which matched, and three tumblers. All of the stemmed glasses and one of the tumblers were in crystal, more expensive than the common flint glass. Sites dating from mid-century contain more glass tablewares of all kinds than the earlier sites, indicating that habits were changing by the time of the gold rushes. The later Cumberland Street deposits re-analysed by Tim Murray and Penny Crook included numerous tumblers and stemmed glasses, with two of the houses having eight tumblers each and the Winches having 10, along with six stemmed glasses, three of which were part of a matching set (Crook et al. 2005). All of their neighbours had at least one stemmed glass as well, some with two or three. The Government House tip at the Conservatorium of Music site also had 10 tumblers and four stemmed glasses, which in comparison to the Winches seems quite modest. It is even more modest when compared with the assemblage from the Martins at Viewbank, which included no less than 13 tumblers and 25 stemmed glasses. It is unusual to have more stemware than tumblers and while Sarah Hayes admits that it might be due to the greater fragility of stemmed glasses she argues it reflects a genuine preference for using that style. Only two households at Paradise, the Buzzas and the McGhies, disposed of drinking vessels, represented by a single vessel at each site, but these were too fragmented to determine if they were tumblers or stemmed glasses.

Techniques for making mass-produced press-moulded glass tablewares were introduced in the United States in the 1820s and in England in 1834. Further improvements in technology in the 1860s and 1870s made a wide range of patterns and styles available from that time (Jones et al. 1989:34). The cargo of the *Eglinton* included a range of pressed glass objects including bowls, mugs, milk jugs, egg cups, plates and salt cellars (Stanbury 2003:160–163). While this indicates that such goods were becoming available in Australia by mid-century, they do not seem to become numerous until the end of the century, as the households at Paradise and Port Albert had the greatest number and variety of pressed glass. Most of the households at Paradise had several decorative bowls while the Thomases at Port Albert also had a large quantity of pressed glass bowls, with fragments of at least eight different vessels present. The Paradise and Port Albert examples are all highly fragmentary, but such bowls could have held any number of things. If they were used at the table they might have held jams or jellies, butter, pickles or salads, extending the complexity and ornamentation of the meals served.

The glassware complemented the many ceramic tablewares in use. Archaeological analysis of tableware has emphasised ware types and patterns, and more recently has started to consider the vessels themselves, their variety of forms and whether they were part of matched sets. The literature on this even within Australia is substantial and readers are referred to Brooks (2005) for an extended discussion, but a few trends can be highlighted. The British settlement of Australia coincided with the English ceramic industry's introduction of inexpensive, good-quality white-bodied earthenwares, so that ceramics were always used here by all classes in preference to the older habits of using wooden, pewter, porcelain or tin-glazed earthenware dishes. Transfer prints were available from the beginning, in items for the table as well as for tea. Edge-decorated plates with a moulded rim and a band of blue or green were widespread until the 1830s, as were cheap and cheerful bowls and mugs decorated with industrial slipware designs such as mocha and cat's eye. These all occur in the early deposits at Cumberland/Gloucester Streets and at the Adventure Bay whaling stations. By the 1840s they had largely gone and most tablewares were decorated with transfer-printed designs. Of the 47 plates found at Lake Innes, occupied in the 1830s and 1840s, only two were shell edged, and there were none at Bean's Parsonage from the 1850s.

Along with the British white-bodied wares early colonists made use of porcelain manufactured in China for the export trade. Porcelain was a prominent part of the cargo of the *Sydney Cove*, and approximately 250 kg of fragments were excavated from the wreck site, all decorated with hand-painted designs in underglaze blue and overglaze polychrome "famille rose" patterns (Staniforth 2003:86–95; see Chapter 4). In addition to teawares and toiletry wares the assemblage included at least 182 dinner or soup plates and 48 octagonal hot-water dishes (plates with a reservoir beneath that held hot water for keeping the meal warm). Neither the dinnerwares nor the teawares seem to have been sent as sets, although matching services were being made in China by this time. Rather, the intention seems to be that they were to be sold individually. Until the work by Mark Staniforth and Mike Nash (Staniforth and Nash 1998) on the *Sydney Cove* assemblage, Chinese export porcelain was frequently misidentified during cataloguing, but it is now known to have occurred on a number of early settlement sites including First Government House and Lilyvale in Sydney, Elizabeth Farm and other sites in Parramatta, Norfolk Island, and Risdon Cove, Wapping, and the Private Secretaries Residence in Van Diemen's Land (Staniforth 2003:97). It has also been found at Adventure Bay, at Lake Innes, and at Bean's parsonage, and seems to have been in widespread use throughout the Australian colonies until at least the 1840s.

The most popular transfer-printed patterns have been Blue Willow, Rhine and Asiatic Pheasant, all of which occur frequently around Australia and were reasonably inexpensive to purchase. Blue Willow was one of the earliest transfer-printed designs available while Rhine was available from at least 1852 and Asiatic Pheasant from 1834. Later in the century other patterns become more common, including Fibre, Cable and Marble. Further study is needed to identify fashion trends on ceramics in Australia, similar to that done in the United States (Samford 1997). One trend that has become apparent is the lack of popularity here of the white granite patterns that dominated American markets from the 1850s (Lawrence 2003b:23–26). While Americans increasingly favoured plain white vessels with comparatively unobtrusive moulded decoration, Australia, along with other parts of the British Empire, continued to prefer colourful transfer prints. Research by Alasdair Brooks has shown that white granite appears in small quantities on Australian sites from ca. 1845–1890, and particularly those occupied in the 1860s (Brooks 2005:56–60). During this period the American Civil War interrupted the pottery trade to North America, leaving British manufacturers without access to their largest market. Exports to Australia increased significantly during this period and the implication drawn by Brooks is that manufacturers were dumping pottery in Australia that was intended for the American market. Archaeological evidence for this comes from Viewbank, where numerous white granite vessels in the Berlin Swirl pattern have been found. A maker's mark from the firm Liddle, Mayer and Elliot dates this to the period 1861–1862 when the Civil War was at its height. Berlin Swirl has been found at other sites, including Bean's parsonage, where it is evidence for a brief occupation after the Bean family left in 1859 and before the house burned down in 1861. Brooks notes, however, that as yet no white granite is known to have been found in Australia with marks that pre-date 1861.

At most sites for which minimum number and set information is available, a variety of patterns have been recovered, suggesting that laying a table with matching dishes was not always a priority (Table 11.3). The transfer-printed wares in the *Eglinton* cargo indicate something of the availability of sets. Some patterns, such as "Anemone", were available in multiple pieces that could have made up breakfast, dinner or tea services. Others, such as "Gothic Ruins", only had pieces for dinner services (Stanbury 2003:94–105). As with teawares, it is possible to compare dinnerwares found at Australian sites in order to trace the extent of matching sets and dinner services. Most sites considered had at least some dishes that were either part

Table 11.3 Tablewares from selected sites

	Matching	Serving vessels	Number of sets	Type of service
QLD-Kirkes	–	–	–	–
QLD-Turks	–	–	–	–
CuGl Glou 97 (1)	–	✓	–	–
CuGl Cara 003	–	✓	–	–
CuGl Cara 005	–	✓	–	–
CuGl Cumb 126	–	✓	–	–
CuGl Glou 93	–	✓	–	–
CuGl Glou 101	–	✓	–	–
QLD-Bartletts	✓	–	1c	–
QLD-Buzzas	✓	–	1c	–
QLD-Plastows	✓	–	1c	–
Dolly's Creek	✓	–	1c	–
Whaling	✓	–	2c	–
CuGl Cara 001	✓	✓	1	1t
CuGl Glou 97 (2)	✓	✓	1	1bf
QLD-McGonnells	✓	–	2	–
CuGl Cumb 122	✓	✓	2	2bf
QLD-McGhies	✓	–	2	1t, 1bf
CuGl Cumb 124	✓	✓	2	2bf
QLD-Shuttleworths	✓	✓	2	1bf, 1t
Pt Albert	✓	✓	5	1t, 7 bf
Pt Ad. McKays	✓	✓	6	3t, 2bf, 1d
Bean	✓	✓	7	5t, 2bf
Pt Ad. Farrows	✓	✓	10	4t, 6bf
Viewbank	✓	✓	30	8t, 1bf, 10d

c = complementary but not matching dishes; t = tea set; bf = breakfast set (plates and matching teawares); d = dinner set (plates and serving vessels) of the same set (matching exactly in ware and decoration) or that were complementary (pieces of a common pattern such as Willow that did not match but were close enough to pass as a set). The only exceptions were six of the Cumberland/Gloucester Streets sites and two of the Paradise households. Of those households with sets, most had sets that matched exactly and were probably purchased at the same time, although a few had complementary sets comprised of dishes in the same pattern but not an exact match. Based on the available data, it appears that the presence and number of sets is strongly associated with social status. Those with only complementary sets, which include three of the Paradise households, the households at Dolly's Creek and the whaling stations, are those sites most strongly identified with labouring or working-class people. These households also owned the smallest number of sets, most with only one each. At the whaling stations the sets consisted of plates in the Willow and shell edge patterns, both so common, inexpensive and widely available that it is likely they represent similar purchases by different men in the whaling gangs. The next group consists of those with matching sets but only one or two sets. This group includes the higher status Paradise families such as the Shuttleworths and the McGhies as well as the Winches at 124 Cumberland Street and three of their neighbours. The final group consists of those households which had a large number of sets, most of which matched and were probably purchased at one time, together with several complementary sets. The Thomas family at Port Albert had five sets and their friends the Beans had seven, while in Port Adelaide the McKays had six sets and the Farrows had ten. The Martins at Viewbank had no less than 30 sets.

Matching sets, particularly those that included serving vessels such as platters and tureens, as well as a variety of forms for each table setting, allowed the table to be laid with greater formality. This in turn created the opportunity to serve more complex meals and to engage in more elaborate rituals of etiquette. In New York, Diana di Zerega Wall and Robert Fitts have argued that in addition to the display of manners required at middle-class meals, having matching sets reinforced the bonds between family members who were dining together (Fitts 1999; Wall 1991). Such rituals were deeply embedded in the genteel habitus but they were less important among the labouring classes. For the working households in this sample, matching sets may have been used or not but it appears that a more important part of their dining ritual was the use of serving vessels. All of the Cumberland/Gloucester Streets assemblages included serving vessels of some kind, whether or not matching sets were present. It seems that symbolically distinguishing between food preparation and serving the meal was significant and required specialised dishes, even if the diners used unmatched plates. At Paradise only three of the households had serving vessels, all of which had matching sets as well, but six of the eight Paradise households had pressed glass dishes, so it may be that these served a similar function. Large serving dishes also played a decorative role in many working-class homes, where the kitchen dresser provided space for the prominent display of colourful dishes. Dressers were features of rural homes in the British Isles as well, and continued in use into the last decades of the twentieth century in both Australia and the United Kingdom (Webster 1999).

Tobacco

Taking tobacco, either as snuff, chewing tobacco or smoked in pipes or cigars, was a popular nineteenth-century indulgence. In Australia the most common archaeological evidence of tobacco use are fragments of moulded white kaolin (pipe clay) smoking pipes. Flasks and tins that contained snuff and spittoons associated with chewing tobacco have yet to be identified archaeologically here, although they have been found on sites in the United States and Canada (Reckner and Brighton 1999). This may be due in part to lack of expertise but it is also an indication of distinctive patterns of tobacco use in Australia. Historians of tobacco in Australia, Robin Walker and Ian Tyrell, have both noted that consumption patterns here differed markedly from those in the United States and the United Kingdom. While the majority of adult males in Australia used tobacco in the nineteenth century (some estimates put the figure as high as 80 percent), overwhelmingly they smoked it in pipes. Chewing tobacco never became popular, and while some snuff was taken in genteel circles, it was never as widespread as smoking tobacco. There is some evidence that the genteel preferred cigars as they did in Britain (Walker 1984:4, 29–30), but except for a few years during the gold rushes cigars never accounted for more than 10 percent of the tobacco market here. Tyrell argues from this that the popularity of the clay pipe was one mark among many of Australians' egalitarian attitudes (Tyrrell 1999:4–5). The relatively smaller consumption of cigars, which were also more expensive than pipe tobacco, certainly indicates that only a small proportion of the population adopted this as a mark of gentility. Cigarettes, first popularised as a result of the Crimean War in the 1850s, did not become a significant part of the Australian market until the 1890s, and even by the end of the century accounted for only 10 percent of the market. In the First World War the inclusion of cigarettes in the rations provided to soldiers paved the way for the dominance of this form of tobacco use.

In the United States tobacco became caught up in the temperance movement of the second half of the nineteenth century, and as native-born, middle-class white Americans were pressured to abandon the habit its use became part of the stereotypically degenerate behaviour assumed of (largely Irish and German) immigrants and the poor (Reckner and Brighton 1999:69). In Australia, where a large portion of the population was of Irish origin, the temperance movement generally was less persuasive, so these associations were less powerful and tobacco generally suffered less opprobrium, although its use was circumscribed by gender. While nearly all men smoked, tobacco use by women was strongly marked by distinctions of class and race. In the first half of the century convict and ex-convict women smoked pipes, a habit which some attributed to customs in Ireland and others claimed was fostered by the convict system itself (Walker 1984:11, 14). It was never socially permissible for genteel women to smoke, although taking snuff was one sign of gentility among both men and women. As the century progressed and convictism receded, it became less acceptable for white women of any class to smoke (Tyrrell 1999:6). As a strongly gendered activity smoking itself became a symbol of masculinity, hedged about by conventions that emphasised its male associations. Men did not smoke around women, so they withdrew to separate rooms or out-of-doors for a smoke after dinner, and the smoky atmosphere of pubs both kept women away and marked them as male spaces. In contrast, Aboriginal women used tobacco, as did Aboriginal men, and this was another sign of their separateness. Tobacco use was encouraged by missionaries and squatters alike as it was recognised that dependency could be used to manipulate behaviour (Walker 1984:15–17). The prohibition of tobacco only became part of the moral reform agenda around the turn of the twentieth century, and then only because the growing popularity of cigarettes in the 1890s made smoking more accessible to juveniles and there were fears it would stunt their growth (Tyrrell 1999:16–33).

Against this background of custom and use it is unsurprising that fragments of clay tobacco pipes have been found so often on Australian sites. They have received less attention than other forms of ceramics, but analysts have pointed to several areas in which closer study of pipe fragments can inform us about colonial behaviour and culture. The primary concerns of early clay pipe studies were to establish descriptive typologies and identify manufacturers (Dane and Morrison 1979; Wilson and Kelly 1987). Reviewing some of the early assemblages, Ian Jack (1986a) identified the importance of Scottish manufacturers in supplying the Australian market, and this dominance has subsequently been confirmed by the study of pipes from other sites (Courtney 1998:127). A demolition deposit at First Government House in Sydney, dating to the 1850s, was unusual as it contained a significant quantity of pipes of Dutch origin (Wilson and Kelly 1987:5–6). Gojak and Stuart (1999) extended this work to outline directions for further research, including closer studies of pipes made either in Australia or specifically for the colonial market, the role of pipes as markers of ethnicity, pipe use by Aboriginal people, and the potential for more finely detailed chronologies. They refer specifically to the issue of rates of consumption and the life-cycle of clay pipes, which Kris Courtney also identified with her observations about usewear on the pipes from Little Lon (Courtney 1998:126).

Before any of these issues can be discussed the methodology of clay pipe analysis must be considered. One of the earliest analytical approaches to clay pipes was as an aid to dating (Binford 1978; Harrington 1978; Oswald 1961). The form of the pipes, and more importantly the diameter of the pipe stem holes, was found to change regularly through time and these have been used extensively to date assemblages in North America and the United Kingdom from the seventeenth and eighteenth centuries. By the nineteenth century, however, both the form and the stem hole diameter of pipes had largely stabilised, meaning that neither method has proven useful in the Australian context. After Jim Allen's pioneering work at Port Essington in the 1960s in which he used the Harrington/Binford method to get dates up to 70 years too early (Allen 2008:77), analysts here have tended to ignore these methods, concentrating instead on decoration and manufacturers. Approaches to quantifying the numbers of pipes in an assemblage is also an issue that has received some attention (Bradley 2000:126; Dane and Morrison 1979:2–3; Gibbs 1995:274; Lawrence 2006b:380). As with glass and other ceramic forms, the fragility of pipes results in large quantities of fragments that can make it difficult to determine the number of complete objects represented in an assemblage. This in turn can obscure data on use and disposal on sites. Ideally, minimum pipe counts will be established using diagnostic features, either the stem/bowl junction or the mouthpiece. Allen used a combination of bore diameter and assumed an average stem length at Port Essington in order to arrive at a minimum number, but this technique was not widely adopted (Allen 2008:76).

Pipes were made in New South Wales from 1804, and pipes made by Joseph Elliot of Market Wharf have been found on sites in Tasmania as well as in New South Wales. The Sydney tobacco merchant Hugh Dixson had pipes made to order by Scottish manufacturers, and his pipes have been found in Victoria, Tasmania and New South Wales. Robyn Stocks (2008) has analysed a number of distinctive reed-stem pipes with carved facetted bowls excavated from early sites in Sydney and Parramatta and believes that they are the product of Sydney potter Thomas Ball (ca. 1800–1823). At Cadman's Cottage in Sydney Gojak found a large number of "Irish" dudeen pipes with thick walls and rouletted rims, several of which had Irish slogans such as shamrocks, "ERIN GO BRAGH" (Ireland Forever), and "Cork" moulded on them. The assemblage dates to the 1860s and 1870s when the site was used as part of the Sydney Sailors' Home and Gojak suggests that the pipes may reflect the nationalism and sectarianism then prevalent among the large Irish-born component of the workforce in the colonial maritime and transport industry (Gojak 1995; Gojak and Stuart 1999:45).

Other patterns of use may be associated with institutional settings, where tobacco played (and continues to play) an important role as one of the few indulgences available to inmates. Walker discusses the ways in which prison authorities attempted to control access to tobacco as part of the system of rewards and punishments, and how this was subverted by the prisoners who used tobacco as a form of currency. It may not be a coincidence then that three of the largest assemblages of clay pipes in Australia are from institutional contexts. The prisoners' barracks at Port Arthur had 1,055 fragments representing a minimum number of 188 pipes (Dane and Morrison 1979), the convict hospital at Parramatta had at least 1,148 pipes (Stocks 2008:41), and Hyde Park Barracks in Sydney, used first to house male convicts and then as a home for destitute women, had 4,105 fragments, possibly the largest assemblage in the country (Davies 2011; Table 11.4). Almost one third of the Hyde Park Barracks pipes were from deposits associated primarily with elderly and destitute women, providing strong evidence for smoking among lower-class women in Australia into the 1880s. Casella also found clay pipe fragments at the Ross Female Factory in Tasmania (Casella 2001a:33). These were concentrated in the solitary cells area of the prison, where the removal of privileges such as tobacco was part of the punishment, leading Casella to argue that the clay pipes are indicative of a clandestine economy of resistance among the prisoners.

Pipes were also numerous, though in smaller quantities, on whaling sites in Tasmania and at Cheyne Beach in Western Australia, all places of work for labouring men (Gibbs 1995:274–275; Lawrence 2006b:155, 162). The military encouraged tobacco use as a means of alleviating strain and inuring men against dreadful conditions, and colonial employers also appreciated those qualities. Despite the

Table 11.4 Total number of clay pipe fragments from selected sites

	Total fragments
Qld Shuttleworths	1
Qld Kirkes	1
Qld Buzzas	1
Lake Innes Site 9	2
Qld Turks	2
Qld McGhies	3
Viewbank	4[a]
Port Albert	6[a]
Qld McGonnells	6
Bean	18
Ross Female Factory	27[a]
Dolly's Creek	42
Lake Innes Site 7	59
Lake Innes Site 2	70
CuGl Glou 97	84
Lake Innes Site 3	126
CuGl Glou 101	148
CuGL Cumb 124	148
Lake Innes Site 5	163
CuGl Cribbs 4	178
CuGl Glou 93	184
CuGl Cumb 128	213
Lagoon Bay	223
Lake Innes Site 6	267
CuGl Cara 003	268
CuGl Cara 001	332
Cheyne Beach	411
First Government House demolition	447
Camp Street Ballarat	544
Adventure Bay	655
Port Arthur Prisoners Barracks	1,055
Convict Hospital Parramatta	1,148
CuGl Cara 005	2,165
Hyde Park Barracks	4,105

[a]indicates sites recorded with minimum number of pipes

large military presence in the convict colonies as British regiments did tours of guard duty, there have been few excavations of military sites, so the smoking habits of colonial soldiers cannot be assessed. Although a substantial collection of clay pipes was recovered from the marines' settlement at Port Essington, Jim Allen argues that based on the dating evidence of the pipes some at least should be attributed to the 1870s cattle stations in the area (Allen 2008:77). All of these institutional and working sites have greater quantities of pipes than assemblages from domestic sites. Directly comparable figures are difficult to obtain, but most of the households Graham Wilson (1999) identified at Cumberland/Gloucester Streets had fewer than 200 pipe fragments each, while the sites at Lake Innes occupied by convict and ticket-of-leave workers had even smaller assemblages with between 60 and 260 fragments (Connah 2007). Only 42 fragments in total were recovered from Dolly's Creek, but the risks of smoking down the mines meant that miners were more likely to take their tobacco as snuff (Walker 1984:15–17). At Paradise there were less than two dozen pipe fragments in total, but this may also reflect the popularity of cigarettes by that time. Tellingly, however, the sites that had more genteel ceramic assemblages, the Thomases and the Beans in Gippsland and the Martins at Viewbank, also had very small assemblages of clay pipes, with only four pipes represented at Viewbank, nine at the Beans and six at the Thomases.

The archaeological distribution of clay pipe fragments reflects the cultural patterns of smoking behaviour. By and large people did not smoke pipes in their homes, women because they generally did not smoke at all and men because they did not smoke pipes or they smoked elsewhere. Middle-class men may have smoked cigars in dedicated smoking rooms away from the women of the household while working-class men smoked out-of-doors. Men of all classes smoked in pubs and clubs and while at work. Men and women in institutions smoked a great deal, sometimes in secret, as a means of dealing with boredom, of resisting authority and of obtaining some fleeting pleasure in a grim situation.

Some indication of individual consumption rates is provided by employment contracts in the whaling industry. Station owners and ships' captains made tobacco available from the "slops", a system of credit purchase used during the whaling season for personal items such as clothing and toiletries (see Chapter 5). At the end of the season the men's debts were deducted from their pay, and the resulting documents record individual consumption habits. The records make no mention of the pipes themselves, which must have been either supplied by the men or provided free with the tobacco, as they sometimes were in pubs. On James Kelly's ship the *Amity* in 1841, a pound (500 g) of tobacco cost three shillings and sixpence, which lasted most men between 6 and 8 weeks (Lawrence 2006b:121). Store accounts from pastoral stations around Armidale in New South Wales also provide insight into consumption rates. In that area, six and a half ounces of tobacco lasted about 3 weeks, which is similar to the whalers. A pipe lasted about 3 weeks as well, suggesting that the whalers would have needed two or three pipes for their pound of tobacco (Walker 1984:15–17). Staining on the Hyde Park Barracks pipes also sheds light on consumption habits. Davies (2010) found that 88 percent of the bowls from the deposits associated with male convicts and later visitors to the Barracks showed only light staining, consistent with use of short duration. In contrast, almost two-thirds of the bowls from the women in the destitute asylum showed heavy blackening inside and out, while several had also been repaired (Fig. 11.6). This reflects careful curation and intensive use among women who had only limited opportunities to replace lost or broken pipes. The pipes from the early phases of the Parramatta convict hospital, a period when pipes were scarce in the colony, likewise show signs of heavy use (Stocks 2008).

Excavations at Casselden Place recovered part of what has been interpreted as a grocer's stock (Williamson 2004c:197–198). It is a large batch of broken stems and bowls, all apparently unused and restricted to only three forms. It was recovered

Fig. 11.6 Heavily used and stained clay tobacco pipe from the Hyde Park Barracks Destitute Asylum in Sydney, occupied between 1862 and 1886 (photo P. Davies)

from subfloor deposits in a back room of the building, possibly where the broken fragments were swept when the batch was dropped. The shop occupied a building called Cornwall's Corner at the intersection of Lonsdale and Little Leichardt Streets. Nearly all the pipes recovered from the site that can be dated to its use as a grocery (1874–1882) have been attributed to Duncan McDougall of Glasgow, indicating that the grocer dealt exclusively with this firm either directly or through a wholesaler. Pipes identical in form and decoration to those recovered from the shop have been found elsewhere on the Casselden Place site, but only from allotments along Little Leichardt Street. Christine Williamson suggests that this shows the purchasing habits of local residents who bought their pipes and tobacco at the corner shop. Another bulk collection of identical pipes was recovered from the site of the *Eglinton* (1852) off the coast of Western Australia (Stanbury 2003:128–129). Myra Stanbury identified fragments of at least 124 pipes with a distinctive oak leaf and acorn pattern, a motif favoured by London manufacturers. The stems are unmarked but the initials "H" and "C" on the spur suggest that they were made by Hannah Cox, who was making pipes from at least 1832 to 1853. It is clear that the analysis of the distribution and use of clay pipes has considerable potential to shed new light on Australian smoking habits.

Dress and Ornament

Clothing is intimately tied to social identity, conforming to and signalling codes of behaviour shaped by gender, status and ethnicity. Clothing is highly recyclable and carefully curated, so it leaves only a few archaeological traces, most notably buttons and other fastening devices, sometimes footwear, and in rare circumstances fabric. Tools used to make clothing such as pins, needles and other needlework items are also found and occasionally pieces of jewellery. For the most part these are objects that have been lost rather than worn out or deliberately thrown away, and they enter the archaeological record accidentally between floorboards or in corners of yards. Documentary sources are generally much more informative about the history of dress, but the archaeological record of clothing-related items can be revealing of behaviour, pointing to the gender and status of site occupants, sometimes to occupations and hobbies, and sometimes to patterns of activity on sites as well.

Buttons are perhaps the most common clothing-related item recovered, but they are not numerous in most assemblages so few have been studied in detail. Sam George analysed buttons from the Prisoners' Barracks at Port Arthur, comparing them to the slightly earlier buttons from the Tasmanian whaling stations (George 1999). She found the buttons were simple and sturdy sew-through forms in bone and wood, reflecting the plain clothes of men accustomed to hard manual labour. On the whaling sites there were also many bronze shanked buttons, possibly because this was a durable material that could withstand the wet conditions that the whalers frequently experienced. In Parramatta Robyn Stocks (2008) has documented blanks used in the local manufacture of bone buttons similar to some of those analysed by George. Jennie Lindbergh analysed an assemblage from late nineteenth-century households at the CSR site in Sydney (Lindbergh 1999). Here too most of the buttons were plain sew-through varieties in mother-of-pearl, bone and copper-alloy and represent the kinds of buttons used on underwear, shirts and children's clothing. Some fancier black glass buttons were used on men's waistcoats while pressed copper-alloy buttons with inscriptions such as "Best Ring Edge" and "Excelsior" were probably used on trousers or suspenders of men's work clothing.

The distribution of button types within the CSR site was also revealing. The remains of eight two-storey brick houses were excavated, all with two or three rooms on the ground floor. All of the houses had large quantities of buttons when compared with other excavated Sydney sites, from around 70 to nearly 400 buttons in each assemblage. In each case the majority of the buttons were recovered from the kitchen area, and particularly from clusters around the hearth and in front of the windows. Dressmaking pins and thimbles were also found in the assemblages. Mary Casey, who excavated the site, has interpreted this pattern as the result of women using the kitchens for sewing (Casey 2004). She compared the distribution of artefacts between the houses to examine the possibility of commercial sewing, that is, piecework employment by a seamstress or tailor rather than normal household sewing. She found that while all the kitchens had more sewing items than other parts of the houses, one house in particular had much larger assemblages of buttons, beads and hooks-and-eyes, as well as pins. Where most of the other houses had less than 100 pins, House 15 had more than 1,500, and where most had less than a dozen hooks-and-eyes, House 15 had over 100. Casey argues that the quantity, variety and distribution of sewing goods in this house, which also included more specialised tools, is strong evidence for commercial sewing activity. She also notes that such a conclusion is only possible because of the opportunity in this case to compare the distribution of artefacts between several households.

When Lilyvale, a site of six terrace houses in the Rocks, was excavated in 1989 more than 4,000 sewing-related items were found, including pins, thimbles, thread-winders, bodkins and needles but not including buttons and other clothing items (Lydon 1993b). At the time of excavation the director, Wendy Thorpe, and Jane Lydon, who analysed the sewing artefacts, believed that sampling methods and taphonomic factors probably accounted for the quantity and distribution patterns of sewing artefacts, most of which were found in two houses. Now that more sites have been excavated around Australia and it is possible to compare patterns more broadly, the distinctive nature of the Lilyvale assemblage is apparent and does seem to suggest professional sewing activity.

At Paradise Kate Quirk was also able to compare distributions between houses, enabling her to identify distinctive patterning in the clothing-related artefacts. The Plastows were cobblers and had the largest number of heel-plates from boots or shoes. An unusually large collection of hooks and eyes and the largest collection of buttons lead Quirk to argue that someone in the McGonnells' household may have been taking in laundry. However, the assemblage at the Bartlett house, where Catherine Bartlett worked as a dressmaker, is relatively modest and does not seem to reflect her occupation at all when compared with those of her neighbours. The assemblage that stands out for Quirk is that of the Turks, which had the largest and most varied range of dress artefacts related to women, which included decorative glass buttons, a hat pin, a purse frame and two brooches. Quirk suggests that this reflects Alice Turk's attention to her wardrobe as a measure of the family's genteel status. She argues that this was a strategic investment for a middle-class family who owned a quartz-crushing battery and had an itinerant goldfields lifestyle that would have made it more difficult to maintain other, less portable genteel equipment such as tea sets and household ornaments (Quirk 2008b:236–238).

Grace Karskens and Nadia Iacono analysed the assemblage of clothing and jewellery items from the Cumberland/Gloucester Streets site, drawing attention to the ways in which men in the Rocks were also accentuating their appearance in the late nineteenth century (Iacono 1999; Karskens 1999:160–161). The assemblage included pocket watches and the Albert chains used to attach them to waistcoats, elaborate collar studs and solitaires (a more decorative style of cuff-link), and even non-prescription eyeglasses that must have been worn purely to lend a more dignified appearance. A similar range of men's fashion accessories was recovered in Melbourne at Casselden Place. Barney Mezey's analysis of the jewellery items from Casselden Place indicates that the assemblage contains a higher proportion of valuable and fashionable pieces than comparable sites in Sydney (Mezey 2005:86–87). In particular, articles of men's and women's jewellery made of gold and semi-precious stones were more common at Casselden Place, suggesting a higher disposable income and/or greater access to good-quality items, both possibly a legacy of the gold rush. It seems the women at Casselden Place had different taste in jewellery too, as both brooches and jet mourning jewellery were more popular at Casselden Place than in the Rocks.

Whole and fragmentary pieces of leather footwear are another clothing-related item found on many sites. Footwear has not received a great deal of attention archaeologically, but changes in manufacturing techniques and fashion have the potential to reveal information about dates, social status and income levels (Veres 2005). Hand-made footwear had given way to mechanised mass production by the end of the nineteenth century, but repairs continued to be made by hand. Analysis of an assemblage of leather from the Lysterfield Boys Farm in outer Melbourne, dating from 1935 to 1946, showed that while the boots were machine-made, repairs were done locally and probably by the boys themselves as part of their training in trades (Veres 2005:95). Both the Cumberland/Gloucester Streets and Casselden Place leather assemblages also include both repaired shoes and parts of shoes and leather scraps to indicate home-made repairs (Bower 1999:127; Porter and Ferrier 2004:334).

Needlework tools such as dressmaking pins, thimbles, scissors and bobbins all provide evidence for the daily work of making and repairing clothing and household linen. These tasks, as well as decorative needlework such as embroidery and lace-making, were central to the construction of female identity in the nineteenth century. Men also worked as tailors and several were listed among the residents at Cumberland/Gloucester Streets and at Casselden Place, but sewing was more closely associated with women. Poor women worked as seamstresses, taking in piecework to earn an income or making lace or beadwork for sale. Women at the Hyde Park Barracks Destitute Asylum sewed their own clothing and bed linen. An assemblage of almost 7,000 sewing-related items, including pins and needles, cotton reels, thimbles, bobbins, crochet hooks and textile fragments, suggests the scale and range of work done by women in the institution. Most of the work was done by hand-stitching, although the purchase of two second-hand sewing machines, in 1878 and 1880, made some of the work a little easier. Strands of plaited straw, and a palm-leaf shredding tool, indicate that hat-making was also practised in the Asylum (Crook and Murray 2006:72–76).

More affluent women had the leisure time to produce fancywork, embroidering, crocheting, and beading the cushion-covers, lampshades, tablecloths and antimacassars that adorned the fashionable Victorian drawing room. Many scholars have traced the connections between needlework, femininity and social class (e.g. Beaudry 2006a:4–5; Kingston 1977:102; Lydon 1993b:129; Maynard 1994:127; Parker 1984:11; Russell 1994:97–98). Before mechanisation around 1850, hand-sewing was a necessity, and all young girls, regardless of status, were instructed in its mysteries. It represented a respectable source of income for the poor and a productive occupation for the genteel for whom work was morally fulfilling and to be idle was anathema. Mary Casey and Kate Quirk have used distribution patterns of buttons and sewing objects to identify households where needlework may have been a source of income, but the assemblage from Viewbank shows the material culture of sewing in a more leisured household.

Lucy Martin and her five daughters used sewing tools that were remarkably similar to those used by the women in inner Melbourne and the Rocks. If the Martin women had ornamental thimbles in precious metals or with inscriptions, these have not entered the archaeological record. Those recovered are plain copper-alloy forms, including one child-sized thimble used by one of the girls when she was young. In comparison, the thimbles at Lilyvale were highly decorated. More than 63 thimbles were found among the six houses at the site, bearing inscriptions that urged good behaviour, such as "Reward for Industry", celebrated events and popular personalities such as "Princess Royal" and "Heroes of England", and more sentimental messages like "Forget Me Not" and "I Love You" that suggest tokens given to friends or lovers (Lydon 1993b:132). The utilitarian thimbles and needles at Viewbank could have been used by the Martin women or by their servants in dress-making and plain sewing tasks. Other items indicate that some of the needlework done by the Martins was of a more decorative nature. Three lace-making bobbins were found and one flat bone needle of the kind used in netting or doily-making. Bobbins have also been found at inner-city sites but in much smaller proportions. At Casselden Place the ratio of bobbins to pins is 1:92, while at Viewbank it is 1:28, suggesting that proportionately more time was spent by the Martin women on decoration than on plain sewing.

Health and Hygiene

Medical treatment was a grim business during much of the nineteenth century. Scientific understanding of disease was limited, and doctors relied for treatment on purging, bleeding and heavy doses of drugs. Wealthy patients were treated at home, while hospitals were the resort of the poorest and most desperate. At the Melbourne Hospital, the screams and cries of patients could be heard by anyone on the streets outside (Pensabene 1980:23). European-trained doctors competed with homeopaths, herbalists, Chinese and Indian medical men and various "quacks" for authority to treat the sick (Martyr 2002). The bacteriological discoveries of Louis Pasteur and Robert Koch in the 1860s and 1870s, however, led to a greater understanding of disease, especially in relation to public health and surgery. Better control of water and food-borne diseases and the advent of antiseptic surgery resulted in dramatic decreases in mortality rates. Anaesthesia and antiseptics gradually altered the community's perception of hospitals from slaughterhouses to life-saving institutions. By the early twentieth century almost every organ of the human body was subject to surgery. In less than a century, medicine had moved from its medieval origins to something recognisably modern.

Archaeological material has the potential to provide valuable insight into private responses to illness, medicine and hygiene. Medicine containers, for example, are common on archaeological sites from the nineteenth century, especially for patent and proprietary medicines. Today labels such as "Mrs Winslow's Soothing Syrup" and "Pink Pills for Pale People" may sound comical, but in the absence of effective medical treatment for most ailments, people sought whatever means they could to help themselves. Hundreds of balsams, elixirs, essences, remedies and tonics were commercially available, many containing substantial, even dangerous, quantities of alcohol and opium (British Medical Association 1909; Finch 1999). Building on work at Five Points in New York City (Bonasera and Rayner 2001), Kirsty Graham identified the types of ailments claimed to be treated by products advertised in the Melbourne *Argus* newspaper between 1850 and 1900 (Graham 2005). She found that one third of all advertisements recorded were for "cure-alls", compounds that claimed to cure many complaints from respiratory problems to digestion, and even cancer. Of the products aimed at more specific complaints, gastrointestinal treatments were the most numerous, followed by those that treated joint problems, chronic diseases, respiratory infections, "female irregularities", nerve problems, and treatments for infants and children.

Matching the medicine container with the ailment it claimed to treat can shed light on the lives of the inhabitants of archaeological sites. The deposit at 124 Cumberland Street in the Rocks contained an unusual concentration of pharmaceutical vessels, which included at least four identical light blue, wide-mouthed bottles made by the Aire and Calder glassworks in Castleford, England, and believed to contain Epsom salts (Carney 1999b). Penny Crook and Tim Murray have suggested that these bottles may have been purchased in an effort to treat one of the residents of the house, George Puzey (Murray and Crook 2005:99–100, 104). Epsom salts were taken in the nineteenth century as both a laxative and as a treatment for dysentery and rheumatism. Puzey, a 36-year-old labourer with a young family, died at the Tarban Creek Lunatic Asylum in 1863. For a year before his death he had suffered from seizures or fits of some kind, probably caused by his work at the Gas Works. His case notes at the Asylum indicate that he and his wife had been trying desperately to treat his condition at home, and the Epsom salts bottles are almost certainly related to that treatment.

As medical knowledge improved and the public health movement successfully achieved stricter regulation of patent medicines, many of the popular nineteenth-century nostrums disappeared. Evidence from Henry's Mill, however, indicates that people continued to treat themselves in the early twentieth century, particularly when living in isolated or remote areas where medical help could be distant or expensive (Davies 2001). Davies excavated fragments of at least 35 patent or proprietary medicine bottles from the site, including examples of D B Jenner's Cough Balsam, Mother Siegel's Syrup and Wood's Great Peppermint Cure. Most of the bottles were advertised to cure chest infections and assist with infants' and children's ailments, suggesting the dominant health concerns at the site. There were also glass phials and small bottles that appear to have contained homeopathic preparations. Chests of homeopathic medicines could be purchased by mail order, along with instruction booklets and homeopathic guide-books to "self-health". These artefacts reveal how individuals and families at the mill responded when illness struck. In a cold and wet environment, with doctors and hospitals simply too far away, people could often do little more than dose themselves and their children with commercial remedies and hope for the best.

Personal hygiene was always important in colonial Australia, and became more so as the implications of germ theory became increasingly well known. Early combs were made of organic materials and might not be expected to survive archaeologically, but several wooden and tortoiseshell comb fragments have been found from pre-1835 deposits at the Cumberland/Gloucester Streets site (Iacono 1999). After the invention of vulcanite (hard rubber) in 1839, combs were mass-produced in this material, and Nadia Iacono notes that most combs at the site come from post-1850s deposits. Lice combs in archaeological assemblages are sometimes taken to indicate lack of cleanliness, but tools to get rid of them clearly suggest concern for hygiene rather than lack of it. Iacono notes that while some nit combs are present at Cumberland and Gloucester Streets, most combs are standard grooming aids. At Casselden Place a range of clothes and hair brushes were recovered in addition to men's and women's combs, decorative hair combs and nit combs (Porter and Ferrier 2004:334–337). Again, most were of vulcanite or other manufactured material and were probably inexpensive. They were found in all parts of the site, indicating that they were in general use.

Toothbrushes are less common at both sites, but as they were generally made of bone it may be that poor preservation is an issue. At Casselden Place 29 toothbrushes were found and only 16 at Cumberland and Gloucester Streets, leading Iacono to suspect that this might be one of the boundaries of personal hygiene for Rocks residents. Unfortunately at present it is not possible at either site to compare evidence for toothbrushes with information about toothpastes and powders, which were commercially available in highly decorative ceramic containers. It is possible that sticks or even fingers could be used to apply the powders, but it may also be that tooth brushing was one of the behaviours that marked out the middle classes. At Viewbank the Martins' tip produced 16 toothbrushes, equal to the quantity from the whole of Cumberland and Gloucester Streets. Only one toothpaste jar was recovered, which seems an inadequate amount of toothpaste for such a lot of toothbrushes.

Washbasins, ewers and chamber pots are also important for the maintenance of personal hygiene. A large portion of the porcelain artefacts excavated from the *Sydney Cove* (1797) cargo consisted of toiletry items. Globular bottles for holding washing water, chamber pots and lids, and fragments of deep basins or washbowls all have matching patterns and appear to have been intended to form sets (Staniforth and Nash 1998:21). Transfer-printed ewers, hand basins and chamber pots also formed part of the *Eglinton*'s (1852) cargo, although the excavated examples are not part of matched sets (Stanbury 2003:121–122).

Washbasins, soap dishes and pitchers were found from every phase at the Cumberland/Gloucester Streets site, with toothpaste containers appearing from the 1860s (Wilson 1999:322). At Casselden Place nearly 400 fragments of chamber pots were found, but only 38 fragments of washbowls. Both forms would have been available in tin and enamel as well as ceramic, but the quantities of chamber pots in particular suggest that these were necessary pieces of household equipment. There were also fragments of soap dishes and toiletry boxes to assist with keeping clean. Records from South Australian insolvency cases indicate that by the 1850s most people felt that toiletry sets and washstands were possessions they could not do without (Young 1992:18). Once again the Viewbank assemblage points to the ways the genteel Martin family was able to take general practices one step further. Three ewers and four chamber pots were recovered from the site. The ewers and one of the chamber pots were in a matching transfer-printed flown-black "Marble" pattern, and suggest that the bedrooms had matching toiletry sets (Hayes 2008:332–333).

Childhood

By the nineteenth century it was generally understood that childhood was a discrete phase of life that was distinct from adulthood. Children needed protection and nurturing through their early years in preparation for adult responsibilities. Toys, games and educational equipment played an important role in this process, with mass production making these goods more widely and cheaply available as time went on. Archaeologists are now more aware of the interpretive potential of the range of childhood-related items recovered from Australian sites. Peter Davies and Adrienne Ellis (2005:15) remind us that even children in literate society produce few written records of their own, and material culture used by children presents a unique source of information about childhood from the child's point of view. At the same time, however, many items that archaeologists identify with childhood were acquired for children by adults and reflect adult views of what was appropriate. Drawing a parallel with early studies of gender, Joanna Derevenski (2000:8–11) notes that archaeologists have tended to overlook children if no identifiable "child" artefacts are present. This ignores the agency of children in negotiating and manipulating all categories of material culture, including spatial relationships within a site.

Although not archaeologically obvious, children were present at many of the sites we excavate and were highly visible in homes and public spaces. Children were numerous in early convict society, to the surprise of some observers, accounting for more than a third of the population in the Rocks in the early 1820s (Karskens 1997:106). Little schooling was available in this period, and most children had entered the workforce by around 12 years of age, although children as young as 7 or 8 were useful workers on farms (Kociumbas 1997:46–51; Molony 2000:68). Despite their large and welcome presence, Grace Karskens notes that there were relatively few child-related items recovered from the early deposits at Cumberland and Gloucester Streets, particularly when compared with the abundance found later in the century (Karskens 1999:56–57). There were some limestone marbles and a few pieces of ceramic dolls, but little else, and Karskens speculates that this may be one of several areas in which Rocks residents followed more traditional, pre-modern practices. Parents in the Rocks were not averse to spending money on other goods such as china and clothing, so the lack of spending on toys reflects a more pragmatic form of affection that centred on the provision of food, shelter, clothing and training.

By the second half of the nineteenth century toys and other goods for children were common in the deposits (Karskens 1999:179). This included dolls and tiny tea sets, lead soldiers, horses and carriages, and more than 800 marbles made of stone, porcelain, glass and terracotta (Iacono 1999:76–77). Game pieces including dice, dominoes and chess pieces could have been used by adults or children, but small thimbles and a ring were meant for children's hands and ornaments featuring figures from nursery rhymes were probably meant for children too. Children also had the use of special tableware, mugs, soup plates, bowls and side dishes bearing instructional text such as "lessons for youth on Industry, Temperance and Frugality" or with the letters of the alphabet (Wilson 1999:316). A similar range of goods was found at Casselden place and in apparently similar quantities (Porter and Ferrier 2004:295).

Dolls and toy soldiers seem emblematic of "good" girls and "rough" boys, and Laurie Wilkie (2000) has discussed the ways that childhood items may have been used by parents to reinforce ideal roles based on gender as well as socio-economic status and race. The overtly didactic tone of the moralising china certainly supports this interpretation. Davies and Ellis, however, note that advertising material did not ascribe gender or even age to toys such as tea sets, marbles and guns until the first quarter of the twentieth century (Davies and Ellis 2005:16).

The Martin family at Viewbank included five daughters and one son, and the toys could have been used by all of them. For the most part the childhood-related items at Viewbank are very similar to those of Casselden Place and Cumberland and Gloucester Streets. Robert (Willy) Martin had a bone china mug with "Robert" written in gilt letters, and one of the children had a similar mug with the words "A Pres[ent]...for//A good [boy/girl]..." (Hayes 2008:162). There were marbles and a toy gun, dolls and a small tea set, as well as dominoes, a die and gaming pieces (Hayes 2008:255–257, 319). The dolls are expensive and at least some appear to have been made in the 1860s, suggesting that they were bought for the Martin girls as teenagers.

By the first years of the twentieth century toys were less expensive and even more numerous than at earlier sites, blurring the boundaries between middle-class and working-class play that Rebecca Yamin has described in New York and New Jersey (Yamin 2002). When the Coach and Horses Hotel at Ringwood, in the hills east of Melbourne, burnt down in 1908, the publican's daughter, little Mary Ellen O'Meara, lost no less than 16 dolls, five more than were recovered from the whole of Casselden Place (A. Barker 2007:66). She also lost six tea sets while her four brothers lost at least eight sets of marbles and the baby lost three glass infant feeders. Anita Barker concludes that although the family was far from well-off, the cost of toys had fallen so much that even good-quality dolls imported from Germany were within the means of most people (Barker 2007:82). Dolls were advertised by a number of retailers at threepence for a china-headed doll and three shillings for a jointed doll with sleeping eyes. Tea sets, skipping ropes, bags of marbles and rubber balls could also be had for only a few pence, equivalent to the cost of a loaf of bread.

The children at Paradise enjoyed an equally wide range of toys. The Bartlett children were adult in age but six of the seven households with younger children had toys, moralising china, or writing slates and slate pencils, and most had several types of items. The Paradise children had china head dolls and fine tea sets and, like the O'Meara children, sought out the round glass stoppers from Codd-style soda water bottles to use as marbles. All the households, with the exception of the Plastows and the Bartletts, had writing materials, i.e. slate boards and pencils, indicating the importance placed on education among the hard-working parents of this town in which evangelical Protestantism was a dominant force. Toys and slates were also numerous at Henry's Mill, occupied between 1904 and 1927 (Davies and Ellis 2005; see Chapter 8). Each of the three houses excavated had either slate pencils or toys or both, with two of the houses each having nearly 40 child-related items. Again, the dolls and some of the marbles were high-quality and relatively expensive, indicating the value that parents placed on obtaining toys that would please their children.

Abundant as these toys seem to have been, they represent only a fraction of the playthings probably used by children on these sites. Organic materials such as wooden trains, skipping ropes and rag dolls would not survive archaeologically, while the potential for play in other, mundane household objects is lost to adult eyes. Claudia Haagen (1994) has documented a wide range of toys traditionally used by Aboriginal children, most of which are made of organic materials and would leave no archaeological trace. Peter Davies was able to use oral histories to recapture some of the play activities at Henry's Mill, which included "kick the can" and building cubby houses in the bush, making fishing nets from old flywire screens and bows and arrows from green sticks. It was these toys they had made themselves, in fact, whose loss was most keenly felt when the mill burnt out in 1927 (Davies 2006a:81–82). More subtle traces of artefact associations and spatial patterning can also give clues to the activities of children. At Dolly's Creek there were no overt signs of children but the evidence of subsistence food gathering in the faunal remains is probably an indication of children's work in hunting rabbits, herding goats and collecting eggs (Lawrence 2000:94). Laurie Wilkie found evidence of a similar household reliance on children's subsistence labour among enslaved families in the Bahamas (Wilkie 2000:108–109).

An unusual distribution of spoons found at Moran's Farm near Melrose in South Australia is also probably the result of children playing (Lawrence 2001b). Six silver-plated teaspoons were recovered from the subfloor deposits of the house, which seemed a large number to accidentally lose in a farmhouse that was only occupied between 1880 and 1915 and had an otherwise unremarkable assemblage (Fig. 11.7). An elderly informant later revealed that when he was young he got into trouble for poking his mother's spoons down behind the skirting boards, and it is quite likely that this is what one of the nine young Moran girls was doing. There is nothing unusual about the spoons themselves and it is only the chance of their strange context that marks them out as temporary playthings. The girls had a good collection of store-bought toys including tea sets, dolls, marbles and one of the newly invented teddy bears, but they had other treasures too. Also found at the site was a copper token given to school children in 1900 to mark the departure of colonial troops for the South African War. One of the girls had punched a hole in the token so it could be worn on a chain around her neck.

Some writing materials, particularly slate pencils and writing slates, have been commonly identified with children and are widespread on Australian sites (Davies 2005c). They were inexpensive at a time when most paper was imported and costly, and partly for that reason they were a central part of the education process in schools.

Fig. 11.7 Teaspoons and tablewares recovered from Moran's Farm, South Australia (photo S. Lawrence)

In 1911, retailer Anthony Hordern and Sons advertised boxes of 100 slate pencils for only 4½ pence, while a 5 × 7 inch writing slate cost only 2 pence. In schools, monitors distributed slates and pencils at the beginning of the day and collected them again at the end, but as Davies notes, worn pencil stubs could easily fall through floor cracks and be lost. This may be one reason why fragments of slate pencils are so much more common on most sites than are fragments of slates. By the end of the nineteenth century it was recognised that the common schoolroom practice of spitting on slates and wiping them with a sleeve was a good way to spread infection, and so education and health officials tried removing slates from schools. Evidence from Henry's Mill, however, where 52 fragments of slate pencil and 11 fragments of writing slate were found, indicates that slates were still used in the 1920s, and other reports indicate that even after the Second World War slates disappeared only slowly.

Although slates are most commonly associated with children, they could also have been used by adults for domestic lists or accounts and by tradesmen doing quick figuring. Ted Higginbotham (2005) has used slates excavated from the rural settlement of Cadia in New South Wales as evidence of adult literacy, observing that slate items were ubiquitous among the higher status households in the community but absent from the households of poor, single men. The fact that slates are so widespread is evidence not only of children but of the importance that authorities and parents alike placed on literacy and education in colonial Australia.

Money

Coins and currency provided a vital medium of exchange between individuals, one which linked private life with wider colonial society and economy. British authorities, however, regarded the first convict settlements in Australia as penal outposts, so there was initially no legal monetary system. Nevertheless, people still wanted to trade with each other, so the age-old system of barter soon appeared, especially with the exchange of wheat, meat, sugar and rum. Commercial life was also established quickly, with a Commissariat (Government) Store established to purchase and distribute rations. At the same time, soldiers drew their pay and spent it, and ships arrived to trade. In the first few years, the most valuable and reliable means of exchange were Paymasters' Bills and Treasury Bills (known as "sterling"), but these were generally issued for large amounts so they were unsuited for small, everyday transactions. Promissory notes and I.O.U.s (known as "currency") also changed hands, but these were heavily discounted according to the creditworthiness of the issuer (Hainsworth 1981:58). Foreign coins arrived haphazardly in officers' purses and convicts' pockets and achieved local acceptability and legal recognition for a brief time (Butlin 1953:4). These coins came from the trading ports between England and Australia and included Spanish dollars and reals, Brazilian reis, rupees from Madras and Calcutta, and duits from the Dutch East Indies (Johnson 1999:247–252). Archaeological evidence from the First Government House site includes two copper farthings from early in the reign of George II (1730–1739), which could have been carried privately in the First Fleet (Boland 1987:6). The small quantity of coins available and their fluctuating value, however, meant that it was difficult in the early years of settlement for many people to plan ahead and create a store of value for future needs (Karskens 1997:164–165).

The amount of coins in circulation increased in December 1800, when £500 arrived on the *Porpoise* in the form of 132,000 copper coins. These, and halfpennies and farthings, are commonly found on archaeological sites in Australia up to the mid-nineteenth century and were legal tender until being recalled in 1868. Governor Macquarie also tackled the coinage problem by purchasing 40,000 Spanish silver dollars from the *Samarang* in 1812. He ordered the convict forger, William Henshall, to cut out a round section from the middle of each Spanish dollar, which ensured the coins would be of reduced value outside New South Wales. The centre section from each dollar was known as a "Dump" and was valued at 15 pence, while the outer section of the coin was valued at 5 shillings and was known as a "Holey Dollar". The coins circulated widely in the colony until around 1829, by which time British sterling had become the official medium of exchange.

More than 260 coins were recovered during excavations at the Cumberland/Gloucester Streets site in the Rocks. Most of these were English farthings and halfpennies, along with a few Spanish and Brazilian coins (Johnson 1999:271–277). The coins were almost all of small value and suggest that the occasional loss of a coin was not a major concern for local residents. A similar pattern of lost coins of low denomination was also apparent at the Casselden Place site in Melbourne (Tucker et al. 2004). The Rocks excavations also yielded 23 brass

Chinese coins known as "cash", which were never legal currency and were instead used as gambling counters in games of *fan-tan* (see Chapter 9). The coins probably arrived in Sydney with Chinese immigrants from the 1850s onwards, but their abundance in the area suggests that the game may have been widespread among Europeans as well (Johnson 1999:246).

By the middle of the nineteenth century, however, there was still a lack of coins of small denominations for people to buy goods on a daily basis. Beginning around 1849, merchants such as grocers and pawnbrokers began issuing their own copper tokens to customers. These trade tokens served as an unofficial, though widely accepted coinage (Crellin 2006:76). Examples from Casselden Place include tokens issued by Coles Book Arcade and by Hide and De Carle Grocers and Wine Merchants of Melbourne. Tokens and coins are the kinds of small, useful items that are more likely to be lost than thrown away, and archaeologically they are more likely to be recovered from subfloor and yard deposits than rubbish pits. A project conducted in collaboration with metal detectorists demonstrates some of the patterning of their loss. Archaeologist Jodi Turnbull (2006) used detailed records kept by one Victorian metal detecting club which made regular excursions to the goldfields districts while prospecting for gold. Turnbull analysed the type of objects they found and the spatial distribution of those objects, and discovered that whereas archaeological excavations that focus on house sites and dumps recover few tokens, tokens are among the most frequent artefacts found by detectorists. She attributes this to the "off-site" survey methods they use, in which they cover large areas of ground by walking grids, in the same way as archaeologists. Surveying the landscape in this way, the detectorists find objects lost by people out and about in their daily business, of which tokens falling from pockets are a classic example.

Conclusion

Historical archaeology reveals private, even intimate details about individual and family life. In this chapter we have seen how people laid their tables and the kinds of food they set out and the smoking and drinking they enjoyed. We have also seen a little of the clothing worn by working people, an area of Australian cultural life that has long been obscure to historians (Maynard 1994:91), as well as the toys children played with, changing responses to medicine and hygiene, and the money used to purchase the array of consumer goods increasingly available in the nineteenth and early twentieth centuries. Careful study of artefacts recovered from deposits such as cesspits and underfloor spaces provides unique insight into at least some of the material goods that people acquired, consumed and eventually discarded. This focus is very specific, shining a light on the behaviour of a few households which by chance have become the subjects of archaeological inquiry. As we have tried to show here, however, the discipline of historical archaeology is now able to move beyond these limited and specific studies. The growing number of carefully documented assemblages from around the country enables us to adopt a wider perspective. We are now able to compare and contrast the material lives of individuals, households and neighbourhoods between rural and urban areas, from colony to colony, between working class, middle class and the well-to-do, as well as to see how responses to the material world changed throughout the nineteenth century and beyond. In this way historical archaeology is beginning to fulfil its potential, bridging the gap between the generalising observations of historians and detailed archaeological studies of artefact assemblages to reveal wider patterns in human behaviour. We still have a long way to go. A focus on the archaeology of the middle classes, for example, has barely begun, and as we argue in the final chapter, the archaeology of the twentieth century deserves much greater attention. Nevertheless, we have shown here how careful study of the mundane and domestic provides access to issues of much wider social, economic and cultural importance.

Chapter 12
Death

Archaeologists have long been intrigued by the remains of the dead. Because skeletons, grave goods and cemeteries represent *deliberate* disposal, unlike the incidental discard of everyday items, mortuary material can bring us a step closer to the lives and intentions of people and places in the past. Along the way, archaeologists have developed many different approaches to studying the dead. Human bones, for example, can provide evidence of age, sex, diet and disease. Grave goods have been extensively studied as art objects, or ritual symbols, or as expressions of social status. Gravestone inscriptions and artwork can reveal attitudes to death and the survival of the soul. In one famous study, James Deetz (1977) identified the changing frequency of headstone designs in New England cemeteries from the 1680s to the 1820s and linked the popularity of these motifs with changes in contemporary religious views. In Britain, Sarah Tarlow (1999) used graveyard memorials from Orkney to explore changing attitudes to death and bereavement since the sixteenth century, while Harold Mytum (2004) has described the many possible approaches to studying mortuary monuments of the historic period. Recent views of mortuary archaeology in the United States (LeeDecker 2009; Veit et al. 2009) highlight the potential of graves and cemeteries to shed new light on the changing role of religion in people's lives and the importance of symbolism in burial treatments.

In Australia, cultural historians have examined various aspects of death. Pat Jalland (2002), for example, provides a detailed history of death, grief and mourning between 1840 and 1918, although she excludes the earlier convict period as of "limited relevance". A more recent study describes ways of death in Australia during the twentieth century (Jalland 2006). Griffin and Tobin (1982) described the funeral service and undertaking business, while Robert Nicol (1994) has examined funerals and cemeteries in South Australia. Joy Damousi (1999) studied wartime bereavement, and Simon Cooke (1991) has examined suicide and cremation. Ken Inglis (1998) has investigated war memorials, and Helen MacDonald (2005) has recently compared the history of human dissection in Britain and Tasmania.

There has also been a great deal of archaeological work done on the skeletal remains of prehistoric Aboriginal people, as well as on the political and ethical dimensions of such research, and on consultation and reburial (e.g. Du Cros 2002:117–141; Fforde 2004:94–118; Meighan 1992; Pardoe 1988; Webb 1987). While scientists have expressed fear that reburying bones after analysis is the same

S. Lawrence, P. Davies, *An Archaeology of Australia Since 1788*,
Contributions To Global Historical Archaeology, DOI 10.1007/978-1-4419-7485-3_12,
© Springer Science+Business Media, LLC 2011

Fig. 12.1 Cemetery at Stanley in north-western Tasmania (photo P. Davies)

as destroying them (Mulvaney 1991), descendants and religious leaders are often more concerned with cultural and religious values and in ensuring respect for the dead. There has also been a growing interest in Australia in grave-markers as arte-facts, as evidence of taste, class and aspirations. Lavelle and Mackay (1987), for example, argued that as the nineteenth century progressed and Australians became more comfortable with national identity, British and European symbols were aug-mented or replaced with such local motifs as eucalyptus sprigs and waratahs. The antiquities of Egypt and the classical world have also influenced funerary mon-uments and memorials to the war dead (Merrillees 1990). In the Adelaide Hills, Donald Pate (2005) identified a range of variables affecting gravestones in early cemeteries (1836–1865) that may relate to the social identities of the deceased. These include the different types of stone (slate, marble, sandstone) and the form of inscription, as well as the size, style and location of memorials. Rural cemeteries are also important for preserving vegetation that represents natural landscapes at the time of European arrival (Lindenmayer et al. 2005:17) (Fig. 12.1).

Most archaeological work done on graves and cemeteries from the historical period, however, has occurred as salvage excavation ahead of development. In these circumstances, the primary aims have been to determine the location of unmarked graves, establish the identity of individual skeletons, and to learn as much as possi-ble about age and sex profiles, health and mortality. Graves and cemeteries, however, are also important for understanding early Australian mortuary practices. To what extent, for example, were burial customs imported from Britain, and how much local adaptation occurred? How did attitudes to death and bereavement change through time, and what physical expression did this receive? Were there differences in burial treatment based on social status, on ethnicity, or religious beliefs? How were convicts treated in death, and those who died far from settlement and cemetery? In this chapter we will look at examples of mortuary archaeology in Australia to try to answer some of these questions. Much of the available evidence relates to marginal and voiceless groups within society, such as criminals and convicts, orphan children, murder victims and ethnic minorities.

Responses to Death

Early colonial settlers in Sydney brought with them an attitude to death and dying that was generally direct and accepting. With life expectancy less than 50 years, death was a common and familiar event. The rituals of grief and mourning were pre-industrial, marked by the expression of anger, anguish or wild hilarity at the wake, largely unconcerned with propriety and emotional restraint (Karskens 1998:36). People who died in their homes were attended by the women of the household. As doctors could do little, even to alleviate pain, they were normally only summoned to confirm that death had occurred. The corpse was an object of respect rather than shame, carefully laid out, washed and dressed in a shroud or winding sheet. Attended by friends and relatives, the funeral processions of both important and humbler persons wound on foot through the streets to the burial ground at the edge of the town. Commercial funerals did not appear until the late 1820s.

As the nineteenth century progressed, the Victorian ideal of the "good death", imported by British and Irish migrants via Evangelical Protestantism, came to be influential in colonial Australia, especially among the middle and upper classes. The good death required piety and fortitude in the face of physical suffering (Jalland 2002:51–68). Ideally, it took place in the family home, surrounded by loved ones, with the dying person farewelling family members, comforted by the prospect of a family reunion in heaven. Emotions were restrained, with grief expressed in formal and polite ways. Funerals and graves were often elaborate and expensive. Such an ideal, however, was harder to sustain in working-class households, where the necessary space, time, wealth and servants were normally unavailable. Among rural farmers, the notion of a good death was also fragile, especially among families living tough and isolated lives.

The good death was also prominent in Catholic households, where the role of the priest and the tradition of the sacraments provided spiritual strength to the dying and their families. The priest administered confession and absolution, followed by the last Eucharist and extreme unction. The ceremonies of the Catholic Church performed by the priest at the deathbed were formally ritualized, and depended less on the faith and participation of family members. This helped to maintain priestly influence in a New World society far removed from traditional church communities in England and Ireland.

An important element of the good Christian death included visiting the graves of family members. Graves served as sites for mourning and remembrance, for meditation, and for Christian devotional ritual. They became shrines that kept alive the memory of the loved one (Jalland 2002:144). Families were thus anxious to buy grave plots in perpetuity and opposed the closure of old graveyards, especially if bodies were to be removed. Popular Christian belief held that disturbance to the body of the deceased jeopardized his or her awakening on the Last Day and thus eternal life (Ariès 1981:31–32). This concern for the sanctity of the burial also fed contemporary horror at human dissection by anatomists, and hampered the introduction of cremation.

The Australian colonies used a mix of both churchyard cemeteries and municipal cemeteries to dispose of the dead. Awareness of the need for public sanitation grew increasingly important as the nineteenth century progressed, and removing burial grounds safely to the edge of settlement was common. Garden cemeteries also became popular. Inspired by the Père-Lachaise cemetery in Paris, garden cemeteries had flourished in Britain and the United States during the nineteenth century (Curl 2000:69–108). Among the first examples in Australia were the Boroondara Cemetery in Melbourne (established 1858) and the Rookwood Necropolis in Sydney, which opened in 1867. Carefully arranged and cultivated, such cemeteries were intended as places of beauty, providing inspiration for life and the opportunity for peaceful reflection (Spicer 1991).

By the early twentieth century, however, there was a growing reaction against the pomp, high cost and perceived excesses of funerals and monuments that characterized the nineteenth century. Memorial parks and lawn cemeteries became increasingly popular. Lawn cemeteries were characterized by grassy swards where the grave sites had been levelled to the surface, and memorials were restricted to unobtrusive monuments or plaques set in the ground. These cemeteries were (and are) clean, uncluttered, hygienic and low maintenance, but also rigid, uniform and impersonal (Griffin and Tobin 1982:71–72). Among the first of these was Enfield in Adelaide, established in the 1940s (Nicol 1997). Such places also reflected a changing response to death. Dying was being taken out of the home and placed in the professional hands of doctors, hospitals and the funeral industry. In contrast to the immediacy and starkness of death for previous generations, death was becoming remote and unspoken, but perhaps no less feared.

Cremation also became popular in this period. A product of the late Victorian era, the debate in Australia over cremation was fierce, waged over issues of health and hygiene, religion, aesthetics and economics. Australia's first cremation of a European took place on Sandringham beach near Melbourne in 1895, and the first crematorium opened in Adelaide in 1903. Early prejudice against cremation gradually waned, and by the 1990s it had become the preferred method of disposing of the dead for more than half the Australian population (Griffin and Tobin 1982:110; Nicol 2003).

Old Sydney Burial Ground

There is little documentary evidence of burial practices in early Sydney, but excavation of the Old Sydney Burial Ground, Sydney's first substantial cemetery, has
provided striking evidence of graves and memorials from the beginning of European
settlement in the area. Located near the current corner of George and Druitt Street,
it was in use between 1792 and 1820 (Fig. 12.2). Most of the 2,266 documented
burials were of convicts or ex-convicts, although soldiers from various regiments
in Sydney were also buried there, along with their family members. There were
no apparent denominational divisions, although the military tended to be buried in
clusters according to regiment. Wealthier families, however, often had graveyards at
their homesteads, while the Domain originally contained one or two graves as well
(Harris 1978 [1807]). Interments in the burial ground were performed with Church
of England rites regardless of individual denomination, as there was no Catholic
priest in Australia until 1803, when James Dixon began working as a chaplain. By
1820 the cemetery was full, and a new burial ground was set aside in Devonshire
Street at Brickfield Hill (now the site of Sydney's Central Railway Station).

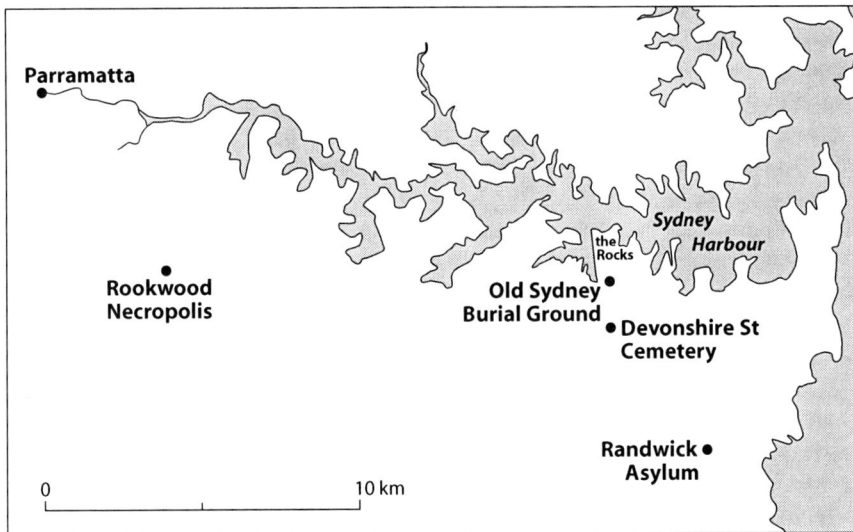

Fig. 12.2 Map of Sydney showing location of mortuary sites mentioned in text

Following its closure, the burial ground was neglected and fell into disrepair, and
in the late 1860s the Sydney Town Hall was constructed on the site (Karskens 1998).
Remains identified at the time of construction were re-buried at the Rookwood
Necropolis, established south of Parramatta in 1867, but with almost half a century of decay and vandalism having obscured the location and identity of graves,

many burials were left behind. Redevelopment of the area in 1974 and 1991 resulted in disturbance to 11 graves, all of which were subject to archaeological salvage (Birmingham and Liston 1976; Lowe and Mackay 1992). Further work was undertaken by Casey and Lowe in 2003 and 2008, which involved the investigation of another 50 burials (City of Sydney 2008). The excavation of graves and vaults revealed important evidence about the transfer of burial practices and customs from Britain to Australia during the early period of European settlement.

Two main forms of burial were represented. The first consisted of substantial brick-lined tombs, measuring up to 2.5 m long, 1.5 m wide and over 1.5 m high. Roofs were of vaulted brick or hardwood beams. Several of the tombs featured doorways that had been bricked up after use. In one tomb the coffin had been placed on four brick piers above the clay floor, separated from the earth, perhaps to symbolically defy the inevitability of decay. Humbler graves consisted of a wooden coffin inserted into a hole barely wider than the coffin itself. Some were held together with wooden pegs, others with nails. The coffins were made of Australian red cedar, either single pieces or narrow planks, and left rough on the underside. At least two coffin lids were decorated with rows of brass tacks, a reflection of the rows of coffin nails employed by the wealthy in the eighteenth century as protection against grave-robbery and as status symbols. The coffins were generally aligned east-west, with the head at the western end of the coffin, facing east. This had been the established Christian tradition in Europe since the fourteenth century (Ariès 1981:14). The original intention was to permit the deceased to face Jerusalem in preparation for the Last Judgement, a tradition transferred from Britain to New South Wales. In many later cemeteries, however, this strict alignment was often not observed.

There was no evidence for large burial pits at the cemetery, as used in England at the time to bury the bodies of paupers. Instead, the brick vaulted tombs, coffin burials and headstones all indicate individual care and respect for the dead. Separate tombs represented a symbolic housing for the body of the deceased and protection from disturbance. Intactness of the body of the deceased was important because it was believed to retain its identity and so accompany the soul to heaven. Nevertheless, skeletal remains recovered archaeologically from the burial ground were generally fragmentary, so little could be learned about the biology of individual interments. With the exception of a fragmentary headstone belonging to ex-convict Elizabeth Steel, who died in 1795, the identification of graves is generally unknown.

In these early days in Sydney, however, memorialization of the dead was not limited to a headstone in a cemetery. During excavation at the Rocks in 1994, archaeologists uncovered a memorial plaque carved on a pre-1823 rock cutting. It reads

Sacred
to the Loving Memory
of
[indecipherable]
who departed this Life
[17 or 27] October [1793 or 180?9]

Despite high-resolution photography, the name of the deceased and the exact date could not be determined (Karskens 1999:60–61). The plaque would have stood at the rear of a house in Gloucester Street. With no evidence of a grave or tomb, it seems the plaque was a memorial rather than a grave-marker. The person may have died at sea, or perhaps a carved gravestone at the burial ground was too expensive for the family and the sandstone close to home offered a good substitute as a memorial and reminder.

Convicts

How were convicts treated in death? In New South Wales, historian Grace Karskens (1998) notes that the way a dead convict was buried owed more to whether he or she had family or friends to arrange the funeral, than to the individual's civil status. The bodies of strangers and "friendless" prisoners were buried with little ceremony in only shrouds or sheets.

In Van Diemen's Land, contemporary accounts stressed the inhumanity of convict deaths and mass burials in common graves. William Gates, for example, a Canadian rebel convicted of treason and transported to Van Diemen's Land in 1840, observed that "the convict is not allowed a decent interment – but to the hole in the earth, when indeed their bodies were not snapped up for the operator and dissecting room" (Gates 1961 [1850]:63). Linus Miller was an American citizen and member of the Patriot Army that attempted to "liberate" the people of Upper Canada from British oppression in 1838 (Pybus and Maxwell-Stuart 2002:65–71). He also recorded his experiences as a convict in Van Diemen's Land and at Port Arthur, observing that:

> When a prisoner died, his remains were dissected, put into a rough coffin in a state of *perfect nudity*... carried to the wharf by four men, placed in a boat, and amid the jeers and curses of the boatmen, conveyed to the landing place at the Isle of the Dead. Here it is left until the clergymen arrives, when it is bourne to the grave, the burial service read, and the body committed to the dust, there to remain until the morning of the resurrection (quoted in Ross 1995:64).

Despite Miller's disapproval of the methods used, it is evident that some care was taken in burying convicts. Typically, the deceased was placed in a coffin, which was taken to the burial ground, and then lowered into the grave. A service was read and the grave was filled in. An autopsy may have been performed if the cause of death was not obvious, but there are no documented examples of deliberate medical dissection at Port Arthur. Convict graves were also occasionally marked. On the Isle of the Dead, for example, sandstone headstones mark the final resting place of nine convicts. However, this accounts for only about 2 percent of the estimated 426 convict burials on the island (Tuffin 2005:7). Others were sometimes marked with a wooden post or cross, but it remains unclear on what basis convict graves were commemorated or left unmarked.

Mass burials of convicts also appear to have been isolated events. On Norfolk Island, for example, a long hump of turf at the eastern edge of the settlement's burial ground, known locally as "Murderers Mound", is said to be the last resting place of 12 convicts hanged after an uprising in 1846 that left four people dead. Otherwise, convicts who died on the island were buried in single graves (Dalkin 1974:24–28, 90–91). There are also claims for communal burials on the Isle of the Dead at Port Arthur (Peacock 1985:12; Ross 1995:33–36). Geophysical surveys, however, have revealed that the island is dotted with closely spaced single interments rather than large mass graves (Links 2004).

Although secondary offenders in the Australian colonies were sent to places like Port Arthur and Port Macquarie, most convicts worked as labourers for free settlers or on government projects (Chapter 2). It was rare for burial grounds to be set aside specifically for convicts. Those who died while under sentence were buried in parish cemeteries scattered throughout the colony. Richard Tuffin (2005) has identified more than 40 places in Tasmania where convicts were buried, including 23 graveyards attached to parish churches. It was costly and difficult to transport the dead long distances, so convicts were generally buried in the district in which they worked and died. At St. David's Burial Ground in Hobart, for example, there were more than 800 convict interments (Tuffin 2005:14). The majority of convicts were buried among the greater mass of free settlers in cemeteries across Van Diemen's Land.

Mortality and Cemeteries

Patterns of dying have changed significantly in Australia over the years. For much of the nineteenth century, infant and young adult mortality was high, and average life expectancy was relatively low. Babies frequently died from poor nutrition, diarrhoea and diphtheria (McCalman 2005). From around the 1880s, however, due largely to improvements in public health, the average age at death increased and mortality rates for infants and children declined. Nevertheless, women remained at risk from complications in pregnancy, childbirth and puerperal fever. Throughout the nineteenth century, women in their 30s had a substantial risk of dying from a combination of childbearing, overwork, exhaustion and poor diet. Male mortality was even higher, due to violence, suicide and industrial accidents, often linked with alcohol abuse (Jalland 2002:6). Despite these causes, however, the most important cause of death for both men and women in the nineteenth century was tuberculosis ("consumption" or phthisis). During the twentieth century, overall mortality rates fell, but women generally had a longer life expectancy. Death from accident and acute diseases became less common, replaced by death from chronic illnesses, such as heart disease and cancer (Lopez and Ruzicka 1977).

Cadia

Mortality patterns in Australia in the later nineteenth and early twentieth century are broadly represented in the skeletal remains from the cemetery at Cadia. The small rural community is located about 20 km south-west of Orange in New South Wales, on the inland slopes of the Great Dividing Range. Salvage excavation of the cemetery took place in 1997 and 1998 ahead of mining development. Although the living descendants were concerned that the remains of their ancestors be reburied as soon as possible after excavation, skeletal analysis still permitted a number of general conclusions about the health of individuals buried at the site (Lazer 2001).

Excavation revealed the remains of at least 111 individuals, buried in the cemetery between 1864 and 1927. Almost half of all the bodies were those of infants. The next most prevalent group were the elderly. Historical records about the causes of death at Cadia indicate that infants and small children in the cemetery tended to die quickly from diseases like whooping cough and gastroenteritis. These causes are consistent with the skeletal record, where the infant skeletons showed no signs of bone modification, which is consistent with a relatively short period of illness prior to death.

The skeletons also provided insights into the general health of the community. For example, there was a distinct separation in height between males and females, with males being taller than females. This suggests that the people buried at Cadia had adequate diets and were in relatively good health during the period of bone growth. Well-developed muscle attachments on the long bones of both men and women also indicate that these individuals were physically active during life. This is to be expected for a rural community with many people involved in mining. Dental health, however, was generally poor, with a high rate of tooth decay and tooth loss during life. About one third of the adult sample had lost all or most of their teeth prior to death. Some children at 3 years of age had cavities (Lazer 2001:58). Tooth problems in this period were generally treated with extraction. When all the teeth were removed, they could be replaced with dentures. In addition, nine adult males had teeth wear patterns consistent with clenching a pipe stem between the teeth.

The skeletons from Cadia thus represent the health and mortality of a rural mining community in the later nineteenth and early twentieth century. There was a very high rate of death for young children, who succumbed quickly to the prevalent childhood diseases of the time. The age-at-death profile suggests, however, that if infants survived the first year or two of life, they had a good chance of living a normal lifespan. There were also a higher proportion of adult males to females in the cemetery, typical of mining settlements of the era.

St. Mary's, Adelaide

A similar pattern of mortality was detected during the investigation of human remains from a burial ground at St. Mary's Anglican Church in Adelaide (Anson 2004; Anson and Henneberg 2004). Redevelopment of the site resulted in the recovery in 2002 of 70 human skeletons from unmarked graves, dating from 1847 until the early twentieth century. The remains were reburied in a concrete crypt within the cemetery after analysis, and they remain accessible for further investigation (Fig. 12.3). Most of the sample consisted of sub-adults, and 29 individuals were infants aged less than 1 year at death. Analysis of the skeletal material and historical sources revealed that children were dying from infections including pneumonia

Fig. 12.3 Installation of concrete rainwater tank at St. Mary's Cemetery in Adelaide to accommodate human skeletal remains (photo T. Anson)

and tuberculosis, exacerbated in some cases by poor nutrition and anaemia. Dental hygiene was also very poor, and little help was available for tooth decay beyond simple extraction. One 8–9-year-old girl apparently died from congenital syphilis, contracted in the womb from her mother. Adults ranged in age from 18 to 59 years at death, and most of the skeletons showed signs of various infections, along with bone lesions that indicate lives of hard physical work. One man may have had leprosy. This part of the cemetery had long been known as the "paupers' section", and it was also used for the interment of many stillborn and newborn babies. Those buried at St. Mary's had struggled through the early years of establishing the settlement of Adelaide. Their mortal remains reveal that those who survived infancy generally looked forward to lives of robust physical health. Infants, however, were vulnerable to a range of infections, and died in numbers which are almost unthinkable today.

Parramatta Convict Hospital

The remains of six perinatal infants were discovered during excavations at the Parramatta Convict Hospital site in 2005–2008 (Donlon et al. 2008). The skeletons were buried in a small area at the rear of the hospital building, dating from ca. 1800 to ca. 1840, and probably represent the infants of convict mothers who had been confined at the convict hospital. The skeletal material is unusual because it is often assumed that the bones of perinates (who died around the time of birth) preserve very poorly compared with adult bones and teeth (Baker et al. 2005:3). These skeletons are thus highly significant for the light they shed on responses to the death of infants in the early decades of European settlement in New South Wales. They ranged in age from about 24 weeks to 40 weeks in utero, suggesting that the infants were stillborn or that they survived birth but died shortly afterwards. The young ages of the skeletons, however, prevented any clear determination of sex to be made. Two skeletons were buried in a shallow double grave, oriented east–west, and dating to 1800–1818, indicating that at least some care and attention was paid to their disposal. Three other perinates, however, from a slightly later period, were discarded in a pit, and another in a storage cellar. The excavators suggest that this cruder pattern of disposal may represent the increasing medicalization of births in hospitals, with the rapid removal of the dead infants from their mothers and their deposition into an open rubbish pit nearby (Donlon et al. 2008:81).

Randwick Destitute Children's Asylum Cemetery, Sydney

The Benevolent Society of New South Wales established an asylum for destitute children at Paddington in Sydney in 1852, but the institution was moved to a new site at Randwick in 1858. It provided care for children abandoned by their parents, or those whose parents were "vagrant, drunk or disorderly" and judged unfit to care for their offspring. There were also children of widowers and widows and parents needing help due to poverty or sickness. The intention was to provide not only a home for the children but a sound and useful education as well, and to train them in useful habits of industry. Over the years about 2,500 children passed through its doors. The Randwick Asylum operated until 1915, when the site was requisitioned for use as a military hospital. It remained a repatriation hospital until 1953 when it became the Prince of Wales Hospital. Redevelopment of the site in the 1990s resulted in an extensive archaeological programme to salvage the children's cemetery in the grounds of the asylum, with 65 burials recovered and recorded (Austral/Godden Mackay 1997). The results revealed aspects not only of child mortality, but attitudes to child welfare and the practice of philanthropy in the later nineteenth century.

A "culture of poverty" was emerging more visibly in Sydney by the 1840s and 1850s. There was growing dislocation caused by the gold rush, by higher prices, and men leaving their families. Children were reported roaming the streets, alone, with siblings or in gangs. Begging and pick-pocketing were reported. Boys sold newspapers, fruit, flowers and matches, while some older girls worked as prostitutes to survive. The approach to dealing with the colony's destitute children grew out of social and economic changes in Britain during the eighteenth century that resulted in the "moralisation" of poverty. Moralists distinguished the deserving poor – the aged, ill, widowed or deserted families, from the undeserving poor – able-bodied but idle and immoral. It was believed that the children of the latter held the same attitude and needed to be separated from their parents and taught to become moral, industrious citizens. This was best done within the confines of an institution, where the children could also be isolated from the corrupting influences of the outside world (Garton 1990:90–92). There was an associated concern to exclude the "undeserving" poor, and this was best achieved by administering the institution by philanthropic members of society.

By the 1870s the Randwick asylum accommodated more than 700 children. It included a receiving house, a hospital, and cottages for employees, and extensive vegetable gardens on the 60-acre site. The children ate a regular diet of milk, meat (boiled or baked), soup and vegetables, along with bread, tea and porridge for breakfast. They had both formal schooling and work to do. Boys worked in the garden and in various jobs around the asylum. Girls worked in the laundry and kitchen, and helped with general cleaning (Ramsland 1986:80–83). Religious instruction was also provided. Around the age of 14 the children were apprenticed out under the supervision of the asylum's subscribers. In the 1880s some children were also boarded out with individual families. The asylum children were not prisoners, but management generally resisted returning them to their families. A number of children escaped from the institution, but whether it was because of ill-treatment, boredom, or a wish to return to their family is uncertain. The Randwick environment was rural at the time and road access was difficult, making it hard for families to visit as well.

The cemetery was located about 300 m away from the main buildings of the asylum, laid out discretely behind a dune crest, in an area considered unsuitable for gardening or agriculture. A more prominent location would have reflected poorly on the level of health care provided, an important consideration for an institution that relied heavily on public subscription for its continued operation. In addition, the administrators may have thought it necessary to separate the young inmates from such an obvious expression of death. There was also a strongly held belief that "miasmas" arising from the noxious decay in burial grounds were associated with outbreaks of disease. The location of the cemetery in a well-ventilated part of the grounds may have been a response to such concerns.

The cemetery was divided along sectarian lines, with Protestants buried in graves at the northern end and Catholics in the southern end. A significantly larger area of land was reserved for Protestant interments. The excavators identified a similar pattern at Sydney's Rookwood Necropolis, and speculate that it may relate to an under-representation of Catholics in both the Randwick asylum and in wider society, and reflect the dominant religious tone of the day (Austral/Godden Mackay 1997 vol. 1:86). On this basis it appears that 122 of the deceased children were members of the Church of England and 52 were Roman Catholics.

The first burial took place on October 20, 1863. Francis Martin, aged 3 years, had died of dysentery and convulsions. His father was dead, and his mother, Ann, was recorded as "an abandoned character". The burial register is filled with similar sad stories. All together, about 175 children died and were buried in the Randwick Asylum cemetery. The final interment, in 1891, was of Grace Caiels, aged 10 years. Although management was obliged to notify the next of kin when the death of an inmate occurred, there is no evidence that this took place. Burial within the cemetery was thus attended only by employees of the asylum, rather than by relatives of the deceased. The managers took the view that as the "dissolute" parents of the inmates had not cared for their children while they were alive, they would care even less when they were dead.

Although the burials were not marked with crosses or headstones, excavation revealed that graves were arranged in north–south rows with individual burials aligned east–west. In New South Wales, the regulation of east–west burial alignments was established by Governor Macquarie in 1820, based on long-standing British traditions (*Sydney Gazette* 29 January 1820). All of the graves excavated in the asylum cemetery were single graves. There were no mass burials even during periods of epidemic when many deaths occurred in short periods of time. In 1867, for example, 78 children buried in the cemetery died from measles and whooping cough.

Coffins were made from 1-inch boards of local timber. Some were painted black or treated with lamp black, while a few may have been painted blue (Fitzgerald and Golder 1994:37). All of the coffins were fixed using screws or nails rather than pegs or staples. There were no metal fittings such as handles or name plates, and no evidence that the coffins had internal lining. Kerfed timbers in some coffins, however, suggest that these were manufactured commercially. Most of the deceased were buried in the traditional manner, with the head to the west, facing east. Only some of the burials yielded buttons or pins, suggesting that most of the deceased children were buried simply in sheets or nightshirts. No personal possessions were found except for a single set of rosary beads in the hand of one of the burials.

Soil conditions had seriously damaged many of the bones in the graves, limiting the information that could be recovered from them. It was noted, however, that indicators of stress on bone development were common. This indicates that children suffered from stress, commonly between 0 and 3 years and before most of them arrived at the asylum. These results suggest that the diet in the asylum was adequate and probably an improvement for many. Unfortunately, many of the children did not have enough opportunity to benefit from this improved diet before their untimely deaths.

Bush Graves

Not everybody who died in Australia was buried in a cemetery. In isolated areas, lone graves had to suffice. The "bush death" was an important element of national identity in the late nineteenth century. Pat Jalland (2002:5) has described the idealized bushman's death as masculine, heroic and sometimes violent, as the explorer, bushranger or gold miner died of thirst in a hostile environment. More commonly, however, people in the bush died from the same prosaic causes as those in other places, including childbirth, disease caused by malnutrition and unclean water, and accidents. Bush deaths and burials were influenced by popular customs and the beliefs of working people. Isolation from the support and rituals of family, church and community reinforced a secular tradition of death and interment. Most funerals were simple, with a deep respect for the dead, and, in the absence of a priest or minister, lacking in formalized ritual (Jalland 2002:243–262).

The archaeological evidence for such bush deaths is widespread, but faint. A recent project in Victoria documented 36 lone graves and small cemeteries in Gippsland (Kaufman and Thompson 2004; Rogers and Helyar 1994). Most were associated with almost-forgotten mining camps and remote alpine grazing properties. Some graves were group family burials and others were individual interments, and many had low fences of wrought iron or timber to mark their position clearly. The authors note, however, that the region almost certainly contains many more lone graves and small burial grounds (Kaufman and Thompson 2004:9, 15). Such places are important for their association with early farming and mining activity, and in revealing responses to death before official local cemeteries were surveyed.

In Western Australia, Yvonne and Kevin Coate (1986) have recorded over 2,000 "lonely graves". These were burials outside registered cemeteries or churchyards, often on settlers' properties, on mining leases, and by the roadside. Burials often took place at the site of death in isolated areas because in the hot climate bodies had to be buried quickly. The use of wooden slabs or crosses to mark such graves was common where timber was plentiful and stone was either not available or there was no one with the skills to carve it. Sometimes living trees were used as memorials as well. Many headstones have long since been lost through ageing, fire, weather and neglect, while some plots were never marked to begin with. Nevertheless, the context of such graves and headstones, combined with available historical evidence, reveals important stories about remote lives and hardship. All too often, it also tells of the short lives and early deaths of children and infants, evidence of women and children that belies the masculine stereotypes of the bush.

Violent Death

Batavia, *Western Australia*

Archaeologists have also investigated cases of murder and execution. The events surrounding the wreck of the *Batavia* off the Western Australian coast in 1629, for example, formed a dramatic and brutal chapter in the early European history of Australia. The recovery of several bodies associated with the ship also provides insight into the mutiny and massacre that occurred. The *Batavia* was a newly built Dutch merchant vessel of the *Verenigde Oost-indische Compagnie* (VOC), the United East India Company, under the command of Francisco Palsaert. Seven months out of Amsterdam, the ship was wrecked on Morning Reef in the Houtman Abrolhos Islands, off the coast of Western Australia, on 4 June 1629. There were more than 300 men, women and children on board, and more than 40 people drowned trying to swim to shore. The survivors reached small islands nearby along the reef, where another 20 or so people soon died of thirst and illness.

Palsaert led a search for water to the arid Australian coastline, about 70 km away. Finding none, he sailed a longboat with crew to the headquarters of the VOC at Batavia (modern Jakarta, Indonesia) to raise help. Palsaert returned to the Abrolhos Islands 3 months later to find that the under-merchant Jeronimus Cornelisz had led a bloodthirsty mutiny on the small islands. In an orgy of violence, Cornelisz and his men had robbed, raped and murdered many of the survivors. The only resistance was from a group of soldiers based on West Wallabi Island who, led by Wiebbe Hayes, fought off attacks by the mutineers. About 125 people were killed, including sailors, soldiers and civilians of various nationalities and social backgrounds, and women and children. Cornelisz and his followers were captured and tried on the islands. Seven mutineers, including Cornelisz, were hanged (Dash 2002).

Following their rescue and a partial salvage of the *Batavia* the 77 survivors sailed on to Batavia and resumed their lives. The victims of the mutineers, however, remained on the islands, many in shallow graves. The archaeology of the shipwreck site itself has been extensively investigated and described by Jeremy Green (1989). Skeletons of a dozen or more victims have also been uncovered on the islands. These bear signs of illness and malnutrition earlier in life, as well as evidence for blows to the skull and jaw inflicted by swords, axes and clubs. A well-preserved skeleton (known as BAT A15507) found on Beacon Island was that of a male, almost 6-foot tall, aged 30–39 years. His teeth and jaw were badly diseased, perhaps the result of scurvy. A 2-inch cut mark on the skull showed that he had probably died after being struck on the head with a sword. Unfortunately, the identity of the man remains a mystery, as his wounds do not tally with the descriptions of individuals in Palsaert's journal (Dash 2002: 248–249; Pasveer et al. 1998).

Further research by the Western Australia Maritime Museum has also focused on a mass grave on Beacon Island (Gibbs 2003a; Pasveer et al. 1998; Paterson and Franklin 2004). The multiple burial contained the remains of three adult males, a teenager, a child and an infant. Several were buried with clothing and personal items including buttons, a thimble, parts of a pewter spoon and twisted copper jewellery wire. The grave itself was shallow and circular, and given the position of the bodies, appears to have been scooped out by hand, rather than carefully dug with tools to form a steep-sided grave. This suggests the hasty disposal of a group of corpses, although it remains unclear whether the grave was dug by mutineers trying to hide their crimes or by other survivors out of decency.

The archaeologists have also tried to identify who was buried in the grave. Using age and sex profiles and contemporary accounts of the massacre, they conclude that the three adults and one youth were probably Passchier van den Enden (gunner), Jacob Hendricxsz (carpenter), an English soldier named Jan Pinten and an unnamed cabin boy. The child and infant could have died of natural causes or have been murdered in early days. There was little or no skeletal evidence of trauma, although the archaeologists point out that murder by drowning or a cut throat, both common on the islands, would not necessarily leave visible marks on the bones (Paterson and Franklin 2004:74).

The *Batavia* mutiny was a dark beginning to European history in the region. The burials of victims are among the earliest European terrestrial sites in Australia. There is potential for much further archaeological work on the islands, recording the graves of victims, and perhaps the traces of structures erected by the survivors. As a postscript, it is ironic that the first recorded white "settlers" in Australia were Wouter Loos and Jan Pelgrom. Both were exiled on the West Australian coast in November 1629 as punishment for their role in the mutiny of the *Batavia* (Dash 2002:211).

The Police Garage, Melbourne

In 1999–2000 archaeologists conducting salvage excavations at the former Police Garage in Melbourne uncovered an intact human burial, together with the incomplete remains of a further two individuals (Hewitt 2003; Hewitt and Wright 2004). The Garage, built in 1937, was on the site of the former Melbourne Gaol Men's Hospital, part of a major prison complex in Melbourne's legal precinct established from 1841. In addition to the burials the excavations revealed a complex matrix of wall footings, drains, paved surfaces, cesspits and introduced fill. The human remains confront us with the mortality of those executed by the State. Investigation also highlights, however, some of the problems that can arise in reconciling bio-archaeological evidence with a contradictory and inadequate historical record.

The concrete floor slab of the garage sealed the stone foundations of the gaol hospital, as well as several yard areas and two small mortuary buildings ("dead houses"). A yard area to the south of the hospital was used to bury condemned, hanged individuals. All the burials were supposedly exhumed in 1937 when the Police Garage was built, and the remains reburied at Pentridge, a prison located on what was then Melbourne's northern outskirts. However, excavation revealed a wooden coffin (F85) at shallow depth, only 0.8 m below the original surface (Fig. 12.4). Both the grave and coffin had been packed with quicklime. Nearby but slightly deeper was a second burial pit (F86) containing the remains of two coffins and a quantity of human bones. Subsequent analysis of F86 could reveal only that

Fig. 12.4 Grave F85 at the Old Melbourne Gaol, thought to be that of George Farrow Blunderfield, hanged for murder in 1918 (photo G. Hewitt)

the remains were from a grave incompletely exhumed in 1937 when the Garage was built. The skeleton in F85, however, was anatomically complete. The quicklime added to the coffin, rather than hastening decomposition of the body, had temporarily slowed decay of soft tissue and permanently enhanced the survival of bone. After analysis the remains were reinterred in two plots at Fawkner Cemetery in northern Melbourne in April 2002. In addition, excavation also revealed a burial pit containing the skeletons of six dogs. These appear to have been used in the 1870s for medical experiments relating to antidotes for snake bites (Buckley 2003, Six dogs: a saga of snakes, dogs and medical byways. BA (Honours) dissertation, Archaeology Program, La Trobe University, Melbourne, unpublished).

Archaeologist Geoff Hewitt and forensic anthropologist Richard Wright grappled with the skeletal, archaeological and documentary evidence to determine the identity of the individual buried in F85. The biological evidence indicated a Caucasoid male of medium stature (ca. 5 feet 9 inches), aged 26–45 years. Bone pathologies on the legs and vertebrae suggested he may have endured pain in the back and hips, perhaps the result of hard labour carrying heavy loads. Damage to bones of the neck was consistent with sub-aural hanging where the knot was placed below the ear. This method brought death by massive trauma and slow strangulation, whereas when the knot was placed under the chin, the "long drop" hanging tended to sever the spinal cord and result in instant death.

In contrast to the skeletal evidence, however, historical records relating to the number, location, timing and identity of burials at the gaol were patchy and often contradictory. This was compounded by the exhumation and reburial of individuals at Pentridge Prison in northern Melbourne, changes of land tenure within the gaol precinct, demolition of curtain walls in 1929 and construction of the Police Garage in 1937. It also remains uncertain exactly when burial within the gaol grounds began. Hewitt and Wright used the forensic evidence of age, height and medical condition to narrow down a list of seven possible identities from more than 50 executions. Details from army and prison medical reports, along with mug shots and post-mortem examinations, permitted a probable, although not certain, identification of the remains with George Farrow Blunderfield alias Arthur Oldring, who was convicted of a double murder and hanged in 1918.

The bodies of prisoners who died while "inside" but who were not under sentence of death were normally released to families for private disposal. Burials of the condemned, however, were treated differently, especially after the 1855 *Act to Regulate the Execution of Criminals*, which stipulated that the body should be buried within the gaol where the execution took place. Punishment came to be symbolically extended beyond the time of death. Individual identity was forfeited, funerary rites in the presence of loved ones were denied, and quicklime was used in the grave with the intent to destroy the body. It is also clear that written records relating to treatment of the bodies of executed prisoners were very poorly and inconsistently maintained. When it comes to reattaching identities to the remains of the deceased, such records could not be taken at face value. Tensions between archaeological evidence and the written record demanded a continual reappraisal of questions and data, to challenge existing narratives and achieve a more nuanced understanding of the past.

Chinese Burials

Reverence for the ancestors is an important feature of traditional Chinese culture and religion. Disposal of the dead, via complex funerary ritual, is central to the process, with a strong belief in the continuity between this world and the afterlife (De Groot 1967; Smith 2006:60–63). Traditional burial in south-eastern China, where most nineteenth-century migrants to Australia originated, was ideally a three-stage process. To begin with, the body was buried according to proper ritual for seven to 10 years, until the flesh decayed from the bones. Then the bones were exhumed, cleaned and reinterred in a large ceramic vessel, which was placed on a hillside outside the ancestral village. The third stage was to remove the urn containing the bones of the deceased to a family vault (Watson 1988:208). The container helped to prevent the bones from "mingling" with the earth, and maintained the spirit of the ancestor. In Cantonese practice, women received much the same ritual treatment in death as men. As women were outside the ancestral lineage, however, their bones were exhumed, cleaned and reinterred as a mark of respect, but without the weight of spiritual benefit to the living (Martin 1988:176).

In the nineteenth century it was very important for overseas Chinese to return to their village to die, or else to have their remains sent back to their birthplace. Dying in Australia, however, where men were far removed from their native village, meant that some accommodation to local conditions was usually necessary. Without family nearby, Chinese miners and workers, who were usually men, relied on district associations (tongs) to ensure that proper funeral rituals were performed. The association was also the agency that would return the bones to the home village for reinterment (Abraham and Wegars 2003:58; see Chapter 9). There is archaeological evidence to attest to the repatriation of remains, but not all Chinese who died here were so fortunate, and colonial cemeteries in many parts of Australia still contain Chinese burials, some with markers bearing Chinese characters and some without. In isolated areas, such as parts of Western Australia for example, Chinese often had to abandon traditional practice and accept ordinary Australian funerals instead (J. Ryan 1991:9).

Grave-markers were used both as a focus for ritual observances by descendants and to indicate the position of the burial for those who came later to disinter the bones. Grave-markers were usually made of stone in nineteenth-century Australia, although wood was sometimes used instead. At the mining settlement of Pine Creek in the Northern Territory, sheets of iron were reused as markers with characters punched on for identification (Jack 1995). The text on the markers included the name of the individual, the date of death, and, crucially, the name of the person's home village. Texts were either in Chinese, English or a combination of the two. It is important to note, however, that many poorer people often did not reach the final stage of reburial, and remained in an unmarked grave.

Chinese cemeteries often include a number of structures, including the altar or memorial shrine, and the burner. Altars provided a focus for collective ceremonies that could not, due to circumstances, be held for individual burials. The markers served as generalized memorials acknowledging the sanctity of the site for the whole

Fig. 12.5 Chinese burner at the Maldon Cemetery in Victoria (photo S. Lawrence)

community (Abraham and Wegars 2003:63). Burners were brick or stone structures, often 2 m or more in height (Fig. 12.5). They were used for the ritual burning of the dead person's private belongings, and for burning paper copies of money, clothing, housing and other objects that would serve the dead in the afterlife. In return, the living expected to receive wealth and good luck. Historian Ian Jack (1995:303) has noted that burners in Australia tend to be much more elaborate than those found in the United States.

Lindsay Smith identified and recorded eight Chinese cemeteries in the southern highlands of New South Wales, six of which were associated with major centres of Chinese settlement (Smith 2006). The cemeteries were situated according to the principles of *feng shui*, located on mountain slopes with flanking ridges and overlooking flowing water. Smith located around 140 burials, most of which were shallow pits from which the remains of the deceased had been exhumed and sent home to China. Only four Chinese headstones were preserved, along with an intact brick burner at Tumut. Towns with cemeteries also had temples, and the two were key indicators of the status of the settlement as a "central place" within the local settlement network. Both Chinese and western miners abandoned the area by the end of the nineteenth century, but those faint shadows in the grass indicate that the Chinese community remained faithful to their dead and that the ancestors were not forgotten.

In the Buckland Valley of north-eastern Victoria historians and archaeologists have worked together to identify a former cemetery that served the large Chinese population of that once-thriving goldfield. From 1853 to the early twentieth century, the narrow mountain valley along the Buckland River was the scene of one of Victoria's richest alluvial diggings (Talbot 2004). At its peak in 1854 the area was rushed by around 6,000 people, almost all Europeans, competing for the shallow surface gold. By 1857, however, as the rush receded, around 2,500 Chinese miners had arrived in the valley while only 500 Europeans remained, reinforcing fears by the latter of being outnumbered by the Chinese. In that year the valley achieved notoriety when a group of white miners attacked members of the Chinese community, burning homes and businesses, killing up to 20 men and driving the survivors to seek refuge in towns nearby. The Buckland Riots and a similar attack at Lambing Flat in New South Wales in 1861 are nationally significant for their role in the later development of the White Australia Policy, racially based legislation that shaped Australian migration policy for several generations (Curthoys 2001). The Buckland cemetery contains hundreds of Chinese burials, only four of which are still commemorated by stone markers bearing Chinese characters. Many other markers may have been taken away by visitors as souvenirs, while wooden markers have been lost to decay and bushfire (Talbot 2004:156). There were also rumours, however, of a separate Chinese cemetery on a nearby hillside. Historians Diann Talbot and Kevin Wong Hoy found documentary evidence to pinpoint the location, which, like the cemeteries in the New South Wales highlands, appears to have been selected based on the principles of *feng shui*. Geophysical survey carried out by Fiona Links from the University of Tasmania revealed evidence for at least 50 features interpreted as likely graves at the site (Links and Lawrence 2004). More recent disturbance to the cemetery, including road works and vegetation growth, makes it impossible to detect if any of these were later exhumed. However, the site has now become a focus for the living. The Chinese Australian Family Historians of Victoria and the Alpine Shire council have jointly erected a cairn on the site which commemorates not only the anonymous dead, but also the Buckland Riots (Wong Hoy 2007).

Frequently treated as outcasts in life, the Chinese in Australia were also marginalized in death. Chinese funerary practices that involved feasting and bonfires were regarded as "heathenish" by European observers, who preferred a more solemn interment. The Chinese dead were also often buried in separate "alien" sections of local cemeteries. Nevertheless, Chinese cemeteries, grave-markers, burners and tombs expressed important personal and social relationships between this world and the next. They were also an accommodation to the realities of life in the present. Traditional beliefs and practices persisted, but were modified as circumstances changed in a foreign context, reflecting the resilience and adaptability of the overseas Chinese.

The Great War

The First World War was a turning point in the way Australians responded to death. More than 60,000 Australians were killed in the conflict, one in every five of those who went away. Historian Ken Inglis (1998:91–92) indicates that two out of every three Australians in uniform were killed or wounded, all in the space of just 4 years. While today Gallipoli is remembered as the bloody baptism of Australian nationhood, the Western Front was much more deadly, with three out of every four Australians who died killed on the battlefields of France and Belgium. The mass slaughter of young men and the untold grief of families left a deep scar on an entire generation, a pain exacerbated by the global influenza pandemic of 1918–1921, the 1930s Depression, and the onset of the Second World War. Pat Jalland (2006:42) argues that the sheer scale of human loss at the time undermined Christian faith in a benevolent God, and prompted a growing secularism, especially among non-Catholics. Nevertheless, commemoration of the war dead occurred in numerous ways, ranging from battlefield cemeteries and Shrines of Remembrance to Rolls of Honour in schools and halls, trees planted in Avenues of Honour, memorial gardens, and thousands of inscribed monuments in towns and suburbs throughout Australia (Holmes et al. 2008:146–153; Inglis 1998; Lake 2006).

The anguish of many families was made worse by not having a body to grieve over, or even the certainty of knowing whether a loved one had died. About 25,000 Australians killed in action were never identified and have no known grave (Jalland 2002:305). Families suffered agonies in not knowing but fearing the worst, imagining smashed bodies and terrible violence. They were denied the solace of grieving without a body to bury or a grave to visit. Many corpses could only be commemorated by group memorials to the missing, like that at Lone Pine at Gallipoli, where the names of 4,228 Australians are inscribed, and at Ypres in Belgium where more than 6,000 fallen Australian soldiers are remembered on the Menin Gate memorial (Jalland 2006:90).

A major archaeological project in France has investigated a mass grave of Australian and British soldiers. The Battle of Fromelles, in north-eastern France, took place on 19–20 July, 1916. It was the first major offensive on the Western Front involving soldiers from the First Australian Imperial Force. The result was disastrous. In just one night the Australians suffered 5,533 casualties to the German machine gunners, while the British lost 1,547 killed or wounded. The German ranks included a young Adolf Hitler, then aged 27 (Corfield 2009; Lindsay 2007:48–54, 143). In recent years, intensive historical research by Melbourne schoolteacher Lambis Englezos suggested that around 400 Australian and British soldiers killed in the battle had been buried in eight rectangular pits at Pheasant Wood, near the village of Fromelles, in the days following the battle. In 2007 a geophysical survey was conducted by a team from Glasgow University in an attempt to locate the burial pits at the site. A full scale excavation was conducted by Oxford Archaeology in 2009 to exhume the soldiers from the group burial and reinter them with full military honours. A total of 250 burials were recovered (Army Fromelle Project 2009). In this way, archaeology becomes part of the memorialization process. Careful excavation has been combined with military and family history to separate the anonymous war dead and return individual identities to the men who lost their lives in the service of nation and empire.

Contemporary Aboriginal Traditions

Graves are also a crucial part of Aboriginal memory and the ongoing cultural attachment to place. As we argued in Chapter 3, Aboriginal culture of the past 200 years is not simply a degraded or eroded version of pre-1788 life. Rather it has engaged with white Australia to combine tradition with change, and graves are an important part of this process. Traditional Aboriginal practices regarding the dead varied considerably across Australia, and included burial, cremation and secondary burial (Attenbrow 2002:139–142; Donlon 1998; Haglund 1976; Hiatt 1969; Hope 1998). Archaeologist Denis Byrne (1998) has described how burial practices have changed in Aboriginal communities in New South Wales over the last 200 years. Until the nineteenth century, Aboriginal graves were often marked by the presence of trees carved with designs to commemorate the person buried, in a similar way to the European use of headstones. As more Aboriginal people adopted Christianity, the new beliefs merged with traditional practices; smoking ceremonies were often carried out at funerals, and the deceased were buried in a crouched or sitting position. The traditional bark wrapping around the body was replaced with the blanket that had kept the person warm in life. Objects placed in the grave also reflected the new circumstances of people's lives and included flaked bottle glass, clay tobacco pipes, coins and crockery (Byrne 1998:12). Relatively few Aboriginal graves, however, have conventional headstones, and many places where Aboriginal people were buried were never formally gazetted as cemeteries. This means that descendants have often had to rely on memories passed down from parents and grandparents to recall the locations of graves and burial places.

Massacre sites are also places of intense emotional importance for Aboriginal communities. The slaughter of Aboriginal men, women and children was a brutal part of the expansion of European settlement in the nineteenth century, although bold resistance was also part of the Aboriginal response. Nevertheless, it has been estimated that up to 20,000 Aboriginal people died across Australia as a direct result of white violence (Broome 1994:74). There was often a conspiracy among the white perpetrators to hide the evidence, which involved burning the bodies and removing skulls as "souvenirs". In many cases, the location of human remains, and often the massacre site itself, are only vaguely known, preserved as shadowy rumours by later generations (Byrne 1998:17). Notwithstanding such silences, there have been hundreds of massacre sites documented around Australia over the years, including more than 100 in the Western District of Victoria alone (Clark 1995).

One of the most infamous examples was the Myall Creek massacre of June 1838, when 11 station hands were tried for the murder of at least 28 Aboriginal people in northern New South Wales, and seven were convicted and hanged. The case provoked outrage in the white community, steeped in the belief of European racial superiority and the conviction that Aboriginal people were "savages". There followed 160 years of silence, in which generations of Australians knew and cared little about such events (Murray 2004c:204–210). In 2000, however, a memorial was established on a hill overlooking the massacre site, in a process during which descendants of both perpetrators and victims publicly acknowledged what had happened.

Conclusion

Australia's changing attitudes to the dead have been traced by examining changes in the processes surrounding exhumation (Karskens 2003a). At the Old Sydney Burial Ground, the bodies were unceremoniously dug up in 1869 and reburied in a mass plot, partly in fear of the foul "miasmas" they were believed to emit. Many bodies were left behind, however, to be found haphazardly over the next 140 years. A few decades later, when the Devonshire Street Cemetery was cleared to make way for Sydney's Central Railway Station, the Public Works Department took control of the project. They removed 30,000 bodies with efficient care and wiped the site clean. The Point Frederick Cemetery at Gosford on the central coast of New South Wales was transformed into a Pioneer Park in the 1970s, replacing an untidy, overgrown "mess" with a planned and controlled suburban showpiece. Most of the gravestones were rearranged for aesthetic reasons, and gardens were built over the dead, who by now were simply ignored.

By the 1990s, excavation at the Destitute Children's Cemetery at Randwick was carried out by professional archaeologists, which meant that the *bodies* of the deceased had once again become significant, not for the threat of disease or for spiritual reasons, but for their value as objects of science. Elaborate protocols were put in place to safeguard the interests of the many stakeholders involved, including the dead children themselves, to ensure their remains were treated with care and respect. Karskens argues that this recent shift in sentiment, where reverence has replaced earlier pragmatism, owes much to efforts to return and rebury the remains of Aboriginal ancestors. The respect demanded by Indigenous people for the human remains of their ancestors has flowed into the non-Aboriginal cultural arena, with the bones of Asylum children reinterred with the respect understood to be their due. The archaeology of the dead thus reminds us not only of our own mortality, but also of the strength and fragility of the social groups within which we and our forebears have lived.

Chapter 13
The Twentieth Century and Beyond

This book has focused on the archaeology of Australia's colonial past, an emphasis which reflects a number of developments in the history of the discipline in this country. The first practitioners of historical archaeology in the 1960s and 1970s were literally breaking new ground. One of their concerns was to establish the legitimacy of an archaeology of European settlement, at a time when most archaeology in Australia focused on the ancient Near East and Mediterranean worlds, or on deep time and the first arrival of Australia's original inhabitants and their adaptations to different regions and environments. This resulted, in part, in the investigation of places of early European arrival, including seventeenth-century Dutch shipwrecks, first settlements along the coast (both failed and successful) and the archaeology of convictism. Research interests quickly widened and deepened, but the colonial period remained in favour, reinforced perhaps by a sense that any place of more recent date, especially after 1900, somehow lacked the archaeological interest or potential of earlier periods. The result has been that the archaeology of this more recent past remains largely neglected in Australia. In Victoria (and until recently in New South Wales), for example, a 50-year rolling date defines archaeological sites in heritage legislation, which means that many places which post-date the Second World War are now formally recognised and protected in law for their archaeological value. With the exception of places significant to Indigenous Australians, however, it is unusual to find dedicated archaeological studies of sites and landscapes from the last 100 years, although archaeologists in Britain and the United States have begun to record sites of the recent and contemporary past, expanding the notion of "an archaeology of us" originally developed by Richard Gould and Michael Schiffer (1981; see Buchli and Lucas 2001; De Silvey 2006; Harrison and Schofield 2009; Holtorf and Piccini 2009; McAtackney et al. 2007; McVarish 2008; Schofield 2009; Schofield and Johnson 2006; Stratton and Trinder 2000). In this final chapter we challenge this reluctance to engage with the archaeology of the twentieth century on its own terms and argue that the very closeness and familiarity of this period offers opportunities and challenges unlike any other in the human past.

The twentieth century was characterised by global wars, mass human migrations and genocide. It was also dominated by dramatic innovation and technological change. Automobiles, aircraft and space travel transformed notions of distance and movement, while radio, television, personal computers and the internet created

S. Lawrence, P. Davies, *An Archaeology of Australia Since 1788*,
Contributions To Global Historical Archaeology, DOI 10.1007/978-1-4419-7485-3_13,
© Springer Science+Business Media, LLC 2011

new media for communication and information. Supermarkets and shopping malls replaced the corner shop and the high street, and cities devoured the countryside. The physical landscape of the twentieth century is still mostly with us and mostly still in its original use. This landscape, from factories and freeways to airports and housing estates, connects us with the past in crucial ways and helps in understanding the major changes that have occurred in the last 100 years. This material is not merely a shabby, recent intrusion, but should be recognised for representing an extraordinary period in the human story. The archaeological record of the twentieth century bears witness to remarkable economic, social and technological vitality, evidence which merits careful and detailed analysis. How much of this landscape we demolish, and how much we recognise and retain for its "heritage" value, will become a matter of increasing concern, as more and more structures and buildings disappear and memories of them are lost (Bradley et al. 2004).

In 1993, historian Susan Marsden asked why archaeologists in Australia had ignored the twentieth century, noting that except for the early settled districts around Sydney and Hobart, "this country has been Australian for much longer than it was colonial" (Marsden 1993:142). Archaeological investigation is important, she argued, because the pace of change during this period was so great that particular objects, manufacturing processes, buildings and structures have been rapidly superseded and abandoned, altered or destroyed. Several recent studies have responded to the challenge she posed (e.g. Allison 1998, 2003; Davies 2006a; Gorman 2005; Grimwade 1998; Prangnell 1999, 2002; Taksa 2005; Veres 2005), while a focus has also emerged on battlefield archaeology (e.g. De La Rue 2005; Cameron and Donlon 2005; Jung 2005) but the twentieth century remains a secondary consideration for most practitioners. For many, the period represents "modern disturbance" or even "overburden" (see Matthews 1999), although studies of late-nineteenth-century places often elide into the early decades of the twentieth century. Study of this period, however, can draw upon not only an abundant historical record, but also artefacts, buildings, living memories, film and photos to provide a picture of recent places and landscapes of a depth and detail unrivalled for any other period.

While archaeologists have often neglected the twentieth century, a focus on this "unloved modern" heritage has developed in recent years among historians, architects, planners and museum curators (Jones 2002; Smith and Akagawa 2009). There has also been a growing focus in Australia on intangible heritage and social identity and the ways in which people confer or inscribe meaning on places and objects. This approach shifts the emphasis away from fabric and places as having *inherent* meaning towards the idea of cultural heritage as a field of cultural and social action (Byrne et al. 2001). Places may be significant for seasons of attachment and memory, even though there is no physical manifestation of this connection. We have seen in Chapter 3 how Indigenous Australians maintain strong cultural links with places that are important in the recent past, although often little is left that is identifiably "Aboriginal" about such sites (Byrne and Nugent 2004). In this way cultural identity is dynamic and inventive, drawing eclectically on the past to employ memories, symbols and language to forge ongoing relationships with the past in the present. Nevertheless, an archaeology of the twentieth century must confront the overwhelming materiality of the past 100 years. In the remainder of this chapter we identify some themes and materials from the recent past that will benefit from detailed archaeological scrutiny in the years ahead.

In Chapter 8 we examined some of the early manufacturing industries in colonial Australia and observed the value of archaeological remains for understanding the development of industrial sites, landscapes, processes and products. Manufacturing in Australia expanded during the twentieth century into the production of thousands of products, with local industry protected by a complex array of tariffs, quotas and subsidies. Manufacturing dominated many suburbs in Melbourne, Sydney, Adelaide, Newcastle and elsewhere, with factory workers making everything from cars and machinery to furniture, paint, chemicals, clothing, boots and many other goods. By the 1950s manufacturing accounted for around 28 percent of Australia's economy (Anderson 1987:166; Carroll 1987). As tariff protection was removed from the 1970s, however, Australian manufacturers struggled to compete with cheaper imports, and local industries declined. Plant and equipment was abandoned or discarded, while factories and warehouses were demolished, converted into apartments or adapted to other industries. Much can still be learned, however, from the physical remains of factories that operated until relatively recently. Machinery, for example, can reveal continuity and change in manufacturing processes and the extent to which local practices became outmoded in an environment of limited international competition or where technology transfer permitted the upgrading and modernising of operations. Equipment can reveal the extent to which batch production was replaced by continuous production and manual handling shifted to automated handling, while transport links demonstrate the scale and efficiency of bringing materials in and sending products away to market. Offices and facilities for workers illustrate the changing nature of labour relations and the impact of the union movement on improving the conditions of work. Changing structures and spaces also reflect the movement of women into the paid workforce in large numbers and the new opportunities for women that factory work represented.

There are perhaps few better symbols of material life in the twentieth century than the automobile. Not only has the car changed the way we live, work, travel and socialise; it has structured the growth of towns and cities and continues to do so. Suburbanisation arose with railways in the nineteenth century, but private cars entrenched the growth of suburban living in the twentieth century. The car also created a vast array of associated infrastructure, including roads and highways and freeways, petrol stations, car parks, garages and drive-ins, while car assembly and manufacturing plants employed thousands of workers in Adelaide, Melbourne and Geelong. In rural areas, rusty old vehicles on farms represent the changing nature of machinery and movement and the changing scale of farming operations (Simpson and Simpson 1988; Smith 2005). This is all now so commonplace as to seem unremarkable. As Graeme Davison (2004) points out in *Car Wars*, however, the triumph of the automobile was the result of powerful historical forces, involving governments and planning authorities, car manufacturers and consumers themselves. The car became much more than a machine in which to travel from A to B, emerging as a status symbol, an emblem of material success and a catalyst for changing sexual values (Pickett 1998). The tension between privacy inside the car while stuck in very public traffic has become a central motif of modern living. Archaeology is well placed to explore how this dependence on the car emerged, how it varied from place to place and the role of the car at the intersection between personal and public life in the twentieth century.

The increasing domination of private cars by the mid-twentieth century also undermined public transport services. Tram systems, for example, were common in Australian capital cities up to this time, while trams also operated in Launceston, Kalgoorlie, Rockhampton, Newcastle, Broken Hill, Ballarat, Bendigo and Geelong. Sydney's tram network included 290 km of track by the 1920s and conveyed millions of passengers every year (Bowdon and Campbell 2009). As mass car ownership and freeways burgeoned in the 1950s, however, most tram systems in Australia were dismantled, with Melbourne alone retaining and developing its network. Some of these systems still operate in a limited way as tourist trams, and the surviving infrastructure includes elements of rail networks, tram cars, depots and maintenance sheds and power plants. The remains, often obscured by later development, can help to reveal how public transport shaped work and travel patterns, the geography of industry and relationships between suburbs and city centres.

The rise of the automobile was also central to major changes in shopping in the twentieth century and the growing focus on the culture of consumption. An archaeology of shops and retailing has enormous potential for revealing the changing nature of distributing, marketing and selling products to consumers (Crook 2000). Department stores, for example, emerged in the 1870s and 1880s and became increasingly prominent from the turn of the century, selling thousands of product lines from large, often multi-storey premises. Stores such as Horderns and David Jones in Sydney, John Martins in Adelaide and Myer and Coles in Melbourne sold clothing for the whole family, along with haberdashery, fabrics, stationery, toiletries, hardware and furniture, and many stores had cafes or restaurants as well as theatres, hair salons and art galleries. Customers came by tram or train to these large stores in the central business district not only to buy items on a shopping list but also to enjoy the experience of browsing aisles stocked with lavish displays of consumer goods. Shopping was on its way to becoming a fashionable leisure activity, and a distinctly gendered one, as shops were designed to appeal to middle-class women whose purchases helped to mark the social standing of their families (Kingston 1994:26). Arcades of smaller shops in city centres and in the suburbs were also part of this development, selling choice merchandise for discerning customers. Awnings and colonnades along shop fronts provided welcome protection from sun and rain and a place to promenade and admire window displays. The coming of the automobile, however, meant that the supporting posts restricted parking spaces, while goods in windows could not be seen from passing cars. Shop awnings were dismantled and shelter for pedestrian customers at street level disappeared. Streetscapes were transformed to accommodate the increasing numbers and importance of private motor vehicles.

The 1920s and 1930s witnessed other changes in retailing as well, including chain stores, self-service, pre-packaged goods, refrigerated displays, aggressive promotion, credit purchase and the decline of home delivery. The general store of the nineteenth century had offered opportunities for small business owners of modest capital and involved much family labour and long hours. Its gradual demise in the twentieth century meant the loss of long wooden counters, large jars full of sweets, bins full of tea, flour and sugar, and neatly stacked shelves. Chain stores set new standards of cheapness and economy and were attractive to working-class shoppers. Personal service declined, and the merchandise was expected to sell itself, which reinforced the importance of individual packaging and advertising. These patterns were strengthened in the decades following the Second World War, when supermarkets emerged in Australia and rapidly gained in popularity for their size, convenience and the sense of modernity and freshness they promoted (Symons 2007:205–216). Shopping by car was now the accepted way to purchase most goods. The end of the twentieth century saw the massive growth and domination of suburban shopping malls, with their vast car parks, food courts and cinema complexes. Malls also replaced the older shopping streets as community hubs, often featuring municipal libraries, health centres and child-care facilities. Shopping, leisure and community services were still located together, but they had been redistributed to the suburbs, in the midst of where people lived. They serve as intensely material symbols of modern life, with consumers and retailers far removed from the factories and farms where products are created.

Automobiles brought widespread change that penetrated every domain of social and economic life. Space exploration did not bring such extensive change, but it constituted a profound shift in our understanding of the universe and represents one of the great achievements of the twentieth century. Most of the initiative and work done in space exploration took place overseas, but Australia has its own archaeology of space. Observatories and telescopes were set up at several locations in Australia, including Tidbinbilla near Canberra and Parkes in western New South Wales, locations valued for their isolation and lack of background light and also for their position in the southern hemisphere. They have always worked closely with NASA and been involved in tracking all of NASA's missions, including the moon landings and the space shuttle. At Woomera in outback South Australia the British government established a facility for testing guided missiles in 1946, while nuclear testing was conducted between 1952 and 1963 at Emu Field and Maralinga in South Australia and on the Monte Bello Islands off the Western Australian coast. There is no doubt that these places and their material culture will be important heritage places for future generations, but at present their heritage aspects are little regarded (Gorman 2005).

Sport is a significant domain of Australian cultural and social life that has a strong material signature, but has lacked an archaeological focus. Horse-racing, hunting, cricket and fighting were popular pastimes for much of the colonial period (Cumes 1979), and authorities reserved public land as parks for sports and leisure (Wright 1989). By the twentieth century most metropolitan and country areas boasted a racecourse and a host of fields for cricket and the various football codes. Spectators were not forgotten, with grandstands built for watching the action. Public swimming pools and tennis courts were also constructed in many places, providing opportunities for practice and the emergence of the first generations of professional sports men and women. Ample land meant that golf courses were popular, creating landscapes that were both cultivated and natural, both public and enclosed. Numerous sports have been played and enjoyed in Australia over the years, fostered by the climate, open space, leisure time, cultural preference and economic opportunity. Sporting facilities encouraged participation, which required further amenities, which encouraged even more participation, and the Australian love affair with sport rolled on. Sports required equipment, and often uniforms, all of which changed in response to various factors. Archaeology is well placed to consider the role of sport in Australian society over the last 100 years and to examine how the growth of professionalism has affected amateur, community-level sports in terms of facilities, equipment and even rule changes. The material culture of team supporters, from buttons, clothing and scarves in team colours to the massive banners made by cheer squads, is all part of potential archaeologies of AFL football, the rugby codes and cricket that remain to be attempted.

Some of the most profound changes in Australian culture since white settlement have happened in the decades following the Second World War, brought about by waves of migration from many parts of the world and by the rise of feminism. Both of these areas have a substantial and fascinating material signature. After the Second World War new migration policies targeted people displaced by the conflict, including those from the Baltic states and from southern and central Europe, in part to provide a source of labour for large infrastructure projects like the Snowy Mountain Scheme in New South Wales and the hydro-electric schemes in Tasmania (both of which also present ideal archaeological studies). This resulted in the arrival of large numbers of people from non-English-speaking backgrounds. They required immediate practical assistance in the form of the migrant hostels noted in Chapter 9, but thereafter spread across Australia bringing new foods, new ways of eating and drinking and the growth of café society, and new suburban landscapes as they established their own clubs and associations, built and decorated houses in styles familiar to them and established gardens that reflected the countrysides they had left behind.

Feminism was the other quiet revolution of this period. Socially, women demanded and achieved great gains in access to education and jobs and in equal pay for equal work. Combined with the contraceptive pill, introduced in 1961, birth rates fell and the size of families declined with two or at most three children entrenched as the norm. The material effects of these changes should be visible in workplaces, as outlined above, and also in homes that were reconfigured to make kitchens more efficient and more open to the other living areas of the house. Women were no longer the quiet servants to be isolated in small kitchens at the back of the dwelling.

An archaeology of the twentieth century is at its most compelling when it investigates the social uses of material culture. Mass production led to higher levels of material possessions among even the poorest groups in the twentieth century. What uses, values and meanings did these possessions have in a capitalist economy, and how did these change through time? As the production of goods became increasingly removed from the home and replaced with objects manufactured in distant factories, the values associated with these goods also altered, becoming less personal, less a link with the past and more a means of engaging with consumer culture. This trend was well in evidence by the nineteenth century, but intensified during the twentieth century, until in many people's lives there was almost a complete disjunction between the spheres of production and consumption. At the same time, however, this homogenising trend was counteracted by the embrace of diversity and pluralism, as individuals and communities continually redefined themselves in the face of distant institutions through the medium of material culture (Miller 1995). The spatial and material architecture of people's lives in the twentieth century was thus fundamentally transformed, and archaeology has an important role to play in documenting these changes and their meanings in people's lives.

The very idea of "rubbish" in the twentieth century also needs to be examined, given the competing pressures of consumption (acquisition), thrift (reuse) and hygiene (discard) constantly tugging at householders' responses to the material world. As Gavin Lucas (2002) reminds us, notions of rubbish in the nineteenth century distinguished between bodily waste, food remains, inorganic refuse such as bottles and cans, and ashes, even though these materials were often discarded together, especially in cesspits and rubbish pits. By the twentieth century, expanding production of containers for food, drink and numerous other domestic items increased the amount of waste to be dealt with, a situation exacerbated by the growing number of people living close together in urban and suburban areas. Disposable paper (and later, plastic) packaging emphasised cleanliness and the single use of goods, strengthening the relationship between consumption, hygiene and discard. Local councils removed much household waste to landfill sites, while other materials were incinerated in the backyard or hoarded in sheds or under houses. In addition, the provision of large-scale water supply and sewage systems, and the growing popularity of indoor bathrooms and toilets, also permitted a greater focus on personal cleanliness and the separation of bodily hygiene from domestic waste. Modern ideas about rubbish thus relate to a whole series of changes affecting personal and domestic economies in the early twentieth century, including the purchase and use of goods, domestic and personal hygiene, recycling, hoarding and discard. In Chapter 10 we discuss how the first stages of these changes have shaped the archaeological record of our cities, with the construction of large-scale municipal tips and the installation of sewage systems, but the trajectory of change, particularly at the personal level, requires further study.

Investigating the social meanings of material culture also depends on a good understanding of the basic chronology and changing designs of the many common and utilitarian artefacts used in this period. In an Australian context, however, studies that rely on the careful post-excavation analysis of items from well-documented twentieth-century sites are rare. Items such as electrical fittings and bathroom fixtures, kitchen cookware, children's toys, items of personal hygiene, consumer electronics and office stationery can all reveal a great deal about the lives of individuals and how they engaged with the material world. One immediate shift seen in the archaeological record is the decline of Britain as the major source of imported goods and the increasing importance of Asian and American imports. New materials play an even larger role. Artefact studies from colonial Australia are dominated, as we

have seen in previous chapters, by ceramics, glass and bone, materials which preserve well in archaeological contexts. The twentieth century, however, saw the rise
of plastics as one of the fundamental fabrics of modern consumer society, often
replacing older manufacturing materials such as iron, glass, wood and clay, but
archaeologists have barely begun to come to terms with this now ubiquitous material
(Mossman 1997; Springate 1997). The products that could be created from plastic
were almost endless and added enormously to the comfort and convenience of everyday domestic life. Most plastics do not biodegrade, although they do photo-degrade,
with prolonged exposure to sunlight breaking down the polymer chains that hold
plastic together, resulting in smaller and smaller pieces. One result is the growing
pollution of waterways and oceans, while another is that buried plastics tend not to
decay and remain accessible for archaeological study.

Plastics generally represent a range of artificial, mouldable substances, including
many types of resins, polymers, cellulose products and proteins. The first successful
plastic was celluloid, developed in New York in 1869 using plant cellulose and later
used in photographic film. German chemists discovered casein in 1897, using skim
milk and formaldehyde, and casein knitting needles were widely used during the
First World War to knit woollen comforts for soldiers. In 1907, Leo Baekeland, a
Belgian chemist working in the United States, invented Bakelite, the first synthetic
plastic. Bakelite was the first heat-resistant plastic, and it was soon widely used in
electrical products such as telephones, light fittings and ashtrays. Synthetic rubber
(neoprene) was developed in the late 1920s, and by 1930 Perspex was in production as a rugged substitute for glass. Nylon appeared in 1935, first developed as a
substitute for silk, but then used in rope, parachutes, brush bristles and many other
products. Cellophane became popular as a packaging material from the 1930s as
well. In the 1940s, other now-familiar plastics also came into production, including
polystyrene foam (for insulation), PVC piping, epoxy resin adhesives and polyester
clothing. By this stage petroleum had come to be the main source of raw material for
plastics. The manufacture of plastic products, which commonly involved extrusion
and moulding, was well suited to automatic machinery, which led to high output and
low cost. Plastics thus gained a reputation for cheapness but also for poor quality.
Nevertheless, they were used in the manufacture of some of the signal products of
the twentieth century, including vinyl records, audio and video cassettes, sunglasses,
plastic drink bottles and wheely bins (Stratton and Trinder 2000:17).

Plastics were not the only new material developed in the twentieth century.
Aluminium, for example, produced from the mineral bauxite, is strong, lightweight
and corrosion resistant, and it competed with steel and plastics for use in aircraft
bodies, packaging and refrigerators. Concrete reinforced with steel gained increasing acceptance as a building material after 1900, as it became widely used in the
construction of bridges and large buildings (Cowan 1998:90–97). Wood came to
be used in new ways as well, including ply, chipboard and laminates. Asbestos, a
mineral mined extensively in Western Australia, was widely used for fire-resistant
packing materials and for insulation, along with brakes for motor vehicles and
cheap wall panels and roofing tiles. Growing appreciation of the carcinogenic
nature of asbestos fibres from the 1970s, however, led to a dramatic reduction in

its use. Asbestos building materials are commonplace in the upper layers of many archaeological sites, constituting an ongoing danger for archaeologists.

One of the most important technologies to emerge in the late twentieth century was the computer. In 50 years we have seen computer hardware shrink in size from machines that occupied entire buildings to those too small to be seen with the naked eye. Digital technologies have infiltrated almost every sphere of public and private life. Alongside such rapid growth, however, has been a massive obsolescence in hardware and software. Generations of now defunct computers have become a disposal problem, but an archaeology of computing will be invaluable for understanding the dramatic transformation of information processing in such a short space of time and the growing penetration of digital technologies into lived human experience. Historians and archivists have expressed alarm for years that so much important electronic information is not being retained, managed and migrated. This is also a concern for archaeologists, not just for the loss of significant historical material, but also for the loss of machines with which to read it. The importance of keeping even a few machines "alive" was illustrated clearly in the United States a few decades ago. Information gathered for the 1960 U.S. Census was stored on computer tapes of a type and format that became obsolete within a few years. By 1990, there were only two machines in the world still capable of reading the data. One of the devices, already regarded as a relic, was in the Smithsonian Institution and the other was in Japan (Basbanes 2003:275). If a computer record cannot be read, then for all practical purposes it ceases to exist.

Michael Stratton and Barrie Trinder (2000:5) argue that people hunger for the kind of understanding which archaeologists can bring to the physical remains of the past 100 years. Houses, factories, objects and landscapes from the twentieth century are close and familiar to us, not remote in time and exotic. They speak directly to us of our own past, something our parents and grandparents helped to build and create. If heritage consists of those things from the past we value the most, and which we use to create social identities, then an archaeology of the twentieth century becomes central to understanding of who we are as individuals and as a wider community. Material from the recent past has immediacy and a vitality lacking for earlier periods. We approach it with enthusiasm or distaste or disinterest, not because it is foreign, but because it is ours.

References

Abraham, Terry and Priscilla Wegars (2003)˄Urns, bones and burners: overseas Chinese cemeteries. *Australasian Historical Archaeology* 21:58–69.

Adam-Smith, Patsy (1982) *The Shearers*. Nelson, Melbourne.

Adams, William H. (2003) Dating historical sites: the importance of understanding time lag in the acquisition, curation, use and disposal of artifacts. *Historical Archaeology* 37(2): 38–64.

Allen, Jim (1969) *Archaeology and the History of Port Essington*. Unpublished Ph.D. dissertation, Research School of Pacific Studies, Australian National University, Canberra.

Allen, Jim (1973) The archaeology of nineteenth-century British imperialism: an Australian case study. *World Archaeology* 5(1):44–60.

Allen, Jim (2008) *Port Essington: The Historical Archaeology of a North Australian Nineteenth-Century Military Outpost*. Studies in Australasian Historical Archaeology 1, Australasian Society for Historical Archaeology and Sydney University Press, Sydney.

Allen, Jim and Jane Lennon (1978) *Report to the Commonwealth Department of Construction on the Archaeology of Norfolk Island*. Commonwealth Department of Construction, Canberra.

Allen, Jim and Rhys Jones (1980) Oyster Cove: archaeological traces of the last Tasmanians and notes on the criteria for the authentication of flaked glass artefacts. *Papers and Proceedings of the Royal Society of Tasmania* 114:225–233.

Allison, Penelope (1998) The household in historical archaeology. *Australasian Historical Archaeology* 16:16–29.

Allison, Penelope (2003) The Old Kinchega homestead: household archaeology in outback Australia. *International Journal of Historical Archaeology* 7(3):161–194.

Ames, Kenneth L. (1986) Meaning in artefacts: hall furnishings in Victorian America. In: Dell Upton and John Michael Vlach (eds.), *Common Places: Readings in American Vernacular Architecture*, pp. 240–260. University of Georgia Press, Athens, GA.

Anderson, Kym (1987) Tariffs and the manufacturing sector. In: Rodney Maddock and Ian W. McLean (eds.), *The Australian Economy in the Long Run*, pp. 165–194. Cambridge University Press, Cambridge.

Anderson, Fiona (2002) *The Quick and the Dead: Live Fencing of Spring Hill Parish, Victoria*. Unpublished BA (Honours) dissertation, Archaeology Program, La Trobe University, Melbourne.

Anderson, Ross (2004) Whaling and colonial trade: evidence on the Shipwreck Cheviot (1827–1854). *The Bulletin of the Australasian Institute for Maritime Archaeology* 28:1–10.

Anderson, Ross (2006) The Convincing Ground: a case study in frontier and modern conflict. *The Bulletin of the Australian Institute for Maritime Archaeology* 30:137–147.

Anderson, Ross, Cassandra Philippou and Peter Harvey (2006) Innovative approaches in underwater cultural heritage management. In: Mark Staniforth and Michael Nash (eds.), *Maritime Archaeology: Australian Approaches*, pp. 137–150. Springer, New York, NY.

S. Lawrence, P. Davies, *An Archaeology of Australia Since 1788*,
Contributions To Global Historical Archaeology, DOI 10.1007/978-1-4419-7485-3,
© Springer Science+Business Media, LLC 2011

Anson, Tim J. (2004) *The Bioarchaeology of the St. Mary's Free Ground Burials: Reconstruction of Colonial South Australian Lifeways*. Unpublished Ph.D. dissertation, Department of Anatomical Sciences, University of Adelaide, Adelaide.

Anson, Tim J. and Maciej Henneberg (2004) A solution for the permanent storage of historical skeletal remains for research purposes: a South Australian precedent that keeps scientists and the church community happy. *Australian Archaeology* 58:15–18.

Ariès, Phillipe (1981) *The Hour of our Death*. Translated by Helen Weaver, Knopf, New York, NY.

Armstrong, Henry J. (1901) *A Treatise on the Law of Gold-Mining in Australia and New Zealand*, 2nd edition. Charles F. Maxwell, Melbourne.

Army Fromelle Project (2009) Army Fromelle Project. Electronic document, http://www.defence. gov.au/army/fromelles/Fromelles-home.asp. Accessed 1 June 2009.

Arnold, Ken (1990) *A Victorian Thirst*. Crown Castleton Publishers, Maiden Gully, VIC.

Ash, Aidan (2007) *The Maritime Cultural Landscape of Port Willunga, South Australia*. Adelaide, Department of Archaeology, Flinders University, Adelaide.

Atkinson, Alan (1988) *Camden*. Oxford University Press, Melbourne.

Attenbrow, Val (2002) *Sydney's Aboriginal Past: Investigating the Archaeological and Historical Records*. UNSW Press, Sydney.

Attwood, Bain (2009) *Possession: Batman's Treaty and the Matter of History*. The Miegunyah Press, Melbourne, VIC.

Auhl, Ian (1980) *Burra and District: A Pictorial Memoir*. Investigator Press, Hawthorndene, SA.

Austral Archaeology (1992) *Archaeological Report on the Rookery Site*. Report submitted to Corporation of the City of Adelaide, Adelaide.

Austral Archaeology (1997) *Point Puer Historical Archaeological Survey Report*. Report submitted to Port Arthur Historic Site Management Authority, Tasmania.

Austral/Godden Mackay (1997) *POW Project 1995: Randwick Destitute Children's Asylum Cemetery*, 4 vols. Report submitted to Eastern Sydney Area Health Service, Heritage Council of NSW and the NSW Department of Health.

Australian Government (2008) *Australian Convict Sites: World Heritage Nomination*. Department of the Environment, Water, Heritage and the Arts, Canberra.

Bagshaw, Anthony (2001) *Message in a Bottle: The Contribution of Private Bottle Collections to the Archaeological Record*. Unpublished BA (Honours) dissertation, Archaeology Program, La Trobe University, Melbourne.

Bairstow, Damaris (1986) Hydraulic power and coal loading at Newcastle harbour, New South Wales. *The Australian Journal of Historical Archaeology* 4:57–66.

Bairstow, Damaris (2003) *A Million Pounds, A Million Acres: The Pioneer Settlement of the Australian Agricultural Company*. D. Bairstow, Cremorne, New South Wales.

Baker, Brenda J., Tosha L. Dupras and Matthew W. Tocheri (2005) *The Osteology of Infants and Children*. Texas A&M University Press, College Station, TX.

Banner, Stuart (2007) *Possessing the Pacific: Land, Settlers and Indigenous People from Australia to Alaska*. Harvard University Press, Cambridge, MA.

Baram, Uzi and Lynda Carroll (2000) The future of the Ottoman past. In: Uzi Baram and Lynda Carroll (eds.), *A Historical Archaeology of the Ottoman Empire: Breaking New Ground*, pp. 3–32. Kluwer/Plenum, New York, NY.

Barker, Anita (2007) *From the Ashes: Children at the Coach and Horses Hotel*. Unpublished BA (Honours) dissertation, Archaeology Program, La Trobe University, Melbourne.

Barker, Bryce (2007) Massacre, frontier conflict and Australian archaeology. *Australian Archaeology* 64:9–14.

Basbanes, Nicholas (2003) *A Splendor of Letters: The Permanence of Books in an Impermanent World*. HarperCollins, New York, NY.

Bate, Weston (1978) *Lucky City: The First Generation at Ballarat 1851–1901*. Melbourne University Press, Melbourne.

Bate, Weston (1988) *Victorian Gold Rushes*. McPhee Gribble/Penguin Books, Melbourne.

Bean, Charles E. W. (1963 [1910]) *On the Wool Track*. Sirius Books, Sydney.

Beaudry, Mary (2006a) *Findings: The Material Culture of Needlework and Sewing*. Yale University Press, New Haven, CT.

Beaudry, Mary (2006b) Stories that matter: material lives in 19th century Lowell and Boston, Massachusetts. In: Adrian Green and Roger Leech (eds.), *Cities in the World 1500–2000*, pp. 249–268. Maney Publishing and the Society for Post-Medieval Archaeology, Leeds.

Beck, Wendy and Margaret Somerville (2005) Conversations between disciplines: historical archaeology and oral history at Yarrawarra. *World Archaeology* 37(3):468–483.

Beckett, Jeremy (1987) *Torres Strait Islanders: Custom and Colonialism*. Cambridge University Press, Cambridge.

Beeston, John (1994) *A Concise History of Australian Wine*. Allen and Unwin, Sydney.

Belich, James (2009) *Replenishing the Earth: The Settler Revolution and the Rise of the Anglo-World, 1783–1939*. Oxford University Press, Oxford.

Bell, Peter (1987) *Gold, Iron and Steam: The Industrial Archaeology of the Palmer Goldfield*. James Cook University, Townsville, Queensland.

Bell, Peter (1990) Continuity in Australian timber domestic building: an early cottage at Burra. *The Australian Journal of Historical Archaeology* 8:3–12.

Bell, Peter (1995) Chinese ovens on mining settlement sites in Australia. In: Paul MacGregor (ed.), *Histories of the Chinese in Australasia and the South Pacific*, pp. 213–229. Museum of Chinese Australian History, Melbourne.

Bell, Peter (1998a) *Early Bricks and Brickwork in South Australia*. Department for Environment, Heritage and Aboriginal Affairs, City of Adelaide, Adelaide.

Bell, Peter (1998b) The fabric and structure of Australian mining settlements. In: A. Bernard Knapp, Vincent C. Pigott and Eugenia W. Herbert (eds.), *Social Approaches to an Industrial Past: The Archaeology and Anthropology of Mining*, pp. 27–39. Routledge, London.

Bender, Barbara (2001) Introduction. In: Barbara Bender and Margot Winer (eds.), *Contested Landscapes: Movement, Exile and Place*, pp. 1–18. Berg, Oxford.

Bentham, Jeremy (1962 [1787]) Panopticon; or, the inspection-house. In: John Bowring (ed.), *The Works of Jeremy Bentham*, vol. 4, pp. 37–172. Russell and Russell, New York, NY.

Bersten, Ian (1999) *Coffee, Sex and Health: A History of Anti-Coffee Crusaders and Sexual Hysteria*. Helian Books, Sydney.

Bickford, Anne (1971) James King of Irrawang: a colonial entrepreneur. *Journal of the Royal Australian Historical Society* 57:40–57.

Bickford, Anne (1991) The Australian ICOMOS charter (the Burra charter) and first government house. In: Graeme Davison and Chris McConville (eds.), *A Heritage Handbook*, pp. 38–42. Allen and Unwin, Sydney.

Bierce, Ambrose (1996) *The Devil's Dictionary*. Wordsworth Reference, London.

Binford, Lewis R. (1978) A new method of calculating dates from Kaolin pipe stem samples. In: Robert Schuyler (ed.), *Historical Archaeology: A Guide to Substantive and Theoretical Contributions*, pp. 66–67. Baywood, Farmingdale, New York, NY.

Birmingham, Judy (1973a) Recent archaeology of Flinders Island. *Australian Natural History* 17(10):328–331.

Birmingham, Judy (1973b) Wybalenna, the Tasmanian Aboriginal settlement on Flinders Island. In: Government Statist (ed.), *Tasmanian Yearbook*, pp. 10–13. Commonwealth Bureau of Census and Statistics, Tasmanian Office, Hobart.

Birmingham, Judy (1976) The archaeological contribution to nineteenth-century history: some Australian case studies. *World Archaeology* 7(3):306–317.

Birmingham, Judy (1984) *300 Queen Street Melbourne*. In association with Allom Lovell Sanderson, Archaeological and Archival Report to the Australian Department of Housing and Construction, Melbourne.

Birmingham, Judy (1990) A decade of diggings: deconstructing urban archaeology. *The Australian Journal of Historical Archaeology* 8:13–22.

Birmingham, Judy (1992) *Wybalenna: The Archaeology of Cultural Accommodation in Nineteenth Century Tasmania*. Australian Society for Historical Archaeology, Sydney.

Birmingham, Judy (1997) Fieldwork in contact archaeology, Central Australia. In: Cameron Petrie and Sam Bolton (eds.), *In the Field: Archaeology at the University of Sydney*, pp. 1–12. Sydney University Archaeological Methods Series 4, Sydney.

Birmingham, Judy (2000) Resistance, creolization or optimal foraging at Killalpaninna Mission, South Australia. In: Robin Torrence and Anne Clarke (eds.), *The Archaeology of Difference: Negotiating Cross-Cultural Engagements in Oceania*, pp. 360–405. Routledge, London.

Birmingham, Judy and Carol Liston (1976) *Old Sydney Burial Ground*. Studies in Historical Archaeology No. 5, Sydney.

Birmingham, Judy and Dennis Jeans (1983) The Swiss family Robinson and the archaeology of colonisations. *The Australian Journal of Historical Archaeology* 1:3–14.

Birmingham, Judy, Ian Jack and Dennis Jeans (1979) *Australian Pioneer Technology*. Heinemann Educational Australia, Melbourne.

Birmingham, Judy, Ian Jack and Dennis Jeans (1983) *Industrial Archaeology in Australia: Rural Industry*. Heinemann Publishers Australia, Melbourne.

Birrell, Ralph W. (1998) *Staking a Claim: Gold and the Development of Victorian Mining Law*. Melbourne University Press, Melbourne.

Birt, Peter (2004) "The Burra": archaeology in a small community in South Australia. In: Paul A. Shackel and Erve J. Chambers (eds.), *Places in Mind: Public Archaeology as Applied Anthropology*, pp. 153–169. Routledge, New York and London.

Birt, Peter (2005) *A Dugout Time Capsule: The Rescue Excavation of a Dugout, Mitchell Flat, Burra, 2004. An Interim Report*. Report submitted to Heritage South Australia, The National Trust of South Australia Burra Burra Branch and the Regional Council of Goyder.

Blainey, Geoffrey (1966) *The Tyranny of Distance*. Sun Books, Melbourne.

Blainey, Geoffrey (1978) *The Rush that Never Ended*, 3rd edition. Melbourne University Press, Melbourne.

Blainey, Geoffrey (1982) *A Land Half Won*, revised edition. Macmillan, Melbourne.

Blainey, Geoffrey (1993) *The Peaks of Lyell*. St. David's Park Publishing, Hobart, Tasmania.

Blainey, Geoffrey (2003) *Black Kettle and Full Moon: Daily Life in a Vanished Australia*. Viking, Melbourne.

Bogle, Michael (2008) *Convicts: Transportation and Australia*, revised edition. Historic Houses Trust of New South Wales, Sydney.

Boland, Pat (1987) *Report on Coins Found at First Government House Site*. Report submitted to Heritage and Conservation Branch, Department of Planning, New South Wales Government. Heritage Resource Services, ANUTech, Canberra.

Bolton, Geoffrey (1992) *Spoils and Spoilers: A History of Australians Shaping their Environment*, 2nd edition. Allen and Unwin, Sydney.

Bonasera, Michael and Leslie Rayner (2001) Good for what ails you: medicinal use at five points. *Historical Archaeology* 35(3):49–64.

Bonyhady, Tim (2000) *The Colonial Earth*. Melbourne University Press, Melbourne.

Boow, J. (1991) *Early Australian Commercial Glass: Manufacturing Processes*. Department of Planning, New South Wales, Sydney.

Borschmann, Greg (1999) *The People's Forest: A Living History of the Australian Bush*. The People's Forest Press, Blackheath, New South Wales.

Bose, Sugata (2006) *A Hundred Horizons: The Indian Ocean in the Age of Global Empire*. Harvard University Press, Cambridge, MA.

Bourdieu, Pierre (1984) *Distinction: A Social Critique of the Judgement of Taste*. Harvard University Press, Cambridge, MA.

Bowdler, Sandra (2002) Hunters and traders in northern Australia. In: Kathleen D. Morrison and Laura L. Junker (eds.), *Forager-Traders in South and Southeast Asia: Long Term Histories*, pp. 168–184. Cambridge University Press, Cambridge.

Bowdon, Caroline B. and Annie Campbell (2009) Shooting through like a Bondi Tram. *Australian Heritage* 15:22–26.

Bowen, Alister (2004) Gippsland's Chinese fish-curing industry: an ongoing archaeological study. *Gippsland Heritage Journal* 28:45–50.

Bowen, Alister (2006) Excavations at a Chinese fish curing site near Port Albert, Victoria. *Archaeology in Oceania* 41(1):37–41.

Bowen, Alister (2007) *A Power of Money: The Chinese Involvement in Victoria's Early Fishing Industry*. Unpublished Ph.D. dissertation, Archaeology Program, La Trobe University, Melbourne.

Bower, Rebecca (1999) Leather artefacts report. In: Richard Mackay (ed.), *The Cumberland/ Gloucester Streets Site, The Rocks, Archaeological Investigation Report Volume 4 Specialist Artefact Reports Part 2*. pp. 15–124. Godden Mackay Logan, Sydney.

Bradley, A., Victor Buchli, G. Fairclough, Dan Hicks, J. Miller and John Schofield (2004) *Change and Creation: Historic Landscape Character 1950–2000*. English Heritage, London.

Bradley, Charles S. (2000) Smoking pipes for the archaeologist. In: Karlis Karklins (ed.), *Studies in Material Culture Research*, pp. 104–133. The Society for Historical Archaeology and Parks Canada, Pennsylvania.

Brand, Ian (1993) *The Port Arthur Coal Mines, 1833–1877*. Regal Publications, Launceston, Tasmania.

Braudel, Fernand (1981) *The Structures of Everyday Life*. Collins, London.

Brett, Judith (2005) Relaxed and comfortable: the liberal party's Australia. *Quarterly Essay* 19:1–79.

Briggs, Asa (1968) *Victorian Cities*. Harmondsworth, London.

Briggs, Susan (2000) *Blood in the Street: An Archaeological Examination of a Commercial Faunal Assemblage from Lot 8-12 Divett St, Port Adelaide*. Unpublished BA (Honours) dissertation, Department of Archaeology, Flinders University, Adelaide.

Briggs, Susan (2005) *Portonian Respectability: Working Class Attitudes to Respectability in Port Adelaide Through Material Culture 1840–1900*. Unpublished Ph.D. dissertation, Department of Archaeology, Flinders University, Adelaide.

British Medical Association (1909) *Secret Remedies: What they Cost and What they Contain*. British Medical Association, London.

Broadbent, James (1984) *Elizabeth Farm Parramatta: A History and a Guide*. Historic Houses Trust of New South Wales, Sydney.

Broadbent, James, Suzanne Rickard and Margaret Steven (2003) *India, China, Australia: Trade and Society 1788–1850*. Historic Houses Trust of New South Wales, Sydney.

Brockwell, Sally, Tom Gara, Sarah Colley and Scott Cane (1989) The history and archaeology of Ooldea soak and mission. *Australian Archaeology* 28:55–78.

Brodie, Allan, Jane Croom and James O. Davies (2002) *English Prisons: An Architectural History*. English Heritage, Swindon, UK.

Brooks, Alisdair (2005) *An Archaeological Guide to British Ceramics in Australia 1788–1901*. Australasian Society for Historical Archaeology and La Trobe University, Sydney.

Brooks, Alisdair and Graham Connah (2007) A hierarchy of servitude: ceramics at Lake Innes Estate, New South Wales. *Antiquity* 81(311):133–147.

Brooks, Alasdair, Hans-Dieter Bader, Susan Lawrence and Jane Lennon (2009) Ploughzone archaeology on an Australian historic site: a case study from South Gippsland, Victoria. *Australian Archaeology* 68(1):27–44.

Broome, Richard (1994) Aboriginal victims and voyagers, confronting frontier myths. *Journal of Australian Studies* 42:70–77.

Broomham, Rosemary (1987) *First Light: 150 Years of Gas*. Hale and Iremonger, Sydney.

Brown, Steve, Steven Avery and Megan Goulding (2004) Recent investigations at the Ebenezer mission cemetery. In: Rodney Harrison and Christine Williamson (eds.), *After Captain Cook: The Archaeology of the Recent Indigenous Past in Australia*, pp. 147–170. Alta Mira, Walnut Creek, CA.

Brown-May, Andrew and Shurlee Swain (eds.) (2005) *The Encyclopedia of Melbourne*. Cambridge University Press, Melbourne.

Buchli, Victor and Gavin Lucas (eds.) (2001) *Archaeologies of the Contemporary Past*. Routledge, London.

Buckley, Robin L. (2003) *Six Dogs: A Saga of Snakes, Dogs and Medical Byways*. Unpublished BA (Honours) dissertation, Archaeology Program, La Trobe University, Melbourne.

Bullers, Rick (2005) *Convict Probation and the Evolution of Jetties at Cascades, the Coal Mines, Impression bay and Saltwater River, Tasman Peninsula, Tasmania: An historical perspective*. Maritime Archaeology Monographs and Reports Series No. 7. Department of Archaeology, Flinders University, Bedford Park, South Australia.

Burke, Heather (1999) *Meaning and Ideology in Historical Archaeology: Style, Social Identity and Capitalism in an Australian Town*. Kluwer/Plenum, New York, NY.

Burningham, Nick (1994) Aboriginal nautical art: a record of the Macassans and the pearling industry in Northern Australia. *Great Circle* 16(2):139–151.

Busch, Jane (1987) Second time around: a look at bottle reuse. *Historical Archaeology* 21: 67–80.

Butlin, Noel G. (1994) *Forming a Colonial Economy, Australia 1810–1850*. Cambridge University Press, Melbourne.

Butlin, Sydney J. (1953) *Foundations of the Australian Monetary System 1788–1851*. Melbourne University Press, Melbourne.

Buxton, Gordon Leslie (1967) *The Riverina 1861–1891: An Australian Regional Study*. Melbourne University Press, Melbourne.

Byrne, Denis (1997) Deep nation: Australia's acquisition of an indigenous past. *Aboriginal History* 20:82–107.

Byrne, Denis (1998) *In Sad but Loving Memory: Aboriginal Burials and Cemeteries of the Last 200 Years in NSW*. NSW National Parks and Wildlife Service, Hurstville, New South Wales.

Byrne, Denis (2003a) The ethos of return: erasure and reinstatement of Aboriginal visibility in the Australian historical landscape. *Historical Archaeology* 37(1):73–86.

Byrne, Denis (2003b) Segregated landscapes: the heritage of racial segregation in New South Wales. *Historic Environment* 17:13–17.

Byrne, Denis (2004) An archaeology of attachment: cultural heritage and the post-contact. In: Rodney Harrison and Christine Williamson (eds.), *After Captain Cook: The Archaeology of the Recent Indigenous Past in Australia*, pp. 135–146. Altamira, Walnut Creek, CA.

Byrne, Denis, Helen Brayshaw and Tracy Ireland (2001) *Social Significance: A Discussion Paper*. Cultural Heritage Division, NSW National Parks and Wildlife Service, Hurstville, New South Wales.

Byrne, Denis and Maria Nugent (2004) *Mapping Attachment: A Spatial Approach to Aboriginal Post-Contact Heritage*. New South Wales Department of Environment and Conservation, Hurstville, New South Wales.

Byrne, Maureen (1976) *Ross Bridge, Tasmania*. Australian Society for Historical Archaeology, Sydney.

Byrne, Maureen and Ian Jack (1979) Excavations at Elizabeth farm house, Parramatta. *The Artefact* 4(3 and 4):57–61.

Cameron, David and Denise Donlon (2005) A preliminary archaeological survey of the ANZAC Gallipoli battlefields of 1915. *Australasian Historical Archaeology* 23:131–138.

Campbell, Janet (1997) Eighteenth century wooden clubs from HMS *Pandora*: a preliminary analysis. *The Bulletin of the Australian Institute for Maritime Archaeology* 21:1–8.

Campbell, Janet and Peter Gesner (2000) Illustrated catalogue of artefacts from the HMS *Pandora* Wrecksite excavations 1977–1995. *Memoirs of the Queensland Museum Cultural Heritage Series* 2(1):53–159.

Campbell, Judy (1983) Smallpox in Aboriginal Australia, 1829–1831. *Historical Studies* 20: 536–556.

Campbell, Judy (2002) *Invisible Invaders: Smallpox and Other Diseases in Aboriginal Australia 1780–1880*. Melbourne University Press, Melbourne.

Cannon, Michael (1988) *Australia in the Victorian Age: Life in the Cities*. Viking O'Neill, Melbourne.

Cantwell, Anne-Marie and Diana di Zerega Wall (2001) *Unearthing Gotham: The Archaeology of New York City*. Yale University Press, London.

Capon, Joanna (1993) Decorative plasterwork in New South Wales, 1800–1939. *Australasian Historical Archaeology* 11:43–51.

Carney, Martin (1999a) A cordial factory at Parramatta, New South Wales. *Australasian Historical Archaeology* 16:80–93.

Carney, Martin (1999b) Glass and bottle stoppers artefacts report. In: Godden Mackay Heritage Consultants (ed.), *The Cumberland/Gloucester Streets Site, The Rocks, Archaeological Investigation Vol. 4 Specialist Artefact Reports*, pp. 15–124. Godden Mackay Logan, Sydney.

Carroll, Brian (1987) *Australian Made: Success Stories in Australian Manufacturing Since 1937*. Institution of Production Engineers Australian Council, Melbourne.

Casella, Eleanor C. (1997) 'A large and efficient Establishment': preliminary report on fieldwork at the Ross female factory. *Australasian Historical Archaeology* 15:79–89.

Casella, Eleanor C. (2000a) Bulldaggers and gentle ladies: archaeological approaches to female homosexuality in convict-era Australia. In: Robert A. Schmidt and Barbara L. Voss (eds.), *Archaeologies of Sexuality*, pp. 143–159. Routledge, London.

Casella, Eleanor C. (2000b) Doing trade: a sexual economy of 19th century Australian female convict prisons. *World Archaeology* 32(2):209–221.

Casella, Eleanor C. (2001a) Every procurable object: A functional analysis of the Ross factory archaeological collection. *Australasian Historical Archaeology* 19:25–38.

Casella, Eleanor C. (2001b) Landscapes of punishment and resistance: a female convict settlement in Tasmania, Australia. In: Barbara Bender and Margot Winer (eds.), *Contested Landscapes: Landscapes of Movement and Exile*, pp. 103–118. Berg, Oxford.

Casella, Eleanor C. (2001c) To watch or restrain: female convict prisons in 19th century Tasmania. *International Journal of Historical Archaeology* 5(1):45–72.

Casella, Eleanor C. (2002) *Archaeology of the Ross Female Factory: Female Incarceration in Van Diemen's Land, Australia*. Queen Victoria Museum, Launceston, Tasmania.

Casella, Eleanor C. (2005) Prisoner of his majesty: postcoloniality and the archaeology of British penal transportation. *World Archaeology* 37(3):453–467.

Casella, Eleanor C. (2006) Transplanted technologies and rural relics: Australian industrial archaeology and questions that matter. *Australasian Historical Archaeology* 24:65–75.

Casella, Eleanor C. (2007) *The Archaeology of Institutional Confinement*. University Press of Florida, Gainesville, FL.

Casella, Eleanor C. and Clayton Fredericksen (eds.) (2001) *Australasian Historical Archaeology Special Issue: Archaeology of Confinement*. Australasian Society for Historical Archaeology, Sydney.

Casey and Lowe Associates (1995) *Archaeological Excavation, Paragon Iron Foundry, Bulwara Road, Pyrmont*. Report submitted to Meriton Apartments, Sydney.

Casey and Lowe Associates (2000) *Archaeological Investigation, CSR Site, Pyrmont (Jacksons Landing)*. Report submitted to Lend Lease Development, Sydney.

Casey and Lowe Associates (2006) *Archaeological Investigation: 109–113 George Street, Parramatta*. Report Submitted to Landcom, Sydney.

Casey, Mary (1998) Gender in historical archaeology 1991–1995: the impact of the first women in archaeology conference. In: Mary Casey, Denise Donlon, Jeannette Hope and Sharon Wellfare (eds.), *Redefining Archaeology: Feminist Perspectives*, pp. 68–76. ANH Publications, Research School for Pacific and Asian Studies, Australian National University, Canberra.

Casey, Mary (1999) Local pottery and dairying at the DMR Site, Brickfields, Sydney, New South Wales. *Australasian Historical Archaeology* 17:3–37.

Casey, Mary (2004) Falling through the cracks: method and practice at the CSR site, Pyrmont. *Australasian Historical Archaeology* 22:27–43.

Casey, Mary (2005a) Material culture and the construction of hierarchy: the Conservatorium site rubbish dump. *Australasian Historical Archaeology* 23:97–114.

Casey, Mary (2005b) The road to controversy. In: Jane Lydon and Tracy Ireland (eds.), *Object Lessons: Archaeology and Heritage in Australia*, pp. 148–166. Australian Scholarly Publishing, Melbourne.

Casey, Mary (2006) Remaking Britain: establishing British identity and power at Sydney Cove, 1788–1821. *Australasian Historical Archaeology* 24:87–98.

Cathcart, Michael (2009) *The Water Dreamers: The Remarkable History of our Dry Continent.* Text Publishing, Melbourne.

Catrice, Daniel (1998) A processing industry in the forest: Kurth Kiln. *Historic Environment* 14(1):4–9.

Chamberlain, Susan (1988) *The Hobart Whaling Industry 1830–1900.* Unpublished Ph.D. dissertation, Department of History, La Trobe University, Melbourne.

Chan, Henry, Ann Curthoys and Nora Chiang (eds.) (2001), *The Overseas Chinese in Australasia: History, Settlement and Interactions.* National Taiwan University and Australian National University, Canberra.

City of Sydney (2008) Old Sydney Burial Ground. Electronic document, http://www.cityofsydney. nsw.gov.au/AboutSydney/HistoryAndArchives/OldSydneyBurialGround.asp. Accessed 17 March 2008. City of Sydney.

Clark, Ian D. (1995) *Scars in the Landscape: A Register of Massacre Sites in Western Victoria 1803–1859.* Aboriginal Studies Press, Canberra.

Clarke, Anne (2000a) The "Moormans Trowsers": Macassan and Aboriginal interactions and the changing fabric of indigenous social life. In: Sue O'Connor and Peter Veth (eds.), *East of Wallace's Line: Studies of Past and Present Maritime Cultures of the Indo-Pacific Region*, vol. 16, pp. 315–335. Modern Quaternary Research in Southeast Asia.

Clarke, Anne (2000b) Time, tradition, and transformation: the negotiation of cross-cultural engagements on Groote Eylandt, Northern Australia. In: Robin Torrence and Anne Clarke (eds.), *The Archaeology of Difference: Negotiating Cross-Cultural Engagements in Oceania*, pp. 142–182. Routledge, London.

Clarke, Anne and Alistair Paterson (2003) Cross-cultural archaeology: an introduction. *Archaeology in Oceania* 38(2):49–51.

Clarke, Anne and Ursula Frederick (2008) The mark of marvellous ideas: Groote Eylandt rock art and the performance of cross-cultural relations. In: Peter Veth, Peter Sutton and Margo Neale (eds.), *Strangers on the Shore: Early Coastal Contacts in Australia*, pp. 148–164. National Museum of Australia, Canberra.

Clarke, Philip A. (2008) *Aboriginal Plant Collectors: Botanists and Australian Aboriginal People in the Nineteenth Century.* Rosenberg, Kenthurst, New South Wales.

Coate, Yvonne and Kevin Coate (1986) *Lonely Graves of Western Australia & Burials at Sea.* Hesperian Press, Carlisle, Western Australia.

Colley, Sarah (1997) A pre-and post-contact Aboriginal shell midden at Disaster Bay, New South Wales South Coast. *Australian Archaeology* 45:1–20.

Colley, Sarah (2002) *Uncovering Australia: Archaeology, Indigenous People and the Public.* Allen and Unwin, Sydney.

Colley, Sarah and Anne Bickford (1996) "Real" Aborigines and "real" archaeology: Aboriginal places and Australian historical archaeology. *World Archaeological Bulletin* 7:5–21.

Collins, David (1975 [1798]) *An Account of the English Colony in New South Wales*, 2 vol. 1975 facsimile edition. A. H. and A. W. Reed, Sydney.

Comber, Jillian (1995) The Palmer goldfield. *Australasian Historical Archaeology* 13:41–48.

Conkey, Margaret W. and Janet D. Spector (1984) Archaeology and the study of gender. In: Michael B. Schiffer (ed.), *Advances in Archaeological Method and Theory*, pp. 1–38. Academic, New York, NY.

Connah, Graham (1986) Historical reality: archaeological reality. Excavations at Regentville, Penrith, New South Wales, 1985. *The Australian Journal of Historical Archaeology* 4:29–42.

Connah, Graham (1988) *The Archaeology of Australia's History*. Cambridge University Press, Cambridge.

Connah, Graham (1994) Bagot's Mill: genesis and revelation in an archaeological research project. *Australasian Historical Archaeology* 12:3–55.

Connah, Graham (1997) *The archaeology of Lake Innes House: Investigating the visible evidence 1993–1995*. New South Wales National Parks and Wildlife Service, Sydney.

Connah, Graham (1998) The archaeology of frustrated ambition: an Australian case study. *Historical Archaeology* 32(2):7–27.

Connah, Graham (2001) The Lake Innes estate: privilege and servitude in nineteenth-century Australia. *World Archaeology* 33(1):137–154.

Connah, Graham (2007) *The Same Under a Different Sky? A Country Estate in Nineteenth-Century New South Wales*. BAR International Series 1625, Oxford.

Connah, Graham (2009) Lake Innes: identifying socioeconomic status in the archaeological record. *Historical Archaeology* 43(3):82–94.

Connah, Graham, Michael Rowland and Jillian Oppenheimer (1978) *Captain Richards' House at Winterbourne: A Study in Historical Archaeology*. Department of Prehistory and Archaeology, University of New England, Armidale, New South Wales.

Connell, J.E. (1987) Cornish beam engines in early South Australian mining. In: Jonathon Selby (ed.), *South Australia's Mining Heritage*, pp. 17–36. Department of Mines and Energy South Australia and the Australasian Institute of Mining and Metallurgy, Adelaide.

Convict Trail (2003) Convict trail: caring for the great North Road. Electronic document, http://www.convicttrail.org/. Accessed 6 May 2009.

Cooke, Simon (1991) Death, body and soul: the cremation debate in New South Wales, 1863–1925. *Australian Historical Studies* 24(97):323–339.

Corfield, Robin S. (2009) *Don't Forget Me, Cobber: The Battle of Fromelles*. The Miegunyah Press, Melbourne.

Coroneos, Cosmos (1995) Why is that hole so big? An analysis of expenditure versus gain in alluvial gold mining. *Australasian Historical Archaeology* 13:24–30.

Coroneos, Cosmos (2004) Port Arthur's maritime legacy. In: Richard Tuffin, Greg Jackman and Julia Clark (eds.), *A Harbour Large Enough to Admit a Whole Fleet*, pp. 79–99. Port Arthur Occasional Papers No. 1, Port Arthur Historic Sites Management Authority, Port Arthur, Tasmania.

Cosgrove, Denis E. (1984) *Social Formation and Symbolic Landscape*. Croom Helm, London.

Cott, Nancy F. (1977) *The Bonds of Womanhood: 'Woman's Sphere' in New England 1780–1835*. Yale University Press, New Haven, CT.

Couchman, Sophie (1995) The Banana trade: its importance to Melbourne's Chinese and Little Bourke Street, 1880s–1930s. In: Paul MacGregor (ed.), *Histories of the Chinese in Australasia and the South Pacific*, pp. 75–90. Museum of Chinese Australian History, Melbourne.

Courtney, Kris (1998) *Piece Pipes: Clay tobacco Pipes from the Site of 'Little Lon', Melbourne, Australia*. Unpublished M.A. dissertation, Department of Fine Arts, Classical Studies and Archaeology, and Department of History, University of Melbourne, Melbourne.

Courtney, Kris and Ian J. McNiven (1998) Clay tobacco pipes from Aboriginal middens on Fraser Island, Queensland. *Australian Archaeology* 47:44–53.

Coutts, Peter (1976) An approach to the investigation of colonial settlement patterns: whaling in Southern New Zealand. *World Archaeology* 7:291–305.

Coutts, Peter (1981) *Victoria's First Official Settlement, Sullivans Bay, Port Phillip*. Victoria Archaeological Survey, Melbourne.

Coutts, Peter (1984) *Captain Mills' Cottage, Port Fairy, Victoria*. Victoria Archaeological Survey, Melbourne.

Coutts, Peter (1985) *Report on Archaeological Investigations at the (1826) Settlement Site – Corinella*. Victoria Archaeological Survey, Melbourne.

Cowan, Henry J. (1998) *From Wattle and Daub to Concrete and Steel: The Engineering Heritage of Australia's Buildings*. Melbourne University Press, Melbourne.

Cozzolino, Mimmo and G. Fysh Rutherford (1990) *Symbols of Australia.* CIS Educational, Melbourne.

Crawford, Ian M. (2001) *We Won the Victory: Aborigines and Outsiders on the North-West Coast of the Kimberley.* Fremantle Arts Centre Press, Fremantle, Western Australia.

Crellin, Andrew (2006) Turning an honest penny: Australia's early coinage. *Australian Heritage* 4:74–78.

Cremin, Aedeen (1989) The growth of an industrial valley: Lithgow. *The Australian Journal of Historical Archaeology* 7:35–42.

Cronin, Kathryn (1982) *Colonial Casualties: Chinese in Early Victoria.* Melbourne University Press, Carlton.

Crook, Penny (2000) Shopping and historical archaeology: exploring the contexts of urban consumption. *Australasian Historical Archaeology* 18:17–28.

Crook, Penny (2005) Quality, cost and value: key concepts for an interpretive assemblage analysis. *Australasian Historical Archaeology* 23:15–24.

Crook, Penny (2009) *Superior Quality: Exploring the nature of cost, quality and value in historical archaeology.* Unpublished Ph.D. Dissertation, Archaeology Program, La Trobe University, Melbourne.

Crook, Penny, Laila Ellmoos, and Tim Murray (2003a) *Assessment of Historical and Archaeological Resources of the Hyde Park Barracks, Sydney.* Volume 4 of the Archaeology of the Modern City Series, Historic Houses Trust of New South Wales, Sydney.

Crook, Penny, Laila Ellmoos, and Tim Murray (2003b) *Assessment of Historical and Archaeological Resources of the Paddy's Market Site, Darling Harbour, Sydney,* Volume 1 of the Archaeology of the Modern City Series, Historic Houses Trust of New South Wales, Sydney.

Crook, Penny, Laila Ellmoos, and Tim Murray (2005) *Keeping Up with the McNamaras: A Historical Archaeological Study of the Cumberland and Gloucester Streets Site, The Rocks, Sydney.* Volume 8 of the Archaeology of the Modern City Series, Historic Houses Trust of New South Wales, Sydney.

Crook, Penny and Tim Murray (2004) The analysis of cesspit deposits from the Rocks, Sydney. *Australasian Historical Archaeology* 22:44–56.

Crook, Penny and Tim Murray (2006) *An Archaeology of Institutional Refuge: The Material Culture of the Hyde Park Barracks, Sydney, 1848–1886.* Volume 12 of the Archaeology of the Modern City Series, Historic Houses Trust of New South Wales, Sydney.

Crosby, Eleanor (1978) *Survey and Excavation at Fort Dundas, Melville Island, Northern Territory, 1975.* Australasian Society for Historical Archaeology, Sydney.

Culican, William and J. Taylor (1975) *Fossil Beach Cement Works, Mornington, Victoria: An Essay in Industrial Archaeology.* Refulgence Publishers, Deception Bay, Queensland.

Cumes, James W.C. (1979) *Their Chastity was not too Rigid: Leisure Times in Early Australia.* Longman Cheshire/Reed, Melbourne.

Cummins, Roger D. (1989) Scouring the clip: boom and burn on Woolscour Lane. *The Australian Journal of Historical Archaeology* 7:23–28.

Cumpston, John S. (1964) *Shipping Arrivals and Departures, Sydney, 1788–1825.* Roebuck Society Publication No. 23, Canberra.

Curl, James S. (2000) *The Victorian Celebration of Death.* Sutton, Stroud, UK.

Curthoys, Ann (2001) "Chineseness" and the Australian identity. In: Henry Chan, Ann Curthoys and Nora Chiang (eds.), *The Overseas Chinese in Australasia: History, Settlement and Interactions,* pp. 16–29. Interdisciplinary Group for Australian Studies, National Taiwan University, Taipei, and Centre for the Study of the Chinese Southern Diaspora, Australian National University, Canberra.

Dalkin, Robert Nixon (1974) *Colonial Era Cemetery of Norfolk Island.* Pacific Publications, Sydney.

Damousi, Joy (1997) *Depraved and Disorderly: Female Convicts, Sexuality and Gender in Colonial Australia.* Cambridge University Press, Cambridge.

Damousi, Joy (1999) *The Labour of Loss: Mourning, Memory and Wartime Bereavement in Australia.* Cambridge University Press, Cambridge.

Dane, Alexandra and Richard Morrison (1979) *Clay Pipes from Port Arthur 1830–1877.* Department of Prehistory, Research School of Pacific Studies, Australian National University, Canberra.

Daniels, Kay (1993) The flash mob: rebellion, rough culture and sexuality in the female factories of Van Diemen's Land. *Australian Feminist Studies* 18(Summer):133–150.

Dargavel, John (1995) *Fashioning Australia's Forests.* Oxford University Press, Melbourne.

Dash, Mike (2002) *Batavia's Graveyard.* Weidenfeld and Nicholson, London.

Davey, Christopher J. (1986) The history and archaeology of the North British Mine site, Maldon, Victoria. *The Australian Journal of Historical Archaeology* 4:51–56.

Davidoff, Leonore and Catherine Hall (1987) *Family Fortunes: Men And Women of the English Middle Class 1750–1850.* Hutchison, London.

Davidson, Andrew P. and Khun Eng Kuah-Pearce (2008) Introduction: diasporic memories and identities. In: Khun Eng Kuah-Pearce and Andrew P. Davidson (eds.), *At Home in the Chinese Diaspora: Memories, Identities and Belongings*, pp. 1–11. Palgrave Macmillan, New York, NY.

Davidson, Iain, Christine Lovell-Jones and Robyne Bancroft (eds.) (1995) *Archaeologists and Aborigines Working Together.* University of New England Press, Armidale, New South Wales.

Davies, Martin and Kristal Buckley (1987) *Archaeological Procedures Manual: Port Arthur Conservation and Development Project.* Department of Lands, Parks and Wildlife, Hobart.

Davies, Peter (1999) Henry's Mill: the archaeology and history of an Otways sawmill settlement. In: John Dargavel and Brenda Libbis (eds.), *Australia's Ever-Changing Forests IV*, pp. 247–259. Centre for Resource and Environmental Studies, Australian National University, Canberra.

Davies, Peter (2001) A cure for all seasons: health and medicine in a Bush community. *Journal of Australian Studies* 70:63–74.

Davies, Peter (2002) A little world apart: domestic consumption at a Victorian forest sawmill. *Australasian Historical Archaeology* 20:58–66.

Davies, Peter (2004) Glass and stoneware containers. In: *Casselden Place (50 Lonsdale Street, Melbourne) Archaeological Investigations Research Archive Report, Volume 3(i): Artefact Reports.* Godden Mackay Logan/La Trobe University/Austral Archaeology, pp. 225–288. Report submitted to Industry Superannuation Property Trust and Heritage Victoria, Melbourne.

Davies, Peter (2005a) The children are running wild: uncovering childhood at a forest sawmill settlement. In: Michael Calver (ed.), *A Forest Conscienceness*, pp. 75–83. Millpress, Rotterdam.

Davies, Peter (2005b) Space and structure at an Australian timber camp. *Historical Archaeology* 39(4):59–72.

Davies, Peter (2005c) Writing slates and schooling. *Australasian Historical Archaeology* 23:63–69.

Davies, Peter (2006a) *Henry's Mill: The Historical Archaeology of a Forest Community.* Archaeopress, Oxford.

Davies, Peter (2006b) Mapping commodities at Casselden Place, Melbourne. *International Journal of Historical Archaeology* 10(4):343–355.

Davies, Peter (2009) French Island Ruins: an archaeology of chicory production in Western Port, Victoria. *The Artefact* 31:4–13.

Davies, Peter (2011) Destitute women and smoking at the Hyde Park Barracks, Sydney. *International Journal of Historical Archaeology* 15(1): in press.

Davies, Peter and Adrienne Ellis (2005) The archaeology of childhood: toys from Henry's Mill. *The Artefact* 28:15–22.

Davies, Peter and Susan Lawrence (2003) The Gabo Island Jetty Shed. *The Bulletin of the Australasian Institute for Maritime Archaeology* 27:19–24.

Davison, Graeme (1978) *The Rise and Fall of Marvellous Melbourne.* Melbourne University Press, Melbourne.

Davison, Graeme (1978) Sydney and the bush: an urban context for the Australian legend. *Historical Studies* 71:191–209.

Davison, Graeme (2000) Colonial origins of the Australian home. In: Patrick Troy (ed.), *A History of European Housing in Australia*, pp. 6–25. Cambridge University Press, Cambridge.

Davison, Graeme (2003) The archaeology of the present: 'excavating' Melbourne's post-war suburbs. In: Tim Murray (ed.), *Exploring the Modern City: Recent Approaches to Urban History and Archaeology*, pp. 41–64. The Historic Houses Trust of New South Wales and the Archaeology Program, La Trobe University, Melbourne.

Davison, Graeme (2004) *Car Wars: How the Car Won our Hearts and Conquered our Cities*. Allen and Unwin, Sydney.

Davison, Graeme, David Dunstan and Chris McConville (eds.) (1985) *The Outcasts of Melbourne: Essays in Social History*. Allen and Unwin, Sydney.

Dawdy, Shannon Lee (2000a) Preface. *Historical Archaeology* 34(3):1–4

Dawdy, Shannon Lee (2000b) Understanding cultural change through the vernacular: creolization in Louisiana. *Historical Archaeology* 34(3):107–123.

Deetz, James (1977) *In Small Things Forgotten*. Anchor Books, New York, NY.

De Groot, Jan Jakob Maria (1967) *The Religious System of China: Its Ancient Forms, Evolution, History and Present Aspect*. 6 vols. Ch'eng Publishing, Taipei.

De La Rue, Colin (2005) The battle for North Australia: The archaeology of a World War Two airfield. In: Patricia Bourke, Sally Brockwell and Clayton Fredericksen (eds.), *Darwin Archaeology: Aboriginal, Asian and European Heritage of Australia's Top End*, pp. 96–105. Charles Darwin University Press, Darwin.

Delgado, James P. (1990) Ships were constantly arriving: the Hoff Store site and the business of maritime supply and demand in gold rush San Francisco. In: Allen G. Pastron and Eugene Hattori (eds.), *The Hoff Store Site and Gold Rush Merchandise from San Francisco, California*, pp. 25–33. Society for Historical Archaeology, Pleasant Hill, CA.

Delgado, James P. (2009) *Gold Rush Port: The Maritime Archaeology of San Francisco's Waterfront*. University of California Press, Berkeley.

Dening, Greg (2004) *Beach Crossings: Voyaging Across Times, Cultures and Self*. The Miegunyah Press, Melbourne University Publishing, Melbourne.

Dent, John (2002) *Yorktown: Manmade Structures*. West Tamar Historical Society, Launceston, Tasmania.

Derevenski, Joanna Sofaer (ed.) (2000) *Children and Material Culture*. Routledge, London.

De Silvey, Caitlin (2006) Observed decay: telling stories with mutable things. *Journal of Material Culture* 11(3):318–338.

Deutsher, Keith M. (1999) *The Breweries of Australia: A History*. Lothian Books, Melbourne.

Dickens, Charles (1852a) The harvest of gold. *Household Words* 113:213–218.

Dickens, Charles (1852b) Off to the diggings! *Household Words* 121:405–410.

Dingle, Anthony E. (1978) Drink and drinking in nineteenth century Australia. *Monash Papers in Economic History* 6:1–31.

Dingle, Anthony E. (1980) The truly magnificent thirst: an historical survey of Australian drinking habits. *Historical Studies* 19(75):227–249.

Dobbin, Christine (1996) *Asian Entrepreneurial Minorities: Conjoint Communities in the Making of the World-Economy 1570–1940*. Curzon, Richmond, Surrey, UK.

Donlon, Denise (1998) Mortuary practices and the sex ratio of Australian Aboriginal skeletal remains in the Sydney Basin, coastal New South Wales, Australia. In: Mary Casey, Denise Donlon, Jeanette Hope and Sharon Wellfare (eds.), *Redefining Archaeology: Feminist Perspectives*, pp. 221–226. Research School of Pacific and Asian Studies, The Australian National University, Canberra.

Donlon, Denise, Mary Casey, Wolfgang Hack and Christina Adler (2008) Early colonial burial practices for perinates at the Parramatta convict hospital, NSW. *Australasian Historical Archaeology* 26:71–83.

Douglas, Alistair (1999) Excavations at Rainbow Quay, an 18th-century Whale Rendering Plant, Rotherhithe, London. *Post-Medieval Archaeology* 33:179–193.

Douglass, William A. (1998) The mining camp as community. In: A. Bernard Knapp, Vincent C. Pigott and Eugenia W. Herbert (eds.), *Social Approaches to an Industrial Past: The Archaeology and Anthropology of Mining*, pp. 97–108. Routledge, London.

Drew, Greg J. (1987) Talisker mine, 1862–1872, its history and heritage. In: Jonathon Selby (ed.), *South Australia's Mining Heritage*, pp. 41–62. Department of Mines and Energy South Australia and the Australasian Institute of Mining and Metallurgy.

Drew, Greg (1988) *Discovering Historic Burra, South Australia*. South Australia Department of Mines and Energy, National Trust of South Australia and the Burra Mine Museum, South Australia.

Du Cros, Hilary (2002) *Much More than Stones and Bones: Australian Archaeology in the Late Twentieth Century*. Melbourne University Press, Melbourne.

Du Cros, Hilary and Laurajane Smith (eds.) (1993) *Women in Archaeology: A Feminist Critique*. Research School of Pacific Studies, Australian National University, Canberra.

Du Cros and Associates (1997) *Former Ebenezer Mission Reserve, Site Conservation and Management Plan*. Report submitted Aboriginal Affairs Victoria and Goolum Goolum Aboriginal Cooperative, Melbourne.

Duncan, Brad (2004) Risky business, the role of risk in shaping the maritime cultural landscape and shipwreck patterning: a case study application in the Gippsland region, Victoria. *The Bulletin of the Australian Institute for Maritime Archaeology* 28:11–24.

Duncan, Brad (2006) *The Maritime Archaeology and Maritime Cultural Landscapes of Queenscliffe: A Nineteenth-Century Australian Coastal Community*. Unpublished Ph.D. dissertation, School of Anthropology, Archaeology and Sociology, James Cook University, Townsville, Queensland.

Dunstan, David (1985) Dirt and disease. In: Graeme Davison, David Dunstan and Chris McConville (eds.), *The Outcasts of Melbourne: Essays in Social History*, pp. 140–171. Allen and Unwin, Sydney.

Dunstan, Keith (1968) *Wowsers: Being an Account of the Prudery Exhibited by Certain Outstanding Men and Women in Such Matters as Drinking, Smoking, Prostitution, Censorship and Gambling*. Cassell Australia, Melbourne.

Dyos, Harold J. and Michael Wolff (eds.) (1973) *The Victorian City: Images and Realities*. Routledge and Kegan Paul, London.

Edwards, Hugh (2007) The story of pearling in the north west. *Australian Heritage* 6:75–82.

Egan, Geoff (1999) London, axis of the Commonwealth? In: Geoff Egan and Ronald L. Michael (eds.), *Old and New Worlds: Historical/Post-Medieval Archaeology Papers from the Societies' Joint Conferences at Williamsburg and London (1997) to Mark Thirty Years of Work and Achievement*, pp. 61–71. Oxbow Books, London, in association with the Society for Historical Archaeology and Society for Post-Medieval Archaeology.

Egloff, Brian J. (1984) Cultural resource management, a view from Port Arthur historic site. *The Australian Journal of Historical Archaeology* 2:73–79.

Egloff, Brian J. (1994) From Swiss family Robinson to Sir Russell Drysdale: towards changing the tone of historical archaeology in Australia. *Australian Archaeology* 39:1–9.

Emmett, Peter (1996) WYSIWYG on the site of first government house. In: Sue Hunt (ed.), *Sites: Nailing the Debate: Archaeology and Interpretation in Museums*, pp. 107–122. Historic Houses Trust of New South Wales, Sydney.

English, Anthony J. (1990) Salted meats from the wreck of the *William Salthouse*: archaeological analysis of nineteenth-century butchering patterns. *The Australian Journal of Historical Archaeology* 8:63–69.

Evans, Ian (1980) *The Lithgow Pottery*. The Flannel Flower Press, Sydney.

Evans, Kathryn (1993) *Shore-Based Whaling in Tasmania Historical Research Project, Volume 1: A Social and Economic History*. Department of Parks and Wildlife Tasmania, Hobart.

Evans, Peter (1994) *Rails to Rubicon: A History of the Rubicon Forest*. Light Railway Research Society of Australia, Melbourne.

Ewins, Neil (1997) *'Supplying the Present Wants of Our Yankee Cousins': Staffordshire Ceramics and the American Market 1775–1880.* City Museum and Art Gallery, Stoke-on-Trent.

Fabian, Sue and Morag Loh (1980) *Children in Australia: An Outline History.* Hyland House, Melbourne.

Fahey, Warren (2005) *Tucker Track: The Curious History of Food in Australia.* ABC Books, Sydney.

Fairbairn, Andrew (2007) Seeds from the slums: archaeobotanical investigations at Mountain Street, Ultimo, Sydney, New South Wales. *Australian Archaeology* 64:1–8.

Fallowfield, Tom (2001) Polynesian fishing implements from the wreck of HMS *Pandora*: a technological and contextual study. *The Bulletin of the Australian Institute for Maritime Archaeology* 25:5–28.

Farrer, Keith T.H. (1980) *A Settlement Amply Supplied: Food Technology in Nineteenth Century Australia.* Melbourne University Press, Melbourne.

Faull, Jim (1987) The Cornish Miner in South Australia. In: Jonathan Selby (ed.), *South Australia's Mining Heritage*, pp. 139–142. Department of Mines and Energy, South Australia and the Australasian Institute of Mining and Metallurgy, Adelaide.

Female Factory (2009) Cascades Female Factory Historic Site. Electronic document, http://www.femalefactory.com.au/. Accessed 6 May 2009. Female Factory Historic Site Ltd.

Ferguson, Leland (1992) *Uncommon Ground: Archaeology and Early African America, 1650–1800.* Smithsonian Institution Press, Washington.

Ferrier, Åsa (2004) The Mjoberg collection and contact period Aboriginal material culture from North-East Queensland's rainforest region. In: Rodney Harrison and Christine Williamson (eds.), *After Captain Cook: The Archaeology of the Recent Past in Australia*, pp. 18–35. Altamira, Walnut Creek, CA.

Fetherling, Douglas (1997) *The Gold Crusades: A Social History of Gold Rushes, 1849–1929*, revised edition. University of Toronto Press, Toronto.

Fforde, Cressida (2004) *Collecting the Dead: Archaeology and the Reburial Issue.* Duckworth, London.

Finch, Lynette (1999) Soothing Syrups and Teething Powders: Regulating Proprietary Drugs in Australia, 1860–1910. *Medical History* 43:74–94.

Finding Sydney (2008) *Final Report: The Search to Find and Identify the Wrecks of HMAS Sydney (II) and HSK Kormoran.* Finding Sydney Foundation, Perth, Western Australia.

Fitts, Robert K. (1999) The archaeology of middle-class domesticity and gentility in Victorian Brooklyn. *Historical Archaeology* 33(1):39–62.

Fitzgerald, Shirley (1987) *Rising Damp: Sydney 1870–90.* Oxford University Press, Melbourne.

Fitzgerald, Shirley (1997) *Red Tape Gold Scissors.* State Library of New South Wales Press, Sydney.

Fitzgerald, Shirley and Hilary Golder (1994) *Pyrmont and Ultimo Under Siege.* Hale and Iremonger, Sydney.

Flanders, Judith (2003) *The Victorian House: Domestic Life from Childbirth to Deathbed.* Harper Perennial, London.

Fletcher, Brian H. (1976) *Landed Enterprise and Penal Society: A History of Farming and Grazing in New South Wales Before 1821.* Sydney University press, Sydney.

Fletcher, Brian H. (1979) Sir John Jamison in New South Wales 1814–1844. *Journal of the Royal Australian Historical Society* 65(1):1–29.

Fletcher, Roland J. (1992) Time perspectivism, Annales, and the potential of archaeology. In: A. Bernard Knapp (ed.), *Archaeology, Annales, and Ethno-History*, pp. 34–49. Cambridge University Press, Cambridge.

Flood, Josephine (2004) *Archaeology of the Dreamtime: The Story of Prehistoric Australia and its People*, revised edition. J. B. Publishing, Marleston, South Australia.

Flowers, E. (1967) Innes, Archibald Clunes. In: A.G.L. Shaw and C.M.H. Clark (eds.), *Australian Dictionary of Biography Volume 2: 1788–1850, I-Z*, pp. 3–4. Melbourne University Press, Melbourne.

Ford, Geoff (1995) *Australian Pottery: The First 100 Years*. Salt Glaze Press, Wodonga, VIC.

Ford, Julie (2004) *The Archaeology of Aircraft Losses in Water in Victoria, Australia During World War Two*. Maritime Archaeology Monograph and Reports Series No. 1, Flinders University, South Australia.

Foucault, Michel (1977) *Discipline and Punish: The Birth of the* Prison. Penguin, London.

Fraser, Hugh M. and Ray Joyce (1986) *The Federation House: Australia's Own Style*. Lansdowne, Sydney.

Frawley, Kevin (1993) Logging technology and forest cutting practices. In: John Dargavel and Sue Feary (eds.), *Australia's Ever-Changing Forests II*, pp. 143–163. Centre for Resource and Environmental Studies, Australian National University, Canberra.

Frederick, Ursula (1999) At the centre of it all: constructing contact through the rock art of Watarrka National Park, central Australia. *Archaeology in Oceania* 34:132–144.

Frederick, Ursula (2000) Keeping the land alive: changing social contexts of landscape and rock art production. In: Robin Torrence and Anne Clarke (eds.), *The Archaeology of Difference: Negotiating Cross-Cultural Engagements in Oceania*, pp. 300–331. Routledge, London.

Fredericksen, Clayton (2005) Single-men's quarters at Fannie Bay Gaol: an archaeology of hard drinking and mateship? In: Patricia Bourke, Sally Brockwell and Clayton Fredericksen (eds.), *Darwin Archaeology: Aboriginal, Asian and European Heritage of Australia's Top End*, pp. 59–74. Charles Darwin University Press, Darwin.

Freeman, Michael (1999) *Railways and the Victorian Imagination*. Yale University Press, New Haven, CT.

Freeman, Peter (1999) Confinement in Bonegilla migrant camp, Victoria. *Historic Environment* 14(2):39–44.

Frost, Alan (1994), *Botany Bay Mirages: Illusions of Australia's Convict Beginnings*. Melbourne University Press, Melbourne.

Frost, Alan (2003) *The Global Reach of Empire: Britain's Maritime Expansion in the Indian and Pacific Oceans, 1764–1815*. The Miegunyah Press, Melbourne.

Frost, Lionel (2001) The Correll family and technological change in Australian agriculture. *Agricultural History* 75(2):217–241.

Frost, Warwick (2002) Migrants and technological transfer: Chinese farming in Australia, 1850–1920. *Australian Economic History Review* 42(2):113–131.

Fullagar, Richard and Lesley Head (2000) Archaeology and native title in Australia: national and local perspectives. In: Ian Lilley (ed.), *Native Title and the Transformation of Archaeology in the Postcolonial World*, pp. 25–34. University of Sydney Oceania Monograph 50, Sydney.

Gale, S.J., R.J. Haworth, D.E. Cook and N.J. Williams (2004) Human impact on the natural environment in early colonial Australia. *Archaeology in Oceania* 39(3): 148–156.

Ganter, Regina (1994) *The Pearl-Shellers of Torres Strait: Resource Use, Development and Decline, 1860s–1960s*. Melbourne University Press, Melbourne.

Garton, Steven (1990) *Out of Luck: Poor Australians and Social Welfare 1788–1988*. Allen and Unwin, Sydney.

Gates, William (1961 [1850]) *Recollections of Life in Van Diemen's Land*, Facsimile edition. Part I. Review Publications, Dubbo, New South Wales.

Gaughwin, Denise (1992) Trade, capital and the development of the extractive industries of northeast Tasmania. *Australasian Historical Archaeology* 10:55–64.

Gaughwin, Denise (1995) Chinese settlement sites in North-East Tasmania. In: Paul MacGregor (ed.), *Histories of the Chinese in Australasia and the South Pacific*, pp. 230–248. Museum of Chinese Australian History, Melbourne.

Gaynor, Andrea (2006) *Harvest of the Suburbs: An Environmental History of Growing Food in Australian Cities*. University of Western Australia Press, Perth.

Gemmell, Warwick (1986) *And So We Graft from Six to Six: The Brickmakers of New South Wales*. Angus and Robertson Publishers, Sydney.

George, Sam (1999) *Unbuttoned: Archaeological Perspectives of Convicts and Whalers' Clothing in Nineteenth Century Tasmania.* Unpublished BA (Honours) dissertation, Archaeology Program, La Trobe University, Melbourne.

Gesner, Peter (1991), *Pandora: An Archaeological Perspective.* Queensland Museum, South Brisbane.

Gesner, Peter (2000) HMS Pandora project – a report on stage 1: five seasons of excavation. *Memoirs of the Queensland Museum Cultural Heritage Series* 2(1):1–52.

Gesner, Peter (2007) *HMS Pandora* (1791): pursuit of the *Bounty.* In: Michael Nash (ed.), *Shipwreck Archaeology in Australia*, pp. 39–50. University of Western Australia Press, Crawley, Western Australia.

Gibbs, Martin (1995) *The Historical Archaeology of Shore Based Whaling in Western Australia 1836–1879.* Unpublished Ph.D. dissertation, Department of Anthropology, University of Western Australia, Perth.

Gibbs, Martin (1997) The technology of colonial ore processing in Western Australia: the Warribanno lead smelter. *Australasian Historical Archaeology* 15:55–65.

Gibbs, Martin (1998) Colonial boats and foreign ships: the history and archaeology of nineteenth century whaling in Western Australia. In: Susan Lawrence and Mark Staniforth (eds.), *The Archaeology of Whaling in Southern Australia and New Zealand*, pp. 36–47. The Australasian Society for Historical Archaeology and The Australian Institute for Maritime Archaeology Special Publication No. 10.

Gibbs, Martin (2001) The archaeology of the convict system in Western Australia. *Australasian Historical Archaeology* 19:60–72.

Gibbs, Martin (2002) Maritime archaeology and behaviour during crisis: the Wreck of the VOC Ship Batavia. In: John Grattan and Robin Torrence (eds.), *Natural Disasters, Catastrophism and Cultural Change*, pp. 66–86. Routledge, New York, NY.

Gibbs, Martin (2003a) The archaeology of crisis: Shipwreck survivor camps in Australasia. *Historical Archaeology* 37(1):128–145.

Gibbs, Martin (2003b) Nebinyan's song – the Aboriginal whalers of South-Western Australia. *Aboriginal History* 27:11–20.

Gibbs, Martin (2005a) The archaeology of subsistence on the maritime frontier: Faunal analysis of the Cheyne Beach Whaling Station 1845–1877. *Australasian Historical Archaeology* 23:115–122.

Gibbs, Martin (2005b) Watery graves – when ships become places. In: Jane Lydon and Tracey Ireland (eds.), *Object Lessons: Archaeology and Heritage in Australia*, pp. 50–70. Australian Scholarly Publishing, Melbourne.

Gibbs, Martin (2006) Maritime archaeology at the land-sea interface. In: Mark Staniforth and Michael Nash (eds.), *Maritime Archaeology: Australian Approaches*, pp. 69–82. Springer, New York, NY.

Gibbs, Martin and Rodney Harrison (2008) Dynamics of dispersion revisited? archaeological context and the study of Aboriginal knapped glass artefacts in Australia. *Australian Archaeology* 67:61–68.

Gilchrist, A. (ed.) (1951) *John Dunmore Lang, Chiefly Autobiographical 1799 to 1878*, 2 vols, Jedgarm, Melbourne.

Gleeson, Janet (1998) *The Arcanum: The Extraordinary True Story of the Invention of European Porcelain.* Bantam Press, London.

Godden Mackay (1992) *Little Pier Street Precinct – Archaeological Excavation.* Report submitted to the Darling Harbour Authority, Sydney.

Godden Mackay Logan (1999) *The Cumberland/Gloucester Streets Site, The Rocks: Archaeological Investigation Report*, 4 vols. Report submitted to the Sydney Cove Authority, Godden Mackay Logan, Sydney.

Godden Mackay Logan (2004) *Camp Street, Ballarat: Excavation Report.* Report submitted to Ballarat City Council, Victoria.

Godden Mackay Logan (2007) *Highlands Marketplace, Mittagong (Part of the Former Fitz Roy Iron Works) – Archaeological Investigation Report*. Report submitted to Fabcot Pty Ltd, Sydney.

Godden Mackay Logan, La Trobe University and Austral Archaeology (2004) *Casselden Place (50 Lonsdale Street, Melbourne) Archaeological Excavations Research Archive Report*. Report submitted to Industry Superannuation Property Trust and Heritage Victoria, Melbourne.

Goffman, Erving (1959) *The Presentation of Self in Everyday Life*. Doudleday, New York, NY.

Gojak, Denis (1988) Gara River: an early hydro-electric scheme in Northern New South Wales. *The Australian Journal of Historical Archaeology* 6:3–11.

Gojak, Denis (1995) Clay tobacco pipes from Cadmans Cottage, Sydney, Australia. *Society for Clay Pipe Research Newsletter* 48:11–19.

Gojak, Denis (1998) An historical and archaeological overview of the whaling industry in New South Wales and Norfolk Island. In: Susan Lawrence and Mark Staniforth (eds.), *The Archaeology of Whaling in Southern Australia and New Zealand*, pp. 11–20. The Australasian Society for Historical Archaeology and The Australian Institute for Maritime Archaeology Special Publication No. 10.

Gojak, Denis (2001) Convict archaeology in New South Wales: an overview of the investigation, analysis and conservation of convict heritage sites. *Australasian Historical Archaeology* 19: 73–83.

Gojak, Denis and Caitlin Allen (2000) The fighting ground creek quartz roasting pits and the early importation of gold processing technology into Australia 1850–1860. *Australasian Historical Archaeology* 18:29–38.

Gojak, Denis and Nadia Iacono (1993) The archaeology and history of the Sydney Sailors Home, The Rocks, Sydney. *The Bulletin of the Australian Institute for Maritime Archaeology* 17(1):27–32.

Gojak, Denis and Iain Stuart (1999) The potential for archaeological studies of clay tobacco pipes from Australian sites. *Australasian Historical Archaeology* 17:38–49.

Gollan, Anne (1978) *The Tradition of Australian Cooking*. Australian National University Press, Canberra.

Gollan, Anne (1988) Salt pork to take away. In: Verity Burgmann and Jenny Lee (eds.), *Making a Life: A People's History of Australia*, pp. 1–17. McPhee Gribble with Penguin Australia, Melbourne.

Goodman, David (1994) *Gold Seeking: Victoria and California in the 1850s*. Allen and Unwin, Sydney.

Gorman, Alice C. (2005) The cultural landscape of interplanetary space. *Journal of Social Archaeology* 5(1):85–107.

Gosden, Chris and Lesley Head (1994) Landscape – a usefully ambiguous concept. *Archaeology in Oceania* 29(3):113–116.

Gould, Richard A. (ed.) (1983) *Shipwreck Anthropology*. University of New Mexico Press, Albuquerque.

Gould, Richard A. (2000) *Archaeology and the Social History of Ships*. Cambridge University Press, Cambridge.

Gould, Richard A. and Michael Schiffer (eds.) (1981) *Modern Material Culture: The archaeology of Us*. Academic, New York, NY.

Graham, Kirstienne (2005) The archaeological potential of medicinal advertisements. *Australasian Historical Archaeology* 23:47–54.

Graham, Marjorie (1979) *Printed ceramics in Australia*. Australian Society for Historical Archaeology, Sydney.

Green, Adrian and Roger Leech (eds.) (2006) *Cities in the World 1500–2000*. Maney, Leeds, UK.

Green, Jeremy (1989) *The loss of the Verenigde Oostindische Compagnie retourschip BATAVIA, Western Australia (1629)*. BAR International Series 489, British Archaeological Reports, Oxford.

Green, Jeremy (2004) *Maritime Archaeology: A Technical Handbook*, 2nd edition. Academic, San Diego, CA.

Greer, Shelley (1995) *The Accidental Heritage: Archaeology and Identity in Northern Cape York.* Unpublished Ph.D. dissertation, Department of Anthropology and Archaeology, James Cook University, Townsville, Queensland.

Greer, Shelley, Rodney Harrison and Susan McIntyre-Tamwoy (2002) Community-based archaeology in Australia. *World Archaeology* 34(2):265–287.

Gresswell, Dan A. (1890) *Report on the Sanitary Condition and Sanitary Administration of Melbourne and Suburbs.* Board of Public Health, Government Printer, Melbourne.

Griffin, Graeme M. and Des Tobin (1982) *In the Midst of Life. . .: The Australian Response to Death.* Melbourne University Press, Melbourne.

Griffiths, Tom and Libby Robin (eds.) (1997) *Ecology and Empire: Environmental History of Settler Societies.* University of Washington Press, Seattle.

Grimwade, Gordon (1998) The Canning Stock Route: Desert stock route to outback tourism. *Australasian Historical Archaeology* 16:70–79.

Grimwade, Gordon (2003) Gold, gardens, temples and feasts: Chinese temple, Croydon, Queensland. *Australasian Historical Archaeology* 21:50–57.

Grimwade, Gordon (2004) Japanese Pearlers' bath-house, Thursday Island, Torres strait. *Memoirs of the Queensland Museum, Cultural Heritage Series* 3(1):379–386.

Grimwade, Gordon (2008) Crispy Roast Pork: using Chinese Australian Pig Ovens. *Australasian Historical Archaeology* 26:21–28.

Haagen, Claudia (1994) *Bush Toys: Aboriginal Children at Play.* Aboriginal Studies Press, Canberra.

Haglund, Laila (1976) *An Archaeological Analysis of the Broadbeach Aboriginal Burial Ground.* University of Queensland Press, St. Lucia, Queensland.

Hainsworth, David R. (1981) *The Sydney Traders: Simeon Lord and his Contemporaries 1788–1821.* Melbourne University Press, Melbourne.

Hammerton, A. James and Alistair Thomson (2005) *Ten Pound Poms: Australia's Invisible Migrants.* Manchester University Press, Manchester.

Hancock, William K. (1972) *Discovering Monaro: A Study of Man's Impact on his Environment.* Cambridge University Press, Cambridge.

Harrington, Jean C. (1978) Dating stem fragments of seventeenth and eighteenth century clay tobacco pipes. In: Robert L. Schuyler (ed.), *Historical Archaeology: A Guide to Substantive and Theoretical Contributions*, pp. 63–65. Baywood, Farmingdale, New York, NY.

Harrington, Jane (1996) The lime-burning industry in Victoria: an occupance approach. *Australasian Historical Archaeology* 14:19–24.

Harrington, Jane (2000) *An Archaeological and Historical Overview of Limeburning in Victoria.* Heritage Council Victoria, Melbourne.

Harris, John (1978 [1807]) letter to Mrs King 25 October (1807). In: *Historical Records of New South Wales* 6, p. 347. Lansdown Slattery and Company, Mona Vale, New South Wales.

Harris, E. Jeanne, Geoff Ginn and Cosmos Coroneos (2004) How to dig a dump: strategy and research design for investigation of Brisbane's nineteenth-century municipal dump. *Australasian Historical Archaeology* 22:15–26.

Harrison, Rodney (2000) Challenging the 'authenticity' of antiquity: contact archaeology and native title in Australia. In: Ian Lilley (ed.), *Native Title and the Transformation of Archaeology in the Postcolonial World*, pp. 35–53. University of Sydney Oceania Monograph 50, Sydney.

Harrison, Rodney (2002a) Archaeology and the colonial encounter: Kimberley spear points, cultural identity and masculinity in the North of Australia. *Journal of Social Archaeology* 2(3):352–377.

Harrison, Rodney (2002b) Australia's iron age: Aboriginal post-contact metal artefacts from Old Lamboo Station, Southeast Kimberley, Western Australia. *Australasian Historical Archaeology* 20:67–76.

Harrison, Rodney (2002c) Nowadays with glass: regional variation in Aboriginal bottle glass artefacts from Western Australia. *Archaeology in Oceania* 35:34–47.

Harrison, Rodney (2003) The archaeology of 'lost places': ruin, memory and the heritage of the Aboriginal diaspora in Australia. *Historic Environment* 17:18–23.

Harrison, Rodney (2004a) Contact archaeology and the landscapes of pastoralism in the north-west of Australia. In: Tim Murray (ed.), *The Archaeology of Contact in Settler Societies*, pp. 109–143. Cambridge University Press, Cambridge.

Harrison, Rodney (2004b) *Shared Landscapes: Archaeologies of Attachment and the Pastoral Industry in New South Wales*. University of New South Wales Press, Sydney.

Harrison, Rodney (2006) An artefact of colonial desire? Kimberley points and the technologies of enchantment. *Current Anthropology* 47(1):63–88.

Harrison, Rodney and John Schofield (2009) Archaeo-ethnography, auto-archaeology: introducing archaeologies of the contemporary past. *Archaeologies* 5(2):185–209.

Harrison and Christine Williamson (2004) *After Captain Cook: The Archaeology of the Indigenous Recent Past in Australia*. AltaMira Press, Walnut Creek, CA.

Harvey, Peter (1999) *Clonmel: Disaster to Recovery*. Heritage Victoria, Melbourne.

Hassam, Andrew (2000) *Through Australian Eyes: Colonial Perceptions of Imperial Britain*. Melbourne University Press, Melbourne.

Hayes, Sarah (2004) *A Forgotten Landscape: An historical archaeology of the first settlement in the north of Tasmania*. Unpublished BA (Honours) dissertation, Archaeology Program, La Trobe University, Melbourne.

Hayes, Sarah (2007) Consumer practice at Viewbank homestead. *Australasian Historical Archaeology* 25:87–103.

Hayes, Sarah (2008) *Being Middle Class: An Archaeology of a Gentility in Nineteenth-Century Australia*. Unpublished Ph.D. dissertation, Archaeology Program, La Trobe University, Melbourne.

Hayes, Sarah (2009) *Glenrowan Siege Archaeological Project Artefact Report*. Report submitted to Dig International and Heritage Victoria, Melbourne.

Head, Lesley and Richard Fullagar (1997) Hunter-gatherer archaeology and pastoral contact: perspectives from the Northwest Northern Territory, Australia. *World Archaeology* 28(3):418–428.

Head, Lesley and Pat Muir (2007) *Backyard: Nature and Culture in Suburban Australia*. University of Wollongong Press, Wollongong, New South Wales.

Hemming, Steve, Vivian Wood and Richard Hunter (2000) Researching the Past: Oral History and Archaeology at Swan Reach. In: Robin Torrence and Anne Clarke (eds.), *The Archaeology of Difference: Negotiating Cross-Cultural Engagements in Oceania*, pp. 331–359. Routledge, London.

Heritage Victoria (2000) *Victoria's Shipwreck Graveyard*. Heritage Victoria, Melbourne.

Herman, Morton (ed.) (1965) *Annabella Boswell's Journal*. Angus and Robertson, Sydney.

Hewitt, Geoff (2003) The former Russell Street Police Garage, Melbourne: a study in the application of documentary sources to archaeological interpretation. *The Artefact* 26:11–31.

Hewitt, Geoff and Richard Wright (2004) Identification and historical truth: the Russell Street Police Garage Burials. *Australasian Historical Archaeology* 22:57–70.

Hiatt, Betty (1969) Cremation in Aboriginal Australia. *Mankind* 7(2):104–119.

Higginbotham, Edward (1987) The excavation of buildings in the early township of Parramatta, New South Wales, 1790–1820s. *The Australian Journal of Historical Archaeology* 5:3–20.

Higginbotham, Edward (2005) *Report on the Archaeological Excavation of Part of Cadia Mining Village, Near Orange, N.S.W.* Report submitted to Cadia Holdings Pty Ltd, Edward Higginbotham and Associates Pty Ltd, Haberfield, New South Wales.

Hill, David (2007) *The Forgotten Children*. Random House, Sydney.

Hill, Valerie (1998) The Welsh village, near Castlemaine, Victoria: a study of people in the landscape. *Australasian Historical Archaeology* 16:60–69.

Hill, Valerie (2003) *The Port Phillip Pastoral Frontier: A Study in Historical Archaeology*. Unpublished Ph.D. dissertation, Archaeology Program, La Trobe University, Melbourne.

Hirst, John (1975) Distance in Australia-was it a tyrant? *Historical Studies* 16:435–447.

Hirst, John (1978) The pioneer legend. *Historical Studies* 18:316–337.

Hirst, John (1983) *Convict Society and its Enemies: A History of Early New South Wales*. George Allen and Unwin, Sydney.

Hirst, John (1988) Egalitarianism. In: Samuel L. Goldberg and Francis B. Smith (eds.), *Australian Cultural History*, pp. 58–77. Cambridge University Press, Cambridge.

Holden, Robert (1999) *Orphans of History: The Forgotten Children of the First Fleet*. Text Publishing, Melbourne.

Holmes, Kate (1983) Excavations at Arltunga, Northern Territory. *The Australian Journal of Historical Archaeology* 1:78–87.

Holmes, Kate (1989) Arltunga: a minor goldfield in arid Central Australia. *The Australian Journal of Historical Archaeology* 7:43–49.

Holmes, Katie, Susan K. Martin and Kylie Mirmohamadi (2008) *Reading the Garden: The Settlement of Australia*. Melbourne University Publishing, Melbourne.

Holtorf, Cornelius and Angela Piccini (eds.) (2009) *Contemporary Archaeologies: Excavating Now*. Peter Lang, Bern.

Hooper, F.C. (1967) *Prison Boys of Port Arthur*. F.W. Cheshire, Melbourne.

Hope, Jeanette (1998) Making up stories: bias in interpretations of Aboriginal burial practices in southern Australia. In: Mary Casey, Denise Donlon, Jeanette Hope and Sharon Wellfare (eds.), *Redefining Archaeology: Feminist Perspectives*, pp. 239–245. Research School of Pacific and Asian Studies, The Australian National University, Canberra.

Horn, C.M. and W.P. Fradd (1987) Gold mining in South Australia, the first fifty years. In: Jonathon Selby (ed.), *South Australia's Mining Heritage*, pp. 63–100. Department of Mines and Energy South Australia and the Australasian Institute of Mining and Metallurgy, Adelaide.

Hosty, Kieran (2006) Maritime museums and maritime archaeological exhibitions. In: Mark Staniforth and Michael Nash (eds.), *Maritime Archaeology: Australian Approaches*, pp. 151–162. Springer, New York.

Hosty, Kieran and Iain Stuart (1994) Maritime archaeology over the last twenty years. *Australian Archaeology* 39:9–19.

Howard, John (1973 [1777]) *Prisons and Lazarettos*. Patterson Smith, Montclair, NJ.

Howard, Mark (1998) The Imlay brothers' account book, 1837–1840. *Tasmanian Historical Research Association Papers and Proceedings* 45(4):229–236.

Howe, Daniel Walker (1975) American Victorianism as a culture. *American Quarterly* 27(5): 507–532.

Howell-Meurs, Sarah (2000) Nineteenth century diet in Victoria: the faunal remains from Viewbank. *Australasian Historical Archaeology* 18:39–46.

Howitt, William (1972 [1855]) *Land, Labour and Gold, or, Two Years in Victoria with Visits to Sydney and Van Diemen's Land*, Facsimile edition, Sydney University Press, Sydney.

Hudson, Kenneth (1976) *The Archaeology of Industry*. The Bodley Head, London.

Hughes, Helen (1964) *The Australian Iron and Steel Industry 1848–1962*. Melbourne University Press, Melbourne.

Hughes, Janet and Estelle Lazer (2000) Importance of "historic sites" on Heard Island for protection of scientific resources and environmental management of a world heritage site. *Papers and Proceedings of the Royal Society of Tasmania* 133(2):71–77.

Hughes, Robert (1986) *The Fatal Shore: A History of the Transportation of Convicts to Australia, 1787–1868*. Collins and Harvill, London.

Hugo, Graeme (2003) Changing patterns of population distribution. In: Siew-Ean Khoo and Peter F. McDonald (eds.), *The Transformation of Australia's Population, 1970–2030*, pp. 185–218. UNSW Press, Sydney.

Humphery, Kim (1997) *Point Puer: Images and Practices of Juvenile Imprisonment in Convict Australia*. Report submitted to the Port Arthur Historic Site Management Authority, Tasmania.

Hunter, Dard (1957) *Papermaking: The History and Technique of an Ancient Craft*, 2nd revised edition. Alfred A. Knopf, New York, NY.

Hyslop, Anthea (1976) Temperance, Christianity, and Feminism: the Woman's Christian Temperance Union of Victoria, 1887–97. *Historical Studies* 17(66):27–49.

Iacono, Nadia (1999) Miscellaneous artefacts report. In: *The Cumberland/Gloucester Streets Site, The Rocks: Archaeological Investigation Report, Volume 4(2) Specialist Artefact Reports.* Godden Mackay Heritage Consultants, pp. 11–118. Godden Mackay Logan, Sydney.

Ignatieff, Michael (1978) *A Just Measure of Pain: The Penitentiary in the Industrial Revolution 1750–1850.* Macmillan, London.

Inglis, Ken S. (1998) *Sacred Places: War Memorials in the Australian Landscape.* The Miegunyah Press and Melbourne University Press, Melbourne.

Insoll, Timothy (1999) *The Archaeology of Islam.* Blackwell Publishers, Oxford.

Ioannou, Noris (1986) *Ceramics in South Australia 1836–1986: From Folk to Studio Pottery.* Wakefield Press, Adelaide.

Ioannou, Noris (1987) A German potter in the Barossa Valley, South Australia, c. 1850–1883. *The Australian Journal of Historical Archaeology* 5:29–40.

Ioannou, Noris (1995) *The Barossa Folk: Germanic Furniture and Craft Traditions in Australia.* Craftsman House, Sydney.

Ireland, Tracy (1996) Excavating national identity. In: Sue Hunt (ed.), *Sites, Nailing the Debate: Archaeology and Interpretation in Museums,* pp. 85–106. Museum of Sydney, Sydney.

Ireland, Tracy (2002) Giving value to the Australian historic past: historical archaeology, heritage and nationalism. *Australasian Historical Archaeology* 20:15–25.

Ireland, Tracy (2003) "The absence of ghosts": landscape and identity in the archaeology of Australia's settler culture. *Historical Archaeology* 37(1):56–72.

Ireland, Tracy (2004) The Burra charter and historical archaeology: reflections on the legacy of Port Arthur. *Historic Environment* 18(1):25–28.

Ireland, Tracey and Mary Casey (2006) Judy Birmingham in conversation. *Australasian Historical Archaeology* 24:7–16.

Isaac, Rhys (1982) *The Transformation of Virginia 1740–1790.* W.W. Norton, New York, NY.

Isaacs, Jennifer (1987) *Bush Food: Aboriginal Food and Herbal Medicine.* Lansdowne, Sydney.

Isaacs, Jennifer (1990) *Pioneer Women of the Bush and Outback.* Lansdowne, Sydney.

Jack, R. Ian (1979) Introduction. In: Judy Birmingham, R. Ian Jack and Denis Jeans (eds.), *Australian Pioneer Technology: Sites and Relics,* pp. 1–10. Heinemann Educational Australia, Melbourne.

Jack, R. Ian (1986a) Clay tobacco pipes exported from Scotland to Australia in the nineteenth century: some preliminary observations. *Historic Clay Tobacco Pipe Studies* 3:124–134.

Jack, R. Ian (1986b) Man's impact on a riverscape: The Hawkesbury-Nepean Valley, New South Wales. In: Graeme K. Ward (ed.), *Archaeology at ANZAAS Canberra,* pp. 56–63. Canberra Archaeological Society, Canberra.

Jack, R. Ian (1995) Chinese cemeteries outside China. In: Paul Macgregor (ed.), *Histories of the Chinese in Australasia and the South Pacific,* pp. 299–306. Museum of Chinese Australian History, Melbourne.

Jack, R. Ian (2006) Historical archaeology, heritage and the University of Sydney. *Australasian Historical Archaeology* 24 19–24.

Jack, R. Ian and Aedeen Cremin (1994) *Australia's Age of Iron: History and Archaeology.* Oxford University Press/Sydney University Press, Melbourne.

Jack, Ian, Kate Holmes and Ruth Kerr (1984) Ah Toy's garden: A Chinese market garden on the Palmer River Goldfield, North Queensland. *The Australian Journal of Historical Archaeology* 2:51–58.

Jackman, Greg (1995) "No good is to be found in the granite": aspects of the social maintenance of mining concepts on Blue Tier tin-field, Tasmania. *Australasian Historical Archaeology* 13: 49–58.

Jackman, Greg (1997) *An Archaeological Survey of the Blue Tier Tin-Field.* Report submitted to Forestry Tasmania, Hobart.

Jackman, Greg (2001) Get thee to Church: hard work, Godliness and tourism at Australia's first rural reformatory. *Australasian Historical Archaeology* 19:6–13.

Jackman, Greg (2009) From stain to saint: ancestry, archaeology, and Agendas in Tasmania's convict heritage – a view from Port Arthur. *Historical Archaeology* 43(3):101–112.

Jackson, R.V. (2005) *Daughters of the Poor*. Australian Scholarly, Melbourne.

Jalland, Pat (2002) *Australian Ways of Death: A Social and Cultural History 1840–1918*. Oxford University Press, Melbourne.

Jalland, Pat (2006) *Changing Ways of Death in Twentieth-Century Australia: War, Medicine and the Funeral Business*. University of New South Wales Press, Sydney.

James, Lawrence (2006) *The Middle Class: A History*. Little, Brown, London.

Jeans, Dennis N. (ed.) (1984) *Australian Historical Landscapes*. George Allen and Unwin, Sydney.

Jeans, Dennis N. (1988) World systems theory: a theoretical context for Australian historical archaeology. In: Judy Birmingham, Damaris Bairstow and Andrew Wilson (eds.), *Archaeology and Colonisation: Australia in the World Context*, pp. 57–63. The Australian Society for Historical Archaeology, Sydney.

Jeans, Dennis N. and Peter Spearitt (1980) *The Open-Air Museum: The Cultural Heritage of New South Wales*. Unwin, Sydney.

Jeffery, Bill (1990) Realising the cultural tourism potential of South Australian shipwrecks. *Historic Environment* 7(3–4):72–76.

Johnson, A. Wayne (1999) Coins, medals and tokens artefact report. In: Godden Mackay Heritage Consultants (ed.), *The Cumberland/Gloucester Streets Site, The Rocks: Archaeological Investigation Report, Volume 4(2) Specialist Artefact Reports*, pp. 241–284. Godden Mackay Logan, Sydney.

Jones, David (2009) *Thirsty Work: The Story of Sydney's Soft Drink Manufacturers*. David Jones, Riverwood, New South Wales.

Jones, David S. (ed.) (2002) *20th Century Heritage: Our Recent Cultural Legacy*. Australian ICOMOS Secretariat, Melbourne.

Jones, Eric and Geoffrey Raby (1989) The fatal shortage – establishing a European economy in New South Wales, 1788–1805. In: John Hardy and Alan Frost (eds.), *Studies from Terra Australis to Australia*, pp. 153–167. Australian Academy of the Humanities, Canberra.

Jones, Lewis and Peggy Jones (1990) *The Flour Mills of Victoria 1840–1990*. The Flour Millers' Council of Victoria, Melbourne.

Jones, Michael, Susan Lawrence and Michelle Denny (1997) *The Rookery Archaeological Excavation Project*. Report submitted to The Kinsman Group, Adelaide.

Jones, Olive (2000) A guide to dating glass tableware: 1800–1940. In: Karlis Karklins (ed.), *Studies in Material Culture Research*, pp. 141–232. Society for Historical Archaeology, Pennsylvania.

Jones, Olive and E. Ann Smith (1985) *Glass of the British Military ca. 1755–1820*. National Historic Parks and Sites Branch, Parks Canada, Ottawa.

Jones, Olive, Catherine Sullivan, George Miller, E. Ann Smith, Jane E. Harris and Kevin Lunn (1989) *The Parks Canada Glass Glossary for the Description of Containers, Tableware, Flat Glass, and Closures*. Studies in Archaeology, Architecture and History, Parks Canada, Ottawa.

Jones, Paul (2005) The view from the edge: Chinese Australians and China, 1890 to 1949. In: Charles Ferrall, Paul Millar and Keren Smith (eds.), *East by South: China in the Australasian Imagination*, pp. 46–69. Victoria University Press, Wellington, New Zealand.

Jones, Philip (2007) *Ochre and Rust: Artefacts and Encounters on Australian Frontiers*. Wakefield Press, Kent Town, South Australia.

Jones, Philip and Anna Kenny (2007) *Australia's Muslim Cameleers: Pioneers of the Inland 1860s–1930s*. Wakefield Press, Kent Town, South Australia.

Jones, Siân (1999) Historical categories and the praxis of identity: the interpretation of ethnicity in historical archaeology. In: Pedro Paulo A. Funari, Martin Hall and Siân Jones (eds.), *Historical Archaeology: Back From the Edge*, pp. 219–232. Routledge, London.

Jung, Silvano (2005) Archaeological investigations of the World War Two Catalina flying boat wreck sites in East Arm, Darwin Harbour: an appraisal of results. In: Patricia Bourke, Sally

Brockwell and Clayton Fredericksen (eds.), *Darwin Archaeology: Aboriginal, Asian and European Heritage of Australia's Top End*, pp. 85–95. Charles Darwin University Press, Darwin.

Jupp, James (ed.) (2001) *The Australian People: An Encyclopedia of the Nation, its People and Their Origins*. Cambridge University Press, Cambridge.

Karskens, Grace (1984) The Convict Road station site at Wiseman's Ferry: an historical and archaeological investigation. *The Australian Journal of Historical Archaeology* 2:17–26.

Karskens, Grace (1986) Defiance, deference and diligence: three views of convicts in New South Wales road gangs. *Australian Journal of Historical Archaeology* 4:17–28.

Karskens, Grace (1997) *The Rocks: Life in Early Sydney*. Melbourne University Press, Melbourne.

Karskens, Grace (1998) Death was in his face: dying, burial and remembrance in early Sydney. *Labour History* 74:21–39.

Karskens, Grace (1999) *Inside the Rocks: The Archaeology of a Neighbourhood*. Hale and Iremonger, Sydney.

Karskens, Grace (2001) Small things, big pictures: new perspectives from the archaeology of Sydney's Rocks neighbourhood. In: Alan Mayne and Tim Murray (eds.), *The Archaeology of Urban Landscapes: Exploring the Archaeology of the Modern City*, pp. 69–88. Cambridge University Press, Cambridge.

Karskens, Grace (2003a) Raising the dead: attitudes to European human remains in the Sydney region c. 1840–2000. *Historic Environment* 17:42–48.

Karskens, Grace (2003b) Revisiting the worldview: the archaeology of convict households in Sydney's Rocks neighbourhood. *Historical Archaeology* 37(1):34–55.

Karskens, Grace (2009) *The Colony: A History of Early Sydney*. Allen and Unwin, Crows Nest, New South Wales.

Karskens, Grace and Susan Lawrence (2003) The archaeology of cities: what is it we want to know? In: Tim Murray (ed.), *Exploring the Modern City: Recent Approaches to Urban History and Archaeology*, pp. 89–112. Museum of Sydney, Sydney.

Karskens, Grace and Wendy Thorpe (1992) History and archaeology in Sydney: towards integration and interpretation. *Journal of the Royal Australian Historical Society* 78(3 and 4):52–75.

Kaufman, Rob and Lorraine Thompson (2004) *Lone Graves of Gippsland Pilot Heritage Study*. Report submitted to Heritage Victoria, Melbourne.

Kenderdine, Susan (1992) From riverboats to wrecks: a guide to the archaeology of historic shipping on the River Murray, South Australia. In: *Muddy Waters: Proceedings of the First Conference on the Submerged and Terrestrial Archaeology of Historic Shipping on the River Murray*. Department of Environment and Natural Resources, South Australia.

Kenderdine, Susan (1993) Muddy waters: accessing the cultural landscape of the River Murray. *The Bulletin of the Australian Institute for Maritime Archaeology* 17(2):11–16.

Kenderdine, Susan (1994a) *Historic Shipping on the River Murray: A Guide to the Terrestrial and Submerged Archaeological Sites in New South Wales and Victoria*. Report submitted to Department of Planning, New South Wales, Department of Planning and Development, Victoria, and Murray Darling Basin Commission, Sydney.

Kenderdine, Susan (1994b) Revelations about river boats and 'rotten rows': a guide to wreck sites of the River Murray. *The Bulletin of the Australian Institute for Maritime Archaeology* 18(1):17–28.

Kenderdine, Susan (1995) *Historic Shipping on the River Murray: A Guide to the Terrestrial and Submerged Archaeological Sites in South Australia*. Report submitted to State Heritage Branch, Department of Environment and Land Management, Adelaide.

Keneally, Thomas (1998) *The Great Shame: A Story of the Irish in the Old World and the New*. Random House, Milson Point, New South Wales.

Kerr, James S. (1984) *Design for Convicts: An Account of Design for Convict Establishments in the Australian colonies During the Transportation Era*. Library of Australian History in association with the National Trust of Australia (New South Wales) and the Australian Society for Historical Archaeology, Sydney.

Kiddle, Margaret (1963) *Men of Yesterday: A Social History of the Western District of Victoria 1834–1890*. Melbourne University Press, Melbourne.

Kingston, Beverley (1977) *My Wife, My Daughter and Poor Mary Ann: Women and Work in Australia*. Nelson, Melbourne.

Kingston, Beverly (1994) *Basket, Bag and Trolley: A History of Shopping in Australia*. Oxford University Press, Melbourne.

Kirkby, Diane (1997) *Barmaids: A History of Women's Work in Pubs*. Cambridge University Press, Cambridge.

Knapp, A. Bernard (1992) Archaeology and annales: time, space and change. In: A. Bernard Knapp (ed.), *Archaeology, Annales and Ethnohistory*, pp. 1–21. Cambridge University Press, Cambridge.

Knapp, Gerrit and Heather Sutherland (2004) *Monsoon Traders: Ships, Skippers and Commodities in Eighteenth-Century Makassar*. KITLV Press, Leiden.

Kociumbas, Jan (1997) *Australian Childhood: A History*. Allen and Unwin, Sydney.

Koppi, Anthony J., Brian G. Davey and Judy M. Birmingham (1985) The soils in the old vine-yard at Camden Park Estate, Camden, New South Wales. *The Australian Journal of Historical Archaeology* 3:24–30.

Kostoglou, Parry (1995) *Shore Based Whaling in Tasmania Archaeological Research Project*, 2 vols. Tasmanian Parks and Wildlife Service, Hobart.

Kostoglou, Parry (1998) When whaling was a war: an examination of conflict in Tasmanian Bay Whaling. In: Susan Lawrence and Mark Staniforth (eds.), *The Archaeology of Whaling in Southern Australia and New Zealand*, pp. 103–110. The Australasian Society for Historical Archaeology and the Australian Institute of Maritime Archaeology Special Publication No. 10, Canberra.

Kostoglou, Parry (2003) *York Town Historic Site: Archaeological Component of Historic Heritage Conservation Management Plan*. West Tamar Historical Society, Launceston, Tasmania.

Kostoglou, Parry and Justin McCarthy (1991) *Whaling and Sealing Sites in South Australia*. Australian Institute for Maritime Archaeology Special Publication No. 6, Fremantle, Western Australia.

Lake, Marilyn (1986) The politics of respectability: identifying the Masculinist context. *Historical Studies* 22(86):116–131.

Lake, Marilyn (2006) Monuments of manhood and colonial dependence: the cult of Anzac as compensation. In: Marilyn Lake (ed.), *Memory, Monuments and Museums: The Past in the Present*, pp. 43–57. Melbourne University Press, Melbourne.

Lampard, Susan (2004) Urban living: the respectable of Jane Street, Port Adelaide. In: Deborah Arthur and Adam Paterson (eds.), *National Archaeology Students Conference: Explorations, Investigations and New Directions*, pp. 26–32. Flinders Press, Flinders University, Adelaide.

Lampard, Susan (2006) Approaches to faunal analysis: a Port Adelaide comparative case study. *The Artefact* 29:22–33.

Lampard, Susan (2009) The ideology of domesticity and the working-class women and children of Port Adelaide, 1840–1890. *Historical Archaeology* 43(3):50–64.

Land Conservation Council (1996) *Historic Places Special Investigation South-Western Victoria, Descriptive Report*. Land Conservation Council, Melbourne.

Lavelle, Siobhan and Richard Mackay (1987) Burial grounds: Kitsch memorials or serious under-takings? In: Judy Birmingham, Damaris Bairstow and Andrew Wilson (eds.), *Archaeology and Colonisation: Australia in the World Context*, pp. 173–186. Australian Society for Historical Archaeology, Sydney.

Lawrence, Susan (1993) Turner's Paddock: nineteenth century refuse and the growth of consumer society. Paper presented at the Australasian Society for Historical Archaeology Conference, Adelaide.

Lawrence, Susan (1995) Poor man's diggings: subsistence mining in the nineteenth century. *Australasian Historical Archaeology* 13:59–68.

Lawrence, Susan (2000) *Dolly's Creek: An Archaeology of a Victorian Goldfields Community.* Melbourne University Press, Melbourne.

Lawrence, Susan (2001a) After the Gold Rush: material culture and settlement on Victoria's central goldfields. In: Iain McCalman, Alexander Cook and Andrew Reeves (eds.), *Gold: Forgotten Histories and Lost Objects of Australia,* pp. 250–266. Cambridge University Press, Cambridge.

Lawrence, Susan (2001b) The Boer war and a family farm: Melrose, South Australia. In: Aedeen Cremin (ed.), *1901: Australian Life at Federation: An Illustrated Chronicle,* pp. 5–7. UNSW Press, Sydney.

Lawrence, Susan (2001c) Foodways on two colonial whaling stations: archaeological and historical evidence for diet in nineteenth-century Tasmania. *Journal of the Royal Australian Historical Society* 87(2):209–229.

Lawrence, Susan (2003a) At home in the bush: material culture and Australian nationalism. In: Susan Lawrence (ed.), *Archaeologies of the British: Explorations of identity in Great Britain and its colonies 1600–1945,* pp. 211–223. Routledge, London.

Lawrence, Susan (2003b) Exporting culture: archaeology and the nineteenth century British empire. *Historical Archaeology* 37(1):20–33.

Lawrence, Susan (2003c) Introduction: archaeological perspectives on the British and their empire. In: Susan Lawrence (ed.), *Archaeologies of the British: Explorations of Identity in Great Britain and its Colonies 1600–1945,* pp. 1–13. Routledge, London.

Lawrence, Susan (2005) Colonisation in the industrial age: the landscape of the Australian Gold Rush. In: Eleanor C. Casella and James Symonds (eds.), *Industrial Archaeology: Future Directions,* pp. 279–298. Springer, New York, NY.

Lawrence, Susan (2006a) Artifacts of the modern world. In: Jane Balme and Alistair Paterson (eds.), *Archaeology in Practice: A Student Guide to Archaeological Analysis,* pp. 362–388. Blackwell, Oxford.

Lawrence, Susan (2006b) *Whalers and Free Men: Life on Tasmania's Colonial Whaling Stations.* Australian Scholarly Publishing, Melbourne.

Lawrence, Susan, Alisdair Brooks and Jane Lennon (2009) Ceramics and status in regional Australia. *Australasian Historical Archaeology* 27:67–78.

Lawrence, Susan, Kevin Hoey and Catherine Tucker (2000) Archaeological evidence of ore processing at the Howqua Hills Goldfield. *The Artefact* 23:9–21.

Lawrence, Susan and Nick Shepherd (2006) Historical archaeology and colonialism. In: Dan Hicks and Mary Beaudry (eds.), *The Cambridge Companion to Historical Archeology,* pp. 69–86. Cambridge University Press, Cambridge.

Lawrence, Susan and Catherine Tucker (2002) Sources of meat in colonial diets: faunal evidence from two nineteenth century Tasmanian whaling stations. *Environmental Archaeology* 7: 23–34.

Lawson, W. (1971) A history of industrial pottery production in New South Wales. *Journal of the Royal Australian Historical Society* 57:17–39.

Lazer, Estelle (2001) *Report on the Excavation of the Cadia Cemetery, Cadia Road, Cadia, NSW, 1997–98. Vol. 4: Skeletal Report.* Edward Higginbotham and Associates, Report submitted to Cadia Holdings, New South Wales.

Lazer, Estelle and Angela McGowan (1990) *Heard Island Archaeological Survey 1986–1987,* revised 2nd edition. Department of Architectural and Design Science, University of Sydney, Sydney.

Leckey, John A. (2004) *Low, Degraded Broots? Industry and Entrepreneurialism in Melbourne's Little Lon 1860–1950.* Australian Scholarly Publishing, Melbourne.

LeeDecker, Charles H. (2009) Preparing for an afterlife on Earth: the transformation of mortuary behavior in nineteenth-century North America. In: Teresita Majewski and David Gaimster (eds.), *International Handbook of Historical Archaeology,* pp. 141–157. Springer, New York, NY.

Lennon, Jane (1998) History, cultural heritage and the regional forest assessment process. *Australian Journal of Environmental Management* 5:38–46.

Leone, Mark P. (1988) The Georgian order as the order of merchant capitalism in Annapolis, Maryland. In: Mark P. Leone and Parker B. Potter (eds.), *The Recovery of Meaning: Historical Archaeology in the Eastern United States*, pp. 235–261. Smithsonian Institution Press, Washington, DC.

Leone, Mark P. (2005) *The Archaeology of Liberty in an American Capital: Excavations in Annapolis*. University of California Press, Berkeley, CA.

Lewis, Miles (1977) *Victorian Primitive*. Greenhouse Publications, Melbourne.

Lewis, Miles (2008) Australian building: a cultural investigation. Electronic document, http://www.mileslewis.net/australian-building. Accessed 23 January 2009.

Lightfoot, Kent (1995) Culture contact studies: redefining the relationship between prehistoric and historical archaeology. *American Antiquity* 60(2):199–217.

Lilley, Ian (ed.) (2000) *Native Title and the Transformation of Archaeology in the Postcolonial World*. University of Sydney Oceania Monograph 50, Sydney.

Lilley, Ian (2004) Diaspora and identity in archaeology: moving beyond the Black Atlantic. In: Lynn Meskell and Robert W. Preucel (eds.), *A Companion to Social Archaeology*, pp. 287–312. Blackwell, Oxford.

Lindbergh, Jennie (1999) Buttoning down archaeology. *Australasian Historical Archaeology* 17:50–57.

Lindenmayer, David, Mason Crane and Damian Michael (2005) *Woodlands: A Disappearing Landscape*, CSIRO, Melbourne.

Lindsay, Patrick (2007) *Fromelles, the Story of Australia's Darkest Day: The Search for our Fallen Heroes of World War One*. Hardie Grant Books, Melbourne.

Links, Fiona (2004) *Isle of the Dead Archaeo-Geophysical Investigations: Preliminary Results*. Report submitted to Port Arthur Historic Site Management Authority, Tasmania.

Links, Fiona and Susan Lawrence (2004) *Geophysical Investigation of a 19th Century Chinese Cemetery, Buckland, Victoria*. Report submitted to Heritage Victoria, Melbourne.

Little, Barbara (1969) The sealing and whaling industry in Australia before 1850. *Australian Economic History Review* 9(2):109–127.

Livingston, K.T. (1996) *The Wired Nation Continent: The Communication Revolution and Federating Australia*. Oxford University Press, Melbourne.

Lopez, Alan D. and Ladisley T. Ruzicka (1977) The differential mortality of the sexes in Australia. In: Neil D. McGlashan (ed.), *Studies in Australian Mortality*, pp. 75–94. Environmental Studies Occasional Paper 4, University of Tasmania, Tasmania.

Lowe, Anthony and Richard Mackay (1992) Old Sydney Burial Ground. *Australasian Historical Archaeology* 10:15–23.

Lucas, Gavin (2002) Disposability and dispossession in the twentieth century. *Journal of Material Culture* 7(1):5–22.

Lucas, Linda (2002) *Glass Bottle Recycling in Victoria*. Unpublished BA (Honours) dissertation, Archaeology Program, La Trobe University, Melbourne.

Lydon, Jane (1993a) Archaeology in the Rocks, Sydney, 1979–1993: from Old Sydney Gaol to Mrs Lewis' boarding house. *Australasian Historical Archaeology* 11:33–42.

Lydon, Jane (1993b) Task differentiation in historical archaeology: sewing as material culture. In: Hilary du Cros and Laurajane Smith (eds.), *Women in Archaeology: A Feminist Critique. Research Papers in Archaeology and Natural History*, pp. 129–133. Research School of Pacific Studies, Australian National University, Canberra.

Lydon, Jane (1995) Boarding houses in the Rocks: Mrs Anne Lewis' privy, 1865. *Public History Review* 4:73–88.

Lydon, Jane (1996) Sites: archaeology in context. In: Sue Hunt (ed.), *Sites, Nailing the Debate: Archaeology and Interpretation in Museums*. pp. 139–162. Museum of Sydney, Sydney.

Lydon, Jane (1999) *Many Inventions: The Chinese in the Rocks 1890–1930*. Monash Publications in History, Monash University, Clayton, VIC.

Lydon, Jane (2001) The Chinese community in the Rocks area of Sydney: cultural persistence and exchange. In: Henry Chan, Ann Curthoys and Nora Chiang (eds.), *The Overseas Chinese in Australasia: History, Settlement and Interactions*, pp. 117–124. Interdisciplinary Group for Australian Studies, National Taiwan University, Taipei, and Centre for the Study of the Chinese Southern Diaspora, Australian National University, Canberra.

Lydon, Jane (2004) This civilising experiment: photography at Coranderrk Aboriginal station during the 1860s. In: Rodney Harrison and Christine Williamson (eds.), *After Captain Cook: The Archaeology of the Recent Indigenous Past in Australia*. pp. 59–74. Altamira, Walnut Creek, CA.

Lydon, Jane (2005) *Eye Contact: Photographing Indigenous Australians*. Duke University Press, Durham, NC.

Lydon, Jane (2009) Imagining the Moravian mission: space and surveillance at the former Ebeneezer mission, Victoria, Southeastern Australia. *Historical Archaeology* 43(3):5–19.

Lydon, Jane, Alisdair Brooks and Zvonka Stanin (2004) Archaeological investigations of the mission-house, Ebenezer mission, Victoria: report to Heritage Victoria and Aboriginal Affairs Victoria. Report submitted to Centre for Australian Indigenous Studies, Faculty of Arts, Monash University in association with Goolum Goolum Aboriginal Cooperative and the Wotjobaluk Native Title Claimant Group, Melbourne.

MacDonald, Helen (2005) *Human Remains: Episodes in Human Dissection*. Melbourne University Press, Melbourne.

MacGregor, Paul (ed.) (1995) *Histories of the Chinese in Australasia and the South Pacific*. Museum of Chinese Australian History, Melbourne.

Macknight, Campbell (1976) *The Voyage to Marege': Macassan Trepangers in Northern Australia*. Melbourne University Press, Melbourne.

Macknight, Campbell (1998) *Low Head to Launceston: The Earliest Reports of Port Dalrymple and the Tamar*. Historical Survey of Northern Tasmania, Launceston.

Macknight, Campbell (2008) Harvesting the memory: open beaches in Makassar and Arnhem Land. In: Peter Veth, Peter Sutton and Margo Neale (eds.), *Strangers on the Shore: Early coastal contacts in Australia*, pp. 133–147. National Museum of Australia, Canberra.

Mac Sweeney, Naoíse (2009) Beyond ethnicity: the overlooked diversity of group identities. *Journal of Mediterranean Archaeology* 22(1):101–126.

Markus, Thomas A. (1993) *Buildings and Power: Freedom and Control in the Origins of Modern Building Types*. Routledge, London.

Marquis-Kyle, Peter and Meredith Walker (1992) *The Illustrated Burra Charter: Making Good Decisions About the Care of Important Places*. Australia ICOMOS, Canberra.

Marsden, Susan (1993) What's wrong with the twentieth century? Why has it been ignored by archaeologists? *Australasian Historical Archaeology* 11:142–144.

Martin, Emily (1988) Gender and ideological differences in representations of life and death. In: James L. Watson and Evelyn S. Rawski (eds.), *Death Ritual in Late Imperial and Modern China*, pp. 164–179. University of California Press, Berkeley, CA.

Martyr, Phillipa (2002) *Paradise of Quacks: An Alternative History of Medicine in Australia*. Macleay Press, Sydney.

Matthews, Keith (1999) Familiarity and contempt. The archaeology of the 'modern'. In: Sue Tarlow and Susie West (eds.), *The Familiar Past? Archaeologies of Later Historical Britain*, pp. 155–179. Routledge, New York, NY.

Mawer, Granville A. (1999) *Ahab's Trade: The Saga of South Seas Whaling*. Allen and Unwin, St. Leonards, New South Wales.

Maynard, Margaret (1994) *Fashioned from Penury: Dress as Cultural Practice in Colonial Australia*. Cambridge University Press, Cambridge.

Mayne, Alan (1982) *Fever, Squalor and Vice: Sanitation and Social Policy in Victorian Sydney*. University of Queensland Press, St. Lucia, Queensland.

Mayne, Alan (1993) *The Imagined Slum: Newspaper Representation in Three Cities, 1870–1914*. University of Leicester Press, Leicester.

Mayne, Alan (2006) Big notes from a Little street: historical research at Melbourne's "Little Lon". *International Journal of Historical Archaeology* 10(4):317–329.

Mayne, Alan and Susan Lawrence (1998) An ethnography of place: imagining 'Little Lon'. *Journal of Australian Studies* 57:93–107.

Mayne, Alan and Susan Lawrence (1999) Enthographies of place: a new urban research agenda. *Urban History* 26(3):325–348.

Mayne, Alan and Tim Murray (eds.) (2001) *The Archaeology of Urban Landscapes: Explorations in Slumland*. New Directions in Archaeology. Cambridge University Press, Cambridge.

Mayne, Alan, Tim Murray and Susan Lawrence (2000) Historic sites: Melbourne's 'Little Lon'. *Australian Historical Studies* 31:131–151.

McAtackney, Laura, Matthew Palus and Angela Piccini (2007) *Contemporary and Historical Archaeology in Theory: Papers from the 2003 and 2004 CHAT Conferences*. Archaeopress, Oxford.

McCalman, Janet (1982) Class and respectability in a working-class suburb: Richmond, Victoria, before the Great War. *Historical Studies* 20:90–103.

McCalman, Janet (2005) 'All just melted with heat': mothers, babies and 'hot winds' in colonial Melbourne. In: Tim Sherratt, Tom Griffiths and Libby Robin (eds.), *A Change in the Weather: Climate and Culture in Australia*, pp. 104–115. National Museum of Australia Press, Canberra.

McCarthy, Justin (1988) The new gold mountain: Chinese trade networks in Northern Australia. In: Judy Birmingham, Damaris Bairstow and Andrew Wilson (eds.), *Archaeology and Colonisation: Australia in the World Context*, pp. 139–148. The Australian Society for Historical Archaeology, Sydney.

McCarthy, Justin (1989) *Archaeological Investigation: Commonwealth Offices and Telecom Corporate Building Sites, The Commonwealth Block, Melbourne, Victoria*. Report submitted to The Department of Administrative Services and Telecom Australia, Melbourne.

McCarthy, Justin (1995) Tales of the Empire city: Chinese miners in the Pine Creek region, Northern Territory, 1872–1915. In: Paul Macgregor (eds.), *Histories of the Chinese in Australasia and the South Pacific*, pp. 191–202. Museum of Chinese Australian History, Melbourne.

McCarthy, Justin and Parry Kostoglou (1986) Pine Creek heritage zone archaeological survey. Report submitted to The National Trust of Australia, Northern Territory.

McCarthy, Mike (1993) *Settlers and Sawmillers: A History of West Gippsland Tramways and the Industries they served, 1875–1934*. Light Railway Research Society of Australia, Melbourne.

McCarthy, Michael (2000) *Iron and Steamship Archaeology: Success and Failure on the* SS *Xantho*. Kluwer/Plenum, New York, NY.

McCarthy, Michael (2004) Historic aircraft wrecks as archaeological sites. *The Bulletin of the Australian Institute for Maritime Archaeology* 28:81–90.

McCarthy, Michael (2007) SS *Xantho* (1872): treasure from the scrapheap. In: Michael Nash (ed.), *Shipwreck Archaeology in Australia*, pp. 157–170. University of Western Australia Press, Crawley, Western Australia.

McCarthy, Michael (2008) The Australian contact shipwrecks program. In: Peter Veth, Peter Sutton and Margo Neale (eds.), *Strangers on the Shore: Early coastal contacts in Australia*, pp. 227–236. National Museum of Australia, Canberra.

McConville, Chris (1985) Chinatown. In: Graeme Davison, David Dunstan and Chris McConville (eds.), *The Outcasts of Melbourne: Essays in Social History*, pp. 58–68. Allen and Unwin, Sydney.

McDonald, Jo (2007) *Dreamtime Superhighway: An Analysis of the Sydney Basin Rock Art and Prehistoric Information Exchange*. Terra Australis 25, Pandanus Books, Research School of Pacific and Asian Studies, Australian National University, Canberra.

McDonald, Jo (2008) Rock art and cross-cultural interaction in Sydney. In: Peter Veth, Peter Sutton and Margo Neale (eds.), *Strangers on the Shore: Early Coastal Contacts in Australia*, pp. 94–112. National Museum of Australia, Canberra.

McGillivery, Angus R. (2004) From sods to seed-beds: cultivating a familiar field at Port Jackson. *Journal of Australian Colonial History* 5:1–29.

McGowan, Angela (2000) On their own: towards an analysis of sealers' sites at Heard Island. *Papers and Proceedings of the Royal Society of Tasmania* 133(2):61–70.

McGowan, Barry (1996) The typology and techniques of alluvial mining: the example of the Shoalhaven and Mongarlowe goldfields in Southern New South Wales. *Australasian Historical Archaeology* 14:34–45.

McGowan, Barry (2001) Mullock heaps and tailing mounds: environmental effects of alluvial goldmining. In: Iain McCalman, Alexander Cook and Andrew Reeves (eds.), *Gold: Forgotten Histories and Lost Objects of Australia*, pp. 85–100. Cambridge University Press, Cambridge.

McGowan, Barry (2003) The archaeology of Chinese alluvial mining in Australia. *Australasian Historical Archaeology* 21:11–17.

McGowan, Barry (2004) The Chinese on the Braidwood goldfields: historical and archaeological opportunities. *Journal of Australian Colonial History* 6(1):35–58.

McGowan, Barry (2005) Chinese market gardens in Southern and Western New South Wales. *Australian Humanities Review* 36. Electronic document. http://www.australianhumanitiesreview.org accessed 21 September 2010.

McGowan, Barry (2006) *Fool's Gold: Myths and Legends of Gold Seeking in Australia*. Lothian Books, Sydney.

McGuire, Randall (1982) The study of ethnicity in historical archaeology. *Journal of Anthropological Archaeology* 1:159–178.

McGuire, Randall and Robert Paynter (eds.) (1991) *The Archaeology of Inequality*. Basil Blackwood, Cambridge, MA.

McPhee, Ewen (2001) A preliminary examination of the history and archaeology of the pearl shelling industry in Torres Strait. *The Bulletin of the Australian Institute for Maritime Archaeology* 25:1–4.

McVarish, Douglas C. (2008) *American Industrial Archaeology: A Field Guide*. Left Coast Press, Walnut Creek, CA.

Mearns, David L. (2009) *The Search for The Sydney: How Australia's Greatest Maritime Mystery was Solved*. Harper Collins, Sydney.

Meighan, Clement W. (1992) Some scholars' views on reburial. *American Antiquity* 57(4): 704–710.

Meinig, Donald W. (1962) *On the Margins of the Good Earth: The South Australian Wheat Frontier, 1869–1884*. J. Murray, London.

Merrington, Peter (2003) Staging history, inventing heritage: the 'new pageantry' and British imperial identity 1905–35. In: Susan Lawrence (eds.), *Archaeologies of the British: Explorations of Identity in Great Britain and its Colonies 1600–1945*, pp. 239–258. Routledge, London.

Merrillees, Robert S. (1990) *Living with Egypt's Past in Australia*. Museum of Victoria, Melbourne.

Mezey, Barney (2005) *Reflections on Casselden Place Through its Jewellery*. Unpublished BA (Honours) dissertation, Archaeology Program, La Trobe University, Melbourne.

Middleton, Angela (2008) *Te Puna: The Archaeology and History of a New Zealand Mission Station, 1832–1874*. Unpublished Ph.D. dissertation, Department of Anthropology, University of Auckland, New Zealand.

Miller, Daniel (1995) Consumption studies as the transformation of anthropology. In: Daniel Miller (ed.), *Acknowledging Consumption: A Review of New Studies*, pp. 264–295. Routledge, London.

Mills, Jenny (1986) *The Timber People: A History of Bunnings Limited*. Bunnings Limited, Perth, WA.

Milner, Peter (1985) The Barwon paper mill, Fyansford. *Heritage Australia* 4(1):18–21.

Milner, Peter (1997) Beam pumping engines in Victoria. *Australasian Historical Archaeology* 15:40–54.

Mitchell, Scott (1994) *Culture contact and indigenous economies on the Cobourg Peninsula, Northwestern Arnhem Land.* Unpublished Ph.D. dissertation, Faculty of Arts, Northern Territory University, Darwin, Northern Territory.

Mitchell, Scott (1996) Dugongs and dugouts, sharp tacks and shellbacks: Macassan contact and Aboriginal marine hunting on the Cobourg Peninsula, Northwestern Arnhem Land. *Bulletin of the Indo-Pacific Prehistory Association* 15(2):181–191.

Mitchell, Scott (2000) Guns or Barter? Indigenous exchange networks and the mediation of conflict in post-contact Western Arnhem Land. In: Robin Torrence and Anne Clarke (eds.), *The Archaeology of Difference: Negotiating Cross-Cultural Engagements in Oceania*, pp. 182–214. Routledge, London.

Mitchell, Scott (2005) A poor man's show: historic archaeology of the Bynoe Harbour Chinese community. In: Patricia Bourke, Sally Brockwell and Clayton Fredericksen (eds.), *Darwin Archaeology: Aboriginal, Asian and European Heritage of Australia's Top End*, pp. 49–58. Charles Darwin University Press, Darwin.

Molony, John (2000) *The Native-Born: The First White Australians.* Melbourne University Press, Melbourne.

Moorhouse, Geoffrey (1999) *Sydney: The Story of a City.* Harcourt, New York, NY.

Moran, Vivienne and Mark Staniforth (1998) The AIMA/NAS Part 1 Training Program. *The Bulletin of the Australian Institute for Maritime Archaeology* 22:137–138.

Morgan, Peter (1991) *Glass Bottles from the William Salthouse.* Unpublished BA (Honours) dissertation, Archaeology Department, La Trobe University, Melbourne.

Morris, Colleen (2001) Chinese market gardens in Sydney. *Australian Garden History* 12(5):5–8.

Morwood, Michael J. and D.R. Hobbs (1997) The Asian connection: preliminary report on Indonesian trepang sites on the Kimberley coast, NW Australia. *Archaeology in Oceania* 32:197–206.

Mossman, Susan (ed.) (1997) *Early Plastics: Perspectives 1850–1950.* Leicester University Press, London.

Moyal, Ann M. (1984) *Clear Across Australia: A History of Telecommunications Since 1788.* Nelson, Melbourne.

Mrozowski, Stephen, Grace Ziesing and Mary Beaudry (1996) *Living on the Boott: Historical Archaeology at the Boott Mills Boardinghouses, Lowell, Massachusetts.* University of Massachusetts Press, Amherst, MA.

Muir, Anne-Louise (2003) Ceramics in the collection of the Museum of Chinese Australian History, Melbourne. *Australasian Historical Archaeology* 21:42–49.

Muir, Anne-Louise (2008) *Kitchen Ch'ing: Chinese Archaeological Ceramics in Victoria.* Unpublished MA dissertation, Archaeology Program, La Trobe University, Melbourne.

Mullins, Steve (2001) Australian pearl-shellers in the Moluccas: confrontation and compromise on a maritime frontier. *The Great Circle* 23(2):3–23.

Mulvaney, John (1991) Past regained, future lost: the Kow Swamp Pleistocene burials. *Antiquity* 65:12–21.

Mulvaney, John (1996) Musing amidst the ruins … . *Australasian Historical Archaeology* 14:3–8.

Murphy, Karen (2007) Mill Point archaeological project: July (2007) field season. *Newsletter of the Australasian Society for Historical Archaeology* 37(4):12–16.

Murray, Tim (1988) Beyond the ramparts of the unknown: the historical archaeology of the Van Diemen's Land company. In: Judy Birmingham, Damaris Bairstow and Andrew Wilson (eds.), *Archaeology and Colonisation: Australia in the World Context*, pp. 99–108. The Australian Society for Historical Archaeology, Sydney.

Murray, Tim (1993) The childhood of William Lanne: contact archaeology and Aboriginality in Tasmania. *Antiquity* 67(256):504–519.

Murray, Tim (1996) Contact archaeology: shared histories? shared identities? In: *Sites, Nailing the Debate: Archaeology and Interpretation in Museums.* pp. 199–213. Museum of Sydney, Sydney.

Murray, Tim (2004a) The archaeology of contact in settler societies. In: Tim Murray (ed.), *The Archaeology of Contact in Settler Societies*, pp. 1–16. Cambridge University Press, Cambridge.

Murray, Tim (ed.) (2004b) *The Archaeology of Contact in Settler Societies*. Cambridge University Press, Cambridge.

Murray, Tim (2004c) In the footsteps of George Dutton: developing a contact archaeology of temperate Aboriginal Australia. In: Tim Murray (ed.), *The Archaeology of Contact in Settler Societies*, pp. 200–225. Cambridge University Press, Cambridge.

Murray, Tim (2006) Integrating archaeology and history at the 'Commonwealth Block': 'Little Lon' and Casselden Place. *International Journal of Historical Archaeology* 10(4):395–413.

Murray, Tim and Alan Mayne (2001) Imaginary landscapes: reading Melbourne's 'Little Lon'. In: Alan Mayne and Tim Murray (eds.), *The Archaeology of Urban Landscapes: Explorations in Slumland*, pp. 89–105. Cambridge University Press, Cambridge.

Murray, Tim and Penny Crook (2005) Exploring the archaeology of the modern city: issues of scale, integration and complexity. *International Journal of Historical Archaeology* 9(2): 89–110.

Murray-Smith, Stephen (1973) Beyond the pale: the Islander community of Bass Strait in the 19th century. *Tasmanian Historical Research Association Papers and Proceedings* 20(4): 167–200.

Myers, Sarah (2002) *Archaeological Excavation of Site H7822–1363, Cohen Place, Melbourne, China Town*. Report submitted to Deal Corporation, the Heritage Council of Victoria and the Chinese Museum Melbourne.

Mytum, Harold (2004) *Mortuary Monuments and Burial Grounds of the Historic Period*. Kluwer/Plenum, New York, NY.

Nash, Mike (1990) Survey of the historic ship *Litherland* (1834–1853). *The Bulletin of the Australian Institute for Maritime Archaeology* 14(1):13–20.

Nash, Mike (1998) A survey of the Tasmanian shore-based whaling industry. In: Susan Lawrence and Mark Staniforth (eds.), *The Archaeology of Whaling in Southern Australia and New Zealand*, pp. 21–28. The Australasian Society for Historical Archaeology and The Australian Institute for Maritime Archaeology Special Publication No. 10.

Nash, Mike (2001) *Cargo for the Colony: The 1797 wreck of the merchant ship* Sydney Cove. Navarine Publishing, Hobart.

Nash, Mike (2003) *The Bay Whalers: Tasmania's Shore-Based Whaling Industry*. Navarine, Canberra.

Nash, Mike (2004) History of the Port Arthur Dockyards. In: Richard Tuffin, Greg Jackman and Julia Clark (eds.), *A Harbour Large Enough to Admit a Whole Fleet*, pp. 39–55. Port Arthur Occasional Papers No. 1, Port Arthur Historic Sites Management Authority, Port Arthur, Tasmania.

Nash, Mike (2005) Investigation of a survivor camp from the *Sydney Cove* shipwreck. *The Bulletin of the Australasian Institute for Maritime Archaeology* 29:9–24.

Nash, Michael (2006) *The Sydney Cove Shipwreck Survivors Camp*. Flinders University, Adelaide.

Nash, Mike (2007) A survey of maritime infrastructure at the Sarah Island penal settlement. *The Bulletin of the Australian Institute for Maritime Archaeology* 31:91–104.

Nash, Mike (2009) *Sydney Cove: The History and Archaeology of an Eighteenth-Century Shipwreck*. Navarine Publishing, Hobart.

Nash, Mike and Ross Anderson (2007) *Cheviot* (1854): Whalers and Merchants. In: Mike Nash (ed.), *Shipwreck Archaeology in Australia*, pp. 123–132. University of Western Australia Press, Perth, WA.

National Shipwrecks Database (2009) Australian national shipwrecks database. Electronic document, http://eied.deh.gov/nsd/public. Accessed 17 June 2009. Department of the Environment, Heritage, Water and the Arts, Australian Government.

Nicholas, Stephen (ed.) (1988) *Convict Workers: Reinterpreting Australia's Past*. Cambridge University Press, Cambridge.

Nicol, Robert (1994), *At the End of the Road: Government, Society and Disposal of Human Remains in the Nineteenth and Twentieth Centuries.* Allen and Unwin, Sydney.

Nicol, Robert (1997) *Fairway to Heaven: The Story of Enfield, Australia's First Lawn Cemetery.* Enfield General Cemetery Trust, South Australia.

Nicol, Robert (2003) *This Grave and Burning Question: A Centenary History of Cremation in Australia.* Adelaide Cemeteries Authority, Adelaide.

Niemeier, Jutta (1995) The changing role of the See Yup Temple in Melbourne, 1866–1993. In: Paul MacGregor (ed.), *Histories of the Chinese in Australasia and the South Pacific,* pp. 327–340. Museum of Chinese Australian History, Melbourne.

Nutley, David (1995) More than a shipwreck: the convict ship *Hive* – Aboriginal and European contact site. *The Bulletin of the Australian Institute for Maritime Archaeology* 19(2): 17–26.

Nutley, David (2003) A river in time: following the course of influences on Manning River history. *The Bulletin of the Australian Institute for Maritime Archaeology* 27:67–70.

O'Brien, Anne (1988) *Poverty's Prison: The Poor in New South Wales 1880–1918.* Melbourne University Press, Melbourne.

O'Farrell, Patrick (1987) *The Irish in Australia.* New South Wales University Press, Kensington, New South Wales.

O'Keefe, Mary (1999) The inconstant shipwreck, Wellington, New Zealand. *The Bulletin of the Australian Institute for Maritime Archaeology* 23:121–125.

Orser, Charles E. (1988) *The Material Basis of the Postbellum Tenant Plantation: Historical Archaeology in the South Carolina Piedmont.* University of Georgia Press, Athens, GA.

Oswald, Adrian (1961) The evolution and chronology of English clay tobacco pipes. *Archaeological Newsletter* 7 (3):55–62.

Oxley, Deborah (1996) *Convict Maids: The Forced Migration of Women to Australia.* Cambridge University Press, Cambridge.

Pardoe, Colin (1988) The cemetery as symbol: The distribution of prehistoric Aboriginal burial grounds in Southeastern Australia. *Archaeology in Oceania* 23(1):1–16.

Parker, Roszika (1984) *The Subversive Stitch: Embroidery and the Making of the Feminine.* The Women's Press, London.

Parkes, Rebecca (2009) Traces of the cameleers: landscape archaeology and landscape perception. *Australasian Historical Archaeology* 27:37–45.

Parliament of Victoria (1874) Mineral statistics of Victoria for the year 1873. In: *Papers Presented to Parliament (Victoria)* 2(8).

Pasveer, Juliette, Alanah Buck and Marit van Huystee (1998) Victims of the *Batavia* mutiny: physical anthropological and forensic studies of the Beacon Island skeletons. *The Bulletin of the Australian Institute for Maritime Archaeology* 22:45–50.

Paszkowski, Lech (2001) Poles. In: James Jupp (ed.), *The Australian People: An Encyclopedia of the Nation, Its People and Their Origins,* pp. 621–623. Cambridge University Press, Cambridge.

Pate, F. Donald (2005) Population expansion in early Adelaide reflected in gravestones and cemetery monuments 1836–1865. In: Pam Smith, F. Donald Pate and Robert Martin (eds.), *Valleys of Stone: The Archaeology and History of Adelaide's Hills Face,* pp. 56–68. Kopi Books, Belair, South Australia.

Paterson, Adam (2004) If it ain't broke, why fix it? A comparative historical and archaeological study of the technological development of tryworks at shore based whaling stations, 1550–1871. In: Deborah Arthur and Adam Paterson (eds.), *National Archaeology Students Conference: Explorations, Investigations and New Directions,* pp. 69–79. Flinders Press, Flinders University, Adelaide.

Paterson, Alistair (2003) The texture of agency: an example of culture-contact in central Australia. *Archaeology in Oceania* 38(2):52–65.

Paterson, Alistair (2005) Early pastoral landscapes and culture contact in Central Australia. *Historical Archaeology* 39(3):28–48.

Paterson, Alistair (2006) Towards a historical archaeology of Western Australia's Northwest. *Australasian Historical Archaeology* 24:99–111.

Paterson, Alistair (2008) *The Lost Legions: Culture Contact in Colonial Australia*. AltaMira Press, Lanham, MA.

Paterson, Alistair and Andrew Wilson (2000) Australian historical archaeology: retrospects and prospects. *Australian Archaeology* 50:81–89.

Paterson, Alistair and Daniel Franklin (2004) The 1629 mass grave for *Batavia* victims, Beacon Island, Houtman Abrolhos Islands, Western Australia. *Australasian Historical Archaeology* 22:71–78.

Paterson, Alistair, Nicholas Gill and M. Kennedy (2003) An archaeology of historical reality? A case study of the recent past. *Australian Archaeology* 57:82–89.

Payton, Philip (2001) Cornish. In: James Jupp (ed.), *The Australian People: An Encyclopedia of the Nation, its People and Their Origins*, pp. 227–234. Cambridge University Press, Cambridge.

Peacock, Margaret (1985) *Margaret Peacock's Isle of the Dead*. Isle of the Dead Publications, Port Arthur, Tasmania.

Pearce, Helen R. (1976) *The Hop Industry in Australia*. Melbourne University Press, Melbourne.

Pearson, Michael (1983) The technology of whaling in Australian waters in the 19th century. *The Australian Journal of Historical Archaeology* 1:40–54.

Pearson, Michael (1984) The excavation of the Mount Wood Woolscour, Tibooburra, New South Wales. *The Australian Journal of Historical Archaeology* 2:38–50.

Pearson, Michael (1985) Shore-based whaling at Twofold Bay: one hundred years of enterprise. *Journal of the Royal Australian Historical Society* 71(1):3–27.

Pearson, Michael (1990) The lime industry in Australia – an overview. *The Australian Journal of Historical Archaeology* 8:28–35.

Pearson, Michael (1993a) 'All that glisters. . .': assessing the heritage significance of mining places. *Australasian Historical Archaeology* 13:3–10.

Pearson, Michael (1993b) The good oil: eucalyptus oil distilleries in Australia. *Australasian Historical Archaeology* 11:99–107.

Pearson, Michael and Barry McGowan (2000) *Mining Heritage Places Assessment Manual*. National Trust and the Australian Heritage Commission, Canberra.

Pearson, Warwick (1996) Water power in a dry continent: the transfer of watermill technology from Britain to Australia in the nineteenth century. *Australasian Historical Archaeology* 14: 46–62.

Pearson, Warwick (1997) Water-powered flour mills in nineteenth-century Tasmania. *Australasian Historical Archaeology* 15:66–78.

Pearson, Warwick (1998) Water-powered flourmilling on the New England tablelands of New South Wales. *Australasian Historical Archaeology* 16:30–44.

Peel, Lynette (1974) *Rural Industry in the Port Phillip Region 1835–1880*. Melbourne University Press, Melbourne.

Pensabene, Tony (1980) *The Rise of the Medical Practitioner in Victoria*. Health Research Project Research Monograph 2, The Australian National University, Canberra.

Peters, Sera Jane (1997) Archaeological wines: analysis and interpretation of a collection of wines recovered from the *William Salthouse* Shipwreck (1841). *Australasian Historical Archaeology* 14:63–68.

Phillips, Peter J. (1980) *Redgum and Paddlewheels: Australia's Inland River Trade*. Greenhouse, Melbourne.

Pickard, John (2009) *Illustrated Glossary of Australian Rural Fence Terms*. Heritage Branch, New South Wales Department of Planning, Sydney.

Pickering, Paul A. (2001) The finger of God: Gold's impact on New South Wales. In: Iain McCalman, Alexander Cook and Andrew Reeves (eds.), *Gold: Forgotten Histories and Lost Objects of Australia*, pp. 37–51. Cambridge University Press, Cambridge.

Pickett, Charles (ed.) (1998) *Cars and Culture: Our Driving Passions*. Powerhouse Publishing and HarperCollins, Sydney.

Piddock, Susan (2007) Slate, slate everywhere slate: the cultural landscape of the Willunga Slate Quarries, South Australia. *Australasian Historical Archaeology* 25:5–18.

Piddock, Susan and Pauline O'Malley (2006) From Cornwall to South Australia: the Delabole Quarry and village. In: Pam Smith, F. Donald Pate and Robert Martin (eds.), *Valleys of Stone: The Archaeology and History of Adelaide's Hills Face*, pp. 361–379. Kopi Books, Belair, South Australia.

Piddock, Susan, Pam Smith and F. Donald Pate (2009) A changed landscape: horticulture and gardening in the Adelaide hills face zone, South Australia, 1836–1890. *Historical Archaeology* 43(3):65–81.

Pigott, Loius (1995) The surgeon's equipment from the wreck of HMS *Pandora*. *The Bulletin of the Australian Institute for Maritime Archaeology* 19(1):23–28.

Piper, Andrew (1988) Chinese diet and cultural conservatism in nineteenth-century southern New Zealand. *The Australian Journal for Historical Archaeology* 6:34–42.

Plomley, Norman J.B. (ed.) (1987) *Weep in Silence: A History of the Flinders Island Aboriginal Settlement*. Blubber Head Press, Hobart.

Plomley, Brian and Kristen A. Henley (1990) The Sealers of Bass Strait and the Cape Barren Island Community. *Tasmanian Historical Research Association Papers and Proceedings* 37(2 and 3):37–136.

Porter, Bernard (2004) *The Absent-Minded Imperialists: Empire, Society and Culture in Britain*. Oxford University Press, Oxford.

Porter, Jenny (2004) Blackfellow's Waterhole: a study of culture contact. *The Artefact* 27:77–90.

Porter, Jenny and Asa Ferrier (2004) Miscellaneous artefacts. In: *Casselden Place (50 Lonsdale Street, Melbourne) Archaeological Investigations Research Archive Report, Volume 3(ii): Artefact Reports*. Godden Mackay Logan/La Trobe University/Austral Archaeology, pp. 289–432. Report submitted to Industry Superannuation Property Trust and Heritage Victoria, Melbourne.

Powell, Joseph M. (1970) *The Public Lands of Australia Felix: Settlement and Land Appraisal in Victoria 1834–91, with special reference to the Western Plains*. Oxford University Press, Melbourne.

Powell, Joseph M. (ed.) (1973) *Yeomen and Bureaucrats: The Victorian Crown Lands Commission, 1878–1879*. Oxford University Press, Melbourne.

Powell, Joseph M. (1976) *Environmental Management in Australia 1788–1914*. Oxford University Press, Melbourne.

Poynter, John (2003) *Mr Felton's Bequests*. The Miegunyah Press, Melbourne.

Praetzellis, Adrian (1999) The archaeology of ethnicity: an example from Sacramento, California's Early Chinese district. In: Geoff Egan and Ron L. Michael (eds.), *Old and New Worlds: Historical/Post Medieval Archaeology Papers from the Societies' Joint Conferences at Williamsburg and London 1997 to Mark Thirty Years of Work and Achievement*, pp. 127–135. Oxbow, Oxford.

Praetzellis, Adrian and Mary Praetzellis (2001) Mangling symbols of gentility in the Wild West: case studies in interpretive archaeology. *American Anthropologist* 103(3):645–654.

Praetzellis, Mary and Adrian Praetzellis (2004) *Putting the "There" There: Historical Archaeologies of West Oakland*. Report submitted to California Department of Transportation.

Prangnell, Jonathon (1999) *'Intended solely for their greater comfort and happiness': historical archaeology, paternalism and the Peel Island Lazaret*. Unpublished Ph.D. dissertation, Department of Anthropology and Sociology, University of Queensland, Brisbane.

Prangnell, Jonathon (2002) The archaeology of the Peel Island Lazaret: part 1: survey. *Queensland Archaeological Research* 13:31–38.

Prangnell, Jonathon, L. Cheshire, and Kate Quirk (2005) *Paradise: Life on a Queensland Goldfield*. University of Queensland Archaeological Services Unit and Burnett Water, Brisbane.

Prangnell, Jonathon and Kate Quirk (2009) Children in Paradise: growing up on the Australian goldfields. *Historical Archaeology* 43(3):38–49.

Presland, Gary (2008) *The Place for a Village: How Nature has Shaped the City of Melbourne.* Museum Victoria, Melbourne.

Prickett, Nigel (2002) *The Archaeology of New Zealand Shore Whaling.* Department of Conservation, Wellington.

Prossor, Lauren (2008) *Consumer Practice and Respectability in Gippsland ca 1840–1900.* Unpublished BA (Honours) dissertation, La Trobe University, Melbourne.

Proudfoot, Helen, Anne Bickford, Brian Egloff and Robyn Stocks (1991) *Australia's First Government House.* Allen and Unwin, with Department of Planning, Sydney.

Proudley, Ray (1987) *Circle of Influence: A History of the Gas Industry in Victoria.* Hargreen Publishing Company in association with Gas and Fuel Corporation of Victoria, Melbourne.

Pullman, Sandra (2001) Along Melbourne's rivers and creeks. *Australian Garden History* 12(5): 9–10.

Pybus, Cassandra and Hamish Maxwell-Stuart (2002) *American Citizens, British Slaves: Yankee Political Prisoners in an Australian Penal Colony 1839–1850.* Melbourne University Press, Melbourne.

Queen Victoria Museum and Art Gallery (1983) *Port Arthur Pottery.* Queen Victoria Museum and Art Gallery, Launceston, Tasmania.

Quirk, Kate (2008a) The colonial goldfields: visions and revisions. *Australasian Historical Archaeology* 26:13–20.

Quirk, Kate (2008b) The Victorians in 'Paradise': gentility as social strategy in the archaeology of colonial Australia. Ph.D. dissertation, Department of Anthropology, University of Queensland, Brisbane.

Rains, Kevin (2003) Rice bowls and beer bottles: interpreting evidence of the overseas Chinese at a Cooktown dumpsite. *Australasian Historical Archaeology* 21:30–41.

Rajkowski, Pamela (1987) *In the Tracks of the Camelmen.* Angus and Robertson Publishers, Sydney.

Ramsland, John (1986) *Children of the Back Lanes: Destitute and Neglected Children in Colonial New South Wales.* University of NSW Press, Sydney.

Ranson, Don and Brian J. Egloff (1988) The Application of Earth-Resistivity Surveys to Australian Archaeological Sites. *The Australian Journal of Historical Archaeology* 6:57–73.

Rathje, William L. (1977) In Praise of Archaeology: Le Project du Garbage. In: Leland G. Ferguson (ed.), *Historical Archaeology and the Importance of Material Things*, pp. 36–42. Society for Historical Archaeology Special Publication No. 2, Lansing, Michigan.

Rathje, William L. and Cullen Murphy (1992) *Rubbish! The Archaeology of Garbage.* University of Arizona Press, Tucson, AZ.

Read, Peter (2000) *Belonging: Australians, Place and Aboriginal Ownership.* Cambridge University Press, Cambridge.

Reckner, Paul E. and Stephen A. Brighton (1999) Free from all vicious habits: archaeological perspectives on class conflict and the rhetoric of temperance. *Historical Archaeology* 33(1): 63–86.

Reynolds, Henry (1982) *The Other Side of the Frontier: Aboriginal Resistance to the European Invasion of Australia.* Penguin Books, Ringwood, VIC.

Reynolds, Henry (1989) *Dispossession: Black Australians and White Invaders.* Allen and Unwin, Sydney.

Reynolds, Henry (1995) *Fate of a Free People.* Penguin, Ringwood, VIC.

Richards, Nathan (1998) Inferences from the study of iron and steamship abandonment: a case study from the Garden Island ships' graveyard, South Australia. *The Bulletin of the Australian Institute for Maritime Archaeology* 22:75–80.

Richards, Nathan (2005) The archaeological examination of watercraft abandonment in Australia: a retrospective. *The Bulletin of the Australian Institute for Maritime Archaeology* 29:61–76.

Richards, Nathan (2008) *Ships' Graveyards: Abandoned Watercraft and the Archaeological Site Formation Process.* University Press of Florida, Gainesville, FL.

Richards, Oline (2001) Chinese market gardening: a Western Australian postscript. *Australian Garden History* 13(1):19–21.

Richards, Rhys (2002) Pacific whaling 1820 to 1840: port visits, "shipping arrivals and departures" comparisons, and sources. *The Great Circle* 24(1):25–39.

Riches, Libby (2003) *True Places: Native Title and the Archaeology of Aboriginal Land.* Unpublished Ph.D. dissertation, Archaeology Program, La Trobe University, Melbourne.

Riches, Libby (2004) Legislating the past: native title and the history of Aboriginal Australia. In: Rodney Harrison and Christine Williamson (eds.), *After Captain Cook: The Archaeology of the Recent Indigenous Past in Australia*, pp. 105–119. Altamira, Walnut Creek, CA.

Ringer, Ron (2008) *The Brickmasters 1788–2008.* Dry Press, Horsley Park, New South Wales.

Ritchie, Neville (1981) Archaeological interpretation of alluvial gold tailing sites, Central Otago, New Zealand. *New Zealand Journal of Archaeology* 3:57–69.

Ritchie, Neville (1986) *Archaeology and History of the Chinese in Southern New Zealand During the Nineteenth Century: A Study of Acculturation, Adaptation and Change.* Unpublished Ph.D. dissertation, Department of Anthropology, University of Otago, Dunedin.

Ritchie, Neville (1993) Form and adaptation: nineteenth century Chinese miners' dwellings in Southern New Zealand. In: Priscilla Wegars (ed.), *Hidden Heritage: Historical Archaeology of the Overseas Chinese*, pp. 335–373. Baywood, New York, NY.

Ritchie, Neville and Ray Hooker (1997) An archaeologist's guide to mining terminology. *Australasian Historical Archaeology* 15:3–29.

Ritchie, Neville and Stuart Park (1987) Chinese coins down under: their role on the New Zealand goldfields. *The Australian Journal of Historical Archaeology* 5:41–48.

Robson, Lloyd (1983) *A History of Tasmania: Volume I, Van Diemen's Land from the Earliest Times to 1855.* Oxford University Press, Melbourne.

Rogers, Janette G. and Nelly Helyar (1994) *Lonely Graves of the Gippsland Goldfields and Greater Gippsland.* J.G. Rogers, Moe, VIC.

Ronayne, Jarlath (2002) *First Fleet to Federation: Irish Supremacy in Colonial Australia.* Trinity College Dublin Press, Dublin.

Ross, Lynette (1995) *Death and Burial at Port Arthur 1830–1877.* Unpublished BA (Honours) dissertation, Department of History, University of Tasmania, Hobart.

Rowney, Barry (1984) Kapunda-Burra South Australia. In: Dennis N. Jeans (ed.), *Australian Historical Landscapes*, pp. 86–99. George Allen and Unwin, Sydney.

Rowse, Tim (1998) *White Flour, White Power: From Rations to Citizenship in Central Australia.* Cambridge University Press, Cambridge.

Russ, Rodney (2007) History, exploration, settlement and past use of the Sub-Antarctic. *Papers and Proceedings of the Royal Society of Tasmania* 141(1):169–172.

Russell, Lynette (2004) 'Either, or, neither, nor': resisting the production of gender, race, and class dichotomies in the pre-colonial period. In: Eleanor Conlin Casella and Chris Fowler (eds.), *The Archaeology of Plural and Changing Identities: Beyond Identification*, pp. 33–51. Springer, New York, NY.

Russell, Lynette (2005) Kangaroo Island sealers and their descendants: ethnic and gender ambiguities in the archaeology of a creolised community. *Australian Archaeology* 60:1–5.

Russell, Penny (1994) *A Wish of Distinction.* Melbourne University Press, Melbourne.

Ryan, Jan (1991) Chinese burials in Western Australia in the nineteenth century. *Studies in Western Australian History* 12:8–16.

Ryan, Lyndall (1981) *The Aboriginal Tasmanians*, first edition. University of Queensland Press, St. Lucia, Queensland.

Ryan, Lyndall (1996) *The Aboriginal Tasmanians*, 2nd edition. Allen and Unwin, Sydney.

Safran, William (2004) Deconstructing and comparing diasporas. In: Waltraud Kokot, Khachig Tölölyan and Carolin Alfonso (eds.), *Diaspora, Identity and Religion: New Directions in Theory and Research*, pp. 1–29. Routledge, London.

Samford, Patricia M. (1997) Response to a market: dating English underglaze transfer-printed wares. *Historical Archaeology* 31(2):1–30.

Schaffer, Kay (1988) *Women and the Bush, Forces of Desire in the Australian Cultural Tradition.* Cambridge University Press, Cambridge.

Schmitt, David (1992) The Gembrook Kurth Kiln. In: Tom Griffiths (ed.), *Secrets of the Forest*, pp. 172–176. Allen & Unwin, Sydney.

Schofield, John (ed.) (2009) *Defining Moments: Dramatic Archaeologies of the Twentieth Century.* Archaeopress, Oxford.

Schofield, John and William G. Johnson (2006) Archaeology, heritage and the recent and contemporary past. In: Dan Hicks and Mary C. Beaudry (eds.), *The Cambridge Companion to Historical Archaeology*, pp. 104–122. Cambridge University Press, Cambridge.

Scholes, Paul A. (1979) *Bendigo Pottery.* Lowden, Kilmore, VIC.

Searle, Suzette (1991) *The Rise and Demise of the Black Wattle Industry in Australia.* Division of Forestry, CSIRO, Canberra.

Seddon, George (1997) *Landprints: Reflections on Place and Landscape.* Cambridge University Press, Cambridge.

Serle, Geoffrey (1963) *The Golden Age: A History of the Colony of Victoria 1851–1861.* Melbourne University Press, Melbourne.

Sheldrick, Janis (2005) Goyder's Line: the unreliable history of the line of reliable rainfall. In: Tim Sherratt, Tom Griffiths and Libby Robin (eds.), *A Change in the Weather: Climate and Culture in Australia*, pp. 56–65. National Museum of Australia Press, Canberra.

Shueard, Hallett and David Tuckwell (1993) *Brewers and Aerated Water Manufacturers in South Australia 1836–1936.* H. Shueard and D. Tuckwell, Stepney, SA.

Sikari, Chris (2003) *An Archaeological Exploration of Nineteenth-Century Steamships.* Unpublished BA (Honours) dissertation, Archaeology Program, La Trobe University, Melbourne.

Silberman, Neil A. (1989) Tobacco pipes, cotton prices, and progress. In: Neil A. Silberman (ed.), *Between Past and Present: Archaeology, Ideology and Nationalism in the Modern Middle East*, pp. 228–243. Henry Holt, New York, NY.

Silliman, Stephen W. (2005) Culture contact or colonialism? Challenges in the archaeology of native North America. *American Antiquity* 70(1):55–74.

Simmonds, P.L. (1854) *The Commercial Products of the Vegetable Kingdom.* T.F.A. Day, London.

Simons, Alison and Maddy Maitri (2006) The food remains from Casselden Place, Melbourne, Australia. *International Journal of Historical Archaeology* 10(4):357–374.

Simpson, Margaret and Phillip Simpson (1988) *Old Farm Machinery in Australia: A Fieldguide and Sourcebook.* Kangaroo Press, Kenthurst, NSW.

Singleton, Theresa A. (1995) The archaeology of slavery in North America. *Annual Review of Anthropology* 24:119–140.

Sluga, Glenda (1988) *Bonegilla: A Place of No Hope.* Melbourne University History Monograph No. 5, University of Melbourne.

Sluga, Glenda (2001) Bonegilla reception and training centre. In: James Jupp (ed.), *The Australian People: An Encyclopedia of the Nation, Its People and Their Origins*, pp. 72–73. Cambridge University Press, Cambridge.

Smith, Anita and Krystal Buckley (2007) Convict landscapes: shared heritage in New Caledonia. *Historic Environment* 20(2):27–32.

Smith, Anita and Wendy Beck (2003) The Archaeology of No Man's Land: Indigenous Camps at Corindi Beach, Mid-North Coast New South Wales. *Archaeology in Oceania* 38(2):66–77.

Smith, Diane M. (2005) *Meaning, Purpose and Social Memory: The Archaeology of Farm Graveyards of Vehicles and Machinery.* Unpublished Ph.D. dissertation, Department of Archaeology, Flinders University, South Australia.

Smith, Frederick H. (2007) *The Archaeology of Alcohol and Drinking.* University Press of Florida, Tallahassee, FL.

Smith, Ian (2002) *The New Zealand Sealing Industry.* Department of Conservation, Wellington.

Smith, Jean (2007) Glass. In: Graham Connah (ed.), *The Same Under a Different Sky? A Country Estate in Nineteenth-Century New South Wales*, pp. 195–203. Archaeopress, Oxford.

Smith, Laurajane and Natsuko Akagawa (eds.) (2009) *Intangible Heritage*. Routledge, London.

Smith, Lindsay M (1998) *Cold Hard Cash: A Study of Chinese Ethnicity in Archaeology at Kiandra, New South Wales*. Unpublished MA dissertation, Department of Archaeology and Anthropology, Australian National University, Canberra.

Smith, Lindsay M. (2003) Identifying Chinese ethnicity through material culture: archaeological excavations at Kiandra, NSW. *Australasian Historical Archaeology* 21:18–29.

Smith, Lindsay M. (2006) *Hidden Dragons: The Archaeology of Mid to Late Nineteenth-Century Chinese Communities in Southeastern New South Wales*. Unpublished Ph.D. dissertation, School of Archaeology and Anthropology, Australian National University, Canberra.

Smith, Pamela A. (2001) Station camps: identifying the evidence for continuity and change in post-contact Aboriginal sites in the South Kimberley, Western Australia. *Australian Archaeology* 53:23–31.

Smith, Pamela A. (2006) Dry-stone walls and water wheels: managing water in colonial South Australia. In: Pam Smith, F. Donald Pate and Robert Martin (eds.), *Valleys of Stone: The Archaeology and History of Adelaide's Hills Face*, pp. 69–92. Kōpi Books, Belair, SA.

Smith, Pamela A. (2007) Water management systems in colonial South Australia. *Australasian Historical Archaeology* 25:19–32.

Smith, Pamela A. and F. Donald Pate (2006) The Adelaide Hills Face Zone 1836–1936: a significant cultural landscape. In: Pam Smith, F. Donald Pate and Robert Martin (eds.), *Valleys of Stone: The Archaeology and History of Adelaide's Hills Face*, pp. 1–16. Kōpi Books, Belair, SA.

Smith, Pamela A., F. Donald Pate and Robert Martin (eds.) (2006) *Valleys of Stone: The Archaeology and History of Adelaide's Hills Face*. Kōpi Books, Belair, South Australia.

Smith, Pamela A. and Richard M. Smith (1999) Diets in transition: hunter-gatherer to station diet to the self-select store diet. *Human Ecology* 27(1):115–134.

Smith, Tim (2000) Up periscope: submarine AE2 makes first contact. *The Bulletin of the Australian Institute for Maritime Archaeology* 24:9–20.

Smith, Tim (2008) Managing an Australian midget: the Imperial Japanese Navy Type a Submarine M24 at Sydney. *The Bulletin of the Australian Institute for Maritime Archaeology* 32:79–89.

Smith, Tim and Chloe Weir (1999) The Whaling Wreck site potential of New South Wales. *The Bulletin of the Australian Institute for Maritime Archaeology* 23:40–45.

Sneddon, Andrew (2006) Seeing slums through rose-coloured glasses: the Mountain Street site, Sydney and its limitations in the search for vanished slum communities. *Australian Archaeology* 63:1–8.

Souter, Corioli (2003) Port of refugees: archaeology and oral history of WII flying boat wrecks in Broome, Western Australia. *The Bulletin of the Australian Institute for Maritime Archaeology* 27:115–120.

Souter, Corioli (2006a) *Archaeology of the Iron Barque Sepia – An Investigation of Cargo Assemblages*. Unpublished MA dissertation, Department of Archaeology, University of Western Australia.

Souter, Corioli (2006b) Cultural tourism and diver education. In: Mark Staniforth and Michael Nash (eds.), *Maritime Archaeology: Australian Approaches*, pp. 163–176. Springer, New York, NY.

Spicer, Chrys (1991) Boroondara: Australia's first landscaped garden cemetery. *Heritage Australia* 10(2):3–7.

Springate, Megan E. (1997) Cellulose Nitrate Plastic (Celluloid) in archaeological assemblages: identification and care. *Northeast Historical Archaeology* 26:63–72.

Stanbury, Myra (1994) Mother-of-pearl shell cultivation: an early 20th century experiment in the Montebello Islands, Western Australia. *The Great Circle* 16(2):90–120.

Stanbury, Myra (2003) *The Barque Eglinton: Wrecked Western Australia 1852: The History of Its Loss, Archaeological Excavation, Artefact Catalogue, and Interpretation*. Australasian Institute for Maritime Archaeology, Fremantle, WA.

Staniforth, Mark (1997) The archaeology of the event – the annales school and maritime archaeology. In: Denise C. Lakey (eds.), *Underwater Archaeology*, pp. 17–21. The Society for Historical Archaeology, Philadelphia, Pennsylvania.

Staniforth, Mark (1998) Three Whaling Station sites on the West Coast of South Australia: Fowler's Bay, Sleaford Bay and Streaky Bay. In: Susan Lawrence and Mark Staniforth (eds.), *The Archaeology of Whaling in Southern Australia and New Zealand*, pp. 57–63. The Australasian Society for Historical Archaeology and the Australian Institute for Maritime Archaeology Special Publication No. 10, Canberra.

Staniforth, Mark (2003) *Material Culture and Consumer Society: Dependent Colonies in Colonial Australia*. Kluwer/Plenum, New York, NY.

Staniforth, Mark (2008) European-Indigenous contact at shore-based whaling sites. In: Peter Veth, Peter Sutton and Margo Neale (eds.), *Strangers on the Shore: Early coastal contacts in Australia*, pp. 124–132. National Museum of Australia, Canberra.

Staniforth, Mark (2009) Shipwreck cargoes: approaches to material culture in Australian maritime archaeology. *Historical Archaeology* 43(3):95–100.

Staniforth, Mark, Susan Briggs and Chris Lewczak (2000) Unearthing the invisible people: European families and Aboriginal people at South Australian Whaling Stations. *Mains'l Haul* 37(3 and 4):12–19.

Staniforth, Mark and Mike Nash (1998) *Chinese Export Porcelain from the Wreck of the* Sydney Cove *(1797)*. The Australian Institute for Maritime Archaeology Special Publication No. 12, Gundaroo, New South Wales.

Stanin, Zvonka (2004a) From Li Chun to Yong Kit: a market garden on the Loddon, 1851–1912. *Journal of Australian Colonial History* 6:15–34.

Stanin, Zvonka (2004b) *Preliminary Archaeological Investigation of Chinese Residential Sites on the Mt. Alexander Diggings*. Report submitted to Heritage Victoria and Parks Victoria, Melbourne.

Stankowski, Katrina (2003) *Polish Hill River: Cultural Identity from Material Remains*. Unpublished MA dissertation, Department of Archaeology, Flinders University, South Australia.

Stankowski, Katrina (2004) A Pole apart? Polish and German material culture in South Australia. *Australasian Historical Archaeology* 22:4–14.

Starr, Fiona (2001) Convict artefacts from the civil hospital privy on Norfolk Island. *Australasian Historical Archaeology* 19:39–47.

Staski, Edward (1990) Studies of ethnicity in North American historical archaeology. *North American Archaeologist* 11(2):121–145.

Steele, Dominic (1999) Animal bone and shell artefacts report. In: *The Cumberland/Gloucester Streets Site, The Rocks, Archaeological Investigation Vol. 4(2) Specialist Artefact Reports*. Godden Mackay Heritage Consultants, pp. 141–237. Godden Mackay Logan, Sydney.

Stenning, Eve (1993) Nothing but gum trees: textile manufacturing in New South Wales, 1788–1850. *Australasian Historical Archaeology* 11:76–87.

Stevens, Christine (2002) *Tin Mosques and Ghantowns: A History of Afghan Cameldrivers in Australia*. Paul Fitzsimons, Alice Springs, NT.

Stine, Linda F. (1990) Social inequality and turn of the century farmsteads: issues of class, status, ethnicity and race. *Historical Archaeology* 24(4):37–49.

Stocks, Robyn (2008) New evidence for local manufacture of artefacts at Parramatta, 1790–1830. *Australasian Historical Archaeology* 26:29–44.

Stone, Derrick I. and Donald S. Garden (1978) *Squatters and Selectors*. Reed, Sydney.

Strachan, Shirley (1986) *The History and Archaeology of the* Sydney Cove *Shipwreck (1797): A Resource for Future Site Work*. Occasional Papers in Prehistory 5, Department of Prehistory, Australian National University, Canberra.

Strachan, Shirley (2000) *Silts in the Sight Glass: Protectors and Raiders of the SS City of Launceston*. Heritage Victoria, Melbourne.

Stratton, Michael and Barrie Trinder (2000) *Twentieth Century Industrial Archaeology*. E and FN Spon, London.

Stuart, Iain (1987) A history of the Victorian brick industry: 1826–1920. *Australian Archaeology* 24(June):36–40.

Stuart, Iain (1989a) *An Historical Archaeological Survey of Wilsons Promontory*. Victoria Archaeological Survey, Melbourne.

Stuart, Iain (1989b) Why did the Hoffman Brick and Pottery works stop making bricks? *Australasian Historical Archaeology* 7:29–34.

Stuart, Iain (1993) Bottles for Jam? An example or recycling from a post-contact archaeological site. *Australian Archaeology* 36:29–34.

Stuart, Iain (1997a) Cultural landscapes as an analytical tool: analysing squatting landscapes. *Historic Environment* 13(3/4):23–28.

Stuart, Iain (1997b) Sea rats, bandits and roistering buccaneers: What were the Bass Strait Sealers really like? *Journal of the Royal Australian Historical Society* 83(1):47–58.

Stuart, Iain (1998) Sealing and whaling seascapes. In: Susan Lawrence and Mark Staniforth (eds.), *The Archaeology of Whaling in Southern Australia and New Zealand*, pp. 98–102. The Australasian Society for Historical Archaeology and the Australian Institute for Maritime Archaeology Special Publication No. 10, Canberra.

Stuart, Iain (1999) *Squatting Landscapes in South-Eastern Australia (1820–1895)*. Unpublished Ph.D. dissertation, Prehistoric and Historical Archaeology, University of Sydney, Sydney.

Stuart, Iain (2005) The analysis of bricks from archaeological sites in Australia. *Australasian Historical Archaeology* 23:79–88.

Stuart, Iain (2007) The surveyors' lot: making landscapes in New South Wales. *Australasian Historical Archaeology* 25:43–55.

Svenson, Geoff (1994) *Marginal People: The Archaeology and History of the Chinese at Milparinka*. Unpublished MA dissertation, University of Sydney, Sydney.

Symons, Michael (2007) *One Continuous Picnic: A gastronomic history of Australia*, 2nd edition. Melbourne University Publishing, Melbourne.

Taksa, Lucy (2005) The material culture of an industrial artifact: interpreting control, defiance, and everyday resistance at the New South Wales Eveleigh railway workshops. *Historical Archaeology* 39(3):8–27.

Talbot, Diann (2004) *The Buckland Valley Goldfield*. Speciality Press, Albury, NSW.

Tarlow, Sarah (1999) *Bereavement and Commemoration: An Archaeology of Mortality*. Blackwell, Oxford.

Taylor, Angela (1998) *A Forester's Log: the Story of John le Gerche and the Ballarat-Creswick State Forest, 1882–1897*. Melbourne University Press, Melbourne.

Taylor, Peter (1980) *An End to Silence: The Building of the Overland Telegraph Line from Adelaide to Darwin*. Methuen Australia, Sydney.

Taylor, Rebe (2002) *Unearthed: The Aboriginal Tasmanians of Kangaroo Island*. Wakefield Press, Kent Town, SA.

Tench, Watkin (1961 [1793]) *A Complete Account of the Settlement at Port Jackson*. In: Laurence F. Fitzhardinge (ed.), *Sydney's First Four Years*, pp. 123–300. Angus and Robertson, Sydney.

Terrell, Michelle M. (2005) *The Jewish Community of Early Colonial Nevis: A Historical Archaeological Study*. University Press of Florida, Gainesville, FL.

Terry, Linda and Jonathan Prangnell (2009) Caboonbah homestead 'Big Rock' or 'Little Britain'. A study of Britishness in late nineteenth and early twentieth century rural Queensland. *Australasian Historical Archaeology* 27:18–28.

Terry, Martin (2005) The voyage. In: Patricia T. Macdonald (ed.), *Exiles and Emigrants: Epic Journeys to Australia in the Victorian Era*, pp. 74–89. National Gallery of Victoria, Melbourne.

Thomas, Nicholas (1991) *Entangled Objects: Exchange, Material Culture, and Colonialism in the Pacific*. Harvard University Press, Cambridge, MA.

Tilley, Christopher (1994) *A Phenomenology of Landscape: Places, Paths and Monuments*. Berg, Oxford.

Timms, Peter (2006) *Australia's Quarter Acre: The Story of the Ordinary Suburban Garden*. The Miegunyah Press, Melbourne.

Torrence, Robin and Anne Clarke (eds.) (2000) *The Archaeology of Difference: Negotiating Cross-Cultural Engagements in Oceania*. Routledge, London.

Townrow, Karen (1989) *Survey and Excavation of Historic Sites on Macquarie Island*. Occasional Paper No. 20, Department of Lands, Parks and Wildlife, Tasmania, Hobart.

Townrow, Karen (1990) Lovely Linoleum. *Research Bulletin* 14. The Australian Society for Historical Archaeology, Sydney.

Townrow, Karen (1997) *An Archaeological Survey of Sealing and Whaling Sites in Victoria*. Heritage Victoria, Melbourne.

Tracey, Michael (1997) Archaeological evidence for a horse-drawn tramway at Bawley Point, NSW. In: John Dargavel (ed.), *Australia's Ever-Changing Forests III*, pp. 188–209. Centre for Resource and Environmental Studies, Australian National University, Canberra.

Tuck, James A. and Robert Grenier (1989) *Red Bay, Labrador: World Whaling Capital, AD 1550–1600*. Atlantic Archaeology, St. John's, Newfoundland.

Tucker, A.L. (1899) Royal Commission on State Forests and Timber Reserves, 4th Progress Report: Wombat Forest: its resources, management and control. In: *Papers Presented to Parliament (Victoria)* vol. 3(25). Government Printer, Melbourne.

Tucker, Catherine, Mark Dunn and John Sharples (2004) Coins and medallions. In: *Casselden Place (50 Lonsdale Street, Melbourne) Archaeological Investigations Research Archive Report, Volume 3(ii): Artefact Reports*. Godden Mackay Logan/La Trobe University/Austral Archaeology, pp. 717–726. Report submitted to Industry Superannuation Property Trust and Heritage Victoria, Melbourne.

Tuffin, Richard (2005) *Isle of the Dead Comparative Study: Death and Burial of Convicts Under Sentence in Van Diemen's Land*. Report submitted to Port Arthur Historic Site Management Authority, Tasmania.

Tuffin, Richard (2008) 'Where the vicissitudes of day and night are not known': convict coal mining in Van Diemen's Land, 1822–1848. *Tasmanian Historical Studies* 13:35–61.

Tuffin, Richard, Greg Jackman and Julia Clark (eds.) (2004) *A Harbour Large Enough to Admit a Whole Fleet*. Port Arthur Occasional Papers No. 1, Port Arthur Historic Sites Management Authority, Tasmania.

Turnbull, Jodi (2006) *Pure Gold: Collaboration Between Archaeologists and Detectorists*. Unpublished BA (Honours) dissertation, Archaeology Program, La Trobe University, Melbourne.

Ulm, Sean, Tony Eales and Sarah L'Estrange (1999) Post-European Aboriginal occupation of the Southern Curtis Coast, Central Queensland. *Australian Archaeology* 48:42–43.

Tyrrell, Ian (1999) *Deadly Enemies: Tobacco and its opponents in Australia*. University of New South Wales Press, Sydney.

Vader, John (1986) *Red Cedar: The Tree of Australia's History*. Reed, Frenchs Forest, New South Wales.

Vader, John (2002) *Red Gold: The Tree That Built a Nation*. New Holland, Frenchs Forest, NSW.

Vader, John and Brian Murray (1975) *Antique Bottle Collecting in Australia*. Ure Smith, Sydney.

Veit, Richard F., Sherene B. Baugher and Gerard P. Scharfenberger (2009) Historical archaeology of religious sites and cemeteries. *Historical Archaeology* 43(1):1–11.

Veres, Maya (2005) Introduction to the analysis of archaeological footwear. *Australasian Historical Archaeology* 23:89–96.

Vermeer, Andrea C. (2009) Men-women and children: gender and the structuring of historical archaeology. In: Teresita Majewski and David Gaimster (eds.), *International Handbook of Historical Archaeology*, pp. 319–331. Springer, New York, NY.

Verrocchio, Jacqueline (1998) *Historic Tobacco Kilns in the Rural City of Wangaratta*. Rural City of Wangaratta, Wangaratta, VIC.

Vines, Gary (1993a) *Farm and Dairy*. Melbourne's Living Museum of the West and the Department of Planning and Development, Melbourne.

Vines, Gary (1993b) *Meat and By-Products*. Melbourne's Living Museum of the West and the Department of Planning and Development, Melbourne.

Vivian, Helen (1985) *Tasmania's Chinese Heritage: An Historical Record of Chinese Sites in North East Tasmania*. Australian Heritage Commission, Queen Victoria Museum and Art Gallery, Launceston, Tasmania.

Voss, Barbara and Rebecca Allen (2008) Overseas Chinese archaeology: historical foundations, current reflections, and new directions. *Historical Archaeology* 42(3):5–28.

Wace, Nigel and Bessie Lovett (1973) *Yankee Maritime Activities and the Early History of Australia*. Research School of Pacific Studies Aids to Research Series, No. A/2, Australian National University, Canberra.

Walden, Sue (1995) The tin fields of North-East Tasmania-a regional variation. In: Paul Macgregor (ed.), *Histories of the Chinese in Australasia and the South Pacific*, pp. 177–188. Museum of Chinese Australian History, Melbourne.

Walker, Murray (1979) *Pioneer Crafts of Early Australia*. Macmillan, Melbourne.

Walker, Robin (1984) *Under Fire: A History of Tobacco Smoking in Australia*. Melbourne University Press, Melbourne.

Wall, Diana DiZerega (1991) Sacred dinners and secular teas: constructing domesticity in mid-19th-century New York. *Historical Archaeology* 25(4):69–81.

Walsh, Gerald P. (1963) The geography of manufacturing in Sydney, 1788–1851. *Business Archives and History* 3(1):20–52.

Wang, Gungwu (1992) *Community and Nation: China, Southeast Asia and Australia*. Asian Studies Association of Australia in association with Allen & Unwin, Sydney.

Wang, Sing-Wu (2001) Chinese immigration 1840s–1890s. In: James Jupp (ed.), *The Australian People: An Encyclopedia of the Nation, Its People and Their Origins*, pp. 197–204. Cambridge University Press, Cambridge.

Ward, David (1976) The Victorian slum: an enduring myth? *Annals of the Association of American Geographers* 66(2):323–336.

Ward, Ian, Peter Larcombe and Peter Veth (1998) Towards new process-oriented models for describing wreck disintegration: an example using the Pandora Wreck. *The Bulletin of the Australian Institute for Maritime Archaeology* 22:109–114.

Ward, Ian, Peter Larcombe and Peter Veth (1999) A new process-based model for wreck site formation. *Journal of Archaeological Science* 26:561–570.

Ward, Russel (1958) *The Australian Legend*. Oxford University Press, London.

Waterhouse, Richard (2005) *The Vision Splendid: A Social and Cultural History of Rural Australia*. Fremantle Arts Centre Press, Fremantle, WA.

Waterson, Duncan B. (1968) *Squatter, Selector and Storekeeper: A History of the Darling Downs, 1859–93*. Sydney University Press, Sydney.

Watson, Don (1984) *Caledonia Australis: Scottish Highlanders on the Frontier of Australia*. Collins, Sydney.

Watson, Rubie S. (1988) Remembering the dead: graves and politics in Southeastern China. In: James L. Watson and Evelyn S. Rawski (eds.), *Death Ritual in Late Imperial China*, pp. 203–227. University of California Press, Berkeley, CA.

Webb, Stephen (1987) Reburying Australian skeletons. *Antiquity* 61:292–296.

Webster, Jane (1999) Resisting traditions: ceramics, identity, and consumer choice in the outer Hebrides from 1800 to the present. *International Journal of Historical Archaeology* 3(1): 53–73.

Wegars, Patricia (1988) The Asian comparative collection. *The Australian Journal of Historical Archaeology* 6:43–48.

Wegars, Patricia (2003) From old gold mountain to new gold mountain: Chinese archaeological sites, artefact repositories and archives in Western North America and Australasia. *Australasian Historical Archaeology* 21:70–83.

Wegner, Jan (1995) Winding engines on the Croydon Goldfield: what the documents don't say. *Australasian Historical Archaeology* 13:11–17.

Westerdahl, Christer (1992) The maritime cultural landscape. *International Journal of Nautical Archaeology* 21(1):5–14.

Whitaker, Anne-Marie (2004) From Norfolk Island to Foveaux Strait: Joseph Foveaux's role in the expansion of whaling and sealing in early nineteenth century Australasia. *The Great Circle* 26(1):51–59.

Wileman, Julie (2005) *Hide and Seek: The Archaeology of Childhood.* Tempus, Stroud, Gloucestershire, UK.

Wilkie, Laurie (2000) Not merely child's play: creating a historical archaeology of children and childhood. In: Joanna Sofaer Derevenski (eds.), *Children and Material Culture*, pp. 100–113. Routledge, London.

Wilkie, Laurie (2003) *The Archaeology of Mothering: An African-American Midwife's Tale.* Routledge, New York, NY.

Williams, Michael (1974) *The Making of the South Australian Landscape.* Academic, London.

Williamson, Christine (2004a) Contact archaeology and the writing of Aboriginal history. In: Tim Murray (ed.), *The Archaeology of Contact in Settler Societies*, pp. 176–199. Cambridge University Press, Cambridge.

Williamson, Christine (2004b) Finding meaning in the patterns: the analysis of material culture from a contact site in Tasmania. In: Rodney Harrison and Christine Williamson (eds.), *After Captain Cook: The Archaeology of the Recent Past in Australia*, pp. 76–101. Altamira, Walnut Creek, CA.

Williamson, Christine (2004c) Clay pipes. In: *Casselden Place (50 Lonsdale Street, Melbourne) Archaeological Investigations Research Archive Report, Volume 3(i): Artefact Reports.* Godden Mackay Logan/La Trobe University/Austral Archaeology, pp. 157–228. Report submitted to Industry Superannuation Property Trust and Heritage Victoria, Melbourne.

Wilson, Andrew (1988) A failed colonial squire: Sir John Jamison at Regentville. In: Judy Birmingham, Damaris Bairstow and Andrew Wilson (eds.), *Archaeology and Colonisation: Australia in the World Context*, pp. 123–138. The Australian Society for Historical Archaeology, Sydney.

Wilson, Graham (1999) Ceramics and tobacco pipes artefact report. In: *The Cumberland/ Gloucester Streets Site, The Rocks, Archaeological Investigation Report Volume 4 Specialist Artefact Reports Part 1*, pp. 205–366. Godden Mackay Logan, Sydney.

Wilson, Graham and Martin Davies (1980) *Norfolk Island: Archaeological Survey, Kingston-Arthur's Vale Region.* Report submitted to Department of Housing and Construction, Commonwealth Government Australia, Canberra.

Wilson, Graham and Peter Douglas (2005) *Castle Hill Heritage Park: Archaeological Excavation Report for the Stage 1 Redevelopment Area.* Archaeological and Heritage Management Solutions. Report submitted to Baulkham Hills Shire Council, New South Wales.

Wilson, Graham and Alexandra Kelly (1987) *Preliminary Analysis of Clay Tobacco Pipes from the First Government House site, Sydney.* Department of Planning, Sydney.

Wolski, Nathan and Tom Loy (1999) On the invisibility of contact: residue analyses on Aboriginal glass artefacts from Western Victoria. *The Artefact* 22:65–73.

Wong, Anna (1999) Colonial sanitation, urban planning and social reform in Sydney 1788–1857. *Australasian Historical Archaeology* 17:58–69.

Wong Hoy, Kevin (2007) Murder, Manslaughter and Affray: making a cold case of the Buckland Riot, 4 July 1857. In: Keir Reeves and David Nichols (eds.), *Deeper Leads: New Approaches to Victorian Goldfields History*, pp. 131–155. Ballarat Heritage Services, Ballarat, VIC.

Woodhouse, Monte C.A. (1993) Elements of a pastoral landscape: Holowiliena, South Australia, in 1888. *Australasian Historical Archaeology* 11:88–98.

Wright, Clare (2003) *Beyond the Ladies Lounge: Australia's Female Publicans.* Melbourne University Press, Melbourne.

Wright, Ray (1989) *The Bureaucrats' Domain: Space and the Public Interest in Victoria 1836–84.* Oxford University Press, Melbourne.

Wright, Ray (1992) *A People's Counsel: A History of the Parliament of Victoria 1856–1990*. Oxford University Press, Melbourne.

Wurst, LouAnn (2006) A class all its own: explorations of class formation and conflict. In: Martin Hall and Stephen W. Silliman (eds.), *Historical Archaeology*, pp. 190–208. Blackwell, Oxford.

Wylie, Jerry and Richard E. Fike (1993) Chinese opium smoking techniques and paraphernalia. In: Priscilla Wegars (ed.), *Hidden Heritage: Historical Archaeology of the Overseas Chinese*, pp. 255–303. Baywood, New York, NY.

Yamin, Rebecca (1997) Lurid tales and homely stories of New York's notorious five points. *Historical Archaeology* 32(1):74–85.

Yamin, Rebecca (2002) Children's strikes, parents' rights: Paterson and five points. *International Journal of Historical Archaeology* 6(2):113–126.

Yang, Mayfair Mei-hui (1994) *Gifts, Favours, and Banquets: The Art of Social Relationships in China*. Cornell University Press, Ithaca, New York, NY.

Yee, Glenice (2006) *Through Chinese Eyes: The Chinese Experience in the Northern Territory 1874–2004*. Glenice Yee, Parap, NT.

Yong, C.F. (1977) *The New Gold Mountain: The Chinese in Australia 1901–1921*. Raphael Arts, Richmond, SA.

Young, Gordon (1985) Early German settlements in South Australia. *The Australian Journal of Historical Archaeology* 3:43–55.

Young, Gordon, Ian Harmstorf and Donald Langmead (1977) *The Barossa Survey*. Report by the School of Architecture, South Australia Institute of Technology, and the Department of History, Adelaide College of Advanced Education, for the Australian Heritage Commission, Canberra.

Young, Linda (1992) Comfort and decency: furniture and equipment in Adelaide homes. In: Brian Dickey (ed.), *William Shakespeare's Adelaide 1860–1930*, pp. 14–26. Association of Professional Historians, Adelaide.

Young, Linda (1997) *The Struggle for Class: The Transmission of Genteel Culture to Early Colonial Australia*. Unpublished Ph.D. dissertation, Faculty of Social Sciences, Flinders University of South Australia, Adelaide.

Young, Linda (2003) *Middle Class Culture in the Nineteenth Century: America, Australia and Britain*. Palgrave Macmillan, New York, NY.

Yu, Sarah (1999) Broome Creole: Aboriginal and Asian partnerships along the Kimberley Coast. *Queensland Review* 6(2):58–73.

Yuan, Chung-Ming (2001) Chinese in White Australia 1901–1950. In: James Jupp (ed.), *The Australian People: An Encyclopedia of the Nation, its People and Their Origins*, pp. 204–206. Cambridge University Press, Cambridge.

Zipfel, Claudia (2002) *Linking Places: Constructing an Aboriginal Social Landscape in the Wimmera Region of North-Western Victoria*. Unpublished BA (Honours) dissertation, Archaeology Program, La Trobe University, Melbourne.

Zipfel, Claudia (2007) Welcome to Bonegilla: refurbishing a camp and reshaping ideas. *History* 92:7–9.

Index

Note: The letters 'f' and 't' following the locators refer to figures and tables respectively.